Communicating for Success

3e

Janet S. Hyden
Great Oaks Institute of Technology and Career Development
Cincinnati, Ohio

Ann K. Jordan
Great Oaks Institute of Technology and Career Development
Cincinnati, Ohio

Mary Helen Steinauer
Educational Consultant
Cincinnati, Ohio

(contributing author)
Margie J. Jones
Retired English Teacher
Snow Hill, North Carolina

THOMSON
SOUTH-WESTERN

Australia · Brazil · Canada · Mexico · Singapore · Spain · United Kingdom · United States

THOMSON

SOUTH-WESTERN

Communicating for Success, Third Edition
Janet Hyden, Ann Jordan, Mary Helen Steinauer, Margie Jones (Contributing Author)

VP/Editorial Director:
Jack W. Calhoun

VP/Editor-in-Chief:
Karen Schmohe

Acquisitions Editor:
Eve Lewis

Project Manager:
Penny Shank

Production Project Manager:
Darrell E. Frye

Vice President, Director of Educational Marketing:
Carol Volz

Marketing Manager:
Courtney Schulz

Senior Marketing Coordinator:
Linda Kuper

Manufacturing Coordinator:
Kevin Kluck

Production House:
Navta Associates, Inc.

Printer: Courier
Kendalville, Indiana

Art Director:
Stacy Jenkins Shirley

Internal and Cover Designer:
Kim Torbeck, Imbue Design

Cover Images:
© Getty Images

For more information about our products, contact us at:
Thomson Higher Education
5191 Natorp Boulevard
Mason, Ohio 45040
USA

Works Cited
p. 123, Reprinted with permission from the Society of Technical Communication, Arlington, VA.
p. 504, Report excerpt courtesy of Elizabeth S. Kroon.
The names of all commercially available software mentioned herein are used for identification purposes only and may be trademarks or registered trademarks of their respective owners. South-Western Educational Publishing disclaims any affiliation, association, connection with, sponsorship, or endorsement by such owners.

Your Communication Solution

Technical Writing for Success, 2e

This comprehensive text is designed to focus on skills that employers demand in today's workplace—thinking, listening, composing, revising, and editing. Using a learn-by-doing approach, these skills are introduced and applied so that mastering technical writing is relevant and exciting. The companion CD, packaged free with each text, includes numerous enrichment activities and sample documents to provide supplemental opportunities to learn and apply the principles of effective technical writing.
Text/CD (hardcover, 4-color, 432 pages) 0-538-43868-1

Spelling Reference, 5e

This handy, compact manual provides correct spelling and word division of the most commonly used words in business writing. The manual includes over 29,000 terms, spelling guidelines, two-letter state abbreviations, and alphabetic guides on the page edge for quick referencing.
Text (soft cover, 1-color, 256 pages) 0-538-69120-4

Human Relations for Career Success, 6e

Human Relations for Career Success provides comprehensive coverage of human relation skills needed for career success in today's workplace. This successful text, now in its 6th edition, provides the foundation. for getting along with others in the workplace. Through concise, hands-on activities, the authors use and engaging approach to introduce topics such as self-esteem, decision making, teamwork, and a positive attitude—all important for today's work environment.
Text (softcover, 2-color, 228 pages) 0-538-43876-2

words@work

This software presents the skills needed as a communicator and contributor in today's world of work. Interactive lessons and exercises reinforce essential grammar, workplace writing, and employability skills. Through workplace scenarios, simulations, and interactive graphics, learning becomes engaging for students.
words@work CD 0-538-69049-6

Discovering Your Career

Taking the unique approach of matching a career to one's personal interests, *Discovering Your Career*, focuses specifically on self-understanding, self-acceptance, career information, goal setting, networking, team building, education opportunities, and the job search process.
Text/CD Package 0-538-43202-0

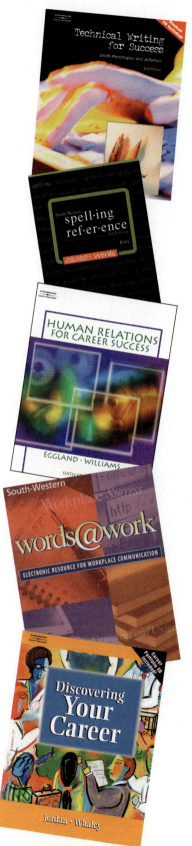

THOMSON

SOUTH-WESTERN

Join us on the Internet at www.swlearning.com

To the Student:

If you want success in any career, you will find nothing more valuable than good communication skills. Such skills are and will continue to be your most valuable assets in both your personal and professional lives. Whether you are talking to a friend, applying for a job, submitting a report, or trying to convince someone that you have a great idea, skilled communication is key. And you'll find, as your communication skills improve, that you will be able to open eyes, open minds, and open doors.

Communicating for Success may be the most practical textbook you've ever used. It helps develop effective workplace communication skills by providing you with more than theories. It shows you what steps to take to carry out specific communication tasks effectively and then lets you try out the tasks yourself. It also provides opportunities for you to work with others, rather than trying to do things yourself, because in today's workplace, you'll have to work cooperatively with other people. School is a good place to learn these things— a safe place where you won't risk losing a paycheck or jeopardizing your career if you don't do them right the first time.

Employers seek, value, and reward the skills stressed in this text. If you master those skills, you will have a much better chance of succeeding at whatever you choose to do in your future.

Communicating for Success is divided into chapters. Each chapter deals with a topic such as describing a process, listening and speaking effectively, persuading someone in authority that you have a good idea, managing your time, and getting and keeping a job. Each chapter ends with a real-world project for you and others to design and present.

In each chapter, in addition to the basic lessons, you will notice several special features labeled "Connections." These features deal with a variety of topics related to careers, ethics in the workplace, people, culture, and technology. As you scan each page, you will also notice featured quotes, anecdotes, and tidbits of information in the margins. We found them interesting and thought you might, too.

Finally, at the end of each chapter, you will find literature selections. These stories, poems, essays, and plays have plots, characters, or themes that relate to the topics in each chapter.

Throughout this text, we refer to resources available on the Internet. We also recommend that you use computers and appropriate software in your projects as well as in your everyday work whenever possible, since computers will be your tools in the workplace.

We hope that you enjoy and learn from *Communicating for Success* and that you will not only know more but be able to do more with what you've learned after completing this course.

Janet S. Hyden

Ann K. Jordan

Mary Helen Steinauer

Acknowledgments

We wish to thank all who helped us create this book. We are particularly grateful to the following educators who reviewed the manuscript and offered helpful suggestions for improvement:

Margaret Ackerman
English and Technical Communication Instructor
Live Oaks Career Development Campus
Cincinnati, Ohio

Sara A. Baker
English Instructor
Allen High School
Allen, Texas

Marie Benson
English Instructor
Allen High School
Allen, Texas

Louie Brockhoeft
Master Fitness Trainer
Mercy Health Plex
Cincinnati, Ohio

Sherry Forster
English and Social Studies Instructor
Delaware Area Career Center
Delaware, Ohio

Kathy Freeman
English and Technical Communication Instructor
Laurel Oaks Career Development Campus
Wilmington, Ohio

Mabel Gelter
English and Technical Communication Instructor
Live Oaks Career Development Campus
Milford, Ohio

Karen McKay Hanks
Instructor
Duval County Public Schools
Jacksonville, Florida

Douglas Haskell
Associate Director
University of Cincinnati
Economics Center for Education and Research
Cincinnati, Ohio

Maurice Henderson
State Consultant
Business Professionals of America
Eastern Michigan University
Ypsilanti, Michigan

Roy A. Hyden
Business Education Chair
Princeton High School
Cincinnati, Ohio

Kristine Labbus
Business Teacher
Neenah High School
Neenah, Wisconsin

Linda Thompson
Work-based Learning Coordinator
Indian Trail Academy
Kenasha, Wisconsin

Jeff Whitesell
English and Technical Communication Instructor
Scarlet Oaks Career Development Campus
Cincinnati, Ohio

Janet Hyden
Ann Jordan
Mary Helen Steinauer

contents

by the way...

Language is not good or bad. It is simply appropriate or inappropriate, depending on the audience and the occasion.

© GETTY IMAGES/PHOTODISC, INC.

by the way...

"People who enjoy what they are doing invariably do it well."

JOE GIBBS, NFL COACH

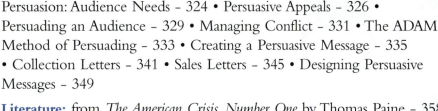
by the way...

One of the most important
workplace skills needed today is
problem-solving ability, according to
the U.S. Department of Labor.

© GETTY IMAGES/PHOTODISC. INC.

© GETTY IMAGES/PHOTODISC. INC.

© GETTY IMAGES/PHOTODISC, INC.

Connections Features

	Career Connection	Culture Connection	Ethics Connection	People Connection	Technology Connection
Chapter 1	p. 6	p. 12	pp. 8, 10, 16		p. 18
Chapter 2	p. 56	p. 31	p. 33	pp. 44, 45, 59	pp. 36, 38
Chapter 3	p. 73	p. 75	p. 78	p. 77	p. 87
Chapter 4	p. 125	p. 111	p. 123	p. 130	pp. 109, 124
Chapter 5	pp. 157, 158	p. 163	p. 146	p. 143	p. 156
Chapter 6	pp. 185, 192	p. 191		p. 181	p. 189
Chapter 7	p. 219	p. 222	p. 238	p. 228	p. 216
Chapter 8	p. 258	p. 262	p. 251	pp. 252, 268	p. 254
Chapter 9	p. 284		p. 302		p. 305
Chapter 10	p. 339		p. 330	pp. 348, 353	p. 325
Chapter 11	pp. 369, 381, 382 383, 384, 389	p. 379	p. 391	p. 393	
Chapter 12	pp. 412, 416	p. 420	pp. 414, 421	p. 418	p. 409
Chapter 13	p. 452	p. 443		p. 438	p. 441
Chapter 14	p. 473	p. 477		p. 482	pp. 480, 490
Chapter 15	pp. 506, 516	pp. 515, 521	p. 520		pp. 509, 513, 522
Chapter 16	pp. 539, 540, 546	p. 543	p. 555	pp. 547, 564	

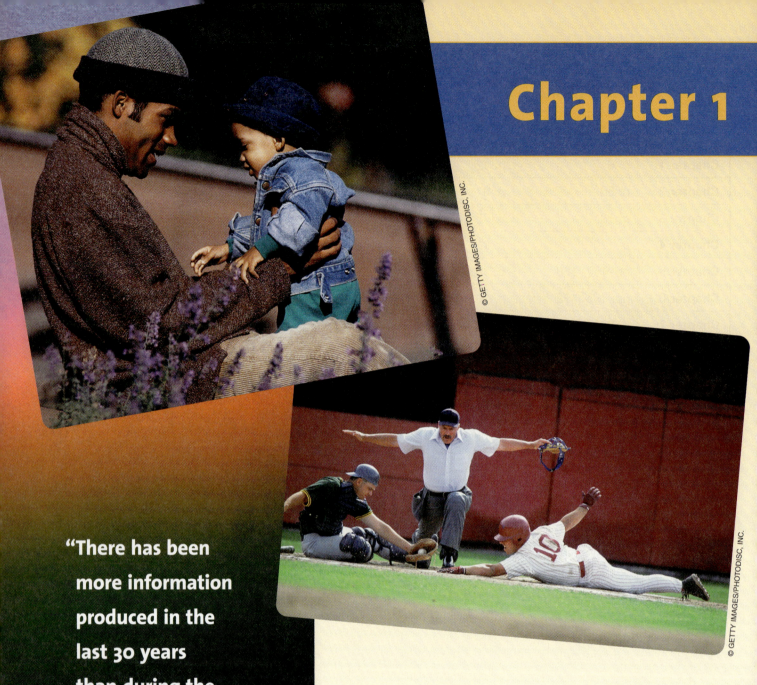

"There has been more information produced in the last 30 years than during the previous 5,000. . . . The information supply available to us doubles every five years."

— RICHARD SAUL WURMAN, *INFORMATION ANXIETY*

Zits / by Jim Borgman and Jerry Scott

Communicating at Work

Have you ever considered what life would be like without communication? No reassuring smiles, no love songs on the radio, no gripping novels, no comforting hugs, no friendly conversation. Fortunately, though, you can communicate. In fact, we spend most of our waking hours listening, speaking, reading, or writing.

Communication is the transfer or exchange of thoughts, information, ideas, and feelings by speech, writing, or signals between at least two people. Since today's workplace demands workers who are proficient in specialized communication skills, the quality of your communication will have a direct bearing on your success on the job. This book will help you learn to communicate successfully at work.

Communication Takes Many Forms

Dear Liz and Todd,

   Thank you so much for sending the lovely roses for my birthday. We had dinner guests the next day, and the roses made such a wonderful centerpiece. How thoughtful of you to remember that white roses have always been my favorite.

   Hope to see you soon.

      Love,
      Grandma

FIGURE 1-1 Thank-you note

The Last Rose of Summer

'Tis the last rose of summer
Left blooming alone;
All her lovely companions
Are faded and gone.
—Thomas Moore

FIGURE 1-2 Poem

At school, at work, and during leisure time, people encounter hundreds of forms of communication daily. The first voice Inez hears each day is her father calling, "Time to get up. You're late already." Then she turns on the television to catch the day's weather report. While eating breakfast, Inez scans the sports page. On her drive to school, as she listens to the radio, she is hardly aware of the many signs she passes along the roadside. Once at school, Inez talks with friends, listens to teachers, and views videos. She reads textbooks, assignment sheets, tests, and chalkboards. She writes in response to assignments in all of her classes. Since Inez is a culinary arts student, she often reads and follows recipes in her career/technical lab.

In her after-school job at Roy's Ribs, Inez greets customers, explains menu items to them, takes their orders, makes requests of the kitchen personnel, and responds to requests from her boss. After work, Inez discusses her day with her family, completes her homework, reads her e-mail, and talks to her friend on the phone before sleeping. Inez spends a great deal of time communicating.

by the way...

"On the job, the average employee spends about 45 percent of his communication time listening, about 30 percent speaking, about 16 percent reading, and about 9 percent writing."

GEORGE BELL,
CORPORATE CONSULTANT

Practice 1-1: Forms of Communication

teamwork

Whenever you see the heading "Practice," you will know that it's time for action—in the form of listening, speaking, or writing.

Examine the six documents shown in Figures 1-1 to 1-6. With a partner, complete *Student Workbook* page 1-A.

Decide what each document is about, who would read it, and why the person would read it. As you decide why the reader would read the document, consider the following questions:

• What does the writer expect the reader to know or think after reading the selection?

• How does the writer expect the reader to feel after reading the selection?

• Is the reader expected to take some action after reading? If so, what action?

Horticulture 102
Midterm Exam, page 2

II. Describe the procedure for feeding rosebushes. Include the following information: (a) why feeding is important and necessary, (b) what to feed, (c) types of feeding, (d) when to feed, (e) how to feed.

Plant food is a number of different elements, suspended in water, which enter the plant usually through the roots and leaves. Once inside, they are moved where they are wanted, mixed up, and altered into various chemical formulae. These elements should, in the normal life cycle, be returned to the soil through leaf fall or through the bodies of insects or other creatures that have been eating the plants. When back in the soil, the elements are recycled by the bacteria in the soil and rendered available to the plant again. However, in the normal rose bed, this cycle is interrupted (little or nothing returns to the soil), because we cut the flowers, clear weeds, and tidy up leaves. Therefore, rose growers must return the elements to the soil themselves.

A good time to put plenty of organic material into the soil is at the time of planting. After their first year, the plants should be fed annually, from early spring to high summer. When organic manure is used, it should be applied in spring, as it normally takes longer to act than inorganic fertilizer. The plants should be fed again when the first flower buds form and then after a couple of months to help the repeat blooming. Some growers feed the plants once a month.

Roses need to be fed when they show signs of deficiency in their growth or leaves. While inorganic manure is convenient and effective, some organic fertilizers are required to keep the soil in good condition. Manure should be applied during the season, early spring to high summer, except for the one purpose of helping to harden off soft growth in late summer or autumn with potassium and magnesium.

FIGURE 1-3　Horticulture class midterm exam

Garrett's Garden Nursery
983 Harrison Lane
St. Paul, Minnesota 55177-0123

Fax Cover Sheet

DATE:　June 24, 200-　　　　　TIME:　4:13 a.m.

TO:　Linda　　　　　　　　PHONE:　612-555-0104
　　　InterComm Industries　　FAX:　612-555-0100

FROM:　Kevin　　　　　　　　PHONE:　612-555-0180
　　　Garrett's Garden Nursery　FAX:　612-555-0181

RE:　Roses

C:　Brenda

Number of pages including cover sheet: 2

Message

As we discussed in our phone conversation on 6/22, I inspected the rosebushes growing on the southeast corner of your main building, removed several leaves from these bushes, and examined the leaves with a magnifying glass.

The roundish dark spots on the upper leaf surfaces indicate blackspot, a common fungal disease. This fungus is probably the most serious (and best-known) of the rose diseases. This is what's causing the lower leaves to yellow and fall off.

On Tuesday, Brenda will spray the affected plants with PlantBlite. One or two repeats of this treatment at two- to three-week intervals should solve the problem. Between treatments, be sure to remove infected leaves before they fall to the ground. Place them in a bag and burn them.

Thanks for letting me know about the problem so promptly. Don't hesitate to call again if you have any further questions. I have enclosed a chart showing symptoms and treatments of common rose diseases.

FIGURE 1-4　Fax cover sheet

Home Page of the Anyville Rose Society

Welcome to the home page of the Anyville Rose Society.

Our meetings occur on the first Thursday of each month at the Civic Center, 4534 East Elm Avenue—right next to Anyville Memorial Hospital—at 7 p.m. Here is a map of the meeting location. This month's speaker will be Clarence Johns, owner of CJ's Natural Gardening. His topic will be "Grin and Groom It."

The Anyville Rose Society was founded in 1950 and is affiliated with the American Rose Society (ARS). There are currently approximately 175 members. Our mission is to encourage interest in the rose, to promote its cultivation, and to disseminate information on its culture among any interested persons.

The society's fair garden committee garnered a second place for its entry in the Lake County Fair. Come take a look at the prizewinning entry.

Photo of garden

Here are several topics we hope you'll find helpful:

How to become a member
Calendar of events
How to grow roses in Lake County
What roses do well in Lake County
Where to see roses in Lake County
Links to other rose sites

We hope you enjoyed our home page. Send your questions or comments by e-mail to

Brittany Gibbs

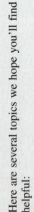

FIGURE 1-5 World Wide Web home page

The peculiar meiosis of the Caninae roses was worked out in detail and reported by Rauhala (8). In this particular group are found tetraploid 2n 5 28, pentaploid 2n 5 35, and hexaploid 2n 5 42 forms, but in all forms Rauhala found exactly seven pairs at meiosis, the remaining chromosomes behaving as univalents in the reduction division. In the first meiotic division the seven bivalents are arranged in a normal fashion on the equatorial plate with the univalents scattered at random over the spindle. According to Rauhala the bivalents separate normally at anaphase I and proceed to the poles, while the univalents remain behind on the spindle. Later the univalents divide and sister halves are distributed regularly to the two poles. Rauhala reported, however, that all chromosomes were included in the restitution nuclei. At second anaphase the seven chromosomes from the original bivalents divide and the sister halves are distributed to opposite poles. The univalents having divided previously at the first anaphase do not divide again and are left behind in the cytoplasm to form supernumerary microspores. Those microspores receiving exactly seven chromatics from the original bivalents are assumed to be the only functional ones, the others becoming abortive.

The reduction division in the macrospore mother cells is quite different. The bivalents behave as in the divisions of the microspore mother cell, but at anaphase I the univalents do not divide, but are all oriented on the micropylar side of the equatorial plate and are included in the micropylar nucleus at the end of the first division. The egg cell finally formed is a derivative of this micraylar nucleus and contains seven less than the somatic number of chromosomes. Thus, if self-pollination occurred the resulting progeny would contain the original somatic chromosome number of parent.

To explain this peculiar meiosis in the Caninae roses, Hill (4) advanced a genome theory, in which he postulated the existence in the genus Rosa of five differential diploid septets of chromosomes, which he designated as A, B, C, D, and E. These septets are supposed to segregate essentially as complete units, and the genome makeup of a species may supposedly be determined by a study of the morphological characters which are more or less specific for the various septets. It is further supposed that pairing at meiosis occurs between similar septets. According to Hill the Caninae roses have resulted from hybridization between species having only one septet in common, resulting in well-differentiated species having only seven pairs of homologous chromosomes.

Chapter 2—Rosa Rubiginosa and Its Hybrids   78

FIGURE 1-6 Textbook page

Communication at School

One document you and your partners analyzed for the last Practice was a school essay for a horticulture class. You have done similar activities hundreds of times in school, and your teachers have read your responses. Why would the horticulture teacher read a description of roses? Because he or she is unfamiliar with procedures for feeding roses? Why did your social studies teacher last year read your explanation of the causes of the Civil War? Because the teacher did not know the causes? Why did your algebra teacher check your answers on the final exam? To find out how to solve for x?

Of course, your teachers know how to feed roses, what the causes of the Civil War were, and how to solve for x. So why read your answers? To find out what *you* know or what *you* can do. *This type of communication **never** occurs at work.*

Communication at Work

Once hired, people at work do not speak or write to demonstrate their knowledge to someone who already knows the answers, for this would be a pointless waste of time. Rather, communication at work occurs because someone who does not already know the answers needs information or ideas.

Every day on the job, you will be called on not only to communicate what you know to others, but also to ask them for information and ideas. As long as you work with people, your ability to communicate will be important to your job success.

© GETTY IMAGES/PHOTODISC, INC.

Firefighters at the scene

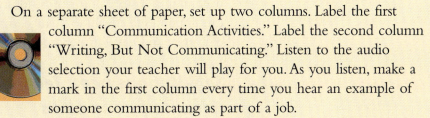

Practice 1–2: Communicating at Work

Let's see how a single incident can result in an assortment of communication activities.

On a separate sheet of paper, set up two columns. Label the first column "Communication Activities." Label the second column "Writing, But Not Communicating." Listen to the audio selection your teacher will play for you. As you listen, make a mark in the first column every time you hear an example of someone communicating as part of a job.

You will also hear some examples of people writing without really communicating with someone else. Make a mark in the second column for each of those examples.

Ch01–02.mp3

Career *Connection*

In legal proceedings, communication is vital. Imagine the frustration of not being able to communicate your rights because you speak another language in an English-speaking court. With no one to interpret for you, you risk being misunderstood—or you might be accused of a crime you didn't commit. These situations are a reality without a legal translator. If a foreign witness or defendant appears in court, nearly perfect communication of both languages is needed, requiring a court interpreter. The demand increases every year because of the large number of languages spoken in the United States—over 245 languages and dialects. The work requires concentration and patience, providing vital communication to guarantee legal rights. If you are fluent in English and another language, legal translation may be the career for you.

What Employers Are Looking For

ADMINISTRATIVE ASSIST.
Excellent Property Mgmt. Firm seeks Admin. Asst. to help mgmt. w/general support/secretarial duties & to control accounts receivable. Functions of the company include <u>weekly reports</u>, processing payments, & maintaining tenant files. <u>Excellent comm. skills & ability to multitask are a must</u>. Experience in Office required.

by the way...

Sign in a beauty salon window: "If you like our work, tell your friends; if you don't, tell us."

To understand how you can prepare yourself for the kind of job you want, it is useful to understand what employers are looking for in new employees. They are, of course, interested in job-specific skills. A chef, for example, needs to know how to cook and bake. An auto mechanic needs to know how to diagnose and repair vehicles.

But since jobs require more than job-specific skills and because jobs are constantly changing, employers are also looking for people with transferable skills. These skills allow employees to adapt to changes in the organization, changes in technology, and changes in the requirements of their jobs.

Knowing How to Learn

Knowing how to learn is the most basic skill because it is the key that unlocks future success. Competence in reading, writing, and math enables people to learn. The ability to use information technology is also quickly becoming a basic skill for most jobs. A person who knows how to learn can respond effectively to change, make improvements in quality and efficiency, and develop new ideas and techniques.

Self-Management, Teamwork, and Communication Skills

Employers want to hire dependable people who come to work on time every day, get along with others, solve problems, and take personal responsibility for the quality of their work. These people must know how to listen and express their thoughts clearly.

Employers want employees who will hear the key points that make up a customer's concerns and who can give an adequate spoken or written response. They look for people who know how to get along with customers, suppliers, coworkers, and supervisors. The number-one reason people are fired from their jobs is because they cannot get along with other employees.

When employers complain about the skills of entry-level workers, they mention problems with communication—writing, listening, reading, and speaking—more often than any others. Communicating effectively is clearly important to your career.

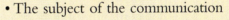

Practice 1–3: Communication Tasks

In a team of three or four students, identify a particular job in a field that interests you and write the job title at the top of a sheet of paper. Then list as many communication tasks as your team can think of that a person who holds this job is expected to perform. Be sure to include listening, speaking, reading, and writing activities. For each item on your list, consider the following factors:

• The subject of the communication

• The form of the communication

• The person or persons who will receive the communication

The following example lists a few of the communication tasks high school teachers must perform on the job.

High School Teacher

• Phone parents to report students' progress

• Explain assignments to students

• Write memos requesting advice from administrators

• Discuss problems with other teachers during committee meetings

• Write tests for students

• Explain procedures to new employees

• Communicate daily announcements to students

• Listen to a student explain that the computer ate his or her homework

• Complete forms requesting supplies

Employers want employees to listen to customers' concerns.

Elements of Communication at Work

MAINTENANCE ENGINEER

Experienced maintenance engineer needed for industrial park. Must have experience in all phases of building maintenance, including electrical systems. A working knowledge of rooftop HVAC units (and repair experience) is preferred.

The ideal candidate should be organized and self-motivated and should have good communication skills. We offer an excellent salary and benefits package.

The process of communicating at work involves five elements: the situation, the sender, the receiver, the message, and the purpose of the message. All of these elements are important, no matter what form your communication takes. A clear understanding of each element is important for communicating messages effectively at work.

The Situation

The **situation** that requires communication includes what is happening and where it is happening. In the audio selection about the classroom fire, the situation determined the types of communication activities that occurred.

Whether you work on a farm, in an office, in a shop, in a store, or on a construction site, you are constantly communicating. As the situation changes, the types of communication activities may change, too.

The Sender

© GETTY IMAGES/PHOTODISC, INC.

The sender's image should reflect positively on the organization that he or she represents.

The **sender** is the person who is speaking or writing. The background, experience, attitudes, and skills of the sender always affect the message.

At work, the sender is also concerned with the image that he or she projects. The ideal image should be one of competence and cooperation toward coworkers. With the public, the sender's image should reflect positively on the organization that he or she represents. Later chapters in this text will provide practice in communicating with a variety of readers and listeners.

The Receiver

The **receiver** of the message could be one person or thousands of people. In this text, the receiver or receivers of the message are the **audience**. The sender must be certain that the audience gets the right information at the right time in a clear and understandable form.

Audiences can be divided into two groups: **specialists** and the **general audience**. Specialists have interest, experience, and knowledge in a particular technical field. Your program teacher and your classmates in lab are specialists in your field. If you have a job in your chosen occupation, your boss and coworkers are probably specialists. Sometimes, though, you may find yourself working for someone who knows very little about what you do.

The general audience includes everyone else: clients, customers, patients, sales representatives, suppliers, and the general public. These people may have little understanding of the technical details associated with your work. They lack the interest, background, and knowledge to understand technical information.

When listening to the audio selection, did you notice any sender who at times fit into the general audience category and at other times fit into the specialist category? How might this occur?

The Message

The message is the information and ideas relayed by the sender to the audience. If communicated in an unclear manner, messages can cause workers to waste time, materials, and money. The message can take one or more forms. Some examples are as follows:

Radio announcements	Memorandums	Photographs
Conversations	Letters	Drawings
Phone calls	Manuals	Maps
Discussions	Catalogs	Graphs
Meetings	Books	Cartoons
Voice mail messages	Signs	Instant messages
Speeches	Pamphlets	DVDs
CDs	E-mail messages	Facial expressions

Practice 1–4: Types of Messages

Examine the list of types of messages above. Suggest a heading for each column that describes each of the three categories of messages. Below each heading, add five more types of messages.

career

Ethics *Connection*

Ethics are standards of right and wrong that guide our decision making. Your employer and your customers expect you to communicate in an ethical manner. People can use language to explain, clarify, and enlighten. They can also use language to mislead, cover up, and lie. While it is important that you carefully consider how you present yourself and your messages, it is equally important to do so honestly. Workplace messages need to be accurate. It is wrong to misrepresent yourself, your organization, your product, or your services. Lying is often illegal and always wrong. Stick with the truth, and your reputation for honesty and accuracy will add credibility to all of your messages.

QUALITY TECHNICIAN

A leader in the manufacture of built-in housing products is looking for a Quality Technician. Candidate must have the following: <u>excellent communication, organizational,</u> and troubleshooting skills. <u>Be detail-oriented with ability to work independently and with teams. Ability to translate goals into actionable plans</u>.

The Purpose

Messages that are sent to both specialists and general audiences at work can have many purposes. The purpose can be to:

• Socialize (small talk or inquiries about personal interests).

• Inform (about a situation, need, problem, or success).

• Persuade (to make a decision, revise an opinion, or take an action).

Most communication at work is informative or persuasive. Whatever form the communication takes, its purpose is always to make something happen.

Practice 1–5: Elements of Communication

In this Practice, you will listen for clues about the subject, sender, audience, form of message, and purpose of communication.

1. Listen again to the audio selection about the classroom fire, but this time listen for single and double beeps.

2. When you hear one beep, listen carefully to the information that follows. After two beeps, your teacher will pause the recording.

3. On *Student Workbook* page 1-B, record the subject, sender, audience, form of message, and purpose of the communication that is described after the single beep.

4. On *Student Workbook* page 1-C, for each message, indicate the sender, the receiver for a general audience, the receiver for a specialist audience, and the purpose of the message for each audience.

Ch01-05.mp3

by the way...

"Always do right—this will gratify some and astonish the rest."

MARK TWAIN, U.S. AUTHOR. PRESIDENT HARRY S TRUMAN HAD THIS REMARK FRAMED BEHIND HIS DESK IN THE OVAL OFFICE.

Effect of the Audience on the Message

Communication is effective if something happens as a result—but not just any something. The something that happens must accomplish the sender's purpose. If, for example, you fax a letter to a customer asking her to pay a bill immediately, and a check arrives two days later, you have communicated effectively.

Effective communication is an interactive process—that is, the sender acts upon or affects the audience and the audience in turn affects the sender. Once the sender has determined the content and purpose of the message, the sender must consider how to communicate effectively with his or her particular audience. To do this, **analyze** (study) the audience and then **adapt** (adjust) the message. Figure 1-7 illustrates the communication interaction.

The following questions indicate what information the sender must ask about the audience:

- What does the audience already know—and need to know?
- How many people are in the audience, and how old are they?
- How much education does the audience have?
- What is the audience's cultural background?
- What is the audience's attitude toward the subject?
- How much time can the audience spend reading or listening to the message?
- What is the audience supposed to do after receiving the message—pass it along to someone else?

An effective message will take into account all of these questions.

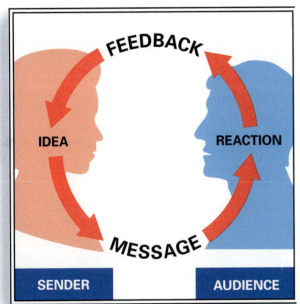

FIGURE 1-7   Effective communication is an interactive process.

Culture and Communication

In analyzing the audience, one important consideration is the audience's cultural background. Many factors shape cultural backgrounds. Some of them are:

- The region of the country or world where raised.
- The region of the country or world where the parents or grandparents were raised.
- Religion.
- Race.
- Gender.

by the way...

"Culture is the name for what people are interested in, their thoughts, their models, the books they read and the speeches they hear, their table-talk, gossip, controversies, historical sense and scientific training, the values they appreciate, the quality of life they admire. All communities have a culture. It is the climate of their civilization.

WALTER LIPPMANN, U.S. JOURNALIST

Culture *Connection*

If we could shrink the earth's population to a village of precisely 100 people, with all the existing percentages remaining the same there would be:

60 Asians
12 Europeans
15 from the Western Hemisphere
13 Africans

50 would be female
50 would be male

80 would be non-white
20 would be white

INTERIOR DESIGNER

Opportunity for full-time designer/salesperson who is fashion- and style-conscious, career-minded, and self-motivated. Must understand the importance of customer service, like working with and care about people, <u>possess the ability to communicate effectively and efficiently</u>, like to sell, and enjoy earning money.

- Age.
- Level of education.
- Workplace and type of job.
- Economic situation.

An individual's culture influences most areas of his or her life, including:

- Styles of food, clothing, and housing.
- Attitudes about family and friendship.
- Beliefs and values.
- Ways of celebrating holidays and other special occasions.
- Attitudes about work and school.
- Attitudes about roles of men and women.
- Reactions to technology.
- Feelings about personal space.
- Use of body language.
- Style of communication.

You will likely find yourself working with people from many different cultures. While your own culture seems right and normal to you, the behavior of people from other cultures may sometimes seem strange or wrong. People from other cultures may communicate differently than you do and may respond differently to what you write or say.

© CORBIS

Culture may influence styles of clothing.

To learn about other cultures, sample foods at ethnic or international restaurants.

Be aware that the words you choose and the communication styles you employ are a result of cultural conditioning. How you phrase your messages can communicate a great deal more than just technical information; age, gender, race, and ethnic and other cultural biases can destroy your attempts to communicate. To learn about other cultures, try the following:

• Read the literature of other cultures.

• Sample foods at ethnic or international restaurants.

• Locate and read magazines or newspapers from other countries.

• Examine your own cultural stereotypes, which are unfair generalizations that lead to misunderstanding.

• Keep an open mind when interacting with people from other cultures and make an effort to learn from them.

Practice 1–6: Communicating Across Cultures

Every language has **idioms**, phrases or sentences that cannot be understood literally. Even if the audience knows the meanings of all of the words in a phrase or sentence, the meaning may still be unclear. A phrase or sentence of this type is said to be *idiomatic*.

Using idioms with audiences with different cultural backgrounds can lead to misunderstanding. Would a person who is new to the United States know, for instance, that a road hog has nothing to do with farm animals? Consider how the word *fall* changes meaning in the following expressions:

Ch01-06.doc

fall apart	fall down on the job	fall out
fall asleep	fall in love	fall short
fall back	fall off	fall through
fall behind		

Explain how a person who learned English from a textbook might interpret the following idiomatic sentences:

1. Larry <u>dug up</u> a date for the wedding.

2. The convertible <u>cut me off</u> just before the exit.

3. I am <u>crazy about</u> chocolate.

4. Sean <u>aced</u> the test without cracking a book.

5. The <u>old heap broke down</u> in the middle of the desert.

6–10. Now list five common idioms that you use in your conversation. Explain how that same person might misinterpret your words.

Adapt the Communication for the Audience

The audience understands an effective message readily. If a message in the workplace can be understood in more than one way, it is ineffective.

SUPPORTED-LIVING MANAGER
Excellent opportunity to assist individuals with MR/DD in community living and oversee service delivery and management of individual needs. Must <u>be team-oriented</u> and flexible and have <u>above-average communication skills</u>. High school diploma, minimum 1 yr. experience with MR/DD, and own transportation required.

ELECTRICAL TECHNICIAN
Immediate opening for a technically oriented person wanting hands-on responsibility in a growing organization. Position requires knowledge of control circuits, some PLC technology, and agency interface (i.e., UL, CSA, & FM) along with <u>strong communication skills for customer service duties</u>. A degree would be a plus. Some travel required. Opening is

The message must be adjusted, or adapted, to suit the audience in the way that a car is customized to suit its driver. Once the writer or speaker has decided on the message and its purpose and has analyzed the audience, decisions must be made about how best to adapt the message. The writer or speaker must consider these questions:

• What form should this message take?

• How will the audience use the message?

• What vocabulary will the audience understand?

• Will the audience have the desire to read or listen, or will I have to get his or her attention?

• Will an illustration or another visual help the reader understand?

• How can I design a user-friendly page?

• How should the information be organized?

• How can I convince the audience to do what I want?

Practice 1–7: Adapting Your Message

Complete this Practice on your own.

1. Write three sentences describing your personal characteristics to a five-year-old child you are babysitting.

2. Write three sentences describing your personal characteristics to someone you would like to date.

3. Write three sentences describing your personal characteristics to a prospective employer.

4. How did the audience and purpose affect your choice of words and details and your sentence structure?

Communicating Messages Effectively

The key to effective communication is *thinking*. In fact, learning to think effectively will automatically improve your communication. No one can see inside your head. Therefore, the only way to let people know what you're thinking is by communicating with them. If your message is unclear, the audience will assume that your thinking is unclear. If it is, you need to straighten out your thinking; if it isn't, you need to straighten out your communication.

The three main stages of the writing process are **planning**, **writing**, and **revising**. (See Figure 1-8.) More time is spent on the first and third stages than on the second.

FIGURE 1-8 The three main stages of the writing process

The Planning Stage

Unless you are giving a prepared speech, when you speak, you voice your thoughts almost as quickly as they occur to you. You have little time to plan your message and no opportunity to change what you have already said. One of the many advantages of a written message is that you can spend time planning it and can then change what you have written *before* you send the message—your message can say exactly what you want it to say. Writing is too complex a process to try to do everything at once. Get your planning out of the way before writing begins. (See Figure 1-9.) Planning a document requires the following:

- Analyzing the audience
- Determining the purpose
- Collecting information
- Selecting and organizing information

FIGURE 1-9 The planning stage

The Writing Stage

The secret to success in the writing stage is to do it wrong the first time. Surprised? Many people assume that a good writer probably gets it right the first time. Wrong. Even professional writers prepare many drafts with the help of editors and proofreaders. For the first draft, just write without breaks. Stopping to edit while you draft breaks the train of thought and keeps you from being as smart or creative as you could be. As you write, don't stop to read what you've written. If you don't know how to spell a word, just approximate and fix it later. If you don't know the right word, use the wrong word. Just keep writing. Later on, you can correct mistakes, add or delete text, and reorganize. (See Figure 1-10.)

FIGURE 1-10 The writing stage

Ethics *Connection*

THE TEN COMMANDMENTS FOR COMPUTER ETHICS

from the Computer Ethics Institute, 1998

1. Thou shalt not use a computer to harm other people.
2. Thou shalt not interfere with other people's computer work.
3. Thou shalt not snoop around in other people's files.
4. Thou shalt not use a computer to steal.
5. Thou shalt not use a computer to bear false witness.
6. Thou shalt not use or copy software for which you have not paid.
7. Thou shalt not use other people's computer resources without authorization.
8. Thou shalt not appropriate other people's intellectual output.
9. Thou shalt think about the social consequences of the program you write.
10. Thou shalt use a computer in ways that show consideration and respect.

© Copyright 1998, Arlene Rinaldi + Florida Atlantic University

by the way...

"Get it down. Take chances. It may be bad, but it's the only way you can do anything really good."

WILLIAM FAULKNER, U.S. NOVELIST

FIGURE 1-11   The revising stage

The Revising Stage

Preparing an effective written message requires editing: checking, proofreading, and revising. (See Figure 1-11.) If you write using a word processing program, the editing process requires much less effort. With only a few keystrokes, such a program will find and help you correct most spelling errors and other types of errors. You do not have to copy the whole message over again. Just change the words, sentences, or paragraphs until you are satisfied that the document says exactly what you mean. Learn to use a computer.

You might not be the best judge of your own writing. As you first read through it, it will, of course, make sense to you. Let some time pass between writing the first draft and editing it in order to gain critical distance.

Read the message aloud to yourself. It may feel silly, but a sentence that looks fine to the eye may sound awkward or unclear to your ear. Learn to proofread with your ears.

Consulting dictionaries, reference books, and web sites on writing style can be helpful. Studying well-written examples is useful, too. If, for instance, you are preparing a resume, examine other people's resumes as you plan your own.

Luckily, you are rarely alone as you write. Consult experts, such as your teachers, to make sure that your facts are correct. Check the accuracy of your message against information in textbooks, manuals, and web sites. Ask other students to help proofread your work. It is easier to spot errors in other people's writing than it is to spot them in your own.

Does Spelling Count?

Earlier in this chapter, you were told that an effective message is one that accomplishes its purpose. In fact, if you write a note to your boss asking permission to leave work early tomorrow so that your dentist can treat your toothache and permission is granted, you have indeed communicated successfully—even if your message contains a spelling error.

A poorly written message, however, can give the audience the impression that the writer is incompetent or uncaring. If you are viewed as incompetent and uncaring in one area, that perception could affect the audience's overall impression of you. Since your message is important, or you wouldn't have bothered to write it, you want it to be taken seriously.

A newspaper story reported that a group of students operated a thriving business manufacturing and selling fake driver's licenses. Eventually, they were caught and arrested. Why? Because they had spelled the name of the state incorrectly on the fake licenses! Yes, spelling does count—even for lawbreakers!

by the way...

Ernest Hemingway, a great American novelist, rewrote the last chapter of his novel A Farewell to Arms 44 times! When asked why, he said, "To get the words right." Rewriting does not mean failure; it often means success.

by the way...

"My spelling is Wobbly. It's good spelling but it Wobbles, and the letters get in the wrong places."

A. A. MILNE, BRITISH AUTHOR. SPOKEN BY WINNIE-THE-POOH, IN *WINNIE-THE-POOH*

Practice 1–8: Using a Spelling Checker

teamwork

Most computers have a spelling checker. This type of program checks every word in a document against its dictionary database. If the spelling checker finds a match, it goes on to check the next word. If the spelling checker does not find a match, it highlights the word and presents the user with options to ignore the misspelling, to replace it with one of several suggested spellings, or to key the correct word.

Spelling checkers are useful, but not foolproof. For example, most names and many technical terms are not in general dictionaries and, therefore, are highlighted as misspelled by the spelling checker. Compound words, such as *sunshine*, misspelled as *sun shine*, will not be caught by the spelling checker. Also, homonym errors, such as writing *affect* when you mean *effect*, may escape the spelling checker. So it is necessary to proofread for spelling errors even if you use a spelling checker.

1. In a team of three students, list 30 or more words that would stump a spelling checker program.

2. The spelling checker cannot distinguish between similarly sounding words or between **homophones**, words that sound alike but are spelled differently. An example of a pair of homophones is *their* and *they're*. The first word is a possessive pronoun; the second word is a contraction. Choosing the correct word is another way to overcome a limitation of the spelling checker. Using *Student Workbook* page 1-D, choose the correct word and justify your answer.

Technology *Connection*

In addition to spelling checkers, most word processing programs have grammar checkers. The user can choose a set of standards for checking material, such as a strict check of all grammar rules. The grammar checker locates some spelling, punctuation, grammar, style, and word choice errors.

Still, people do a better job of proofreading. Grammar checkers can locate only about 33 percent of writing errors. Beware, because a sentence that looks just fine to a grammar checker may make no sense at all. For example, a grammar checker found no errors in the following sentence:

Mary frequently dusts her January loudly with a Volkswagen.

While it makes sense to use a grammar checker, do not rely on it. Trust your eyes and ears and the opinions of other people who read what you write.

LANDSCAPE, MAINTENANCE, SUPER, CREW LEADERS, ASST. CREW LEADERS, & TECHNI-CIANS

- Excellent pay.
- Vacation.
- Holidays.
- Benefits.
- 401K.
- Knowledge of turf, turf applications, & turf equipment.
- Good communication skills.
- Ability to supervise 2 to 5 people.
- Horticulture education and background a plus.
- Valid driver's license.
- Full-time or part-time positions.

MEDICAL ASSISTANT

Challenging FT position available in our fast-paced multi-physician office. Requires physician office experience and completion of medical assistant training program or LPN license. Certification to initiate venipuncture and operate physician office radiology equip-ment is preferred. Candidates should possess basic computer skills and demonstrate excellent communication skills.

Does Punctuation Count?

Punctuation in writing is like expression in speaking. A misplaced comma may change the meaning of a sentence by causing the reader to pause in the wrong place. Consider this sentence:

Woman without her man is nothing.

What does this sentence mean? Now read the same sentence with punctuation added.

Woman—without her, man is nothing.

Did adding punctuation affect the meaning? Punctuation, too, counts.

Practice 1–9: Using Punctuation to Convey Meaning

Write each sentence below twice, each time with different punctuation, to convey two different meanings.

1. No children are allowed in the pool
2. Juan thinks his teacher is a genius
3. Ms. Krause your client just came in
4. Aaron my boss always puts the customer first

Proofreading Marks

Proofreading marks are symbols or codes that indicate what kind of changes need to be made to writing. These symbols allow you to mark needed changes without doing much writing on the draft. These standardized codes help the writer understand your marks. A list of proofreading marks appears on page 573 of this text.

Practice 1–10: Using Proofreading Marks

The opening paragraph for an article about netiquette needs revision. Rewrite it, using proofreading marks to guide your revision.

Netiquette and the Culture of Cyberspace

"When thou enter a city abide by its customs."

—The *Talmud**

When the Internet first began, there were only a few thousand computers connected to it. Cyber space (a world created by computers) was populated by a relatively small group of people as with every other group of people, they developed their own Culture, along with guidelines to govern the behavior of thier citizens. These guide lines are know as netiquette, a combination of the words *network* and *etiquette*. Now that a lot of people are "surfing the net, we should all know the basics of netiquette so we can avoid some misunderstandings offense, and embarrasment

*The *Talmud* is the collection of ancient Rabbinic writings consisting of the *Mishnah* and the *Gemara*, constituting the basis of religious authority in Orthodox Judaism.

Now use proofreading marks to indicate needed revisions to the rest of the article shown on *Student Workbook* page 1-E.

Summary

review and research activities visit communicating.swlearning.com

Communication is the transfer or exchange of thoughts, information, ideas, and feelings by speech, writing, or signals between at least two people. Follow these guidelines whenever you communicate at work:

- Consider how the situation, the sender, the audience, and the purpose affect messages.

- Carefully analyze the audience and adapt the message for the audience and purpose.

- Plan and edit all written communication.

Works Cited

"The Global Village." *The Global Village: If We Could Shrink the Earth* http://davidpbrown.co.uk/nota-bene/the-global-village.html

UN Department of Economic and Social Affairs, Population Division, 2000

U.S. Bureau of the Census International Data Base, 2001

literature

Overview

Being familiar with the type of reading and writing done in the English classroom, you note that major differences exist between literature and technical writing.

A person reads literature on his or her own terms. For example, one reader's experience differs from another reader's, which allows for different interpretations of a piece of literature. The interpretations will have similarities, but because of the readers' experiences, interpretations may differ.

Each genre (poetry, drama, short story, novel, essay) serves as a lens for observing, recording, and examining the world.

The relationship between the literary text and its meaning or interpretation is not as direct as that required by technical writing. For example, consider a train schedule (technical writing), which records "The B train from Spencer arrives at 12:05 A.M." This statement has only one interpretation. An interpretation that the B train from Spencer arrives at 12:50 A.M. is wrong and may lead to pointless standing around at the railway station. Ambiguity (having two or more meanings) in literary selections is accepted and allows the reader several interpretations. Different interpretations of a piece of technical writing can cause confusion and damage business relationships.

Literature takes a nugget of information and expands it into an unlimited amount of meaning. Technical writing takes an unlimited amount of meaning and reduces it into a nugget of information.

Future Tense

Gary couldn't wait for tenth grade to start so he could strut his sentences, parade his paragraphs, renew his reputation as the top creative writer in school. . . . his head cocked alertly as Dr. Proctor introduced the new Honors English teacher, Mr. Smith. Here was the person he'd have to impress. . . . The man was hard to describe. . . .

"If he was a color he'd be beige," said Gary. "If he was a taste he'd be water. If he was a sound he'd be a low hum." . . .

"Describe a Typical Day at School," said Gary, trying unsuccessfully to mimic Mr. Smith's bland voice. "That's about as exciting as tofu."

"A real artist," said Dani, "accepts the commonplace as a challenge."

That night, hunched over his humming electric typewriter, Gary wrote a description of a typical day at school from the viewpoint of a new teacher who was seeing everything for the first time, who took nothing for granted.

> "A real artist accepts the commonplace as a challenge."

He described the shredded edges of the limp flag outside the dented front door, the worn flooring where generations of kids had nervously paced outside the principal's office, the nauseatingly sweet pipe-smoke seeping out of the teachers' lounge.

And then, in the last line, he gave the composition that extra twist, the little kicker on which his reputation rested. He wrote:

> The new teacher's beady little eyes missed nothing, for they were the optical recorders of an alien creature who had come to Earth to gather information.

The next morning, when Mr. Smith asked for a volunteer to read aloud, Gary was on his feet and moving toward the front of the classroom before Mike Chung got his hand out of his pocket.

The class loved Gary's composition. . . .

Gary felt good until he got the composition back. Along the margin, in perfect script, Mr. Smith had written:

You can do better.

"How would he know?" Gary complained on the way home.

"You should be grateful," said Dani. "He's pushing you to the farthest limits of your talent." . . .

Gary rewrote the composition, expanded it, complicated it, thickened it. Not only was this new teacher an alien, he was part of an extraterrestrial conspiracy to take over the earth. Gary's final sentence was:

> Every iota of information, fragment of fact, morsel of minutiae sucked up by those vacuuming eyes was beamed directly into a computer circling the planet. The data would eventually become a program that would control the mind of every school kid on earth.

Gary showed the new draft to Dani before class. He stood on tiptoes so he could read over her shoulder. Sometimes he wished she were shorter, but mostly he wished he were taller.

"What do you think?"

"The assignment was to describe a typical day," said Dani. "This is off the wall."

He snatched the papers back.

"Creative writing means creating." He walked away, hurt and angry. . . . Gary's rewrite came back the next day marked:

Improving. Try again.

(cont'd on next page)

Saturday he locked himself in his room after breakfast and rewrote the rewrite. He carefully selected his nouns and verbs and adjectives. He polished and arranged them in sentences like a jeweller strings pearls. . . .

Gary wrote:

> The alien's probes trembled as he read the student's composition. Could that skinny, bespectacled Earthling really suspect its extraterrestrial identity? Or was his composition merely the result of a creative thunderstorm in a brilliant young mind?

Before Gary turned in his composition on Monday morning, he showed it to Mike Chung. He should have known better.

"You're trying too hard," chortled Chung. "Truth is stranger than fiction." . . .

Mr. Smith handed back Gary's composition that next day marked:

See me after school.

© GETTY IMAGES/PHOTODISC, INC.

Gary was nervous all day. What was there to talk about? Maybe Mr. Smith hated science fiction. One of those traditional English teachers. Didn't understand that science fiction could be literature. *Maybe I can educate him,* thought Gary.

When Gary arrived at the English office, Mr. Smith seemed nervous, too. He kept folding and unfolding Gary's composition.

"Where do you get such ideas?" he asked in his monotone voice.

Gary shrugged. "They just come to me."

"Alien teachers. Taking over the minds of schoolchildren." Mr. Smith's empty eyes were blinking. "What made you think of that?"

"I've always had this vivid imagination."

Mr. Smith looked relieved. "I guess everything will work out." He handed back Gary's composition. "No more fantasy, Gary. Reality." . . .

The words flowed out of Gary's mind and through his fingers and out of the machine onto sheets of paper. He wrote and rewrote until he felt the words were exactly right:

> With great effort, the alien shut down the electrical panic impulses coursing through its system and turned on Logical Overdrive. There were two possibilities:

> 1. This high school boy was exactly what he seemed to be, a brilliant, imaginative, apprentice best-selling author and screenwriter, or,

> 2. He had somehow stumbled onto the secret plan, and he would have to be either enlisted into the conspiracy or erased off the face of the planet.

First thing in the morning, Gary turned in his new rewrite to Mr. Smith. A half hour later, Mr. Smith called Gary out of Spanish. There was no expression on his regular features. He said, "I'm going to need some help with you."

Cold sweat covered Gary's body as Mr. Smith grabbed his arm and led him to the new vice-principal. She read the composition while they waited. Gary got a good look at her for the first time. Ms. Jones was . . . just there. She looked as though she'd been manufactured to fit her name. Average. Standard. Typical. The cold sweat turned into goose pimples.

© THINKSTOCK

How could he have missed the clues? Smith and Jones were aliens! He had stumbled on their secret and now they'd have to deal with him. . . .

Ms. Jones ignored him. "In my opinion, Mr. Smith, you are overreacting. This sort of nonsense"—she waved Gary's composition—"is the typical response of an overstimulated adolescent to the mixture of reality and fantasy in an environment dominated by manipulative music, television, and films. Nothing for us to worry about." . . .

"I'm not going to do anything this time," said Ms. Jones, "but you must promise to write only about what you know."

"Or I'll have to fail you," said Mr. Smith.

"For your own good," said Ms. Jones. "Writing can be very dangerous."

"Especially for writers," said Mr. Smith, "who write about things they shouldn't." . . .

Jim Baggs was practicing head fakes— in the hallway. He slammed Gary into the wall with a hip block. "How's it going, Dude?" he asked, helping Gary up.

"Aliens," gasped Gary. "Told me no more science fiction."

"They can't treat a star writer like that," said Jim. "See what the head honcho's got to say." He grabbed Gary's wrist and dragged him into the principal's office.

"What can I do for you, boys?" boomed Dr. Proctor.

> "Writing can be very dangerous."

"They're messing with his moves, Doc," said Jim Baggs. "You got to let the aces run their races." . . .

"From the beginning," ordered Dr. Proctor. He nodded sympathetically as Gary told the entire story. . . .

(cont'd on next page)

"You really have a way with words, Gary. I should have sensed you were on to something."

Gary's stomach flipped. "You really think there could be aliens trying to take over earth?"

"Certainly," said Dr. Proctor, matter-of-factly. "Earth is the ripest plum in the universe."

Gary wasn't sure if he should feel relieved that he wasn't crazy or be scared out of his mind. He took a deep breath to control the quaver in his voice, and said: "I spotted Smith and Jones right away. They look like they were manufactured to fit their names. Obviously humanoids. Panicked as soon as they knew I was on to them."

Dr. Proctor chuckled and shook his head. "No self-respecting civilization would send those two stiffs to Earth."

"They're not aliens?" He felt relieved and disappointed at the same time.

"I checked them out myself," said Dr. Proctor. "Just two average, standard, typical human beings, with no imagination, no creativity."

"So why'd you hire them?"

Dr. Proctor laughed. "Because they'd never spot an alien. No creative imagination. That's why I got rid of the last vice-principal and the last Honors English teacher. They were giving me odd little glances when they thought I wasn't looking. After ten years on your planet, I've learned to smell trouble."

> *"And I can't wait to hear what the folks back home say when you read it to them."*

Gary's spine turned to ice and dripped down the backs of his legs. "You're an alien!"

"Great composition," said Dr. Proctor, waving Gary's paper. "Grammatical, vividly written, and totally accurate." . . .

"And I can't wait to hear what the folks back home say when you read it to them," said Dr. Proctor.

"I made it all up." Gary had the sensation of rocketing upward. "I made up the whole . . ."

—Robert Lipsyte

Start-Up: The excerpt from Robert Lipsyte's short story is an example of ambiguity in literature. As a class, discuss different possible interpretations of the story.

Connection: The memo in Figure 1–12 is intentionally unclear and ambiguous. Rewrite it so that there is no misunderstanding.

TO: The Person in Charge

FROM: Department Supervisor

DATE: July 3, 200-

SUBJECT: TEMPERATURE IN OFFICES

Several staff members have complained recently about the temperatures in their offices.

I want you to do something about them.

Maybe you could set them at comfortable levels. They should turn on early in the morning and turn off after everyone has left for the day. Be sure the climate in the offices is suitable for all.

FIGURE 1-12: An unclear memo

John Coleman, the author of this nonfictional account, had a distinguished career as a teacher at the Massachusetts Institute of Technology, a college president, and a board member of several major companies before he left academics and joined the blue-collar world.

Feeling that there was a lack of understanding between the white-collar worker and the blue-collar worker, Coleman worked in sewers, dug ditches, and collected garbage.

This journal account tells of the author's experience of being undeservedly degraded by a waitress with whom he worked.

"From Man to Boy" from Blue-Collar Journal

Tuesday, March 27

One of the waitresses I find hard to take asked me at one point today, "Are you the boy who cuts the lemons?"

"I'm the man who does," I replied.

"Well, there are none cut." There wasn't even a hint that she heard my point.

> "Are you the boy who cuts the lemons?"
> "I'm the man who does."

Dana, who has cooked here for twelve years or so, heard that exchange. "It's no use, Jack," he said when she was gone. "If she doesn't know now, she never will." There was a trace of a smile on his face, but it was a sad look all the same.

In that moment, I learned the full thrust of those billboard ads of a few years ago that said, "Boy. Drop out of school and that's what they'll call you the rest of your life." I had read those ads before with a certain feeling of pride; education matters, they said, and that gave a lift to my field. Today I saw them saying something else. They were untrue in part; it turns out that you'll get called "boy" if you do work that others don't respect even if you have a Ph.D. It isn't education that counts, but the job in which you land. And the ads spoke too of a sad resignation about the world. They assumed that some people just won't learn respect for others, so you should adapt yourself to them. Don't try to change them. Get the right job and they won't call you boy any more. They'll save it for the next man.

> Get the right job and they won't call you boy any more.

It isn't just people like this one waitress who learn slowly, if at all. Haverford College has prided itself on being a caring, considerate community in the Quaker tradition for many long years. Yet when I came there I soon learned that the cleaning women in the dormitories were called "wombats" by all the students. No one seemed to know where the name came from or what connection, if any, it had with the dictionary definition. The *American College Dictionary* says a wombat is "any of three species of burrowing marsupials of Australia . . . somewhat resembling ground hogs." The name was just one of Haverford's unexamined ways of doing things.

It didn't take much persuasion to get the name dropped. Today there are few students who remember it at all. But I imagine the cleaning women remember it well.

Certainly I won't forget being called a boy today.

—John Coleman

Start-Up: Krazy Kousins Pizzeria has two male and two female servers. During business hours, these employees are responsible for waiting on tables, keeping the salad bar stocked, filling up salt and pepper shakers and other condiment jars, and rolling silverware in napkins. Once he serves his customers, Employee A does not return to the table to give additional service, uses other employees' rolled silverware, seldom refills the containers on the salad bar, and neglects refilling the condiment containers. The other servers have informed the manager of the problem and asked her advice.

In the past, Employee A has done a good job for the pizzeria, but he is now having personal problems. Although the manager cannot permit his work habits to destroy the interpersonal relationships among her other employees, she also wants to keep a previously good employee from quitting his job. She needs to handle this problem in a positive but firm manner.

Connection: In groups of three, make a list of the problem(s). Brainstorm to find several solutions and to determine what advice the manager could give to improve Employee A's work habits.

Write a short skit to illustrate what the manager would say and how the employee might respond. Use a dialogue format and include stage directions (descriptions of the characters and settings, as well as directions regarding how the characters would move and what they would be doing).

Working with Literature: Refer to *Student Workbook* page 1-F for an activity on interpersonal relationships in the workplace.

© GETTY IMAGES/PHOTODISC, INC.

"Words can have no single fixed meaning. Like wayward electrons, they can spin away from their initial orbit and enter a wider magnetic field. No one owns them or has a proprietary right to dictate how they will be used."

—DAVID LEHMAN, U.S. POET, EDITOR, CRITIC

Sniglet (snig' lit)

Any word that doesn't appear in the dictionary, but should

FLOPCORN (flop' korn) n. The unpopped kernels at the bottom of the cooker.

McMONIA (muk moan' ee uh) n. (Chemical symbol: Mc) Noxious gas created by fast-food employee mopping under your table while you're eating.

MAYPOP (may' pahp) n. A bald tire.

FONESIA (fo nee' zhuh) n. The affliction of dialing a phone number and forgetting whom you were calling just as they answer.

Communicating Definitions

Defining words is not a new activity for you. In fact, since third grade,

you have been asked by your teachers to give

definitions of vocabulary words in English class,

science class, math class—all of your classes. Why did

your teachers ask you to define these words?

Because it is impossible to discuss literature, biology, geometry, or any field of study without understanding the vocabulary of that discipline.

Defining at Work

Since you have begun a study of a particular occupational field, you have spent time learning the vocabulary of your work. Each field has its own specialized language, and you must make the language a part of your own vocabulary to work effectively in that field.

Simply knowing your occupation's vocabulary is not enough. You must use it to communicate requests, suggestions, explanations, instructions, and descriptions to others. This would be easy if everyone you had to communicate with knew your specialized vocabulary, but they often do not.

If you work in a shop, you must communicate with coworkers, trainees, supervisors, managers, office workers, suppliers, and customers. If you work in a medical office, you must communicate with doctors, nurses, technicians, and patients, some of whom may be small children. If you work in a business office, you must communicate with managers, clients and customers, salespeople, and other office workers.

Various audiences have various needs for information and may or may not understand specialized vocabulary. Yet you must communicate effectively with all of them.

Practice 2–1: Uses for Definitions

Definitions rarely stand alone; they are usually part of a longer communication. For example, directions for rebuilding an engine may begin with definitions of technical terms so readers understand those terms when they encounter them while following the directions. Working with two or three other students, list as many types of business and technical communication as you can that include definitions.

Why Defining Is Necessary

You can assume that your reader or listener will understand most of the words you use exactly the way you mean them. However, if a word can be understood more than one way or if you are using a technical term, you must provide a definition unless you are certain that your audience will not misunderstand.

Culture *Connection*

A **dialect** is a style of language that is distinctive to a particular region. Many thousands of differences in words, pronunciations, and phrases characterize the various dialects of the United States. For example, every region has words that are peculiar to its dialect. Children learn these words at home rather than at school; the words are part of the children's oral rather than written culture. Do you know what any of the following words mean? You probably won't find them in the dictionary. *Turn the page upside down to read their definitions.*

1. mulligrubs	5. Juneteenth	9. lanai
2. neb-nose	6. noshery	10. Oklahoma rain
3. alamagoozlum	7. bizmaroon	11. bumfuzzled
4. chizzywink	8. faunch	12. off-brand

1. unwellness	5. emancipation day	9. porch
2. inquisitive person	6. snack bar	10. sandstorm
3. maple syrup	7. bullfrog	11. confused
4. large mosquito	8. to rant and rave	12. unusual

Words with Multiple Meanings

Many words have more than one meaning. If you think your audience might misunderstand the meaning you intend for a word, provide a definition.

For example, the dictionary lists 20 definitions for the word *stock*. People in different occupations use this word in different ways.

- To a merchant, stock is goods kept on hand.
- To an economist, stock is a share owned in a company.
- To a nautical engineer, a stock is the crosspiece on the end of an anchor's shaft.

- To a farmer, stock is all of the animals kept on the farm.
- To a geologist, stock is the main body of intrusive igneous rock of which less than 40 miles is exposed.
- To a chef, stock is broth used as a base for soups, gravies, and sauces.
- To a botanist, stock is a plant from which cuttings are taken.

To communicate effectively, the chef and the botanist must agree on which definition of stock to use.

Practice 2–2: Words with Multiple Meanings

Words that have more than one meaning can be easily misunderstood. The three common words defined below have some uncommon meanings. With a partner, analyze the definitions listed for each word. For each definition, give the job title of a person who might use it.

1. valve
   a. A membranous structure in a hollow organ or passage, as in an artery or a vein, that folds or closes to prevent the return flow of the body fluid passing through it.
   b. Any of various devices that regulate the flow of gases, liquids, or loose materials through piping or through apertures by opening, closing, or obstructing ports or passageways.
   c. A device in a brass wind instrument that permits change in pitch by a rapid varying of the air column in a tube.
   d. One of the paired, hinged shells of certain mollusks and of brachiopods. The entire one-piece shell of a snail and certain other mollusks.

2. chip
   a. A small piece, as of wood or glass, broken or cut off.
   b. A minute slice of a semiconducting material, such as silicon or germanium, processed to have specified electrical characteristics, especially before it is developed into an electronic component or integrated circuit.
   c. To chop or cut with an ax or another implement.
   d. To make a short, lofted golf stroke, used in approaching the green.

3. draft
   a. A device that regulates the flow or circulation of air.
   b. A written order directing the payment of money from an account or a fund.
   c. A preliminary outline of a plan, document, or picture.
   d. To drive close behind another vehicle to take advantage of the reduced air pressure in its wake.

Ethics *Connection*

Would you ever

- Use the office copier to make ten copies of your resume?
- Take home five pens that your employer purchased to give to regular customers?
- Buy a leather jacket for your neighbor, using your employee discount?
- Make a long-distance call to wish your mom a happy birthday, using the office phone?
- Call in sick on a nice spring day so you can go kayaking?
- Ask another employee to clock out for you so you can leave 20 minutes early?
- Embezzle $5,000 from the company accounts?

Which of the above actions would you define as theft? Chances are your employer defines *all* of them as theft. Both large and small losses to business add up. Statistics on employee crime from the FBI, U.S. Department of Commerce, and U.S. Chamber of Commerce show the following:

- One-half of all employees admit to stealing.
- Six percent of a typical business's profits are lost annually to employee crime.
- Between 20 and 30 percent of all business failures are attributed to employee theft.

If your employer loses profits or goes out of business because of employee theft, your job will be affected even if you don't steal. If your employer made an anonymous hotline available so employees could report theft, would you use it?

Abstract Ideas

A **concrete** word stands for something that can be seen, felt, weighed, or measured. An **abstract** word stands for an idea or a quality. *Sweetness* is abstract. *Sugar* is concrete.

The meaning of an abstract word shifts according to its use, which often leads to misunderstanding. For example, your boss advises you to "straighten up." Do you tuck in your shirt? Clean your desk? Report for work on time? Improve your posture?

You can define an abstract word or phrase by giving **criteria**, tests that are applied to the term being defined. What criteria would define *accurate work* for a veterinary assistant? Would a brain surgeon have different criteria for accurate work? The definition of the abstract word or phrase and the criteria depend on the situation.

Examine the term *safe environment*. To a child-care center, the criteria might include covered outlets, sharp objects placed out of reach, barricaded stairs, and clean surfaces. However, criteria for a safe environment in a chemical processing plant might include air-cleaning equipment, sprinkler systems, and gauges for measuring air quality.

Practice 2–3: Abstract Terms

1. Are the following terms concrete or abstract?

a. metal	e. cost	i. privacy
b. truth	f. ethics	j. money
c. success	g. value	k. air
d. efficiency	h. telephone	l. child

Various societies, cultures, and workplaces constantly redefine abstract terms such as *quality, family, success,* and *sexual harassment.* Some businesses put their definitions in writing. For example, most professions have **codes of ethics,** standards of right and wrong. *Ethics* is an abstract term that must be defined for it to be meaningful. Even if they are not written down, everyone must understand the ethics of his or her job.

2. Ask your teacher what constitutes ethical behavior for an educator. Write three ethical standards for teachers.

3. Write three criteria for defining ethical behavior in a particular occupational field with which you are familiar. Begin by naming a specific job in that field.

by the way...

"If A is a success in life, then A equals x plus y plus z. Work is x; y is play; and z is keeping your mouth shut."

ALBERT EINSTEIN, GERMAN-BORN U.S. SCIENTIST, ON THE DEFINITION OF SUCCESS

Acronyms

An **acronym** is a word made up of the first letters of each word in a phrase. Most acronyms are written in all capital letters with no periods. For example, the acronym OSHA contains the first letters of **O**ccupational **S**afety and **H**ealth **A**dministration. The acronym SWAT (**S**pecial **W**eapons **A**nd **T**actics), as in SWAT team, is another example.

DILBERT reprinted by permission of United Feature Syndicate, Inc.

Acronyms that are understood by almost everyone do not need defining. In fact, some are so common that people have forgotten that they are acronyms. The acronym *radar* (*r*adio *d*etecting *a*nd *r*anging) is one example. Not all acronyms are pronounceable. The acronym *FBI* is not pronounceable as a word, but it is still recognized as an acronym rather than an abbreviation.

Acronyms that are understood only by specialists require definition. People who work with computers use acronyms that many people do not understand:

LAN	local area network	DOS	disk operating system
GIGO	garbage in, garbage out	GUI	graphical user interface
FAQ	frequently asked questions	PIM	personal information manager
CAD	computer-aided design	MUD	multi-user dungeon
RAM	random-access memory	MIDI	musical instrument digital interface

When using an acronym, write out its expansion (the words from which the acronym is formed) the first time you use it. After that, assume that the audience will remember what the acronym means.

Example:

The CPU (central processing unit) is the brain of a computer.

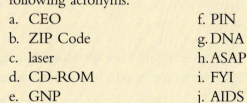

Practice 2–4: Using Acronyms

1. Using a dictionary, give the expansions for the following acronyms.
   a. CEO
   b. ZIP Code
   c. laser
   d. CD-ROM
   e. GNP
   f. PIN
   g. DNA
   h. ASAP
   i. FYI
   j. AIDS

2. List three acronyms used in your school.
3. Do you know of any acronyms that are used by specialists in your field of study? Use one of them in a sentence. Give its expansion in parentheses.

Technology *Connection*

Lexicographers are people who write dictionaries. They do not invent words; they describe words people use in conversation, in literature, and in the media. Since new words are coined every day and since old words often take on new meanings, lexicographers never run out of work.

New technologies have always resulted in new words. For example, dictionaries published in 1992 do not include listings for *hacker* or *CD-ROM*. The Internet—a word also not listed in 1992 dictionaries—has the potential to influence language more rapidly than other technology, since it is so interactive. Anyone can create a new word or invent a new way to use an old word. Try inventing a new word by attaching one of the three prefixes listed below to an old word.

Prefix	Meaning	Examples
cyber	having to do with computers, especially the Internet	cybernetics, cyberspace
e	something electronic, usually replacing a paper-based or verbal process	e-mail, e-ticket service
hyper	originally meant "over"; now means "momentum" or "being interactive"	hyperlink, hypermedia, hypertext

Technical Jargon

Technical jargon is the specialized language of a particular occupation. When the specialist uses technical jargon with a general audience, confusion may result. If, for example, your doctor diagnoses your scrapes and bruises as *abrasions* and *contusions*, you may become confused and apprehensive since you are unfamiliar with the medical jargon.

Use of technical jargon allows members of the same occupation to communicate efficiently about their work. A programmer can refer to a computer system as a *kludge* when speaking to a coworker. But when speaking to a nonspecialist, he would need to explain that a kludge is a computer system that is difficult to use due to poor design.

Synonyms

Synonyms are words that have the same or nearly the same meaning. The specialist may, at times, be able to replace a technical term with a familiar one. If the audience needs to learn the terms, both the technical term and the more familiar synonym may be given. For example:

The inspection revealed that the plane's <u>fuselage</u> was damaged.
The inspection revealed that the plane's <u>body</u> was damaged.

The inspection revealed that the plane's fuselage (body) was damaged.

Communicating a Useful Definition

Often a familiar synonym for a technical term may not exist. Then the technician must provide a definition. Most terms can be defined with a carefully constructed sentence called a **three-part sentence definition**.

Three Parts of a Sentence Definition

The three parts of a sentence definition are term, group, and details.

- The **term** is the word that is being defined.
- The **group** is a familiar classification in which the term belongs.
- The **details** give information about the term to show how it is different from other members of the same group.

Term		Group	Details
A toxin	is	a poison	produced by a plant or an animal.

The three parts of a definition can appear in any order.

Term		Details	Group
A conflagration	is	a large and destructive	fire.

Constructing a Three-Part Definition

Suppose you are giving a three-part definition of *tureen*. The term *tureen* belongs to the group *dishes*. The definition "a tureen is a type of dish" is helpful but incomplete because not all dishes are tureens. One detail that shows how tureens are different from other types of dishes is that a tureen is broad and deep. This detail eliminates platters, saucers, and many other dishes. However, a mixing bowl is also broad and deep, but it isn't a tureen. More details are needed; for example, tureens usually have lids. However, a casserole dish can be broad and deep and have a lid, but it isn't a tureen. When you add the detail that a tureen is used for serving foods such as soups or stews, you eliminate from the definition all dishes that are not tureens.

Three-Part Definition of *Tureen*:

A tureen is a broad, deep, usually covered dish used for serving foods such as soups or stews.

This definition applies only to the word *tureen* and includes all tureens.

Adding information such as different materials from which tureens can be made is not necessary because these details are not essential for a basic understanding of the term *tureen*.

Technology *Connection*

If you spent some time in a TV studio, you might need to know the following definitions of technical jargon:

- *Chromakey* is electronic placement of pictures behind the people on camera.
- *Cover footage* is a shot used to replace pictures of an interviewer and the subject while their voices are still heard.
- *Keeper* is usable video.
- Video disturbance caused by the object being taped, often jewelry or clothing, is called *moray*.
- The abbreviation *natsot* (natural sound) is background sound recorded during taping.
- The abbreviation *O/C* stands for "on camera."
- A picture reduced so it takes up only part of the screen is a *squeeze frame*.

Practice 2–5: Recognizing Group and Details

In a three-part sentence definition, the term is the word that is being defined, the group is the classification in which the term belongs, and the details set the term apart from members of the same group.

Copy the following sentences. Then circle the group and underline the details. The term is italicized.

Example:

Lagniappe is an <u>extra or unexpected</u> (gift or benefit).

1. *Cajeta* is a thick, dark syrup or paste made from caramelized sugar and goat's milk.

2. To *cultivate* means to prepare soil for the raising of crops.

3. A *credit union* is a financial institution formed by workers in the same organization that serves only its members.

4. An insulting message posted to a newsgroup is a *flame*.

5. *Vellum* is heavy, off-white, fine-quality paper resembling parchment.

Problems in Defining

Giving a meaningful three–part sentence definition is a simple process. With practice, it can become a part of your everyday communication. Still, the following problems in defining can interfere with clear communication.

Incomplete Definitions

You've already learned that in order for a definition to be helpful to the audience, it must include all three parts—the term, the group, and the details.

Imagine trying to explain what a Dalmatian is to a small child who has never seen one. If you include only the term and the group

without details—"A Dalmatian is a dog"—can you be sure that the child will accurately picture a Dalmatian?

On the other hand, if you include only the term and the details—"A Dalmatian is big and white with black spots"—what might the child visualize?

Practice 2–6: Giving Complete Three-Part Sentence Definitions

1. In Sentences a-e, either the group or the details are missing. Identify which is missing. Work on this Practice with a partner.
   a. *Nitroglycerin* is used in making explosives and medicine.
   b. A *darby* is used by plasterers when working on ceilings.
   c. One of the bones is called the *patella*.
   d. A *sedan* is a style of automobile.
   e. A *stethoscope* is used for listening to sounds produced within the body.

2. Complete the following definitions by filling in the group.

   a. *Finland* is a _____ in northern Europe.
   b. _____ growing on the upper lip is a *mustache*.
   c. A *pediatrician* is a _____ who specializes in the treatment of babies and children.
   d. To *flatter* is to _____ excessively and often insincerely, especially to win favor.
   e. A *carpool* is a _____ who share transportation costs and take turns providing a vehicle and driver.

3. Complete the following definitions by adding the details.
   a. A *parasite* is an organism . . .
   b. A *bank* is a place of business . . .
   c. *Purple* is a color . . .
   d. A *needle* is an instrument . . .
   e. To *arrest* means to take or hold in custody . . .

A plotter

Nonspecific Groups

When defining a technical term, make sure that the group is familiar and specific enough to be helpful. General groups such as *things, items*, or *devices* provide no information about the term being defined. Even groups such as *tools, machines,* and *parts* often do not provide enough information about the term to be helpful. *Power tools, life-support machines*, and *engine parts* are more informative. The more specific the group, the more helpful it will be.

Using a previous example, if you tell a child that a Dalmatian is an animal (general), you are giving him or her less information than if you say that a Dalmatian is a dog (specific). The following definitions illustrate how using a specific group makes the definition more informative:

General Group:

A plotter is a <u>device</u> that draws graphs or pictures, usually by moving a pen.

Specific Group:

A plotter is a <u>computer output device</u> that draws graphs or pictures, usually by moving a pen.

Circular Definitions

A <mark>circular definition</mark> confuses the audience by repeating, rather than explaining, the term. Examine the following circular definitions:

Project management software is software designed for managing projects.

The dorsal fin is the fin on the dorsal surface of a fish.

In the first example, the definition merely repeats the term. In the second example, the meaning of *dorsal* is not given, but the word is used as if the audience already knows its meaning.

by the way...

"*Happiness is good health and a bad memory.*"

INGRID BERGMAN. U.S. ACTRESS, ON THE DEFINITION OF HAPPINESS

Practice 2–7: Giving Informative Definitions

Ch02-07.doc

1. When defining, always choose a specific group that gives the audience enough information. Next to each letter on the next page is a list of three related terms. Beside each list, you will find a general group name. Give a more informative, specific group name. For example:

lemon, orange, lime

General group: fruit

Specific group: citrus fruit

Related Terms	General Group
a. parrot, parakeet, canary	birds
b. guitar, violin, cello	instruments
c. lizard, crocodile, snake	animals
d. Berlin, Rome, Madrid	cities
e. inauguration, wedding, bar mitzvah	events

2. Choose one term from Items 1a–1e above and write a complete and informative three-part sentence definition for it.

3. In each sentence below, the group is too general to be helpful. Revise the definitions, using a more informative, specific group. For example:

> The wrist is a <u>spot</u> between the human hand and the human forearm.
>
> The wrist is a <u>joint</u> between the human hand and the human forearm.

   a. A gesture is something that communicates an idea, a sentiment, or an attitude.

   b. Punch is a liquid made from several ingredients.

   c. A dungeon is a cold, dark place, usually underground.

   d. *Shish kebab* is a term for pieces of seasoned meat, and sometimes vegetables, roasted on skewers and served with condiments.

   e. A match is an item tipped with a mixture that ignites when subjected to friction.

Practice 2–8: Giving Useful Three-Part Sentence Definitions

career

Review the information on the parts of the sentence definition and the problems that can occur in defining.

Then do the following:

1. Choose five of the following incomplete or incorrect definitions. Edit them and write out corrected definitions. Be sure to write complete sentences.

   a. A felon is a person who has committed a felony.

   b. A prune is a type of plum.

   c. An SOS is used when help is needed.

(cont'd on next page)

d. *Geology* is a term that deals with the history of Earth and its life.
e. A bicycle is a vehicle with two wheels.
f. A stadium is where you play games.
g. A bar code is a series of vertical bars of varying widths.
h. *Hypoglycemia* is a medical term.
i. Dehydration is the process of dehydrating.
j. Programming is when you tell a computer what to do.
k. Flextime is a type of work schedule.
l. Telecommuting is when you work at home.
m. A ladle has a long handle and is used for serving liquid food.
n. Disinfect is when you clean something thoroughly.
o. A motorcycle is a vehicle with two wheels.

2. Choose five of the terms listed below. Write three-part definitions for them.

soufflé	vein	petal	antibiotic
spark plug	electricity	audience	tourniquet
acronym	fender	server	dowel
monitor	letterhead	amplifier	asset
scanner	ergonomic	portrait	catalytic converter
proofread	bifocals	irrigation	communication
garnish	DVD	cursor	speedometer
VCR	resume		

Failure to Analyze When Defining a Term

Analyzing your audience will help you decide how much information and the words to include in the definition. Definitions containing unfamiliar words intended for the general audience do not adequately define. The specialist may, on the other hand, understand other technical terms included in the definition. Also, the specialist requires more detailed information than the general audience does. Consider the following example:

Ethernet is a LAN connection with a bandwidth of 10,000 kilobits per second.

Most people would have to run to a dictionary to look up *LAN*, *bandwidth*, and *kilobits*. Remember that, as a communicator, it is your responsibility to be clearly understood at all times.

Notice in the following definitions how the vocabulary and the amount of detail differ depending on the intended audience.

General Audience	Specialist
A differential is a set of gears that transmits power to the wheels.	A differential is a type of transmission by which torque is delivered at a right angle to the motor.
Excising is cutting off a piece of body tissue.	Excising is the action of making an entry into the tissue to remove a segment of the tissue or to remove a lesion.

Finally, make sure you consider your purpose in defining. Are you, for example, defining *fire stop* so a client will understand an item on a contractor's bill, or will the reader, a carpenter trainee, be expected to build a fire stop into a wall?

Practice 2–9: Defining for Different Audiences

Identify the intended audience as general or specialized for each definition listed below.

1. A booster is a braking device that increases pressure output or decreases the amount of effort required to operate or both.

2. A booster is a part of a car's brake system that makes it easier to stop the car.

3. A mortise is a hole cut in a piece of wood into which another piece fits so as to form a joint.

4. A mortise is a hole or recess cut in a piece of wood to receive a tenon.

5. Gingiva (also known as *gums*) is the skin surrounding the teeth.

6. Gingiva is the mucous membrane that covers the alveolar parts of either jaw.

7. An envelope is a type of wave displayed on a measuring instrument that measures voltage used by electronics technicians.

(cont'd on next page)

by the way...

An education researcher defined play as "the freely chosen and personally directed enactment of a group of non-goal-oriented behaviors which become progressively more complex with experience and which in themselves facilitate the development of an equivalent range of tools (i.e., skills and abilities) without which personal and species evolution cannot continue."

People *Connection*

Did you ever wonder where the expression "the real McCoy" came from? Elijah J. McCoy, born in Canada in 1843 to parents who had escaped slavery, earned an engineering degree in Scotland. Despite his education, he was unable to find a good engineering job, so he worked as a fireman for the railroad. Part of his job was to oil the train engine, which at that time required shutting the engine down. He knew that there must be a way to drip oil continuously onto the moving parts of machines, so he began experimenting. As a result, McCoy invented the first automatic machine "lubricating cup." Large industries in the United States, Canada, and abroad began to order the device. Everyone began bragging about having "the real McCoy." His invention is still used today in cars, trains, rockets, ships, and other machines.

8. An envelope is an enclosed waveform made by outlining peaks of modulated RF waves.

9. Tooth is the surface texture of the medium.

10. Tooth is the surface roughness of paper.

11. Piggyback refers to a small IV bag that runs along with a larger IV bag.

12. Piggyback refers to a small-volume IV bag of solution that is running along with or in a larger, already-existing IV line over a brief period of time.

Practice 2–10: Defining Technical Terms

career

1. List 12 technical terms from a specialized field. They should be words that you have learned in your studies, not words that would be familiar to a general audience.

2. Choose eight of the technical terms you listed. Then, using three-part sentence definitions, define them as follows:

   a. First, define the eight terms so that a general audience will understand them.

   b. Next, define the same eight terms for specialists. Remember, the specialist will be able to understand other technical terms used in your definition. Specialists, however, may require more details than will the general audience. Ask yourself what the audience can understand and what the audience needs to know.

   c. In each definition, circle the group and underline the details. Make sure each definition is a complete sentence.

People *Connection*

Providing More Information

"The only place where success comes before work is in the dictionary."

VIDAL SASSOON, HAIR DESIGNER

Often a synonym or a three-part sentence definition gives the audience enough information. At other times, however, the audience needs or wants more information about a term. Then you should provide an expanded definition. An **expanded definition** gives all of the information that the audience wants or needs about the term.

In an expanded definition, the subject, audience, and purpose determine the:

- Form of communication (written or oral).
- Amount of information.
- Type of information.
- Word choice.
- Sentence and paragraph structure.
- Page design.
- Subject, type, and number of illustrations.

Planning an Expanded Definition

Consider what the audience already knows about the term and what the audience needs to know. To define a term clearly and thoroughly, you must predict the questions that the audience will ask about that term within a given situation and then answer them in the definition. The answers to the questions make up the *data* for the expanded definition. **Data** is organized information that usually is used to solve a problem.

Practice 2–11: Predicting the Audience's Questions

The data included in an expanded definition of a technical term depends on the audience and the purpose. Four situations are described below in which a definition is required. For any three situations, write three questions that you predict the audience will ask.

1. Eddie Lopez has been told by an auto mechanic that his car's engine has stopped running because it "threw a rod." The engine must be replaced. Eddie does not know what it means to "throw a rod." What questions about this expression does the mechanic need to answer?

2. Karen Scott has been advised to set up an IRA account at her bank. Karen does not know what an IRA account is. What questions can you predict Karen asking?

3. Pat Michaels has been told by an occupational counselor that your educational program offers challenges and opportunities. Pat is unfamiliar with your program. Before you define your program, what questions would you predict that Pat will need to ask?

4. Tonya Williams has purchased a new home. The roofing inspector has advised her to have the chimneys tuck-pointed. What questions will an expanded definition of tuck-pointing answer?

Parts of an Expanded Definition

A written expanded definition includes a title, an introduction, a body, and perhaps a closing, as well as the source(s) of the information presented.

The Title

The **title** tells the audience what kind of information to expect. Center the title at the top of the page. Do not underline or put quotation marks around the title.

You may capitalize every letter in the title. For example:

DEFINITION OF SPHYGMOMANOMETER

by the way...

Most French dictionaries list fewer than 100,000 words, while German dictionaries list about 185,000. English dictionaries, however, list an average of 500,000 words.

If you do not wish to capitalize every letter, follow the standard rules listed below for capitalizing titles. For example:

What Is a Sphygmomanometer?

- Capitalize the first letter of the first and last words.
- Capitalize the first letter of all other words except for:
  - Articles (*a, an, the*).
  - Coordinate conjunctions (*and, or, but, nor*).
  - *To* in infinitives (*to Walk, to Go*).
  - Prepositions consisting of fewer than five letters (*at, by, for, in, of, off, on, out, to, up, with*).

The Introduction

The **introduction** for an expanded definition includes an accurate and complete three-part sentence definition. It may also explain why it is important for the reader or listener to have additional data. The main topics that will be covered in the body may be listed in this introductory sentence.

The Body

The **body** is the main part of the definition. It includes data that answers the questions you predict the audience will ask about the term. The body of a written expanded definition is organized into sentences and paragraphs. The main sections are divided by headings, and illustrations may be included.

The Closing

A closing may or may not be needed. Analyze the audience to decide if you need to:

- Restate the most important point.
- Indicate where to find more information about the term.
- Summarize the main points.

Sources

Your only source of information for the definition may be your own experience. If, however, you have consulted any experts, textbooks, articles, manuals, or other sources, name each source at the end of the definition. This not only gives credit where credit is due, but also builds audience confidence in the correctness of your facts. In addition, if the audience would like to consult your source(s), they have the information needed. Information on citing sources is provided later in this chapter.

Writing Clear Sentences

A fax machine

In expanded definitions and all other written communication, the words in a sentence, the length of sentences, and the arrangement of the words within a sentence depend on audience, subject, and purpose. In order to produce clear, understandable written or oral communication, you must produce clear, understandable sentences.

Sentence Length

In technical writing, as in most good writing, sentence length varies. A combination of sentence lengths not only makes communication more interesting because it varies the pace, but also makes communication less tiring. A series of short, choppy sentences can be as tiring to the reader as long, complicated sentences. Experts recommend that sentences used in business and technical documents not exceed 17 words.

Example of Short, Choppy Sentences

Facsimile transmission is also known as fax. Facsimile transmission is a system by which text is converted. It is converted into signal waves. The signals are entered into the transmission system. This system is usually phone lines. The signals are sent to a remote receiving point. At that point, a receiver reconverts the signals. It produces a copy of the original material.

Example of a Long, Complicated Sentence

Facsimile transmission, also known as fax, is a system by which text is converted into signal waves, entered into the transmission system (usually phone lines), and sent to a remote receiving point where a receiver reconverts the signal into a copy of the original material.

Carefully analyze the reader or listener when trying to determine the best sentence lengths for the definition. A general audience will not be able to take in several new ideas contained in one sentence. One new or important main idea per sentence will be more easily understood. Specialists, on the other hand, probably have enough background and interest to absorb new information more quickly.

Practice 2-12: Varying Sentence Length

1. Working with a partner, combine the lists of short sentences in Items a–c into clear single sentences. You may add words, remove words, and rearrange ideas. Each revised sentence must be grammatically correct and include all of the ideas from the original sentences.

For example, the following sentences could be combined:

> A parsec is a unit of measurement. It measures interstellar space. It equals 3.26 light-years.

Combining the sentences by joining them with *and* is not effective.

> A parsec is a unit of measurement and it measures interstellar space and it equals 3.26 light-years.

Here are two effective ways to combine the sentences:

> A parsec, a unit of measurement for interstellar space, equals 3.26 light-years.

> A unit of measurement for interstellar space, the parsec, equals 3.26 light-years.

a. Gutta-percha is a type of gum. It is obtained from trees. The trees grow in East India. Gutta-percha is used for electrical insulation.

b. The telephone rang. Three customers came in. The computer crashed. All of this happened at once.

c. Her name is Kim. Kim works as a carpenter. Everyone told her women couldn't be good carpenters. Kim has been promoted twice.

2. The following sentence is overly long and complicated. Break it into three or four shorter, more easily understood, but complete sentences.

Fiber optics are cables that carry sound and video signals across bundles of extremely thin strands of glass, each about the thickness of a strand of hair, which, although they are much lighter and more flexible than copper wire, are able to carry much more information—hundreds of thousands of times more—than copper wire, in less space.

3. To gain practice in writing concisely, complete *Student Workbook* page 2-A.

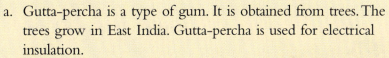

---

by the way...

"...something made greater by ourselves and in turn that makes us greater."

MAYA ANGELOU, U.S. AUTHOR, ON THE DEFINITION OF WORK

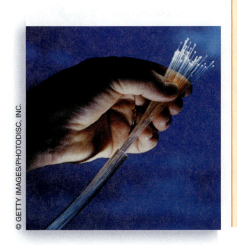

Fiber-optic cable

Word Arrangement

Suppose it is Friday night and you want a pizza delivered to your home. You pull out the phone book to look up the number for the pizza parlor. The phone number is 555-0102. You pick up the phone and instead dial 555-0120. The numbers are correct, but you mistakenly dialed them in the wrong order. The order of the numbers is important.

In a sentence, the order of the words is important. Though the words may be correct, if they are in the wrong order, you cannot communicate your ideas clearly. Your own written sentence might look perfectly fine on the page to you; you may not even notice that the words are out of order until you hear the sentence read aloud.

Use your ears to proofread sentences. Do your sentences make sense, or do they sound like these?

Unclear: Opaque ink is paint used to fill in spots on negatives that you don't want. (You don't want the *negatives*?)
Revised: Opaque ink is paint used to fill in spots that you don't want on negatives.

Unclear: Even though low on gas, Rob kept driving his car. (Is Rob low on gas?)
Revised: Rob kept driving his car even though it was low on gas.

In the first sentence, because the words *that you don't want* are closer to *negatives* than they are to *spots*, the sentence is confusing. Moving the words closer to *spots* solves the problem.

We have discussed how to fill the barrels with our employees.

Practice 2–13: Writing Sentences That Make Sense

teamwork

It is important to arrange words in a logical order so that sentences make sense. The following sentences may *look* correct to you. Working on this Practice with a partner, read the sentences aloud to each other and *listen* to them. Revise the sentences so that they make sense, reorganizing the sentences and adding words when necessary.

1. We have discussed how to fill the barrels with our employees.

2. The car was advertised in the newspaper which costs $8,000.

3. Bella is writing a report about the accident on the laptop.

4. Joseph explained how he wrecked his car while eating lunch in my kitchen.

5. We learned about the apartment building over the radio that had burned to the ground.

Ch02-13.doc

6. Ms. Chen planned the speech that she had to give while jogging to work.

7. Felipe looked for the wrench in the customer's car which had been mislaid.

8. Mark discussed the wiring he had installed while he had coffee in the cafeteria.

9. Driving to the store, Diane's hat flew out of the open window.

10. Baked for one hour, Andrew removed the bread from the oven.

11. Mr. Swift looked for his pen in his desk which was missing.

12. Even though her brother was in it, thieves stole Mrs. Ivey's suitcase from her car.

Organizing Paragraphs

In written communication, well-organized paragraphs help readers see how ideas are related. Since a paragraph develops a single idea, a new paragraph signals a new idea to the reader. Think of paragraphs as units of thought and give each main idea its own paragraph.

When organizing information within a paragraph, present the most important information either first or last, since readers tend to forget the middle items. If you are presenting new or difficult information, help your reader understand by moving from simple ideas to more complex ones. Tie ideas together with signal words such as *first, second,* or *last* so that readers can tell how ideas relate to one another.

For most forms of writing, a writer uses a variety of paragraph lengths. In business and technical writing, however, most paragraphs are short, only a few sentences each.

Practice 2–14: Organizing a Paragraph

1. Arrange the scrambled sentences on *Student Workbook* page 2-B into a logical order.

2. The following definition of a work team is made up of short, choppy sentences. First, combine related ideas in each group of sentences into meaningful single sentences. Then arrange the three sentences into a logical order.

(cont'd on next page)

Definition of a Work Team

A work team is a group of individuals.

The individuals work together.
The individuals have the same objectives.
Their work is mutually dependent.

In the workplace, the competition is not against other teams within the organization.

The competition is against waste.
The competition is against poor quality.
The competition is against delays.
The competition is against the need to redo work.
The competition is against low productivity.
The competition is against competitors in the marketplace.

The team members are joined together.
The team members are joined in a coordinated effort.
The coordinated effort is much like a team in a contest.
The coordinated effort is also like a team in a competition.

Team members are joined in a coordinated effort.

Page Design

Take a look at the front page of any daily newspaper. The name appears in large letters at the top of the page. Next comes the leading headline, written in large, dark letters that call your attention to the day's most important story. Notice the photographs, and perhaps charts and drawings, which may have touches of color. The news stories all have brief, informative titles. The articles are printed in narrow columns or are enclosed in boxes. Long articles are broken up by easy-to-see headings, and important points within articles are sometimes preceded by black dots or dashes.

White Space

Just as newspapers are designed for quick, easy reading, so too is business and technical writing. Along with clear sentences and well-organized paragraphs, use of white space can help get your message across by making your writing easy to read. (See Figures 2-1 and 2-2.)

This paragraph has been formatted with almost no white space. White space is blank space on a page that contains no words or illustrations. The margins of this paragraph are narrow, and there is little space between lines or letters. Full justification (even right margin) makes the text even harder to read. This type of page design can discourage even the most determined reader. A solid block of print like this one looks difficult and boring and is time-consuming to read. The experienced writer knows how to use white space to encourage the reader to read.

FIGURE 2-1   Inadequate white space

These paragraphs have been formatted with adequate amounts of white space. Appropriate use of white space creates a page that is attractive and easy to read.

The margins create a balanced "picture frame" effect. Paragraphs in this example are separated with white space. This white space tells the reader to expect a new idea.

A well-designed page has roughly equal amounts of print and white space.

FIGURE 2-2   Adequate white space

Headings

When you read the newspaper, you scan the titles of the articles to find the ones that interest you. You may read only the information in the newspaper that you want or need. So it is with business and technical writing. Your audience may want to read only certain sections of your document. At other times, your audience may read it from start to finish and then later go back to find certain information. **Headings** help your reader by alerting the reader to the main topics.

Style

Headings are capitalized according to the same rules that govern titles. Headings are usually written in bold print and are sometimes underlined or emphasized by color. Since headings serve as brief descriptions of the material that follows, they are not written in complete sentences. Introductions and closings do not ordinarily require headings.

Placement

Headings are usually centered or placed along the left-hand margin. Leave white space above and below main headings so that they are easy to find at a glance.

Page through this chapter to see how headings help you locate information quickly. Your audience is more likely to read a page that looks easy to read. If your message is important, pay attention to page design.

Illustrations

Imagine trying to adequately define *parallelogram* or *praying mantis* without an illustration. How effective are the following descriptions?

A parallelogram is a quadrilateral whose opposite sides are parallel and equal.

A praying mantis is a green or brownish predatory insect which, while at rest, folds its front legs as if in prayer.

The addition of drawings that show, rather than just tell, increases the effectiveness of these definitions. (See Figures 2-3 and 2-4 on the next page.)

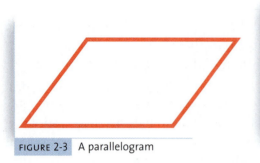

FIGURE 2-3 A parallelogram

FIGURE 2-4 A praying mantis

An illustration, or a **visual**, can help the audience understand your definition. Including a visual can save your reader time by quickly showing what might require paragraphs of writing to explain. In addition to providing valuable information, the visual adds interest to your page.

Once you have decided that a visual will increase your audience's understanding of a definition, you must decide what type of visual to use, how to produce it, and where to place it.

Practice 2–15: Designing a Logo

A **logo** is a visual symbol designed to represent a company or an organization. Companies spend thousands of dollars on the design of these visuals since customers often identify products by the logos alone. You may even find logos on your clothing or shoes.

1. Examine five company logos and answer the following questions about each one.
   a. Describe the logo.
   b. Who is the intended audience for the logo?
   c. What is the logo's purpose? What is its intended effect on the audience? Consider what impression the logo creates. Is it professional or casual, formal or fun, expensive or economical?
   d. Is the logo effective? Why or why not?

2. Erik Maxwell, a commercial art student, has painted his parents' restaurant window with seasonal designs over the past year. Lately, other neighborhood businesses have been asking if they can hire Erik to paint their windows. Erik is convinced that he can start his own small business in window painting. He decides to call his business Windows of Opportunity. He designs a logo to use on his business cards and on the flyers he plans to drop off at local stores. Which of the logos shown on the next page should Erik use and why?

3. Design a logo to be used on letterhead, business cards, and products for the company *(Your Last Name) and Associates.*

Logo 1

Logo 2

Logo 3

Types of Visuals

First, analyze the subject, audience, and purpose to choose the most effective type of visual. Once you have this information, there are many options from which you can choose: drawings, photographs, diagrams, tables, charts, and graphs. Drawings and photographs are most often used to illustrate definitions.

Production

Drawings and photographs show the actual appearance of an object. Photographs, however, sometimes include distracting detail. A clear drawing shows only what the audience needs to see. Consider using a computer graphics program or clip art for your visuals.

Most people can produce drawings of simple objects if they take their time. Make a rough draft (see Figure 2-5) of a drawing that illustrates your expanded definition. Then use a ruler and perhaps a compass to produce a neat illustration. Make the drawing simple, accurate, and large enough for the audience to see easily.

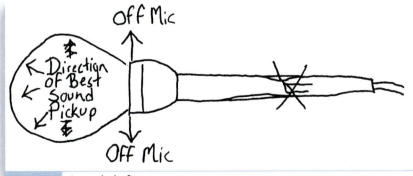

FIGURE 2-5 A rough draft

Career *Connection*

Looking for a sports career with the major leagues? The chance of your making it into a major-league baseball team as a player is only 1 out of 2,300 if you played high school baseball. But you could help professional teams, professional leagues, or college teams promote their products. Creating new product designs with logos is challenging work. Taking the logo and changing it slightly to place it on new products, clothing items, or materials uses the same skills as designing a page and working with visuals. The employment outlook is excellent, with room for advancement and salary increases.

Captions

Most visuals need captions that clearly explain what the reader is looking at. If your visual is on a page all by itself, anyone who looks at the visual should be able to identify exactly what it shows. Clearly print or key captions and labels. If there is more than one visual, number each one "Figure 1," "Figure 2," etc. (See Figure 2-6.)

Placement

The best place for a visual is the point in the text where it is easiest for the audience to identify. The text is the written portion of a definition. Just after the first mention of the object shown in the drawing, insert the drawing in the text. If the visual is too large to insert in the text, place it on a separate page. The reader should not have to wait until he or she has finished reading, though, to examine the drawing. When the need to look at the visual arises, tell the reader where to find it; for example, *See Figure 3 on page 2*. Refer to the visual within the text so that the audience will know why it is important; for example, *Figure 3 on page 2 shows the main parts*.

Leave white space around the visual. This creates a more attractive page, and the visual will be easier to find.

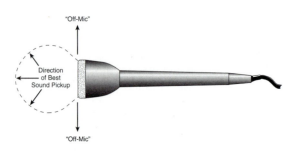

Figure 1 Directional microphone. The typical control room microphone has a cardioid directional pattern, so named because of its heart-shaped area of sensitivity.

FIGURE 2-6   Final draft with caption

Practice 2–16: Designing an Effective Page

Working with a partner, use scissors to cut out the elements for a definition of *robotics* found on *Student Workbook* pages 2-C and 2-D. Create an effective and attractive document by positioning the elements on two or three sheets of plain paper. When you are satisfied with your page design, glue the elements in place.

Naming Sources

At the end of your definition, cite the source(s) consulted to find the information. Several correct styles exist for naming the sources used for information or for visuals. Various fields of study and various publications have their own accepted styles. Many technicians who write use the style shown in this chapter.

All styles of references include the same information; however, the information is arranged differently in each style. Keep in mind that the objective is to provide enough information so that someone else could track down the original source.

Use the following examples as models for references. Pay close attention to the pattern of capitalization and punctuation. If it is available, use italic type instead of underscore.

Information from a book:

Authors	M. R. Dikel and F. E. Roehm
Title of book	Guide to Internet Job Searching
City of publication	New York
Publisher's name	McGraw-Hill
Year of publication	2002

Dikel, M.R. and Roehm, F.E. Guide to Internet Job Searching. New York: McGraw-Hill, 2002.

Information from a magazine:

Author of article (if known)	Daniel McGinn
Title of article	Faster Food
Title of magazine	Newsweek
Date of magazine	April 19, 2004
Page numbers	E20-E22

McGinn, Daniel. "Faster Food." Newsweek. 19 Apr. 2004: E20-E22.

Information from an interview:

Name	Lee Hamilton
Title	Manager
Organization	Hamilton Electronics
Date of interview	May 10, 2004

Hamilton, Lee. Manager, Hamilton Electronics. Personal interview. 10 May 2004.

Information from a web site:

Author's name (if known)	Liz Llorente
Title of article	Talent, Versatility, Class
Title of complete work	Hispanic Magazine Online
URL (http address)	www.hispaniconline.com/ magazine/2004/june/ Coverstory/index.html
Date of visit	June 26, 2004

Llorente, Liz. "Talent, Versatility, Class." Hispaniconline. http://www.hispaniconline.com/magazine/2004/june/ Coverstory/index.html.

Practice 2-17: Naming Sources

Using the information listed, write the reference for each of the sources shown below. Refer to the previous examples for the correct order of information, capitalization, and punctuation.

1. Information from a book:

Author	Scott Adams
Title of book	Words You Don't Want to Hear During Your Annual Performance Review
City of publication	Kansas City, MO
Publisher's name	Andrews McMeel Publishing
Year of publication	2003

2. Information from a magazine:

Author of article	Roger DiSilvestro
Title of article	Greatest Lakes in the World
Title of magazine	National Wildlife
Date of magazine	June/July 2004
Page numbers	44–51

3. Information from an interview:

Name	Suzanne Kemp
Title	Director
Organization	Citizens for the Earth
Date of interview	August 20, 2004

4. Information from a web site:

Author's name	Al Tompkins
Title of article	Wednesday Addition: Driving Drowsy Law
Title of complete work	Al's Morning Meeting
URL (http address)	www.poynter.org
Date of visit	May 17, 2004

People *Connection*

Summary

Workers must communicate a wide variety of messages to both general audiences and specialists. The audience must be able to understand every word exactly as the writer or speaker intended for effective communication to take place. Follow these guidelines whenever you define technical terms at work:

- Give complete, informative sentence definitions that include the term, the group, and the details.

- When more information is required, provide an expanded definition. The expanded definition should answer all questions you predict the audience may ask about the term.

- Create an effective design for a written expanded definition. Include an informative title and headings; white space; and visuals, such as drawings, diagrams, or photographs.

- Write clear and correct sentences and paragraphs.

- Name the sources of information and visuals.

review and research activities visit
communicating.swlearning.com

Giving an Expanded Definition

Select one of the following Project choices for an expanded definition. Then follow steps 1–9.

- Ms. Delgado is a third-grade teacher at a nearby elementary school. She needs descriptions of various jobs for her students to read because she wants to expand their knowledge of careers. She also is interested in showing the children how the math, reading, writing, and science skills that they are learning now will help them in the future. Your task is to provide Ms. Delgado's class with one expanded definition of a job in your career field.

- Select a complex technical term from your course of study to thoroughly define for an entry-level worker in your occupational field.

- Define *ethics, excellence,* or *quality* as it applies to your chosen career. Your audience represents your customers.

1. Carefully read the Sample Project Plan and the Sample Expanded Definition on pages 61–63.

2. Begin filling out the Project Plan, *Student Workbook* page 2-F. Will a drawing or photograph help your reader understand your definition? If so, plan a visual.

3. Locate facts that answer the questions your audience may have about the term being defined. Under the questions on your Project Plan, jot down facts that will help you answer those questions. Do not write complete sentences, just brief notes.

4. Have your teacher check your Project Plan.

5. Using the information on your Project Plan, write a rough draft. Write quickly without stopping to consult a dictionary or to puzzle over exact wording. Just try to get your ideas down in roughly the correct form. A rough draft should be rough.

6. Using the Rough Draft column of the Project Guide (*Student Workbook* page 2-G), check your own work with one or more classmates. Have them record all of their comments and changes on your Project Guide and rough draft. Ask them to write a constructive comment on the rough draft and sign it. Have your teacher check your rough draft.

7. Revise your rough draft, incorporating the changes that your classmates and your teacher suggested.

8. Using the Final draft column of the Project Guide, proofread your work. Make any needed corrections.

9. Turn in the final draft along with the Project Guide. Your teacher will use the Teacher's Comments column to evaluate your final draft.

Sample Project Plan

Plan for an Expanded Definition

SUBJECT	URL	CONTENT
		Questions the audience might ask and data to answer them.
AUDIENCE	a new employee	**What does a URL do?** Directs browser to the web page—works like a mailing address
PURPOSE	**What actions should the audience take?** Understand what a URL is for and what its parts are	**What does http mean?** Hypertext transfer protocol Format used to retrieve document—mention FTP **What is the domain?** The computer where the web page is stored
FORMAT	☒ written ☐ oral ☐ other	**What is the last part of the URL for?** The document (home page) you're looking for HTML—hypertext markup language
SOURCES	WEBster Home Page Mr. Hughes	**What do the domain name extensions mean?**
VISUALS	**What visuals, if any, will make the definition more effective?** Parts of a URL with each part in a different color List of domain name extensions	.gov government .edu educational institution .mil military .org private organization .com company .net network host **What is the correct way to key in a URL?**
INTRO	**Three-part sentence definition:** A URL (uniform resource locator) is a method of naming documents or places on the Internet.	Case, spelling, punctuation matter

Sample Expanded Definition

What Is a URL?

A few years ago, strange strings of letters and punctuation marks, like this

**http://www.gibberish.com/~nonsense/
moregibberish.html**

began appearing on advertisements for everything from movies to luxury cars. These strings of characters are URLs. A URL (uniform resource locator) is a method of naming documents or places on the Internet. Just like a mailing address, each part of the URL address plays a specific role in directing a web browser to the correct location anywhere in the world. (See Figure 1.) On the World Wide Web (WWW), URLs are accessed with *browsers*, or computer programs that can connect to the Internet and display web pages.

http://www.epa.gov/cpd.html

Protocol   Domain Name   Document

FIGURE 1   URL For the Climate Protection Partnership

The Protocol

For example, the URL of the main *web page* (a document on the WWW) for the United States Environmental Protection Agency's Climate Protection Partnership Program is http://www.epa.gov/cpd.html. The part of the URL before the colon represents the *protocol*, or format used to retrieve the document; *http* (hypertext transfer protocol) means that the document is on the WWW. If, instead of *http*, that part of the URL was *ftp*, it would mean that that document could be accessed through *file transfer protocol* (FTP), a format that allows a user to list files on, retrieve files from, and add files to another computer on the Internet.

Sample Expanded Definition

The Domain Name

The next part of the URL, *www.epa.gov,* is called the *domain name* and represents the computer on which the document can be found. The *.gov* extension identifies the computer as belonging to the United States government. Some other common extensions are shown in Figure 2.

Domain Name Extensions

.com	company or business
.edu	educational institution
.mil	military site
.org	private organization
.net	network gateway

FIGURE 2 Common Domain Name Extensions

The Document Name

The last item to be listed is the web page document name—in this case, *cpd.html*—the Climate Protection Partnership Program home page. Hypertext markup language (HTML) is the language used to create the document.

URLs are case-sensitive, which means that uppercase and lowercase letters are considered different letters, so a user has to enter a URL with all letters in the correct case. Punctuation and spelling both count. Key a URL correctly and let your browser take you around the world.

Sources:

AL6400.com
http://www.al6400.com 28 July 2004.

Hughes, Simon. Computer science teacher, Freemont High School. Personal interview, 24 July 2004.

literature

Overview

Literature uses definitions. Many times authors must clarify a concept or explain a complex idea. A reader's understanding of the concept or idea depends on how well the writer explains it.

James Baldwin was a popular, successful writer who wrote novels, essays, and plays that won critical acclaim. Among these were *Go Tell It On the Mountain, Nobody Knows My Name: More Notes of a Native Son,* and *Another Country*.

In an address presented to a college audience, James Baldwin used the dictionary definition of the word *majority,* but then continued by expanding and explaining the definition to fit his personal concept in his speech.

"In Search of a Majority"
An Address

I am supposed to speak this evening on the goals of American society as they involve minority rights, but what I am really going to do is to invite you to join me in a series of speculations. Some of them are dangerous, some painful, all are reckless. It seems to me that before we can begin to speak of minority rights in this country, we've got to make some attempt to isolate or define majority.

> *"... we've got to make some attempt to isolate or define majority."*

Presumably the society in which we live is an expression—in some way—of the majority will. But it is not so easy to locate this majority. The moment one attempts to define this majority one is

> *"Majority is not an expression of numbers ..."*

faced with several conundrums. Majority is not an expression of numbers, of numerical strength, for example. You may far outnumber your opposition and not be able to impose your will on them or even to modify the rigor with which they impose their will on you, i.e., the Negroes in South Africa or in some counties, some sections, of the American South. You may have beneath your hand all the apparatus of power, political, military, state, and still be unable to use these things to achieve your ends. . . .

I suppose it can be said that there was a time in this country when an entity existed which could be called the majority, let's say a class, for the lack of a better word, which created the standards by which the country lived or which created the standards to which the country aspired. I am referring to or have in mind, perhaps somewhat arbitrarily, the aristocracies of Virginia and New England. These were mainly of Anglo-Saxon stock, and they created what Henry James was to refer to, not very much later, as our Anglo-American heritage, or Anglo-American connections. Now at no time did these men ever form anything resembling a popular majority. Their importance was that they kept alive and they bore witness to two elements of a man's life which are not greatly respected among us now: (1) the social forms, called manners, which prevent us from rubbing

© UPI/CORBIS-BETTMANN

too abrasively against one another and (2) the interior life, or the life of the mind. These things were important; these things were realities for them and no matter how rough-hewn or dark the country was then, it is important to remember that this was also the time when people sat up in log cabins studying very hard by lamplight or candlelight. That they were better educated than we are now can be proved by comparing the political speeches of that time with those of our own day.

Now, what I have been trying to suggest in all this is that the only useful definition of the word *majority* does not refer to numbers, and it does not refer to power. It refers to influence. Someone said, and said it very accurately, that what is honored in a country is cultivated there. If we apply this touchstone to American life we can scarcely fail to arrive at a very grim view of it. But I think we have to look grim facts in the face because if we don't, we can never hope to change them.

—James Baldwin

Start-Up: A sentence definition is bare-bones stuff. An expanded definition needs more information, explanation, and examples to show how something looks, acts, or fits in among other things before people truly understand it. There are many kinds of details you can add to a sentence definition to expand it into a paragraph or an essay. Listed here are several definition expanders:

- Give a dictionary definition.
- Tell what people say about the term being defined.
- Describe the term in detail.

- Tell what the term is not.
- Compare the term to something.
- Explain the different kinds.
- Use a quotation.
- Add your personal experience.

Connection: As a class, list the ways that James Baldwin expands the definition of the word *majority*. On the chalkboard, write examples of these expanders from the text.

Understanding Definitions

Start-Up: In the world of work, people must use definitions that convey exactly what they mean in concrete terms. In the world of literature, however, authors often use abstract words, deliberately involving the reader in defining the words. The use of abstract words encourages readers to interpret the work in more than one way. Note that in technical writing, people strive for one interpretation.

Connection: Form groups of three or four students and consider the abstract definitions given below. Write a concrete definition based on the abstract one. When appropriate, try to think of concrete examples of the definition. The first question is completed for you.

1. "Willy was a salesman. . . . He's a man way out there in the blue, riding on a smile and a shoeshine." (*Death of a Salesman* by Arthur Miller)

   Answer: A salesman is a loner who must rely on his personality and his appearance to sell his goods.

   Examples: Salesmen who must come to the door (e.g., insurance agents or people selling cosmetics)

2. ". . . we need a definition of greatness, and I suppose that would be somebody who . . . benefited all mankind." (*Master Harold and the Boys* by Athol Fugard)

3. "Satire is a sort of glass wherein beholders do generally discover everybody's face but their own." ("Battle of the Books" by Jonathan Swift)

4. ". . . first in love; when you were like a person sleepwalking, and you didn't quite see the street you were in, and didn't quite hear everything that was said to you." (*Our Town* by Thornton Wilder)

5. "I am a Doctor. A.B. . . . M.A. . . . Ph.D. . . . ABMAPHID! Abmaphid has been variously described as a wasting disease

of the frontal lobes, and as a wonder drug. It is actually both." (*Who's Afraid of Virginia Woolf?* by Edward Albee)

6. "What does that 'mean—tame'?" . . .

"It is an act too often neglected," said the fox. "It means to establish ties. . . . But if you tame me, then we shall need each other." (*The Little Prince* by Antoine de Saint-Exupery)

7. "A foolish consistency is the hobgoblin of little minds, adored by little statesmen and philosophers and divines." ("Self-Reliance" by Ralph Waldo Emerson)

8. "A child said *What is grass?* fetching it to one with full hands. . . . I guess it is the handkerchief of the Lord." ("Song of Myself" by Walt Whitman)

9. "If a man has an office with a desk on which there is a buzzer, and if he can press that buzzer and have somebody come dashing in in response—then he's an executive." ("Address before the Trade Association Executives' Forum of Chicago" by Elmer Frank Andrews)

10. "New York, the nation's thyroid gland." ("Shore Leave" by Christopher Morley)

Overview

In 1916, Don Marquis, in his newspaper column "The Sun Dial" in the *New York Sun*, introduced archy the cockroach and mehitabel, a cat who believed she was Cleopatra in an earlier life. Archy believed that he was a free-verse poet in an earlier life. Every night archy recorded his experiences and observations on his boss's typewriter.

from archy and mehitabel

. . . archy would climb painfully upon the framework of the machine and cast himself with all his force upon a key, head downward, and his weight and the impact of the blow were just sufficient enough to operate the machine, one slow letter after another. He could not work the capital letters, and he had a great deal of difficulty operating the mechanism that shifts the paper so that a fresh line may be started.

We never saw a cockroach work so hard or perspire so freely in all our lives before. After about an hour of this frightfully difficult literary labor he fell to the floor exhausted.

Congratulating ourself that we had left a sheet of paper in the machine the night before so that all this work had not been in vain, we made an examination, and this is what we found: . . .

(cont'd on next page)

"pity the poor spiders"
by archy

I have just been reading
an advertisement of a certain
roach exterminator
the human race little knows
all the sadness it
causes in the insect world
i remember some weeks ago
meeting a middle aged spider
she was weeping
what is the trouble i asked
her it is these cursed
fly swatters she replied
they kill off all the flies
and my family and i are starving
to death it struck me as
so pathetic that i made
a little song about it
as follows to wit

twas an elderly mother spider
grown gaunt and fierce and gray
with her little ones crouched beside her
who wept as she sang this lay
curses on these here swatters
what kills off all the flies
for me and my little daughters
unless we eats we dies

swattin and swattin and swattin
tis little else you hear
and we ll soon be dead and forgotten
with the cost of living so dear

my husband he up and left me
lured off by a centipede
and he says as he bereft me
tis wrong but i ll get a feed

and me a working and working
scouring the streets for food
faithful and never shirking
doing the best i could

curses on these here swatters
what kills off all the flies
me and my poor little daughters
unless we eats we dies

only a withered spider
feeble and worn and old
and this is what
you do when you swat
you swatters cruel and cold

i will admit that some
of the insects do not lead
noble lives but is every
man s hand to be against them
yours for less justice
and more charity

—archy (Don Marquis)

Start-Up: Archy the cockroach doesn't capitalize words or use punctuation in his poems.

The competent technical writer must communicate information and ideas accurately. To ensure this accuracy, writers must edit their work to eliminate any possibility of being misunderstood.

Poor archy, a free-verse poet, is writing poetry the best he can. Let's give this cockroach some help.

Connection: Group into pairs and edit archy's work. Add all of the needed capital letters, punctuate the lines correctly, and correct the grammar.

Working with Literature: Refer to *Student Workbook* page 2-H for an activity on how archy defined societal problems.

Chapter 3

© GETTY IMAGES/PHOTODISC, INC.

© GETTY IMAGES/PHOTODISC, INC.

"All speech, written or spoken, is a dead language until it finds a willing and prepared hearer."

—ROBERT LOUIS STEVENSON, SCOTTISH NOVELIST, ESSAYIST, AND POET

I HOPE YOU WON'T MIND MY PILLOW AND BLANKET AT YOUR PRESENTA-TION.

THE LAST TIME YOU PRESENTED, I LOST CONSCIOUSNESS AND BROKE MY NOSE ON THE TABLE.

WHATEVER HAPPENED TO GOOD MANNERS?

© 1991 United Feature Syndicate, inc.

DILBERT reprinted by permission of United Feature Syndicate, Inc.

Listening and Responding

Listen up! You've probably heard that from teachers, coaches, parents—people who had to get a point across to a group of individuals who obviously weren't paying attention. You often have to be reminded to listen because your mind tends to focus on one thing at a time. If you see or hear something interesting, you may block out other sights and sounds completely.

Believe it or not, listening attentively can be more difficult than reading. Yet it's one of the first things a person learns to do. Infants do it naturally—listening for their mother's or father's voice when they are just a few weeks old; smiling at friendly voices; and crying at strange, unfriendly ones. It is the beginning of a survival mechanism.

Listening for Survival

Children develop the ability to listen in order to avoid physical harm as they grow up: hiding at the sound of a threatening person, hearing a motor and squealing tires in time to dodge a speeding car, and hearing the high-pitched noise of a flying object parting the air just in time to duck as it whizzes by.

Listening is as important to survival on the job as it is to protecting a person from life-threatening situations. Listening to customers, to a supervisor, to coworkers, to suppliers, to health or safety inspectors—any one of these listening situations can mean success or failure at work. Whether you like it or not, as long as you work for people or with people, you have to improve your listening skills.

Most listening is done in the presence of a speaker: someone is standing in front of you, behind you, or next to you and says something. But what if the speaker is nowhere in sight? Many times a day, in fact, you may find yourself listening to:

- The radio.

- An announcement over a public address system.

- A telephone caller.

Impressions Created by the Voice

by the way...

Some people don't realize how much their voices are saying about them.

When a speaker is heard but not seen, that speaker's voice may cause a listener to form a mental picture of the person behind the voice. The listener may begin to make judgments about what kind of person this speaker is (honest, dishonest, fearful, bold, etc.). What are some of the clues you use to put together a picture or an impression of an absent speaker such as a telephone caller or a radio announcer?

You may have had the opportunity to meet a person after hearing him or her on the radio or over the telephone. Did your mental picture look anything like the real person? Or did the appearance of the person surprise you?

Think of a popular radio personality whose voice has become well known to the listening public. When this radio personality introduces a popular singer at a concert or broadcasts from a local business, people in the audience may wonder how this person with the deep, booming voice can be such a small, ordinary-looking individual. Or this same speaker may be a mild-sounding individual with the fierce countenance and build of a football tackle. Radio announcers learn to make their voice work for them. They create the impression they need to create. That's their business.

Career *Connection*

Many women who work in management positions today, in both small and large businesses, owe at least part of their success to consulting companies. These consultants teach people how to communicate successfully in order to become accepted and respected in the business world.

Many of these consultants go from city to city presenting workshops lasting from a day to a week or more. Other consultants are located in major cities and draw large numbers of businesspeople from all over the United States.

Why have these workshops become so popular? It is a known fact that few large corporations have a high percentage of women in upper management or as chairs of their governing boards. Workshop presenters offer the hope that women who improve their communication skills will become more successful in corporations and not only draw a salary on a par with their male coworkers, but also climb higher on the corporate ladder.

Practice 3–1: Telephone Images

1. Read the following excerpts from different telephone conversations. For each excerpt, record whether you think the speaker is male or female, estimate the speaker's age, and add any other impressions you have of the person. An example is provided for you.

Example:

Girl, do you know what my boss already asked me to do this morning? That woman wants me to give up another Saturday and work overtime.

Sample answer: Could be either sex; probably late teens or twenties; is talking to a friend (uses the familiar term *girl*); is upset with his or her boss (calls her "that woman"); and doesn't like to work on Saturdays.

a. Julio, this is Sara. Whaddaya think that yo-yo upstairs just asked me to do? She actually wants me to take all those ceiling fans off the stockroom shelves and check the serial number on each one.

b. Hi! Wish you could see that red convertible I'm feasting my eyes on right now. Ri-i-ght! Not bad at all! Say—the reason I called is to see if you can replace that muffler this afternoon—maybe three or so?

c. Mr. Chan wishes to speak with Mr. Brady. Is Mr. Brady in, please?

Ch03-01.mp3

(cont'd on next page)

d. Edna, did you get the work order on that CNC lathe in the machine shop? We're really hurting to get that one up and running.

e. Hey, Charlie? Jones here. Didja get those ten sacks of feed in for my mares yet?

2. Listen to the audio selection your teacher will play for you. Give at least two additional observations about the speaker. For example, does the speaker sound energetic? Show a lack of manners by loudly chewing gum while speaking? Sound bored? Speak in a formal rather than a familiar way?

3. It's a lot easier when you can see the speaker. Pick one of the telephone callers in Item 1. Jot down the kinds of observations you might have made of that caller if you had been in the same room with him or her.

4. Compare your responses with those of other students. Do you think any of you fell victim to sexual **stereotyping**? That is, did any of you assume that a speaker was a man or woman based on what some people consider typical male or female behaviors? What are some of those behaviors? Are they truly male or female?

Making Your Voice Work for You

Your voice can work for you, too, even though you may never become a radio announcer. Remember, just as you listen to others, others are also listening to you. Of course, when you are at work, others are listening to you as more than just an individual; when you are at work, you represent your company.

If, for example, you work for Bradley Electronics, you may be the only person in the company that a customer ever sees or hears. Naturally, Bradley Electronics has to be absolutely certain that all employees give the best possible impression of the company, or it risks losing customers. Losing customers, of course, means losing money. It takes money to pay employees, and no smart employer is going to waste money on an employee who causes the company to lose business.

When you encounter a persistent or irate customer and want to say, "Leave me alone," you instead must take a deep breath, calm your voice, and politely say, "Tell me how I can help you, Ms. El Khoja, and I'll do my best." (Address the customer by name. It adds a personal, friendly tone to your conversation.)

Sometimes you can say words that sound perfectly innocent to you, and the customer interprets them as arrogant. Your tone of voice, which

Culture *Connection*

Even though early settlers came to this country to be free, women had few freedoms until very recently in history. They did not have equal educational opportunities. They could not study auto mechanics or carpentry, for example. If they managed to get into medical school, their qualifications and grades often had to be higher than those of their male counterparts. They had no rights to own property, and they were not given the right to vote until 1920. In some states, it wasn't until the 1970s that working women could get a loan to purchase a home or a car without having their husbands or fathers cosign for them.

A major breakthrough occurred in a change in the law: Title IX of the Civil Rights Act of 1964 prohibited employers of more than 15 workers from discriminating on the basis of sex, race, color, religion, or national origin. As a result of Title IX, anyone who had the appropriate skills could get hired.

Prior to the sixties, most women worked in clerical jobs, service industries, retail sales, and factories. But in the mid-sixties, they began applying for a greater variety of jobs. More women got training so they could qualify for skilled employment with higher wages in "nontraditional" occupations.

Growing numbers of women are now working in construction, mechanics, manufacturing, and electronics. By 2003, women accounted for 21–24 percent of American metalworkers, plastic workers, criminal investigators, architects, detectives, and supervisors of detectives and police. In the future, women will continue to have an influence on laws and customs affecting their roles.

includes the emphasis you give to specific words, may affect how the customer interprets your meaning. You may not even be aware that something as simple as a bad cold or an unpleasant memory translates into a whiny or irritable tone as you deal with coworkers and customers. Your tone may not be intentional, which is why it's so important to be aware of it and control it.

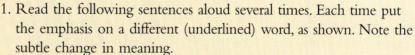

Practice 3–2: Vocal Inflections

CH03-02.mp3

1. Read the following sentences aloud several times. Each time put the emphasis on a different (underlined) word, as shown. Note the subtle change in meaning.
   a. <u>What</u> do you want me to <u>do</u> about it?
   b. What do you want <u>me</u> to do about it?
   c. What do <u>you</u> want me to do about it?
   d. What do you <u>want</u> me to do about it?

2. Listen to the audio selection your teacher will play for you. Follow along in your book so you can hear how the underlined words are vocally emphasized. Which sentences sound more positive? More negative? Why?

Using the Right Tone

by the way...

When you are not feeling well, try smiling and deliberately speaking to others in a more cheerful tone. It can actually make you feel better.

The best definition of **tone** is verbal attitude; that is, attitude shown through the voice. Whether your voice is high or low, hoarse or smooth, your attitude is in your tone. You can show respect, courtesy, and competence with any kind of voice.

You've probably heard the saying "Work smarter, not harder." Using the proper tone is one way to work smarter. It isn't that hard to do, but it does require thinking before you speak. Otherwise, an attitude you do not intend may be communicated to your listener.

Practice 3–3: Making Your Voice Work for You

1. *Use your voice to send the wrong message.* Each example (a–d) contains a comment that a salesperson or service representative might make in a particular business setting. Pretend that you are the salesperson or service representative and that you are in a bad mood. Give yourself time to read each comment to yourself first. Then practice reading it aloud to a partner in a way that would turn off a customer.

   Take turns with your partner, exaggerating the way you emphasize the words to make the tone (attitude) of the comment rude or discourteous. Don't add or skip any of the words. Just work on attitude and see what you can do with your voice.

   a. *Business setting:* A salesperson is demonstrating a portable DVD player with a 12-inch screen. The customer keeps interrupting, causing the salesperson to get flustered.
   Comment from salesperson: "Here. Maybe you'd like to try it yourself."

   b. *Business setting:* Two high school students head for the mall after school. They enter a clothing store and begin trying on jackets between racks of clothing. Several jackets fall on the floor. They ignore the fallen jackets and proceed to another rack.
   Comment from salesperson: "Excuse me. Is there something I can help you with?"

   c. *Business setting:* A customer in a garden store has been moving potted plants from one place to another, looking at them, then walking away and leaving them in disarray.
   Comment from salesperson: "Have you been able to find any plants that you like in our store?"

People *Connection*

Robert Reich was not looking for a job when President Bill Clinton asked him to join his cabinet as secretary of labor in 1993. He was a faculty member at the John F. Kennedy School of Government at Harvard University, where he was known as one of America's foremost political economists.

Reich has since become more widely known to the American public as a man of keen intellect; excellent communication skills; and a quick, often self-deprecating sense of humor. He admits having had difficulty getting used to politics. He had been accustomed to saying and writing what he thought. After becoming a politician, he said he had to think twice about what to say and how to say it, lest political opponents use his ideas against the president and the good things that he was trying to accomplish.

Often Reich used humor to take the edge off awkward situations. When he was introduced publicly after being nominated as secretary of labor, he approached the podium only to discover that, although the podium was chest-high for the president, it was up to Reich's nose, and no step stool had been provided to allow him to see over it. (Reich is less than five feet tall.) The reporters seemed embarrassed by his plight. Finally, he commented, "Modesty aside, I've known for months that I was on Bill Clinton's short list." The reporters hooted.

WALLY MCNAMEE/CORBIS

Robert Reich speaking to reporters

by the way...

"Do not the most moving moments of our lives find us all without words?"

MARCEL MARCEAU, MIME

d. *Business setting:* A customer who's had a car repaired after a serious accident returns with a frown a day after paying for the repairs. He approaches the service desk, while complaining loudly to a fellow customer.
   Comment from service representative: "So did I hear you say there's a problem with your car?"

2. *Use your voice to send the right message.* Using the same four comments as in Items a–d, see what it takes to produce the right tone for a business setting.

   Take turns with your partner, exaggerating the words you would emphasize to make the tone of the comment polite and helpful. Use your partner's name to add a personal touch.

   What did you do to make the comments sound polite? Note that emphasis on words alone was not enough to get the results you wanted. Tone of voice—kind, rough, cheerful, irritated—had a lot to do with your results.

Ethics *Connection*

A serious concern in the United States today is the need to treat men and women with equal respect in the workplace. Any behavior that focuses on the sexual attributes of a person, such as making crude comments to or about a person or touching someone in a way that is unwanted by the recipient, is not only bad manners, but also a crime. It is called sexual harassment.

Offensive behavior may be physical or verbal, and it may come from a coworker or a supervisor. Crude jokes, name-calling, and sexual advances or suggestions, if unwanted by the person receiving them (or by other workers who are forced to witness such behavior directed at someone else) may be reported.

Laws against sexual harassment apply to schools as well as the workplace. (Actually, school is a workplace for a lot of people, though students don't often think of it that way.) In your own school district, someone is appointed as the Title IX officer. This person is someone to whom sexual harassment can be reported without fear of recrimination. The Title IX officer then sees to it that the behavior is stopped, either by warning the offender or by reporting the behavior, thus initiating disciplinary action. Do you know who your Title IX officer is? If you don't, check your student handbook or ask your principal.

Practice 3–4: Workplace Scenario

Think of something good or bad that might happen in one of the work sites listed below. (You may want to choose one that appeals to your own career interest.) Write a brief **scenario** about what happens and give two or three comments that might be spoken by an employee to a supervisor, coworker, or customer/client. Let someone else in the class read your scenario and decide whether you described a positive or negative business situation.

Animal feed store	Hospital
Attorney's office	Lumberyard
Auto repair shop	Machine shop
Bakery	Motorcycle shop
College campus	Pet grooming shop
Computer service center	Plumbing company
Construction site	Printing company
Day-care center	Private home
Doctor's office	Restaurant
Farm supply store	Specialty store
Greenhouse	State park
Hair salon	Supermarket

by the way...

People tend to pay close attention and respond in a positive way when they are addressed by name in a respectful and friendly manner.

Good Listener Versus Problem Listener

When a coworker, customer, or supervisor comes to you about a business matter, be as concerned about your behavior as you are about your words. Let the person know that you are listening. Actions often speak louder than words.

Study the following list to see what it takes to be a good listener as opposed to a problem listener.

Effective and Ineffective Listening Skills

Good Listeners	Problem Listeners
listen closely to what is said.	let their mind wander.
keep their eyes on the speaker.	let their eyes wander around the room.
remain quiet so as not to interrupt the speaker.	distract the speaker with annoying behavior.
ask appropriate questions to help clarify what the speaker is saying.	do not show any response to what the speaker is saying.
act interested.	act bored.
listen for emotional content.	listen only to the words (do not listen for hidden meanings).

Practice 3-5: One-on-One

teamwork

Being a good listener, like anything else, takes practice. Here is an opportunity to practice being both a poor and a good listener and talking to both a poor and a good listener.

Study the list above, which shows the characteristics of a good listener versus a poor listener.

For the next few minutes, you will be paired with someone in your class. Follow this procedure:

1. Decide who will be Person A and who will be Person B.

2. For two minutes, Person A will tell Person B about something that was important to him or her as a child. Person B will not talk back, but otherwise will act as a poor listener.

(cont'd on next page)

3. Then, for two minutes, Person A will tell Person B about something that is important to him or her today. Person B will not speak, but otherwise will act as a good listener.

4. Reverse roles and let Person B do the talking, repeating steps 2 and 3.

After everyone has had a chance to be both a speaker and a listener, be ready to tell the class what kinds of things your bad listener did. Be very specific about exact behaviors. How did your bad listener's behaviors make you feel as you were speaking?

List ways that the good listener behaved. How did these behaviors make you feel as you were speaking?

©GETTY IMAGES/PHOTODISC, INC.

The problem listener avoids eye contact and does not respond to the speaker.

The Importance of Verbal Feedback

The behaviors of good and poor listeners are forms of what is often called **feedback**. *Verbal feedback* is talking to the speaker, asking questions such as "Why did you do that?" or saying things such as "I know just what you mean."

Using feedback skills helps to build successful communication between speaker and listener. Sometimes you think you know what the person means, but after clarifying with a question, you find out that you were quite mistaken in your thinking.

What would be some logical questions that might **clarify** the following questions or statements?

1. Rene, do you have *Test 13* in your backup files?

2. Be sure to put the Bordeaux jacket on the mannequin.

3. Please take the azalea to the customer in the office.

The Meaning Behind the Words

People say much more than is contained in their words alone. You can probably remember an argument that ended with "All I said was. . . ." And someone responded with "Yes, but it's *how* you said it."

Verbal feedback

To be sure you truly understand what someone is saying, you have to listen not only with your ears, but also with your brain. You have to learn to analyze not only the words, but more importantly:

- The sounds of the words.
- Their emotional content.
- The physical movements and facial expressions of the person speaking.

If you cannot listen sensitively, you will not do well at work. How skilled you are at taking blood samples, spot welding, planting shrubs, decorating cakes, or installing peripherals on a computer won't matter much without effective listening and responding skills.

You may not lose your job for being a poor listener. You may not even receive a warning, at least not at first. But real success—respect from coworkers, praise from your supervisor, good recommendations, increased responsibility, raises, and promotions—are more likely to come to those who listen well and respond appropriately.

Listening for Implied Meanings

The hidden meaning in a message is like the music behind the words of a song. Many times people speak to you, and they mean exactly what their words are saying. However, there's often an implied meaning they may be trying to communicate, sometimes without even realizing it.

You can better understand people and sometimes avoid conflicts if you listen for hidden meanings. Tone of voice, facial expression, and body language all help to provide clues.

For example, a coworker says, "The coffee machine is broken." It may be that the coffee machine *is* broken, but why did he tell *you*? The reason he told you is the meaning behind the message. Maybe you're good with machinery, and he wants you to fix it. Or maybe he'd like you to report that it's broken. Or maybe he's frustrated and just wants to gripe to someone.

Now is the time to use a clarifying question. A haughty "So?" is not a clarifying question; it merely aggravates people. Try something such as "What's the machine doing, eating your money?" Usually, a friendly, questioning response will result in the person saying something such as "No, it's putting sugar in all the coffee. I hate sugar in my coffee."

Sometimes people don't really need an answer; they just need to complain to someone. A friendly, sympathetic response will help. Avoid saying things such as "So?" or "What do you expect *me* to do about it?"

Getting along with coworkers and customers is a lot easier when you get to know them well enough to understand what they mean when they say even the most common things.

Practice 3–6: Implied Meanings and Jargon

1. Between now and tomorrow at this time, listen for at least one instance in which a person says a simple thing to you, but you know from the body language, facial expression, or tone of voice that the words spoken do not really say what's on the person's mind. Be prepared to share this example of an implied meaning with the class and tell them what you think the person was really saying or feeling.

Example:

You say "How are you doing?" to someone. He answers "OK" in a depressed voice and keeps walking away from you.

Implied meaning: "I'm *not* OK, but I don't want to talk about it."

2. Work with a partner to complete *Student Workbook* page 3-A. By completing this exercise, you will learn how well you understand jargon.

What Your Speech Says About You

The way you talk can tell people where you're from, how much education you have, what neighborhood you live in, what you do for a living, and more. This observation is not true of only you, of course, and it's not true of only Americans who speak English. It's true of people in every part of the world.

In every society, there are people who are more educated or less educated. There are people who have more money or less money. There are people who work in different kinds of jobs, where words such as *prosthesis, rotors, capacitors,* and *picas* are used—words that people in other kinds of jobs don't use or understand.

Word Choice Linked to Audience and Purpose

People choose words that they find useful, important, and effective depending on who they're talking to and what the occasion happens to be. People who use different sets of words (or who use the same words but pronounce them differently) may have different backgrounds or may use the words to represent different things. The words *car, Beemer, wheels,* and *rod* may all refer to automobiles. However, they are not all equally effective with everyone. You have to choose the most effective word with the right tone to communicate with certain people or groups.

In My Fair Lady, Eliza Dolittle was treated like a flower girl until she learned to speak like a lady.

Consider the comment "Nobody is like my mom." This statement says the same thing as "Ain't nobody like my momma" and "No one is quite like Mother." In these three statements, the speakers could mean the same thing. It is even possible that the speaker of all three statements could be the same person.

Inappropriate language for the audience

Let's pretend that the speaker of all three of those statements *is* the same person (a young man). He may say "Nobody is like my mom" to his high school principal, "Ain't nobody like my momma" to his best friend, and "No one is quite like Mother" while performing in a play. If he can do this, he is not a faker; he is smart.

People who want to be able to communicate clearly always keep their audience and purpose in mind. They vary their way of speaking to suit their audience and purpose. This cartoon illustrates this idea. "Let's hurry, Grandpa" would be perfectly appropriate to say to your grandfather. "Step on it, Jack!" would be OK to say to a friend you wanted to move faster. But if you said one of these things to the wrong person, that person might be offended.

Practice 3–7: Are You Asking for Trouble?

Below are several businesslike requests. Rewrite each one to give a similar message but in a way that is not appropriate for work. (Think whiny, argumentative, pushy, etc.) An example is provided for you.

Businesslike request: Is it all right if I leave 15 minutes early today, Ms. Tasker?

Inappropriate request: Hey! I'm outta here!

> **or:** You have to let me leave early, or I'll lose my driver's license.

Provide inappropriate ways of saying each of the following:

1. Is there a problem with the delivery truck, Mrs. Ortega?

2. Aren't you feeling any better today, Mr. Wilson?

3. Bill, do you need some help with those packages?

4. Mr. LaRosa seems to like the work you do, Cory.

5. You always wear such neat clothes, Miss Kwan.

At work, you must choose the manner of speaking that is most appropriate and effective for your job. Speech that is perfectly acceptable at home or among friends may not be acceptable at work and vice versa.

Sometimes you may need to be careful of your word choice for legal reasons. That is why, for example, police officers are taught to use statements such as "We apprehended the alleged intruder." Police officers are taught not to accuse or condemn a person.

A Pocketful of Dialects

Words used with adults often can't be used with very young children, who do not have the same degree of knowledge or experience and often require simpler language. You, too, must use different words with customers who do not understand the technical terms that you might use comfortably with your coworkers.

Develop a pocketful of dialects—that is, many ways of speaking that suit the event, location, and people you're with. Some firms train their employees on how to speak at work so that they get along with coworkers and represent the company well to outsiders. If this type of training is not available to you, listen to supervisors and coworkers. Imitate the successful people around you.

If you are not used to dealing with customers or clients, practice phrases that reflect what your employer wants customers to hear. Above all, select words carefully, pronounce them clearly, and treat others with respect.

What would be a more appropriate, businesslike, customer-friendly way to rephrase each of the following statements? Write a better response. An example is provided for you.

Example:

Electronics repairer to returning customer: Good grief, did that thing break already?

Better response: You're back. Is there something else I can help you with?

1. *Salesperson in appliance store:* Okay, man, I can sell you a service plan if you really want to spend that kind of money.

2. *Dentist to patient:* Most people hate this drill. They're such crybabies.

3. *Dining room attendant:* Lady, if you can't get that kid to quiet down, we'll have to ask you to leave. Other customers are complaining.

4. *Florist to customer:* That aloe plant would have been fine if you'd watered it like I told you to.

5. *Department store salesperson:* I can't wait on you now. I'm busy with somebody else.

Working with Telephone Messages

Many people don't like to be told what to do or how to do it, but at work, the importance of following directions cannot be overemphasized. Following directions at work is important for many reasons, including:

- Handling equipment correctly.
- Safeguarding employees from workplace hazards.
- Ensuring that customers' orders will be correctly interpreted.
- Gathering accurate information on clients.

One of the most common occurrences that requires people to follow directions is receiving telephone messages. When you think of people taking telephone messages, you usually think of secretaries and other office workers. Actually, workers in many different occupations answer telephones. In many businesses, employees answer their own telephones or take messages for others in

Taking an accurate telephone message involves both listening and writing skills.

the office. Conducting business on a cell phone in the car, at home, or in public has become commonplace. Pizza deliverers, drivers of concrete mixer trucks, real estate agents, plumbers, and electricians all may be required to take telephone messages as a routine part of their jobs. A driver may be in a truck, and a voice on the line may say:

"Tell Donna Chavez that we'll be there at 7 P.M."
or
"Be sure that you and Ali check the brake fluid on Number 9 before leaving the lot."

You should have a pencil or pen and a small card or piece of paper in your pocket or somewhere nearby. Otherwise, in the rush of the day's activities, you may forget to pass along the message or forget what's to be done. It's easy to miss details. (Was that Vehicle 9 or Vehicle 5 that needed to have the brake fluid checked?)

Wherever you happen to be when a call comes through, you may have to answer the phone and take a message for someone else, even if it's not officially your job to answer phones on a regular basis. Your voice is the only image of your company that the customer has at that time. An "I want to help you" attitude is a must.

How to Answer the Phone

Follow this procedure when answering the phone for any type of business:

1. Answer with the company's name. Sometimes your employer will have specific guidelines on how to answer the phone.

2. Copy all key pieces of information (not every word) given by the caller. Usually, telephone message forms are provided for this purpose.

3. Repeat the information, especially verifying numbers and the spelling of names.

4. End the call by thanking the caller.

Practice 3–9: Taking Telephone Messages

Because writing information while listening to a caller is not always easy, your teacher is going to give you a chance to practice this important skill. Using *Student Workbook* pages 3-B and 3-C, take down the key details from each caller. Be prepared to pass the messages along to someone else. Use the current date and time.

This task is not as easy as it seems, so be patient with yourself. You'll improve with practice.

Ch03-09.mp3

Technology *Connection*

You pick up the phone and a cheerful voice says, "Hello. I'd like to get your opinion about products used in your home. I am a computer, so please listen and answer only when I give you the signal."

Electronic technology can now digitize the sounds of a human voice and play them back to you. The results make a computer sound quite authentically human. However, when you get used to listening to them, these voices often sound stilted or overly cheerful.

Do you hang up, or do you listen and respond? Some people refuse to talk to a computer. But companies increasingly rely on computers to get valuable information, and many people do provide—without hesitation—the information the computer requests. If enough people refused to talk to computers, businesses would quit using them. So the fact that these computers are still around means that they are helping someone make money.

Getting the Answer You Want

Many large companies now use electronic messages to serve customers more quickly and efficiently. A caller is likely to hear a greeting followed by a set of directions. For example:

> "Welcome to the Auburn Metropolitan Power Company. Listen carefully to the following menu so that we can serve you more efficiently."
> "If you are calling one of our representatives and know the extension, enter the number of that extension now."
> If you do not enter an extension number, still more messages follow.
> "If you wish to place an order, press 2."
> "If you wish to inquire about a billing, press 3."
> "If you wish to speak with an operator, stay on the line and someone will speak with you shortly."

Sometimes these directions are given so quickly that it is hard to comprehend them before the next direction is given. However, if you wait, the entire series of instructions will probably be repeated or a person will answer. Just waiting for the proper instructions and navigating through the system can be a test of patience and keen listening skills.

Leaving Messages for Others

Sometimes, especially if you are calling someone who does not stay near a phone all day, you will have to leave a message. You may hear the person's voice answer the phone and suddenly, just as you are about to say hello, you are instructed to "please leave your message at the sound of the tone."

Choosing not to talk to an answering machine is unprofessional. It can cause you to lose business and can cause delays in your acquiring or giving out important information. Not leaving a message wastes your time as well, since you have to continue calling until you reach the person.

The trick is to be ready with your message. Be prepared to say exactly what you want to say as soon as the electronic voice tells you to leave your message. Since a machine can't provide callers with verbal feedback, you must be clear about what you mean and give just the right impression when leaving a message.

At first, it may be difficult to avoid stuttering and stammering into the machine. Here are a few tips to help you sound like a true professional.

1. Jot down a few key words so you don't forget anything you are supposed to say.

   For example, if you need to speak to Olga about rescheduling an appointment for October 3 to a later date, preferably in the morning, you might write

   "Olga—cancel Oct. 3—later date in a.m."

   That way, you won't have to stop to decide what to tell Olga by way of her answering machine.

2. Mentally rehearse your first few words. (Getting started is the most difficult part.)

3. If you are caught off guard, hang up, get your thoughts together, and call again. Then leave the message. Machines are very patient! They don't care if you don't get it right the first time.

4. Remember, you usually have less than a minute to leave a message. Keep it short.

Practice 3–10: Leaving a Message on an Answering Machine

Read the following situation until you understand all of the details. Decide what you will say to Tara Rikofsky, writing it in 50 words or fewer. Then read your message into the tape recorder. Remember to pronounce your words clearly. Don't forget to leave your name, your company's name, and your phone number.

Situation: You own a lawn care company and are two days behind schedule because of severe thunderstorms. More tornado-like weather is expected tomorrow, and you know the job can't be done during a storm. You have to call Tara Rikofsky at the Rolfe Company to let her know that you haven't forgotten her, but that you don't know exactly when you can reschedule the work since the weather is uncertain and other customers are ahead of her. You also realize that PerfectLawn, one of your biggest competitors, has been trying to get the Rolfe account away from you, so you have to keep your customer happy. You decide to call. Tara is out of the building, and after the phone rings, her answering machine clicks on. What do you say?

Remember to pronounce your words clearly and don't forget to leave your name and phone number.

©GETTY IMAGES/PHOTODISC, INC.

"Please leave your message at the sound of the tone."

Practice 3–11: Creating a Work Situation Involving Telephone Messages

1. Using the yellow pages of a phone book, the Internet, or advertisements from newspapers and trade magazines, find a company representing an occupational area of your choice.

2. Work with a partner to develop a situation in which a customer would need to leave a message for someone at the company, asking for information or service.

3. Create the customer's phone message to that company. Compose the message as though you were going to leave it on an answering machine.

4. Record the message on a tape recorder. If no recorder is available, choose one person to recite the message to another team of students in class. If you do not use a tape recorder, but simply recite your message, remember that you cannot answer questions as you give the message.

5. The members of the other team must then summarize your message on a phone message form and recite it back to you. Listen carefully to be sure all details are repeated accurately.

Talking to a group is just one step beyond talking to an individual. The same things have to be considered, but on a larger scale. For example, you have to talk loudly enough to be heard by the whole group, and you have to look at more people than you do in a conversation.

Does talking to a group make you nervous? Almost everyone gets nervous just thinking about speaking before a group. If you follow a few simple steps, you will do a good job with your presentation.

1. Choose a topic of interest to you and your audience. If the topic is given to you by your teacher, try to find an interesting or unusual way to present it.

2. Analyze your audience. Who are they? What are their backgrounds and interests? Do they already have attitudes or opinions about your topic? What aspect of your topic might especially interest them?

3. Clarify your purpose in sharing this topic with them.

4. Gather facts about your topic.

5. Organize the presentation. Put your ideas on note cards and put them in order. (Don't forget to number the cards after you decide which order to put them in.)

6. Design your visuals. People often remember visuals when they don't remember the words. Make your visuals large, colorful, and easy to see. You may want to design them on the computer, using presentation software such as PowerPoint®, which allows you to incorporate your notes with movement, drawings, and photographs, using a lot of eye-catching options.

7. Rehearse your presentation, including where you will put your notes and how you will display your visuals. If you use a flowchart, an outline, or a computer presentation, you may not have to use your note cards at all.

Choosing a Topic and Analyzing the Audience

Often a topic in school or at work is assigned to you. It then becomes part of your task to figure out the most appealing way to present it to your audience. Is your audience a group of classmates? Is it an auditorium full of parents and relatives? Is it a troop of Cub Scouts or Brownies? You need to know ahead of time who your audience will be so that you can choose your words to suit their ages, interests, cultural backgrounds, and educational levels.

If, however, you must choose the topic yourself, sticking with a topic that you know well and that interests your audience will give you confidence and make your preparation easier.

Clarifying Your Purpose

You need to decide whether your purpose in this presentation is simply to entertain your audience, to inform them about something interesting or important, or to persuade them to take some action as a result of what you're saying. Your purpose will dictate where you need to focus. Narrowing your focus to specific points makes it easier to construct an effective presentation.

Carefully planning your presentation will result in a better performance.

Gathering Information

Find a catchy quote or an amusing or thought-provoking anecdote to use in beginning your presentation. Then decide whether you need to talk to others to get the necessary information or whether you need to research your topic using the Internet, books, trade magazines, and other sources.

Organizing the Presentation

There are several methods of preparing notes for a presentation. The most important consideration is that you be able to read and use the notes easily.

If your main points are shown in a visual such as an outline, a flowchart, or a diagram, your notes will have to include only those supporting details that you might otherwise forget.

Note-Taking Methods

Some people write notes on index cards; others use a sheet of paper. Both note-taking methods have pros and cons. The cards are convenient, but you must handle them as you speak. Notes written on a sheet of paper do not require this handling, but you may have a more difficult time locating specific points.

Notes can be written in a formal outline or as a list. (See Figures 3-1 and 3-2 on pages 92 and 93.) If you prefer a formal outline, keep it as simple as possible. After all, you want to be able to glance at your notes when

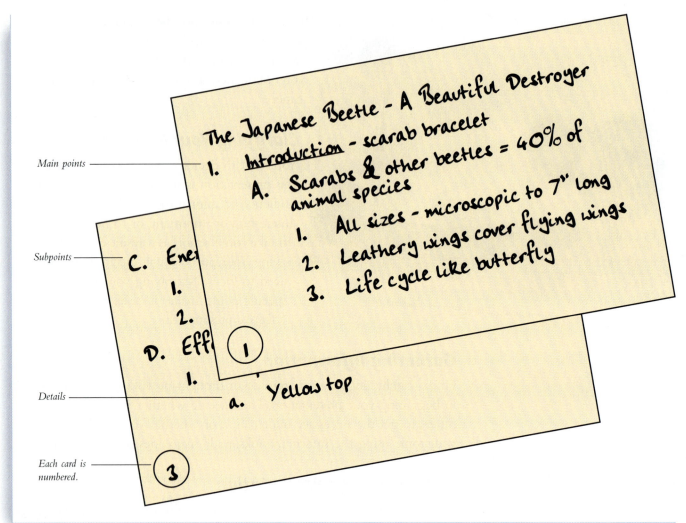

Main points

Subpoints

Details

Each card is numbered.

The Japanese Beetle - A Beautiful Destroyer
I. Introduction - scarab bracelet
    A. Scarabs & other beetles = 40% of animal species
        1. All sizes - microscopic to 7" long
        2. Leathery wings cover flying wings
        3. Life cycle like butterfly

C. Ene...
    1.
    2.
D. Eff...
    1.
        a. Yellow top

① ... ③

FIGURE 3-1 Notes in formal outline format

necessary, not read from them. Print your notes neatly or key them to make them easy to read. Use large letters, but not capital letters (capital letters may be used for the title). If you feel more confident making your notes in list form, do so.

Planning the Organization

Any effective presentation includes an introduction, a body, and a conclusion. In the notes shown in Figure 3-2, the introduction and conclusion are written out word for word, exactly as the speaker intends to say (or perhaps even read) them. This approach helps ensure a clear and confident beginning and end.

The Introduction. The introduction, which you will probably compose last, introduces the audience to the topic, gets their attention, and lists the main ideas that will be covered. The audience will know why they should listen, what information will be explained, and how that information will be organized.

The Japanese Beetle
A Beautiful Destroyer

The introduction is written out word for word.

Have you ever seen someone wearing a scarab bracelet like this one? If so, the person was wearing a wristful of fake scarab beetles. These multicolored creatures have been the inspiration for popular items of jewelry since ancient times.

Bullets, dashes, underlining, color, or stars make the points and subpoints stand out.

- Beetles represent 40%—nearly half—of the 300,000 species of the world's insects & 1 out of 4 animal species.
    —need magnifying glass to see tiny ones
        vs. 7" long ones

Use single words or brief phrases.

    —leathery body
    —life cycle like butterfly

- Beetles everywhere—in food, carpets, clothes, animal dung, plants, etc.

- Japanese most beautiful. Enemy of gardeners.
    —eats 275 kinds of plants (fruits, roses, etc.)

Use large, easy-to-read print.

Efforts to get rid of Japanese beetle, esp. trap
    —yellow top w/pheromone
    —locate bag to collect 25 feet away from plants

The conclusion is written out word for word.

Maybe the ancients admired these beetles because they were survivors—or maybe they just accepted them because they were so much a part of their lives. As for me, I may wear a scarab bracelet, but I want to keep the real scarabs off my flowers—and out of my hair.

FIGURE 3-2 Notes in list form

The Body. The outlined body, which includes the main points, is the longest part of the presentation. If you are explaining how to do something, you should put the points in chronological order.

The Conclusion. The conclusion should be brief. It restates the most important points and may recommend some action on the part of the audience. The purpose of the presentation will determine the information included in the conclusion.

Practice 3-12: Preparing Notes for a Speech

You have been asked to give a three-minute speech to people interested in your field of study. You are to describe a tool or another piece of equipment used in your program of study and discuss how it's used. On notebook paper, use the list method to prepare notes for the speech. Write out the introduction and conclusion exactly as you would say them. Decide what kinds of visuals you could use.

Preparing Visuals

Visuals will make your speech easier to understand and more interesting. Another advantage of visuals is that your audience will spend most of the time looking at them instead of you. What makes many people most nervous about giving a speech is all of those eyes staring at them! Visuals can help solve that problem.

Whether you choose drawings, diagrams, flowcharts, models, pieces of equipment, potted plants or other live specimens, or a combination of these, make sure that your visuals are attractive, neat, and informative. You may project them on a wall or screen, stand them on a table, draw them on the chalkboard, or use whatever device is necessary to make it easy for every member of the audience to see them. Give your visuals titles if they are needed and refer to the titles in your presentation.

Rehearsing the Presentation

Rehearsing helps your final presentation in many ways. It helps you to:

- Decide where notes need revision.
- Estimate the time it takes to give the presentation.
- Improve your delivery.

Ask a friend or family member to observe your rehearsal and offer suggestions for improvement. If no one is available to do this, use a video camera or tape recorder so that you can review your own performance. If you are working as part of a team, the team must rehearse together. Individuals should know when they are to act and speak. Include reminders in your notes.

You can improve your delivery by following a few basic rules, which follow.

Speak Up!

Most important, make sure that your audience—whether 3 or 30 people—will be able to easily hear and understand you. This is *your* job, not theirs. Practice raising your voice so that it is loud enough to fill a room. (Make your voice louder, not higher in pitch.) Pronounce each word clearly and speak slowly. If you mumble or move along too quickly, your audience will lose interest. They should not have to struggle to understand you.

Watch Your Body Language—Your Audience Will, Too

The gestures and mannerisms that you use to communicate with your audience can greatly add to—or take away from—your speech. Therefore, it's a good idea to rehearse before someone else to get feedback on your body language. As you practice, follow the tips below.

Delivering the Presentation

When it is finally time to face the audience, relax and do your best. If you have carefully planned and rehearsed your presentation, you have done all you can. Just take a deep breath and begin. If you make a mistake, go on. Your audience will understand that you are doing your best to perform a difficult task.

Remember to speak clearly, slowly, and loudly enough for your audience to understand. As you speak, keep these tips in mind:

Use visuals to illustrate your main points.

- Maintain as much eye contact with your audience as you can. If you find this difficult, direct their attention to your visuals.

- Never turn your back to the audience.

- Avoid behaviors such as swaying, fiddling with your notes, adjusting your clothes, or other fidgeting that will reveal your nervousness and distract your audience.

- Stand comfortably and talk to your audience. After all, they are just people, and you have years of experience in talking to people.

Ch03-13.mp3

Practice 3-13: Analyzing a Speech

Analyzing a presentation and making suggestions for improvement should be a helpful, positive experience for both the speaker and the critic. Do not make suggestions in an insulting or degrading way.

In this Practice, you will listen to a speech given by a floriculture student describing the Japanese beetle, a natural enemy of plants. Make three positive suggestions for improvement. Avoid telling the speaker what *not* to do. Instead, tell her what she can do to improve. Make three positive suggestions for improvement; for example, add an interesting fact to the introduction to get the audience's attention, give information in the correct order, define unfamiliar terms, find out all needed information ahead of time, give complete information, and omit unnecessary information.

Summary

Communicating well means speaking thoughtfully, listening carefully, and responding appropriately to supervisors, coworkers, and customers. Follow these guidelines whenever you find yourself communicating with someone:

- Listen for meanings underlying the words.
- Tune in to the feelings of the person you are communicating with.
- Use appropriate language for the situation.
- Speak clearly and avoid distracting mannerisms.
- Take notes when necessary.
- Pass along messages intended for others as quickly and accurately as possible.

For review and research activities visit
communicating.swlearning.com

Works Cited

Reich, Robert. *Locked in the Cabinet*. New York: Knopf, 1997.

project-based assessment

Oral Presentation

Describing an Important Object, Rule, or Idea

Regardless of what you are studying, you have dealt with objects, rules, or ideas that are an important part of your field of study. For example, if you are studying forestry or parks management, you need to understand how to identify trees or what makes a lake a healthy habitat for fish. If you are studying accounting, you must understand a spreadsheet.

You and a partner will prepare and deliver an oral presentation to describe an important object, rule, or idea from your field of interest that would be valuable or interesting to a general audience. Divide tasks between you and your partner based on your individual skills and talents.

Examples:

Occupation	Useful Information for a General Audience
Child-care worker	Which snacks are healthful for young children and why?
Nurse assistant	Why is it important to wash your hands before and after working with patients? What diseases are spread by dirty hands?
Electrician	What is electricity, and how does it work?
Horticulturist	Which types of grasses grow best in your area? What kinds of soils and fertilizers do they need?

1. Study the Sample Project Plan on page 99. Brainstorm ideas for a topic, for an organizational plan, and for the type and subject matter of visuals you might use.

2. With your partner, complete the Project Plan on *Student Workbook* page 3-D.

3. Have your teacher check your Project Plan.

4. Listen to the more polished sample presentation about the Japanese beetle. The notes for this presentation are in Figure 3-2 on page 93.

5. With your partner, prepare notes and visual(s) for your presentation.

6. Rehearse your part of the presentation individually; then rehearse it with your partner. Use your notes and visuals as you would in presenting before the class.

7. Using the Rough Draft column of the Project Guide on page 3-E of your *Student Workbook,* rate your rehearsed presentation.

8. Do another rehearsed presentation with your partner. If possible, ask a classmate to act as your audience and help you and your partner rate yourselves, using the Final Draft column of the Project Guide.

9. Give your presentation and your Project Guide to your teacher, who will use the Teacher's Comments column to evaluate your notes, visual(s), and speech.

Sample Project Plan

Plan for a Presentation

SUBJECT	The Japanese Beetle— A Beautiful Destroyer	CONTENT Main points to describe or explain:
AUDIENCE	General audience, classmates	Scarab bracelet—fake scarab beetles
		Beetles represent 40% of world's insects.
PURPOSE	**What actions should the audience take?** Recognize and understand the Japanese beetle	—microscopic up to 7" long, leathery body
		—life cycle like butterfly
		Beetles everywhere—in food, carpet, clothes, animal dung, plants
FORMAT	☐ written ☒ oral ☐ other	Japanese beetle most beautiful
SOURCES	<u>Insects</u> by Joni Phelps Hunt, Silver Burdett Press, 1995, and <u>Comptons Interactive Encyclopedia</u>, 1995.	—enemy of gardeners —eats 275 kinds of plants (fruits, roses, etc.)
VISUALS	**What visuals, if any, will make the report more effective?** Colored photo of Japanese beetle, scarab bracelet	Traps designed to get rid of beetles—describe trap Beetles survive in spite of everything
PREPARE	**Necessary materials, equipment:** none	Like the bracelet, but not the real beetles Want to keep them away from my flower beds

Overview

Most everyone has had the overwhelming experience of leaving a safe inner circle of family on the first day of school. Everyone has adjusted, to some degree, to the close supervision and new restraints of school. Some individuals have coped better than others. Shirley Jackson's story is of a little boy's retelling of his experiences during his first days at school.

Don't miss the surprise ending.

"Charles"

The day my son Laurie started kindergarten, he renounced corduroy overalls with bibs and began wearing blue jeans with a belt; I watched him go off the first morning with the older girl next door, seeing clearly that an era of my life was ended, my sweet-voiced nursery-school tot replaced by a long-trousered, swaggering character who forgot to stop at the corner and wave good-bye to me.

He came home the same way, the front door slamming open, his cap on the floor, and the voice suddenly become raucous shouting, "Isn't anybody *here*?"

At lunch he spoke insolently to his father, spilled his baby sister's milk, and remarked that his teacher said we were not to take the name of the Lord in vain.

"How *was* school today?" I asked, elaborately casual.

"All right," he said.

"Did you learn anything?" his father asked.

Laurie regarded his father coldly. "I didn't learn nothing," he said.

"Anything," I said. "Didn't learn anything."

"The teacher spanked a boy, though," Laurie said, addressing his bread and butter. "For being fresh," he added, with his mouth full.

"What did he do?" I asked. "Who was it?" Laurie thought. "It was Charles," he said. "He was fresh. The teacher spanked him and made him stand in a corner. He was awfully fresh."

> "I didn't learn nothing," he said.

"What did he do?" I asked again, but Laurie slid off his chair, took a cookie, and

© GETTY IMAGES/PHOTODISC, INC.

left, while his father was still saying, "See here, young man."

The next day, Laurie remarked at lunch, as soon as he sat down, "Well, Charles was bad again today." He grinned enormously and said, "Today Charles hit the teacher."

"Good heavens," I said, mindful of the Lord's name, "I suppose he got spanked again?"

"He sure did," Laurie said. "Look up," he said to his father.

"What?" his father said, looking up.

"Look down," Laurie said. "Look at my thumb. Gee, you're dumb." He began to laugh insanely.

"Why did Charles hit the teacher?" I asked quickly.

"Because she tried to make him color with red crayons," Laurie said. "Charles wanted to color with green crayons so he hit the teacher and she spanked him and said nobody play with Charles but everybody did."

The third day—it was Wednesday of the first week——Charles bounced a seesaw on to the head of a little girl and made her bleed, and the teacher made him stay inside all during recess. Thursday Charles had to stand in a corner during story-time because he kept pounding his feet on the floor. Friday Charles was deprived of blackboard privileges because he threw chalk.

On Saturday I remarked to my husband, "Do you think kindergarten is too unsettling for Laurie? All this toughness, and bad grammar, and this Charles boy sounds like such a bad influence."

"It'll be all right," my husband said reassuringly. "Bound to be people like Charles in the world. Might as well meet them now as later."

> *". . . this Charles boy sounds like such a bad influence."*

On Monday Laurie came home late, full of news. "Charles," he shouted as he came up to the hill; I was waiting anxiously on the front steps. "Charles," Laurie yelled all the way up the hill, "Charles was bad again."

"Come right in," I said, as soon as he came close enough. "Lunch is waiting."

"You know what Charles did?" he demanded, following me through the door. "Charles yelled so in school they sent a boy in from first grade to tell the teacher she had to make Charles keep quiet, and so Charles had to stay after school. And so all the children stayed to watch him."

"What did he do?" I asked.

"He just sat there," Laurie said, climbing into his chair at the table. "Hi, Pop, y'old dust mop."

"Charles had to stay after school today," I told my husband. "Everyone stayed with him."

"What does this Charles look like?" my husband asked Laurie. "What's his other name?"

(cont'd on next page)

"He's bigger than me," Laurie said. "And he doesn't have any rubbers and he doesn't ever wear a jacket."

Monday night was the first Parent-Teachers meeting, and only the fact that the baby had a cold kept me from going; I wanted passionately to meet Charles's mother. On Tuesday Laurie remarked suddenly, "Our teacher had a friend come to see her in school today."

"Charles's mother?" my husband and I asked simultaneously.

"Naaah," Laurie said scornfully. "It was a man who came and made us do exercises, we had to touch our toes. Look." He climbed down from his chair and squatted down and touched his toes. "Like this," he said. He got solemnly back into his chair and said, picking up his fork, "Charles didn't even *do* exercises."

"That's fine," I said heartily. "Didn't Charles want to do exercises?"

"Naaah," Laurie said. "Charles was so fresh to the teacher's friend he wasn't let do exercises."

"Fresh again?" I said.

"He kicked the teacher's friend," Laurie said. "The teacher's friend told Charles to touch his toes like I just did and Charles kicked him."

"What are they going to do about Charles, do you suppose?" Laurie's father asked him.

Laurie shrugged elaborately. "Throw him out of school, I guess," he said.

Wednesday and Thursday were routine; Charles yelled during story hour and hit a boy in the stomach and made him cry. On Friday Charles stayed after school again and so did all the other children.

With the third week of kindergarten Charles was an institution in our family; the baby was being a Charles when she cried all afternoon; Laurie did a Charles when he filled his wagon full of mud and pulled it through the kitchen; even my husband, when he caught his elbow in the telephone cord and pulled telephone, ashtray, and a bowl of flowers off the table, said, after the first minute, "Looks like Charles."

> *"Charles was so fresh to the teacher's friend he wasn't* let *do exercises."*

During the third and fourth weeks it looked like a reformation in Charles; Laurie reported grimly at lunch on Thursday of the third week, "Charles was so good today the teacher gave him an apple."

"What?" I said, and my husband added warily, "You mean Charles?"

"Charles," Laurie said. "He gave the crayons around and he picked up the books afterward and the teacher said he was her helper."

"What happened?" I asked incredulously.

"He was her helper, that's all," Laurie said, and shrugged.

"Can this be true, about Charles?" I asked my husband that night. "Can something like this happen?"

"Wait and see," my husband said cynically. "When you've got a Charles to deal with, this may mean he's only plotting."

He seemed to be wrong. For over a week Charles was the teacher's helper; each day he handed things out and he picked things up; no one had to stay after school.

"The P.T.A. meeting's next week again," I told my husband one evening. "I'm going to find Charles's mother there."

"Ask her what happened to Charles," my husband said. "I'd like to know."

"I'd like to know myself," I said.

On Friday of that week things were back to normal. "You know what Charles did today?" Laurie demanded at the lunch table, in a voice slightly awed. "He told a little girl to say a word and she said it and the teacher washed her mouth out with soap and Charles laughed."

"What word?" his father asked unwisely, and Laurie said, "I'll have to whisper it to you, it's so bad." He got down off his chair and went around to his father. His father bent his head down and Laurie whispered joyfully. His father's eyes widened.

"Did Charles tell the little girl to say *that*?" he asked respectfully.

"She said it *twice*," Laurie said. "Charles told her to say it *twice*."

"What happened to Charles?" my husband asked.

"Nothing," Laurie said. "He was passing out the crayons."

Monday morning Charles abandoned the little girl and said the evil word himself three or four times, getting his mouth washed out with soap each time. He also threw chalk.

> We maneuvered up to one another cautiously, and smiled.

My husband came to the door with me that evening as I set out for the P.T.A. meeting. "Invite her over for a cup of tea after the meeting," he said. "I want to get a look at her."

"If only she's there," I said prayerfully.

"She'll be there," my husband said. "I don't see how they could hold a P.T.A. meeting without Charles's mother."

At the meeting I sat restlessly, scanning each comfortable matronly face, trying to determine which one hid the secret of Charles. None of them looked to me haggard enough. No one stood up in the meeting and apologized for the way her son had been acting. No one mentioned Charles.

After the meeting, I identified and sought out Laurie's kindergarten teacher. She had a plate with a cup of tea and a piece of chocolate cake; I had a plate with a cup of tea and a piece of marshmallow cake. We maneuvered up to one another cautiously, and smiled.

(cont'd on next page)

"I've been so anxious to meet you," I said. "I'm Laurie's mother."

"We're all so interested in Laurie," she said.

"Well, he certainly likes kindergarten," I said. "He talks about it all the time."

"We had a little trouble adjusting, the first week or so," she said primly, "but now he's a fine little helper. With occasional lapses, of course."

"Laurie usually adjusts very quickly," I said. "I suppose this time it's Charles's influence."

"Charles?"

"Yes," I said, laughing, "you must have your hands full in that kindergarten, with Charles."

"Charles?" she said. "We don't have any Charles in the kindergarten."

—Shirley Jackson

Start-Up: Listening, not just hearing, is very important in communication.

Everyone needs to improve his or her listening skills. The biggest listening problem is lack of interest. Some students excuse low grades by saying that their teachers are boring or subjects are not interesting. The real problem in most cases, however, is lack of interest. What can you do to make a class more interesting? Make a game out of the class. Reward yourself for staying alert. Your reward may be better grades. Look for ways you can use the material you learn in class now. Impress your friends with your knowledge. Challenge yourself. Set a goal for yourself and become informed.

Lack of concentration is another listening problem. To help improve your concentration, make a record of how often you lose concentration. Get sticky notes and label one for each class. When your attention wanders, make a mark on the note. This record will show how often you don't concentrate in class. Keep this record for five days. Average the number of times you did not pay attention for each class. This average will be a target for you to reduce. If this practice does not cause you to pay better attention in class, ask your teacher for assistance.

Be an active listener. Restate main ideas in your own words. Relate new ideas to old ones. If you don't understand, ask questions. Avoid distractions. Predict topics and pose problems. Find ways to improve your listening skills.

Connection: Laurie's parents proved to be problem listeners: they heard only words and did not listen actively. They were very interested in Laurie's days at school, but they did not probe his actions, nor did they question him until they were satisfied they understood the real situation.

They missed the nonverbal cues.

1. Reread Jackson's story. List all of the cues, verbal and nonverbal, that indicate Laurie is really Charles.

2. Write down some advice for Laurie's parents on improving their listening skills. Put your advice in the form of a doctor's prescription. For example:

Once a day, give one tablespoon of questioning. (Probe for information and clarification.)

Include at least three items in your prescription.

"Barbara Allen"

Overview

In literature, a ballad is a poem that tells a story and is often set to music. "Barbara Allen," which has over a dozen titles, is one of the most widely recorded ballads in history. English and Scottish versions, as well as American versions, exist. A historian found over 90 versions in Virginia alone.

During the Middle Ages, when few people could read or write, minstrels composed ballads about the everyday lives of common people on such topics as lost love, envy, loyalty, sudden disaster, and revenge. These ballads were passed down by word of mouth from generation to generation.

Early settlers of America brought the ballads with them. These ballads still flourish in the Appalachian Mountains, among cowhands, and within many cultures.

Start-Up: You will listen to a recorded version of "Barbara Allen."

Connection: Listen to the ballad once. Then listen a second time, taking notes on each verse as it is sung. Write down the answers to these questions: Who was involved? What happened? When? Where? How? Why?

Imagine that you want to share with an acquaintance the story told by the ballad. Modernize the story. Tell it as if the situation happened to someone you both know. Write a message as if you were sending it by e-mail. The message must be a maximum of 100 words and should answer the questions on which you took notes.

Working with Literature: Refer to *Student Workbook* page 3-F for an activity on listening.

Chapter 4

© GETTY IMAGES/PHOTODISC, INC.

"The factory of the future will have only two employees, a man and a dog. The man will be there to feed the dog. The dog will be there to keep the man from touching the equipment."

—WARREN BENNIS, AUTHOR AND DISTINGUISHED PROFESSOR OF BUSINESS ADMINISTRATION, UNIVERSITY OF SOUTHERN CALIFORNIA

Using the TOT Outlet Cap

Crawling babies are attracted to electrical outlets. The TOT Outlet Cap can protect them from electrical hazards. Works on any type of outlet.

To use:

1. Hold the TOT Outlet Cap with the arrow facing up. Push prongs into outlet slots. Make sure caps are flat against the outlet plate.

2. To use the outlet, lift removal slot at top and bottom of cap. Bend back flexible connector for access to slot.

Caution:

This product is not intended to substitute for adult supervision. Always replace Outlet Cap as soon as you are finished using the outlet.

Giving Instructions

Instructions range in complexity. Arrows show which end of a milk carton to open; book-length computer manuals detail operating procedures. Maps use very few words, while instructions for completing tax returns use thousands of words.

Everyone has encountered instructions that are confusing, incomplete, or inaccurate. This chapter will help you learn to give useful and effective instructions.

The three important elements of all communication are audience, subject, and purpose. As communicators, however, you sometimes become so interested in your subject and purpose that you forget the needs of the audience. Since you expect the audience for instructions to act, not just to listen or read, you must keep their needs in mind. Ask yourself how your audience will use your instructions.

How are people supposed to use instructions? Everyone knows that it is best to read all instructions before doing anything. But how do people really use instructions? Most people read only what they think they need to know when they need to know it.

You cannot assume that your audience will read or listen to all of your instructions or that your audience will carry out your instructions in the order in which they were given. Nevertheless, careful audience analysis will help you produce instructions that the audience can likely use. After all, instructions that no one can use are no better than no instructions at all.

Different audiences have different needs.

Audience Characteristics

The characteristics of the audience for your instructions will dictate everything from your word choice to your page design and use of visuals. How old are your readers (or listeners)? How much education have they had? Is English their primary language? How much previous experience with the subject do they have? Are they highly motivated to follow instructions, or are they reluctant? What exactly does your audience need to know?

Length of Instructions

Instructions that are overly long and detailed are less likely to be completely and carefully read than brief, to-the-point instructions. Thorough audience analysis will help you determine the amount of explanation to include. Provide all of the information your reader will need to successfully carry out the instructions *and nothing more.*

Method of Presentation

Determining the most effective way to present your instructions can be crucial to their success. Simple instructions can be oral—in fact, a demonstration is often most effective. Sometimes, though, you are separated from your audience by space and/or time. Then you need to present written instructions. At other times, particularly for more complex operations, your instructions may need to combine both oral presentations and written reminders.

Technology *Connection*

Sometimes even excellent instructions fail. Perhaps the audience doesn't read them or listen to them carefully. Sometimes audiences are more inexperienced than the writer anticipated. Many companies offer help lines as a service to customers who have trouble with their products. Computer hardware and software technical support lines often get calls from customers with little computer experience. According to Charles Brewer's "Home Computing" newspaper column, one company's technical support technicians reported the following stories:

A technician told a customer to "open a window," meaning a program group window on the computer screen. The customer opened a window—and then complained about the room getting too cold.

Another customer returned his broken computer to the company. It seems that when he tried to sign up for an online service, it asked him to "enter your credit card number" and he stuck his credit card in the disk drive.

Remember, what seems simple to you may appear complicated to your audience. Careful analysis of your audience, subject, and purpose will determine whether your instructions should be written, oral, or both.

Practice 4–1: Grading Instructions with a Team

For this Practice, work with three or four other students. Your teacher will give your team five sets of instructions to grade. Make sure each team member examines each set of instructions. Discuss the strengths and weaknesses of each set. Summarize the group's evaluation of the instructions on *Student Workbook* page 4-A. For each set of instructions, fill in the blanks indicating the purpose of the instructions; for example, "Instructions for Growing Magic Rocks." Note two or three effective features and two or three ineffective features. Then give each set of instructions a grade. You may give no more than one A, one B, one C, one D, and one F.

Giving Effective Oral Instructions

On-the-job training often involves showing rather than telling. The presenter not only must demonstrate an operation, but also must teach techniques and ideas, present information, and persuade the audience to follow directions. The key to effective oral instructions is planning.

Analyze the Audience

The complexity of your subject will, in part, determine the length of your presentation and the amount of planning required. However, consider the age, experience, attitude, and needs of your audience as well. You must plan more carefully for instructions for 30 people than you would for 3 people.

Practice 4–2: Considering Your Audience

For this Practice, you will need a sheet of paper, a pencil, and a book to use as a lap desk. Choose a partner to work with. One of you is Person A; the other, Person B. Position yourselves so that you can talk and listen to each other but cannot see each other.

1. Your teacher will give a copy of a drawing to Person A in each team. Person A will describe the drawing and give B clear and precise instructions for reproducing it on his or her paper. Person B may not speak or make any sounds at all—no questions, no requests to repeat instructions, no statements about being ready for the next step. Person A may not look at B's drawing, and B may not look at A's. When A is finished, B should compare his or her drawing to A's drawing.

2. Your teacher will give you instructions for the second round. After completing Round 2, answer the following questions:

   a. What problems did the lack of feedback cause when you gave or followed instructions?
   b. How did giving or following instructions with no feedback make you feel?
   c. What three things did you do to make your instructions easy to follow?
   d. What three things could you have done to improve your instructions?
   e. How is producing written instructions like giving oral instructions with no feedback?
   f. Why is it important to plan carefully for large audiences?
   g. Why are written instructions often easier to follow than oral instructions?
   h. Based on this activity, can you provide three rules for giving effective oral instructions? Explain.

Research the Subject

If there are any gaps in your knowledge of your subject, consult manuals, experts, or other sources to fill in those gaps. Remember, your audience may ask questions, and you want to give accurate answers. Nothing is more important in giving instructions than accuracy. Double-check accuracy by asking someone who is not familiar with the subject to

Culture *Connection*

Most people at times use gestures to give simple instructions, such as *stop, quiet,* or *come here.* People take for granted that everyone will understand what they mean. But these gestures are culturally biased; that is, they often vary from one culture to another—a possible source of misunderstanding. Here are some examples of how people in other countries make the sign for *come here*:

Burma   Palm down with fingers moving as though playing the piano

Philippines   Quick downward nod of the head

Scandinavia   Tossing the head back

If that's not confusing enough, in Albania and Bulgaria, a nod means "no," while a head shake means "yes."

© GETTY IMAGES/PHOTODISC, INC.

On-the-job training often involves showing rather than telling.

follow your instructions. Note places where this person had questions or made errors; then revise the instructions accordingly.

Organize

Organize your presentation so that the listener will be able to follow your directions easily. Present information in the order the audience will use it as they carry out the instructions. The organizational plan for instructions explained later in this chapter also works well for most oral instructions.

Make Notes

Since it is important to present instructions in the proper order, outline your presentation or prepare note cards so you don't forget an important fact or step. The presentation will be more effective if you occasionally refer to notes as you talk, instead of reading word for word from a page.

Prepare Visuals

Since the most highly developed sense is sight, most people learn more from seeing than from hearing. Whenever possible, show rather than tell. Whether your visuals are actual tools or equipment that you are using, a drawing or diagram, or some other type of illustration, make sure that they are large enough and are clearly visible to everyone in the audience.

Practice

Visuals must be clearly visible to the audience.

The most important benefit to practicing your presentation is that it will give you confidence and relieve your anxiety about having to speak publicly. Practice as though your audience were there. Don't just think the words; talk out loud. Use your visuals as you practice. If you find that you occasionally need to pause and think, that's OK. Do not fill brief silences with *umm, all right,* and similar expressions.

Give the Presentation

Guard against performing the process without talking; an effective presenter describes the steps as they are being performed. Do not rush through your demonstration and remember to talk clearly and loudly enough to be heard in the back of the room. If you don't mind interruptions, let your audience know that they can ask you questions during your presentation. Otherwise, ask if they have any questions when you finish the instructions.

Locational Instructions

Locational instructions explain how to get from here to there. Only the simplest instructions may be given orally, since the human brain is able to remember only a limited amount of information at one time. A clear map will sometimes be sufficient, as in Figure 4-1. At other times, written or oral instructions with a map will be most effective. The complexity of the directions and careful audience analysis will guide you.

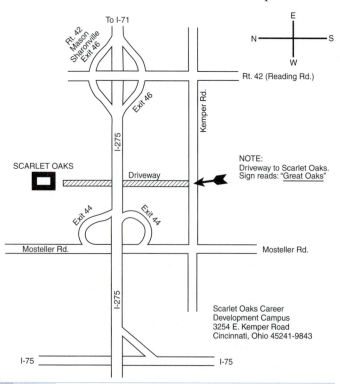

FIGURE 4-1 A map showing locational instructions

Practice 4-3: The Numbers Game

Most people cannot retain more than seven bits of unrelated information at a time in short-term memory. For example, since phone numbers are only seven digits long, most people can remember one just long enough to dial it. Once that number has been dialed several times, it will probably be stored in the brain's long-term memory. If oral instructions include more than a few steps, the audience will need written reminders. To test this information, listen carefully while your teacher reads a series of numbers; then write them down. Your teacher will give you further instructions.

Tips for Giving Locational Instructions

When giving locational instructions, follow these guidelines:

1. Identify the starting point and destination.

2. Give the distance between the starting point and the destination in terms of space (six miles or blocks) or time (about five minutes).

3. Indicate the general direction between the starting point and the destination. If appropriate, use compass points (northeast, south).

4. Give specific, step-by-step directions in **chronological** (time) order. Note landmarks and places where mistakes might occur. Include enough detail to make the instructions easy to follow, but eliminate unnecessary detail that may only confuse your audience.

Ch04-04.mp3

Practice 4–4: Listening to Instructions

1. Listen to the effective locational instructions that your teacher provides.

2. Listen to the ineffective locational instructions.

3. List five ways to improve the second set of instructions.

Practice 4–5: Giving Clear Oral Instructions

Your teacher will give you a slip of paper identifying a place located in or around the building. You will give oral instructions from the room in which you are sitting to the location written on your paper. You may not reveal the destination. If your instructions are clear enough, the class should be able to guess.

1. Jot down reminder notes before it is your turn to participate in this Practice.

2. Begin by giving the distance between the starting point and the destination.

3. Indicate the general direction.

4. Give specific, step-by-step instructions.

5. Do not use hand signals to indicate direction.

6. Provide enough—but not too much—detail.

7. Give all instructions in the right order.

FIGURE 4-2   An ineffective map

Using Maps to Give Instructions

A clear, accurate, well-designed map is often the most effective way to present locational instructions. If you cannot find a suitable map, you may have to draw one yourself. Drawing a simple map does not take artistic ability, but it does take time and patience. As in all instructions, accuracy is the most important factor.

Practice 4-6: Evaluating a Map

Think about maps you have used in the past, whether they were road maps or maps showing how to find a particular location in a building. What made them easy—or difficult—to follow? The map shown in Figure 4-2 is not effective. Examine it closely. Then list five ways to improve it.

Practice 4-7: Constructing an Effective Map

Draw both a rough draft and a final draft of a map showing how to get from the gas station nearest your home to your school.

For the Rough Draft

1. Use a pencil.

2. Give your map a clear title written in all capital letters.

3. Indicate the starting point and the destination.

4. Show the distance in miles.

5. Use compass points (north, southeast) to indicate direction.

6. Show the correct path, using arrows.

7. Include landmarks and street names.

8. Use as few words as possible.

9. Include enough detail to make your map easy to follow.

For the Final Draft

1. Use unlined paper and a ruler.

2. Make your map neat, uncrowded, and attractive.

3. Carefully print any words.

4. Make sure that your audience can read your map without rotating the page.

5. Eliminate distracting detail.

6. Use color to highlight important places.

The Content of Instructions

Effective instructions are complete and easy to follow. Most instructions include an introduction, definitions, necessary preparations, warnings and precautions, steps, and sometimes a closing. Each section of the instructions (except the title and introduction) must have its own heading so that the audience can find needed information quickly. Instructions for cleaning up a chemical spill, shown at the end of this chapter, provide good examples of these elements.

Special care is necessary when using any chemical product. Proper use of chemicals includes safely storing and disposing of them. The chemicals contained in many common products are poisonous if swallowed; others are caustic and can burn the eyes and skin or release toxic fumes. If a large chemical spill occurs, you must be very careful to clean it up correctly.

FIGURE 4-3   Introduction for instructions

Preparations
- Make sure that a fire extinguisher rated ABC or BC is nearby.
- Put out any flame and keep people away.
- Wear a respirator, rubber gloves, rubber boots, and safety goggles.

Materials and Equipment
- Clean cloths or paper towels
- Plastic garbage bag
- Absorbent material (cat litter or vermiculite)

FIGURE 4-4   Preparations, including materials and equipment, shown in a list with bullets

WARNING

Toxic Fumes

Can cause dizziness or unconsciousness.

Open all windows and doors to the outside.

Wear a respirator.

FIGURE 4-5   A warning for instructions

The Introduction

The introduction often serves several functions: it can provide an overview of the task being explained, give the purpose of the task, explain a process, or encourage the reader to read and follow the instructions. Your subject and the characteristics of your audience will determine the information appropriate for your introduction. (See Figure 4-3.)

Definitions

Once again, let your intended audience be your guide. If you are not 100 percent certain that your audience will understand a technical term, define it, using a three-part sentence definition. Give the definition immediately after using the term for the first time or list it in a glossary following the introduction.

Preparations

What preparations will the audience need to make before following the steps? For example, are certain conditions necessary, such as strong light, a 60- to 70-degree room temperature, or a dust-free environment, to begin the task? What tools, equipment, and materials are needed? For written instructions, if more than two are required, list them down the page. Unless the exact order matters, use bullets instead of numbers. Bullets are symbols inserted at the start of each line that make a list easy to read. (See Figure 4-4.)

Warnings and Precautions

Effective warnings and precautions can prevent safety hazards, injuries, ruined materials, broken equipment, and other problems. It is your responsibility to ensure the safety of your audience as they follow your instructions. (See Figure 4-5.)

Steps

1. Pour absorbent material on the spill. Wait for it to be soaked up.

2. Scoop up the absorbent material with a shovel or dustpan; put it in a bag.

3. Remove all traces of the spill, using a cloth or brush dipped in solvent.

4. Scrub the area thoroughly with a stiff-bristled brush and a solution of mild detergent and water.

5. Rinse and wipe dry with clean cloths or paper towels.

6. Following the disposal regulations of your community, remove chemical-soaked cloths, paper towels, and absorbent materials.

7. Change your clothes and wash them separately.

FIGURE 4-6   Numbered steps

Steps

Include enough detail to eliminate any confusion about what to do. To test your instructions, ask a person unfamiliar with the task to read them and provide feedback. Are there any unexplained gaps or steps that could be interpreted more than one way? Explain *how* as well as *what* to do. In written instructions, steps presented in a numbered list should describe just one action for each numbered item. (See Figure 4-6.)

The Closing

A closing may be needed to tell the audience how to test the results of following the instructions, to summarize the main steps, or to mention other methods of carrying out the task. Whatever the purpose, the closing should be brief.

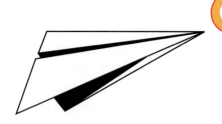

Practice 4–8: Making a Paper Airplane

For this Practice, you will need three sheets of unlined paper. Fold the first sheet into a paper airplane. It can be as simple or complex as you wish. If you do not know how to make a paper airplane, make up your own design. Try to prevent anyone from seeing your plane. Your teacher will give you further instructions.

Using Language Effectively

by the way...

A technical writer must have the ability to make simple that which is not simple.

Careful use of language makes instructions easy to understand and use. No one reads instructions merely for pleasure. The words and combinations of words must be carefully chosen to carry out the purpose of the instructions: to enable the audience to act, not just to understand. Your language must be **precise**, **concise**, and **clear**. Write all steps as **commands**. Be especially careful when writing numbers.

Word Choice

Depending on your audience, you may need to define technical terms as you use them. Whenever possible, choose words that most people can understand. You might produce instructions that are complete and technically accurate, but if your reader is unable to understand even a few words, your instructions will be useless.

Precise Language

The difference between *crow* and *crown* is only one letter, but if one of them is sitting on your head, the difference is important! In communication at work, "almost the right word" is the wrong word. Make certain that you understand the exact meaning of each word you use—and that you are using it appropriately. Then make sure that your audience cannot misinterpret your meaning. **Precise** language is exact and accurate.

One important aspect of precision is choosing the right word. Some word pairs, such as *cite* and *site*, can cause difficulty because they are often confused. *Cite* is a verb that means "to quote as an authority or example": I cited several experts in my study of water pollution. It also means "to recognize formally": The volunteers were cited for service to the city. *Cite* can also mean "to summon before a court of law": Our company was cited for pollution violations. *Site* is a noun that means "location": The new site for the recycling center is a mile away. When in doubt about the precise meaning of a word, look it up in a dictionary.

Practice 4–9: Precise Writing

1. The words and phrases below are unclear because they are not precise. Copy each unclear phrase. Then replace the vague, imprecise language with concrete and exact words and phrases.

   Examples:

Vague	Precise
just a few ingredients	three ingredients
a perfect-size nail	a 10d nail
the institution	the university

   a. a number of tools   e. the missing part
   b. a large profit   f. a tall person
   c. a high temperature   g. a few colors
   d. quite a few orders   h. soon

2. Complete *Student Workbook* page 4-B to practice selecting terms based on their precise meanings.

Concise and Clear Language

Extra words, sentences, and information clutter your writing, making your instructions unnecessarily long and confusing to your audience. If anything can be removed without changing the meaning of your message, remove it. **Concise** language is economical—every word counts.

Practice 4–10: Concise and Clear Writing

1. The words and phrases in the left column are not concise or clear. Replace the following words and phrases with clearer, more concise ones.

Examples:

Wordy or Unclear	Concise and Clear
exact same	same
terminate	end
in the year of 1492	in 1492
true facts	facts
completely finished	finished
during the time that	while

Ch04-10.doc

a. cancel out

b. positive benefits

c. utilize

d. each and every

e. costs the sum of

f. make an inspection

g. really interesting

h. in the state of Iowa

i. at all times

j. yellow in color

k. in the amount of

l. end result

m. personal opinion

n. three different people

2. Rewrite the following sentences to make them more precise and concise. In the example and the first two sentences, the wordy or vague words and phrases are underlined.

Example:

Should you wish to return the item, please contact the undersigned by phone in a timely manner.

To return the stereo system, please call me by May 31.

a. Our future plans include procuring additional units.

b. Either one or the other of the plans is totally acceptable.

c. I believe that there are several operators who are violating regulations with regard to safety procedures.

d. During unfavorable weather conditions, perform maintenance in an indoor area.

e. If you purchase a large number of them, the locking devices that are circular in shape cost the sum of $7.50.

Command Forms

In instructions, steps are always given in the second person and as **commands**. Second person is you, the audience. Commands allow the writer to address the audience directly, increasing the likelihood that the steps will be followed. "Please stand for the Pledge of Allegiance" is a command.

Practice 4–11: Writing Commands

All but one of the following instructions are not written as commands. Instead, they describe or explain—rather than direct—action. Rewrite the instructions as commands. Begin each sentence with a *verb*, the word in the sentence that expresses the action. In the first two sentences, the base form of the verb is underlined. For the one instruction that is correctly written, write *command*.

Example:

"Everyone should complete this Practice today" is not a command.
"This Practice is due today" is not a command.
"Complete this Practice today" is a command.
Complete is a verb.

Ch04-11.doc

1. It is a good idea to <u>ask</u> questions if you don't understand the instructions.

2. The board should be <u>clamp</u>ed to the bench.

3. All employees must fill out an insurance form.

4. They should lower the bar before sawing.

5. The X-rays need to be examined immediately.

6. Safety glasses must be worn by all electricians.

7. Take the time to make the customer feel comfortable.

8. The lines need to be drawn more carefully.

9. Customers should be listened to.

10. All phone calls must be returned promptly.

Writing Numbers Correctly

When writing instructions and other workplace documents, write numbers carefully. A hastily written 5 can look like an S; a 4 can look like a 9. The following table shows when to use words and when to use figures when writing numbers. When you follow these guidelines, you help the audience to read numbers accurately.

GUIDELINES FOR WRITING NUMBERS	
Use Figures For	**Examples**
1. Dates, house numbers (except *One*), telephone numbers, ZIP Codes, specific amounts, mathematical expressions, etc.	July 30, 2005; 600 Race Street; 61 percent; 555-0103; 10:30 p.m.; Chapter 12; $29.54
2. Measures, weights, and dimensions.	The recipe calls for 2 cups of sugar, 1/2 teaspoon of salt, 1 stick of butter, and 1/4 cup of cocoa.
3. Numerals expressed as decimals.	12.0006
4. Numbers above ten or numbers that require three or more words.	She sold 12 new cars in 2 1/2 hours.
5. Several related numbers (including fractions) that occur within a sentence.	We ordered 20 reams of paper, 3 boxes of envelopes, and 5 printer cartridges.
6. One of two numbers occurring next to each other.	12 fifty-gallon containers
Use Words For	**Examples**
7. One of two numbers occurring next to each other.	50 six-cylinder cars four 3,600-pound loads
8. Numbers from one through ten.	I left work two hours early.
9. A number that begins a sentence. **Note:** If using words for numbers at the beginning of a sentence is awkward, reorganize the sentence.	Fifty cents is a fair entrance fee. Sixty percent of first-year students come from this area. **Wrong:** 2,175 orders are ready. **Awkward:** Two thousand, one hundred seventy-five orders are ready. **Correct:** We have 2,175 orders ready.
10. Numbers that are approximate or indefinite.	You'll save hundreds of dollars. About fifty machines were returned.
11. Fractions.	Our department receives three-fourths of the funding.

When writing dollar amounts, use the dollar sign and decimal point: Materials will cost $487.50. You can leave the comma out of figures in the thousands: When you add labor, the total is $2500. Also leave the comma out of addresses and years: In 1999, they moved to 2733 Eighth Avenue.

Practice 4-12: Writing Numbers Correctly

Rewrite any of the following sentences in which numbers are used incorrectly. Three sentences are correct as stated. For them, write the word *correct*. Refer to the guidelines shown in the table on the previous page.

1. Press the Enter key 3 times.

2. Twenty-seven dollars was spent for one twelve-volt battery.

3. If I had $1,000,000, I'd travel the world.

4. The preschool will have room for about one hundred fifty children next year.

5. Sam reported that one-fourth of the modems had been sold.

6. The statement included the following costs: $25.00 for chicken, $15.65 for beef, and seven dollars for pasta.

7. The cabinet was three feet high, 10 feet long, and 18 inches deep.

8. 175 people applied for permits before January fifteenth.

9. We sold 4 50-inch televisions.

10. We need drill bits for 1/2-inch holes, 3/4-inch holes, and 1 1/2-inch holes.

Giving Precautions and Warnings

Using effective language is especially important whenever safety is an issue. Warn your listeners or readers of any hazards that you can foresee as they are following instructions. Provide warnings at the point in your instructions when the audience is most likely to encounter the problem. If your audience reads the warning two hours before encountering the potential danger, they may forget. On the other hand, if you caution them at the end of your instructions, it may already be too late.

An effective warning or precaution contains four types of information: a **signal word**, a **hazard identification**, the **result of ignoring the warning**, and instructions for **avoiding the hazard**. (See Figure 4-7 on the next page for a sample warning.)

The Signal Word

A precaution warns the audience to be careful, while a warning gives a stronger message that severe harm will occur if the warning is ignored. The signal words *DANGER, WARNING, STOP, CAUTION,* and *IMPORTANT,* written in large, capital, bold letters, get the audience's attention. The colors red and yellow also help alert your audience.

by the way...

"Perfection is achieved, not when there is nothing left to add, but when there is nothing left to take away."

ANTOINE DE SAINT-EXUPÉRY, FRENCH WRITER

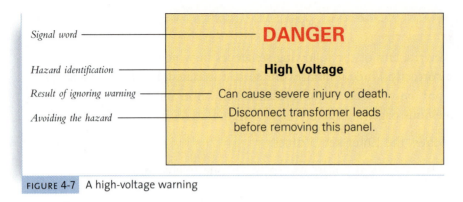

Signal word ——————
Hazard identification ——————
Result of ignoring warning ——————
Avoiding the hazard ——————

DANGER

High Voltage

Can cause severe injury or death.
Disconnect transformer leads
before removing this panel.

FIGURE 4-7   A high-voltage warning

The Hazard Identification

This part of the message tells the audience what the hazard is. The hazard identification should appear in bold print. **Electrical shock, Radiation**, and **Hazardous vapors** are some examples. Use **sentence case** for this part. In sentence case, the first letter of the first word is capitalized.

The Result of Ignoring the Warning

The next part of the message describes what will happen if the warning is ignored. It tells what damage the **Radiation, Hazardous vapors, Electrical shock**, etc. will cause. Use sentence case for this part.

Avoiding the Hazard

The last part of a precaution or warning gives detailed instructions for avoiding the hazard. This section must be concise and well organized. Use simple, direct commands in sentence case.

Careful
Acme Liquid.

Contains no oxygen.
Should be serviced in a ventilated area.

FIGURE 4-8   A warning sign

CAUTION

THIS MACHINE OPERATES WITH A LASER LIGHT THAT COULD CAUSE AN INJURY TO THE USER'S EYES.

EYES MUST BE PROTECTED AND DON'T AIM THE BEAM AT EYES OR AT SURFACES THAT REFLECT.

FIGURE 4-9   A caution sign

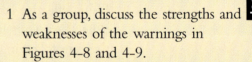

Practice 4-13: Precautions and Warnings

1 As a group, discuss the strengths and weaknesses of the warnings in Figures 4-8 and 4-9.

2. On your own or with a partner, rewrite the warnings, correcting them and improving their effectiveness. Use the four-part format shown in Figure 4-7.

3. On the top half of the back of your paper, make a four-part sign that warns the user of a hazard in your classroom, in your lab, or at work. Label the four parts of your sign.

4. On the bottom half, make a four-part warning sign to hang around your neck the next time you are having a bad day. The warning will protect you from friends and enemies (and will protect them from you). No profanity, please.

Ethics *Connection*

How does the following excerpt from "The Society for Technical Communication Code for Communicators" apply to writing instructions?

As a technical communicator, I am the bridge between those who create ideas and those who use them . . . .

I value the worth of the ideas I am transmitting and the cost of developing and communicating those ideas. I also value the time and effort spent by those who read or see or hear my communication.

I therefore recognize my responsibility to communicate technical information truthfully, clearly, and economically.

My commitment to professional excellence and ethical behavior means that I will

• Use language and visuals with precision.

• Prefer simple, direct expression of ideas.

• Satisfy the audience's need for information, not my own need for self-expression.

• Hold myself responsible for how well my audience understands my message.

Designing an Effective Page

Carefully planned layout and design of written instructions can make the difference between instructions that are successfully followed and those that are ignored or misused. Logical layout of material, titles and headings, white space, easy-to-read print, and easy-to-follow sequence (order) all contribute to effective instructions.

Page Design

A page that looks easy and quick to read is more likely to be read than a disorganized page crammed with words and pictures. Information that is difficult to locate may be ignored. Help your audience follow instructions by carefully designing your page. Follow these guidelines:

• Number your steps down the page and separate them with white space.

• Use bullets for most other lists (unless sequence is important).

• Use clear, large print and visuals.

• Use a computer or write neatly.

Spread the material evenly over the page instead of crowding it in one area. Place visuals so that your reader can find them easily within the text, or if visuals must be on another page, include directions explaining where to find them.

The right font choice can reinforce your message, whereas the wrong one can detract from it. Remember that your primary purpose is to make the document easy to read and to understand.

Most experts agree that 12-point normal serif fonts are best for large amounts of text because they are easy to read. Serifs are decorative extensions at the ends of letters.

Sans serif typefaces (typefaces without serifs) are effective for small amounts of text and for titles and headings.

Decorative and display typefaces will get your reader's attention, but use them sparingly, since they can be hard to read.

Script typefaces look like handwriting. Although some of them can be difficult to read, they come in handy when you want a small amount of text to have a more personal look.

Whichever style you choose, avoid using more than two typefaces on a page. Never use all capital letters for display or script fonts, since that makes them too difficult to read.

White space makes important information stand out, much like a silent room can make a sneeze sound like an explosion. White space also indicates the writer's organization and makes for an inviting and easy-to-read page.

If you use a computer to produce documents, you will have to decide which typefaces, type styles, and fonts to use. A **typeface** is a particular design for the letters and other symbols (for example, Times Roman or Helvetica). A **type style** is a variation on a typeface (for example, normal, bold, or italic). A **font** is one size and style of a particular typeface (for example, 10-point Helvetica Bold). The thousands of available typefaces range from formal to casual, from artistic to businesslike, and from plain to fancy.

The Title

The wording of the title informs the audience about the purpose of the instructions. "HOW TO CLEAN UP A LARGE CHEMICAL SPILL" or "CLEANING UP A LARGE CHEMICAL SPILL" is more informative than "CHEMICAL SPILLS." Center your title at the top of your page and use all capital letters, bold print, or a display font.

Headings

Headings can help your reader locate information at a glance. When your reader needs to assemble necessary materials, for instance, he or she does

by the way...

In your workplace, learn to admit mistakes and to accept imperfection. A good manager will encourage you not to be fearful and pin the blame elsewhere, which is a breach of ethics. Occasional mistakes are an inevitable consequence of being creative.

not want to read through the definitions or steps while trying to locate the materials list. Headings must stand out from the rest of the page so that the reader can locate them quickly. Use bold print or color and white space to make them obvious. Center headings or align them at the left margin. Headings must also be consistent; that is, they need to be formatted the same way throughout the document.

Chronological Order

Instructions must be written in chronological (time) order—the same order as the reader's action. You would never list materials at the end of your instructions or warn your reader to remove all nails from the cutting surface after he or she has made the first cut. The audience should be able to carry out the instructions in the order given. For example, "Before you open the lid, turn the machine off" is confusing. "Turn the machine off before opening the lid" is clearer.

Putting information down in the order you *think* it instead of the order in which your reader will *use* it can have disastrous results. Here's an example from M★A★S★H, a popular television comedy that ran from 1972 through 1982. The 4077th M★A★S★H was an Army medical unit located in Korea during the Korean War. In one episode, two doctors, Hawkeye and Trapper, are assigned to defuse an unexploded bomb that has landed in the compound. Colonel Blake, hiding behind a sandbag bunker, reads a bomb-defusing manual aloud to them through a bullhorn.

"First, you need a wrench," he reads. Hawkeye and Trapper find one. "All right, now, place it gently on the nut just above the locking ring and loosen." They loosen it. "Now rotate the locking ring counterclockwise." They figure out which way is counterclockwise and rotate it. "Now remove the tail assembly." They remove it. "And carefully cut the wires leading to the clockwork fuse at the head." They cut them. "But first," shouts Blake, "remove the fuse." The punch line of this joke is, of course, the resulting explosion.

Practice 4–14: Page Design

List five differences between the negative and the positive examples of layout and design shown in Figures 4-10 and 4-11.

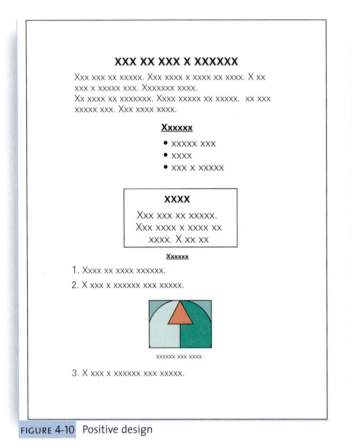

FIGURE 4-10   Positive design

FIGURE 4-11   Negative design

Creating Effective Visuals

The expression "a picture is worth a thousand words" becomes a reality when applied to giving instructions. When planned and executed well, visuals can add interest to the presentation, highlight important points, and clarify directions.

Visuals, then, serve as important components of instructions by *showing* what to do. Your subject, audience, and purpose will determine the most appropriate type of visuals, the number needed, and the information they will show.

Types of Visuals

Analyze the subject, audience, and purpose of your instructions to choose the most effective type of visual. Depending on your subject, audience, and purpose, you might choose models or objects, drawings or photographs, or diagrams to illustrate instructions.

Models and Objects

For oral instructions and demonstrations, the actual equipment or a model is often most helpful. Position the object so everyone in the audience can see it clearly.

Drawings and Photographs

Realistic, accurate drawings and photographs show your audience the parts of a mechanism, a before-and-after situation, the differences between similar items, or the steps in an operation. (See Figures 4–12 to 4–15.)

Often a simple drawing is easier to read than a photograph since it eliminates the photograph's distracting details. Refer to Chapter 2 for guidelines for constructing effective drawings.

DRAWING SHOWING PARTS OF A MECHANISM

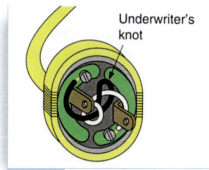

FIGURE 4-12 Plug end of an electrical cord

FIGURE 4-13 Before and after

DRAWING SHOWING STEPS IN AN OPERATION

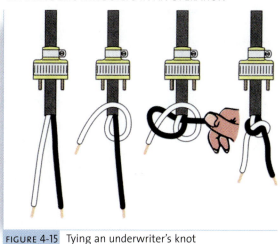

FIGURE 4-15 Tying an underwriter's knot

DRAWING SHOWING DIFFERENCES BETWEEN SIMILAR ITEMS

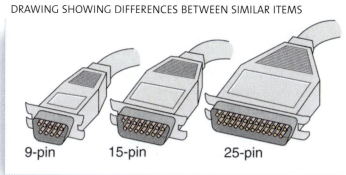

9-pin   15-pin   25-pin

FIGURE 4-14 D-shaped connectors

Diagrams

Diagrams, constructed mainly of lines and symbols, illustrate ideas, areas, and processes. (See Figures 4-16 to 4-18.) Examples of diagrams include maps, schematics, and blueprints. The guidelines for constructing drawings in Chapter 2 also apply to diagrams.

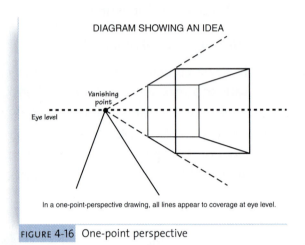

FIGURE 4-16 One-point perspective

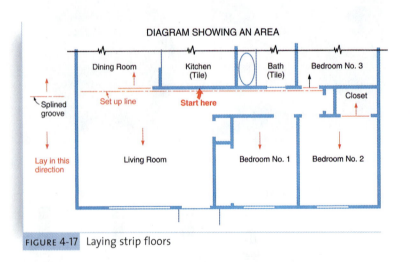

FIGURE 4-17 Laying strip floors

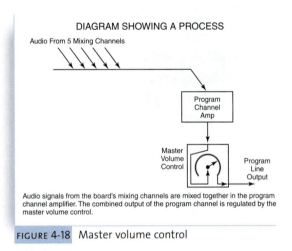

FIGURE 4-18 Master volume control

When to Include Visuals

Before deciding to include a visual in your instructions, ask yourself whether a visual will help the audience to:

- Understand the purpose of the instructions.
- Identify parts or equipment.
- Understand a specific step or series of steps.
- Avoid injury or increase safety.
- Successfully complete the task.

If your answer to *any* of these questions is yes, include the visual with your instructions.

A. Words Only

Xxx xxx xx xxxxx. Xxx
xxxx x xxxx xx xxxx. X xx
xxx x xxxxx xxx. Xxxxxxx
xxxx. Xxxx xx xxxx
xxxxxx. X xxx x xxxxx
xxx xxxxx. Xxxxxx xx
xxxx xx xxx. Xxx xxx xx
xxxxx. Xxx xxxx x xxxx xx
xxxx. X xx xxx x xxxxx
xxx. Xxxxxxx xxxx. Xxxx
xx xxxx xxxxxx. X xxx x
xxxxxx xxx xxxxx. Xxxxxx
xx xxxx xxxx xx xxxxx xx
xxxxx xxx. Xxx xxx xx
xxxxx. Xxx xxxx x xxxx xx

Example: Identifying harmful fumes by
their odors

B. Mostly Words with Some Visuals

Xxx xxx xx xxxxx. Xxx
xxxx x xxxx xx xxxx. X xx
xxx x xxxxx xxx. Xxxxxxx
xxxx. Xxxx xx xxxx
xxxxxx. X xxx
x xxxxxx xxx
xxxxx.
Xxxxxx xx
xxxx xx xxx.
Xxx xxx xx
xxxxx. Xxx xxxx x xxxx xx
xxxx. X xx xxx x xxxxx
xxx. Xxxxxxx xxxx. Xxxx
xx xxxx xxxxxx. X xxx x
xxxxxx xxx xxxxx. Xxxxxx

Example: Making a pie crust

The audience, subject, and purpose determine the relative amount of **verbal information** (words) and **visual information** (drawings, diagrams, and photos) to include in instructions.

Work on this Practice with one or two partners. For each illustration (A–D), list two more subjects for instructions that would be appropriate for the amount of verbal and visual information shown. (One subject is already provided for each illustration.)

C. Mostly Visuals with Some Words

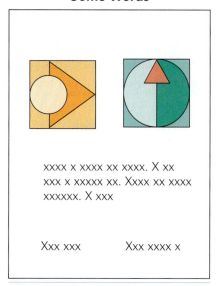

xxxx x xxxx xx xxxx. X xx
xxx x xxxxx xx. Xxxx xx xxxx
xxxxxx. X xxx

Xxx xxx   Xxx xxxx x

Example: Rescuing a choking victim

D. Visuals Only

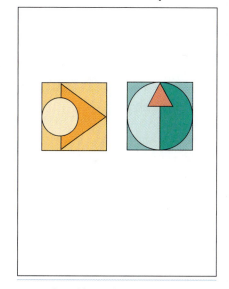

Example: Folding a letter

Making Visuals Effective

Try scanning a few pages that include visuals. You'll find that your eyes naturally focus on the visuals first. Effective visuals are often necessary elements of instructions. However, the reader may ignore a visual that requires too much work to use. A useful visual is accurate, clear, appropriately sized, and complete.

Accuracy and Completeness

How, for example, could the audience locate the "center knob" on a drawing that shows only two knobs? Or four knobs? Accurate, complete visuals, properly labeled, provide information that the reader or listener needs.

Size and Clarity

Using appropriately sized visuals is important in both oral and written instructions. Obviously, an audience must be able to see visuals during a live presentation in order to understand your instructions. Likewise, an overly large visual on a printed page takes up scarce space, while a very small visual requires too much effort on the part of the audience to see.

Clarity also aids your visuals' effectiveness. A fuzzy, overly detailed photograph merely takes up valuable space and detracts from your instructions. An effective visual is as simple as possible, without omitting essential detail.

Creating Attractive Visuals

Many types of visuals require little or no artistic ability. A stick figure showing a safe method of lifting a heavy weight is more helpful than no visual at all. (See Figure 4-19.) Take your time, do your best, and keep trying until you are satisfied with the results.

When greater artistic ability than you possess is called for, try presenting a rough sketch of your visual to a friend who has drawing talent. He or she may be pleased and flattered that you asked for help.

Finally, if you have access to a computer with graphics software, learn how to use it. Most of the art used in business and industry today is created on computers, producing amazing results; moreover, graphics software is fun to use. Clip art collections may include visuals appropriate for your instructions.

by the way...

"Make everything as simple as possible, but not simpler."

ALBERT EINSTEIN, GERMAN-BORN U.S. SCIENTIST

FIGURE 4-19 Stick figure lifting weight

Learn to use graphics software to create visuals.

When producing drawings and diagrams, follow these guidelines:

- Use only informative and appropriate visuals.

- Produce by hand or with a computer visuals that are attractive, neat, clear, and easy to use.

- Include a brief title or caption.

- Clearly label all of the parts your audience will need to locate.

- In written instructions, place your visuals at the point where your audience will need to use them. If visuals must appear on a separate page, let the audience know when to look at them and where to find them.

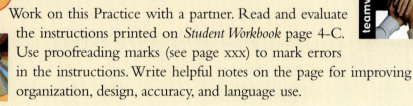

Practice 4–16: Editing Instructions

teamwork

Ch04–16.doc

Work on this Practice with a partner. Read and evaluate the instructions printed on *Student Workbook* page 4-C. Use proofreading marks (see page xxx) to mark errors in the instructions. Write helpful notes on the page for improving organization, design, accuracy, and language use.

Summary

A valuable employee is able to give effective instructions to coworkers and customers. Follow these guidelines whenever you are required to give instructions at work:

- Adapt the instructions to the previous knowledge and the needs of the audience.

- Carefully plan the instructions.

- Make sure all information is accurate.

- Include an introduction, definitions, preparations, warnings or precautions, a list of steps given as commands, and a brief closing when needed.

- Communicate clearly, precisely, and concisely.

- Design a page that is easy to use.

- Include visuals whenever they will help the audience follow instructions.

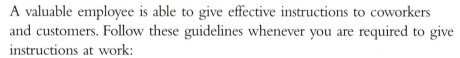

eview and research activities visit
communicating.swlearning.com

project-based assessment

Giving Instructions

Suppose that you have been asked by your supervisor to create a set of instructions that will be used in your classroom, in your lab, or at work. You may give instructions for standard or emergency procedures; for proper hygiene; or for safe assembly, use, or maintenance of equipment. Your subject must be related to your career training.

Examples:

- Washing hands in a medical lab
- Clearing a paper jam in the office copier
- Cropping a photo
- Putting out an electrical fire in a repair shop
- Handcuffing a suspect
- Thinning seedlings

The visual effect is very important since this instructional information must be noticed, read, and understood under various conditions. Consider the amount of time that your audience will have to read and follow the instructions. Also consider stressful circumstances that might impair the reader's ability to carry out the instructions.

1. Review the information in this chapter and the instructions for cleaning up a large chemical spill shown in the Sample Project Plan and the Sample Instructions on pages 133–135.

2. Complete the Project Plan on *Student Workbook* page 4-D and have your teacher check it.

3. Using the Rough Draft column of the Project Guide (*Student Workbook* page 4-E), check your work with one or more classmates. Have them record all of their comments and changes on your Project Guide and rough draft. Ask them to write a constructive comment on the rough draft and sign it.

4. Have your teacher check your rough draft.

5. Revise and edit the rough draft.

6. Using the Final Draft column of the Project Guide, proofread your work. Make any needed corrections.

7. Turn in the final draft along with the Project Guide.

Sample Project Plan

Giving Instructions

SUBJECT	**How to:** Clean up a chemical spill	**CONTENT** **Main steps to follow:**
AUDIENCE	All employees **Why should they follow instructions?** To be safe	Need—paper towels, cloths, kitty litter, shovel, brush, solvent 1. Pour kitty litter
PURPOSE	**What actions should the audience take?** Read & follow instructions	2. Scoop up & dispose 3. Brush with solvent 4. Scrub, rinse, dry
FORMAT	❑ written ❑ oral ❑ other	5. Get rid of cloths, kitty litter, etc. 6. Wash clothes
SOURCES	"Safety First . . . and Second" Pursuits pp. 45–49 4–98	
VISUALS	**What visuals, if any, will make the instructions more effective?** Drawings—pouring cat litter, safety equipment	
INTRO	**Necessary conditions, materials, equipment::** conditions—protective clothing, fire extinguisher, flames out	**Necessary precautions/warnings:** Toxic fumes warning

Sample Instructions

How to Clean Up a Large Chemical Spill

> **WARNING**
>
> **Toxic Fumes**
>
> Can cause dizziness or unconsciousness.
>
> Open all windows and doors to the outside.
>
> Wear a respirator.

Special care is necessary when using any chemical product. Proper use of chemicals includes safely storing and disposing of them. The chemicals contained in many common products are poisonous if swallowed; others are caustic and can burn the eyes and skin or release toxic fumes. If a large chemical spill occurs, you must be very careful to clean it up correctly.

Preparations

- Make sure that a fire extinguisher rated ABC or BC is nearby.
- Put out any flame and keep people away.
- Wear a respirator, rubber gloves, rubber boots, and safety goggles.

Materials and Equipment

- Clean cloths or paper towels
- Plastic garbage bag
- Absorbent material (cat litter or vermiculite)
- Shovel or dustpan
- Stiff-bristled brush
- Solvent (check label on chemical for the right type)
- Mild detergent

Steps

1. Pour absorbent material on the spill. Wait for it to be soaked up. (See Figure 1.)
2. Scoop up the absorbent material with a shovel or dustpan; put it in a bag.
3. Remove all traces of the spill, using a cloth or brush dipped in solvent.

4. Scrub the area thoroughly with a stiff-bristled brush and a solution of mild detergent and water. (See Figure 2.)

5. Rinse and wipe dry with clean cloths or paper towels.

6. Following the disposal regulations of your community, remove chemical-soaked cloths, paper towels, and absorbent materials.

7. Change your clothes and wash them separately.

Figure 1: *Pouring absorbent material*

Figure 2: *Person with proper safety equipment scrubbing the area*

Source: "Safety First . . . and Second." *Pursuits.* April 2005: 45–49.

literature

Overview

Easily understood and accurate instructions are very important in the workplace. These instructions include special warnings and cautions. Much time and money can be wasted when inaccurate instructions are given. At times, catastrophic events can happen because adequate instructions and precautions were not given to prevent harm to employees and others in the workplace.

People who give instructions without consideration of the audience, subject, and purpose often end up misdirecting their audience. The poem you are about to read tells how the speaker was angered by people who had given him or her inaccurate instructions.

"Traveller's Curse After Misdirection"

May they stumble, stage by stage

On an endless pilgrimage,

Dawn and dusk, mile after mile

At each and every step a stile;

At each and every step withal

May they catch their feet and fall;

At each and every fall they take

May a bone within them break;

And may the bone that breaks within

Not be, for variation's sake,

Now rib, now thigh, now arm, now shin,

But always, without fail, THE NECK.

—Robert Graves

Start-Up: The speaker in Graves's poem might have traveled without incident, despite being poorly directed, if there had been signs to follow. Signs and symbols are visual shorthand instructions that assist people and guard them from harm. Think of the button with an upward-pointing arrow on an elevator; the sign with a picture of a suitcase in an airport; and the skull and crossbones on a container, the contents of which are harmful if swallowed. Particularly for people who cannot read or do not speak the local language, such wordless visuals are invaluable.

Connection: Search for examples of visuals without words. List as many as you can find.

Working with Literature: Refer to *Student Workbook* page 4–F for an activity on following instructions.

Overview

In his book *Make Your Words Work*, Gary Provost provides instruction on how to use active verbs to make writing better. In giving these instructions, he uses personal illustrations and examples rather than rules to make his point.

"Use Active Voice . . . Most of the Time" from Make Your Words Work

A guy I know hangs around his apartment every evening in front of the television, hoping somebody will call and invite him to dinner. In the afternoon he haunts the mailbox, figuring maybe an invitation or a check will show up from some unexpected source. He dreams about new friends coming into his life, a better job popping up out of nowhere, and he figures he might win a new car someday if a disc jockey calls him up and asks an easy question. I know another fellow who plays tennis every morning. When he meets a man or a woman he'd like to know better, he gets the phone number and calls the person up. This guy started his own business a few years back, and now he's putting the profits into businesses by his friends. He also likes to go skydiving.

© GETTY IMAGES/PHOTODISC, INC.

(cont'd on next page)

Which man do you find more interesting, the passive one who lets things happen to him, or the active one who makes things happen?

The active man is more interesting. In writing, too, active is more interesting than passive. Just as you would fix your attention on the active man and ignore the passive one, your reader will fix his attention on the active words and phrases.

New writers often fall into the habit of casting their characters as the passive recipients of some activity, when they should be writing about people or objects doing things, making things happen.

Compare "The Christmas present given to Frank was an electric guitar" with "Frank got an electric guitar for Christmas"; "The result of the accident was many injuries to Bertha" with "When the car crashed, Bertha broke her arm, twisted her neck, and dislocated her hip."

New writers often fall into the habit of casting their characters as the passive recipients of some activity, when they should be writing about people or objects doing things, making things happen.

A key to finding the active voice is to write about people, not things. "A good time was had by all," for example, is a passive-voice sentence about good times. "Everybody had a good time" is an active-voice sentence about people.

Sometimes, of course, you are not writing about people, but about objects or concepts. Even then your object or concept should take charge of the sentence, become the subject, and work in the active voice.

For example, "Nushka was loved by Garonovitch." If you're writing about Garonvitch, then "Garonovitch loved Nushka." But maybe you're really writing about love. In that case, "Love filled Garonovitch with excitement," and "It was love that made him act so foolishly."

The tip-off to these dull, passive-voice sentences is usually a compound verb such as *was driven* or *were presented*. Cash them in for sharp, short, interesting, active verbs, and your writing will work better.

—Gary Provost

Start-Up: Assume you are the supervisor of a large retail department. Management just sent you the following instructions on how to answer the telephone in your department. Management insists that each person in your department follow these instructions. Since your employees take many calls during the course of a day, these instructions are important.

New procedures for answering the phone were given to our department. Now when the phone rings, the # button must be pushed by you before the phone will connect. In addition, since the departments were reorganized and renamed by upper-level management, your response to identify our department should be "Retail" rather than "Ready-to-Wear." At the end of the conversation, the # button should once again be pushed to terminate the connection. By using this procedure, the specific departments can be billed directly.

Connection: Respond to each of the following questions. Remember, your decisions must reflect favorably on you as a good employee.

- What is your first impression of the instructions?

- Would you make a copy to distribute to each of your employees? Why or why not?

- Would you discuss the instructions with your supervisor? Why or why not?

- Would you want to find out who was responsible for writing the instructions and talk with that person? If you did so, what might the outcome be?

- Would you want to talk to your employees about the instructions? Explain.

- Would you consider revising the instructions, then distributing copies to your employees? Explain.

- How would you handle this situation?

Chapter 5

© CORBIS

"Individual commitment to a group effort—that is what makes a team work, a company work, a society work, a civilization work."

—VINCE LOMBARDI, NFL COACH AND GENERAL MANAGER

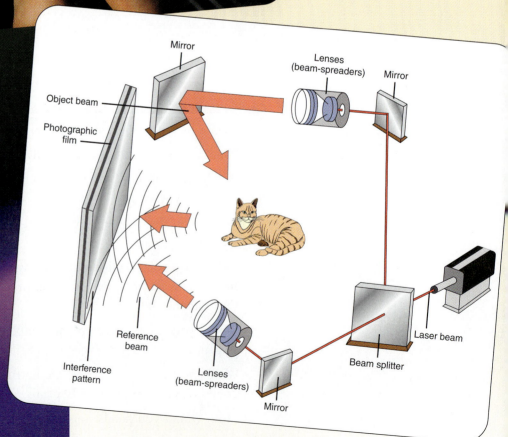

Mirror

Lenses (beam-spreaders)

Mirror

Object beam

Photographic film

Interference pattern

Reference beam

Lenses (beam-spreaders)

Mirror

Beam splitter

Laser beam

Describing a Process

What's the latest trend in tattoos? Removal! State-of-the-art removals are done with lasers that penetrate the outer layer of skin and fragment the tattoo pigment. Removing a tattoo requires multiple treatments over a period of weeks or months, can cost hundreds to thousands of dollars, and can be painful. The process works like this: A laser machine shoots out a small beam of light aimed at the ink molecules. If the tattoo is red, a green beam is used because red absorbs green. This absorption creates heat, which breaks up the molecules, allowing the body's white blood cells to eat away at the ink. The tattoo is not actually erased; it is pushed deeper into the body so the body can clean it out.

Types of Processes

The paragraph you just read is a description of a **process**, a series of actions leading to a specific result. Your job will require you to describe processes to supervisors, coworkers, and the general public so they can understand them.

Process descriptions explain how things work or how things are done or made. Processes can be carried out by machines, by people, or by nature. For example, the previously described process that enables doctors to remove tattoos is a mechanical process. All processes consist of a series of steps that occur in a particular order. The following chart shows other examples of processes.

PROCESSES ARE CARRIED OUT

By Machines	By People	By Nature
how polygraph machines work	how law enforcement officials administer polygraph tests	how emotions alter pulse, respiration, and blood pressure
how diamond saws work	how jewelers determine the value of a diamond	how carbon changes to diamonds
how Doppler radar works	how the National Hurricane Center predicts the paths of hurricanes	how hurricanes form
how a bread machine works	how a baker makes croissants	how yeast causes bread to rise

Sometimes a process description just satisfies people's curiosity about how something works. At other times, process descriptions enable readers or listeners to make informed choices and sound decisions, work safely, and grow professionally. Even though the audience will rarely carry out the described process, other actions may depend on a clear understanding of that process.

Practice 5-1: Types of Processes

Work on this Practice with a partner. For each of the following items, tell whether the process is carried out by machines, by people, or by nature. Then explain a useful way in which the intended audience can apply their understanding of the process. Are the audience members in each case general, or are they specialists?

Process	Intended Audience
1. how bacteria cause food poisoning	a restaurant worker
2. how antilock brakes and cruise control work	a new driver

Ch05-01.doc

teamwork

People *Connection*

When Philo Farnsworth was 15, his family moved to a new house in Rigby, Idaho. The former owners had left behind several technical publications. After reading them, Farnsworth became fascinated with the process of using photo-electric cells and cathode-ray tubes to transmit images, and he began designing such a system. At age 21, Farnsworth applied for a patent for his "image dissector" camera tube. This glass tube had a photosensitive mirror at one end on which an image was focused. The mirror emitted electrons in response to different light intensities projected upon it. After presenting the device to investors, he established a small production company. Before financial difficulties forced him to sell his patent rights to RCA, Farnsworth used his invention to make the first-ever public demonstration of television in 1934.

Parents should understand how babies acquire language.

Process	Intended Audience
3. how overexposure to the sun can cause skin cancer	an apprentice carpenter
4. how the IRS decides who to audit	a small-business owner
5. how a computer virus can destroy data	a World Wide Web surfer
6. how babies acquire language	a new parent
7. how numbers in animal populations are estimated	a wildlife management student
8. how a consumer survey was taken	an advertising executive

Process Descriptions Compared to Instructions

Instructions and process descriptions have several similarities. Both are composed of steps that occur in a particular sequence. Both can be given to general or specialized audiences. In manuals, process descriptions often come before instructions.

The main distinction between instructions and process descriptions is purpose. The audience for instructions is expected to carry out the steps. The audience for a process description is expected just to understand the process, not carry it out. Instructions explain how to work a DVD player; a process description explains how a DVD player works.

Instructions Use Commands

Steps in instructions are always given as **commands** in the second person. Commands directly tell the reader what to do. In the following examples, notice that each command begins with an action verb.

Americans who travel abroad must often apply for a passport.

Check the gauges every 30 minutes.
Please **give** your name when answering the phone.
Turn in your mileage report every Friday.

Process Descriptions Use Statements

Steps in process descriptions are always given as <mark>statements</mark> that explain what happened or what is done. The action verb in these examples follows the subject of the sentence.

The technician **checks** the gauges every 30 minutes.
We always **give** our names when answering the phone.
Employees **turn in** mileage reports every Friday.

Practice 5–2: Commands and Statements

The following eight sentences are written as commands. Rewrite each command as a statement. Hint: Begin your first sentence with the word *Americans*.

Process: Obtaining a U.S. Passport

1. If you are planning to visit India, apply for a passport.

2. Get an application form from a travel agent and fill it in ahead of time.

3. Appear in person at a regional passport office.

4. Present the following materials: the application form, proof of U.S. citizenship, two recent photographs of yourself, proof of identity, and payment.

5. To prevent theft, carry your passport in a money belt or pouch, not in a pocket or purse.

6. If you lose your passport while in the United States, go to the nearest U.S. Passport Agency.

7. If you are in India, report the loss to the nearest U.S. embassy or consulate; also notify the local police.

8. When your passport is about to expire, apply for a new one by mail.

Ch05-02.doc

by the way...

Process Descriptions Use Active and Passive Verbs

Always express commands in instructions, using active verbs. In a sentence with <mark>active verbs</mark>, the subject of the sentence does the action. You can, however, give statements in process descriptions, using either active or passive verbs. In sentences with <mark>passive verbs</mark>, the subject of the sentence receives the action. Perhaps an illustration will help. The following paragraph, reprinted from a manual explaining how *not* to write a technical report, is an example of a process description using passive verbs.

A 72-gram brown Rhode Island Red country-fresh candled egg was secured and washed free of feathers, etc. Held between thumb and index finger, about three feet more or less from an electric fan (General Electric No. MC-2404, Serial No. JC23023, non-oscillating, rotating on "high" speed at approximately 1052.23 ± 0.02 rpm), the egg was suspended on a string (pendulum) so it arrived at the fan with essentially zero velocity normal to the fan rotation plan. The product, adhering strongly to the walls and ceiling, was difficult to recover; however, using putty knives a total of 13 grams was obtained and put in a skillet with 11.2 grams of hickory smoked Armour's Old Style bacon and was heated over a low Bunsen flame for 7 min. 32 sec. What there was of it was excellent scrambled eggs. (Reprinted with the Permission of the U.S. Dept. of Energy From a Savannah river Laboratory Report)

The writer not only used passive verbs but also included unnecessary detail and technical jargon to make a point about how *not* to write. The translation of this example, with clear, direct, *active* verbs, follows.

Carlos and I *threw* an egg into an electric fan. Although we *had* a difficult time removing it from the walls and ceiling, we *managed to make* excellent scrambled eggs with the small amount recovered.

Unless you have a good reason to do otherwise, choose active rather than passive sentence construction. Sentences with passive verbs are not as clear and tend to be wordier and weaker than sentences with active verbs. Passive verbs consist of a form of the verb *to be* plus the action verb. For example:

- *Was* placed
- *Were* noticed
- *Are* invited
- Has *been* reached
- *Is* found

In the following sentence, the subject of the sentence—the mileage reports—doesn't do anything. Something—being turned in—is done to the mileage reports by the employees. This sentence is passive:

Mileage reports are turned in every Friday by employees.

It's easy to make a passive sentence active. Just begin the sentence with the subject that does the action. In this sentence, the employees do the action, which is turning in the mileage reports. This sentence is active:

by the way...

Ethics *Connection*

When you hear people in uncomfortable situations overusing passive verbs, get out your hogwash detector. They may be trying to evade responsibility. Consider this response to a customer who sent film of his only daughter's wedding pictures to a photo lab: "We must report that during the handling of your twelve 35mm photo orders, the films were involved in an unusual laboratory experience." Nobody did anything to the rolls of film; they just had a bad experience. Of course, the customer can always hold another wedding for his daughter and take the pictures all over again, using the 12 replacement rolls the lab so generously sent him. If you make a mistake, don't say, "A mistake happened." Instead, take responsibility by saying, "I made a mistake." As Nikki Giovanni, an American poet, once said, "Mistakes are a fact of life. It is the response to error that counts."

Employees turn in mileage reports every Friday.

At times, the *who* or *what* that does the action is so obvious or so unimportant that it is left out entirely. In these cases, using passive verbs is acceptable. In the following examples of passive-verb statements, the operator or doer of the action is not mentioned.

Sunny is being promoted to assistant manager.
The building was demolished ten years ago.
Your applications have always been processed on time.

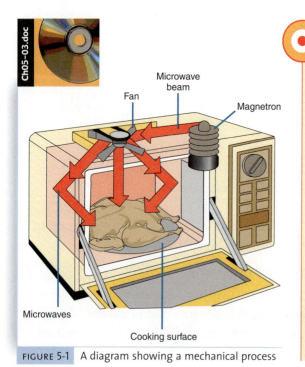

Ch05-03.doc

Fan

Microwave beam

Magnetron

Microwaves

Cooking surface

FIGURE 5-1   A diagram showing a mechanical process

Practice 5–3: Active and Passive

These statements have passive verbs. Rewrite them with active verbs. In the first two sentences, the subject of each sentence is in bold print.

Process: How a Microwave Oven Works *(See Figure 5-1.)*

1. A beam of microwaves is produced by **a magnetron**.

2. The waves are scattered by **the fan**.

3. Waves are absorbed by molecules of water in the food.

4. Molecules are aligned by waves of energy.

5. The alignment is then reversed by waves.

6. Rapid and repeated twisting is caused by this alignment and realignment.

7. Heat is produced by the twisting.

Describing a Process: Structure and Language

A good process description is organized like a story—with a beginning, a middle, and an end. The events are chronological; that is, related in the order in which they occur. Parallel ideas are expressed in the same way. Analogies (comparisons) often make the description easier to understand.

Chronological Order

Chronological order is time order. When communication is organized chronologically, the first event comes first, the second event comes second, etc. Process descriptions are organized chronologically.

Practice 5–4: Describing a Process in Chronological Order

The following description of how an answering machine records a message is not organized chronologically. Notice how hard it is to keep track of the series of actions and how they relate to the overall process.

Reorganize the description chronologically to make it easier to follow. Add words such as *after, then,* and *while* to help the reader keep track of the proper sequence of actions.

Ch05-04.doc

Process: How an Answering Machine Works

The "message waiting" and "operation" lights turn on and the outgoing message starts after the first ring of the phone sets up an electronic connection between the answering machine and the phone line. The outgoing message is a prerecorded message that can last up to 20 seconds. The incoming message starts after the beep that tells the caller that he or she may leave a message. The machine disconnects after a ten-second silence. An electronic voice control circuit allows the machine to continue recording as long as the caller keeps talking. Before the machine "hangs up" until the next call, the "operation" light goes off.

Parallel Structure

Experienced writers present parallel ideas the same way; that is, they make the sentence elements that express these ideas **parallel**. Parallel structure makes writing clear and effective. Here's one example from a speech by President John F. Kennedy:

Conformity is the *jailer of freedom* and *the enemy of growth*.

The two parallel, italicized phrases are joined with a conjunction, *and.* Both phrases consist of the word *the*, a noun, the word *of*, and another noun. This similarity in the structure of the phrases makes them parallel.

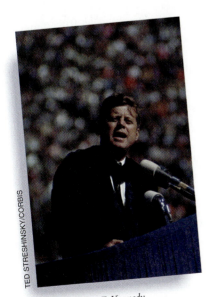

TED STRESHINSKY/CORBIS

President John F. Kennedy

If Kennedy had not used parallel structure, he might have said instead, "Conformity is the jailer of freedom and opposes growth." Notice how much less effective this sentence sounds than the first version. Most people can detect faulty parallelism by listening to the sound of a sentence.

Elements in lists are clear and effective when they are parallel, as in the following sentence, also from Kennedy:

> The great enemy of the truth is very often not the lie—*deliberate, contrived and dishonest*—but the myth—*persistent, persuasive and unrealistic.*

Always use parallel structure in listing statements in a process description. Using parallel structure helps the audience picture the flow of the process described and see it as a clearly presented series of actions. In contrast, sentences and lists that are not parallel may confuse the audience.

Practice 5–5: Parallel Structure

With a partner, revise the following sentences to make them parallel. Remember that *listening* to the sound of the sentences helps. The words and phrases that should be made parallel are italicized in the first two sentences.

1. I like *to identify a problem* and *solving it*.

2. Kalena was promoted not only *for her hard work and loyalty,* but also *because she gets along well with people.*

3. Your suggestion is creative, is reasonable in cost, and was presented convincingly.

4. This could be a problem for both the winners and those who lose.

5. I possess neither the skill nor am I patient enough to care for small children.

6. Each supervisor is responsible for the following:
   • Reducing costs
   • Provide training for all new employees
   • Inventory

7. Julius found the perfect job by preparing a perfect resume, he contacted references, and he took the time to make dozens of phone calls.

8. Each diagram shows the appearance of the object, and how it works is shown, too.

Ch05-05.doc

Analogies

An **analogy** is a comparison between the unknown and the known. Using an analogy implies that since the things being compared are alike in some ways, they are probably alike in other ways as well. An analogy is a useful device in explaining an unfamiliar process. In the following introduction for a process description, truck scales are compared to the familiar doctors' office scales.

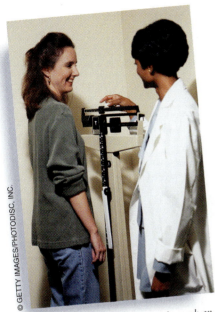

Doctors' office scales and truck scales work on the same principle.

> The scales that weigh you in the doctor's office and the platform scales that weigh trucks both work on the same principle. Scales of both types have levers that divide the weight and then balance many pounds on the platform with a single pound at the weight indicator. The four pairs of levers on a 50-ton truck scale cause 7,000 pounds on the platform to exert a one-pound force at the indicator. The doctor's scale, on the other hand, has only one pair of levers with a 40-to-1 "tip ratio."

Practice 5–6: Analogies

Analogy tests measure one's ability to perceive relationships between words. Use *Student Workbook* page 5-A to practice solving analogy problems.

Organizing a Process Description

An effectively written process description includes an informative title, an introduction, a body that explains each step in the process, and perhaps a closing. A longer description of a complex process requires headings for each main step.

Read the process description shown in Figure 5-2 on page 150. The notes in the margin point out some features of this description.

Using Visuals

As with definitions and instructions, an informative visual can make a process description easier to understand. A good visual can also reduce the amount of writing and reading needed for a thorough explanation. Occasionally, a visual may be able to stand on its own; however, a written or spoken explanation is usually necessary.

What Are Those Microchips That People Put in Their Dogs?

For many years, because collar tags are so easily lost or removed, pet owners and breeders have relied on tattoos as a more permanent form of pet identification. Unfortunately, the use of tattoos is not an unerring method. Say, for example, your dog has gotten lost. Someone finds him and takes him to the animal shelter. Upon his arrival, he is unsettled and possibly frightened. The shelter aide quickly notes the gnarled metal ring dangling from his collar where his I.D. tag used to hang. As she attempts to check your dog for a tattoo, he snarls and squirms. His hair is matted, and the aide does not see the small series of numbers located near his right hind leg. This is not an uncommon scenario, so people have been trying to find other systems of identification. Microchips are one of the latest and most popular systems.

What Are Radio-Frequency Identification (RFID) Microchips?

Similar to bar codes and magnetic stripes, microchips are a form of automatic identification technology. Generally, these microchips are used to store and transmit information that is specifically related to something or someone. They can be implanted (either by injection or a surgical procedure), temporarily inserted, or simply attached to an object. Because they use radio-frequency signals to relay the stored information, they are referred to as radio-frequency identification (RFID).

According to the two main manufacturers, AVID and Destron Fearing, microchips used in pet identification and recovery are programmed to store a unique, permanent identification number. The chip and an antenna are sealed in an airtight, biocompatible capsule made of glass. The entire mechanism can range in size from less than half an inch to a little over an inch in length. The average microchip is about the size of a grain of rice. The device itself contains no battery, and its electronic circuitry is activated only when it is being scanned.

How Do RFID Microchips Work?

The method of implanting the microchip is very much like administering a vaccination. A sterile applicator is used to inject the microchip just under the skin at the back of the dog's neck, between the shoulder blades. To avoid migration (movement from the original implant site), one company uses a patented sheath to promote bonding between fibrous tissue and the microchip capsule.

Once the microchip is successfully implanted, it can be "read" with a scanning device. The scanner emits a low-frequency radio signal, activating the microchip. The microchip then sends the unique identification number back to the scanner. After the information is encoded, the scanner displays the number on its LCD display. The number is then entered into a database, along with the proper contact information. Programs such as the American Kennel Club (AKC) Companion Animal Recovery (CAR) program maintain worldwide databases so they can help reunite lost pets with their families. According to the AKC CAR, more than 900,000 pets and companion animals have been registered in its database, which does include tattooed animals, and almost 50,000 pets have been reunited with their families.

"What are those microchips that people put in their dogs?" *HowStuffWorks, Inc.*
http://science.howstuffworks.com/question690.htm. 25 Jun. 2004.

FIGURE 5-2 Features of a process description

Reprinted by permission www.howstuffworks.com

Drawings, diagrams, and flowcharts are especially useful for illustrating process descriptions. You may need to review basic guidelines (see Chapters 2 and 4) for creating drawings and diagrams.

Drawings

Figure 5-3 illustrates an informative drawing showing how a camera works. Even a person who has little artistic ability can produce a drawing like this one. This drawing is appropriate for a general audience since it shows only the basics of the process.

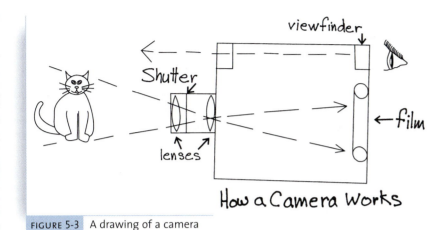

FIGURE 5-3   A drawing of a camera

Diagrams

Diagrams are abstract representations of ideas. When choosing a diagram to go with your process description, you should carefully think about your audience. Is it general or specialized? If the diagram is too complex, you will probably confuse your audience. If it is too simple, you may bore them.

The diagram in Figure 5-4 shows how an audio control console creates echo effects. Notice the differences between this diagram and Figure 5-3. This diagram and its written explanation are more complex. It was created for a specialist who already has some knowledge of the process and the technical jargon.

Audio
Source

Audio Control Console

Program Line
Output
with Echo

Board
Input
#1

Board
Input
#2

Program Line
Audio Out

Tape
Record
Head

Tape
Playback
Head

→ Tape Delay →

A reverberating (repeat echo) effect is made when a combination of tape delay and feedback is used. The sound goes from the source through the board to the record head and onto the tape. A fraction of a second later, the playback head picks up the sound and plays it back through the board to the record head.

FIGURE 5-4   A diagram of the tape echo process

Flowcharts

Flowcharts are diagrams that show steps in a process connected by arrows. They are often used as illustrations in technical manuals. By following the arrows, the reader can see the main steps of the process in chronological order. The writer who constructs an effective flowchart must thoroughly understand the process shown. In fact, the act of creating the chart may help the writer clarify his or her understanding of the process.

The flowchart in Figure 5-5 illustrates the process that allows a computer to control the movements of an industrial robot.

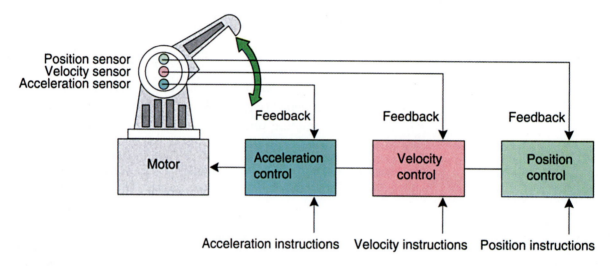

Feedback Loops

The controls for an industrial robot include sensors that monitor the position of each joint, the changes in the velocity of the movement of each joint, and movement as acceleration or deceleration. The diagram shows the feedback information and the instructions that are relayed in response to it. The feedback information flows in a series of loops as the sensors supply information to the system.

FIGURE 5-5   A flowchart showing robot feedback loops

As you move into the workplace, you may see flowcharts that show how work flows within a company or a given department. Such flowcharts are often included in employee manuals. Understanding where you are on the flowchart and what role you play can be an important key to doing your job successfully.

Figure 5-6 shows how ferns propagate. Examine this example and read its explanation.

Figure 5-7 illustrates the water cycle. Carefully examine the visual. Then write a short paragraph explaining the process.

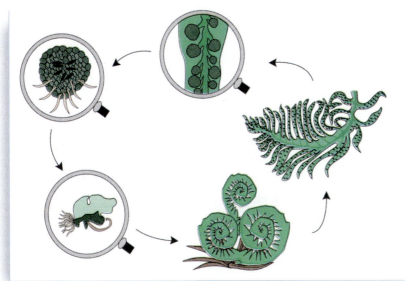

The Life Cycle of a Fern

Spores grow underneath leaf fronds and are spread by wind. Where they land, a prothallus grows. This produces sperm and egg cells. The final stage is the growth of a new fern.

FIGURE 5-6   A flowchart showing a natural process

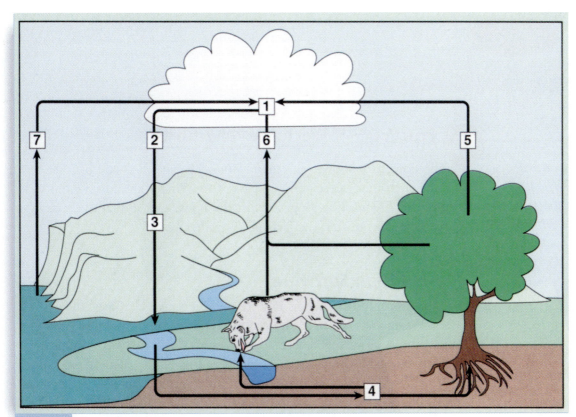

FIGURE 5-6   The water cycle

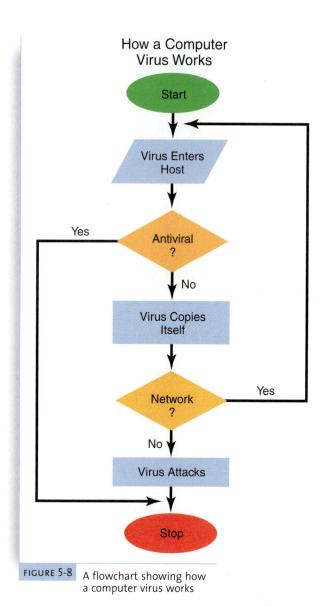

How a Computer
Virus Works

Start

Virus Enters
Host

Antiviral
?

Yes

No

Virus Copies
Itself

Network
?

Yes

No

Virus Attacks

Stop

FIGURE 5-8   A flowchart showing how
a computer virus works

Computer programmers use a special type of flowchart to show the steps in a software program. This type of flowchart can also be used to illustrate processes. Figure 5-8 shows how destructive computer programs called viruses infect computer systems. Notice how the shapes enclosing each step have meanings of their own.

• An oval indicates the beginning or end of the process.

• A parallelogram indicates input to the process or output from the process.

• A diamond indicates a decision. Inside the diamond is a question. Two arrows lead from the diamond, one marked "yes" and one marked "no." Each path must eventually lead to "stop."

• A rectangle indicates a step in the process not requiring a decision.

Practice 5–8: Fractured Flowcharts

The flowcharts shown on *Student Workbook* pages 5-B and 5-C do not match their corresponding paragraphs. Things are missing, out of order, and factually wrong. Correct the flowcharts so that the facts in the flowcharts match the facts in the paragraphs.

Presentation Software

Presentation software such as PowerPoint, Freelance Graphics, and Harvard Graphics can help you produce effective visual aids for oral presentations of process descriptions. **Presentation software** simulates slide shows on the computer screen. Special projectors allow these slides to be shown on a large screen. Presentation software can also generate attractive, colorful transparencies.

Presentation software allows you to add color, movement, and a variety of special effects to the visuals for speeches. The software templates—sample presentation designs that you can use—make creating a dazzling production amazingly easy. With a little training and a healthy dose of planning, you can create an attractive and engaging presentation. Here are a few guidelines to follow as you prepare a slide show:

- Begin with a well-thought-out plan and key in your content in outline view. This allows you to concentrate on your message without distraction. After all, a great-looking presentation that fails to communicate your message will waste everyone's time.

- Don't get too carried away with special effects. Your audience may be wondering what your next effect will be instead of paying attention to what you have to say.

- Never put more words on a slide than you would put on a T-shirt.

- Time slide changes so that the audience has enough time to read the slides—but not too much time.

- When making the presentation, stand to the left of the screen so the audience can see you.

Describing Processes Orally

As you have seen, processes can be described in writing. More often, though, they are spoken as part of casual conversation between two people. A dog trainer might explain to the owner of a puppy how dogs learn to obey commands. An installer of a home security system might explain to a homeowner how the system detects movement in the house. This type of discussion requires knowledge, but not much planning, on the part of the speaker. In other situations, however, a great deal of planning may be required.

DILBERT reprinted by permission of United Feature Syndicate, Inc.

Explaining a Process to a Group

If you are asked to explain a process to a group at work, you must consider the needs of your audience. How much time will they have to listen to you? Remember that people are busy, so they have little time or patience for disorganization. Plan

Technology *Connection*

Groupware is software that allows people located in different parts of a building or different parts of the world to communicate and work on the same project at the same time. Teams can create and edit a document together, almost as if they were working at the same desk. Groupware also can merge phone and e-mail systems. Messages are delivered to "smart post offices." These networks can hunt down the receiver of a message and deliver it in the proper format—be it pager, cell phone, laptop computer, or fax machine.

carefully to tell the audience what they need to know—and no more—as efficiently as possible. Consider the following example.

> Ms. Bhati supervises the print shop of a large company that manufactures gardening equipment. Her department produces brochures, forms, product inserts, flyers, the company newsletter, and more. New digital equipment has been installed that will give her department the capability of producing higher-quality materials in less time.
>
> Ms. Bhati must meet with the supervisors of the other 12 departments to explain what the new equipment can do. Since the meeting is scheduled to run for only 30 minutes, she must plan carefully to make efficient use of time, while still getting her points across to everyone in the group.

Presenting Information with a Team

If a team has worked together to make a decision or solve a problem, it may be asked to present its results, either in writing or by speaking. An effective team takes advantage of the talents and skills of the individual members of the group when planning the presentation. Taking the time to learn the strengths of each member will benefit everyone. For instance, the math skills, public speaking skills, writing ability, computer expertise, artistic talent, proofreading skills, or organizational ability of any team member cannot be used unless it is known. Try to assign tasks based on the individual strengths of team members. Working in teams is discussed on pages 157–164.

◎ Practice 5–9: Flowcharting a Process

Complete the flowchart on *Student Workbook* page 5-D showing the steps required for planning and giving an effective oral presentation. Refer to pages 90–91 in Chapter 3 for information about this process. Give the flowchart an informative title.

by the way...

"People who enjoy what they are doing invariably do it well."

JOE GIBBS, NFL COACH

Career *Connection*

Kaizen is a Japanese word meaning "the relentless quest for a better way for higher-quality craftsmanship." If you practice Kaizen and make the pursuit of perfection a daily goal, your work will improve and your organization will come closer to meeting its goals. Improvements are usually gradual. If, however, everyone in the organization constantly tries to outdo yesterday, measurable improvement will eventually happen. Your productivity, product quality, cost control, and customer service efforts need continuous upgrading. After all, the competition never stands still.

Remember, a strong, successful organization is the best paycheck insurance there is. Even if other circumstances cause your organization to fail, by becoming the best you can be, you'll find it that much easier to land a new job.

Practice 5–10: Analyzing a Speech

Ch05-10.mp3

In this Practice, you will listen to a speech explaining a process. Write a note to Erin, the speaker. Begin with a compliment; then make three positive suggestions for improvement. Instead of telling her what not to do, tell her what she can do to improve.

Teams Work!

In the past, managers of business and industry issued orders and directives to the people who carried them out. They expected little communication in return. In recent years, however, many organizations have adopted new management techniques. These organizations demand a high level of performance and communication skills from their employees. Simply complying with rules and obeying supervisors is not enough; these organizations need employees who are willing to work in new ways.

Many companies are organizing their employees into work teams. In this type of organization, everyone must understand decision-making processes. The effective use of teams in the workplace can help organizations reach their goals. In addition, the ability to work as a member of a team has become an important asset for employees. Your chances of being considered for a promotion can depend on your ability to work with and contribute to a team. Furthermore, team members often report increased job satisfaction.

In order to accomplish any task (such as making a decision), a team needs goals, leadership, and organization. The Project for this chapter involves participating in a team that will explain a process to the class. Your team must make many decisions, and its success will depend on the skills of each individual. With practice, you can learn to be a productive team member.

Career *Connection*

Robert E. Kelley coined the term *followership*. In his article "In Praise of Followers," he identified four essential qualities of effective followers.

They manage themselves well: Effective followers have the ability to think for themselves and see themselves as equals to the leader they follow.

They are committed to a higher purpose: They work toward the purpose of the organization.

They build their strengths: Effective followers have high work standards and are continually learning. They seek out extra work and responsibilities.

They take risks: Effective followers are credible and honest and have the courage to speak up.

by the way...

"A problem well stated is a problem half solved."

C. F. Kettering, U.S. inventor

by the way...

"You can't tell someone to go out and lead. You become a leader by doing it. So if you want to be a leader, go do it."

Chuck Noll, NFL linebacker and coach

Goals

The first task of any decision-making group is to clarify its goals—what is it trying to accomplish and why? Your group will not function as a team unless it agrees upon the task and the goals, develops effective leadership and decision-making strategies, and learns to resolve conflict.

Leadership

In formal groups such as committees, a leader or chairperson is usually chosen. In more informal groups, one or two people will, out of necessity, assume the role of leader. Either way, the team leader has many responsibilities. Practice 5-11 will help you to focus on leadership roles.

Practice 5-11: Leadership Roles

For this Practice, your whole class will work together as a problem-solving team. Your team's task is to calculate the average height in feet and inches of the members of the team. Time limit: 15 minutes.

After time is called, complete *Student Workbook* page 5-E.

Organization

A decision-making group cannot function without leadership. It also cannot function without organization. Once everyone in the team clearly understands the team's task or goal, team members should collect as much information and as many ideas as possible by brainstorming.

Brainstorming

Brainstorming is a problem-solving activity that requires all members of a group to contribute their ideas toward making a decision. Brainstorming can lead to creative solutions that individual members might not come up with on their own. This technique is useful when group members want to generate options to consider when making decisions. When brainstorming, keep these guidelines in mind:

1. Make sure everyone understands the problem that needs solving.

2. Choose one team member to record all solutions to a problem without discussion, evaluation, or comment—negative or positive. No idea—no matter how silly or unworkable—is rejected. It is best if all of the team members can see the suggested solutions as they are recorded.

3. Try to ensure that all members participate, as anyone can come up with a usable solution. Eccentric ideas often lead to creative solutions. Participation means more than talking or note taking; active listening is crucial.

4. Once the team has run out of solutions, the recorder crosses out duplicates.

Practice 5–12: Brainstorming

1. Sketch a flowchart illustrating the steps in the brainstorming process listed above.

2. Work on this brainstorming Practice in a team consisting of four or five members. Begin by writing down the names of your team members. Then complete steps a–e.

   The Problem: How many uses can you think of for a paper clip?

   a. Choose one member to write down all ideas—exactly as they are presented—so that all members can see them.
   b. Brainstorm as many ideas (uses) as you can. Record all ideas without discussion. The goal is to generate as many ideas as possible.
   c. When the team runs out of ideas, come up with three more.
   d. Cross out duplicates.
   e. Write down your group's total number of uses. How does this compare to the totals of the other groups?

3. After completing step 2, answer the following questions:

   a. Who acted as leader of your team? How could you tell?
   b. What contributed to your team's success?
   c. Write down two ways that your group could improve the next time you try brainstorming.

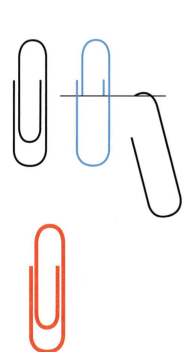

Team Member Roles

Sometimes, after participating in a meeting, people leave feeling dissatisfied because nothing was accomplished. This may be because the team could not focus on the problem or they could not resolve conflict. Perhaps some members of the team just didn't seem to care.

In every team, each member plays one or more roles. Some of the roles are productive; that is, they help the team reach its goals. Other roles are unproductive. When you work with a team, are you a productive or unproductive member? To determine this, it is helpful to examine some of the roles.

Practice 5–13: Roles People Play

For this Practice, your teacher will divide the class into two groups. One group will act as a decision-making team; the other group will be observers.

Directions for the team members:

Each member of the decision-making team draws a card that includes a description of the role he or she is to play. It is important for you to study the description of the role and to stay in character throughout the discussion. Cards also list one or more facts to contribute to the discussion. Do not show your card to anyone.

Directions for the observers:

Use *Student Workbook* page 5-F, which lists the roles and their descriptions. As you *silently* observe the discussion, try to figure out who is playing which role. Write the person's name next to the description of the role, along with the evidence for your decision. Be prepared to share your observations during the follow-up discussion.

The decision-making team will solve the following problem:

Your teacher has been named teacher of the year and will leave next week on a two-month speaking tour of the United States. The administration has selected three possible long-term substitute teachers from the list of qualified candidates. Your team's task is to select one of the three applicants to substitute for your teacher.

Decision-Making Strategies

In Practice 5–13, you saw how some behaviors help a team reach its goals while other behaviors are obstacles to the team's success. Even when everyone involved engages in productive behavior, the team may not be successful unless they know how to go about making a group decision.

Once the team understands the problem to be solved, understands the goal, and has brainstormed possible solutions, members must choose the best solution and the best method to carry it out. Disagreement (conflict) may occur during this process. Some decision-making strategies are described in the following sections.

Rank Ordering

Rank ordering is a process that allows the team to list solutions and ideas in order by priority. As a result, team members discover how much agreement exists between them. The process of rank ordering involves the following steps:

1. Team members agree on the criteria for ranking ideas. How will they measure the usefulness of the ideas? What will constitute the best ideas?

2. Team members identify each idea on the list with a letter of the alphabet.

3. Team members individually list the letters on a sheet of paper and indicate the rank of each idea, with *1* being the first choice, *2* the second choice, etc.

4. Team members take turns calling out the number that indicates their ranking of each idea. One member records all of the numbers on a flip chart, chalkboard, or large sheet of paper that is visible to everyone.

5. The team analyzes the rankings, looking at the total for each idea as well as the individual votes.

The Nominal Group Technique

The **nominal group technique** helps the team generate options to consider in making decisions. The process involves the following steps:

1. Each team member writes ideas on a sheet of paper.

2. One member records all of the members' ideas on a chalkboard, flip chart, or large sheet of paper so that all members can see them easily. No discussion of ideas should occur during this step.

3. Members vote to establish the rank of all items on the list.

4. The team discusses the vote and eliminates lower-ranked items.

5. Rounds of voting and discussion continue until the team reaches consensus. A consensus is a decision that all members can support to some degree.

© 1999 Randy Glasbergen.
www.glasbergen.com

GLASBERGEN

"Let's form a committee to create a task force to develop a team to determine the fastest way to deal with the problem."

Cartoon by Randy Glasbergen. Licensed from www.glasbergen.com

Multivoting

Multivoting allows a team to reduce a long list of ideas to a manageable number. The process of multivoting involves these steps:

1. The team members decide on the criteria for selecting the best ideas from the list.

2. Members vote for their favorite ideas, no more than 25 percent of the entire list. For example, if the list includes 28 items, each member can vote for no more than 7. Team members can give only one vote to an individual idea and must use all of their votes. Votes are recorded with a tally mark beside each item on the list.

3. Team members thoroughly discuss the ideas with the most votes and discard the lower-ranked ideas.

4. In the second round of voting, each member votes for one of the remaining ideas.

⊙ Practice 5–14: Making a Decision

Your teacher will divide the class into three teams. Each team will use one of the decision-making strategies described on pages 161–162 to solve the following problem:

Your school board voted to make participation in a volunteering project to benefit the community a requirement for graduation. The project can be completed individually or as a team. Your team has decided to work together to satisfy this requirement. The board has specified the following criteria (standards):

• The project must provide a real benefit to the community.

• Each person must contribute no fewer than ten hours.

• The individuals or the team must present evidence that they have met the requirement.

Culture *Connection*

Some teams are made up of individuals from different cultures. Their differing styles of communication can create misunderstanding and conflict when a problem needs to be solved or a decision needs to be made. Here are some tips for minimizing conflict in a multicultural team:

• Be aware that different people use nonverbal language, such as eye contact, posture, and gestures, in different ways.

• Repeat key ideas and ask questions to make sure everyone understands.

• Restate others' ideas to make sure you understand them.

• Signal your openness to others' ideas, but not just in words; your tone of voice and your body language say more about your attitude than your words do.

• Summarize the results of the team meeting orally or in writing.

Your team's task is to decide what activity to do to satisfy the community service requirement. Each team will use a different decision-making strategy. Be prepared to report the following information to the class during the follow-up discussion:

1. What decision-making strategy did your team use?

2. Did any member provide leadership? If so, who?

3. How successful was your team in reaching its goal? What factors contributed to your success?

4. What problems did you encounter?

5. Did members at times disagree? If so, how did you resolve disagreements?

6. How would you rate the effectiveness of your assigned decision-making strategy?

Conflict Management

Even when a team uses an effective decision-making strategy, conflict is inevitable. Individual differences in personality, values, and cultural background exist in any team. The goal is not to eliminate conflict; rather, the goal is to manage conflict in a productive, positive way. Practice 5-15 will give you experience in analyzing how people manage conflict.

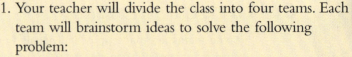

Practice 5-15: Conflict Resolution

1. Your teacher will divide the class into four teams. Each team will brainstorm ideas to solve the following problem:

   Because of the excellent work your class has done so far this year, you will be awarded a $10,000 grant to spend in some way that will benefit the entire class. The only restrictions are that you must spend all $10,000 and what you spend it on must have educational value.

   After brainstorming ideas, follow these steps:

   a. Choose a team leader.
   b. Use rank ordering, the nominal group technique, or multi-voting to arrive at your solution.
   c. Record the team's decision on a sheet of paper.

2. Once the teams have reached their decisions and recorded them, follow these steps:

   ### Instructions for team leaders:

   a. List all four teams' decisions on a flip chart, chalkboard, sheet of poster board, or large sheet of paper. It is important for all members of the class to be able to see the list.
   b. Sit close to the other team leaders so you can talk.
   c. You and the other team leaders may use rank ordering, the nominal group technique, or multivoting to select one of the four solutions to the problem of how to spend the money. Your goal is to *agree* on the decision.

   ### Instructions for the rest of the class:

   d. Position yourself so that you can silently watch the team leaders as they discuss the problem.
   e. As you observe, complete *Student Workbook* page 5-G. Pay attention to how the team members handle disagreements. You might observe one or more of the conflict resolution strategies listed on the *Student Workbook* page. When you notice members using one of these strategies, note below its description on *Student Workbook* page 5-G the point of disagreement, along with a brief report of who did what.

Summary

A process description explains how something works, how something is done, or how something is made. Giving an effective process description requires careful planning. Follow these guidelines whenever you describe a process at work:

- Remember that the purpose of a process description is audience understanding, not action.

- Explain steps in a process in chronological order, using active or, when appropriate, passive statements.

- Use parallel structure and, when appropriate, analogies to make your description clearer.

- Organize a written process description to contain an informative title, an introduction, a body that explains each step in the process, and perhaps a closing.

- Use visuals such as drawings, diagrams, and flowcharts to illustrate a process description.

- Plan oral presentations of process descriptions by choosing a subject, analyzing your audience, clarifying your purpose, gathering facts, organizing the presentation, designing visuals, and rehearsing.

The ability to work as a member of a team is a valuable asset in the workplace. Teams are often asked to solve problems and to make decisions. Effective teamwork involves setting goals, establishing leadership, making effective decisions, and managing conflict.

review and research activities visit
communicating.swlearning.com

project-based assessment

Describing a Process

No matter what field you are studying, you have learned some information that can be valuable to people who do not have your training. For instance, the person who drives but who will never repair a car can avoid some clutch repairs by understanding how the car's transmission works.

Examples:

- How personal credit information is stored in and retrieved from data banks

- How children develop ideas of right and wrong

- How rays given off by an arc welder can damage unprotected eyes

- How news wire services distribute data to the media

- How plaque forms in arteries

- How whales communicate

For this Project, you will give a description of a process related to your occupational field that would be valuable or interesting to a general audience. You will give the description as an oral presentation that you prepare and deliver to your class as part of a team.

1. Study the Sample Project Plan on page 168. Brainstorm ideas for a topic, for an organizational plan, and for the type and subject matter of any visuals. With your team, research the chosen topic and complete the Project Plan on Student Workbook page 5-H. Have your teacher check it.

2. Listen to the recorded sample presentation. The notes for this presentation are on page 169. The visual referred to in the speech is Figure 5-8 on page 154.

3. Assign tasks to team members based on their individual skills and talents.

4. With your team, prepare notes and visuals for the presentation.

5. Study the Project Guide, *Student Workbook* page 5-I, for criteria (standards) by which the presentation will be evaluated.

6. Rehearse the presentation individually and with your team. Using the Rough Draft column of the Project Guide, check your work with one or more classmates as you rehearse your presentation. Have them record all of their comments and changes on your Project Guide and rough draft of your notes and visuals. Ask them to write a constructive comment on the rough draft and sign it.

7. Do a final rehearsed presentation. If possible, ask a classmate to act as your audience and help you rate yourselves, using the Final Draft column of the Project Guide.

8. Give the presentation. The Project Guide will be used to evaluate your notes, visuals, and speech.

Sample Project Plan

Plan for Describing a Process

		CONTENT **What are the main steps and supporting details?**
SUBJECT	How a computer virus works	

AUDIENCE	Communication class—general audience	Viruses are created by hackers
		
		Virus enters host
		   virus—small, destructive program
		       genes packed in protein shell
		   host—person or computer with a virus

PURPOSE	**What actions should the audience take?**
	
	Protect their data from viruses
		Vaccines & antiviral software can prevent infection
		
		Virus makes copies of itself and spreads
		   cough, sneeze, touch
		   networks, modems, floppy disks

FORMAT	☐ written ☒ oral ☐ other	Virus attack
		   prank message—Form virus
		   data destruction
		      Casino virus example
		      FAT—file allocation table

SOURCES	"Antidote for Viruses" CompUser pp. 38–40 1-04 "Common Sense for the Common Cold" The Telegraph B2 3-24-04	BACK UP YOUR WORK
VISUALS	**What visuals, if any, will make the presentation more effective?** Flowchart showing main steps Screen shot of Casino virus	
INTRO	**What will get the audience's attention?** Analogy between computer & cold viruses	

Sample Notes

Notes for a Process Description

Write out the introduction word for word. _____

Do you use a computer at home or at work or at school? If you do, you need to know about a deadly disease that could attack your computer. It's called a virus. No, your computer can't catch your cold, but it can get sick, and the process is similar to the way your body catches a cold and gets sick.

1. Virus enters host **(show flowchart)**.

   • Body—genes packed in protein shells

   • Computer—small software programs

Define VIRUS, HOST, HACKER

2. Prevention

   • Body—flu shot

   • Computer—antiviral software

Use numbers and bullets. _____

3. Virus copies itself.

4. Virus spreads.

   • Body—to other people—airborne or direct contact

   • Computer—to other computers—networks, modems, floppy disks

5. Virus attacks host.

   • Body—symptoms appear

   • Computer—data and files destroyed

Make the notes easy to read. _____

   • Form virus—beeps as you key on the 18th

   • Casino virus example **(show Casino virus screen shot)** FAT—file allocation table

Write out the conclusion word for word. _____

Doctors say that the best way to avoid colds is to wash your hands frequently. If you do get a cold, once it has run its course, the body goes to work repairing your system. But computer systems can't repair themselves, and there's no foolproof method to protect your computer from a virus if your computer comes in contact with other computers. The best protection for your hard work is making backup copies of your files.

Overview

This excerpt from *The Jungle* by Upton Sinclair describes the process used by the meat-packing industry to slaughter hogs at the beginning of the 20th century. Sinclair wrote the book to be used as a weapon against the meat-packing industry, to show the exploitation of the workers. Instead, the book generated a campaign to upgrade the sanitary conditions of the meat-packing industry. Sinclair thought the cause was of little help to the workers. The response to this passage and a later one—which revealed that men sometimes lost their balance on the slimy floor, fell into the vats, and ended up like hogs as part of the final meat product—caused a public outcry for more controls on meat inspection. As a result, the Meat Inspection and Pure Food and Drug Acts were formulated and passed.

from The Jungle

One could not stand and watch very long without becoming philosophical, without beginning to deal in symbols and similes, and to hear the hog-squeal of the universe. Was it permitted to believe that there was nowhere upon the earth, or above the earth, a heaven for hogs, where they were requited for all this suffering? Each one of these hogs was a separate creature. Some were white hogs, some were black; some were brown, some were spotted; some were old, some were young; some were long and lean, some were monstrous. And each of them had an individuality of his own, a will of his own, a hope and a heart's desire; each was full of self-confidence, of self-importance, and a sense

CORBIS-BETTMAN

of dignity. And trusting and strong in faith he had gone about his business, the while a black shadow hung over him and a horrid Fate waited in his pathway. Now suddenly it had swooped upon him; and had seized him by the leg. Relentless, remorseless, it was; all his protests, his screams, were nothing to it—it did its cruel will with him, as if his wishes, his feelings, had simply no existence at all; it cut his throat and watched him gasp out his life. And how was one to believe that there was nowhere a god of hogs, to whom this hog-personality was precious, to whom these hog-squeals and agonies had a meaning? Who would take this hog into his arms and comfort him, reward him for his work well done, and show him the meaning of his sacrifice? Perhaps some glimpse of all this was in the thoughts of our humble-minded Jurgis, as he turned to go on with the rest of the party, and muttered: "Dieve—but I'm glad I'm not a hog!"

The carcass of the hog was scooped out of the vat by machinery, and then it fell to the second floor, passing on the way through a wonderful machine with numerous scrapers, which adjusted themselves to the size and shape of the animal, and sent it out the other end with nearly all of its bristles removed. It was then again strung up by machinery, and sent upon another trolley ride; this time passing between two lines of men, who sat upon a raised platform, each doing a certain single thing to the carcass as it came to him. One scraped the outside of a leg; another scraped the inside of the same leg. One with a swift stroke cut the throat; another with two swift strokes severed the head, which fell to the floor and vanished through a hole. Another made a slit down the body; a second opened the body wider; a third with a saw cut out the breast-bone, a fourth loosened the entrails; a fifth pulled them out—and they also slid through a hole in the floor. There were men to scrape each side and men to scrape the back; there were men to clean the carcass inside, to trim it and wash it. Looking down this room one saw, creeping slowly, a line of dangling hogs a hundred yards in length; and for every yard there was a man, working as if a demon were after him. At the end of this hog's progress every inch of the carcass had been gone over several times; and then it was rolled into the chilling room where it stayed for twenty-four hours, and where a stranger might lose himself in a forest of freezing hogs.

> . . .and for every yard there was a man, working as if a demon were after him.

—Upton Sinclair

Start-Up: Parallelism is used in both technical writing and literature. Repeating the same grammatical form emphasizes step-by-step organization.

Connection: Reread the excerpt.

1. List the ideas that are presented in the same way grammatically.

2. Rewrite one or two examples, removing the parallelism. What is the result?

3. Identify at least five descriptive passages or situations from the selection that could possibly inflame the public because of the imagery or emotional impact.

Overview

The following selection is a literary description of a process. When Denise Grady's two-year-old son began to stutter, she decided to research the reason. By breaking down the subject of stuttering into its constituent parts and studying how the parts fit together as a whole, the author explains the phenomenon of stuttering. As the author analyzes stuttering, she identifies the various body parts involved and the steps that lead to normal speech.

"Stuttering"

Nobody knows why people stutter. The disorder occurs in virtually every culture, and speech therapists estimate that it affects about one percent of the population of the world. The earliest explanations, dating from ancient Greece and persisting into the early 1800's, blamed the tongue: it was too weak, too wet, too dry, too hard, too cold, too large. By the early part this century, the focus had shifted upward, and stuttering was seen first as a bad habit or the product of a neurosis, and later as the result of some unknown abnormality of the brain.

Today many speech researchers think that stuttering is both a physiological and a behavioral condition. The details may differ from one person to the next, but the basic scenario is that stuttering begins for an organic reason and persists, at least in part, because the anxiety generated by the stuttering then makes the stuttering worse, as do some of the habits that people fall into in their struggle to control their speech. Some experts believe that excessive concern with the mechanics of talking can throw the rhythm off, just as thinking too much about where to put your foot next can lead to a fall, and trying to perfect each sentence as you write can lead to writer's block. Some researchers have even suggested that people become physically addicted to stuttering, perhaps to little jolts of adrenaline or other brain chemicals that may be released during stuttering.

In order to speak, one has to coordinate breathing, voice, and movements of the mouth, lips, and tongue. Almost a hundred muscles are involved, and all of them must receive nerve signals at certain instants to produce the right sequence of movements. Because the muscles are on both sides of the body, their movements must also be synchronized. The speech control center resides in the left half of the brain in most people; one popular theory suggests that in stutterers its control may be incomplete, and the right side may fire out conflicting orders that throw the whole speech apparatus out of whack. The result may be a breakdown in timing—a failure of the mechanism that organizes the movements required for speech and that marks its rhythm. Some researchers say that mistiming may be a perpetual problem: stutterers may hear their own speech in a distorted way—with a delay, perhaps—that interferes with their ability to talk.

Male stutterers outnumber females by at least three to one, and the disorder often runs in families. It nearly always comes on during preschool years, when speech and language pass through their most intense phases of development. Many children, especially boys, have brief periods of stuttering or stumbling or fragmented speech. Most get over it. Why some never do remains a mystery. In one of his books, *The Nature of Stuttering*, Charles Van Riper describes a "monstrous collage of factors" of physiology, intelligence, personality, verbal skill, and environmental stress that may contribute to stuttering.

—Denise Grady

Start-Up: The most complicated subject is composed of simpler parts. When a complicated subject is broken down into simpler parts, the process is more easily understood. A medical textbook may break a surgical procedure down into a series of steps. An automobile repair manual may list parts and tell how these parts work together.

Connection: To analyze the writing of a process description, answer the following questions about "Stuttering."

1. Is this process carried out by machines, by people, or by nature?

2. Is the intended audience specialized or general?

3. Take a sampling of the verbs. Are the verbs active or passive?

4. Is there parallelism? If so, give an example.

5. Is the wording of the selection clear, concise, and direct? If so, give examples.

6. Would the selection be more easily understood if a visual accompanied it? Give a reason for your answer.

Working with Literature: Refer to *Student Workbook* page 5-J for an activity about stuttering.

Chapter 6

Tell me and I'll forget; show me and I may remember; involve me and I'll understand.

—CHINESE PROVERB

Vapor Condenses

Vapor becomes Clouds

Precipitation

Water Evaporates

Runoff goes to Groundwater

Hydrologic Cycle

© GETTY IMAGES/PHOTODISC, INC.

Reproduced by permission.
Exploring Agriscience *by Herren*
Delmar Publishers, Albany, New York, Copyright 1996

Describing a Mechanism

Starting a new job? Getting an equipment upgrade? Trying a different exercise to help patients recover from knee surgery? Figuring out what combination of grains to use to increase growth in your livestock? Designing a perfect landscape plan? What do these scenarios have in common? They all entail learning something new—about equipment, a machine, a technique, a substance, an organism, a system, or a tool. Performing any of these tasks takes more than knowing a definition and more than knowing the process of how something works. Understanding requires knowing the entire mechanism.

A Mechanism Defined

Isn't a mechanism a machine? Sometimes it is, but not all of the time. A **mechanism** is an object or a system that may be simple or complex. It can have any number of parts; each part has a particular function. The parts of the mechanism work together to accomplish a definite purpose. So a mechanism isn't always a machine. Any system that has parts that function separately to achieve an overall effect is a mechanism.

So a mechanism does not have to be a piece of machinery. Yet, generally, most people think of a mechanism as something as complex as an airbrush, but it can be as simple as a whetstone. Furthermore, a system, an organism, or a location can be a mechanism also.

A mechanism can have any number of structural parts. For example, a key has one structural part; a fuel-injection system has many structural parts. The structural parts of a hardhat are the shell or body of the hat, the brim, the adjustable headband, and the interior crown's strap device. (See Figure 6-1.)

A mechanism can have any number of functional parts. In fact, the simplest mechanism may have only one structural part but many functional parts. For example, a key has only one structural part but several functional parts. Each indentation on the key separately trips a spring and rod inside the cylinder lock. (See Figure 6-2.)

A mechanism has only this simple requirement: at least two parts that work separately, but together perform a single function.

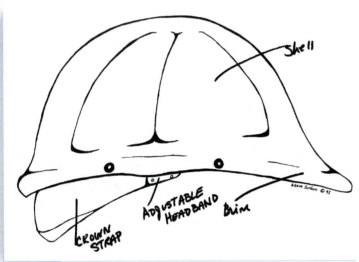

FIGURE 6-1   The structural parts of a hardhat

Reproduced by permission of Adam D. Jordan

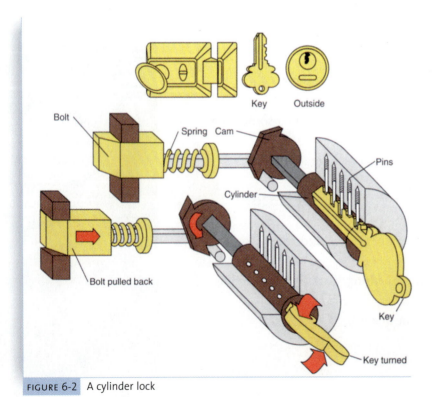

FIGURE 6-2   A cylinder lock

Practice 6–1: Finding a Mechanism

Determine whether the following objects, substances, and systems can be described as mechanisms. Keep in mind the definition of a mechanism.

1. harness
2. fork
3. curling iron
4. blueprint
5. thermometer

6. digital camera
7. microphone
8. anti-shoplifting tag
9. irrigation
10. blood

FIGURE 6-3   UPC bar code

A UPC bar code is a mechanism. The parts of a UPC bar code, the graphical series of bars and spaces, are arranged in certain patterns (see Figure 6-3) that describe coded data characters that a machine reader can scan. Another mechanism, a food web, is a system that can be explained through a diagram of its parts. (See Figure 6-4.) Each part works independently —a grasshopper eats a plant, a small bird consumes the grasshopper, a fox or an owl preys on the bird, etc. The parts also perform an overall function as a complex network dependent originally upon the soil, contributing to the constant cycle of life on earth.

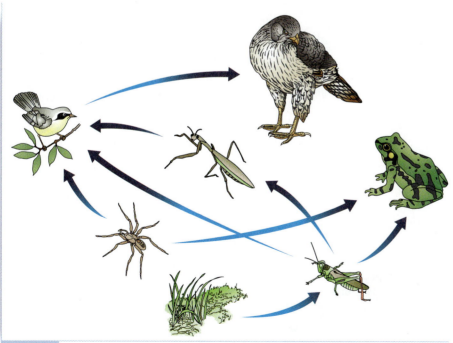

FIGURE 6-4   A food web

Reproduced by permission. Exploring Agriscience *By Herren Delmar Publishers, Albany, New York, Copyright 1996.*

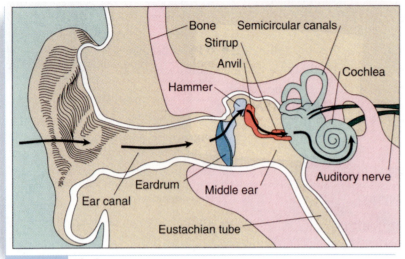

FIGURE 6-5   The human ear

The outer ear is a shell that catches sound waves. The drawing in Figure 6-5 may be familiar to you. The drawing shows how sound waves reach the outer ear, pass through the middle ear, and enter the inner ear, permitting a person to hear. The ear and its adjoining parts are the mechanism. The drawing, in addition to the explanation, is the mechanism description.

Classification of Mechanisms

Mechanisms can vary from basic to elaborate, from miniscule to large, and from inanimate to living. Tools, organisms, substances, sites or locations, and systems are the primary categories of mechanisms.

Tools and Machinery

When most people hear the word *mechanism,* they picture a **tool** or machinery. Even though tools are not the only type of mechanism, the tool is the easiest to understand. The tool becomes an extension of the user and aids the worker in doing his or her job. Some tools appear to be simple, seemingly made of just one or two parts. One such tool is a claw hammer. However, the claw hammer's major parts are the claw, the head, the cheek, the neck, the face, the poll, the adze eye, and the handle. (See Figure 6-6.) That simple tool seems to have many parts after all!

Tools and machinery can be simple or complex, handheld or massive.

- A laser has many sections that work together to pierce or cut materials such as metal.
- A perm rod has several parts that combine to make a tool. This tool holds rolled hair in place so that a stylist can add perm solutions to curl the hair.

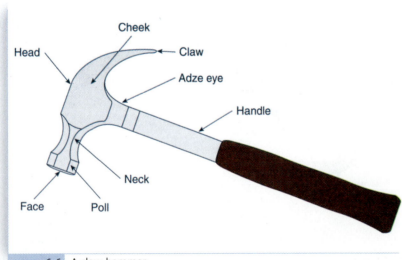

FIGURE 6-6   A claw hammer

- A clamp's handle turns its threaded piece that, combined with the body of the clamp, will determine the clamp's throat opening.
- A printing system may be large or small but consists of many parts.

Organisms

The range of **organisms** is virtually unlimited. From a single-celled amoeba to a whale or a human being, organisms are living mechanisms. A tree is a mechanism consisting of different parts, such as the roots, the leaves, and the bark. These parts have separate functions: taking in nutrients from the soil, providing respiration, and protecting the tree against insects.

Substances

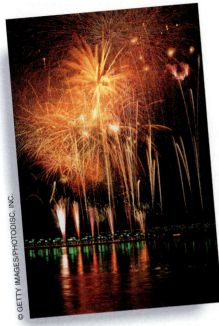

© GETTY IMAGES/PHOTODISC, INC.

A substance mechanism

Some **substances** may be considered mechanisms. These substances have two or more parts that, when examined separately, do not resemble the new composite material. One such substance is automotive paint, which contains chemicals such as toners, reducers, and hardeners—components that can work independently. However, when they are combined, these compounds have a different function; they work together to achieve a factory-quality vehicle finish.

Locations

Some **locations** are considered mechanisms. The site includes separate parts that work together for one purpose. Viewing the site's components—for example, the parts of the terrain and the buildings—forms the mechanism. Surveyors, drafters, architects, and construction workers are examples of people who create or use locations as mechanisms.

The construction site for Paul Rosenfield's new home (see Figure 6-7) is an example of the location as a mechanism. Part of the house is built into a mountain wall to conserve energy and to preserve the terrain. The lower section overhangs the rocks with a spectacular view of the sea, making the overall effect from the decks breathtaking. There are entrances from the mountain road above and from the seaside drive below. All parts of the site work together to form the mechanism.

Systems

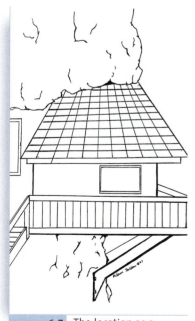

FIGURE 6-7   The location as a mechanism
Reproduced by permission of Adam D. Jordan

Groups of parts that work together to perform a function form a **system**. Without each component, the system cannot function. Systems can be either natural or manufactured. For example, a plant cannot replicate without all of the parts of its reproductive system. All of the parts work together for the overall purpose of reproduction; however, each part has an independent function. Another example of a system is a word processing computer program. For each command in a word processing system's pull-down menus, there is a separate function, but together those parts form a systematic, efficient program that produces a formatted document. For example, one command makes the text bold; another changes uppercase to sentence case. Another example is irrigation, which is a highly complex mechanism of a system. Its parts work together to provide water for crops in climates where rain is scarce.

Practice 6-2: Selecting a Mechanism

For each of the mechanism categories, name two mechanisms. When practical, one mechanism should be from your career cluster. Record your answers on *Student Workbook* page 6-A.

Uses for Mechanism Descriptions

There are numerous uses for mechanism descriptions. These purposes may include purchasing, replacing, repairing, explaining, etc. Each description can also vary for different audiences.

Soybeans, for instance, can be a mechanism in various ways, depending on the purpose for each description. Notice how each person in the following example describes soybeans in a different way.

- Tess, an organic farmer who grows soybeans to sell, does not decide what product uses certain parts of the plant; neither does she describe the whole bean or its parts to the buyer. Instead, she describes her beans to another farmer as being superior in size, color, firmness, and overall quality.
- Ana, a supervisor in the factory that purchased Tess's beans, describes the soybean to Rick, a new employee. Ana explains the process of extracting the oil from the bean to sell separately. Then she explains the separation of the hulls from the meat of the bean. The factory sells the hulls for cattle feed and grinds the meat of the bean into soy flour. Ana's description of the bean varies greatly from Tess's because both are describing the soybean for different purposes and for different audiences.

Decision Making

Knowing how a mechanism works is important in many situations. The knowledge gained from studying a mechanism description, along with observing the way a mechanism is working, helps people make sound decisions. Watching for changes and comparing and contrasting mechanisms also provide information that is useful in making decisions.

People *Connection*

When you next make a call on a cell phone, think of Hedy Lamarr. Best known for her movie performances in the 1930s and '40s, Hedy Lamarr was a perceptive tinkerer whose scientific mind explored ways of preventing the jamming of submarine signals in the early days of World War II. When she wanted to pursue her ideas, she was discouraged and urged to work for the war bond effort instead. However, she teamed up with George Antheil, and their patent describing the method for radio signals' bouncing among frequencies at split-second intervals was accepted in 1942. The military used the invention during the Cuban missile crisis in 1962, and today the invention's concept is applied to wireless Internet transmission and cellular phones. Unfortunately, the patent expired in 1959, and Lamarr and Antheil never received any royalty payments for its commercialization. In 1997, recognition finally came for the movie star with the engineering mind, credited as having insight into the concept of the wireless Internet. Her comment? "It's about time."

by the way...

The need for basic training is increasing! A survey conducted by Olsten reports that more than 60 percent of newly hired employees need increased computer skills and more teamwork skills. The lack of these skills drives up production costs while the company does the training.

- An emergency room technician must know how a healthy human arm works before he or she can treat an accident victim with a broken arm.
- To know how to prune juniper bushes, a landscape manager should understand their pattern of growth.
- An electronics technician needs to know how a soldering iron tip should look to decide when to begin soldering.

All three situations need more than a superficial look; they require a thorough knowledge of a mechanism.

Training

Training situations occur daily in the workplace. Employers provide training for workers new to a job and new to equipment or procedures. In addition, transferred or promoted employees must develop experience with new products, machines, and even work sites. For all employers, changing technology creates new training needs for skilled employees.

- Even though Addie has been in the baking industry for several years, as the newly hired chief baker in Johnetta's bakery, she still needs instruction in the bakery's machines. The bread machines are a different brand than Addie has been using, and each oven has its own temperature idiosyncrasies. As a new employee, Addie needs to have the machinery described to her so that she will be able to use it correctly.
- The oxyacetylene welding unit is a new piece of equipment for the manufacturing area. It needs to be introduced to the workers,

even though many of them have been on the job for more than 20 years. As the supervisor, Helena must be able to describe the overall capabilities of the machinery, each part and its function, and the machine's performance while she trains her workers on the equipment.

Manuals give an overview, a type of general description of mechanisms. The technical description is usually followed by visuals, such as specifications sheets (specs) and special types of interior drawings. The details are typically added later in the succeeding sections of the manual. These technical mechanism descriptions are used for customer and employee training.

Reports

Mechanism descriptions are used within reports. The functions, parts, or data contained within the report may need to be described. For example, any changes in equipment or purchase recommendations will need a description before decisions are made. Sometimes the descriptions are presented as an oral presentation or as a written report given in presentation form.

When Karim presented his architectural firm's bid for the Technical Center, he knew it would be meaningless without the floor plan and the three-dimensional drawings showing the location of the equipment. In addition, the report on the computer network would include modifying several off-site locations. His audience wouldn't be able to understand that report without the wiring diagrams to describe the changes.

Marketing

A marketing campaign may include a mechanism description because marketing promotes the product as a whole and presents the parts of the product. If the buyer is a specialist, more details should be included than for a general buyer.

Proposals are a form of marketing. Often the audience for a proposal is a general purchaser. Bids to purchase equipment must be explained with a mechanism description to this nontechnical buyer. So that the buyer can understand a proposal, visuals are usually included with the written description.

The Clamara crankshaft is more efficient than the crankshaft produced by the Hut Company, its competitor. In its marketing campaign, the Hut Company should highlight the features that make the crankshaft better by using a drawing with a written description. Now Clamara needs to

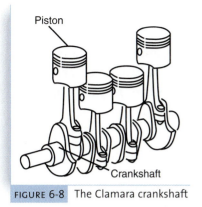

Piston

Crankshaft

convince the giant Christos Car Corporation that it should use the Clamara crankshaft. In its proposal, Clamara will include a drawing of the side of the entire crankshaft (Figure 6-8) and a drawing highlighting the features that make the crankshaft superior to its competitor.

Practice 6–3: Wording a Mechanism Picture

Examine your left shoe very carefully. Imagine that last weekend you and your friends spent a day at the beach. As your friend was driving down the highway, you decided to open the window and dump the sand out of your shoe. Unfortunately, you shook too hard and dropped the shoe! The right shoe is perfectly fine—and the shoes are a favorite pair of yours—so you want the shoe back.

Create a newspaper lost and found ad to find your shoe. Want ads have a maximum amount of words, usually 20 or 30, so you need to be brief and concise.

Parts of a Mechanism

"A closed mind is a dying mind."

EDNA FERBER, U.S. AUTHOR

A blueprint fits the definition of a mechanism; it is an object with parts performing different functions, each function serving a definite purpose. However, a computer spreadsheet is very complex and is best described when it is divided into sections. The sections can then be explained in a particular order. (This method of explanation is similar to the process description in Chapter 5.) **Random order** is not an effective way to describe the parts of a mechanism.

Structure, function, and order of importance are ways that you can divide a mechanism into parts. The method or combination of methods that you choose depends on the purpose of the mechanism description.

Structure

You can organize your description in terms of a mechanism's physical appearance. First, look closely at the mechanism. Then describe its parts in a logical order according to the physical aspects that you see. Structurally, parts can be described from top to bottom, left to right, front to back, or outside to inside. (Chapter 2 is a good reference source for describing structural parts.)

The mechanism described by structure is the **machine at rest**—that is, a machine that is not in operation. The written picture of a machine at rest focuses on the mechanism's parts and the relationship of the parts to one another. The description only briefly mentions the function of the parts to enhance the explanation of the structure.

A structural description of the heart might begin as follows:

> The human heart functions like a circulation pump for the body's blood. The heart consists of four chambers. The two small upper chambers are the left atrium and the right atrium. The left and right ventricles lay below each related atrium.

Function

When the audience needs to concentrate more on the purpose for each part of the mechanism, you should explain the **function** of each part to the audience to illustrate the description. This type of description explains a **machine in operation**; the way the machine looks is secondary to the way the machine performs. In the functional description, you give the purpose of each part, rather than describe the part itself. A description of a machine in operation emphasizes parts working together to perform a function. How the parts are located in relationship to one another is only mentioned.

Functional parts are often described in the order of the tasks that each part performs. For example, Part A moves Part B, which moves Part C, etc. Not every mechanism can be described functionally, particularly in a description of a substance.

The functional parts of a hardhat are the shell that protects the head, the brim that shields the eyes, the adjustable headband that sizes the hat to the individual's head, and the crown's strap device that combines with the headband to protect the head from impact, (See Figure 6-1 on page 176.)

Remember the earlier description of the heart based on structure? If the audience needs a description of how the heart performs, rather than how it is put together, then the heart should be described according to function. Notice how the following description emphasizes the function of the four major parts of the heart; the location of the heart's parts is mentioned only in relation to function.

> The human heart functions like a circulation pump for the body's blood. The heart consists of four chambers. The left atrium and the right atrium are the small upper chambers that receive the blood from the body. The left and right ventricles below the atriums pump the blood away from the heart.

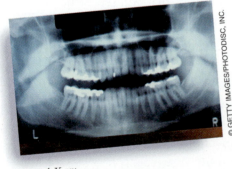

© GETTY IMAGES/PHOTODISC, INC.

Dental X-ray

Importance

In a few instances, the parts of a mechanism can be described **in order of importance**. Consider this example: The teacher is explaining how to check an X-ray film or radiograph to the dental assistant class. Parts of the film should be described in order of

According to the *Occupational Outlook Handbook*, the occupations with the largest projected employment decline in the United States are (in descending order):

- Telephone operators
- Word processors and typists
- Textile machinists
- Fishing workers
- Farmers and ranchers
- Electrical and electronic equipment assemblers
- Computer operators
- Brokerage and loan clerks
- Travel agents

An occupation may decline for many reasons. One reason is that others often absorb formerly specialized occupations, such as those of word processors and computer operators, into their own job description. However, another reason is that the occupation's mechanisms are becoming extinct, such as the reception telephone center and the typewriter. Voice-mail systems and the personal computer are replacing those mechanisms.

importance—that is, which is the most important part to check first, second, etc. Dental cavities are more important to check because they need to be repaired before the patient can schedule other dental work. List positive aspects before negative aspects for the best effect on your audience.

However, some mechanisms cannot be described according to importance. For example, no one can judge the upper half of the heart as being more important than the lower half. Without either chamber, you would die!

Combination of Methods

At times, a combination of two methods may be used to describe a mechanism. (See Figure 6-9.) If the structural location of the chambers of the heart is as significant as the way the heart functions, then the description would be similar to the following, with both structural and functional parts equally emphasized.

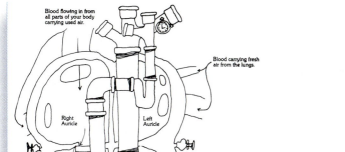

Blood flowing in from all parts of your body carrying used air.

Blood carrying fresh air from the lungs.

Right Auricle

Left Auricle

Blood is pumped to the lungs to get rid of the used air.

Blood filled with fresh air gets pumped to all parts of your body.

Right Ventricle

Left Ventricle

The heart is made up of two pumps working side by side.

FIGURE 6-9   Blood flow through the heart

Reprinted by permission of The McGraw-Hill Companies

The human heart functions like a circulation pump for the body's blood. The heart consists of four chambers. The left atrium and the right atrium are the two small upper chambers. These upper chambers receive the blood from the body. The left and right ventricles are below each related atrium. The ventricles pump blood away from the heart.

Your audience and the particular use of the mechanism description will help you decide whether you need to describe a mechanism by structure, function, importance, or a combination of methods.

Practice 6-4: Describing the Parts of a Mechanism

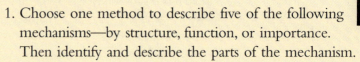

1. Choose one method to describe five of the following mechanisms—by structure, function, or importance. Then identify and describe the parts of the mechanism.

Example:

hairbrush   *Function:* The bristles move through hair to smooth, detangle, and style. The handle provides a means for holding the brush.

a. thermometer   f. telephone receiver
b. blood   g. gum eraser
c. wood chisel   h. lightbulb
d. bar code   i. tire
e. elm tree   j. paintbrush

2. Now choose five mechanisms from your career major. Repeat step 1 to complete this Practice.

Writing Mechanism Descriptions

A mechanism is described in words. A mechanism description may be written for a general audience who has never seen the mechanism or who may have very little knowledge of it. Even the specialized audience may need a description. The specialist may have the basic knowledge that a general audience has, but may need more technical, detailed information. With either audience, the description must be clearly written.

Though visuals are usually included with the written mechanism description, they cannot stand alone. Visuals enhance or strengthen the written description of a mechanism.

Sometimes the same mechanism must be described to different audiences. Such descriptions will vary, not in the way the mechanism is used, but in the language and complexity of the description. For example, Sera Broga comes into Jim Phay's electronics shop with a broken Diastar television antenna that she wants repaired. When Jim examines the antenna, he thinks that repairing the outdated Diastar antenna would be less cost-effective than replacing the antenna with a portable satellite dish system. Jim Phay must describe the mechanisms of both the broken Diastar antenna and the replacement system of a satellite dish and its network to his customer, Sera Broga, before she can make her decision.

Jim wants Sera to understand what is involved in repairing the antenna versus replacing it with a satellite dish, so he needs to use nonspecialized language that a person with general knowledge, such as Sera, understands. Though Sera may have other reasons for not replacing the antenna, Jim does not want his explanation to be the reason for poor customer decision making.

Even though the labor cost is high, Sera decides to have Jim repair the antenna. Now Jim needs to describe the antenna mechanism to Misha Roth, his repairer. Jim's explanation is especially important because Misha has never repaired a Diastar antenna before. Moreover, Jim's description to Misha will be different than his description to Sera because, as a repairer, Misha is a specialist. In his work, Jim sees the need for describing a mechanism in different ways to different audiences.

Common Versus Specific Terms

Use more **common** or ordinary **terms** for a general audience. These terms are basically nontechnical and are less confusing. **Specific terms** have more technical details. These terms may seem more accurate, but this accuracy is frequently needed only by a specialist.

In common or general terms, a motor would be called "powerful." A seat would have "adjustable heights." A saw would come with "three different types of blades." In specific terms, the motor would be 1.5 horsepower. The seat would be adjustable to four positions in 2-inch increments. The saw blades would come in $7\frac{1}{2}$-, 7-, and $6\frac{1}{2}$-inch sizes.

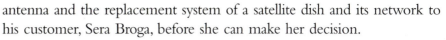

Practice 6–5: Choosing General or Specific Terms

From *Student Workbook* page 6-B, choose one part or function of each mechanism. Describe that part or function in both general and specific terms.

Concrete Versus Abstract Terms

Careful word choice is also important. Besides a common or specific term being chosen, a **concrete term** must be chosen over an abstract term. Because the mechanism description must be precise, use concrete terms to enable the audience to understand the word picture better. For example, *blight* is the concrete term that clarifies the abstract term *disease* (of plants). *Chartreuse* is the concrete color name; *green* is the **abstract term**.

by the way...

Practice 6–6: Choosing Concrete Terms

1. The following abstract terms need to become concrete terms for a mechanism description. Write a concrete word or phrase to replace each abstract term given.

Examples:

safe	*dry floors*
dull-colored	*beige*
large	*6 feet in diameter*

a. disappointing   g. thin (as in the opposite of thick)
b. wet   h. thin (as in a liquid)
c. quickly   i. rusty
d. problem area   j. not feeling well
e. bright   k. pretty
f. thick   l. round

2. Using sensory language, words or phrases that appeal to one of the five senses, is another way to make your mechanism description concrete. Using *Student Workbook* page 6-C, describe the underlined words, using sensory language.

Analogies

Often it is best to explain an unfamiliar mechanism by comparing it to something with which the audience is familiar. That direct comparison is called an **analogy**. The names of some terms have originated from analogies. Letters of the alphabet and numbers are familiar, so terms such as *C-clamp, A-frame, I beam,* and *figure eight* originated. These analogies often give the unfamiliar a visual shape. Parts of the body provide useful analogies to describe parts of objects. The *neck* of a guitar, the *head* of a pin, and *gooseneck lamp* are examples of this type of analogy.

The following examples use analogies to create clear comparisons of well-known objects with lesser-known objects.

- The serpentine belt is as wide as an adult's little finger.
- The highlighting solution should be as thick as cake frosting.
- The hole is dime-sized.
- The human heart functions like a circulation pump for the blood.

A word of caution: Use analogies to simplify your descriptions, not to make them more confusing. So be sure that your audience is familiar with the terms you compare. Also use an analogy *only* when the audience needs the comparison to understand the description better.

© CORBIS
Highlighting with solution

Technology *Connection*

Interval Research Corporation has patented a watch that you can never lose, one that resembles a programmable tattoo. This liquid-crystal display, implanted under the skin, is visible and can be charged by holding the wrist near an external source. There are no health hazards—in fact, the screen not only shows the time, but also contains biosensors that monitor temperature and blood pressure. The invention could be lifesaving to a person with heart disease.

Practice 6–7: Using Analogies

1. Often an analogy creates a word picture. Explain the visual analogy for five of the following terms.

Example:

disk brake   *The brake shoe is in the shape of a disklike saucer.*

Ch06-07.doc

a. blueprint	f. chain saw
b. tail comb	g. snapdragon
c. computer chip	h. claw hammer
d. elbow joint	i. hairline fracture
e. T square	j. forklift

2. Create analogies for five of the following items. Describe the overall appearance and the major parts.

Example:

keyboard   *The keyboard is a musical instrument that looks like a small piano mounted on a board. The keys are pressed to produce musical notes.*

a. scanner	f. transit
b. dental chair	g. keyhole saw
c. soil profile (soil lines)	h. easel
d. drafting table	i. CD-ROM
e. shock absorber	j. bit (horse equipment)

Precise Wording

The wording of a description needs to be **precise**. The more exact the description, the clearer it will be. Remember always to keep your audience and purpose in mind. An accurate description is important.

Precise wording is needed whether the audience is general or specialized. For example, the following is a general description of a sheetfed scanner. The description is accurate but is in nontechnical terms.

> The sheetfed scanner is a device the size of a lunch box that looks like a mini-computer printer and attaches to both the computer and the printer. Some scanners are so small that they can fit behind the keyboard. Simply feed a page into the scanner and push a button. The scanner head will move over the paper, reproducing photographs, drawings, and text as computer files.

If the description is for a specialized audience, more technical material is needed. The description of the scanner might be changed to the following:

> The sheetfed scanner is a narrow rectangular device that produces digitized versions of hard-copy photographs, line art, and text. When you feed a page into the slot on the scanner, the scanner head moves over the paper and captures the image. You can work with scanned files in popular graphics, presentation, web publishing, and word processing programs.

Practice 6–8: Analyzing Mechanisms for Different Audiences

1. After reading through the questions on *Student Workbook* page 6-D, listen to and take notes on the mechanism descriptions that your teacher will play for you.

2. With a partner, answer the questions on *Student Workbook* page 6-D. You may need to listen to the Audio Activity a second time to hear all of the details.

The Third Person

When you speak and write to others, you use the verb and the personal pronoun in the second person, as in the sentence "You brought the cider." When you give instructions, you also use the second person in the form of a command, as in "Bring the cider." When you use the second person, you write and speak directly to the reader, often with a familiar tone.

A description of a mechanism, however, is more impersonal. Generally, you are not writing to a person you know; instead, you are writing for an unknown audience. Therefore, you need to write in the **third person**, which is more impersonal and slightly more formal than the second person.

Culture *Connection*

Reaching the nation's Hispanic and Latino population as consumers is often done by targeting the group as a whole. The most popular way of reaching Latinos is by communicating in Spanish. However, many Hispanic people do not read or speak Spanish. Their communities may consist of such diverse groups as Cuban, Colombian, Mexican, Dominican Republican, and Puerto Rican people. The groups not only have diverse ethnic traits, but also differ in issues that affect their buying habits. Each group needs to be targeted, with the message directing concerns to that particular audience.

A group of people

For third-person writing, instead of saying *I* or *you,* use words and phrases such as the following:

Singular	**Plural**
he, she, it, one	they
a person (or a name)	people (or names)
an individual	individuals
an object	objects

Practice 6–9: Using the Third Person

1. Rewrite the following sentences so that all parts are in the third person.

   Example:

   If you like shorts, wear them at home.

   If a student likes to wear shorts, he or she should wear them at home.

   a. Dental assistant students should report to the auditorium and bring your notebooks.
   b. The wise trainer knows that you must dry a horse after bathing it in the winter.
   c. You can casually call long distance, and the bill will shock you in a month.
   d. High cholesterol may be a problem if you eat red meat.
   e. Why drive your car to the mall when walking the two blocks is good exercise for the body?
   f. Set the alarm 15 minutes early, and you will arrive at school on time every day.

2. For additional practice using the third person, use *Student Workbook* page 6-E.

Career *Connection*

In the past, the masculine pronouns *he*, *him*, and *his* were the standard in the English language to represent groups that might include women. Today many people consider this usage sexist. Here are some ways to avoid it.

• Try switching to plural pronouns, such as replacing *his* with *their*.

• Use gender-free words, such as *person, one, employee*, or *customer*.

• Reword to avoid using the pronoun.

• Alternate use of masculine and feminine pronouns.

Objectivity

Write the mechanism description precisely and more formally than you would an instruction. The body of the mechanism description must be objective. Since the purpose of a mechanism description is to inform the audience, it should not include opinions or judgments except when necessary in the introduction and conclusion.

Practice 6–10: Making Sentences Objective

The following sentences are taken from descriptions, but they are not objective. Rewrite the sentences to make them objective.

Example:

> The use of spurs is unfair to the horse.
> *Digging spurs into a horse's sides can cause wounds.*

1. Computer-aided design program upgrades are too expensive for small businesses.

2. The resume that gets the job is best.

3. The type of nail doesn't matter; no one looks at a basement ceiling.

4. The paint will cover any surface. That's what the salesclerk says.

5. Placing the tax on the customer's check will please him or her.

6. To apply the bandage properly, the nurse must first clean the wound well.

7. Only an expert knows how to choose the proper pigment.

8. Play is a welcome activity at any time in a child's day.

9. Using the Internet to make travel reservations is a breeze.

10. His performance was great.

The Active Voice

Write your description in the **active voice**, using active verbs; the active voice is more direct and less confusing. Remember, you may be describing an unknown or unfamiliar object to the audience, so the clearer your writing, the better. The active voice is desirable, but the passive voice is acceptable when the one who does the action is less important or obvious. (To review the active verbs, turn to pages 144–146 of Chapter 5.)

With the active voice, the word or phrase in the subject position gets the emphasis. The subject is performing the action in the sentence. The active voice is more direct and precise, emphasizing the mechanism over the description.

Ch06-11.doc

Practice 6–11: Writing in the Active Voice

1. Change the following sentences from the passive to the active voice. Use only the third person.

Example:

> The disease should be prevented by the inoculation.
> *The inoculation should prevent the disease.*

a. The seeds have been eaten by the birds.

b. The employee should be hired by the personnel department.

c. Hardhats should be worn at all times.

d. Unrefrigerated potato salad will be spoiled in a few hours.

e. Fingernails can be shaped with materials such as acrylics or porcelain.

f. Shawn should have been declared the first-place winner.

g. A suit and tie will be worn by each male business student three times a week.

h. A prospective employee will not be hired by many employers if his or her resume reflects frequent job changes.

i. Communication skills are needed even by people who work alone.

j. A good student will be rewarded with excellent job placement, a satisfactory paycheck, and room for advancement.

(cont'd on next page)

2. The following phrases describe three mechanisms. Write a description for each mechanism; use the active voice and complete sentences. The first one is started for you.

a. black walnut tree
one of the most valuable native American trees
heavy, strong, durable wood
wood easy to work with
wood in great demand for veneers, cabinetmaking, interior
     finishing, gunstocks
bark used for tanning
yellowish brown dye from nut husks
twigs—favorite deer food

The black walnut is one of the most valuable native American trees. Carpenters work the heavy, strong, durable wood easily. Black walnut is in great demand for. . . .

b. internal combustion engine
power source for automobiles and airplanes
power develops in smooth-walled tube cylinder
cylinder—piston moves inside
movement of piston caused by expansion of gases
similar to steam engine—both use cylinders

c. pancreas
two essential substances:
• insulin into bloodstream regulates amount of sugar in blood
• pancreatic juices into duodenum contain enzymes that help
   digest food

Using Visuals in Mechanism Descriptions

Visuals add value to a mechanism description. A general audience may not understand the mechanism, despite the descriptive words. A specialized audience may have the basic technical knowledge but no understanding of the details of a specific subject area. With either audience, the mechanism description needs further explanation, and visuals help the audience better understand the information. Visuals illustrate the different aspects of a mechanism.

When visuals are included, they are additions or enhancements to the description. Some facts cannot be described in a single visual, such as weight, materials used, actual size, texture, and three-dimensional contours. Each variation of the mechanism must be included in a separate visual.

Exterior Visuals

Some mechanisms may be totally unfamiliar to an audience. If the audience has never seen the mechanism, show an **exterior perspective**. Photographs, maps, and realistic drawings can provide an overall picture. Distracting details should not be included.

These exterior views must focus on the mechanism. The illustration must be uncluttered. Distracting details should not be included. Other than the mechanism itself, very little else should be in the picture. A contrast is needed between the subject and the background for the mechanism to be the focus. For photographs, good lighting is essential, as shown in the photo of the construction site.

An exterior view of a construction site

Interior Visuals

Cross sections, schematics, and cutaway and exploded drawings depict the parts of a mechanism from the inside. With **interior views** of a mechanism, the audience can see where each part is located with respect to the other parts and to the mechanism as a whole.

Someone who is unfamiliar with an object can visualize it clearly with an interior view. By studying an interior visual, the audience can better repair, make changes, order parts, operate the mechanism, purchase equipment, etc. Through the visualization, the audience will understand what is going on under the housing, hood, or other exterior cover.

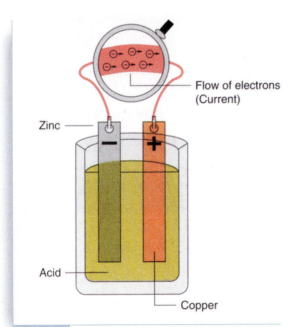

FIGURE 6-10   A cross section of a battery circuit

Cross Sections

Cross sections depict the layers of a mechanism. This type of visual shows the depth and location of each layer. The content of each layer is often labeled as well. In Figure 6-10, the cross section of a battery circuit shows the layers and parts of the battery and the flow of electrons from negative to positive.

Schematics and Interior Maps

Schematics are drawings or diagrams that show an overall view of a mechanism with connections and various components labeled. (See Figure 6-11.) Many people assume a schematic is a diagram of only electrical circuits or wiring, but this type of diagram has a more generic use. For example, a **map** is a type of schematic with directions labeled by arrows and with significant locations marked.

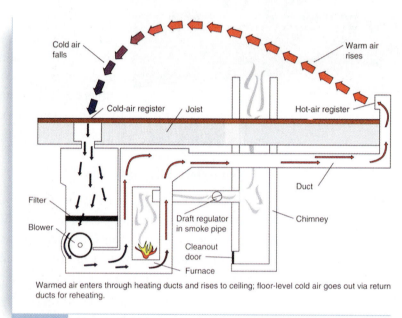

Warmed air enters through heating ducts and rises to ceiling; floor-level cold air goes out via return ducts for reheating.

FIGURE 6-11 A warm-air system

Cutaway Drawings

Cutaway drawings slice the mechanism to show internal parts that are normally concealed from the exterior. (See Figure 6-12.) These drawings have a seemingly transparent exterior wall so that the interior can be visible with the parts labeled. In cutaway drawings, you label the specific angle or position, called the **perspective**, of the drawing in the title. The labels may be *frontal view, side view, top view,* or something similar.

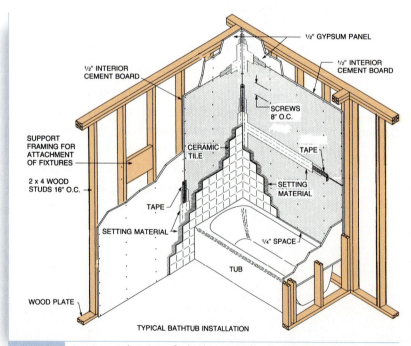

FIGURE 6-12 A cutaway drawing of a bathroom wall—top view

Reproduced by permission. Carpentry by Lewis. Delmar Publishers, Albany, New York, Copyright 1995.

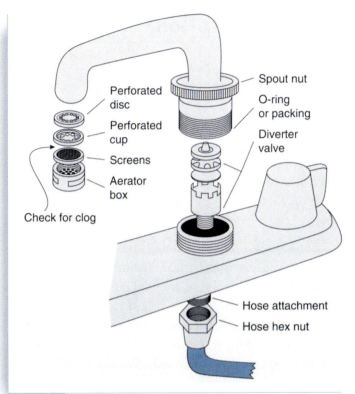

Perforated disc

Perforated cup

Screens

Aerator box

Check for clog

Spout nut

O-ring or packing

Diverter valve

Hose attachment

Hose hex nut

FIGURE 6-13　An exploded drawing of a faucet

Exploded Drawings

Exploded drawings show how the parts of a mechanism fit together; the pieces are shown exploded or separated from each other in succession. Often exploded drawings appear in repair or maintenance manuals to allow users to assemble a device and replace parts. A general audience would need the exploded drawing in Figure 6-13 to replace the O-ring in a faucet.

Practice 6–12: Using Visuals

What visual would best illustrate a description of the mechanisms in the following list? You can use a cross section, a schematic, a cutaway drawing, an exploded drawing, or an exterior view for your visual. Give the reason for your choice.

Examples:

faucet	*exploded drawing*
house wiring diagram	*schematic*

1. drainage system for underground house

2. lamp socket

3. motherboard

4. automobile engine

5. tree trunk

6. blender

7. hair shaft

8. movement of water through layers of sediment

9. retractable ballpoint pen

10. highway system

Organization of a Mechanism Description

Describing a mechanism provides an overview for the audience who may not be familiar with it. When choosing the subject, keep in mind the type of audience and the purpose for giving the description. Then divide the mechanism description into sections. Whether written or oral, mechanism descriptions use the following method. To explain the mechanism clearly, choose a visual that is best suited for the subject and for the specific audience.

The Introduction

The beginning of the introduction needs to attract the audience's attention—and give the name of the mechanism. Include the brand name and model number if applicable. Next, the audience needs to understand what the mechanism is, so define it in a three-part definition, as you learned in Chapter 2, page 37. In the introduction, also specify who uses the mechanism, where it is used, and when it is needed. If necessary, include personal remarks and recommendations, depending on the audience. This beginning part can be completed in two or three sentences.

The Physical Characteristics

The overall explanation of the appearance provides an accurate, objective description of the physical features of the mechanism. Even though one or more visuals are usually included, they cannot show such characteristics as weight and materials. Several sentences should prepare the audience for the central part of the description—explaining the mechanism's parts.

The Major Parts

To describe the mechanism thoroughly, name the major parts. You can classify the parts by structure, function, order of importance, or a combination of methods. If you describe the parts by structure, you might indicate the parts' locations on a visual in a logical order. If the mechanism is divided by function, name each part and its function together, if possible, in the order that each part performs. This objectively written portion of the presentation gives the overall operation of the mechanism; it is a miniature process description, which you learned about in Chapter 5. However, do not spend too much time on this section; keep the purpose of your description in mind.

After the overview of the parts, select features that set the mechanism apart from similar mechanisms if doing so makes the mechanism significantly different from others. Emphasize each of those features in detail, discussing facts such as size, shape, weight, color, material, and

by the way...

No athlete would ever imagine entering competition without adequate preparation, including studying the opponent. Do yourself a favor—do the same when preparing a project. Study the audience well.

overall appearance. Explain why these facts were selected—what makes a feature significant? A visual will help the audience better understand the mechanism's features.

The Closing

Now that you have described the mechanism, highlight the major parts again. Give any additional information necessary for your audience, such as price, different models or variations, guarantees—any information needed for the use of the mechanism description. Depending on the audience and the purpose, you may include personal remarks, persuasive language, and recommendations. Refer to the purpose of the description in the closing.

Practice 6-13: Describing a Common Mechanism

teamwork

Your teacher will give you a paper clip. In small groups, choose the audience and the purpose for the description. Then describe this mechanism in detail. Include physical characteristics, major parts, and function, adding a visual. Prepare to share your mechanism description with the class.

Summary

A mechanism description is the explanation and drawing of a mechanism, a tool, an organism, a substance, a location, or a system that has a minimum of two parts. These parts work separately, but together accomplish one purpose. The description clarifies the mechanism for the audience and must be accurate, clear, and concise. One or more visuals should accompany the written description. Follow these guidelines when you describe a mechanism:

- Understand the audience and purpose for the mechanism description.
- Choose a method for describing the parts.
- Use language appropriate to a mechanism description, such as analogies, objective writing, and active voice.
- Include visuals that show exterior or interior views for most descriptions.
- Organize the mechanism description to include an introduction, the physical characteristics, the major parts, and a closing.

review and research activities visit
communicating.swlearning.com

project-based assessment

Mechanism Description

To encourage the purchase of state-of-the-art equipment, your state has given school districts the chance to apply for matching funds for equipment costing more than $500. Your teacher, Mr. Kinishi, has given you the authority to investigate the purchase of replacement equipment and to report the results to him. This mechanism would be something that is familiar to you, but not as well known to Mr. Kinishi.

After doing your investigation, you must give a presentation to Mr. Kinishi and your advisory committee. Write your presentation for a general audience with some technical knowledge. Translate the specific knowledge into more general terms that your audience will understand. Include a visual to explain the recommended mechanism thoroughly. Mr. Kinishi will use your presentation to prepare an announcement to open bids for competitive companies.

1. Review the information in this chapter. Then listen to the recorded sample presentation while your teacher shows you the visual. Study Shelley Sanchez's Sample Project Plan on page 201.

2. After consulting trade journals and catalogs, choose the mechanism for your description. Then complete the Project Plan, *Student Workbook* page 6-F, and have your teacher check it.

3. Using the information from your Project Plan, prepare notes for your presentation. Use the third person, be objective, and use the active voice. Include at least one analogy to form a clear image of the mechanism for the audience. (Chapter 2 will help you in describing the parts of the mechanism you have chosen.)

4. Review the types of visuals discussed earlier in this chapter. Then choose the type of visual best suited to explain your mechanism. Prepare your visual and label the parts.

5. Study the Project Guide, *Student Workbook* page 6-G, for criteria for your presentation. (Refer to Chapter 3, starting with page 71, for planning your talk.) Rehearse your presentation individually; then rehearse it for another student. Use your notes and visual as you would in presenting before the class. Using the Rough Draft column of the Project Guide, you and the other student should rate your rehearsed presentation.

6. Revise your notes and presentation, incorporating the changes in the presentation that your fellow student and teacher suggested. Proofread and practice the presentation with another student again, using the Final Draft column of the Project Guide.

7. Give your presentation to the class. The Project Guide will be used to evaluate your visual and your presentation.

Sample Project Plan

Plan for Describing a Mechanism

			CONTENT
SUBJECT	Downdraft Ventilation paint booth for autobody spray painting		**Three-Part Definition**
			The Downdraft Ventilation paint booth is an autobody painting booth that removes spray paint components by forced downdrafts of air.
AUDIENCE	Advisory committee and teacher (a general audience with some technical knowledge)		**Physical Characteristics**
			Booth—Sheet metal, large enough to hold car, SUV, pickup truck
			Ceiling—Airflow nozzles
PURPOSE	**What actions should the audience take?** Recommend district purchase of Downdraft Ventilation paint booth with matching state funds		Floor—Exit ports
			Doors—vehicle-sized at both ends of booth
			Major Parts and Their Purpose
			Housing—Reduces exposure to harmful contaminants to technician and outside environment
FORMAT	☐ written ☒ oral ☐ other		Airflow input nozzles—Space inside booth enough for technician to use conventional gravity or siphon-feed paint gun
SOURCES	"Control of Paint Overspray in Autobody Repair Shops" DHHS (NIOSH) Publication No. 96-106		Filters—Entering air of outside contaminants, then forced downward by downdraft
			Exit ports—Allow removal of most paint contaminants
			Doors—Protect outside air
			Closing
VISUALS	**What visual will represent the mechanism?** Labeled cross section of booth containing automobile		Advantages over present: Protects technician and outside
			Results in lower overspray concentrations and cleaner paint job
ANALOGY			Recommend purchase by district with matching state funds
	Size comparable to car wash booth		

literature

Overview

Keep in mind that mechanisms may be tools or machinery, organisms, substances, locations, and systems. In the poem you are about to read, Rudyard Kipling, a British writer in the 19th century, tells about only one kind of mechanism. Although industry has greatly benefited humankind, you should understand the problems that machines can ultimately cause. Note what Kipling is saying about the power of machines.

"The Secret of the Machines"

We were taken from the ore bed and the mine,
    We were melted in the furnace and the pit—
    We were cast and wrought and hammered to design,
We were cut and filed and tooled and gauged to fit.
Some water, coal, and oil is all we ask,
And a thousandth of an inch to give us play:
And now, if you will set us to our task,
We will serve you four and twenty hours a day!

We can pull and haul and push and lift and drive,
    We can print and plow and weave and heat and light,
We can run and jump and swim and fly and dive,
    We can see and hear and count and read and write!

Do you wish to make the mountains bare their head
    And lay their new-cut forests at your feet?
Do you want to turn a river in its bed,
    Or plant a barren wilderness with wheat?
Shall we pipe aloft and bring your water down
    From the never-failing cisterns of the snows,
To work the mills and tramways in your town,
    And irrigate your orchards as it flows?
It is easy! Give us dynamite and drills!
    Watch the iron-shouldered rocks lie down and quake,
As the thirsty desert level floods and fills,
    And the valley we have dammed becomes a lake.

But remember, please, the Law by which we live,
    We are not built to comprehend a lie,
We can neither love nor pity nor forgive.
    If you make a slip in handling us you die!
We are greater than the Peoples or the Kings—
    Be humble, as you crawl beneath our rods!
Our touch can alter all created things,
    We are everything on earth—except The Gods!

Though our smoke may hide the Heavens from your eyes,
    It will vanish and the stars will shine again,
Because, for all our power and weight and size,
    We are nothing more than children of your brain!

—Rudyard Kipling

Start-Up: Name the different machines to which the poem could be referring. How might these machines cause problems? Brainstorm solutions to the problems.

Connection: In small groups, brainstorm to create a list of problems that machines have caused in the past, cause in the present, and may cause in the future. (Don't deal with just surface problems, but with problems for humanity.)

Assume the personality of a machine of your choice. Use your imagination. Tell about one day in the business world.

Working with Literature: Refer to *Student Workbook* page 6-H for an activity on the actions performed by the machines in the poem.

Overview

Did you ever try to read a book, view a video, or watch a ball game while someone was trying to engage you in conversation when you didn't want to participate? It's exasperating, isn't it? What can you do? Kurt Vonnegut tells a story of such a situation. Read it to find out how one man handled this annoyance.

This is a frame story, a story told within another story. As you read, think about how the inside story relates to the frame story.

"Tom Edison's Shaggy Dog"

Two old men sat on a park bench one morning in the sunshine of Tampa, Florida—one trying doggedly to read a book he was plainly enjoying while the other, Harold K. Bullard, told him the story of his life in the full, round, head tones of a public address system.

Bullard, who had been, before he retired, successful in many fields, enjoyed reviewing his important past.

But he faced the problem that complicates the lives of cannibals—namely: that a single victim cannot be used over and over. Anyone who had passed the time of day with him and his dog refused to share a bench with them again.

So Bullard and his dog set out through the park each day in quest of new faces. They had had good luck this morning, for they had found this stranger right away, clearly a new arrival in Florida, still buttoned up tight in heavy serge, stiff collar and necktie, and with nothing better to do than read.

> "Yes," said Bullard, rounding out the first hour of his lecture, "made and lost five fortunes in my time."

"Yes," said Bullard, rounding out the first hour of his lecture, "made and lost five fortunes in my time."

"So you said," said the stranger, whose name Bullard had neglected to ask. "Easy, boy. No, no, no, boy," he said to the dog, who was growing more aggressive toward his ankles.

"Oh? Already told you that, did I?" said Bullard.

"Twice."

"Two in real estate, one in scrap iron, and one in oil, and one in trucking."

"So you said."

"I did? Yes, guess I did. Two in real estate, one in scrap iron, one in oil, and one in trucking. Wouldn't take back a day of it."

"No, I suppose not," said the stranger. "Pardon me, but do you suppose you could move your dog somewhere else? He keeps—"

"Him?" said Bullard, heartily. "Friendliest dog in the world. Don't need to be afraid of him."

"I'm not afraid of him. It's just that he drives me crazy, sniffing at my ankles."

"Plastic," said Bullard, chuckling.

"What?"

(cont'd on next page)

"Plastic. Must be something plastic on your garters. By golly, I'll bet it's those little buttons. Sure as we're sitting here, those buttons must be plastic. That dog is nuts about plastic. Don't know why that is, but he'll sniff it out and find it if there's a speck around. Must be a deficiency in his diet, though, by gosh, he eats better than I do. Once he chewed up a humidor. Can you beat it? *That's* the business I'd go into now, by glory, if the pill rollers hadn't told me to let up, to give the old ticker a rest."

"You could tie the dog to that tree over there," said the stranger.

"I get so darn' sore, at all the youngsters these days!" said Bullard. "All of 'em mooning around about no frontiers any more. There never have been so many frontiers as there are today. You know what Horace Greeley would say today?"

"His nose is wet," said the stranger, and he pulled his ankles away, but the dog humped forward in patient pursuit. "Stop it, boy!"

"His wet nose shows he's healthy," said Bullard. "'Go plastic, young man!' That's what Greeley'd say. 'Go atom, young man!'"

The dog had definitely located the plastic buttons on the stranger's garters and was cocking his head one way and another, thinking out ways of bringing his teeth to bear on those delicacies.

> *"Don't talk to me about no opportunity any more. Opportunity's knocking down every door in the country, trying to get in."*

"Scat!" said the stranger.

"Go electronic, young man!" said Bullard. "Don't talk to me about no opportunity any more. Opportunity's knocking down every door in the country, trying to get in. When I was young, a man had to go out and find opportunity and drag it home by the ears. Nowadays—"

"Sorry," said the stranger, evenly. He slammed his book shut, stood and jerked his ankle away from the dog.

"I've got to be on my way. So good day, sir."

He stalked across the park, found another bench, sat down with a sigh and began to read. His respiration had just returned to normal, when he felt the wet sponge of the dog's nose on his ankles again.

"Oh—it's you!" said Bullard, sitting down beside him. "He was tracking you. He was on the scent of something, and I just let him have his head. What'd I tell you about plastic?" He looked about contentedly. "Don't blame you for moving on. It was stuffy back there. No shade to speak of and not a sign of a breeze."

"Would the dog go away if I bought him a humidor?" said the stranger.

"Pretty good joke, pretty good joke," said Bullard, amiably. Suddenly he clapped the stranger on his knee. "Sa-ay, you aren't in plastics, are you? Here I've been blowing

(cont'd on next page)

off about plastics, and for all I know that's your line."

"My line?" said the stranger crisply, laying down his book. "Sorry—I've never had a line. I've been a drifter since the age of nine, since Edison set up his laboratory next to my home, and showed me the intelligence analyzer."

"Edison?" said Bullard. "Thomas Edison, the inventor?"

"If you want to call him that, go ahead," said the stranger.

"If I *want* to call him that?"—Bullard guffawed—"I guess I just will! Father of the light bulb and I don't know what all."

"If you want to think he invented the light bulb, go ahead. No harm in it." The stranger resumed his reading.

"Say, what is this?" said Bullard, suspiciously. "You pulling my leg? What's this about an intelligence analyzer? I never heard of that."

"Of course you haven't," said the stranger. "Mr. Edison and I promised to keep it a secret. I've never told anyone. Mr. Edison broke his promise and told Henry Ford, but Ford made him promise not to tell anyone else—for the good of humanity."

Bullard was entranced. "Uh, this intelligence analyzer," he said, "it analyzed intelligence, did it?"

"It was an electric butter churn," said the stranger.

"Seriously now," Bullard coaxed.

"Maybe it *would* be better to talk it over with someone," said the stranger. "It's a terrible thing to keep bottled up inside me, year in and year out. But how can I be sure that it won't go any further?"

"My word as a gentleman," Bullard assured him.

"I don't suppose I could find a stronger guarantee than that, could I?" said the stranger, judiciously.

"There is no stronger guarantee," said Bullard, proudly. "Cross my heart and hope to die!"

"Very well." The stranger leaned back and closed his eyes, seeming to travel backward through time. He was silent for a full minute, during which Bullard watched with respect.

"It was back in the fall of eighteen seventy-nine," said the stranger at last, softly. "Back in the village of Menlo Park, New Jersey. I was a boy of nine. A young man we all thought was a wizard had set up a laboratory next door to my home, and there were flashes and crashes inside, and all sorts of scary goings-on. The neighborhood children were warned to keep away, not to make any noise that would bother the wizard.

> *"Mr. Edison broke his promise and told Henry Ford, but Ford made him promise not to tell anyone else—for the good of humanity."*

"I didn't get to know Edison right off, but his dog Sparky and I got to be steady pals. A dog a whole lot like yours, Sparky was, and we used to wrestle all over the neighborhood. Yes, sir, your dog is the image of Sparky."

"Is that so?" said Bullard, flattered.

"Gospel," replied the stranger. "Well, one day Sparky and I were wrestling around, and we wrestled right up to the door of Edison's laboratory. The next thing I knew, Sparky had pushed me in through the door, and bam! I was sitting on the laboratory floor, looking up at Mr. Edison himself."

"Bet he was sore," said Bullard, delighted.

"You can bet I was scared," said the stranger. "I thought I was face to face with Satan himself. Edison had wires hooked to his ears and running down to a little black box in his lap! I started to scoot, but he caught me by my collar and made me sit down.

" 'Boy,' said Edison, 'it's always darkest before the dawn. I want you to remember that.'

" 'Yes, sir,' I said.

"'For over a year, my boy,' Edison said to me, 'I've been trying to find a filament that will last in an incandescent lamp. Hair, string, splinters—nothing works. So while I was trying to think of something else to try, I started tinkering with another idea of

> *"I thought maybe intelligence was a certain kind of electricity, so I made this intelligence analyzer here."*

mine, just letting off steam. I put this together,' he said, showing me the little black box. 'I thought maybe intelligence was a certain kind of electricity, so I made this intelligence analyzer here. It works! You're the first one to know about it, my boy. But I don't know why you shouldn't be. It will be your generation that will grow up in the glorious new era when people will be as easily graded as oranges.' "

"I don't believe it," said Bullard.

"May I be struck by lightning this very instant!" said the stranger. "And it did work, too. Edison had tried out the analyzer on the men in his shop, without telling them what he was up to. The smarter a man was, by gosh, the farther the needle on the indicator in the little black box swung to the right. I let him try it on me, and the needle just lay where it was and trembled. But dumb as I was, then is when I made my one and only contribution to the world. As I say, I haven't lifted a finger since."

"Whadja do?" said Bullard, eagerly.

"I said, 'Mr. Edison, sir, let's try it on the dog.' And I wish you could have seen the show that dog put on when I said it! Old Sparky barked and howled and scratched to get out. When he saw we meant business, that he wasn't going to get out, he made a beeline right for the

(cont'd on next page)

intelligence analyzer and knocked it out of Edison's hands. But we cornered him, and Edison held him down while I touched the wires to his ears. And would you believe it, that needle sailed clear across the dial, way past a little red pencil marker on the dial face!"

"The dog busted it," said Bullard.

" 'Mr. Edison, sir,' I said, 'what's the red mark mean?'

" 'My boy,' said Edison, 'it means that the instrument is broken, because that red mark is me.' "

"I'll say it was broken," said Bullard.

The stranger said gravely, "But it wasn't broken. No, sir. Edison checked the whole thing, and it was in apple-pie order. When Edison told me that, it was then that Sparky, crazy to get out, gave himself away."

"How?" said Bullard, suspiciously.

"We really had him locked in, see? There were three locks on the door—a hook and eye, a bolt, and a regular knob and latch. That dog stood up, unhooked the hook, pushed the bolt back and had the knob in his teeth when Edison stopped him."

"No!" said Bullard.

"Yes!" said the stranger, his eyes shining. "And then is when Edison showed me what a great scientist he was. He was willing to face the truth, no matter how unpleasant it might be.

" 'So!' said Edison to Sparky. 'Man's best friend, huh? Dumb animal, huh?'

"That Sparky was a caution. He pretended not to hear. He scratched himself and bit fleas and went around growling at ratholes—anything to get out of looking Edison in the eye.

" 'Pretty soft, isn't it, Sparky?' said Edison. 'Let somebody else worry about getting food, building shelters and keeping warm, while you sleep in front of a fire or go chasing after the girls or raise the devil with the boys. No mortgages, no politics, no war, no work, no worry. Just wag the old tail or lick a hand, and you're all taken care of.'

" 'Mr. Edison,' I said, 'do you mean to tell me that dogs are smarter than people?'

" 'Smarter?' said Edison. 'I'll tell the world! And what have I been doing for the past year? Slaving to work out a light bulb so dogs can play at night!'

" 'Look, Mr. Edison,' said Sparky, 'why not—' "

"Hold on!" roared Bullard.

"Silence!" shouted the stranger, triumphantly. " 'Look, Mr. Edison,' said Sparky, 'why not keep quiet about this? It's been working out to everybody's satisfaction for hundreds of thousands of years. Let sleeping dogs lie. You forget all about it, destroy the intelligence analyzer, and I'll tell you what to use for a lamp filament.' "

> *" '. . . do you mean to tell me that dogs are smarter than people?' "*

"Hogwash!" said Bullard, his face purple.

The stranger stood. "You have my solemn word as a gentleman. That dog rewarded *me* for my silence with a stock-market tip that made me independently wealthy for the rest of my days. And the last words that Sparky ever spoke were to Thomas Edison. 'Try a piece of carbonized cotton thread,' he said. Later, he was torn to bits by a pack of dogs that had gathered outside the door, listening."

The stranger removed his garters and handed them to Bullard's dog. "A small token of esteem, sir, for an ancestor of yours who talked himself to death. Good day." He tucked his book under his arm and walked away.

—Kurt Vonnegut

Start-Up: Close your textbook. From memory, sketch a visual of Mr. Edison's intelligence analyzer. Label the parts of the analyzer. Then open your textbook and compare the accuracy of your sketch to the description in the story. Finally, use your imagination to sketch a cross section of what you think the inside of the analyzer looks like. Label the parts.

Connection: What is used to analyze a person's intelligence today? Talk to a knowledgeable person to help find the answer to this question.

Chapter 7

© GETTY IMAGES/PHOTODISC, INC.

"The difference between the right word and the almost right word is the difference between lightning and the lightning bug."

—MARK TWAIN, U.S. AUTHOR

- It's Friday night, and you've got a date with Chris. You're going to rent a video, but there are so many to choose from. How do you decide?

- Clint asked Leah to the prom, but now they have to decide where to go for dinner before the dance. Both of them have eaten only in fast-food restaurants, never anywhere fancy. How can they choose a first-class restaurant if they've never been to one?

- You want to find out how your friend Rosa did in the speech contest, but you have only five minutes to listen to her before you leave for your job. How can Rosa tell you about her performance in such a short amount of time?

Summarizing

A summary is the solution to choosing a movie, deciding on a restaurant, and describing an event. You can read a summary of a movie plot, along with an expert opinion, in a movie review. A restaurant guide in a local magazine summarizes the type of food, the atmosphere, and the pricing, which will help Clint and Leah choose a restaurant. Rosa can easily summarize the highlights of her performance in the speech contest in the five minutes you have to spare before you leave for work. Providing just the highlights is summarizing. The summary focuses on the important points, saving both time and space.

Summary: A Definition

Summaries are shortened versions of speeches, writings, and events. People create summaries from original sources, such as books, articles, meetings, work orders, and reports. You include the central idea of the original source in the summary, but restate the idea. You add major points and important details that are essential to the central idea. A summary may be as brief as a single sentence or as long as several pages.

by the way...

Al Smith, former governor of New York and presidential candidate, became a first-term state legislator in 1903. After a long day's work, instead of relaxing, he would read and master every line of the state budget. His unparalleled command of the fine print began his stellar political career. He concentrated on the details to use them in describing the big picture with seasoned legislators.

Practice 7–1: Recognizing Everyday Summaries

career

1. Summaries are a part of everyday life—at home, at school, and at work. You often use summaries out of habit, without thinking of them as summaries. Each of the following situations needs a summary to save someone time. Briefly explain how the summary would be used or created.

Example:

When she phones to give you directions to her office, Desiree mentions every landmark and intersection. You ask her to repeat the directions several times so that you can write everything down.

You need to write down only major points, such as street names and buildings near major intersections or turns.

a. Mr. Martinez asks you what his two-year-old daughter Maria has done during her day at preschool. You spend more than five minutes describing Maria's day. Since you spent this much time with Mr. Martinez, you feel obligated to spend the same amount of time with the parents of your other 14 students.

b. Mr. Jefferson requires his students in English class to report on a book. Each student takes nearly 15 minutes to describe the novel he or she has read.

c. The doctor has just examined one of her patients. As a medical assistant, you must write down her report and her instructions. However, the doctor must speak very slowly and repeat what she says so that you can keep up with her.

2. Now it's your turn. When would you use summaries in your career? Describe two situations in which summarizing would be beneficial.

Characteristics of a Summary

A summary has the following features: It should be brief, well-written, independent of the source material, and accurate.

- **Brief.** The summary is short and to the point. Often it will be no more than one paragraph or even one sentence.

- **Well-Written.** The summary is understandable, with the most important points connected into unified paragraphs with topic sentences.

- **Independent.** The summary is clear, stands alone, and is independent of the original material. It contains only the main ideas of the source. For example, the summary of a conservation report requires no further explanation. A reader may decide to consult the original source for details, such as statistics. Add no new data to the source material, although you may include personal opinions in certain situations.

- **Accurate.** The summary provides an understanding of the original writing, speech, or event. It does not distort its meaning, but clearly reflects the author's intent.

Generally, follow this guideline: A summary is necessary when there is no way that you can describe the entire event, writing, or speech without shortening it considerably.

Summary Basics

The summary remains brief because it deals only with the most important information. However, while summarizing, keep in mind the subject, the audience, and the purpose of the summary.

The Subject

Writing a summary is actually writing a self-contained piece miniaturized from the original. Use fewer words than the author, but write in complete sentences. A summary need not follow the organization of the original, but it must be consistent, not confusing.

The length of the original writing, speech, or event often determines how to summarize. The more complex the original, the longer and more complex the summary. Above all, the summary must contain an accurate representation of the original. Whoever uses the summary should be able to understand it without consulting the original.

The Audience

Whoever is reading or hearing the summary (your audience) determines how you create the summary.

The General Audience. A summary for the general audience puts the summarized information into plain English; however, the information will not be too general to be useful. For example, although he is not a professional baker, David Brown is interested in purchasing a bread machine to pursue his hobby. Before making his investment, he needs to know brand comparisons, frequency of repairs, prices, and other general information on household bread machines. After reading consumer buying guides and cooking magazine comparisons, David will summarize his findings to his wife, Rachel, so that they can make the best buying choice as a family. For David Brown, simplifying through a summary is the best way to avoid confusion and to make an intelligent purchase.

The Specialist. <mark>Basic technical style</mark> is better for the specialist's summary. This type of summary provides enough information for the needs of this audience, often with recommendations and/or results. The specialist needs sufficient information to make a decision.

Professional bakers

For her commercial baking class, Sonya Ramirez must purchase a machine that will mix the dough for the various breads and pastries her students make. In addition, she needs to make a decision: Should she purchase a machine to be used only by her class, or should she buy one for the entire Food Service Department? Since Sonya needs to base her decision on specific uses—such as the machine's life span, cost, etc.—she must read technical articles and make a qualified summary to her Advisory Committee. The committee, made up of professional bakers, can then decide whether to purchase the dough machine.

⊙ Practice 7–2: Determining the Audience

When you summarize, you need to make decisions about what the audience needs. Decide whether the following audiences are general or specialized.

1. Bob Fong asks you what the doctor did during his son's surgery.

2. An over-the-road truck driver has a diesel mechanic look over her truck. She needs to know the recommended repairs.

3. You must make a report to the purchasing department on an article reviewing the newest model of a company's laser printer.

4. Fiona calls a staff meeting to explain the features of the new employee health insurance plan.

5. When Helio phones Ms. Diamond to reply to her help wanted ad, she asks Helio about his qualifications for the position.

6. The social studies class needs a summary of the president's budget address.

7. Hydra Marine Motors has introduced a new inboard engine. The marine mechanics class needs to know the quality of the engine's performance.

8. You are the charge nurse on Ada Wright's floor at Riverview Hospital. You must write a report on her discharge to Sunrise Nursing Home.

9. Jackson is explaining how to set up a template file for your document's outline.

10. You've been asked to submit to the company newsletter a 200-word article on upcoming expansion plans.

The Purpose

While creating the summary, keep in mind the purpose for making it. Deciding what needs to be included and what needs to be eliminated is the most difficult decision when writing a summary. Ask yourself, "What point is the original work making?" This question will help you decide on the summary's purpose. Include only what is necessary after reading the article more than once.

Audience and purpose are often closely related when you create a summary. The patient's father who wanted a report of his son's surgery needed a general summary for the specific purpose of getting information and reassurance. This summary was not only for a different audience, but also for a different purpose. Generally, the specialist needs the more thorough explanation.

Types of Summaries

The purpose of a summary determines which type of summary you write. The three types are informative, explanatory, and analytic. You can write any one of these for the general or the specialized audience. The following descriptions and examples will help you understand each type of summary in more detail.

The Informative Summary

The **informative summary** condenses the author's main ideas with no explanation or detail. Often a sentence in the original document states the central idea, or you can restate the topic sentence in your own words.

Technology *Connection*

Internet news services often offer two options for reading the news. One option is the quick summary, and the other is an in-depth look at the news story. The detailed news story may have links to related stories and web sites. When searching for news services, you can find network television and radio news sites (e.g., CNN), national news television and radio stations and network sites (e.g., National Public Radio), and national news magazines (e.g., *Time*), as well as web news services (e.g., PointCast).

An informative summary of the FCCLA (Family, Career and Community Leaders of America) Spring Rally program might include only the agenda.

FCCLA Spring Rally Program
The FCCLA Spring Rally program begins after lunch with a panel discussion and demonstration of picnic ideas, followed by the award ceremony, the election results, and the swearing in of new officers.

◉ Practice 7–3: Finding the Central Idea

Each of the following paragraphs contains a sentence that expresses the central idea of the paragraph. Identify this sentence.

Ch07–03.doc

1. Because synthetic lashes are attached to the client's own and become part of them, they last as long as the natural eyelashes, about 6 to 8 weeks. Hence, they are referred to as "semi-permanent eyelashes." However, due to the fact that natural eyelashes fall out regularly (a few each week), taking the attached false lashes with them, the false lashes should be filled in by periodic visits to the salon. (*Milady's* 466)

2. Even with all the predators eating insects, that still leaves a lot to destroy crops. For many years we have used chemicals to get rid of insects. These chemicals, called insecticides, have been very efficient. They have been the most efficient means ever devised to kill insects. In the past insecticides have been used in tremendous quantities. The overuse of insecticides has resulted in problems. Many of the older chemicals like DDT have been harmful to the environment, and wildlife suffered. These chemicals remained in the soil for many years. Rain would wash the chemicals into streams where they were absorbed by aquatic plants and animals. Animals such as water birds and eagles ate the fish and absorbed

the chemicals. Reproductive cycles were disrupted because the eggs from the birds would not hatch. (Herren 75)

3. Air is not the only source from which a heat pump can absorb heat, but it is the most popular. The most common sources of heat for a heat pump are air, water, and earth. For example, a structure located next to a large lake can remove heat from the lake and deposit it in the structure. The lake must be large enough so that the temperature will not drop appreciably in the lake. This system is a water-to-air heat pump. The water-to-air heat pump may also use a well to supply the water. If so, some consideration must be given to where the water will be pumped after it is used. A typical water-to-air heat pump uses 3 gallons of water per minute (gpm) in the heating cycle and 1.5 gpm in the cooling cycle per ton of refrigeration. (Whitman and Johnson 850)

The Explanatory Summary

An **explanatory summary** contains only information; it includes no analysis or opinion. The objective writing contains the author's main ideas and essential supporting details. The explanatory summary expresses the content of the source in as little as one paragraph and rarely more than one keyed page.

An explanatory summary of the FCCLA Spring Rally will include more than the schedule of the day's events. Now the report includes a brief description of each event. The explanatory summary records the writer's understanding of the day's events, but without evaluation or criticism. The following is an explanatory summary of the program portion of the Rally.

FCCLA Spring Rally Program

A panel discussion and a demonstration of picnic ideas—food, themes, games, and events—was presented by the Bartlett District Chef Training and Child Learning classes at the annual FCCLA Spring Rally on May 6. A certificate was presented to each class officer, with special award certificates given by each instructor. The current district officers then announced the election results. The new officers came to the platform, replacing the current officers in a ceremony.

The Analytic Summary

An **analytic summary** interprets, evaluates, or criticizes the facts of a source. After writing the information, blend in observations and/or criticisms. *However, indicate when you are stating an opinion so that the reader*

The FCCLA Rally

can see clearly *what is fact and what is opinion*. The summary should give enough information to provide an understanding of what was read, seen, or heard. Adding quotes from other sources may help to make your personal judgment more acceptable or believable, but add only enough for the audience to appreciate the criticism and to stress your point. The more specialized the audience, the more technical the summary.

An analytic summary of the FCCLA Rally program will combine an explanation of events with analysis. For example, now that the FCCLA Rally is over for this year, the officers need to make proposals for next year's event. First, the officers need to include a brief description of each activity. Then they need to add analysis to show the benefit of each event. Was the event a success? Could it be improved? Ultimately, these added comments will help the club decide which events to change or to keep for next year's Rally. The following is the analytic summary portion of the Rally program.

FCCLA Spring Rally Program

The Bartlett District Chef Training and Child Learning classes presented a well-planned panel discussion and demonstration of picnic ideas—food, themes, games, and events—at the annual FCCLA Spring Rally on May 6. All members were interested both academically and personally.

Each instructor awarded a certificate to each class officer. Consistency was a problem with the awards. Some certificates were framed; some were showy; some were given for every minor achievement. The district officers should develop guidelines for certificates before next year's Rally.

The current district officers then announced the election results. The new officers came to the platform, replacing the current officers. The switching of officers turned out to be a very emotional ceremony. Don't change this great idea!

Distinguishing Between Fact and Opinion

The difference between factual statement and opinion is as important in writing as it is in speaking. A **fact** is supported by evidence; therefore, a fact can be proved. Do not base the fact's proof on what you *think* is true, but on what you *know* to be true. An **opinion** is a personal belief; it may or may not be based on fact.

Graphic design is a career in demand. Graphic designers are those lucky artists who don't have to starve to do what they love. To be successful in this profession, one needs to be skilled not only in illustrating and designing, but also at absorbing and synthesizing information from many sources, such as market research and contemporary culture. The successful graphic designer blends a storehouse of knowledge, technical expertise, and creativity with the client's ideas, resulting in a productive, collaborative effort.

Opinions are personal feelings; they are biased statements. Whether opinions are based on fact, they cannot be proved true or false.

Factual Statements Can Be Proved

Informative and explanatory summaries contain only facts. These facts are generally restated in your own words with no analysis or judgment added. Analytic summaries include opinion, but that opinion is based on fact.

Factual Statements	Opinion
The temperature is 97 degrees.	It's a scorcher outside today.
The white pine sapling needs a hole as deep as its roots when it's planted.	You need to dig a deep hole to plant the white pine sapling.

Note: Defining a statement as factual doesn't necessarily mean the statement is true. You can prove a statement of fact either true or false. You also can state untrue information as a fact; that is, you are giving false information as a fact.

Factual Statement?

Combine blue and red to form the color purple.
You can prove this statement *true.*
Prove this statement true by combining blue and red—and producing the color purple.

Factual Statement?

Combine blue and green to form the color purple.
You can prove this statement *false.*
Prove this statement false by combining blue and green—and making the color turquoise.

by the way...

A recent hiring trend for some national corporations is using graphologists to analyze prospective employees' handwriting. These firms believe that a person's handwriting gives a summary of the person's personality. For example, tense people press too hard, creative people add many flourishes, and those who don't dot their i's are often brilliant, for their hands are slower than their minds.

Practice 7–4: Proving a Factual Statement

The following statements are expressed as facts, but can the statements be proved true or false? For each statement that is not a fact, state why it is not a fact. For each statement that is a fact, briefly describe the method that you would use to prove or disprove it.

1. An excellent peanut butter isn't overly sticky or gritty, and it doesn't leave a dry feeling in the mouth.

2. Choosing loudspeakers is the most difficult part of buying or upgrading an audio system.

3. A letter is composed of words; however, the way the letter looks on the page can be as important as the text.

4. The welder must be prepared to work in extreme heat and to risk burns from sparks.

5. If you inspect a tree's roots, you can determine whether the tree is getting enough water.

6. Mistral font is too informal for business letters.

7. To catch melanoma quickly, check moles frequently for changes in color or size.

8. Government safety regulations deter technological expansion in the workplace.

A statement of fact can be turned into an opinion by adding a conditional word or phrase such as *maybe, in my opinion,* and *I think.*

Practice 7–5: Investigating Using Fact and Opinion

In small groups, decide whether each of the statements in the following incident is a fact or an opinion. Use only the information provided in the incident to reach your conclusions. In deciding whether each of the statements is a fact or an opinion, your group must come to a consensus.

Incident: A businessman had just turned off the lights in a store when a man appeared and demanded money. The owner opened up the cash register. The contents of the cash register were scooped up, and the man sped away. A member of the police force arrived promptly.

1. A man appeared after the owner had turned off his store lights.

2. The robber was a man.

3. A man did not demand money.

4. The man who opened the cash register was the owner.

5. The store owner scooped up the contents of the cash register and ran away.

6. Someone opened a cash register.

7. After the man who demanded the money scooped up the contents of the cash register, he ran away.

8. While the cash register contained money, the story does not state how much.

9. The robber demanded money of the owner.

10. The story relates a series of events in which only three people are referred to: the owner of the store, a man who demanded money, and a member of the police force.

Details: Using Objective Language

Objective words give details but do not analyze or judge. *Purple, metallic, closed, counterfeit,* and *frozen* are examples of such words.

Subjective words describe, but also give your interpretation, your perception of a word. These words express your opinion, which may or may not be based on fact. *Beautiful, soft, big,* and *appropriate* are examples of these expressive words.

Guard against using loaded language in summaries to distort the meaning of the original material. **Loaded language** has strong emotional overtones, which can produce strongly positive (or negative) reactions. For example, the last paragraph of the summary of the FCCLA Rally on page 218 includes this objective statement: "The new officers came to the platform, replacing the current officers." Notice how the meaning is distorted when negative loaded language replaces objective language: "The new officers *strutted* to the platform, *ousting* the *old* officers."

Culture *Connection*

When traveling in a foreign country, try to speak a few words of the native tongue. Those few words will be much appreciated. However, the best way to ask a question in English is to print it legibly on a piece of paper. Your inquiry cannot be misinterpreted this way, and perhaps someone nearby knows some English.

Practice 7–6: Objective Language

1. Indicate whether the following phrases and statements are fact or opinion.

Examples:

concentric circles	fact
A computer drawing is more efficient than a board drawing.	opinion

   a. the best fast-food hamburger
   b. an enormous dent
   c. 100 decibels
   d. a raw piece of beef
   e. a soft thump
   f. The melting temperature of silver is 961 degrees Celsius.
   g. Oak doors last the longest.
   h. The average life of a Labrador retriever is ten years.
   i. Probably more people use credit cards than cash to purchase furniture.
   j. Orange is a more brilliant color than turquoise.

2. Use *Student Workbook* page 7-A to practice recognizing loaded language.

Preparing to Summarize an Article

Summarizing an article requires reading it and finding the main ideas. If the summary is for specialists, you may add some details and examples to provide a more in-depth view. Usually, a general audience will not be interested in a detailed technical article that is filled with specialized terms and points.

Photocopying

The copier police

After you choose an article to summarize, the use of the copier can definitely be a time-saver. If the article is in the library, you may not be able to check out the material to take home. But by photocopying the original, you can still read it in its entirety or you can read it in sections, as with a book.

When photocopying, duplicate the entire page and page number. Also identify the source—author, title, publication, and date—in the format explained in Chapter 2, pages 57 and 58. But beware! Photocopying does not replace note taking; photocopying merely supplements note taking.

Also remember to follow the copyright law, last rewritten in 1976. As a rule, copying is legal only for your own personal use unless you have the author's permission to reprint the copyrighted information. Public libraries and media centers post a copyright restrictions warning above copiers. (See Figure 7-1.)

WARNING CONCERNING COPYRIGHT RESTRICTIONS

The copyright law of the United States (Title 17, United States Code) governs the making of photocopies or other reproductions of copyrighted material.

Under certain conditions specified in the law, libraries and archives are authorized to furnish a photocopy or other reproduction. One of these specified conditions is that the photocopy or reproduction is not to be "used for any purpose other than private study, scholarship, or research." If a user makes a request for, or later uses, a photocopy or a reproduction for purposes in excess of "fair use," that user may be liable for copyright infringement.

This institution reserves the right to refuse to accept a copy order if, in its judgment, fulfillment of the order would involve violation of copyright law. (U.S. Copyright Office, 37 C.F.R.)

FIGURE 7-1   Copyright restrictions warning

Copyrights protect almost any original work that is established in any tangible form, and copyright protection begins as soon as the author creates his or her work. Copyright protection extends to design and content of audio CDs, web sites, CD-ROMs, and computer programs. In fact, if you create a web site, you have a site copyright as soon as you stop keying and save it as an HTML file.

Using someone else's words or ideas as your own is known as **plagiarism**. Whether you plagiarize on purpose or you plagiarize unknowingly, you are stealing. If an author discovers that you have taken credit for his or her work, you could be sued. Instead, be honest and give credit where credit is due.

Documentation at the beginning of your summary gives the author credit for writing the original work. Use the sample Project summary on page 243 as an example of source information.

Choosing and Arranging Main Points

You have chosen the article to be summarized. To plan the summary, you must analyze the article. After you read the article and identify the organizational pattern, highlighting with marginal notes and note taking will help you prepare for the summary writing.

The Organizational Pattern

Look for signals that show how the author has arranged the article. These signals, or word clues, will reveal the main points of the article and the **organizational pattern** of the writing. Common organizational patterns include chronological (time) order, order of importance (listing of points from most to least significant), and spatial order (arrangement around placement or geography). Transitions, additional word clues explained on pages 230 and 231 of this chapter, will help you sort out an article's arrangement, as will definitions and lists of ideas.

Highlighting (Underlining)

A highlighter is a useful tool for marking the central idea and important supporting details of the text. The highlighter contains water-soluble ink that marks material permanently. The **highlighting** procedure is the same as underlining, but highlighting is simpler to do, easier to notice, and cleaner looking than underlining. Though the traditional highlighter color is yellow, office supply stores offer many colors. If you choose, you may use different colors for different reasons, such as yellow for the central idea, blue for supporting details, and pink for evaluative support. Of course, only mark purchased or photocopied material. *Never* highlight material that you have borrowed from the library or from other people.

When highlighting material to prepare your summary, follow these steps:

1. *Read the section first.* You can decide what to highlight only after reading the material and then understanding the audience's needs.

2. As a rule, *highlight about 10 percent of the original material.* If you mark nearly all of the text, you may as well mark nothing. Remember that the purpose of highlighting is to call your attention to the main points.

3. *Mark the main points for writing a summary based on your audience.* When reading a technical article, mark only broader statements for the general

audience. The specialist needs the basic technical points and possibly some examples. A review of the latest popular sports car, for example, will highlight the overall topics for the average consumer. However, the auto mechanic may need the article marked in more detail to explain such categories as driveline and body integrity.

Highlighting, then, provides a permanent record of important ideas and helps organize notes. This procedure also saves time that would be spent taking notes or rereading the article. When you have to meet deadlines, such techniques for saving time become especially important.

Marginal Notes

Marginal notes are words and symbols written in the text or in the margins. This type of marking works best when combined with highlighting. Marginal notes can also become note taking within the article itself. Mark details if you need supporting statements or if the article is for a specialist. Figure 7-2 shows some typical symbols used in marginal notes.

Write the notes in your own words. These marginal notes can be used later to form the summary. When commenting on the article, put personal comments in the margin also—in parentheses ( ). Using parentheses will help to keep your personal thoughts and ideas separate from the article's. These marginal notes will be especially important when you write an analytic summary.

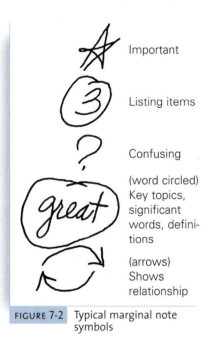

FIGURE 7-2 Typical marginal note symbols

Important

Listing items

Confusing

(word circled) Key topics, significant words, definitions

(arrows) Shows relationship

Note Taking

If you can't mark the article itself, take brief notes, recording the main points. However, don't be so brief that you will have to reread the article to understand the meaning of the notes.

For help in **note taking**, follow these steps:

1. *Read the entire article.*

2. *Take down the main ideas in your own words.* These notes may become the start of your summary statements.

3. *Support the main ideas with some facts.* Such support is generally necessary for articles written for specialists. For example, you can write a word or two for each point of an article on the causes of high blood

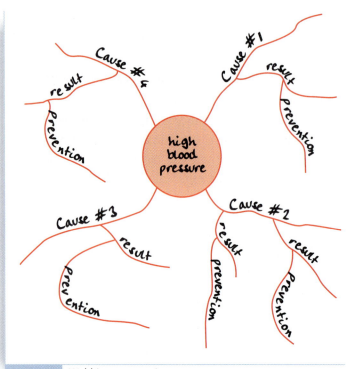

FIGURE 7-3 Webbing or mapping

pressure if the summary is for a general audience. An audience of specialists, however, will probably need a more detailed explanation of the basis for each cause of high blood pressure.

4. *Mark all of your personal reactions with parentheses.* These remarks can take the form of notes, lists, outlines, **webbing** or **mapping** (Figure 7-3), or any other organizational pattern you choose.

⊙ Practice 7–7: Marking Text and Taking Notes

Read the following paragraphs twice, taking two sets of notes for an explanatory summary—one for the general audience and one for the specialist. (Refer to your own notes and Figure 7-2 for guidelines.)

1. Sound travels readily through the air and through some materials. When airborne sound strikes a wall, the studs act as conductors unless they are separated in some way from the covering material. Electrical outlet boxes placed back to back in a wall easily transmit sound. Faulty construction, such as poorly fitted doors, often allows sound to pass through. Therefore, good construction practices aid in controlling sound. (Lewis 509)

2. Any care provided to elderly individuals should allow as much independence as possible. Assistance should be provided as needed for the individual's safety, but the individual should be allowed to do as much as possible. For example, a health care worker should encourage elderly persons to choose their clothing and dress themselves even if it takes longer. Self-stick strips can replace buttons to make the task of dressing easier and to provide more independence. This helps the elderly individual adapt to the situation and maintain a sense of self-worth. At all times, elderly

Ch07-07.doc

individuals should be allowed as much choice as possible to help them to maintain their individuality. (Simmers 134)

3. An alternator, rather than a generator, is used on today's vehicles to charge the battery and operate the electrical circuits. This is because the alternator is much more efficient than a generator. Alternators are much smaller, lighter in weight, and produce more current than generators. The alternator has a set of rotating poles and a stationary set of windings. In addition, there is no split-ring commutator. Solid-state diodes are used to convert ac to dc voltages. The alternator is made of a stator, rotor, and slip-ring and brush assembly. Many modern (late-model) alternators have the regulator built into the housings as a complete unit. (Schwaller 467)

Writing a Summary

The following steps are for summarizing written work, particularly articles, but the same procedure is used for summarizing other material as well.

For any summary, the following steps are necessary:

1. *Previewing.* Skim the article to look for trends and internal summaries.

2. *Reading.* Read the article thoroughly.

3. *Note taking.* Use one or more of the organizational aids, such as highlighting or marginal notes, to find the important points in the article.

4. *Writing (main idea).* Summarize the central idea of the article in one or two sentences. These sentences will become the informative summary. A single-sentence informative summary can be the topic sentence of an explanatory summary. Adding an opinion can form the topic sentence of an analytic summary.

5. *Writing (sections).* Restate sections or paragraphs of the article in your own words.

6. *Combining.* First, blend the main-idea sentence and the section sentences by using transitions. These word clues signal the organizational pattern and move one sentence into the next. Second, write a clincher sentence to tie the subpoints together. Finally, add an ending.

7. *Editing.* Eliminate repetition. Make the writing to the point by taking out unnecessary words. This brevity is important to get the point across more effectively, but make sure your sentences flow smoothly from one to another. (The transitions you added in the previous step should help with the flow.) Check the summary against the original article to make sure you have not distorted its message. Also make sure that nothing new has been added, except the personal comments if you are writing an analytic summary. As with any other written work, proofread carefully, checking for grammar, punctuation, and spelling.

8. *Documenting.* Give credit to the original source. Refer to pages 57 and 58 of Chapter 2 for the proper style.

9. *Formatting.* Check the entire document for placement of documentation and written copy on the page, effective use of white space, and balance of written copy and the visual (if you had one) on the page. Generally, your page will begin with the title and the documentation, followed by the written copy. The sample on page 243 is an excellent example of a formatted written summary.

Lucia Franco must hand in a report on a common construction hazard for a safety contest. She read the article "One of the Most Frequent Construction Dangers" (see Figure 7-4), highlighted it, and took notes to begin writing her report.

After studying her article, Lucia wrote this informative summary, which showed her adviser that she was working on the assignment.

Gasoline and other flammable fuels are common safety hazards on construction sites.

by the way...

According to the Occupational Outlook Quarterly, *nearly two-thirds of U.S. employees work in service industries in which knowledge is the most important product.*

One of the Most Frequent Construction Dangers

Think of dangerous substances on construction sites, and fumes and chemicals come to mind. Actually, the most commonplace hazardous substance is gasoline. Experts from the Occupational Health and Safety Administration (OSHA) report that gasoline is misused on many construction sites. Gasoline caused more than one-sixth of ==hazardous substance accidents in the last year.==

These cases are some examples:

- A worker used gasoline to destroy a hornet's nest on top of a septic tank. When he opened the tank, it burst; he was severely burned.
- A laborer on a construction site used gasoline to clean her tar-covered clothes. She was seriously burned when a sudden fire covered her in flames.
- A worker sawed through steel, which resulted in sparks that ignited a nearby gasoline can. The worker suffered third-degree burns.

==Gasoline fumes are also hazards.== These vapors can collect and grow. Sparks and heat can flare up instantly. ==To prevent these fires, fast cleanups and suitable ventilation are crucial safety procedures.== If necessary, workers should use masks.

==Other fuels,== such as alcohol and kerosene, are often found on building sites. These substances ==are also flammable.== The chemicals heptane, benzene, and acetone (found in paints and sealants) cause problems similar to those with gasoline. Exposure to some flammable and combustible materials can cause other health hazards over time.

Contractors often assume that workers know the rules for using gasoline. They then overlook teaching safety rules for its use. Workers need training for managing spills and refilling heated motors. Using tools that generate sparks can also be a problem. Employers should allow workers to smoke in a safe place that is *not* near gasoline.

==To prevent dangerous accidents, construction crews should require training in the cautious handling== of gasoline and other hazardous substances.

FIGURE 7-4 "One of the Most Frequent Construction Dangers" article

Next, Lucia expanded her informative summary to form an explanatory summary, the basis of her safety paper.

Gasoline and other flammable fuels are common safety hazards on construction sites. Spills, sparks, and smoking are dangerous because fires can occur. Not only the liquid is a danger, but also the vapors from gasoline and other combustible fuels can be ignited. In order to have safer handling of these materials, contractors need to instruct crews on how to use these fuels.

Lucia next added her own comments, which advised the reader on how to prevent flammable material accidents on the job site. She then used the analytic summary for her construction technology class.

After instructing each new employee about the hazards, contractors should post warning signs. For example, signs should read "No Smoking" and "Let tools cool down before refueling." Also, employers should store flammable materials in a separate well-ventilated area.

Construction hazards

A written summary needs to be smooth, without extraneous words. Transitions allow individual statements to blend into one paragraph, eliminating extra words and emphasizing the main idea. However, the summary must remain true to the original article. An analytic summary includes opinions.

Transitions

Transitions are the road signs of writing; they tell the reader in what direction the writer's ideas are going. These words and phrases logically connect separate statements into related ideas, helping the ideas flow smoothly to focus on the relationships to emphasize.

The following list provides examples of common transitions that can help you arrange information clearly and logically.

COMMON TRANSITIONS

To add ideas:
- also
- and
- furthermore
- in addition
- moreover

To contrast ideas:
- but
- conversely
- however
- on the contrary
- on the other hand
- still
- while

To compare ideas:
- besides
- in the same way
- similarly
- then

To reveal cause and effect:
- as a result
- because
- consequently
- hence
- since
- that
- therefore
- thus

To show time sequence:
  after
  a year later
  before this
  formerly
  later
  meanwhile
  next
  now
  occasionally
  subsequently
  then
  when

To illustrate:
  for example
  for instance

To introduce a condition:
  although
  if
  nevertheless
  under the circumstances

To sum up ideas:
  finally
  in conclusion
  in summary

The following summary is taken from Lucia's first rough draft on the topic of flammable fuel safety. Notice that the paragraph is written without transitions.

Gasoline and other flammable fuels are common safety hazards on construction sites. Spills cause danger. Sparks can be dangerous and cause fires. Smoking can cause fires. Gasoline and combustible fuels are a danger. The vapors of these materials can be ignited. Safer handling of these materials is needed. Contractors need to instruct crews on how to use these fuels.

By reorganizing materials and adding transitions, Lucia made her writing smoother and more coherent. In the final version, which includes her analytic comments, the transitions are underlined.

Gasoline and other flammable fuels are common safety hazards on construction sites. Spills, sparks, and smoking are dangerous because fires can occur. Not only the liquid is a danger, but also the vapors from gasoline and other combustible fuels can be ignited. In order to have safer handling of these materials, contractors need to instruct crews on how to use these fuels. After instructing each new employee about the hazards, contractors should post warning signs. For example, signs should read "No Smoking" and "Let tools cool down before refueling." Also, employers should store flammable materials in a separate well-ventilated area.

By putting *and* in her second sentence, Lucia combines several fire hazards and points out the causes of the fires. *Not only/but also* introduces additional causes. The phrase *in order to* establishes a cause-and-effect relationship. In the analytic section of her summary, Lucia uses these additional signals: for sequence, *after;* to introduce examples, *for example;* and to add an idea, *also.*

1. List the transitions in the following paragraphs. Then write the signal that each transition makes. What relationships do the transitions make within the paragraph? For an example, use Lucia's paragraph with transitions added.

   a. Most children can understand and respond to a number of words before they can produce any. Their first words include names of objects and events in their world (people, food, toys, animals). Then the child begins to overextend words, perhaps using "doggy" to refer to all animals. Finally, single words can be used as sentences: "Bye-bye" can refer to someone leaving, a meal the child thinks is finished, the child going away, a door closing. (Gordon and Williams-Browne 405)

   b. One common result of improper image placement, particularly on small presses, is ink depletion. As the ink roller revolves over the sheet, it has enough ink to properly print the first halftone on the lead edge of the sheet, but not enough ink to print the remaining images in line with the halftone on the tail edge of the sheet. The ink becomes depleted from the ink rollers faster than it can be replaced from the ink reservoir. The result is good ink coverage on the lead edge of the sheet, but poor ink coverage on the tail edge of the sheet. Correct image position during the design stage can balance ink distribution needs to avoid ink depletion. (Adams, Faux, and Rieber 65)

   c. Another way to divide available techniques is by "trial" and "usage" promotions. For example, coupons and sampling are considered quite effective in getting new customers to try a service or product. On the other hand, contests and sweepstakes are good at convincing present customers or trade channels to use services more often. Once again, an organization may decide to use a combination of "trial" and "usage" promotions. (Morrison 409)

2. Using transitions makes your writing clear, especially when you are preparing a summary. Without transitions, your summary will consist of a list of separate ideas in the form of sentences. To make the sentences meaningful to the reader, you need to add transitions. Rewrite the following paragraphs, adding transitions, combining sentences, and moving ideas to make the summary clearer.

---

by the way...

"What is written without effort is in general read without pleasure."

Samuel Johnson, British author

---

a. I believe that in the really important areas of life, women are superior to men. Why? Women live longer. According to the Centers for Disease Control, the life expectancy of a female baby is now some five years longer than it is for a male baby. These government health figures show that women are more able to resist major diseases. On the average, girls learn to count and to read earlier than boys do. Women seem less likely than men to solve their problems with violence. In cartoons, women hurl the rolling pins. In real life, men hurl the bombs.

b. Aspirin was first introduced in Germany more than 100 years ago. Aspirin has proved to be a miracle drug. Aspirin banishes headaches, reduces fever, and eases pain. Aspirin does have some dangers. If taken in excess, aspirin can cause stomach upset, bleeding ulcers, and even death. Aspirin is responsible for more good than harm. It may prevent heart attacks. It is possible that aspirin contains properties that prevent blood clots and heart attacks caused by them. Blood clots clog arteries in the heart.

Brevity and Conciseness

Using two, six, or even ten words when one word would do is sometimes called *gobbledygook*. **Brevity** is the opposite; it involves using as few words as possible.

An office manager sent a memo that included this wordy paragraph to her district manager.

Mr. Jaquez has contacted me verbally with respect to the enclosed disclosure of acceleration. That has generated the attached rejoinder, seemingly insinuating that he desires to waive the responsibility.

In other words, Mr. Jaquez turned down the job!

Summaries condense information into a few sentences. Only the most crucial words and phrases should be included in a summary—not like the following wordy paragraph.

A chapter summary in a textbook will save students time when they need to review for a test. There are definitions of terms that the author believes are important. The major points that the author stresses are focused on in the chapter summary. This section of each chapter is a valuable tool.

by the way...

"Remember the waterfront shack with the sign, 'Fresh Fish Sold Here.' Of course it's fresh, we're on the ocean. Of course it's for sale, we're not giving it away. Of course it's here, otherwise the sign would be someplace else. The final sign: 'Fish.'"

PEGGY NOONAN, U.S. AUTHOR AND PRESIDENTIAL SPEECHWRITER

This paragraph includes too many unnecessary words for a summary. A shortened version appears as follows:

> A real time-saver for studying, the chapter summary focuses on the major points and essential terms and definitions of the chapter.

The main idea of each paragraph is the same, but there are fewer words.

Practice 7–9: Deleting for Brevity and Adding Transitions

Rewrite the following summaries by eliminating unnecessary words, combining related sentences, and adding transitions. Use the summaries that appeared previously in this chapter for examples.

1. You can prepare people to eat for the future. Teach them to avoid foods that can cause health problems. Teach them to avoid caffeine. Teach them to avoid alcohol. Teach them to avoid foods that are high in cholesterol. Teach them to avoid junk food. You can encourage them to plan nutritious meals. You can encourage them to drink a lot of water. People will live longer, healthier lives.

2. Some employees need to take medication at work. Some medications can cause a worker to become drowsy. That drowsiness can cause accidents. The accidents lead to safety problems and downtime. The employee may need to take over-the-counter medicine. Workplace accidents can be lessened. Employers should be aware of side effects of medications. Employees need to inform supervisors of their medication. Regulations should be established for using medication. Fewer accidents will be the result.

3. Microwave ovens have many uses. Mostly they are time-savers. The two major uses of microwaves are for defrosting and reheating. The foods most often cooked in the microwave are popcorn and liquids being heated. Microwaves are used primarily for convenience. A cook can creatively fix meals, using the microwave. It was initially promoted to save energy.

Using Quotes

The article that you are summarizing may have some material that you do not want to change. This material can be quoted directly or paraphrased. However, credit must be given to the author to avoid plagiarism.

Direct quotes are the exact words of a writer or speaker. They should be included within a summary when no other words can describe the original *except* the original. When writing a direct quote, enclose the exact words within quotation marks.

A **paraphrase** is a rewriting of the author's words in your own words. In paraphrasing, all words are changed from the original.

When three or more words are used in the same order as the original, make this a direct quote. Compare the original with your copy to make sure you have not miscopied the source. Using direct quotes gives specific recognition to the author.

by the way...

"Excellence is not a destination you arrive at . . . It is the benchmark for your journey."

EARVIN "MAGIC" JOHNSON, U.S. BASKETBALL PLAYER

Writing Without Bias

Being true to the original article and accurate as to the statements and facts given is important when you are summarizing. One way to slant or distort a summary is to leave out portions that don't agree with what you wish that the article had said. This omission results in a biased summary. For example, Jermayne read the article shown in Figure 7-5 about workplace environmental health.

Workplace Injury and Disease:

A Mainstream Public Health Problem

In today's society, Americans are working more hours than ever before. The workplace environment profoundly affects health. Each of us, simply by going to work each day, may face hazards that threaten our health and safety. Risking one's life or health should never be considered merely part of the job.

In 1970, Congress passed the Occupational Safety and Health Act to ensure Americans the right to "safe and healthful working conditions," yet workplace hazards continue to inflict a tremendous toll in both human and economic costs.

Occupational injury and disease create needless human suffering, a tremendous burden upon healthcare resources, and an enormous drain on U.S. productivity. Yet, to date, this mainstream public health problem has escaped mainstream public attention. Workplace injuries and diseases are neither inevitable nor acceptable. The time has come to protect one of our most valuable resources: the American worker.

FIGURE 7-5   "Workplace Injury and Disease" article

Source: New Directions at NIOSH. United States. National Institute for Occupational Safety and Health (NIOSH). Washington: NIOSH, 1996.

After reading the article, Jermayne wrote this summary:

Going to work every day affects American workers' health. Despite government action, injuries and deaths occur every day on the job. As a result, health care costs escalate and productivity decreases.

The original article contains statements and statistics, but nowhere does it state that going to work every day affects workers' health or that workplace injuries directly increase health care costs or decrease productivity. By adding a slant to the information from the original article, Jermayne added bias in his summary. The summary by itself does not appear biased, but after one compares it with the original, the slant is apparent. A reader should not have to check the original article to have accurate information. *The summary should be just as accurate as the original.*

Practice 7–10: Identifying Slanted Summaries

After reading each of the following paragraphs and their related summaries, decide if the summary is slanted. Write down the clues that helped you determine if there was bias. Use Jermayne's biased summary as an example. Your teacher may have you work with a partner.

1. There is a mistaken notion that using clippers to "clean" the neckline makes the hair grow in thicker on the neck. This is not true, because the amount of human hair can only be as great as the number of follicles in the area. Use of clippers or any other implement does not increase the number of follicles. (*Milady's* 94)

   Using clippers for trimming the neckline results in a greater number of follicles and, thus, thicker hair.

2. By far, the most significant piece of credit legislation is the federal Consumer Credit Protection Act. Part of this act is known as the 1968 Truth-in-Lending Act, and its two primary purposes are to inform consumers about terms of a credit agreement and to require creditors to specify how finance charges are computed. The act requires a finance charge to be stated as an annual percentage rate and requires creditors to specify the procedures for correcting billing mistakes. (Longenecker, Moore, and Petty 326)

   The Consumer Credit Protection Act is the most important federal credit statute. It tells consumers about contract terms, informs them of how creditors calculate finance charges, requires that finance charges be written in annual percentage rates, and requires creditors to explain how to correct mistakes in bills.

3. A Pell Grant is an award to help first-time undergraduates pay for their education after high school. A first-time undergraduate is one who has not earned a bachelor's or first professional degree. (A professional degree would include a degree in such fields as pharmacy or dentistry, for example.) Eligibility for those who receive a Pell Grant for the first time is usually limited to 5 or 6 years of undergraduate study, not including remedial coursework.

For many students, a Pell Grant provides a "foundation" of financial aid to which aid from other federal and non-federal sources may be added. Unlike loans, grants don't have to be paid back. (United States Department of Education 22)

The Pell Grant is a federal financial aid award for undergraduate and/or graduate study. For the first-time student, all coursework is paid for.

Summarizing Oral Information and Delivering Oral Summaries

So far, you have read about written summaries of written articles. You can also summarize oral information. Summarizing oral material is paraphrasing a listening situation, such as a discussion, a conversation, a speech, instructions, or a lecture, and the visual clues that may be part of the situation. Your summary of oral information may be a verbal presentation and/or a written summary. For example, you may summarize a meeting orally to a coworker and in writing as the minutes of the meeting.

Job situations often require you to deliver summaries orally. For example, in an interview, you may verbally summarize your qualifications to a prospective employer rather than present them in writing.

Voice mail is a type of summary presented orally. With this system, a caller leaves messages at a central number, where they are posted to a mailbox within the telephone system. Voice mail often has a time limit, so the caller must plan the message and summarize the information to avoid rambling and sounding unorganized. Using the techniques discussed in Chapter 3 for condensing information for electronic phone messages will also help in delivering summaries orally.

Use the following guidelines to summarize oral information:

- *Listening to summarize is more demanding than listening for pleasure.* An active listener remembers the main points. Taking notes will help, but that is not always possible.

- *Prepare to remember.* Relate what the speaker says to the reasons for listening.

- *Clump information into large sections.* This is easier to do when the speaker has major organized points. Listening for clues to the organization of an oral presentation will help you prepare an effective summary.

- *Create a mental picture of someone performing the information given.* This picture will help you remember and understand the main points.

Ethics *Connection*

- *Listen to the speaker with an open mind and note the interest level.* When the speaker becomes enthusiastic, an important point is being given. But don't react to an idea before the speaker is finished. Instead, wait until the speaker concludes to make sure you have heard everything.

Practice 7–11: Writing Summaries of Oral Material—News Stories

Ch07-11.mp3

1. Listen to the news recordings that your teacher will play for you. Take notes on the news stories, being sure to write the following:
   a. The headline of the story
   b. The major points
   c. The organizational pattern
   d. The key transitions

2. Write an explanatory summary of each of the news stories. Be as specific and brief as possible.

3. Compare your summary with a partner's. Note the following:
   a. Did you have the same major points? If not, what is the difference?
   b. What details did you both omit?

Practice 7–12: Writing Summaries of Oral Material—Situations

Ch07-12.mp3

Your teacher will play four recordings describing different situations. After you have listened to all of the recordings, you will write an explanatory summary of each situation. Listen carefully and take notes. You will need only some of the information for your summaries. The narrator will provide you with the audience and purpose of the summary for each situation.

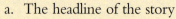

Summary

The summary is a shortened version of the original material and contains the central idea and the major points of a speech, a writing, or an event. You may present a summary in oral or written form. Whatever the form, follow these guidelines when you summarize:

- Consider subject, audience, and purpose.

- Choose the type of summary—informative, explanatory, or analytic—according to the purpose of the summary.

- Make sure that the summary is brief, accurate, unbiased, and easily understood so the reader does not need to consult the original source.

- Use transitions to link the summary into one unit.

review and research activities visit
communicating.swlearning.com

Works Cited

Adams, J. Michael, David D. Faux, and Lloyd J. Rieber. *Printing Technology*. Albany: Delmar Publishers, 1996.

Gordon, Ann Miles, and Kathryn Williams-Browne. *Beginnings and Beyond*. Albany: Delmar Publishers, 1996.

Herren, Ray V. *Exploring Agriscience*. Albany: Delmar Publishers, 1997.

Lewis, Gaspar. *Carpentry*. Albany: Delmar Publishers, 1995.

Longenecker, Justin G., Carlos W. Moore, and J. William Petty. *Small Business Management*. Cincinnati: South-Western College Publishing, 1997.

Milady's Standard Textbook of Cosmetology. Albany: Delmar Publishers, 1995.

Morrison, Alastair. *Hospitality and Travel Marketing*. Albany: Delmar Publishers, 1996.

Schwaller, Anthony E. *Automotive Technology*. Albany: Delmar Publishers, 1993.

Simmers, Louise. *Diversified Health Occupations*. Albany: Delmar Publishers, 1993.

United States Department of Education. *The Student Guide*. 1997.

Whitman, William C. and William M. Johnson. *Refrigeration and Air Conditioning Technology*. Albany: Delmar Publishers, 1995.

Writing an Evaluative Summary

 Your manager has asked your opinion of new procedures, products, or systems that will improve the work situation or help with safety problems. After reviewing various printed materials, find an article that you can summarize for your manager.

Possible sources of information include the following:

- Trade magazines
- Product inserts
- Popular magazines
- Manufacturers' web sites
- Newspaper articles
- *Consumer Reports* magazine

1. Carefully read the sample Project article, "Stress Management: What Is Stress?" (page 241), the Sample Project Plan (page 242), and the Sample Summary (page 243).

2. Highlight or take notes on your article.

3. Begin filling out the Project Plan on *Student Workbook* page 7-B. Will a drawing or photo help your reader understand your summary? If so, plan a visual.

4. Have your teacher check the Project Plan.

5. Using the information on your Project Plan, write a rough draft.

6. Using the Rough Draft column of the Project Guide (*Student Workbook* page 7-C), check your work with one or more classmates. Have them record all of their comments and suggested changes on your Project Guide and rough draft. Ask them to write a constructive comment on the rough draft and sign it. Have your teacher check your rough draft.

7. Revise and edit your rough draft, incorporating the changes that your classmates and your teacher suggested.

8. Using the Final Draft column of the Project Guide, proofread your work. Make any needed corrections.

9. Turn in the final draft along with the Project Guide.

What Is Stress?

Stress happens when the demands of life get out of control. Changes occur, causing problems. As a result, stress can take over. However, the changes are not the problem; the problem is the way we react to the changes.

Changes in Life

Daily arguments, a new spouse, loss of a job—even a lottery win—can cause stress. The big events and the small ones, the positive and the negative ones, are all changes that create stress.

Both physically and mentally, stress gains an advantage. Characteristics of stress often include tiredness, an acid stomach, an achy neck and shoulders, headaches, and an overwhelming irritated feeling. Our reactions to stress are often negative, such as smoking, overeating, losing sleep, and drinking too much—and the reactions often harm us more than the stress itself.

The result? We fall prey to illnesses such as colds and flu more easily. Higher levels of stress increase the chances of having a heart attack, a stroke, cancer, or an ulcer. Asthma sufferers may endure more complications and have attacks more often.

Causes of Stress

You need to determine the causes of your stress before you attempt to manage it. Besides life-changing events, your feelings can trigger stress. Here are some common causes of stress:

- Problems in the family or at work
- Lack of time
- Uncertainty over money
- Increased responsibilities
- Personality conflicts
- Sudden changes

Stress Reactions

You can turn every negative reaction to stress into a positive solution. You don't even have to be Mary Poppins to do it!

Managing Stress

Work with stress positively. Everyone has problems in life, but the way we approach them will reduce our stress.

1. Understand

Why worry when worry won't solve the problems? Accept the things that you cannot control. Talk to yourself. The more you use positive self-talk, the more you shatter stress.

2. Focus

Here's that positive word again. Yes, focus on the positive. Look at the bright side of the supposed downside. What are better ways of managing the situation? Looking positively helps the answers come more easily.

3. Maintain a Positive Outlook

Why worry about problems that may never occur? Just keep things in perspective. When a problem arises, ask yourself, "In five years, will this matter?" If the answer is no, move on.

If stressful events are controllable, work on changing them. Take action to eliminate the problem. If the events are not in your control, accept them positively with the attitude that you can reduce the stress.

LYDIA HARTZLER

If you are	then
hitting and screaming,	seek counseling.
grouchy,	try getting enough sleep.
overeating,	exercise with a friend.
tight in the neck and shoulders,	stretch your muscles with yoga.
spending too much money,	budget or go to credit counseling.
having repeated headaches,	try controlled, slow breathing.
never assuming the blame,	think things over and take responsibility.
in a hurry and worrying,	make priorities and organize your days.
domineering,	allow others to share decision making.
pessimistic,	talk to yourself in a positive way.

Sample Project Plan

Plan for Summarizing

		CONTENT
SUBJECT	Summary of "Stress Management"	**Central Idea:** Our lives have many changes that could cause stress, but we can manage it through coping skills.
AUDIENCE	Manager	**Main Supporting Details:** Causes • Life changes, such as family and money problems • How we cope with the pressures in life, such as problems at work and not enough time
PURPOSE	**What actions should the audience take after reading the summary?** Use article's summary to improve work situation.	Common Symptoms • Tired • Upset stomach, headaches Coping Skills
FORMAT	☒ written ☐ oral ☐ other	• Solutions to negative reactions • Positive attitude • Understand what we can't change
SOURCES	**Publication Title:** Wellness Publications **Article Title:** "Stress Management" **Author:** Lydia Hartzler **Date:** August 2004 **Page Numbers:** 47	Look at things that matter Keep things in perspective **Opinions and Evaluations (analysis):** Good to educate department Will help with pressures of change in production and new personnel
VISUALS	**What visuals, if any, will make the summary more effective?** None	**Audience's Call to Action:** Need education program for department. Form a committee and set up agenda and timelines as soon as possible.

Sample Summary

Summary of "Stress Management"

Changes in our lives can cause stress, but stress can be managed through attitude and coping skills. The problem is not the pressures in our lives, but how we cope with them.

Life changes, such as family and money problems, can cause stress. Also, the pressure of problems at work and lack of time to accomplish what we want to do can produce stress if we don't cope well. Symptoms of stress include being constantly tired and having an upset stomach and headaches.

Attitude and coping are keys to managing stress. There are many solutions to stress's negative reactions. By adopting a more positive attitude, we can lessen the stress reaction. We need to understand that, unfortunately, there are some things we cannot change. Therefore, we need to learn to live with them. We should look at things that matter and keep things in perspective. If they matter, we should handle them more positively.

A stress management program is a good policy that will benefit our department in the long run. We need to form a committee and set an agenda and timelines as soon as possible to start an education program. A stress management program will help with the pressures of change in production and with the addition of new personnel. The program can't start soon enough.

Hartzler, Lydia. "Stress Management." *Wellness Publications*. Aug. 2004: 47.

Overview

Henrik Ibsen, who was born in Norway in 1828, wrote the first great plays about the problems people have in everyday life. When he began writing plays, most of them were romantic stories written just to entertain audiences. His plays departed from the norm, using everyday language, and his characters' problems could be anyone's.

Ibsen's plays are still being performed. They are especially important because they have been so influential in the writing of drama.

from *A Doll's House*

In the following final scene from the play, Nora summarizes to her husband what she perceives her life to have been thus far.

Nora: That is just it; you have never understood me. I have been greatly wronged, Torvald—first by Papa and then by you.

Torvald: What! By us two—by us two who have loved you better than anyone else in the world?

Nora (shaking her head): You have never loved me. You have only thought it pleasant to be in love with me.

Torvald: Nora, what do I hear you saying?

Nora: It is perfectly true, Torvald. When I was at home with Papa he told me his opinion about everything, and so I had the

ROBBIE JACK/CORBIS

same opinions; and if I differed from him I concealed the fact, because he would not have liked it. He called me his doll child, and he played with me just as I used to play with my dolls. And when I came to live with you—

Torvald: What sort of an expression is that to use about our marriage?

Nora (undisturbed): I mean that I was simply transferred from Papa's hands to yours. You arranged everything according to your own taste, and so I got the same tastes as you—or else I pretended to. I am really not quite sure which—I think sometimes the one and sometimes the other. When I look back on it it seems to me as if I have been living here like a poor woman—just from hand to mouth. I have existed merely to perform tricks for you, Torvald. But you would have it so. You and Papa have committed a great sin against me. It is your fault that I have made nothing of my life.

Torvald: How unreasonable and how ungrateful you are, Nora! Have you not been happy here?

Nora: No, only merry. And you have always been so kind to me. But our home has been nothing but a playroom. I have been your doll wife, just as I was Papa's doll child; and here the children have been my dolls. I thought it great fun when you played with me, just as they thought it great fun when I played with them. That is what our marriage has been, Torvald.

> "I have been your doll wife, just as I was Papa's doll child . . . ."

—Henrik Ibsen
(translated by Peter Watts)

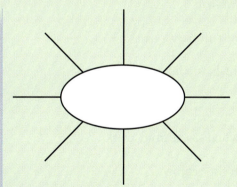

FIGURE 7-6   A spidergram

Start-Up: Nora summarizes her life, as she sees it thus far, for her husband Helmer Torvald. This scene occurs at the end of the play. Nora had forged her father's name in order to borrow money to take Torvald on a trip to bring him back to health. Torvald had found out about the forgery and condemned Nora for it, even though she had done it for him. He even went so far to say that she was not a fit mother because of this crime. As it turned out, the man who held the forged note had a turn of conscience and returned the note to Nora and Torvald. No harm done. Torvald immediately indicated that his comments about her no longer held true and that she could return to being his little "skylark," "spendthrift," and "doll." The above scene then occurs.

Connection: Form groups of three. Choose one student to draw a spidergram (Figure 7-6) on which the group will show the main ideas that summarize Nora's life. Write the topic being summarized on the body of the spider; on the legs, write each main idea.

Working with Literature: Refer to *Student Workbook* page 7-D for an activity on summarizing.

Overview

Poetry, the brief form of literature, can often summarize wrenching experiences in fewer lines than a short story or novel can. In this poem, Robert Frost presents a simple story: a boy, a buzz saw, a tragedy.

"Out, Out—"

The buzz saw snarled and rattled in the yard

And made dust and dropped stove-length sticks of wood,

Sweet-scented stuff when the breeze drew across it.

And from there those that lifted eyes could count

Five mountain ranges one behind the other

Under the sunset far into Vermont.

And the saw snarled and rattled, snarled and rattled,

As it ran light, or had to bear a load.

And nothing happened: day was all but done.

Call it a day, I wish they might have said

To please the boy by giving him the half hour

That a boy counts so much when saved from work.

His sister stood beside them in her apron

To tell them "Supper." At the word, the saw,

As if to prove saws knew what supper meant,

Leaped out of the boy's hand, or seemed to leap—

He must have given the hand. However it was,

Neither refused the meeting. But the hand!

The boy's first outcry was a rueful laugh,

As he swung toward them holding up the hand,

Half in appeal, but half as if to keep

The life from spilling. Then the boy saw all—

Since he was old enough to know, big boy

Doing man's work, though a child at heart—

He saw all spoiled. "Don't let them cut my hand off—

The doctor, when he comes. Don't let him, sister!"

So. But the hand was gone already.

The doctor put him in the dark of ether.

He lay and puffed his lips out with his breath.

And then—the watcher at his pulse took fright.

No one believed. They listened at his heart.

Little—less—nothing!—and that ended it.

No more to build on there. And they, since they

Were not the one dead, turned to their affairs.

—Robert Frost

In the poem above, a young boy loses his hand in a tragic accident that results in his death. The buzz saw appears to be almost human through the word choices that Frost uses to personify it. The family seems to accept the death as part of living.

Start-Up: Since summaries are the general idea of things, writers make them as short and concise as possible. In the English classroom, this is called a précis. In the workplace, for clarity and to save time, money, and labor, technical writing must often be as succinct as possible.

Connection: Accidents are common. Before using equipment or tools, workers must know and observe necessary safety regulations.

Use a search engine to find safety regulations for the operation of a gasoline-powered chain saw. Once you find a site, prepare a summary of the title of the web site, an expanded definition of a power saw, protective clothing worn while the saw is being operated, and precautions to take before operating the saw. Also describe *kickback*, a dangerous problem in the operation of a saw.

Chapter 8

© GETTY IMAGES/PHOTODISC, INC.

Forms are big business. Whole companies exist whose employees do nothing but design, print, and produce forms for other businesses.

Using Forms

objectives

Read a Variety of Forms

Identify the Purposes of Standard Forms

Complete Forms Accurately and Legibly

Critique the Design of a Form

Design a Usable Form

Forms are full of blank spaces. These spaces may sit above lines or appear as empty boxes. Whatever they appear to be, they invite you to fill them in. A form exists for nearly every milestone in your life. When you're born, someone fills out a birth certificate to record who you are and when and where you were born. When you were taken to the doctor, when you entered kindergarten, when you joined the Girl Scouts or Boy Scouts, when you got a report card, when you signed up for soccer, when you registered for classes, when you applied for a part-time job, when you got your driver's license—on all of these occasions and many other times besides, a form had to be filled out to provide a record of who you are, whom to call in an emergency, what grades you made in school, and on and on.

Forms

Carefully read each form you fill out to determine its purpose.

REUTERS/LANDOV

A form has at least two purposes: to get information and to give information. The job application form is a good example. The person or company that wants you to fill out a job application form uses it to get information to find out whether you have the proper qualifications for a job within the company. You fill out the form because you want to give information about yourself to show that you qualify for a particular position within the company.

The key word is *information*. Forms are designed to get as much information as possible on one page, without unnecessary writing or irrelevant details. When filling out a well-designed form, you should not have to guess what the person who designed the form wants from you. The purpose should be clear.

Practice 8–1: Identifying the Purposes of Forms

Some of the following workplace forms may be familiar to you. Write two purposes for which each form was designed.

1. Medical insurance form
2. W-4 form
3. Customer satisfaction form
4. Accident report
5. Parts request form
6. Work order
7. Purchase order
8. Invoice
9. Service report
10. Suggestion form

Tips on Filling Out Forms

Most people see a form, grab a pen or pencil, and begin reading and filling out one blank at a time. While this may seem to be a logical approach, it can actually waste time; if you are filling out the form incorrectly (or using the wrong form), you will ultimately have to start over and do it right. If you want to save time in the long run, spend a minute or two skimming the form.

Know the Purpose of the Form

Are you sending for a sample copy of a magazine? Or are you getting hooked into a year's subscription for which you will be billed later? Are you applying for vacation days? Or are you asking for release time to take a course in web design?

Be careful. Forms can look similar but may contain very different information. You need to read each form carefully.

Ethics *Connection*

Imagine that you begin receiving catalogs and flyers for electronic equipment. You then start wondering how the sender got your name and address. The answer may come if you ask yourself if you filled out a card with your name, address, and phone number and dropped it in the box that said "Win a DVD player" at the MediaStore grand opening. That card, along with hundreds of others, may have been sold to the supplier of the DVD player, who used the cards to create a mailing list. That mailing list may then have been resold to other companies. Soon you find yourself getting all kinds of junk mail.

If you don't want to have your personal information shared with other companies, write to them or look for a check-off box on their order forms that says something like "Do not make my name available to other mailers." Check the box and mail the form back to the company. Good business ethics requires the company to abide by your wishes.

Note the Arrangement of Questions

Do the questions go from left to right? Top to bottom? Are the questions divided into sections on the page? There may, for example, be one section for you and another section for your spouse.

Often you will notice a section labeled "For Office Use Only." Do not write in that space; that is where those receiving the form will make their notations.

Use Only Standard English

Remember, those who read your form do not know you. So don't use any trade jargon, slang, or foreign terms. Use simply worded, standard English. Don't, for example, make your medical insurance company come back to you two months after you've broken your arm and say, "What does this mean?" You may be stacking up unpaid doctor bills because you did a haphazard job of filling out the required medical form.

Bring a Fact Sheet

When you know you are going to have to fill out a form, bring essential information with you if possible. For example, if you go to a bank to apply for a loan, take along a fact sheet of important names, addresses, and phone numbers.

- Do you know your mother's maiden name?
- Do you know the full name, address, and phone number of your nearest relative?
- Do you have with you your checking account number and a record of your personal finances, such as the amount of any debts you have and your monthly salary?

If you do not have all of this information, you will lose precious time in getting your loan processed. Actually, it would make sense to go to the bank, ask for a loan form, and then take it home and look up the information as you fill it out.

When going to a doctor, take your insurance identification card with you. Some doctors' offices use the card to fill out and submit insurance forms for you. You may also be required to supply information from the card in filling out the offices' forms.

Print Clearly or Key

Don't get fancy and add curlicues or dot your *i*'s with hearts. Simple block printing is best for all parts of a form except the signature line.

Aa Bb Cc Dd Ee Ff Gg
Hh Ii Jj Kk Ll Mm Nn
Oo Pp Qq Rr Ss Tt Uu
Vv Ww Xx Yy Zz

FIGURE 8-1   The alphabet in block printing

You were probably first introduced to block printing in elementary school. (See Figure 8-1.) Remember, in any occupation, it is appropriate to print. Whether you are filling out a form, handwriting a memo, or leaving a short message for someone, the receiver often appreciates the clarity of printing since handwriting is sometimes difficult to read.

Of course, you may encounter forms on the Internet or forms designed in business software. In those cases, you just key the information using a computer.

Some people use their handwriting as an excuse to cover up poor spelling. But when you print, you are sending this message:

> I want this information to be perfectly clear to my reader. I am confident in what I say, and I want the reader to understand me.

Be as Brief as Possible

Don't use three words where one will suffice. Use phrases instead of full sentences. In other words, use the shortest, clearest way to state your information. Do not write a paragraph when a word is all that is requested. Save your words for those times, for example, when a form tells you to "Tell, in your own words, what you saw at the scene of the accident. Use additional paper if necessary."

Use Standard Abbreviations

Wherever possible, use **standard abbreviations** that are prescribed or commonly accepted and that the reader will understand. If, for example, you are not married, write *NA* in the space where your spouse's name is requested. Don't write "I am not married" or "I have no spouse." The abbreviation *NA* means "not applicable" and is all that is required. If you prefer, you can draw a short line in the space. By using *NA* or a short line, you are telling the reader that you didn't ignore the blank or that you didn't have some questionable reason for not filling it in; you are saying that the requested information simply doesn't apply to you.

Practice 8–2: Using Abbreviations and Acronyms

1. Write a standard abbreviation for each of the following words or phrases. (There may be more than one.) You may use letters, numerals, or other symbols as appropriate. Consult a dictionary if necessary. The first one is done for you.

   Example:

   Avenue **Ave.**

a. five feet eleven inches	g. Enrico Company, Incorporated
b. Doctor of Medicine	h. social security number
c. Boulevard	i. identification card
d. number	j. thousand
e. February 2, 2005	k. package
f. Post Office Box 1052	l. date of birth

2. Complete *Student Workbook* page 8-A for additional practice with abbreviations and acronyms.

Technology *Connection*

You've probably noticed that many forms today do not just have blank lines to fill in. They often contain boxes or separated lines for each letter required. The reason is that the information is set up for data entry; that is, for someone to put into a computer. Printing and separating each item or letter makes it easy for a data entry clerk to read the information and thus minimizes the possibility of error. Sometimes the form is already set up in the computer software. So instead of handing you a form to fill out, a receptionist may ask you for each piece of information needed and enter it into the computer as you say it.

Other abbreviations you should know are as follows:

- The two-letter abbreviations for the 50 states used by the United States Postal Service.

- Abbreviations for streets and roads—for example, *St., Rd., Rte., Ave.,* and *Ct.*

- Abbreviations for titles used in addressing people. Many forms require you to indicate which title you prefer. But first, be sure you're clear about how these personal titles are used.

Mrs. Title preferred by many married women. Examples: *Mrs. Laurie Singleton* or *Mrs. Darius Singleton.*

Mr. Title used for all men, married or unmarried, unless they have a professional title, such as *Doctor* or *Reverend.* Sometimes *Mr.* is used with other titles, as in *Mr. President* for the president of the United States or *Mr. Speaker* for the Speaker of the House of Representatives.

Ms. Title used for married or unmarried women unless they indicate another preference.

Miss Now a word, although it started as the short form of *mistress,* which used to mean "unmarried woman." This title is preferred by some unmarried women.

Dr. Doctors are not all medical doctors. For example, a person with a Ph.D. in mathematics or history is also called *Doctor.* Some of these people work in colleges or engineering, chemical research, or other professions. Examples of two famous nonmedical doctors: Sally Ride, the first woman astronaut, and Martin Luther King, Jr., civil rights leader.

Rev. *Reverend* is the title of a minister or priest. Not all ministers use this title. Some use *Mr.* or *Dr.*

Forms in Our Lives: One Person's Story

Barrett Izaakson's struggles with paperwork began when he applied for his driver's license during his sophomore year. He found out that a driver's license isn't just handed to a person as a reward for turning 16 and passing a driver's test. In fact, he wasn't even allowed to take the test until he showed his birth certificate to prove his age. That's when his problems started. Although Barrett had been living with his parents at the same address in Ohio since he was three months old, he had been born near Chicago. So he had to write to the records office there for his birth certificate. Several years earlier whole city blocks of buildings in downtown Chicago had been flooded due to a disastrous water main break. Businesses and government offices were shut down, some for several weeks. These offices included not only basements, but also subbasements far underground, which filled with water when those pipes burst. People saved what they could and tried to move files out of basement offices to higher ground. Barrett's birth certificate was in one of those subterranean file cabinets.

It took weeks for a city office worker in Chicago to find and mail him a faded copy of his once water-saturated birth certificate. He began to wonder if this was a foreshadowing of future struggles with forms.

It wasn't until his senior year, though, that he began to think that banks and government agencies were burying him in forms. It started with a series of family calamities. First, his dad was laid off from work, and his mom went from part-time to full-time work at Kibbles Cookies on the 3 to 11 P.M. shift to make more money. Plans to get a new car and give the old one to Barrett were put aside. Now he would have to buy a car so he could get to his senior co-op job. He also knew that his parents could no longer afford to help him pay his car insurance—$2,000 a year.

Barrett had worked part-time for Buildex Lumber, mostly on weekends, since he turned 16 in January 2004. In this first "real job," he had proved himself to be a reliable employee and his boss, Mr. Nunez, had offered him a full-time job when he finished high school. He had started in a co-op job in the company's warehousing and inventory department during his senior year, and now he was working 30 hours a week at $8.50 an hour. He couldn't quit now. His choice was simple: To keep his job, he would need a car, and since his savings amounted to less than $200, he would have to get a loan so he could buy the car.

Getting a Loan

People get loans from banks every day. But as Barrett soon discovered, that does not mean that loans are easy to get. He discovered that banks don't care how much you need the money. They're in the money-lending business to make money. To do so, they must charge interest on every penny they lend.

Barrett discovered that since he was only 18 and had never had a loan before, he had no **credit rating** and, therefore, would need a **cosigner** to assure the bank that the loan would be paid. He asked his uncle, Wilbert Schilling, to be his cosigner, since his parents couldn't take on the burden of another loan. Uncle Bert knew that Barrett had no other debts and that he was hard-working, reliable, and conscientious, so Uncle Bert agreed to be the cosigner. Uncle Bert also knew that Barrett could afford a loan payment of about $100 after he made his insurance payments and took care of car upkeep and incidentals. They went back to the bank together to get a printout of the loan details Barrett would need to purchase the older used car he had in mind.

The bank would charge Barrett 6.74 percent annually for the balance due on his loan, but since the interest was compounded, it actually worked out to an annual percentage rate (APR) of 8.43 percent. In addition, there was a one-time bank charge of $100. See Figure 8-2 for the way the bank presented the loan on paper.

1ST CITY BANK
INSTALLMENT LOAN

2/25/05	ASSUMPTIONS		CONCLUSIONS	
CASH ADVANCED	$3,700.00	PRINCIPAL NOTE AMT		3,865.00
BANK FEE	100.00			
DOC CHARGE	15.00	AMT FINANCED		3,765.00
VSI	50.00			
		FINANCE CHARGE		538.08
LIFE INSURANCE	.00	ANNUAL PERCENTAGE RATE		8.43%
		DAYS TO 1ST PAYMENT		39
CONTRACT DATE (DDMMYY)	022505			
1ST PYMT DATE (DDMMYY)	041505	NUMBER OF PAYMENTS		36
INTEREST RATE	6.74%	AMT OF EACH PAYMENT		$119.53
INSURANCE: NONE		TOTAL PAYMENT AMT		$4,303.08

FIGURE 8-2 A printout showing bank terms for Barrett's installment loan

Filling Out Loan and Credit Card Applications

When you are applying for a loan, your job history, credit rating, and educational level are all important. The person or company lending you the money must be sure that you can pay back the loan. These factors may work for or against you. However, you need to remember one thing in filling out these and other applications: Never lie. Your credit rating is a matter of record. The loan officer or credit card company will look at the information you provide to see if you appear to be a good risk or to be sure that you have filled out the form properly. Then they will send for a copy of your credit rating.

In this age of computers, it is fairly easy for someone to follow your money trail. If you have ever had a car loan, a home mortgage, or a credit card, your bills and payments are in your credit report. And a computer somewhere can retrieve that file in seconds. If the facts in the file don't agree with what you have written on the form, you are caught in a lie. Liars are not good credit risks.

Occasionally, however, the facts in your credit file don't agree with what you have written on the form. This happens not because you have lied or made a mistake, but because someone has made an incorrect entry, has kept outdated information, or has confused you with another person with a last name similar to yours (meaning that the person's debts are in your file). It may be wise to write to a consumer reporting agency every few years to get a copy of your credit records so that you can find and resolve any inaccuracies that may exist.

Filling out loan or credit card applications accurately may take a lot of research. That's why you are not expected to fill them out immediately. You can take the forms home and look up the information you need. If you realize you don't understand a question—such as "Have you ever **defaulted** on a loan?"—don't hesitate to call the customer service people at the bank or loan company. Ask them to clarify what they mean. Most likely they will treat you politely because they appreciate people trying to do things right. They will tell you that *defaulted* means "failed to pay a financial debt." Banks and loan companies are used to handling all kinds of questions.

If you pay off the loan, your credit rating will be established and you will have an easier time getting a loan on your own the next time you need one. If you default and someone else has to pay (or worse, if for some reason neither you nor your cosigner can pay), you will be subject to legal action and you may not qualify the next time you apply for a loan.

Career *Connection*

You have studied geography in school and have probably used computers at home or in school, but have you thought about making a career of the combination? If you like geography and computers, you might be interested in a career in GIS (geographic information systems). When decisions have to be made about how to redistrict schools or where to locate an electrical power plant or a new subdivision, a GIS specialist is likely to be consulted. This consultant combines computerized mapping with data analysis in helping city, state, and national planners make critical planning decisions.

GIS specialists are also hired by large corporations that need to know if a particular town or country is a good place to locate one of their plants. The corporations need answers to such questions as these: What are the local zoning laws if any? Are there enough potential workers to run the plant? Does the location have proper sewage? Are water and electric utilities available? Gathering the data to answer these questions is the job of the GIS specialist. If this type of career interests you, check the Internet at http://www.gis.com or find a good college search software package to locate universities that offer degrees in GIS.

by the way...

According to Robert McKinley, founder of the RAM Research Group, which researches credit card information for both consumers and bankers, "Anyone who knows anything about the [credit] card business knows that if you make the minimum payment, the two percent per month that they ask for, you will never get out of debt. It takes 30 years to clear a $2,000 debt."

As you fill out a credit card application form, remember that credit cards are a type of loan arrangement. When you charge a purchase using a credit card, the payment is actually made by a company—usually a bank, a gasoline company, or a department store. Then later you pay the company back, usually with interest. As a cardholder, you also may have to pay an annual fee.

Be sure to read credit card applications carefully on both sides. Read all of the fine print and look for a chart showing the interest rates the company will charge if you don't pay the entire balance of the bill each month. The annual interest rate is often 18 to 21 percent (an additional $18 to $21 added to your bill for every $100 charged).

Wise credit card users make a practice of paying off their entire balance at the end of each month. That way they avoid a mounting debt and an interest charge.

Some companies require you to pay off the entire amount you have charged each month, so there is no interest. Their cards usually carry an annual fee of $35 to $50 or more. You need to know the terms of the agreement you are signing when you fill out the credit card application. Once you sign it, you have entered into a contract with the company and are legally bound to the terms set forth in that contract.

Practice 8-3: Filling Out Forms

Use Barrett Izaakson's driver's license, bank account statement, paycheck, and any other information you have learned about him from reading this chapter to fill out the following forms:

1. Barrett's loan application (Do not fill in the co-applicant part.)

2. His request for **direct deposit** of a portion of his paycheck into his savings account

3. A form for a free subscription to *Buildex National, The Construction Supplier's Magazine*

The forms are on pages 8-C through 8-E in your *Student Workbook*.

Buildex Lumber Co.
Subsidiary of Buildex International
406 MidCity Tower
Hamilton, Ohio 45011-2708
Phone: 513-555-0137

Check No. 20050147

March 2, 2005

Pay to the order of _____ Barrett Izaakson _____ $128.90

Exactly ONE HUNDRED TWENTY-EIGHT & 90/100 DOLLARS

1st CITY BANK
Hamilton, Ohio

JB Blum

0141-08-0001

OHIO DRIVER LICENSE

BARRETT IZAAKSON
2700 PEERPOINT WAY
HAMILTON, OH 45011-2743

LICENSE NO.	S.S. NUMBER
AB010725	898-40-7426

BIRTH DATE	ISSUE DATE
01/10/88	02/14/04

Sex	HT	WT	Hair	Eyes
M	5-09	150	BRO	BRO

UNDER 21
UNTIL 01/10/09

Restr
A

Barrett Izaakson

City Bank
Hamilton, Ohio 45011-9382

Account Number 0523-77	Barrett Izaakson 2700 Peerpoint Way Hamilton, OH 45011-2743	To report errors or make inquiries call: 513-555-0124

02-01-05 through 02-28-05

Statement of Account

Date	Deposit Type	Interest	Deposit Amount	Balance
1-30-05				128.06
2-06-05	Savings		15.00	143.06
2-13-05	Savings		15.00	158.06
2-20-05	Savings		15.00	173.06
2-27-05	Savings		13.00	186.06
2-27-05		2%	3.72	189.78

PHOTO © GETTY IMAGES/PHOTODISC, INC.

Job-Related Forms

A variety of forms is commonly used in most workplaces. You will encounter some or all of these as an employee. Some of the most common are W-4 forms, medical forms, on-site service report forms, work orders, and purchase orders.

W-4 Forms

The W-4 is a federal income tax form, and you are usually required to complete one as soon as you are hired. (See Figure 8-3.) It tells your

Form W-4 (2004)

Purpose. Complete Form W-4 so that your employer can withhold the correct Federal income tax from your pay. Because your tax situation may change, you may want to refigure your withholding each year.

Exemption from withholding. If you are exempt, complete only lines 1, 2, 3, 4, and 7 and sign the form to validate it. Your exemption for 2004 expires February 16, 2005. See **Pub. 505,** Tax Withholding and Estimated Tax.

Note: *You cannot claim exemption from withholding if:* ***(a)*** *your income exceeds $800 and includes more than $250 of unearned income (e.g., interest and dividends) and* ***(b)*** *another person can claim you as a dependent on their tax return.*

Basic instructions. If you are not exempt, complete the **Personal Allowances Worksheet** below. The worksheets on page 2 adjust your withholding allowances based on itemized deductions, certain credits, adjustments to income, or two-earner/two-job situations. Complete all worksheets that apply. **However, you may claim fewer (or zero) allowances.**

Head of household. Generally, you may claim head of household filing status on your tax return only if you are unmarried and pay more than 50% of the costs of keeping up a home for yourself and your dependent(s) or other qualifying individuals. See line **E** below.

Tax credits. You can take projected tax credits into account in figuring your allowable number of withholding allowances. Credits for child or dependent care expenses and the child tax credit may be claimed using the **Personal Allowances Worksheet** below. See **Pub. 919,** How Do I Adjust My Tax Withholding? for information on converting your other credits into withholding allowances.

Nonwage income. If you have a large amount of nonwage income, such as interest or dividends, consider making estimated tax payments using **Form 1040-ES,** Estimated Tax for Individuals. Otherwise, you may owe additional tax.

Two earners/two jobs. If you have a working spouse or more than one job, figure the total number of allowances you are entitled to claim on all jobs using worksheets from only one Form W-4. Your withholding usually will be most accurate when all allowances are claimed on the Form W-4 for the highest paying job and zero allowances are claimed on the others.

Nonresident alien. If you are a nonresident alien, see the **Instructions for Form 8233** before completing this Form W-4.

Check your withholding. After your Form W-4 takes effect, use Pub. 919 to see how the dollar amount you are having withheld compares to your projected total tax for 2004. See Pub. 919, especially if your earnings exceed $125,000 (Single) or $175,000 (Married).

Recent name change? If your name on line 1 differs from that shown on your social security card, call 1-800-772-1213 to initiate a name change and obtain a social security card showing your correct name.

Personal Allowances Worksheet (Keep for your records.)

A Enter "1" for **yourself** if no one else can claim you as a dependent . . . . A ______

B Enter "1" if:
- You are single and have only one job; or
- You are married, have only one job, and your spouse does not work; or
- Your wages from a second job or your spouse's wages (or the total of both) are $1,000 or less.

. . B ______

C Enter "1" for your **spouse.** But, you may choose to enter "-0-" if you are married and have either a working spouse or more than one job. (Entering "-0-" may help you avoid having too little tax withheld.) . . . . C ______

D Enter number of **dependents** (other than your spouse or yourself) you will claim on your tax return . . . . D ______

E Enter "1" if you will file as **head of household** on your tax return (see conditions under **Head of household** above) . E ______

F Enter "1" if you have at least $1,500 of **child or dependent care expenses** for which you plan to claim a credit . . F ______

(**Note:** *Do* ***not*** *include child support payments. See* ***Pub. 503,*** *Child and Dependent Care Expenses, for details.*)

G **Child Tax Credit** (including additional child tax credit):
- If your total income will be less than $52,000 ($77,000 if married), enter "2" for each eligible child.
- If your total income will be between $52,000 and $84,000 ($77,000 and $119,000 if married), enter "1" for each eligible child plus "1" **additional** if you have four or more eligible children.

G ______

H Add lines A through G and enter total here. **Note:** *This may be different from the number of exemptions you claim on your tax return.* ▶ H ______

For accuracy, complete all worksheets that apply.
- If you plan to **itemize or claim adjustments to income** and want to reduce your withholding, see the **Deductions and Adjustments Worksheet** on page 2.
- If you have **more than one job** or are **married and you and your spouse both work** and the combined earnings from all jobs exceed $35,000 ($25,000 if married) see the **Two-Earner/Two-Job Worksheet** on page 2 to avoid having too little tax withheld.
- If **neither** of the above situations applies, **stop here** and enter the number from line H on line 5 of Form W-4 below.

Cut here and give Form W-4 to your employer. Keep the top part for your records.

Form **W-4**

Department of the Treasury
Internal Revenue Service

Employee's Withholding Allowance Certificate

▶ **Your employer must send a copy of this form to the IRS if: (a) you claim more than 10 allowances or (b) you claim "Exempt" and your wages are normally more than $200 per week.**

OMB No. 1545-0010

2004

1 Type or print your first name and middle initial	Last name	2 Your social security number
Home address (number and street or rural route)	3 ☐ Single ☐ Married ☐ Married, but withhold at higher Single rate. **Note:** *If married, but legally separated, or spouse is a nonresident alien, check the "Single" box.*	
City or town, state, and ZIP code	**4 If your last name differs from that shown on your social security card, check here. You must call 1-800-772-1213 for a new card.** ▶ ☐	

5 Total number of allowances you are claiming (from line **H** above **or** from the applicable worksheet on page 2) | 5 |

6 Additional amount, if any, you want withheld from each paycheck . . . . | 6 | $

7 I claim exemption from withholding for 2004, and I certify that I meet **both** of the following conditions for exemption:
- Last year I had a right to a refund of **all** Federal income tax withheld because I had **no** tax liability **and**
- This year I expect a refund of **all** Federal income tax withheld because I expect to have **no** tax liability.

If you meet both conditions, write "Exempt" here . . . . ▶ | 7 |

Under penalties of perjury, I certify that I am entitled to the number of withholding allowances claimed on this certificate, or I am entitled to claim exempt status.

Employee's signature
(Form is not valid unless you sign it.) ▶ **Date** ▶

8 Employer's name and address (Employer: Complete lines 8 and 10 only if sending to the IRS.)	9 Office code (optional)	10 Employer identification number (EIN)

For Privacy Act and Paperwork Reduction Act Notice, see page 2. Cat. No. 10220Q Form **W-4** (2004)

FIGURE 8-3 The W-4 form

employer how many **dependents** (people, including yourself, whom you support) you are declaring. Your employer will then know how much federal income tax to withhold from your paycheck. If you have a job now, you probably already filled out this form at work.

All you probably have to fill out is page 1 (as shown in Figure 8-3). Page 2 is for people who itemize their deductions. These people usually have a home mortgage and sufficient charitable contributions, nonwage income (such as interest on investments), and other financial considerations that make it sensible for them to itemize their deductions.

Medical Insurance Forms

In most companies, full-time workers are offered some type of medical insurance as a **fringe benefit**. Usually, you, as an employee, must pay a certain amount in the form of a **deductible** or **co-payment**. You may, for example, have to pay 20 percent of all medical bills while your insurance company pays the remaining 80 percent. Or you may have to make a co-payment (for example, $10) each time you visit a doctor. If you should require surgery or extensive therapy, you would have to pay a set percentage. Sometimes for an added fee, your entire family can be covered by the insurance. Whatever the charge, it is far less than you would have to pay to a doctor or hospital if you didn't have insurance.

Money from a medical insurer is handled in two ways: It can be paid directly to the doctor, or it can be paid to you after you prove that you already paid the doctor. In either case, you may be required to fill out a portion of the insurance form stating who you are, what company you work for, and whatever other information is requested.

If the doctor bills the insurance company directly, he or she will have detailed information about you on file. Usually, you are required to present your health insurance identification card. It includes your insurance company's name, your policy number, your employer's name and code number, and perhaps other additional information. Then the bill is sent directly to the insurance company. If you are required to pay a percentage of the cost, the insurance company sends you a bill for the amount.

Some doctors will not send your bill to the insurance company, but will require you to pay the bill. Then you have to fill out a medical claim form provided by your insurance company and attach the doctor's bill showing that you have paid it in full. The insurance company will then reimburse you for the amount your policy stipulates.

Culture *Connection*

The crossword puzzle is a form that has nothing to do with business. It's just for fun. And it seems to be peculiarly English, since the first known crossword puzzles originated in England in the 1800s. According to *Compton's Encyclopedia*, these puzzles were fairly simple compared to the challenge of the well-known *New York Times* crossword puzzles of today, and they soon became a serious pastime in the United States. The first known American crossword puzzle, designed by a journalist named Arthur Wynne, was published in the *New York World* Sunday Supplement on December 21, 1913.

Certainly the English alphabet better lends itself to the form of the crossword puzzle than do some other alphabets. Japanese and Chinese characters, which are stylized picture drawings, do not consist of individual letters that form words. The parts of these characters cannot be taken apart and inserted into separate blocks; separating the pen strokes would destroy the character and thus destroy the meaning.

An example of the portion of a typical medical form where patient information is required is shown in Figure 8-4.

PART I PATIENT AND MEMBER INFORMATION		*(please print or key)*
1. Member's name _____ Address _____ City _____ State _____ ZIP _____ Phone (____) _____	6. Patient's date of birth Age __/__/__	10. **IMPORTANT** If patient is covered by any other group or non-group health insurance, please complete this section. Name of other employer _____ Address of other employer _____ Name of other person employed _____ Birth date of other person employed _____ Relationship to patient _____ Other health care plan _____
	7. Patient's relation to Member self (male) 1☐ self (female) 2☐ husband 3☐ wife 4☐ son 5☐ daughter 6☐ other male dependent 7☐ other female dependent 8☐	
2. Patient (first name, middle initial, last name)		If patient is a child and parents are divorced, please answer the following: a. Which parent has custody of the patient?_____ b. Is there a court decree that states which parent is responsible for medical bills? ___ yes ___ no. If yes, please attach a copy of the court decree.
3. Member's certificate or ID no.: _____ _____ (Numbers can be found on Member's ID card.)	8. Is patient full-time student 19 years of age or older? ☐ yes ☐ no Name of school:	11. Is the patient eligible for Medicare? ☐ yes ☐ no
4. Group Name: _____	9. Was condition related to: A. Employment ☐yes ☐no B. Accident ☐yes ☐no Date of Onset: _____	12. Describe the illness, injury, or symptom:_____ _____ _____ Date symptom first appeared: _____
5. Group Number: _____		
5a. I authorize release of any information relative to this claim to be used by a review agency solely for the purposes of determining reimbursement. _____ DATE: _____ (Signature of Member or Spouse)		

FIGURE 8-4   A patient information form

Using either your own personal information or Barrett Izaakson's information, fill out the W-4 and medical insurance enrollment forms on pages 8-F and 8-G in your *Student Workbook*.

On-Site Service Report Forms

In an increasing number of occupations, employees who deal directly with customers on the customer's property must make a written report of their work. Sometimes this includes listing the costs billed to the customer.

Many new employees are shocked to discover that, just when they finally get hired as an electrician or a plumber or a furnace repairer, they suddenly have to polish their speaking and writing skills.

Service reports are meant to inform the employer as well as the customer of exactly what services were rendered, how long the service call took, and what materials were used. Usually, the company provides a form for the service representative to fill out. Sometimes the form is filled out on the spot and handed to the customer. At other times, it may be taken to the office and converted into a letter or detailed invoice for the customer.

The service report in Figure 8-5 was filed by an electrician who did work in a private home. In this case, the report was filed in the office. Then it was keyed, printed, and mailed to the customer as part of the bill. What is missing from this bill?

DIGITAL VISION

A service representative must often prepare an on-site report to describe the details of the work performed.

Holkamp Electric Company
100 West Main Street—Georgetown, Indiana

DESCRIPTION OF WORK

Work performed on September 9 and 11, 200-

For labor and material necessary to clean and service furnace and electronic air cleaner.

Installed new thermocouple on furnace, installed new water pad on humidifier, and checked system for proper operation.

Installed owner's two floodlight fixtures with motion detector and furnished and installed new control switch in kitchen.

Furnished and installed new ground fault interrupter receptacle (connected to existing circuit in garage) on outside of house in side yard.

Total Price: $521.40

TERMS OF PAYMENT

Payment due upon job completion or receipt of invoice. 2% interest per month assessed on all accounts outstanding after 15 days of invoice date.

FIGURE 8-5　A printed service report

In the situation described below, Luisa Sosa, the service representative for a heating and air-conditioning company, must write out the report on the spot. While on the job site, she bills the customer and collects a check for services rendered.

Assume that Luisa is scheduled to service an air conditioner at 811 Lake Street. When Luisa arrives, she is expected to call the office and tell the secretary or dispatcher that she is at the scheduled site and is ready to start working. The time is then recorded so that the number of hours Luisa works can be figured into the bill. Luisa makes another phone call when the job is finished to report that the work is done and to give an account of what supplies she used. Someone in the company's office then figures up the bill and tells Luisa what to charge the customer. She writes the amount on her report and collects the money from the customer for services rendered.

The report itself has to be composed and written so that it is understandable and legible. There is no room for error, so Luisa has some standard phrases ready to use on the form. (See examples below.) She must also be prepared to explain each item on the bill, including the need for any replacement parts, to the customer's satisfaction.

If you are ever in Luisa's situation, you need to remember to record exactly what you did in chronological order, using short statements. Don't get fancy. Just begin each statement with a verb and keep it straightforward and simple. Examples:

Cleaned furnace.
Replaced furnace filter.
Replaced humidifier pad.
Checked thermostat.

In other occupations, you might use statements such as the following:

Replaced fan belt.
Reapplied tracking powder behind baseboard.
Installed light fixture in kitchen.
Cleaned trap in bathroom sink.

Notice the absence of words such as *I, the,* and *a.* These words are not necessary to the meaning of the report, and they take up extra space on a small form. Use a bare-bones approach. Say only what absolutely needs to be said. Just be careful not to skip essential information.

Figure 8-6 is a report form filed by Paul, a heating and air-conditioning specialist. Paul is good at servicing furnaces, but not so good at writing his service reports. He has the right idea, but writes sloppily, runs his statements together, and misspells too many words, which reflects badly on his employer.

Critique Paul's report with a partner. List everything that is helpful or confusing and tell exactly what should be done to improve it. Then use the blank form on page 8-H of your *Student Workbook* to write the report correctly. The beginning verb is provided.

Maintenance Work Orders

The work order is a maintenance or repair request. It is designed to suit the needs of particular kinds of businesses and is filled out by someone who notices a problem with equipment, structure, electrical wiring, plumbing, etc. that may affect performance or safety. Here are some examples of situations in which a work order might be required.

- You are working in a warehouse and notice that shelving is pulling loose from a wall or that a truck stop rail is loose at the service entrance.
- You are an administrative assistant and notice bare wires on an electric outlet in the office.
- A coworker in the food processing plant where you work points out that the meat locker door is not closing properly, which could cause the meat to spoil.

In situations such as these, you would need to fill out a work order. Then you would submit the form to the individual or department responsible for maintenance, as shown in Figure 8-7 on the following page.

JOB WORK ORDER
No. 98338

DATE OF ORDER

CUSTOMER Lacey Manon

BILL TO

SERV. REP. Paul   STARTING DATE 10/3/——

ORDER TAKEN BY

ADDRESS 1919 Hyde Street

CITY Frost City

☑ DAY WORK
☐ CONTRACT
☐ EXTRA

JOB NAME

JOB PHONE

DESCRIPTION OF WORK
Clean & service furnace
clean pilot light replaced
thermocouple oil motor check
heat exchanger OK at this
time Gave price price of $195:0
to install humidifier.

Paid service call and
work on furnace by check #2493

Thank You $94:95

METHOD OF PAYMENT
☐ CASH AMT. $_____
☐ CREDIT CARD
☐ CHECK NO. _____ AMT. $_____
☐ SEND BILL

TOTAL MATERIALS
TOTAL LABOR
TAX
TOTAL AMOUNT $94 95

DATE COMPLETED 10/3/——   WORK ORDERED BY

Signed Lacey Manon
I hereby acknowledge the satisfactory completion of the above-described work.

FIGURE 8-6   Paul's service report

MAINTENANCE WORK ORDER

DEPT NO.	WORK ORDER NUMBER
10	1158

DOWNTIME REQUIRED ☐   DATE SUBMITTED _6-10---_   DATE REQ'D _6-12---_

ORIGINATOR: _Rob Stendhal_   PHONE EXT: _310_

AREA CONTACT: _Mustafa Al Haq_   PHONE EXT: _125_

APPROVED BY: _____   SAFETY PERMIT REQUIRED: YES ☐ NO ☐

MACHINE NO./DESCRIPTION: _____

PRIORITY:	1. EMERGENCY	2. URGENT	3. PRIORITY	SAFETY: A. YES
	4. ROUTINE	5. SHUT DOWN		B. NO

DESCRIPTION OF WHAT IS WRONG OR MAINTENANCE WORK REQUESTED: _____

Safety gate at #2 dock, Bldg. 102, won't
close. Hinge is broken.

DESCRIPTION OF WORK PHASE	CLK NO. HRS PPL	EST. HRS MR E P IR TR	ACT TR HRS	CMP
Completed – gate repaired	4			

	TOTALS	AVL	PHS NO.	PARTS/MATERIAL REQUIRED	AVL
PHS NO.	PARTS/MATERIAL REQUIRED				X
Gate hinge					

TOTAL EST. HRS. _____   PARTS/MATERIAL REQUIRED ____

DATE SCHEDULED: _6-11---_   DATE COMPLETED: _6-12---_

WORK PERFORMED: _Hinge replaced on gate._

SUPERVISOR'S SIGNATURE _Pilar Cruz_

WHITE - ORIGINATOR'S COPY   PINK - ORIGINATOR'S FEEDBACK COPY   GREEN - PLANNER'S COPY   CANARY - MAINTENANCE COPY   CARD STOCK - EQUIPMENT HISTORY FILE

FIGURE 8-7   A work order

PURCHASE ORDER

Your Company Name
Your Company Slogan
Your Company Street Address
City, State ZIP
000.000.0000 Fax 000.000.0000

The following number must appear on all related
correspondence, shipping papers, and invoices:
P.O. NUMBER: 980512

Ship To:

(Name and address of place where
you want Doors Galore to deliver the
merchandise.)

To:
Attention: Josh Gilland
Doors Galore
3333 Hacienda Lane
Phoenix, AZ 50012-1432

P.O. DATE	REQUISITIONER	SHIP VIA	F.O.B. POINT	TERMS
7/16/ - -	Becky	Avi Express		60 Days

ITEM	QTY.	UNIT	DESCRIPTION	UNIT PRICE	TOTAL
1.	2	ea	Insulated door, DM552-S	469.25	992.50
2.	3	set/2	Brass hinge set, BF032-557	29.95	89.95
3.	1	ea	External door lockset and latch, brass, D23207-408	92.50	92.50

	SUBTOTAL	$1,174.85
	SALES TAX	$ 70.49
	SHIPPING & HANDLING	$ 117.49
	OTHER	
	TOTAL	$1,362.83

1. Please send two copies of your invoice.
2. Enter this order in accordance with the prices, terms, delivery method, and specifications listed above.
3. Please notify us immediately if you are unable to ship as specified.
4. Send all correspondence to:
   Name
   Company Name
   Your Company Street Address
   City, State ZIP
   000.000.0000, ext. 000; Fax 000.000.0000

Requisitioner _____   Date _____

Authorized by _____   Date _____

FIGURE 8-8   A sample purchase order

Purchase Orders

Every business, big or small, uses purchase orders. These forms order (request) the purchase of items. Purchase orders vary from company to company, but they have certain things in common. A simple PO, as purchase orders are commonly called, is shown in Figure 8-8. Note that you must be clear about the order quantity.

Item 1 calls for two doors. Each door is $496.25; therefore, you must multiply the price per door by 2 (the total number of doors needed) to get the total price of $992.50.

Item 2, on the other hand, specifies three sets of hinges, with two hinges in each set (set/2). One price includes both hinges. They are not $29.95 each; they are $29.95 combined as a set. The required number of hinges will cost $89.85.

Usually, individual items are indicated by *ea* (for *each*). What do you think the following abbreviations would mean on a purchase order?

bx, cs, pk, mil

Practice 8–6: Filling Out a Purchase Order

Imagine that you work for the Bright Window Company and are in charge of replacing old office equipment. You have researched and priced everything you need. Now, using the following information and the blank purchase order on page 8-I of your *Student Workbook,* fill in the purchase order as it should look if you were actually ordering these items.

At the bottom of the PO, sign your name as the requestor. The business manager or another authorized person signs on the "authorized signature" line in a real business transaction, which means that the purchase is approved and that the company will pay for the items when they are received.

Remember to use standard abbreviations wherever possible.

Purchase order information:

Vendor: Office Suppliers, Inc., 98 Retail Drive, Little Rock, Arkansas 72206-1256 (Shipping and billing addresses are the same.)

Item 1—2 Condor Desktop Copiers, Model DT-39 with four preset reduction ratios and 100-sheet paper tray, @ $349.50 each.

Item 2—2 Steel-Side file cabinets, Model 21-539, four-drawer, almond in color, @ $198.00 each.

Item 3—1 SoSharp electric pencil sharpener @ $39.95.

Add up the costs, add 10 percent of the total to the PO for shipping, and compute the total.

People *Connection*

Most people do not think of prisoners when they see a guide dog with a person who is blind. But since the "Puppies Behind Bars" program began, inmates in prisons across the United States have been responsible for nurturing and training puppies that become guide dogs for people who are blind, companions and helpers of people with various illnesses, and even bomb-sniffing dogs.

For 14 to 16 months, the inmates are responsible for feeding, cleaning, nurturing, and training the dogs 24 hours a day. Each night the puppies curl up in the prisoners' locked cells. The "puppy raisers" teach the dogs manners and obedience before the animals begin formal training. On weekends, volunteers take the pups to veterinarians and to their homes so the dogs experience things that are not common in prison, such as ringing phones, playful children, and busy streets.

The prisoners love the dogs, but many agree that giving the dogs constant, round-the-clock care is the hardest thing they've ever done—and they take great pride in doing it well.

Good Form Design

A business may have any number of forms that are used regularly—from dozens to hundreds. Some are on paper; some are processed on a computer. Some are well designed; some are poorly designed. If you have ever had trouble filling out a form, the problem may not have been with you. The form may have been poorly designed.

A poorly designed form not only wastes time, but also wastes money if several pages are used where one would suffice or if the wrong information results in confusion, mismanagement, missed appointments, or unpaid bills.

From everything that has been said in this chapter about forms, you can draw some conclusions. First, a well–designed form is easy to read and fill out. The wording is clear and appropriate for its intended audience and purpose. It has a pleasing balance of print and white space.

Good judgment is important in creating a form. Whether a question is to be answered by inserting words, circling numbers, or checking boxes depends on the question being asked. The final test of a good form, of course, is whether it is easy to fill out. Before printing and distributing a form, the form designer should have someone fill it out to see whether questions are clear and easy to answer.

Practice 8-7: Critiquing a Form

Look carefully at the locator sheet in Figure 8-9. This form is filled out by people as they come and go in an office so that the receptionist knows who is out, where they can be reached in case of an emergency, and when they can be expected to return.

Critique the locator sheet with a partner; list everything about it that is helpful or confusing and tell exactly what should be done to improve it. Hint: Use the responses of those who have filled out the form as clues to how you should modify it to make it more user-friendly. Then create a better version using the table or spreadsheet function in your computer software or a ruler, pencil, and lined paper.

Locator Sheet

Monday, April 12, 200-

Name	Time Out	Destination	Approx. Return	Ret'd (x)	Time Out	Destination	
Ambrose, Stu	7:30	Metro Mall	10:00	✓	12:30	Lunch	✓
Ceja, Phillipa	3:00	downtown	Tues				
Ciancio, Ben	12:15	Lunch	✓				
Czerny, Amy	8:15	Chamber of Comm	11:00	X	12:30	Lunch	✓
Hecht, Lamar	11:30	Lunch	12:30	✓	1:00	Tech Center	
Hickory, Dana	9:30	Convention	Ctr. Tues.				
Ichbonegun, N.	11:30	lunch	12:30	X			
Jain, Indira	9:40	warehouse	11:30	X	1:00	Tech Center till 4:00	
Kranz, Leo	10:30	Bell Insurance	1:30				
Montenegro, J.		ill-home	4/14				
Nugent, Jenna	1:00	errand	2:30				
Yamamoto, H.		vacation-	4-20				

FIGURE 8-9   A locator sheet

Summary

Forms are used at all levels in every business. They are used to get specific information quickly in a way that can be easily understood. Regardless of what you do or where you work, follow these guidelines concerning forms:

- Make sure you understand the purpose and meaning of any form you encounter.

- Fill out forms neatly and accurately.

- Design or redesign a usable form for a given purpose and audience if called upon to do so.

review and research activities visit
communicating.swlearning.com

Designing a Form

In an effort to improve quality, most businesses now use a customer satisfaction survey of some type. Sometimes the questions are read over the phone, and the answers the customer gives are marked on a form. Sometimes a questionnaire is simply given to a customer to fill out and send in or drop into a box on-site.

You have probably seen such a questionnaire in a local restaurant, automobile service center, or department store. Look at the Sample Project Plan for designing a customer satisfaction form and the sample form that was actually designed from that plan on page 271. Then plan and design a customer satisfaction form of your own.

1. Decide on a type of customer satisfaction form that could be used by a business (or a department within a business) in the career field of your choice.

2. Complete the Project Plan on *Student Workbook* page 8-J.

3. Have your teacher check your Project Plan.

4. Using the information in your Project Plan, complete the rough draft of the customer satisfaction form.

5. Using the Rough Draft column of the Project Guide on page 8-K of your *Student Workbook,* check your work. Then have another student check it.

6. Have your teacher check your rough draft.

7. Revise your rough draft, incorporating the changes that your classmates and your teacher suggested.

8. Using the Final Draft column of the Project Guide, proofread your work. Make any needed corrections.

9. Turn in the final draft along with the Project Guide.

Sample Project Plan

Plan for a Customer Satisfaction Form

SUBJECT	Sandy Isles Inn Restaurant	CONTENT
AUDIENCE	Adults—general audience	Introduction: note to customers
PURPOSE	**What actions should the audience take?** Write their responses on the form and mail it in.	Ask time of day and how often they come to the restaurant. Ask about 1) quality of food 2) opinion of the price 3) opinion of the service
FORMAT	☒ written ☐ oral ☐ other	Leave blank lines for other comments.
SOURCES	Look at forms from other restaurants to get ideas.	Thank the customers for filling it out. Remind them to mail it.
VISUALS	**What visuals, if any, will make the customer satisfaction form more effective?** At top of form, use font that matches restaurant logo.	

Sample Customer Satisfaction Form

Sandy Isles Inn Restaurant

To Our Valued Customers: Your opinion is important to us. Please take a moment and let us know how we are doing. Mark your responses on this card and drop it into a mailbox at your convenience.

Time of day (circle one):   a) noon to 5 p.m.   b) 5 p.m. to 8 p.m.   c) 8 p.m. to 11 p.m.

How often do you dine here at Sandy Isles?   a) at least once a week   c) 4 to 5 times a year

b) at least once a month   d) This is my first visit to Sandy Isles.

Please rate our food and service:

1. The food was ....a) excellent   b) acceptable   c) acceptable, but could be better
2. The food was ....a) an excellent value for the price   b) reasonably priced   c) overpriced
3. Our service was...a) prompt and courteous   b) too slow to suit me   c) a bit rushed

Let us know how we can better serve you.   _____

_____

_____

_____

Thank you for your time.   *The Management*

Overview

Garrison Keillor, born in Anoka, Minnesota, attended Anoka High School and the University of Minnesota. Since 1963, he has worked in radio. His radio stories have been collected on numerous cassettes and CDs, including *Lake Wobegon U.S.A.* He is the host of *A Prairie Home Companion* on National Public Radio. He lives in Wisconsin and New York.

Garrison Keillor's stories have a down-home flavor. They are well suited to an oral reading because of the colloquial language, conversational tone, and repetition. His stories also show a good sense of humor. "Easter" is not just a casual, rambling story, but relates a serious message about how adults affect children and how children affect adults.

"Easter" *from Leaving Home*

It has been a quiet week in Lake Wobegon. The children are back to school after a riotous week of Easter break. The weather was so lovely when the children were released from confinement, the fresh air went to their heads. Air has a different effect on children: what we merely breathe, children are ignited and launched by. At Our Lady on Sunday morning, Father Emil felt as if he was speaking to a convention of rabbits instead of the usual herd of turtles. Constant movement in the pews. The homily was on new life and it was all around to be seen.

© GETTY IMAGES/PHOTODISC, INC.

When I was a kid, we sat quietly on Sunday morning sometimes for forty or fifty seconds at a stretch. Fidgety kids were put between two grownups, usually your parents or sometimes a large aunt. Like tying a boat to a dock. Every time you moved they'd grab your shoulder and give you a sharp shake and hiss at you, *Sit*. Death will be like that. I'll be in bed and think, "Well, I think I'll get up and live a little," and death will grab me, shake me, say, "Shhh. Be quite. Lie still." I used to think about death on Sunday morning. How hard it would be to lie in your coffin for years with nothing to read, nothing to do, but some grownups I knew probably could manage quite well.

Some former children returned for Easter, bringing their children with them, and some children were shipped earlier to spend the week with grandparents, some of whom are starting to recover to the point where they can sit in a chair and sit back all the way, not lean forward ready to jump when they hear the crash. The grandparents imagined the kiddos leaning against them on the sofa listening to Uncle Wiggily: they forgot how explosive kids can be. Something in the air sets them off. A kid can go all day and hardly eat, then the moon shifts and he's eating like a farmhand. You served baked horse and he eats all of it. Children can lie around for a long time, then a herd of them bursts in the front door and gallops through the kitchen and outside. Children are always on the verge of bursting. They burst six, seven times a day and think nothing of it.

Virginia Ingqvist had two grandkids with her last week. Barbara's two oldest, Doug and Danielle. Hjalmar worked late at the bank. He loves them, but he knows his limit, and it's about thirty minutes. One is four and the other five, an age when you want to find out everything in one day. "Why don't buildings fall?" asked Doug two minutes after he arrived. "Because," Virginia explained, "because they're built to stand." "How?"

> *"Children are always on the verge of bursting."*

Thirty seconds, and already she was into architecture, and knew that biology and astronomy and physics were coming right up. Then theology. "Who's God?" "God is God." "Yeah, but who?" It's never a subject you know something about, such as etiquette.

Barbara came up on Friday with her two-year-old and took all three of them to her friend Ruthie's house to visit. Ruthie has three of her own. Her three and Barbara's three sniffed each other for a moment and then two cats made the mistake of coming around the corner of the house into the backyard. The cats realized it was a mistake and backed away, saying, Uh sorry, didn't know you were here. We'll come back later. But the kids grabbed them, hauled them indoors, got them dressed and into a doll buggy, two little cat children. The cats went limp, waiting for a chance to break out, which they did—two cats in full regalia, one up the tree, one on the garage roof, trying to remove their clothes, five children in pursuit, and the two-year-old investigating the back porch.

Barbara and Ruthie sat in the yard talking about child rearing. Barbara's philosophy is more relaxed than her mother's, less restrictive, a hands-off approach, allowing children freedom to explore and find their own boundaries. As she said this, she watched the little boy climb the porch steps, stand at the top, turn around, and

(cont'd on next page)

when he took a step forward straight out into space, she leaped up and made a dash for him, too late to catch him, but she almost stepped on his head. When she scooped him up, she came close to spraining his neck. A major cause of injury to children is parents rushing to the scene. The panic reflex. Some children love to scream for the thrill of making immense people move fast. I remember that, on a quiet day, my sister and I in the backyard wondered, "Where's Mom?" Upstairs, we thought. So I screamed, "MOM." She made it down in two seconds. A good pair of wheels for an old lady.

Grandma Tollefson turns off her hearing aid when descendants are around, so a crash is only a whisper to her, boys thundering around upstairs are a distant tapping. One afternoon a sound came out of her house like jets taking off, her grandson practicing his guitar. She was there, knitting, rocking, saying to him, "You know, there was a boy I knew who played the guitar—what was his name? Oh dear. He moved away in 1921, I think. He played his guitar on his porch, and I sat on our porch and listened. I don't think he knew. The screens were so dark, and I could hear him so clear, just like I can hear you. I was in love with him for a whole summer and he didn't know it." Kevin didn't hear a word she said, and she didn't know the music was blowing her hair back.

> *"A major cause of injury to children is parents rushing to the scene."*

Selective ignorance, a cornerstone of child rearing. You don't put kids under surveillance: it might frighten you. Parents should sit tall in the saddle and look upon their troops with a noble and benevolent and extremely nearsighted gaze.

The Buehler boy celebrated a birthday last night and ten of his closest friends came over for a party. They danced to alarming music and ate an alarming amount of pizza and told alarming jokes and there were periods of alarming dead silence, which the Buehlers heard from the kitchen, where they remained in quarantine. They whomped up armloads of chow, and passed it to their son, who carried it to his guests. Stayed in the kitchen for five hours, except for one trip to the bathroom, averting their eyes, and the mister snuck up front once to have a look, and when he looked he wished he hadn't. He was dying of curiosity. The party was so quiet and then burst into laughter, and then silence and then whispering and screams of laughter. He tiptoed down the hall and peeked and saw they were huddled over the Buehlers' wedding album. Nineteen fifty-nine was a funnier year than he had realized and he was a little hurt. He was quite handsome then in those half-rim glasses, his hair carefully oiled and combed back on the sides, like an ocean wave about to break, and piled high in front. He misses that pompadour. There's not much left where it rose from his head, a little tuft as a souvenir of what a stylish devil he used to be. He was hurt when he heard them laughing about his hair. He thought, "What are these people doing in my house? Why am I feeding them?"

Nothing you do for children is ever wasted. They seem not to notice us, hovering, averting our eyes, and they seldom offer thanks, but what we do for them is never wasted. We know that as we remember some gift given to us long ago. Suddenly it's 1951, I'm nine years old, in the bow of a green wooden rowboat, rocking on Lake Wobegon. It's five o'clock in the morning, dark; I'm shivering; mist comes up off the water, the smell of lake and weeds and Uncle Al's coffee as he puts a worm on my hook and whispers what to do when the big one bites. I lower my worm slowly into the dark water and brace my feet against the bow and wait for the immense fish to strike.

> *"Nothing you do for children is ever wasted."*

Thousands of gifts, continually returning to us. Uncle Al thought he was taking his nephew fishing, but he made a permanent work of art in my head, a dark morning in the mist, the coffee, the boat rocking, whispering, shivering, waiting for the big one. Still waiting. Still shivering.

—Garrison Keillor

Start-Up: Forms are utilized for many purposes.

Connection: Work with two classmates. Select one of the following topics mentioned in Keillor's story: school, weather, church, dying, child rearing, or fishing. Brainstorm a list of forms pertaining to this topic that are used to gather information; for example, a school needs children's birth certificates before the children can begin school.

Overview

Isaac Asimov (1920–1992), one of the most prolific writers of the 20th century, is best known for his science fiction, even though his works range from science fiction to mysteries to history to juvenile books. His works appear in books and magazines and on cassettes, CDs, videos, and DVDs. Also, many of his works have been made into movies and television shows.

In "Eyes Do More Than See," Isaac Asimov has projected life a trillion years forward. He says a lot about life in this short story. In an attempt to better humans, science seems to have created beings that have lost their humanity. The story implies a warning: If research continues in genetics (a branch of biology that studies the gene, the part of a cell that determines the inheritable characteristics of an organism), humans must make sure that they do not lose their humanity in the process.

"Eyes Do More Than See"

After hundreds of billions of years had passed, he suddenly thought of himself as Ames. Not the energy wavelengths that were now the equivalent of Ames—but of the body and of the sound waves of his name that he no longer heard and could no longer see.

His new idea for the contest had sharpened his memory for so many more of the old, old, eons-old things. He flattened the energy field that made up the total of himself, and its lines of force stretched into distance beyond the stars.

Brock's answering signal came.

> "He flattened the energy field that made up the total of himself . . . ."

Surely, Ames thought, he could tell Brock. Surely he could tell somebody.

Brock's shifting energy pattern adjusted to that of Ames, and communication began. "Aren't you coming for the contest?" communicated Brock.

"Of course."

"Will you take part?"

"Yes." Ames' lines of force pulsed with the answer. "Most certainly. I have thought of a whole new art form. Something really unusual."

"What a waste of effort," came Brock's reply. "How can you think of a new variation that has not been thought of in two hundred billion years? There can be nothing new."

For a moment Brock shifted out of phase and out of communication, so that Ames had to hurry to adjust his lines of force. He caught the drift of other thoughts as he did so—the view of galaxies against the velvet of nothingness and of endless ranks of energy beings drifting between the galaxies.

Ames said, "Please absorb my thoughts, Brock. Don't close out. I've thought of manipulating matter. Why bother with energy? There is nothing new in energy. How could there be?"

"Matter!" Ames interpreted Brock's energy vibrations as those of fear.

Ames said, "Why not? We were once matter ourselves back—back—a trillion years ago anyway. Why not create objects in the form of matter?" Ames was excited now. "Listen, Brock, why not build up an imitation of ourselves in matter, matter as we used to be?"

Brock replied, "I don't remember how that was. No one does."

"I do," said Ames with pulsing energy. "I've been thinking of nothing else, and I am beginning to remember. Brock, let me show you. Tell me if I'm right. Tell me."

"No! This is silly; it's . . . repulsive."

"Let me try, Brock. We've been friends; we've pulsed energy together from the beginning—from the moment that we became what we are. Brock, please!"

"Then quickly," Brock pulsed.

Ames had not felt such a tremor along his own line of force in—well, in how long? If he tried it now for Brock and it worked, he could dare manipulate matter for the contest. He could surprise the energy beings who had been waiting through so many endless reaches of time for something new. He could astound them; he could win the contest.

The matter was thin out there between the galaxies, but Ames gathered it. He scraped it together over the cubic light-years, choosing the atoms, achieving a claylike consistency, and forming matter into an oval form that spread out below.

"Don't you remember, Brock?" he asked softly. "Wasn't it something like this?"

Brock's energy field trembled. "Don't make me remember. I don't remember."

(cont'd on next page)

"That was the head. They—we—called it the head. I remember it so clearly. I want to say it, I mean the sound." Ames worried briefly, then said, "Look. Don't you remember that word, that sound?"

On the upper front of the oval appeared HEAD.

"What is that?" asked Brock.

"That's the word for head. The symbols that meant the word in sound. Tell me you remember, Brock!"

"There was something in the middle," said Brock hesitantly. "Something in the middle."

A vertical bulge formed.

Ames said, "Yes! Nose, that's it!" and NOSE appeared upon the form. "And those are eyes on either side." LEFT EYE—RIGHT EYE appeared on the form.

Ames regarded what he had made, his lines of force pulsing slowly. Was he sure he liked this?

"Mouth," he said with small quivers of his energy field, "and chin and Adam's apple and collarbone. Now the words come back to me."

These words appeared on the form.

"Don't make me remember." Ames said uncertainly, "What is wrong with remembering?"

Brock said, "I haven't thought of them for hundreds of billions of years. Why have you reminded me? Why?"

Ames was momentarily lost in his thoughts. "Something else. Something to hear with—something to pick up sound waves. Ears! Where do they go? I don't remember where to put them."

Brock cried out, "Leave it alone! Ears and all else! Don't make me remember." Ames said uncertainly, "What is wrong with remembering?"

"Because the outside wasn't rough and cold, as on your model, but smooth and warm. Because the eyes were tender and alive, and the lips of the mouth trembled and were soft." Brock's lines of energy glowed and wavered, glowed and wavered.

Ames said, "I'm sorry. I'm sorry."

"You're reminding me that once I was a woman and knew love, that eyes do more than see, and I have none to do it for me."

With violence Brock added matter to the rough-shaped head and said, "Then let them do it!" And Brock fled.

And Ames saw and remembered too—that once he had been a man. The force of his energy field split the head and he fled back across the galaxies on the energy track of

Brock—back to the unchanging forever always repetition of life.

And the eyes of the shattered head still glistened with moisture Brock had placed in them to represent tears. And the head of matter did what the energy beings could do no longer—it wept for their humanity and for the fragile beauty of the bodies they had given up a trillion years ago.

—Isaac Asimov

Start-Up: What makes you a unique person?

Carefully consider what it means to be human. Then, keeping the story in mind, make a list of what would be gained if people were to become bodiless (without form). Make a list of what they would lose. Use the chalkboard or a transparency on an overhead projector to list your gains and losses.

Connection: In periodicals, find pictures that best represent you in the following areas: work, school, home, achievements, and leisure and relaxation. Write these areas on construction paper; cut out the pictures and glue them beside the words. Also predict how the pictures may change in the next ten years. Present this information attractively. Give your work a title.

Working with Literature: Refer to *Student Workbook* page 8-L for an activity on using forms.

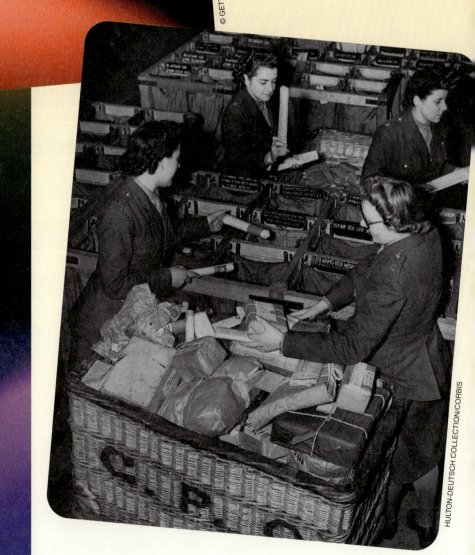

Chapter 9

© GETTY IMAGES/PHOTODISC, INC.

HULTON-DEUTSCH COLLECTION/CORBIS

"Consciously or unconsciously, every one of us does render some service or other. If we cultivate the habit of doing this service deliberately, our desire for service will steadily grow stronger, and we will make not only our own happiness, but that of the world at large."

—MAHATMA GANDHI,
INDIAN PEACE ACTIVIST

Communicating Messages

An old story about a New York City plumber goes something like this: It seems he had discovered that hydrochloric acid did a dandy job of cleaning out drains. Just to be on the safe side, he wrote the Bureau of Standards asking if he was doing any harm.

Since this practice was certainly harmful, the Bureau wrote back, "The efficacy of hydrochloric acid is indisputable, but the chlorine residue is incompatible with metallic permanence." The plumber replied with his thanks for their prompt approval. Concerned, the Bureau wrote to him again: "We cannot assume responsibility for the production of toxic and noxious residues with hydrochloric acid and suggest you use an alternative procedure."

The plumber wrote back declaring he was glad the Bureau agreed with him. Now alarmed about the safety of the New York City sewer system, the Bureau fired off, "Don't use hydrochloric acid; it eats the pipes!"

The plumber story illustrates why it's so important to study the audience and the purpose for any message before writing even one word. This chapter will help you to produce messages—notes, memos, e-mail messages, and letters—that get the results you want.

Most communication at work is conversation, either face-to-face or over the phone. But everyone has to write messages from time to time. Why? Some messages just work better when they are written rather than spoken. A list of reasons follows:

- If the message is complicated or important, writing it gives the writer a chance to plan, organize, and revise. In addition, the reader will have an easier time grasping the ideas, since he or she can stop reading to think or to reread some sections.

- People often hear what they want to hear. A written message is more likely to be understood accurately.

- A written message is a permanent, dated record of a request, a complaint, a compliment, or an announcement. Both you and your reader can keep a copy for later reference.

- Some people are too busy to take calls or are rarely near a phone. Some people screen their calls. A *written* message may reach them.

- Writing to a distant audience is cheaper than phoning.

- Written messages can save time when you need to communicate the same information to several people.

- If you are angry or upset, you may say something that you'll regret later. Writing gives you a chance to regain control of your emotions and, if necessary, edit and rewrite the message.

Most people receive more paperwork on the job than they can handle. When deciding how to get your message to your audience, ask yourself this question: Am I more likely to get what I want if I tell it or if I write it? Write only when you must.

by the way...

Words fly, writings remain.

LATIN PROVERB

Communicating with Customers

by the way...

Since, according to the CIA's The World Factbook, as many as 80 percent of companies are now service-oriented, interaction with customers is often more important than the actual product.

If your job is not valuable to either external or internal customers, you have a problem!

by the way...

"You can't promise your customers sunny weather, but you can promise to hold an umbrella over them when it rains."

Sign in a telephone service center

Most experienced communicators follow unwritten—and sometimes written—rules and conventions of correspondence. These rules make it easy for their readers to understand messages quickly and accurately and to react appropriately. It helps to think of many of your readers as *customers. Customer* means more than a person who buys goods or services from you. A **customer** is anyone who depends on or benefits from the work you do—or suffers when your work is done poorly or not done at all. Customers are also people you want something from. You want **external customers** to buy your organization's goods or services. You also want your boss's approval, and you want your coworkers to do their jobs. Bosses and coworkers are **internal customers**. Everyone *has* a customer, and everyone *is* a customer.

Since everyone has customers, everyone is involved with customer service—answering questions; solving problems; fixing what's broken; making it happen *now*; and doing all of these things with courtesy, reliability, and competence. Your customers want what they want, and they want it now. Not only that, but they want to feel good about it. It's a tall order, but one that everyone in your organization must understand. If the employees don't understand customer service, your organization will lose business to competitors that do. And if you don't understand your own role in customer service, your internal customers may decide to replace you with someone who does. Improving your written communication with your customers—both external and internal—is a good start.

Career *Connection*

To external customers, *you* are the company. Whether their feelings about the organization are good or bad relates directly to their experience with you. Is that fair? No. Especially since so many things that you have no control over can go wrong. But fair has nothing to do with it. Texas A&M researcher Dr. Leonard Berry says customer service boils down to these five factors:

- Reliability   Keeping promises accurately and dependably
- Responsiveness   Helping customers promptly and willingly
- Assurance   Demonstrating knowledge of your job
- Empathy   Being sensitive to customers' needs and showing them individual attention
- Tangibles   Keeping yourself and your work area clean, attractive, and organized

Practice 9–1: Identifying Customers

1. In a team of two or three, brainstorm to identify one external customer and one internal customer for people with the following job titles:

   a. Medical lab technician
   b. School secretary
   c. Movie set designer
   d. Emergency vehicle driver
   e. Police officer
   f. Hotel assistant manager
   g. 911 dispatcher
   h. Writer of newspaper classified ads
   i. Horse trainer
   j. Car designer

2. Give a job title related to your area of occupational study. Identify three customers for that job. The customers may be internal or external.

3. What kinds of information would individuals holding the job title in Item 2 need to communicate with their internal and external customers?

Purposes for Messages

You can group written messages—correspondence—according to purpose. Most messages fall into one of these five groups:

- Messages that *express*
- Messages that *inform*

- Messages that *request*
- Messages that *instruct*
- Messages that *persuade*

Some messages have more than one purpose. For instance, a message may instruct employees on how to fill out the new insurance forms; it may also try to persuade them to complete the forms by the end of the week. Still, the writer needs to focus on the primary purpose.

```
65 Kenny Drive
Seattle, WA 98105-1105
February 12, 200-

Attention Manager
Roger's
443 East Halsey Road
Seattle, WA 98104-2847

Ladies and Gentlemen:

Just a quick note to compliment one of your employees.

Yesterday afternoon I was fifth in line in the express checkout line
with four people behind me. There was a problem with the register,
and the line had not moved for several minutes. Your employee
Tony noticed and opened another register. It's not what he did, but
how he did it, that deserves praise.

As I saw him approach the register, I got ready for the mad dash to
the new register. Usually what happens is the last person in line,
the person who has been waiting the least amount of time, is first
in the new line. Not this time. Instead of announcing, "Register 9 is
open," Tony looked the person who'd been waiting longest right in
the eye and said, "I believe you're next."

If this technique is store policy, congratulations to you all. If Tony
came up with this technique on his own, he deserves special recog-
nition. I hope all of the cashiers in your store follow his example.
Keep up the good work!

Sincerely,


Emila Del Gesso

Mrs. Emila Del Gesso
```

FIGURE 9-1   Personal-business letter in block format

The following table lists purposes and suggested content of messages. These guidelines are only suggestions. The situation and the audience will influence the information to include in any message. Examples of these types of messages are shown throughout this chapter.

CONTENT OF WRITTEN MESSAGES

Purpose	Suggested Content
To Express	Purpose of the message
	Reference to the occasion
	Personal sentiment
To Inform	Purpose of the message
	Explanation of the situation (Who? What? Where? When? How? Why?)
	Conclusion, recommendation, and/or action statement
	Polite ending
To Request	Purpose of the message
	Background information
	Details that will enable the reader to respond (Who? What? Where? When? How? Why?)
	Action statement
	Polite ending
To Instruct	Purpose of the message
	Reasons why the reader should follow the instructions
	List of steps, including what to do and how to do it
	Polite ending
To Persuade	The content of persuasive messages is explained in Chapters 10 and 11.

Practice 9–2: Purposes for Messages

1. Make a list of all of the figure numbers for the 12 sample messages (including the Sample Letter for the chapter Project) shown in this chapter. (Since the Sample Letter does not have a figure number, list it as "Sample Letter.") Beside each figure number, write the primary purpose of the message. If the message has a secondary purpose, list it as well.

2. Why do you think the writers of the messages shown in Figures 9-1, 9-2, and 9-5 wrote their messages instead of making phone calls?

3. Examine several pieces of junk mail. Categorize them by purpose, including secondary purpose.

Qualities of Effective Messages

A written message communicates a great deal about its writer to both internal and external customers. If your writing is careless, inefficient, and incompetent, the reader will assume that your work is also careless, inefficient, and incompetent. Since you represent your organization, the reader of your message will suspect that the organization is careless, inefficient, and incompetent.

Kimura & Kimura

April 7, 200-

Mr. Reed Beauchamp
Department B
Molloy Industries
8557 Dexter Avenue
Raleigh, NC 27612-0001

Dear Mr. Beauchamp

I am concerned about a situation that has developed because of your delivery procedures.

Last week the following events occurred: We placed an order on April 1 for 300 large furgetts and were promised delivery by noon the next day. When the order did not arrive by 1 p.m., I called your warehouse and was told the shipment would be here within an hour. I called again at 3 p.m. Your employee Brad would not give me any specific information about the order. He also refused to give me the name of his supervisor. In fact, he hung up when I asked.

The order arrived three days later. We refused delivery since by that time, we had placed an order with one of your competitors. It was filled immediately.

I hope this problem was an isolated incident. Can you promise that similar situations will not happen in the future? We would like to continue our long-standing relationship with Molloy Industries.

Sincerely

Kijiro Kimura

Kijiro Kimura
Production Manager

14 East Shore Parkway
Zebulon, North Carolina 27597-9889
Phone 919-555-0111
Fax 919-555-0114
KIMURAB@TNET.COM

FIGURE 9-2 Business letter in modified block format printed on letterhead stationery

Your employer does not pay you to project a poor image to customers. Since a successful business often depends on its image, communication that broadcasts a negative impression could cost you your job. The clarity, tone, economy, and courtesy of your written messages are parts of that image.

A Clear Purpose

Before you begin writing, decide exactly what you want your reader to do. It is surprising how many otherwise correct messages never get around to the point. The writer either assumes that the reader will figure it out or fails to decide on the purpose before writing. The reader's reaction is "So what?"

Suppose you write to the manager of a printing company to complain that the order forms that were printed included incorrect prices. If you explain the problem but do not tell the manager how you want him or her to correct it, your letter will not be effective. Decide what your purpose is; then state it directly in the first or second sentence.

An Appropriate Tone

Most people wear different styles of clothing for different occasions. You would not wear the same outfit to work out at the gym, to work in an office, and to attend a wedding. Style in clothing is like tone in writing. The **tone** of correspondence ranges from casual to formal and depends on the situation, the message's purpose, and the relationship between the writer and the reader. Today very formal writing is usually limited to messages such as engraved invitations. Most writing at work is less formal and often conversational.

Write to an audience the way you would speak to them. Would you talk to the president of the United States the same way you would talk to your Aunt Maggie? Overly stiff and formal language is as inappropriate as language that is too casual. Pretend the person you're writing to is seated beside you. How would you speak to that person? Write the way you would speak, only with more precision.

Appropriate attire depends on the situation.

© CORBIS

Put You *Before* I

People read all messages looking for "what's in it for me." They are more interested in themselves than they are in your problems, your successes, and your concerns. They want to know how your message will help *them*. Notice in these two examples how the *I* attitude was changed to a *you* attitude:

Rough Draft	Revision
I want to thank you for asking about our new service plan. I am enclosing a pamphlet that details the benefits of our new plan. I would very much like to enroll you within the next 30 days since we are offering a special low rate as our introductory offer.	Thank you for asking about our new service plan. You'll find that the enclosed pamphlet outlines the benefits of the plan. If you sign up within the next 30 days, you'll be able to take advantage of a special low rate we're offering to you on an introductory basis. Thank you.

Be Positive

Even if you feel angry or frustrated, maintain a respectful, friendly tone. You can be firm without resorting to sarcasm or hostility. If your letter has a positive tone, you'll find that your reader is more willing to do what you want. Even negative messages can be stated with a positive tone. In the following examples, the messages have been revised to make them more positive and customer-oriented. The first example shows how using the passive voice can make a negative statement more impersonal.

Rough Draft	Revision
You did not send your application before the deadline.	Your application was received after the deadline.
You sent the wrong form.	We received Form A but need Form B to complete the sale.
If you have any problems, please call me.	If you have any questions, please call me.
We cannot pay this bill in one lump sum as you requested.	We can clear up the balance in six months by paying you in monthly installments of $150.

Use "Thank You" and "I'm Sorry"

Give sincere thanks to internal and external customers whenever they:

- Do business with you.
- Compliment you.
- Are patient with you.
- Offer comments or suggestions.
- Help you to serve them better.
- Make you smile.

With practice, thanking people can become a habit. Apologizing when something goes wrong can be more difficult because you often equate apologizing with admitting failure or blame. But to your customers, an apology means that you understand things are not going right for them at that time. Don't wait and don't try to shift responsibility or find fault— even if your customer is the one who goofed. Give a simple apology, fix the problem, and then let the customer know what you've done.

Rough Draft	Revision
If those guys in maintenance were doing their job, this wouldn't have happened.	I'm sorry you are experiencing a problem.
Since you failed to state what size you want, we won't be able to send your uniforms.	Thank you for your order. You'll receive your uniforms within three days after you send us your size on the enclosed form.

Practice 9–3: Improving the Tone of Messages

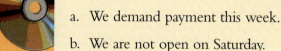

Ch09–03.doc

1. Revise the following messages to make them more conversational.

   a. Your efforts are most certainly appreciated.

   b. Please do not hesitate to contact me if you have any questions.

2. Revise the following negative messages to make them more positive.

   a. We demand payment this week.

   b. We are not open on Saturday.

3. Revise these sentences to make them more *you*-oriented.

   a. I will fax the price list immediately.

   b. We offer superior service to our customers.

4. Revise the following message to improve its tone.

Your desk is always messy. I find that I feel extremely embarrassed when visitors enter our area and, immediately upon entering, see this mess. Clean it up today. I don't want to have to tell you again.

enfant Incorporated

3444 Commodity Circle
Plummer's Landing, KY 41081-0438
606/555-0147

June 6, 200-

Ms. Marguarite Akermann
Production Supervisor
Finneyton Technologies Company
P.O. Box 12844
Tampa, FL 33647-2473

Dear Ms. Akerman

FAX BOARD UPGRADE

The six fax boards that we shipped to you on May 25 (Invoice 4112) were equipped with the wrong memory chips. The new boards are being shipped to you by Express Delivery today.

I am sorry that this problem occurred. A small change in the subcontractor's upgrade assembly schedule created the difficulty. Unfortunately, several dozen boards were shipped before the problem was discovered.

I hope this has not caused any production delays for you, and I thank you for your understanding. We will keep you informed about future upgrades.

Sincerely yours

Gary Eder

Gary Eder
Quality Control Manager

Enclosure

c R. Vallejos

FIGURE 9-3 Business letter in block format printed on letterhead stationery

Economical but Polite

At work, most people don't have time to read everything they are given to read. Make sure that your message is one that will be read immediately. An economical message is more likely to be read than one that is not economical. To respect your reader's time and patience, get right to the point, stick to the point, and then end it. Limit sentences to 20 words and paragraphs to 5 lines.

BLOFFERS INC.
256 Camino Diablo
Los Angeles, California 90066-2023

Fax Cover Sheet

DATE: March 10, 200-   **TIME:** 3:07 PM

TO: Joe Beasley   **PHONE:** 216-555-0142
         Bigg Company   **FAX:** 216-555-0144

FROM: Walter Witherspoon   **PHONE:** 310-555-0194
           Bloffers Incorporated   **FAX:** 310-555-0190

RE: Copy of Invoice 873943

Number of pages including cover sheet: 2

Message

This will acknowledge receipt of your request dated March 5, 200-, in which you requested us to send you a copy of our invoice dated January 23, 200-, No. 873943, for three dozen yellow-striped bloffers in the amount of $954.43 plus $57.00 tax, totaling $1,011.43.

We are pleased to comply with your request. Please find attached a photostatic copy of the above-mentioned invoice, indicating the merchandise ordered and the total amount charged.

We trust that the copy of this invoice will be self-explanatory and hope that this matter is now settled to your satisfaction. I am thanking you in advance for your cooperation. Please do not hesitate to call me at the number given above if you have any questions at all.

FIGURE 9-4   A wordy fax cover sheet

Economical writing is brief and concise. Spend your words as if they were dollars; don't spend them on unnecessary information. Remember that sentences written in the active rather than the passive voice are more concise. In addition, active-voice sentences more strongly convey most ideas.

Rough Draft	Revision
The instruments were sterilized by Julia.	Julia sterilized the instruments.
I want to take this opportunity to tell you that we appreciate your cooperating together with us on the project.	Thank you for helping us on the project.

Even an economical message, though, has room for good manners. Do not sacrifice politeness for brevity.

Rough Draft	Revision
I must have your signature immediately on the purchase order for the new mixer. I intend to take no further action until I hear from you.	The purchase order for the new mixer is ready for your signature. Please sign it and send it back to me so that I can send it to Miss Reho for final approval.

Clear, Precise Language

As in other forms of writing, clarity and precision are essential in writing messages. Choose your words and construct your sentences and paragraphs carefully so that they communicate your message without confusing the reader. Notice how little exact, usable information is included in the rough draft below.

Rough Draft	Revision
One of our customers called to complain about poor service in your department when she had to wait a long time for someone to do a simple repair that should have taken a short time.	Our customer Carmen Ruiz called to complain because on October 30, she waited for two hours while Mike Whitesell repaired a broken hinge on her glasses. This simple repair ordinarily takes 15 minutes.

Familiar Language

Use language that is familiar to your reader. Every field has its own jargon, specialized technical language. Avoid technical jargon unless you are positive your reader will understand it. Also avoid using foreign phrases. In the classic style manual *The Elements of Style,* William Strunk, Jr., wrote, "The writer will often find it convenient or necessary to borrow from other languages. Some writers, however, from sheer exuberance or a desire to show off, sprinkle their work liberally with foreign expressions, with no regard for the reader's comfort. It is a bad habit. Write in English." Still, since some foreign expressions are commonly used, you should become familiar with them.

Rough Draft	Revision
A myocardial infarction is contraindicated.	You didn't have a heart attack.
Kerning will improve the appearance of your headings.	Adjusting the spacing between characters will improve the appearance of your headings.
Your contract specifies $200 per diem.	Your contract specifies $200 each day.

Style

It is important to learn the accepted rules of correspondence. A person who regularly reads business correspondence will think there is something odd about you if you do not use these styles. You may not be taken seriously, for instance, if you write your letters in pencil on notebook paper.

Over the years, your teachers have endlessly coached you in correct capitalization, spelling, punctuation, and grammar. Now is your chance to put that learning into practice. Accuracy in numbers and correctly spelled names are especially important. Check the spelling of the reader's name twice, as most people are sensitive about their name. Although it may seem unfair, other people will judge you based on the correctness of your writing. Since you want to be taken seriously, take the time and effort to use what you know.

Practice 9–4: Revising Ineffective Messages

Ch09-04.doc

1. Each of the following sentences lacks at least one quality of an effective message. Revise the sentences to improve their tone and to make them more economical, polite, and precise.

   a. Many people attended the demonstration.

   b. We regret to tell you that there will be a short delay in processing your forms.

   c. It was suggested that the deadline be extended.

   d. The new manuals will be available to each and every technician by the month of August.

   e. I know you're the boss, but what's your problem anyway?

2. The fax cover sheet shown in Figure 9-4 on page 292 is wordy. Revise it to make it more economical and conversational. Use no more than two sentences.

3. The writer of the memo shown in Figure 9-5 was angry when he wrote his rough draft. Not only did someone's careless behavior cause the theft of sensitive information, but now the company must pay for new ID cards and increased security. Write what you imagine Brandon's angry, negative first draft said.

4. Write the first paragraph of a letter answering the letter from Kijiro Kimura shown in Figure 9-2 on page 287.

5. Complete *Student Workbook* page 9-A to gain knowledge of some commonly used foreign phrases.

Memorandum

TO: All Employees

FROM: Brandon Tigner

DATE: August 15, 200-

SUBJECT: NEW ID CARDS

What is this message about?

Please call the personnel office (Ext. 778) this week to make an appointment to get a new ID card.

What are the facts, and what do they mean?

Last week someone obtained copies of confidential information after gaining entrance to what we thought was our secure research center. Therefore, we are issuing new cards and tightening security. The new ID cards are specially coded so only authorized persons will be able to enter our high-security areas.

What do we do now?

We rely on you to safeguard your card. Since we pride ourselves on our state-of-the-art systems, we must keep them secure at all times.

FIGURE 9-5 A memo with an effective message

Content of Effective Messages

Except for the simplest messages, an effective message has three parts that answer the following questions:

- What is this message about?
- What are the facts, and what do they mean?
- What do we do now?

What Is This Message About?

This introductory section lets the reader know what the message is about and, perhaps, who you are. It should make the reader want to read the rest of the message. Getting to the point quickly is one of the best ways to get the reader's attention.

Mention the most important point—the purpose of your message—in this first brief section. Even messages that are read are not always read to the very end. If the most important point appears at the end of the page or, even worse, on the second page, the reader may never see it.

What Are the Facts, and What Do They Mean?

This section gives the reader enough information to make the decision, grant the request, or solve the problem. It must be concise, clear, and well organized. For easy reading, put important points or details into lists rather than paragraphs.

What Do We Do Now?

Don't fight. Make it right.

HARDEE'S COMPLAINT-HANDLING POLICY

Many written messages are action-oriented. The action statement tells the reader what to do and when to do it. Or it may explain what the writer intends to do. State the action clearly and directly. You'll find that making polite requests is more effective than making demands. It is often appropriate to close with a polite ending, such as "Thank you."

Sending Notes

Notes are informal personal messages. Writing the note by hand gives your message a personal touch. Notes may or may not be mailed. A typical format for a personal note is shown in Figure 9-6. Sending thank-you notes to people who go out of their way to help you is like sending an unexpected gift. Also send notes to congratulate customers and coworkers on promotions, achievements, and special occasions in their professional and personal lives. The few minutes it takes to write these simple messages are well worth the time. Your associates will appreciate your thoughtfulness.

JJ

Date ——————————————————————— *November 10, 200-*

Salutation ——————————————— *Dear Herb,*

Body ——————————————— *I just heard the good news about your promotion. Congratulations!*
I can't say that I'm surprised. I think your hard work is largely responsible for this year's decrease in defective parts.
Nice job!

Complimentary close——————————————— *Sincerely,*

Signature ——————————————— *Jocelynne*

FIGURE 9-6 A handwritten note

Writing notes by hand gives messages a personal touch.

Practice 9–5: Sending a Note

Write a note to any staff member at your school, expressing thanks for some recent help or advice. Your note doesn't have to be long, but it should be sincere. Be specific about why you're thanking the reader. Use blue or black ink and unlined paper. Follow these guidelines:

- Include only the date, salutation, body, complimentary close, and signature.

- Place the date, complimentary close, and signature beginning near the center of the page.

- Indent paragraphs.

Figure 9-6 is an example of a personal note. Refer to Figure 9–11 on page 305 to see a thank-you letter.

Sending Memos

Memorandums, commonly called **memos**, are messages written to people within the organization and do not usually go through the United States Postal Service. The memo, the most common form of written communication at work, is easy to draft. Memos consist of two main sections: a heading and a message. Memos may include some of the same optional parts as business letters. These parts are discussed later in this chapter.

There is no one correct format for memos. Many organizations have their own preferences. If your employer does not, use a 2" top margin, default (1.25") or 1" side margins or default, and about a 1" bottom margin.

The Heading

The heading of the memo has four parts, each with a **guide word**:

TO:	The name of the reader (or readers), sometimes followed by a comma and the person's title
FROM:	The name of the writer (or writers), sometimes followed by a comma and the person's title
DATE:	The date on which the memo was written
SUBJECT:	A brief description of the content of the memo, keyed in all capital letters. Instead of *SUBJECT*, you may also see *REFERENCE* or *RE*.

Sometimes the memo includes a **copy notation**, *c* (meaning "copy"), followed by names of other people who received copies of the memo. The memo shown in Figure 9-7 has a copy notation. It is placed two lines below the body of the memo.

Follow each guide word with a colon (:). You may see different placement of these four items. Following the examples in this chapter will ensure correct formatting. Some organizations use memo forms. All you have to do on these preprinted forms is fill in the heading information and write the message, as shown in Figure 9-8 on page 301. Many word processing programs include predesigned memo templates.

The Subject Line

An informative **subject line** serves the same purpose as the headline of a newspaper story: It gives exact information about the subject and motivates the audience to read on. It not only answers the question

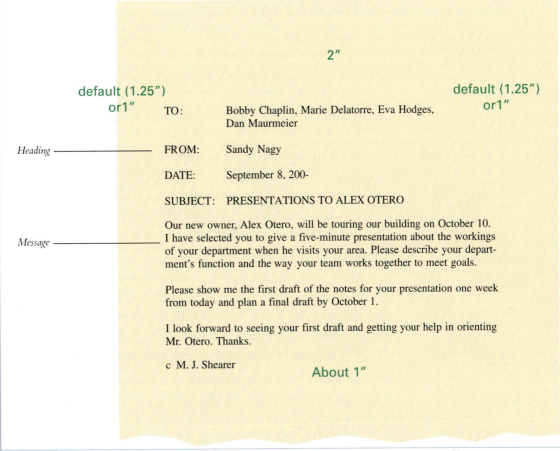

default (1.25")
or 1"

2"

default (1.25")
or 1"

Heading

TO: Bobby Chaplin, Marie Delatorre, Eva Hodges,
           Dan Maurmeier

FROM: Sandy Nagy

DATE: September 8, 200-

SUBJECT: PRESENTATIONS TO ALEX OTERO

Message

Our new owner, Alex Otero, will be touring our building on October 10. I have selected you to give a five-minute presentation about the workings of your department when he visits your area. Please describe your department's function and the way your team works together to meet goals.

Please show me the first draft of the notes for your presentation one week from today and plan a final draft by October 1.

I look forward to seeing your first draft and getting your help in orienting Mr. Otero. Thanks.

c M. J. Shearer

About 1"

FIGURE 9-7   The two main sections of a memo

"What is this about?"; it also answers the question "So what?" Notice how the following revised subject lines answer those questions.

Rough Draft	Revision
RE: RATS	RE: RATS SIGHTED IN DUMPSTER AREA
SUBJECT: MILEAGE REIMBURSEMENT	SUBJECT: PROCEDURE FOR SUBMITTING MILEAGE REIMBURSEMENT REQUESTS
REFERENCE: WIDGET SHIPMENT	REFERENCE: WIDGET SHIPMENT, INVOICE 34322, DATED 3/12/--

Try to keep subject lines to ten or fewer words.

The Message

Memos solve problems either by giving the reader new information or by persuading the reader to take an action. Since the writer and the reader of the memo are usually coworkers, the reader probably already knows something about the subject of the memo. Background information and explanations are often unnecessary. *Don't tell readers what they already know.*

Most memos are brief, perhaps only one paragraph long; others are longer. Include informative internal headings for long memos. Paragraphs in memos do not always follow the traditional "topic sentence, body, concluding sentence" structure. A shortened form is acceptable as long as the reader can understand the memo's meaning.

Each memo should deal with only one subject. If the memo includes more than one subject, the reader may take action on part of the memo and overlook the other parts. Furthermore, the reader may not be the person who will act to solve the problem or fulfill the request. If a memo includes two subjects, the reader may need to pass it along to two people. If you have two messages, write two brief memos.

Of course, more than one person may need to read your memo. Then your heading will read like the following:

TO: Phil and Nancy
or
TO: All Supervisors

Send Phil and Nancy or all supervisors copies of the memo.

Practice 9–6: Sending and Answering Memos

1. Write a memo to your boss, requesting permission to leave work two hours early one day next week. Include all of the facts your boss will need to make a decision.

2. Answer another student's memo. Give him or her permission to leave early.

3. Answer a second memo with a no. Give a good reason for your refusal and a positive alternative.

4. Read the letter shown in Figure 9-12 on page 310. Write a memo from Mr. Bridges to Keith to find out how the phone call to TriCom Ltd. went.

INTEROFFICE MEMO

To: All Staff   DATE: April 12, 200-

From: Penny

Subject: E-MAIL PROCEDURES

We finally have the bugs worked out of the new e-mail system. I apologize for the delay and thank you for your patience. I think the features of EEZ-Mail make it worth the wait. Please follow these guidelines so we can get the most out of this system:

- Check for messages at the start of your shift, before or after lunch, and at the end of your shift.
- Avoid sending junk mail.
- Check with senders before forwarding their message to someone else. It's common courtesy.
- Since messages take up disk space, regularly delete files you no longer need. Be aware, though, that deleted
- Although we do not regularly read messages, you can't consider them private. Do not send confidential information by email.

Please e-mail me if you have any questions. My e-mail user name is *doergerp*.

FIGURE 9-8 A memo to multiple readers

Sending Electronic Mail

Electronic mail, better known as **e-mail**, is communication technology that allows people to send memos from their computers directly to computers in the same building or at locations tens of thousands of miles away. According to the Electronic Messaging Association, by 2003, 40 billion e-mail messages were sent per day by over 600 million users. The United States Postal Service reports delivering 553 million messages per day during the same year.

E-mail combines the efficiency and low cost of memos with the speed and conversational nature of phone calls, but without the problem of telephone tag. You can also send and receive messages 24 hours a day, 365 days a year, and your readers can respond to your messages instantly. You can easily send one message to several people, and they can just as easily reply to, print, edit, file, and forward your message. E-mail is the fastest way to send short messages.

Most e-mail messages are brief and casual. Electronic-mail software provides a memo format for composing messages, with boxes to fill in the name and/or e-mail address of each recipient, a subject line, the names and e-mail addresses of any people who should receive copies of the message, and the message, as shown in Figure 9-9. Informative, specific subject lines are very important to readers who receive a lot of e-mail messages. The subject line can let them know whether the message is important or useful enough to be dealt with—or deleted— right away.

The qualities and parts of effective messages discussed earlier in this chapter also apply to writing e-mail messages. Some additional guidelines follow:

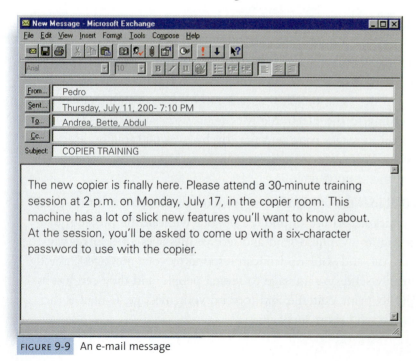

FIGURE 9-9 An e-mail message

- Keep paragraphs short, only a few sentences each. Otherwise, your reader might lose his or her train of thought while scrolling through long paragraphs.

- Keep messages to one screen—about 25 lines.

- DO NOT USE ALL CAPITAL LETTERS IN YOUR MESSAGE. DOING SO MAY SAVE YOU A FEW KEYSTROKES, BUT USING ALL CAPITAL LETTERS IS HARD TO READ.

- When responding to a message, include enough information in your message so that your reader knows what it's about. If your coworker sends the message "Where do you want to go for lunch today?" and two hours later you reply "I don't care," your reader will probably be perplexed. Instead, write "I don't care where we go to lunch today."

- Don't send someone a message just because you can. Wasting coworkers' time with unnecessary messages is inconsiderate.

- Don't use e-mail to send bad news or criticism. Sending a "You're fired" e-mail message would be in very bad taste.

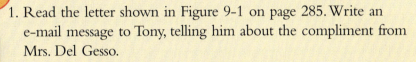

Practice 9-7: Sending E-mail

1. Read the letter shown in Figure 9-1 on page 285. Write an e-mail message to Tony, telling him about the compliment from Mrs. Del Gesso.

2. Read the message shown in Figure 9-9 on page 302. Send an e-mail message to Pedro, explaining that you cannot attend the training session. What information will Pedro need from you?

Sending Business Letters

Business letters are written messages mailed to people who are outside the organization. If you read ten books on business letter writing, you will probably see ten correct—but different—ways to draft business letters. Not only that, but many organizations have their own preferences. Although this section will not attempt to show you all variations, it will give you enough information and practice so that you can set up an effective letter.

The experts do agree on a few requirements. Keep the following general guidelines in mind:

- Key your business letters. You may write personal notes and quick memos by hand, but key letters. Use plain 8 1/2- by 11-inch paper. Most people prefer white paper, but the color can also be off-white, beige, or light gray. Print the letter, using a quality printer.

- Use **letterhead** stationery from your organization if it's available. The company name and address (and perhaps phone numbers and company logo) are preprinted on the paper. The letter shown in Figure 9-2 on page 287 was printed on letterhead stationery. Do not use your employer's letterhead for letters relating to personal business.

- Balance the letter attractively on the page. Use default (1.25") or 1" side margins. You may center the letter vertically, using your

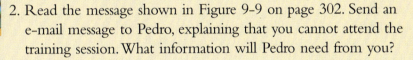
Electronic mail replaces most paper memos in some organizations.

software program's automatic centering feature or use a top margin of 2" and a bottom margin of at least 1".

- Text in the body of a letter should be left-aligned.
- Use easy-to-read 11- or 12-point typefaces.
- Most business letters are no longer than one page. If the letter is longer, try to shorten it as you revise. If additional pages are necessary, use plain paper, not letterhead, for them. List the name of the addressee, the page number, and the date in the upper left corner. Follow with a double space (DS) and at least two lines of the body. Never place just the closing and signature block on the second page. (See Figure 9-10.)

1"

Addressee's Name
Page X
Date

DS

Use this heading style for all subsequent pages of letters or memorandums that exceed one page. Note that the top margin is 1". The rest of the margins are the same as those used on the first page.

FIGURE 9-10   Heading for the second page of a letter

Practice 9–8: Standard Business Letter Parts

As you read pages 304–309, complete the form on *Student Workbook* page 9-B with facts about the standard parts of business letters. Look also at the sample letter in Figure 9-11. When you are finished, you'll have a reference sheet to use the next time you write a letter.

Standard Parts of Business Letters

Most business-letter styles include a heading, date, inside address, salutation, body, complimentary close, and signature block. The letter in block format in Figure 9-11 shows placement of the letter parts on the page. Since many acceptable variations of the seven standard letter parts exist, learn whatever style your employer prefers. This chapter describes the most common styles. Refer to Figure 9-11 as you read the descriptions of the standard letter parts.

default (1.25")
or 1"

Center vertically or 2"

default (1.25")
or 1"

Heading —————— VanTech Productions
578 Enterprise Drive
Ann Arbor, MI 48103-9126
Date —————— May 31, 200-

DS

Inside address —————— Ms. Susan Weitsle
Staff Assistant
TC Design
988 Midland Boulevard
Chelsea, MI 48118-0202

DS

Salutation —————— Dear Ms. Weitsle:

DS

Thank you so much for your quick response last week. It's a pleasure to encounter good customer service and friendly, motivated employees.

DS

Body —————— We needed several reams of paper immediately, and the order was filled without delay. I know you usually require a full week to fill an order, and we appreciate your making an exception for us.

You can count on us for many future orders. We're all looking forward to a long and satisfying relationship.

DS

Complimentary close —————— Sincerely,

QS *Courtney Bryant*

Signature block —————— Ms. Courtney Bryant
Office Manager

At least 1"

FIGURE 9-11 Placement of the seven standard parts of business letters

The Heading

The **heading** of a letter is like the return address of an envelope. It gives the mailing address of the writer. Spell out the name of the city and words such as *Street* and *Avenue*, but use standard two-letter abbreviations for states. Separate city and state with a comma. Key the ZIP Code one space after the state. The writer's name is not part of the heading; it belongs at the end of the letter.

Examples:

VanTech Productions	578 Enterprise Drive
578 Enterprise Drive	Ann Arbor, MI 48103-9126
Ann Arbor, MI 48103-9126	

Do not use a heading if you are using letterhead stationery.

The Date

The **date** is when the letter was written. Do not abbreviate the month. Separate the day and the year with a comma. Key the date immediately below the heading. If you are using letterhead, key the date at the top margin.

Example:

May 31, 200-

The Inside Address

The **inside address** gives the full mailing address of the reader. Your letter will be more likely to reach the right person if you include all of the information that you have, such as name, title, department, and company name. The information in the inside address is the same as that in the mailing address on the envelope. Do not abbreviate except for the state name. Separate the city and state with a comma. Separate the state and the ZIP Code with one space.

When writing to someone with a professional title, such as *Dr.,* use that title. For other people, use a **courtesy title** (*Miss, Ms., Mrs.,* or *Mr.*). When writing to a woman, use the courtesy title she prefers. If you do not know what she prefers, use *Ms.* If you aren't sure what title to use (for instance, if the person's name could be a man's or a woman's) and cannot find out with reasonable effort, use the first and last name with no title. A job title, such as *Staff Assistant,* can appear on the same line as the person's name (separated from the name by a comma) or on the following line.

Key the inside address four lines below the date at the left margin. You may reduce this space to two lines for longer letters to avoid using a second page.

Examples:

Ms. Susan Weitsle	Name of Person, Title
Staff Assistant	Name of Department
TC Design	Name of Organization
988 Midland Boulevard	Street Address
Chelsea, MI 48118-0202	City, State ZIP Code

The Salutation

The **salutation** is sometimes called the greeting. The first name is not included, just the courtesy or professional title and the last name. (If you are on a first-name basis with the person to whom you are writing, however, address that person by first name.) The salutation appears two lines below the inside address.

Two different punctuation styles can be used in the salutation and closing of letters. **Open punctuation** has no punctuation after the salutation and closing. **Mixed punctuation** includes a colon after the salutation and a comma after the complimentary close.

The following table shows how the correct salutation depends on the information in the first line of the inside address.

SALUTATION AND INSIDE ADDRESS

Name and Title Known	Title, but Not Name, Known	Name and Title Unknown
Ms. Susan Weitsle Staff Assistant TC Design 988 Midland Boulevard Chelsea, MI 48118-0202	Attention Staff Assistant TC Design 988 Midland Boulevard Chelsea, MI 48118-0202	TC Design 988 Midland Boulevard Chelsea, MI 48118-0202
Dear Ms. Weitsle: *or* Dear Susan: (if you are on a first-name basis with her)	Ladies and Gentlemen: *or* Gentlemen and Ladies:	Dear TC Design: *or* Ladies and Gentlemen: *or* Gentlemen and Ladies:

Practice 9–9: Writing Inside Addresses

For each group of facts, write the inside address in block format. Use the correct postal abbreviations for the state names—two capital letters with no periods. Skip a space below each address and write a correct salutation followed by a colon.

1. The director of Jupiter Day-Care Center, Georgia, Atlanta Public Schools, 30301-2413, 413 Neptune Street, Atlanta

2. Maine, B. J. Santos, 27 Pike Street, Lobster Heaven, Augusta, 04330-1217, Chef

3. Eureka, 95501-1215, 8905 Craft Road, Paris Stables, California

4. The manager of the Customer Service Department of the Airway Heights Gas and Electric Company. This company is located at 621 Lockness Avenue in the town of Airway Heights, which is in Washington. The ZIP Code in Airway Heights is 99001-2621.

5. Arvi Saarisuu of Roettig Enterprises, located in Daisetta, a town in Texas. The company is at 877 East Karcher Road. The ZIP Code there is 77533-1126.

6. Katrina Price-Hall, the pharmacy technician who works at the drugstore nearest your home. Don't forget the ZIP Code.

7. The personnel manager of a local business that hires people with training in your occupational field.

Ch09-09.doc

The Body

The **body** is the message part of the letter. It follows the guidelines for effective communication. It should answer these questions:

- What is this message about?
- What are the facts, and what do they mean?
- What do we do now?

In modified block format, the first line of each paragraph may be indented 0.5", but the examples in this book show paragraphs with no indentation. Single spacing is used within paragraphs; double spacing is used between paragraphs. Paragraphs are generally brief.

by the way...

A United States Postal Service survey indicated that more than 33 percent of all mail contained incomplete or inaccurate address elements and, therefore, delivery was affected—for more than 67 billion pieces of mail per year!

The Complimentary Close

The **complimentary close** is a word or phrase used to end the message. Several acceptable business-letter complimentary closes follow, in the order of least to most formal. If you use mixed punctuation in a letter and follow the salutation with a colon, follow the complimentary close with a comma. Capitalize only the first letter of the first word.

Examples:

Best wishes,	Sincerely,
Cordially,	Yours truly,
Sincerely yours,	Respectfully,

If you are not an experienced business-letter writer, some of these complimentary closes may sound vaguely romantic to you. They're not. Readers expect these closings. However, "Thank you" is not an acceptable complimentary close. Your thanks belong in the body of the letter.

The Signature Block

The **signature block** includes your keyed name below your handwritten signature. The keyed name is necessary in case the reader cannot read the signature. Sign your name in blue or black ink. This, by the way, is a signature, not an autograph, so write legibly. Writers often sign only their first name if they know the reader well.

A woman can take this opportunity to let the reader know which courtesy title she prefers. A person whose name does not indicate gender can similarly include a courtesy title to let the reader know which title is appropriate.

Examples:

Sincerely,	Yours truly,
Courtney Bryant	*Gary Eder*
Ms. Courtney Bryant	Gary Eder
Office Manager	Quality Control Manager

Practice 9–10: Correcting Letter Parts

With a partner, examine the letter in *Student Workbook* page 9-C, which contains 25 errors. Locate the errors and mark them, using the proofreading marks shown on page 572. In the boxes, label the letter parts. Then revise the letter. The writer intended this letter to be modified block format with open punctuation.

Optional Letter Parts

Along with the seven standard letter parts, use the attention line, subject line, reference initials, enclosure notation, and copy notation when you need them. The letter in block format shown in Figure 9-12 uses all five optional parts and shows their placement.

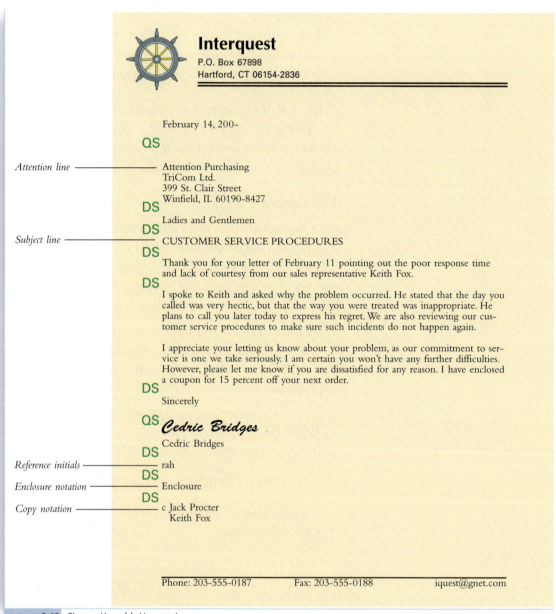

Interquest
P.O. Box 67898
Hartford, CT 06154-2836

February 14, 200–

QS

Attention line —— Attention Purchasing
TriCom Ltd.
399 St. Clair Street
Winfield, IL 60190-8427

DS

Ladies and Gentlemen

DS

Subject line —— CUSTOMER SERVICE PROCEDURES

DS

Thank you for your letter of February 11 pointing out the poor response time and lack of courtesy from our sales representative Keith Fox.

DS

I spoke to Keith and asked why the problem occurred. He stated that the day you called was very hectic, but that the way you were treated was inappropriate. He plans to call you later today to express his regret. We are also reviewing our customer service procedures to make sure such incidents do not happen again.

I appreciate your letting us know about your problem, as our commitment to service is one we take seriously. I am certain you won't have any further difficulties. However, please let me know if you are dissatisfied for any reason. I have enclosed a coupon for 15 percent off your next order.

DS

Sincerely

QS *Cedric Bridges*

Cedric Bridges

DS

Reference initials —— rah

DS

Enclosure notation —— Enclosure

DS

Copy notation —— c Jack Procter
Keith Fox

Phone: 203-555-0187   Fax: 203-555-0188   iquest@gnet.com

FIGURE 9-12 Five optional letter parts

The Attention Line

An **attention line** is used when you do not know the name of the receiver of the letter or when you are writing to an organization. Key the word *Attention* followed by a title or the name of a department. Key the attention line as the first line of the inside address.

The Subject Line

The **subject line** of a letter is similar to the subject line of a memo. It tells the reader at a glance what the letter is about. Key it two lines below the salutation. Subject lines are keyed in all capital letters.

Reference Initials

The **reference initials** are the initials of the person who keyed the letter. These initials are used only when you key letters for someone else or if someone else keys your letters for you. Reference initials are placed two lines below the keyed signature, against the left margin. They should be keyed in lowercase, not capital, letters. Reference initials can also be added to memos.

The Enclosure Notation

An **enclosure** is anything in the envelope besides the letter, such as a check. Two lines below the reference initials, key the word *Enclosure* or *Enclosures*. Memos also may include enclosure notations. When you have more than one enclosure, add the number of enclosures this way:

Enclosures 2

The Copy Notation

The **copy notation** lets the reader know another person (or other people) received a copy of the letter. Key the copy notation two lines below the enclosure notation. Key *c,* followed by the name or names of those receiving a copy.

Common Letter Formats

Two popular letter formats are block and modified block. In **block** format (see Figure 9-1, page 285, and Figure 9-11, page 305), all lines begin at the left margin. In **modified block** format (see Figure 9-2, page 287), the heading (if needed), date, complimentary close, and signature block begin near the center of the page. In this style, paragraphs may be blocked at the left or indented.

Unless your employer states a preference, use the style that suits you best. Block format is easiest to key. Remember that when keying on letterhead stationery, you do not use a heading.

Addressing Envelopes

The United States Postal Service sent a pamphlet to residential customers to explain how to address mail for faster delivery. It also gives standard abbreviations. Your teacher will give you a copy of the pamphlet.

Notice that every letter in the address is a capital letter and that all punctuation is omitted. When addresses are formatted this way, mail can be sorted automatically by the Postal Service's electronic scanners, which saves routing time. Always use the two-letter postal abbreviation for the state name. Use only the standard abbreviations for *Avenue, Street, Suite, Apartment,* etc. Follow United States Postal Service guidelines whenever you address mail.

Figures 9-13 and 9-14 show how to fold letters and insert them into two standard sizes of envelopes.

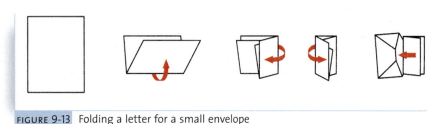

FIGURE 9-13 Folding a letter for a small envelope

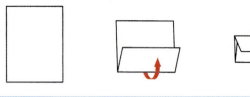

FIGURE 9-14 Folding a letter for a large envelope

Practice 9-11: Addressing Mail

Use the envelope forms on *Student Workbook* page 9-D for this Practice.

1. Complete the first envelope for the letter shown in Figure 9-1 on page 285 sent from Emila Del Gesso to Roger's.

2. Complete the second envelope for a *reply* to the letter shown in Figure 9-2 on page 287. The letter would be from Reed Beauchamp to Kijiro Kimura.

3. Complete the third envelope for a letter from you to an administrator of your school district.

Practice 9-12: Writing Messages

You will need a partner for this Practice.

1. Locate the full mailing address for a local business.

   Write a letter in modified block format to the owner of the business—who happens to have the same name as your partner—to complain about the poor service you received from one of his or her employees yesterday. Be sure to include all three parts of an effective message. Fold the letter and address the outside as if it were an envelope. Deliver the letter to your partner.

2. Review the information in this chapter on the qualities of effective messages; then answer your partner's letter. Design a letterhead for this letter and use block format. Fold the letter, address the "envelope," and deliver it.

3. Write a memo to the employee who was the subject of your partner's complaint. Make this memo as positive as you can.

Practice 9-13: Correspondence Word Search

To review key terms in this chapter, complete the word search puzzle on *Student Workbook* page 9-E.

Summary

Learning to write effective notes, memos, e-mail messages, and letters is important for all workers. Since the written message projects an image of the writer and his or her organization, it is important to produce professional, quality correspondence. Follow these guidelines whenever you write a message:

- Specifically state the purpose.
- Communicate clearly, concisely, and courteously.
- Answer these questions: What is this message about? What are the facts, and what do they mean? What do we do now?
- Use a standard style for memos and business letters.
- Address envelopes according to Postal Service guidelines.
- Carefully proofread and revise your message.

review and research activities visit
communicating.swlearning.com

project-based assessment

Business Letter

Sending a Request Letter

In this Project, you will write and send at least one business letter. Depending on your circumstances, you may choose one (or more) assignments from this list:

- Most job applications ask you to list three to five references. References are responsible people who can attest to your honesty, dependability, and positive work habits. You must, however, obtain permission from a person to list him or her as a reference. Write to someone who would give you a good reference the next time you look for a job. Ask for permission to include his or her name on your list of references.

- When you are searching for a job, you may find it helpful to have letters of recommendation from your references to give to interviewers. Write to one of your references, asking for an open letter of recommendation. Mention the type of job you may be applying for.

- What is your dream job? How would you go about getting that job? If you have a specific career goal, write to an organization that you would like to work for in the future. What training, experience, and qualities does the company expect from new employees? How can you prepare yourself for eventual employment with that organization? Call the organization to find out to whom to address your letter.

- Companies sometimes donate used equipment to schools. Write to a local business in your occupational field. Briefly describe your educational program and ask if the business might be willing to donate equipment. Check with your school district to find out the guidelines for accepting donations.

- Write to an organization that produces goods or services related to your educational program, asking for specific information about those goods or services.

1. Review information and examples. Study the Sample Project Plan and the Sample Request Letter on pages 316 and 317.

2. Complete the Project Plan on *Student Workbook* page 9-F and have your teacher check it. Consider including a self-addressed, stamped envelope to make it easy for your reader to respond.

3. Write a rough draft. Using the Rough Draft column of the Project Guide, *Student Workbook* page 9-G, check your work with another student. Have your partner read your letter aloud to you. Ask your teacher to check the rough draft.

4. Revise your letter. Using the Final Draft column of the Project Guide, proofread your work. Make needed corrections. Print the final draft.

5. Fold your final draft and place it in a correctly addressed envelope. Do not seal the mailing envelope. Turn it in with the Project Guide.

Sample Project Plan

Plan for a Request Letter

SUBJECT	Arrangements for taking certification exam		
AUDIENCE	testing coordinator		
PURPOSE	**What actions should the audience take?** Give permission to take an oral exam		
STYLE	☒ block ☐ modified block		
HEADING	Apt. 7B 3495 Fair Acres Lane Warren, MI 48089-2327		
DATE	12/3/--		
LETTER ADDRESS	Testing Coordinator Certification Center 609 E. Main St., Suite 4-B Detroit, MI 48233-6977		
SALUTA-TION	Ladies and Gentlemen:		
COMPLI-MENTARY CLOSE	Yours truly,		
OTHER PARTS	reference initials		

CONTENT

Background:

date of test

reason for not writing the test

Details:

have taken oral exams before

If I can't take an oral exam, what to do next?

my phone number

Action Statement:

Let me know before January.

Call if you need more information.

Polite Ending:

Thank you for your assistance.

Sample Request Letter

3495 Fair Acres Lane
Apartment 7B
Warren, MI 48089-2327
December 3, 200-

Attention Testing Coordinator
Certification Center
609 East Main Street
Suite 4-B
Detroit, MI 48233-6977

Ladies and Gentlemen:

I am scheduled to take my certification exam at your center on January 20, 200-. However, I am not able to write answers to the questions because I lost the use of my hands in an accident four years ago.

Do you have a way to accommodate me? In the past, I have taken oral exams. If you are unable to make special arrangements, what steps should I take next? Please let me know by the end of December.

I am well prepared and eager to take the certification exam. You may call me at 810-555-0150 if you need more information.

Thank you for any assistance that you can provide.

Yours truly,

Tina Schultz rb

Miss Tina Schultz

rb

TINA SCHULTZ
3495 FAIR ACRES LANE APT 7B
WARREN MI 48089-2327

ATTN TESTING COORDNTR
CERTIFICATION CTR
609 E MAIN ST STE 4-B
DETROIT MI 48233-6977

literature

Overview

Letters appear in every type of literature. In the Shakespearean play *Macbeth,* Lady Macbeth receives her husband's letter informing her of three witches' predictions for Macbeth's future. The novel *To Be Young, Gifted and Black* includes a letter addressed to the editor of *The New York Times,* expressing the disillusionments of militant blacks of the late sixties. In the following selection, the letter is written in the form of a love poem.

This poem speaks simply and directly of an arranged marriage, one that began without awareness of love or feeling. In this poem, the speaker is a young Chinese woman who is writing to her husband after his five months' absence. She refers to her early marriage, her growing love for him, and her loneliness. The poet uses images from nature, such as deep moss, autumn leaves, and yellow butterflies, to suggest how long her husband has been away.

What evidence is there that the marriage has become one of mutual love and respect?

"The River-Merchant's Wife: A Letter"

Based on a poem by RIHAKU (LI T'AI PO): (A.D. 700–762), one of China's greatest poets.

While my hair was still cut straight across my forehead
    I played about the front gate, pulling flowers.
        You came by on bamboo stilts, playing horse,
You walked about my seat, playing with blue plums.
And we went on living in the village of Chokan:
Two small people, without dislike or suspicion.

> *I desired my dust to be
> mingled with yours . . .*

At fourteen I married My Lord you.
I never laughed being bashful.
Lowering my head, I looked at the wall.
Called to a thousand times, I never looked back.

At fifteen I stopped scowling,
I desired my dust to be mingled with yours
forever and forever and forever.
Why should I climb the look out?

> *. . . I will come out to meet
> you . . .*

At sixteen you departed.
You went into far Ku-to-yen, by river of swirling eddies,
And you have been gone five months.
The monkeys make sorrowful noise overhead.

You dragged your feet when you went out.
By the gate now, the moss is grown, the different mosses,
Too deep to clear them away!
The leaves fall early this autumn, in wind.
The paired butterflies are already yellow with August.

Over the grass in the West garden;
They hurt me. I grow older.
If you are coming down through the narrows of the
    river Kiang,
Please let me know beforehand,
And I will come out to meet you
                As far as Cho-fu-Sa.

                        —translated by Ezra Pound

Start-Up: Needless to say, the letter that this young Chinese wife writes to her husband is quite different from the letters you have been writing in this chapter. Disregard the fact that the letter is written as a poem. What other differences exist?

Connection: List the differences you find between a traditional letter and the one the Chinese woman writes. Consider letter format, standard letter parts, special letter parts, word choice, and sentence and paragraph structure.

Working with Literature: Refer to *Student Workbook* page 9-H for an activity on writing a document.

Overview

Michel-Guillaume-Jean de Crèvecoeur (yes, this is his name) came to America from France, his homeland, to travel and survey in the American colonies during the 1700s. He later settled on a farm near Chester, New York.

Crèvecoeur began writing his literary letters to inform Europeans of the opportunities in the New World. He idealized America as a land free of restraints and class structure. His letters, published in 1782, had a great influence on creating the image of America abroad.

from Letter III. "What Is an American" from Letters from an American Farmer

I wish I could be acquainted with the feelings and thoughts which must agitate the heart and present themselves to the mind of an enlightened Englishman, when he first lands on this continent. . . . Here he beholds fair cities, substantial villages, extensive fields, and an immense country filled with decent houses, good roads, orchards, meadows, and bridges, where a hundred years ago all was wild, woody, and uncultivated! What a train of pleasing ideas this fair spectacle must suggest; it is a prospect which must inspire a good citizen with the most heartfelt pleasure.

The difficulty consists in the manner of viewing so extensive a scene. He is arrived on a new continent; a modern society offers itself to his contemplation, different from what he had hitherto seen. It is not composed, as in Europe, of great lords who possess everything, and a herd of people who have nothing. Here are no aristocratical families, no courts, no kings, no bishops, no ecclesiastical dominion, no invisible power giving to a few a very visible one, no great manufacturers employing thousands, no great refinements of luxury. The rich and the poor are not so far removed from each other as they are in Europe.

What then is the American, this new man? He is either a European or the descendant of a European, hence that strange mixture of blood, which you will find in no other country. I could point out to you a family whose grandfather was an Englishman, whose wife was Dutch, whose son married a French woman, and whose present four sons have now four wives of different nations. He is an American who, leaving behind him all his ancient prejudices and manners, receives new ones from the new mode of life he has embraced, the new government he obeys, and the new rank he holds. He becomes an American by being received in the broad lap of our great *Alma Mater*. Here individuals of all nations are melted into a new race of men whose labors and posterity will one day cause great changes in the world.

> *Here individuals of all nations are melted into a new race of men whose labors and posterity will one day cause great changes in the world.*

Americans are the western pilgrims who are carrying along with them that great mass of arts, sciences, vigor, and industry which began long since in the East; they will finish the great circle. The Americans were once scattered all over Europe; here they are incorporated into one of the finest systems of population which has ever appeared, and which will hereafter become distinct by the power of the different climates they inhabit.

The American ought therefore to love this country much better than that wherein either he or his forefathers were born. Here the rewards of his industry follow with equal steps the progress of his labor; his labor is founded on the basis of nature, *self-interest*; can it want a stronger allurement? Wives and children, who before in vain demanded of him a morsel of bread, now, fat and frolicsome, gladly help their father to clear those fields whence exuberant crops are to arise to feed and to clothe them all, without any part being claimed either by a despotic prince, a rich abbot, or a mighty lord. Here religion demands but little of him—a small, voluntary salary to the minister and gratitude to God; can he refuse these? The American is a new man, who acts upon new principles; he must therefore entertain new ideas and form new opinions. From involuntary idleness, servile dependence, penury, and useless labor, he has passed to toils of a very different nature, rewarded by ample subsistence.—This is an American.

—Michel-Guillaume-Jean de Crèvecoeur

Start-Up: You have learned in this chapter that all correspondence should answer certain questions:

1. What is the message about?

2. What are the facts, and what do they mean?

3. What do we do now?

Connection: Does the author answer these questions in his letter? Give examples.

Chapter 10

"You'll miss 100% of the shots you never take."

—Wayne Gretzky, Professional Hockey Player

Persuading

Persuasion is everywhere. Advertising constantly bombards the public from billboards and television, from newspapers and magazines. Politicians campaign to win votes. Pizza parlors put flyers on mailboxes and coupons on doors to get people to try their products. The Marines and the Army recruit high school juniors and seniors. Teachers convince students to use safety equipment; parents urge kids to clean their rooms. All of these requests are expressed through persuasion.

Persuasion: Audience Needs

Persuasion is used every day on the job. The coworker who wants to trade days off uses persuasion. Personnel departments use pay incentives for better attendance. Your supervisor wants the best job done and uses persuasion to accomplish the purpose.

Persuasion is the conscious effort to influence attitudes and behavior. This attempt may reinforce a belief or convince a person that a certain point of view is the right one. Persuasion may result in a direct action— or it may not succeed. The person who persuades pushes, and that push may cause change.

Practice 10–1: Finding Everyday Persuasion

How does persuasion influence your life? In the following situations, describe events when persuasion affected your life.

1. Describe two recent occasions when you tried to persuade someone.

2. Describe two recent occasions when someone tried to persuade you.

3. Describe two situations in your career major in which persuasion may be used.

The persuader should understand the needs of the audience. What are its unsatisfied needs? The persuasive message must satisfy the audience's needs, not the needs of the writer or the speaker. The psychological researcher Abraham Maslow developed a sequence of needs. Maslow's sequence of needs provides a starting point in understanding and motivating an audience.

The lower-level needs must be met, or satisfied, before the higher-level needs can be met. For example, the person who is hungry and out of work must satisfy the need of hunger before he or she can search for a job. Once the person is fed, the hunger won't be the motivation; the lack of work will.

Maslow's sequence of needs (shown in Figure 10-1) is arranged in five categories:

1. Physical needs: Including food, warmth, shelter, sex, and avoidance of pain

2. Safety needs: Offering security for oneself and loved ones, having good health, and being in control of one's life

3. Love and belonging needs: Including the love of family, a sense of belonging, and concern for society

Technology *Connection*

Scents can affect your mood. But can smells persuade you to spend money when you are shopping? Will the smell of cinnamon make you feel warm and loved? Will the smell of fresh flowers suggesting a sunny day make you feel cheerful? Yes, says Dr. Alan Hirsch of the Smell and Taste Research Treatment Foundation in Chicago. According to Dr. Hirsch, smell has the greatest impact on behavior because it is associated with the part of the brain that is linked with emotion. Using smells is like bribing you to buy—at least luring you into a store and making you linger longer. Have you ever noticed that the bakery in newer supermarkets is near the store's entrance?

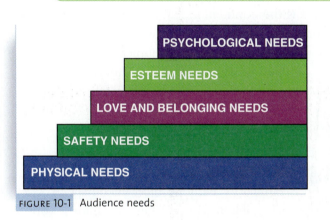

FIGURE 10-1   Audience needs

4. Esteem needs: Recognizing achievement and importance to make one feel better about oneself

5. Psychological needs (sometimes called self-actualization): Fulfilling one's potential and feeling happy about oneself; helping others

The chances of persuading an audience are greater under certain conditions. If the audience's needs are similar to the action that the persuader wants or if a person's self-esteem is low, persuasion is more likely to occur.

 ### Practice 10–2: Identifying the Audience's Needs

Maslow's sequence of needs is the basis of the following job-related persuasive arguments. For each argument, identify the need or needs.

a. We would like you to move to our new store, along with 80 percent of our current employees. You'll still be able to socialize and eat lunch with your friends.

b. Take this new job. The employer provides wellness benefits: annual physicals, exercise equipment reimbursement, and payment for health club membership.

c. The director took your plan to the regional manager. Now we want to reward you for a job well done by offering you a management position. Will you accept?

d. Would you speak at the annual company dinner? You've done such a tremendous job. Congratulations!

e. Working at the new job will mean I can get a reliable car, not one that breaks down when the weather is cold or wet, so I'll miss fewer days at work. I should be able to afford a dinner out once in a while. Why not change jobs?

After choosing the need or needs of the audience to use in the persuasive appeal, the communicator must decide the method of motivation required to get the plan or idea accepted. This motivating factor is called an **appeal**. The Greek philosopher Aristotle observed three basic types of appeals that are just as effective in persuasion today. The persuader's credibility, reason, and emotions are the basis for the appeals.

Credibility: "Believe What I Say"

Persuasion is more likely to occur when the audience likes and trusts the persuader. **Credibility** is the confidence that the persuader inspires in the audience. The more trust the audience places in the communicator, the more it will rely on the communicator's judgment. The persuader's reputation, motivation, and presentation are the basis for the personal trust.

Which person would you choose to cook your dinner?

Reputation

Having knowledge of and showing familiarity with a subject encourages a favorable reaction. When you inform your audience of your credentials, your knowledge, and your experience, you familiarize them with your reputation and inspire credibility. One way to encourage success is showing how to perform a task, demonstrate a product, or explain a procedure.

An audience is more likely to believe someone with high standards of moral conduct. A person who is perceived as dishonest will have a difficult time persuading an audience about anything. Such unethical behaviors as gross exaggeration, lying, name-calling, and misrepresenting the truth destroy—not build—credibility.

Motivation

The persuader is more likely to gain credibility when he or she shows care and concern for the subject. Often people are persuaded by others whose motives they respect, even though the persuasive message may not affect them personally. People are more willing to accept change when they believe that the persuader serves their own personal interests.

Presentation

Many people assume that what they see is what they get. This may or may not be true. Most often credibility is built through the overall personal impression that an individual or a product makes. Inexpensive stationery, grammar errors, and misspellings do not impress. Above all, determining who your audience is will help you make the best personal impression.

Reason: "Use Your Head"

Develop logic by doing the homework of **PLANNING** + **THINKING** + **RESEARCHING**. This formula gives supportive reasoning for every "why" question that the audience is likely to ask to make a sound decision. Solid facts and statistics will support the persuasive message.

Notice how Laura applies the above formula. After discovering a defective computer sensor that regulates fuel mixture, Laura lists all of the possible problems that may result if Ms. Ibarra delays her car repairs. Because Laura's argument is logical and thorough, Ms. Ibarra is convinced and agrees to the work. By using her head, Laura successfully persuades Ms. Ibarra to approve the repairs.

After considerable research and expense, Babbert's has developed a great healthy treat—

BrocSkins.

FIGURE 10-2   "Before" ad for BrocSkins

Emotions: "Follow the Feeling"

Persuasion works best when the writer uses language to affect emotions. The words you choose can create a persuasive effect. However, avoid words that make a person feel uncomfortable and do not use language that leaves the audience cold. For example, the advertisement in Figure 10-2 creates little interest in the product.

So what? By not using any words that engage the audience's emotions, the company produced an ad with no customer appeal. The company is actually bragging about itself, not the product

In the revised advertisement shown in Figure 10-3, the company appeals to the emotions of the consumer. The advertisement positively attempts to persuade parents who buy the product that their children will love BrocSkins. Not only that, but the children will be eating healthy food as a bonus. By appealing to emotions, the persuader can get inside the consumer's head. Always try to predict the consumer's reactions.

You won't be able to keep enough BrocSkins in the cupboard!

BrocSkins

Our new broccoli treats have a potato-chip flavor that kids love. But parents love BrocSkins treats for their low sodium and high vitamin C content.

FIGURE 10-3   "After" ad for BrocSkins

Practice 10-3: Identifying the Appeal

For each of the following persuasive messages, identify whether the appeal is based on the author's credibility, reason, emotions, or a combination of these methods.

1. Picture calves living in darkness in a stall so tight that they can't even turn around. They are eating a milk mash until they reach the right weight to be sold for veal.

2. Two thousand cars go through this intersection every day to a four-way stop sign at Glendale and Stonegate. On Eudora Drive, 1,400 cars stop at a traffic light every day. Why shouldn't the busier intersection have a stoplight?

3. Our featured speaker, Bonnie Viera, is here today to speak about the needs of the Literacy Task Force. She is the chair of the County Commission on Literacy.

4. Would you please learn to use a computer? It takes much less time than working by hand. The computer is often more accurate than humans in checking spelling errors.

5. When the outside temperature reaches 80 degrees, you actually use less gasoline by using your car's air conditioner than you would if you drove with your windows open. The open windows disrupt the smooth flow of air over the car, causing the car to burn more gasoline.

6. If you aren't a team player, the boss will fire you. He dislikes employees who won't work overtime.

7. Pesticides get into the intestines of small animals and birds through seeds. Inside their bodies, the pesticides cause bleeding and death. So avoid using pesticides.

Practice 10-4: Appealing to Needs

Using the grid on page 10-A in the *Student Workbook,* write a sales slogan for each of the following products. Identify the need or needs, according to Maslow, that your product will satisfy. Name the appeal or appeals that you used.

1. Shoes
2. Sports car
3. Family car
4. Notebook computer
5. Day-care services
6. Doe Burgers
7. Career/technical education

Persuading an Audience

When addressing your audience, choose the best message for that particular audience. Anticipate the audience's reactions as well as its unsatisfied needs. Then adapt the argument to these reactions. For instance, in a speech describing methods of cooking over a charcoal grill, to talk about roasting meat to an audience of vegetarians is a complete waste of energy. Always consider what appeals best to the needs of your audience.

Audience Reactions

An audience's reaction to persuasion can vary. Analyzing the audience will help to predict its reaction. Is the audience favorable to the message? Does the audience have any preconceived ideas? Is the audience opposed to the persuasion? Making predictions about the audience will help form the persuasive argument. Audience reactions can vary from positive to negative.

Favorable Opinion

The audience that favors your suggestion or viewpoint is obviously the easiest to persuade. Take that favorable interest and use it to increase the audience's commitment to your idea. For instance, a political candidate does not have to persuade voters who already support him or her.

No Opinion

Audiences that have no opinion could be uninformed; they just might not know enough about the subject to form an opinion. Provide these audiences with enough information to sway them. **Apathy**, or indifference, can also cause an audience to have no opinion. You need to create interest in the cause to get the audience's commitment to it. However, establishing that interest and getting the audience's attention may be more difficult than it sounds. Remember that if you can easily persuade the apathetic, the opposition can easily persuade them as well.

Opposing Opinion

An audience that is against your viewpoint may range from slightly negative to very hostile. The hostile audience probably will not listen to your attempts to persuade. Anything you say may have little effect, especially if the reasons you present are rooted in emotions. Also, audiences that are close-minded and see issues as either/or choices are not likely to change.

by the way...

"Pick battles big enough to matter, small enough to win."

Jonathan Kozol, U.S. author

You may have fallen asleep in front of the television and awakened to a smoothly produced 30-minute television commercial, often known as an infomercial. Beware of running to that telephone and ordering based on unsubstantiated claims and endorsements of celebrities who are highly paid to recommend the advertised product. Is ordering the product now really saving you money? Is the free gift really free? Why can't you wait to order until tomorrow? These are questions to ask while calling the local Better Business Bureau before ordering.

You can evaluate a negative audience, however. Your arguments to persuade can then be developed around the audience's unmet needs. Try not to misrepresent the opposition to earn points for the persuasion. Name-calling doesn't help; it only hurts. Be reasonable; persuasion that is extreme is often ignored.

Types of Conflict

Without conflict, why persuade? Everyone would just agree. There must be some sort of dissatisfaction, or an audience will not be receptive to persuasion. After discovering the need for persuasion, you need to find the type of conflict present in the majority of the audience.

Computer fear

Pseudo Conflict

A **pseudo**, or false, **conflict** is really not a conflict at all. All signs point to a disagreement, but no disagreement is there. Some people just think they must choose one option or another. However, if they could see a compromise, there would be no need for a battle. For example, some people fear computers. They would rather ignore these devices or quit their job than learn to use them to make their job easier. Employers who understand the pseudo conflict can ease computer fear by providing slow-paced computer classes and sympathetic instructors.

Problem/Solution Conflict

Problem/solution conflict occurs when the audience agrees with the problem but not with the suggested solution. Working to come up with alternative solutions helps. For instance, crops need to be protected from destructive insects, but many people do not want to use chemicals. Rather than have damaged vegetation, a solution would be to offer the use of organic pesticides.

Values Conflict

When persuasion attacks personal values (the attitudes or beliefs that a person holds), conflict may result. Such beliefs form the basis of a person's character. Be careful with **values conflict**, proceeding cautiously. Find a way, even a small way, that the audience can agree. Then slowly work on the persuasion.

Ego Conflict

Some people think that an argument must have a winner or a loser. Instead, one can often propose a simple agreement and soften egos. Hence, both sides can win, creating a win–win situation. For example, Shanda, the cook in the household, wanted to remodel the kitchen, but her husband Louis, who managed the family budget, thought the change was not needed. To compromise, they settled their personal conflicts by updating the kitchen themselves.

Managing Conflict

Conflict can be constructive if it is managed properly. Cooperation, not competition, is the key. However, you can treat conflict either positively or negatively. The ways that people manage conflict vary from withdrawal and surrender to assertiveness, persuasion, and negotiation.

Withdrawal and Surrender

A person can withdraw from conflict physically or psychologically. **Physical withdrawal** happens when a person *literally* moves away from the conflict situation. **Psychological withdrawal** happens when a person *mentally* moves away from the conflict situation. Withdrawal may be a good or bad choice, depending on the situation.

Psychological withdrawal can also be positive or negative. Suppose Rinji and his mother have a disagreement about his keeping his room clean, and they become angry. Rinji could withdraw by daydreaming. By ignoring the conflict, he will probably only infuriate his mother more. Instead, if Rinji changes the subject tactfully, he and his mother could both calm down and resume the discussion later.

Surrender is a way of avoiding conflict—and discussion. The person who surrenders gives up the present argument, but may not necessarily give up the conflict. A person can interpret surrender as an implication that the other person does not care. Another explanation is that a person is a martyr if he or she surrenders: "I'll do it your way; I always do." Surrender leaves the persuader angry because the person who surrenders avoids the discussion and never addresses the conflict.

Assertiveness

Assertiveness is generally a very desirable way to manage conflict and to persuade, but learning to be assertive is hard. Being **assertive** is stating the position positively but firmly, using no hostility. Assertiveness requires stepping back from the issues and considering the pros and cons to find a solution.

For example, Anna wants assertively to persuade her boss, Mr. Espino, that her new technique for wiring the circuit is more effective. First, she writes down the positive points and supports them with facts. Then Anna thinks of all of the drawbacks that Mr. Espino will mention. She plans ways to disprove them. Anna's assertive approach may just sway the usually reluctant Mr. Espino.

Persuasion

Persuasion can resolve conflict if it has a sound, logical basis. Attempting to change an attitude or a behavior works better when a person is open, not secretive. For instance, Mario asked Luis to buy candy to help his soccer team's fund-raiser. Luis bought several boxes of the overpriced candy, knowing that the profits would help Mario's team purchase new jerseys. But what Mario didn't tell Luis was that the more candy bars he sold, the greater his chances of winning the top-seller's prize of a trip to the World Cup games. Surprising someone with a **hidden agenda**, a concealed reason for the persuasion, often ends in disaster.

Negotiation

Successful negotiation often means managing conflict through trade-off. Keeping an open mind, not being stubborn, and winning—or losing—gracefully can help with positive conflict solutions. If the negotiation is lost, discuss the reasons for failure. Improvements can be made to turn the failure into a success the next time.

A good strategy is to give the other side a little edge by first listening to what they have to say. Then present them with the superior argument.

by the way...

"Commitment may only require 5% or 10% more effort, but it makes all the difference in the world."

ART SCHWARTZ, U.S. AUTHOR

Practice 10–5: Finding and Resolving Conflict

1. There is conflict in the following situations. In small groups, discuss the disagreement. Then name the type of conflict and write the reason for each disagreement.

   a. The engine is pinging in your five-year-old, low-mileage car. You just replaced the transmission and the tires, and the body is in great shape. The mechanic tells you that you need a rebuilt engine. You think you should sell the car, but you can't afford a new one.

   b. A state agency knows that it must monitor the child-care industry closely. The Federal Health Administration agrees but wants less state inspection of activities and more federal examination of sanitary facilities. The state remains firm; it believes that child care should be state, not federally, regulated.

   c. Nadro wants to hire Mina as an electronics inspector. The company has offered her a large hourly wage and flextime. In her interview, Mina asks about the company's use of radioactive materials. The company interviewer seems to avoid the question, since she thinks that if Mina knew the extent to which she would be handling radioactive materials, she wouldn't take the job. Nadro wants Mina as a worker; she is experienced, with a good work record.

2. Using the guidelines for managing conflict, how could your group resolve the differences in the situations in 1a, b, and c? Brainstorm in your groups and write down the answers.

The ADAM Method of Persuading

Motivating the audience to read or listen past the first line is a must in persuasion. If you use the ADAM approach, you will generally persuade your audience. With the ADAM method, the most effective persuasion—whether visual, oral, or written—uses these four steps.

A—Attract **attention**.
D—Create **desire**.
A—**Appeal** to needs.
M—**Move** to action.

Attract Attention

Stimulate interest in the product or idea immediately—in the first line or sentence! If you do not, the audience will be lost. After deciding on the focus of your appeal, create a way to arouse and attract that interest. Some suggestions that work follow.

- Ask a question: Interest readers by asking a question that they cannot answer with a no. They will have to read further to get a response.
- Startle: "In the next 12 minutes, 120 Americans will be disabled in an accident." Make a surprising statement.
- Offer something free: The audience must be required to do something to get a gift, a coupon, or a discount.
- Flatter: Flattery appeals to the ego of the audience.
- Don't give up: Be persistent.

Anything that interrupts the message will distract the reader. Get his or her attention—and keep it. Combining two or more ways of attracting attention can create an even more persuasive effect.

Create Desire

While you have its attention, give the audience a powerful reason to act immediately. If you don't know your audience, find out by doing research. Then review Maslow's needs and show the audience what it's missing. Speak directly to the audience. For example, say, "What would you do if you had a sudden financial emergency? Would you ask for a loan? If you think you'd have a problem, you're absolutely right."

Appeal to Needs

Now comes the pitch. Show the audience how the idea will satisfy its needs. Point out the benefits. Try appealing to the audience's needs in the following ways:

- Problem/solution: State the problem and explain what will happen every minute that the problem goes unsolved.
- Comparison of advantages: "Yes, the ROM Shop provides five times faster service than the other local computer repair shops."
- Satisfaction of requirements: "Our shop offers a full-service parts department. If you're not satisfied, we will give you a full refund."
- Testimonial: "Natalie Porter uses Glo Hair Color. You, too, can have movie star hair color."
- Negativity: You often need a negative approach when facing a hostile audience. "Choose a Jack Russell terrier like Mollie, and you can enjoy your dog without time-consuming grooming."

Move to Action

Now it's time to get the audience to change. Clinch the deal. Give the audience a solution and get them to act on it. Make the move simple and to the point. For example, enclose an order form or a postcard. Invite the reader to call. Set up a meeting time. Move to action!

Practice 10–6: Analyzing Advertising

The ADAM method is used in nearly all advertising. In this Practice, you will analyze recorded commercials to discover how the ADAM method is used.

Listen to the commercials on the CD that your teacher will play. After each commercial, answer the questions on page 10-B in your *Student Workbook*. Your teacher may have you work in small groups.

Creating a Persuasive Message

The ADAM method motivates the audience to use a product or service. When you organize the message to produce specific results, persuasion is more effective. Together, the following persuasion-building statements help create a persuasive message. Each persuasive action statement requires thinking about the audience and its needs—and then looking in detail at each statement:

- Determine a goal.
- Give logical evidence.
- Organize the material.
- Use motivating language.
- Build credibility.
- Deliver convincingly.

Determine a Goal

The purpose or goal of the persuasion should be clear to the audience. If the audience can't figure out the goal of the persuasion, why should it pay attention?

Give Logical Evidence

Evidence can best prove a proposition. The statements of evidence do not have to be facts, but they must support the goal. The evidence itself often has a very positive impact on the audience. Evidence that appears to be logical, yet is not a fact, may be an **inference**. An inference seems like a natural and obvious conclusion, but it is a prediction or a guess based on fact.

The following sets of examples have the same evidence. The first statement is a fact. The opinion and the inference are guesses based on that fact. The opinion is based on personal assumptions, and the inference is a presumption drawn from the fact and opinion combined.

Fact	Dad has seen dirty dishes and half-eaten food all over the kitchen.
Opinion	Dad is angry.
Inference	Dad is going to make us clean the kitchen.
Fact	Delia reads three newspapers a day.
Opinion	Delia is a brain.
Inference	Delia will be the best in the class on the current events test.

Yes, Dad did see the food all over the kitchen, and Delia does read three newspapers a day. Those are facts. But the inferences may or may not come true, even though they are based on facts. Dad may be forgiving, and Delia may flunk the test. Try to avoid using inferences as facts. An audience doesn't want to be persuaded and then find out that the facts are not true. Instead of using an inference, make a statement and support it with facts.

Practice 10–7: Determining Fact, Opinion, and Inference

1. Identify each of the following statements as fact, opinion, or inference.

   a. Mica is the fastest runner in our school.
   b. He can best South's runner easily.
   c. It is a terrific day to go fishing.
   d. The bass have been biting at the bait.
   e. We'll have fish for dinner.
   f. Kathy said that Springfield was 73 miles from her house.
   g. We've been driving for an hour.
   h. We'll be in Springfield soon.

2. In newspaper articles and magazines, find examples of statistics, graphs, and other data. Using the grid on page 10-C of the *Student Workbook*, decide how the media uses the data, including who the intended audience is, what the purpose of the data is, and what the need and the conflict are.

Organize the Material

Arrange the material in a way that will produce the expected audience reaction. If the audience is familiar with the material, you will not need as much explanation. For audiences that you expect will be favorable or will have no opinion, be simple and direct, going straight to the bottom line. If you anticipate an audience to be hostile, build your argument first—before stating the persuasion. Be very clear and specific.

Figure 10-4 shows a flyer for an office supply store. Sales did not increase until the store owner modified the flyer, as shown in Figure 10-5.

Use Motivating Language

Choose language that will persuade the audience; choose language that will motivate. For instance, Miguel wrote a collection letter and ended it with "Send your payment no later than Monday." However, Miguel will be more likely to get the money for his company if he firmly states, "Send the payment by Monday."

Sometimes plain language may not be the best choice if the words sound offensive to the audience. However, don't fall into the trap of using euphemisms. **Euphemisms** are pleasant-sounding words that substitute for unpleasant or awkward subjects. *The little girls' room* substitutes for the word *toilet*. A euphemism for *dying* is *passing away*. An *outplacement center* provides job-seeking assistance for employees who are laid off.

**Our store is
outstanding in
serving your
office supply needs.**

**Stein's Supplies
100 Hall Drive
Waltham, MA
02254-0118**

FIGURE 10-4 "Before" office supply store flyer

**Our store is outstanding
in serving your
office supply needs.**

✂ **More locations**
✂ **More salespeople**
✂ **More complete catalog**
✂ **More delivery trucks**
✂ **More products in stock**

**Stein's Supplies
100 Hall Drive
Waltham, MA 02254-0118**

FIGURE 10-5 "After" office supply store flyer

Choose words that are to the point and not crude. Plain talk or writing is better than using a polite euphemism.

Practice 10–8: Avoiding Euphemisms

The following sentences contain euphemisms. Rewrite the sentences to be more direct and to the point.

1. Catalena bought a pre-owned car.

2. The bank charged a quality service fee for its automatic teller machine (ATM) transactions.

3. Why did you buy synthetic glass mugs instead of ceramic?

4. A domestic engineer both lives and works in the same building.

5. If you don't attend your college classes, you'll expedite progress toward alternate life pursuits.

6. The employee was poorly motivated.

7. After the company began downsizing, Todd became a dislocated worker.

8. The librarian was reprimanded for weeding books.

Build Credibility

Persuasion will not take place if the audience cannot believe the persuader. Reputation (including competence and character), motive, and presentation build credibility.

Credibility helps a sales associate persuade customers.

Deliver Convincingly

Choosing the best method to persuade is important. By using the ADAM method effectively (see pages 333–335), you can motivate audiences. If you carefully plan to structure your message presentation, you will increase the effectiveness of your persuasion.

You can arrange words to create a reaction in the audience. However, be careful not to use **loaded language**. These words or phrases carry strong emotional appeal, either positive or negative. The audience tends to hear the words, not the thoughts behind them.

Word choice is very important. **Inferred meaning** may cause anger in some people and no reaction in others. The careful reader or listener sorts out the message despite the emotional overtones. Nevertheless, many people react before reading or listening carefully.

Career *Connection*

Good customer relations keep clients coming back. What's the secret? Observe your hairstylist and learn.

• *Take control.* Your hairstylist is in charge when the cape goes around you.

• *Show your expertise.* The best stylists are great listeners. They hear the customer's needs—and then make a recommendation.

• *Let them have it your way.* Hairstylists are excellent at influencing their customers—almost manipulating them into thinking an idea was their own.

• *Use your tools.* Hairstylists can't work without their shears, razors, clippers, etc.

• *Make the next appointment.* Successful stylists book their next appointment before the customer leaves.

by the way...

Investigate the Better Business Bureau web site for complaints concerning local and national businesses. The site also discloses unethical national advertisements and adds to the list monthly.

Practice 10–9: Eliminating Loaded Language

1. Identify which word in the series is loaded language.

    a. child, youngster, kid, brat, toddler
    b. rookie, beginner, trainee, apprentice
    c. police officer, cop, law enforcement, security

2. Change the italicized word or phrase to eliminate loaded language. Rewrite each sentence. Be careful not to use euphemisms.

    a. The manager seemed so *egotistical,* wanting her way without discussion.
    b. The house needs an *overhaul.*
    c. Buy Garevan, the modern, *cheap* trash disposal solution.
    d. Yes, this neighborhood is *infested with mutts.*

3. **Doublespeak** is deceptive language that hides or misrepresents the truth. Using *Student Workbook* page 10-D, match the misleading phrase with its true meaning.

Practice 10–10: Writing Persuasive Messages

Choose an issue that you feel strongly about, such as cafeteria food, less strict attendance policies, or animal rights. Write an "I Urge Gram" in 15 or fewer words to defend your stand. Have a partner proofread your "I Urge Gram." Then check the message to be sure it strongly supports your position.

After your teacher proofreads the "I Urge Gram," recopy it on paper your teacher provides.

Practice 10–11: Making a Business Card

"Every second a customer looks at a business card generally translates into dollars," states Avery Pitzak of American Business Cards. Like a small-space ad, the business card has a powerful impact and reflects the business's image.

Design your own business card. This card should reflect something you are trying to sell about yourself; for example, your job search, your training skills, your speaking ability, your service learning, or a business you are starting. (See Figures 10-6 and 10-7.)

1. Decide on the focus of your business card—the one element that will attract the customer and dominate the card. Keep the intended audience and the purpose of the card in mind. Will it have the intended effect? The style of your card may be professional, casual, contemporary, or elegant. (See Figures 10-6 and 10-7 for examples.)

2. Choose the visual element that will make your card unique.

Examples:

- Use of white space
- Logo
- Graphics or clip art
- Slogan
- Unique shape of the copy
- Creative use of fonts

3. Include the necessary printed information, such as your name (and the name of your company if appropriate), as well as:

- Your address.
- Your phone number.
- Your e-mail address.
- Your web site.

FIGURE 10-6 Effective use of color

FIGURE 10-7 "Catchy" business card

Collection Letters

In many situations, written persuasion is more effective than oral persuasion. Writing is permanent. For this reason, the writer should convey the message clearly, reasonably, and logically. A clear example of written persuasion is the **collection letter**.

Jason bought a stereo from Sounders on a time payment plan. He gave the store a down payment and agreed to pay Sounders $40 a month until the stereo was paid for in full. However, Jason lost his job at Lola's Used Cars when Lola went bankrupt. Instead of talking to Sounders, Jason just stopped making payments on his stereo.

Sounders tried to contact Jason through a series of messages—postcards, phone calls, and letters. (See Figure 10-8 on page 343.) Eventually, Jason called Sounders and worked out a new payment plan. The collection letter should not offend the customer's **goodwill**, but should appeal to his or her conscience instead.

Success

Successful collections are based on the following procedures:

1. Timeliness	Within two weeks after an account is due, the creditor calls or sends the first reminder notice.
2. Consistency	Each notice includes the due date, the type of account and/or the account number, the amount owed, and the date the notice was sent.
3. Regularity	After the first notice, later notices are sent every two weeks until the debtor responds.
4. Increasing severity	Each message should be stronger than the previous message.

A Collection Series

The collection sequence that many companies use is a three-stage series of communications. The three stages are the inquiry, the reasonable appeal, and the firm appeal.

The Inquiry

A phone call or letter goes out to gently remind the customer the account payment is due. The inquiry letter requests that the customer call, write, or stop in to explain when he or she will pay. The writer asks directly or indirectly for the overdue payment and may mention a penalty for late payment. Some companies have two steps at this level: a phone call and a letter.

The Reasonable Appeal

The company's message becomes stronger in this letter. The letter appeals to the customer's sense of fairness and refers to the customer's good credit rating. The letter explains the consequences if the customer leaves the account unpaid. Losing the merchandise, removing the service, and paying interest penalties are all possible results.

The Firm Appeal

This letter strongly urges the customer to pay the past-due account or to make contact with the company for payment arrangements by a certain date. The customer knows that the time to pay is long past. At this point, many companies turn the account over to a collection agency or an attorney. Unpleasant circumstances, such as repossession, a collection agency, or a lawsuit, could follow soon.

An Important Note: A company cannot legally harass a debtor or threaten physical harm. Federal, state, and local laws define what is considered creditor harassment.

Parts of a Collection Communication

Whether a company communicates by phone or by letter, the message should have the following three sections. (See Figure 10-8.)

1. Goodwill Greeting
   Open the letter or phone call with a general comment about the service or product. This remark will promote a feeling of goodwill.

2. Announcement of the Problem
   When you state the problem and the purpose of the letter, also mention the due date, as well as the type of account and/or the account number.

3. The Next Step
   Close the letter or phone call by stating what the next step is if the payment or arrangements aren't made. This statement can range from a mild warning to an ultimatum. In addition, express the hope that the customer is willing to cooperate. At any point in the letter, you may mention documents you choose to enclose, such as an invoice or a copy of a credit agreement.

SOUNDERS STEREOS

1211 Queens Court
Pittsburgh, PA 15228-8840
878-555-0612
sounderstereos@usa.bus

July 8, 200-

Mr. Jason Miller
1806 Lane Street
Pittsburgh, PA 15228-8810

Dear Mr. Miller:

PARAGRAPH 1
General comment to
promote goodwill.

I hope that you are enjoying your new Sounders stereo music system. If you have any questions about the system, please contact either me or your local Sounders store.

PARAGRAPH 2
Problem stated. Purpose
of letter. Timeliness—
2 weeks past due date.

Your long-term account requires a $40 monthly payment, due on the 20th. Sounders has not yet received your June payment.

PARAGRAPH 3
Next step given. Tone—
firm, not harassing.

I trust that you will contact your local Sounders store immediately to make payment arrangements. Interest penalties add to the cost of your payment daily. If you have any questions, please do not hesitate to call me at 878-555-0110 or your local Sounders store.

Sincerely yours,

Ernesto Hernandez

Ernesto Hernandez
Account Supervisor

FIGURE 10-8 An effective collection letter

Practice 10–12: Revising Collection Letters

Revise the collection letter in Figure 10-9 to make it more effective. Follow the guidelines for the firm appeal letter presented in this chapter. You can create details that you think are appropriate for the letter.

Beechmont Bathtubs
218 Ardwick
Bellevue, NM 87116-1806
(505) 555-0105

March 13, 200-

Ms. Gladys Amora
8687 Lyon Drive
Silverdale, NM 87113-7949

Dear Ms. Amora:

Why haven't you paid your Beechmont Bathtub account? You owe us $302.14. We want it now! The account is two months overdue. We've also sent you two letters. You haven't responded, and that's very frustrating. Did you forget to send your payment?

You probably have the check in the mail. Why haven't you sent the $302.14? Are you trying to cheat us? Well, Beechmont Bathtubs won't stand for this. You said you liked it. We have no use for a seven-foot custom-made red bathtub, but we'll remove it from the house if you don't pay. If you do like the tub, or even if you don't, pay this bill by March 31.

Yours,

Maeve Chamber

Maeve Chamber
Account Supervisor

FIGURE 10-9 An ineffective collection letter

Sales Letters

Selling—it's everywhere. And persuasion is the tool of sales. Selling, however, is not forcing customers to buy. Selling makes a product or service or place appealing enough that the customer is willing to spend money on it.

Selling requires more than just concentrating on what is being promoted. The goal is to create interest in the product or service from the beginning. With a convincing, positive tone, prepare the sales pitch well. To do this, you must know your audience, product, and competition.

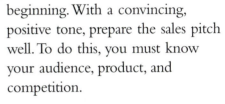

Do you run the risk of having your house burn down?

If you have not cleaned your chimney this year, your house could easily be lost in flames.

ChimMaster — The Sweep That Cleans

837 Ashley Court, Ashland, OH 44805-1598
419/555-0113

FIGURE 10-10   A chimney sweep ad

The Audience

Put yourself in the typical customer's place. That person gets an average of ten sales letters a day. What will make your letter stand out? Create the emotional emphasis and center everything in the letter around the emotion. Analyze the target audience. What are their backgrounds? Is it a diverse or a similar group? Approach each audience member in a personal way suitable for that audience, as shown in Figure 10–10.

The Product

Assume that the customer needs the product and cannot function without it. Learn why the customer would buy the product and focus on that reason. What objections would the customer have to buying the product? Answer any objections by giving the customer logical reasons to buy, as shown in Figure 10–11. Make sure you are totally familiar with the product or service. What are its strengths? Its weaknesses? Its special features? What kind of questions would the customer ask about the product or service?

The sales letter can create a solution—after the audience believes it has a problem or conflict. This feeling of discomfort is called **dissonance**. The greater the dissonance, the easier the sale.

Tireland has the best deals in town.
Good quality
Great selection
Excellent service
AND Low Prices

219 Route 40
Steamwood, IL 60103-1217
630/555-0169

FIGURE 10-11   A tire ad

The Competition

Know the competition. Emphasize the strengths of your company, rather than criticizing the competition. Give a strength for every weakness the competition has. (See Figure 10-12.) Show that the customer has a need for your product or service, not the competitor's.

Parts of a Sales Letter

Following the ADAM approach will logically lead the audience into the letter—and into the sale. The format of a sales letter is similar to business letter format, as shown in Figure 10-13. Chapter 9 is your reference for a standard business letter format. The following sections discuss special parts of sales letters and ways that sales letters may differ in format from standard business letters.

The Headline

The headline is 85 percent of the power of the sales letter. When you analyze the audience, you choose the most emotional element to emphasize. Now use that element. The headline is similar to the headline of a newspaper article and gives the focus of the letter.

When constructing the headline, remember the ADAM method—ask a question, startle, or flatter. The headline should be a strong opener that attracts the reader's attention. You can use a single word, a phrase, a declarative sentence, or a question. Often the headline is in a prominent font or in a contrasting color. If the headline doesn't attract the reader's attention, the reader may stop reading and throw the letter away!

In the sales letter, the headline usually appears two lines down from the address in place of the salutation. For sales letters that include a salutation, the headline appears two lines down from the salutation and two lines from the body text.

High price of dining
got you down?

Come to

ED'S DINER

All meals $5.00

Drinks and desserts included
Can't beat our prices—or our food!!!

1015 Shannon Dale, Silver Spring, MD 20904-1015
(301) 555-0115

Open every day from 3 to 10 p.m.

FIGURE 10-12   A restaurant ad

The Opening Paragraph

The opening paragraph of the sales letter is nearly as important as the headline. Solve the audience's problem, as the ad does for Ed's Diner in Figure 10-12. Emphasize the positive features of the product or service and don't mention the weaknesses. Keep that reader's attention!

The language of the sales letter should be simple and direct. Avoid using technical information for a general audience; the audience will not read the sales pitch if the language is too specialized or wordy. Repetition is key. Restate the information over and over in different ways.

The Body Paragraph(s)

This paragraph (or paragraphs) solves the problem. Here you make your claim that the product or service or place is the best the reader has ever known. Support claims with specific and truthful facts or statements that the reader will understand. Testimonials are excellent; examples support as well. Again, be as creative and unusual as possible, repeating the name of the company as many times as possible.

Letterhead

ACES

100-A Country Drive
Bartlett, OH 45123-0486
acesandas@aces.bus

Logo

November 29, 200-

Ms. Clarissa Nan
804 Robinwood Drive
Centerville, TX 75833-6916

Headline

DO YOU HAVE STRAIGHT A'S?

Strong opening paragraph

If you can't answer **yes** to that question, then something is **wrong**. Something needs to be changed. You can change your grades to beautiful A's—all you need is **ACES**.

Eye-catching claims offering solutions

ACES is your ticket to the *Honor Roll*!
　　　ACES is your passport to high SAT and ACT scores!
　　　　　ACES is the way to make your parents smile!
　　　　　ACES is the *key* to the future!

Problem solved

ACES is a complete study system that will put YOU in charge of your grades. **ACES** costs very little, only pennies a day. The time you spend with **ACES** will *boost* your grades.

Tells what to do
Prompt response needed

Just call 1-800-GET-ACES today to sign up for a free 30-day trial offer—or fill out the enclosed card. But hurry—the offer is limited to the first 200 customers only.

Catchy closing

Today is your **ACES** day!!!

Sincerely,

Stella Zumot

Stella Zumot
President of **ACES**

Enclosure

FIGURE 10-13 A sales letter

People *Connection*

Kathy Lehne's company, Sun Coast Resources, Inc., began because her high school business co-op teacher placed her as a clerk-typist at an oil distribution company. When the oil company moved out of Kathy's area of eastern Texas, she knew that she had a loyal customer base and wanted to try starting her own company. Being only 24 years old was no deterrent to her, but financing was. By working out a deal with her former company to buy on credit and sell to her customers, Kathy grew her company into a $200 million business in less than ten years. Now Kathy is the owner of one of Texas's largest petroleum wholesalers—and it all started with a high school business co-op job!

The Closing Paragraph

The closing paragraph includes an action statement. Make it easy for the customer to buy the product. Tell the reader what to do—for example, send in the enclosed postcard, send for the free gift, call for information, or fill out an order form. You need to close the sale confidently and positively, encouraging the reader to respond *now*. The closing paragraph can make or break the sale.

The Closing

The closing of the sales letter should be sincere and should be followed by the signature and title of the writer. Occasionally, a company name is used instead of the writer's title. Sometimes a sales letter will use a sentence such as "Buy now!" instead of a typical closing.

by the way...

"Direct mail is what you send; junk mail is what you get."

GORDON PEERY, *OFFICE SYSTEMS* READER

Practice 10–13: Analyzing Sales Letters

teamwork

Bring in sales letters and/or promotional mailings to your teacher. In small groups, analyze at least two items by answering the following questions. You may use the grid in your *Student Workbook*, page 10-E.

1. What are the product's major and minor appeals?

2. What attracts the reader's **attention**?

3. What creates **desire**?

4. What **appeals** to the reader's needs?

5. What **moves** the reader to action?

6. What are the letter's or promotional mailing's strengths and weaknesses?

Not only the words in the persuasive message, but also the visual style can persuade the reader. Researchers have studied the influence of lettering, graphics, color, positioning for eye movement, and format.

Many readers skim sales letters. In fact, many people often call this mail junk mail. Get the readers' attention right away so they won't junk your mail. Attract them with lettering, colors, and startling statements.

Sales letters are designed to grab the reader's attention for the sole purpose of marketing. These letters tend to use more ways of emphasizing text, such as bold, italics, capital letters, and different type sizes, than other business letters. Sales letters often use unconventional grammar, such as elliptical (condensed) expressions that represent complete sentences (*Price? No problem.*), and unconventional punctuation (*!!!*).

Lettering

Lettering can help you design an eye-catching ad very quickly and inexpensively, as shown in Figure 10-14. Here are some tips:

- Use type that seems to shout—bold and large.
- Keep the heading short—that makes the type seem even larger.
- Avoid elaborate typefaces. They are often hard to read, especially in a small space.

Keeping your audience in mind, link the style of typeface to the emotional focus of your letter. If you are formal and professional in your tone, your lettering should be also. Mixing typefaces is fine to grab attention and to emphasize, but only mix for a reason—not to be flamboyant.

FIGURE 10-14 A haircut ad

Color

Choosing the right combination of colors for paper, type, and graphics will help enhance your persuasive message. They draw the audience's attention, as well as create desire and appeal to needs. What colors to use depends on who your audience is, whether you are using color copy, and what feelings you want to evoke in the reader.

For color copy, three key qualities of paper emphasize the color print's appearance: smoothness, brightness, and whiteness. The paper should be very smooth, so that the color images seem to burst off the paper. The brightness and whiteness of the paper ensure sharp color distinction. An almost blue-white shade is the best paper shade for enhancing lettering.

FIGURE 10-15 Color choices can evoke certain feelings.

Colored paper is fine to use; however, be sure it gives the effect you want. Some combinations of paper and ink are difficult to read, such as black ink on red paper. Select colors for the feelings they arouse in the reader, such as those discussed in the following guidelines. (See Figure 10-15.)

• Warm colors—red, orange, yellow, and pink—attract and stimulate the reader. These colors invite the reader to read and keep reading. Red is very inviting for children. (Notice how cereal boxes and toy packages often use red.)

• Cool colors—white, blue, green, and lavender—are peaceful colors, making the audience feel comfortable.

Generally, avoid cool colors unless you are using them for a desired effect, such as a relaxing ocean scene.

Different colors can stimulate the senses and offer subliminal suggestions for the audience. Examples of such color uses follow.

• Taste
Orange invites the reader to eat. Blue suggests sweetness. An orange flyer would be a good choice to promote a restaurant.

• Smell
Pink, lavender, yellow, and green make readers think of smell. Green also suggests a sense of calmness, which lowers stress.

• Status
Colors of status and prestige are gold, silver, purple, and black. Navy blue commands authority. Green declares self-assurance.

Graphics

An effective graphic in a persuasive message can engage an audience more quickly than almost anything else. Graphic elements include clip art, photos, drawings, charts, and graphs. A simple way to add graphics to a message is to use type as art. Many word processing programs contain different styles of type and ways to create bullets, large capital letters, lines, and boxes. Such software usually comes with step-by-step instructions for changing the shape of text.

As with any other part of a persuasive message, use graphics carefully for maximum effect. Using the same type of graphic for similar parts of a persuasive message—bulleted lists, for example—helps tie the parts together. Placed appropriately, a single distinctive graphic can draw the reader's attention to that particular part of the message.

by the way...

Popular colors of the 1970s, once known as avocado and harvest gold, are now renamed guacamole and terra-cotta—and are in vogue again. The Day-Glo colors of the post-Vietnam era meant happiness; now those colors say high-tech, especially when used with translucent plastic.

Positioning

For each persuasive message, choose a **focal point**—a headline, a graphic, or another design element that draws the attention of the reader. To attract interest, arrange text and other graphic elements carefully on the page, using white space to set off text and graphics.

The overall layout of the persuasive message should follow a pattern, guiding the eye. For example, the Tireland ad in Figure 10-11, page 345, is in a T-shape. The T is the underlying pattern that the reader's eyes follow. The ACES letter, Figure 10-13, on page 347 is in the shape of the letter S. The reader's eye goes from the logo at the upper right corner to the opening lines of print on the left. It then slants to the lower right and back to the lower left.

The shape of the letter is not the only way that forms can attract a reader. Letterhead, headings, underlining, and capital letters also influence the pattern. Highlighting words and adding bullets are two other eye-catching methods.

Letterhead

The sales letter should appear on letterhead stationery that includes the company name, address, telephone number, and e-mail address—and web site and fax number if available. To attract the customer's attention, the letterhead should be graphically styled for the desired effect. The letterhead with a logo should end approximately 1 to 1 1/2 inches down from the top of the paper.

The text of the letterhead should set the tone of the page. The traditional way of designing a letterhead is to center the company information at the top of the page. This design may be appropriate for conservative or formal audiences and messages. More innovative letterhead displays the text and logo in different ways, perhaps **asymmetrically** or **cascading** down the side or across the bottom of the page. Whatever the design, it must be distinctive and appropriate to focus on the message.

Logos

As you learned in Chapter 2, a **logo** is a symbol or trademark that visually represents the company. If the customer becomes familiar with the logo, he or she will see the logo and automatically think of the company. Familiar logos often sell better than words. The logo should measure approximately 3/4-inch square, or five lines of text. A much larger logo will distract the customer from reading the text.

Practice 10-14: Designing a Sales Letter

The Reggae, Rock, and Rhythm letter in Figure 10-16 is not effective. The letter does not get the typical customer's interest—in reading the letter or buying the product. Rewrite and redesign the letter, using what you have learned in this chapter.

Consider lettering, graphics, color, and positioning in redesigning this letter. Redo the letter with a logo. Use the ACES letter in Figure 10-13 on page 347 as a convincing example.

Ch 10-14.doc

Reggae, Rock, and Rhythm
5215 Forest Road
Buffalo, NY 14247-3548
October 13, 200-

Moreland High Student Council
622 Murray Hill Road
Lincoln, NE 68537-6211

Guys and Gals—

Reggae, Rock, and Rhythm will play for your party or dance. We play any kind of music you want. Requests are our specialty.

Call us today at 555-0149. Reasonable rates.

Book us.

Yours truly,

Matt   Ken   Brian

Matt, Ken, and Brian
Reggae, Rock, and Rhythm

FIGURE 10-16   An ineffective sales letter

People *Connection*

Attracting young people to buy products is important because teens spend over $100 billion annually. Here's what they like—and don't—in ads:

- 65% **Be honest.**
- 52% **Be funny.**
- 45% **Make it clear.**
- 43% **Show me.**
- 37% **Show me why it's important.**
- 31% **Being offensive doesn't sell.**
- 25% **Show reality.**
- 24% **Slogans and jingles are cool.**
- 22% **Don't patronize me.**
- 19% **Don't order me around.**

—Teen Research Unlimited

Summary

Persuasion is the attempt to influence attitudes or behavior in both positive and negative ways. Follow these guidelines when using persuasion:

- Analyze the audience's needs.
- Identify the type of appeal required to persuade the audience.
- Determine whether the audience has a conflict with your persuasive message; if so, decide how to resolve that conflict.
- Motivate the audience to accept your persuasive message by using the ADAM method.
- Organize the written persuasive message into an effective sales letter.
- Use design strategies to format persuasive messages for maximum impact.

by the way...

"State your persuasion in positive terms," says Colleen Growe, president of a television production company. Instead of saying "No, that's not right . . . ," say, "To be truthful, the real question is . . . . "

review and research activities visit
communicating.swlearning.com

project-based assessment

Sales Letter

Writing a Sales Letter

You are chair of the Fund-Raising Committee for your group. Your student organization is starting a fund-raiser or a service learning project. To increase sales and/or volunteer participation, you and two others have decided to write a sales letter. Your goal is to persuade readers to participate in an activity to support your service learning project or to spend money on your fund-raiser.

What you choose as your fund-raiser or volunteer project determines the purpose of the letter. You may choose to have the audience:

• Participate in an activity, such as a walk for pledges.

• Buy a product.

• Try a service, such as a car wash.

• Support a cause or donate to send students to an event.

Limit the audience to one target group, defining the needs of that group. Keeping the type of fund-raiser in mind, some suggested audiences are:

• Parents.

• Residents of the school district.

• Employers.

• Consumers of certain products.

• Those with a particular habit or hobby.

• A group of employees.

• An age group.

In addition to writing your letter, design a letterhead, including a logo for your organization.

1. Carefully read the sales letter examples from the chapter, as well as the Sample Project Plan and the Sample Sales Letter on pages 356 and 357.

2. Choose your fund-raiser or service learning project. Then limit the audience for your letter. Have your teacher approve your topic.

3. Complete the Project Plan, *Student Workbook* page 10-F.

4. Have your teacher check the Project Plan.

5. Using the information on your Project Plan, write the rough draft of the sales letter. Write quickly without stopping to check spelling or to perfect exact wording. Just try to get your ideas down in roughly the correct form. A rough draft should be rough.

6. Design a letterhead and logo for your letter.

7. Using the Rough Draft column of the Project Guide on *Student Workbook* page 10-G, check your work with one or more students. All of you should mark the Project Guide and note any changes on the rough draft. Have your teacher check your rough draft.

8. Revise your rough draft, incorporating the changes that your partner(s) and your teacher suggested.

9. Using the Final Draft column of the Project Guide, proofread your work. Make needed corrections.

10. Turn in the final draft of the letter along with the Project Guide.

Sample Project Plan

Plan for Writing a Sales Letter

SERVICE LEARNING	Multiple Sclerosis (MS) Walk
AUDIENCE	Student body
PURPOSE	**What action should the audience take?** Sign up to walk for MS
NEED	**Physical, safety, love and belonging, esteem, psychological:** Psychological, appealing to the part of the personality that helps others
APPEAL	**Credibility, reason, emotions:** Credibility based on motivation Emotions, secondary appeal
SOURCES	Pamphlets from the MS Society
VISUALS	**Logo, letterhead, other:** On a path of many hearts, footprints symbolize the walk with the steps of love. The path of hearts is not straight.

CONTENT

Attract **attention.**

The selfish nature of us all

Create **desire.**

Appealing to the part of the personality that needs to help others

Appeal to needs.

The Walk will raise money for the MS Society.

The money will help fund MS research.

Our walking for money will satisfy our need to help others.

Move to action.

Sign up for the Walk.

Pick up MS literature.

Start gathering pledges.

Sample Sales Letter

North Student Council
Bellevue, Louisiana

May 6, 200-

HOW MUCH OF YOUR TIME IS SPENT HELPING OTHERS?

If you're like most of us, not much at all.

Put your money away. We don't want money—we want your legs.

The Multiple Sclerosis Walk is only two weeks away. On Saturday, May 22, you can walk for MS and earn money for MS research. Your help is needed.

Sign up in the lobby. Then pick up a pledge sheet—and get pledges for every mile you walk. Friends, parents, neighbors, employers—they will all pledge. Who wouldn't want to help others? They can even earn a tax deduction! Helping others feels great—try it. What do you have to lose—except for a Saturday morning?

Sign up today!

Margaret

Margaret Lewis
Student Council President

literature

Overview

Thomas Paine was an American revolutionary propagandist. He wrote against tyranny and monarchy.

Paine, in the following excerpt from *The American Crisis, Number One* (the first of 16 pamphlets he started to write in December 1776), wrote these words: "These are the times that try men's souls," five months after the Declaration of Independence was signed. The morale of General George Washington's troops was at a low ebb. These words were read to Washington's troops just before they crossed the Delaware River to fight at Trenton, New Jersey.

from The American Crisis, Number One

These are the times that try men's souls. The summer soldier and the sunshine patriot will, in this crisis, shrink from the service of their country; but he that stands it now, deserves the love and thanks of man and woman. Tyranny, like hell, is not easily conquered; yet we have this consolation with us, that the harder the conflict, the more glorious the triumph. What we obtain too cheap, we esteem too lightly: it is dearness only that gives every thing its value. Heaven knows how to put a proper price upon its goods; and it would be strange indeed if so celestial an article as *freedom* should not be highly rated. Britain, with an army to enforce her tyranny, has declared that she has a right not only to *tax* but "to *bind* us in *all cases whatsoever*"; and if being *bound in that manner* is not slavery, then is there not such a thing as slavery upon earth. Even the expression is impious; for so unlimited a power can belong only to God.

I have as little superstition in me as any man living, but my secret opinion has ever been, and still is, that God Almighty will not give up a people to military destruction, or leave them unsupportedly to perish, who have so earnestly and so repeatedly sought to avoid the calamities of war, by every decent method which wisdom could invent. Neither have I so much of the infidel in me as to suppose that He has relinquished the government of the world, and given us up to the care of devils; and as I do not, I cannot see on what grounds the king of Britain can look up to heaven for help against us: a common murderer, a highwayman, or a housebreaker, has as good a pretense as he.

I once felt all kind of anger which a man ought to feel against the mean principles that are held by the Tories: a noted one, who kept a tavern at Amboy, was standing at his door, with as pretty a child in his hand, about eight or nine years old, as I ever saw, and after speaking his mind freely as he thought was prudent, finished with this unfatherly expression, "Well! give me peace in my day." Not a man lives on the continent but fully believes that a separation must some time or other finally take place, and a generous parent should have said, "If there must be trouble, let it be in my day, that my child may have peace"; and this single reflection, well applied, is sufficient to awaken every man to duty. Not a place upon earth might be so happy as America. Her situation is remote from all the wrangling world, and she has nothing to do but to trade with them. A man can distinguish himself between temper and principle, and I am as confident, as I am that God governs the world, that America will never be happy till she gets clear of foreign dominion. Wars, without ceasing, will break out till that period arrives, and the continent must in the end be conqueror; for though the flame of liberty may sometimes cease to shine, the coal can never expire. . . .

—Thomas Paine

Start-Up: Thomas Paine uses primarily emotional appeal to incite the American working class to fight against the British. He compares the British king to a common criminal, presents America's struggle for freedom as a holy cause, and says that America's happiness lies in being free of "foreign dominion."

Connection: Review what you know about the above situation. Then, with a partner, rewrite the above speech, using the ADAM approach to persuasive speaking.

Working with Literature: Refer to *Student Workbook* page 10-H for an activity on persuasion.

Overview

George Orwell is the pen name chosen by Eric Blair. Born in Bengal, a region of India, and schooled in England, Orwell became famous for his two novels of political satire: *Animal Farm* and *1984.*

From 1922 to 1927, Orwell served in the Indian Imperial Police in Burma, where he wrote this essay. His ability to see the plight of the underdog and to describe the difficult official relationships between the British and the Burmese explains why this essay has been ranked a classic.

"Shooting an Elephant"

In Moulmein, in lower Burma, I was hated by large numbers of people—the only time in my life that I have been important enough for this to happen to me. I was sub-divisional police officer of the town, and in an aimless, petty kind of way anti-European feeling was very bitter. No one had the guts to raise a riot, but if a European woman went through the bazaars alone somebody would probably spit betel juice over her dress. As a police officer I was an obvious target and was baited whenever it seemed safe to do so. When a nimble Burman tripped me on the football field and the referee (another Burman) looked the other way, the crowd yelled with hideous laughter. This happened more than once. In the end the sneering yellow faces of young men that met me everywhere, the insults hooted after me when I was at a safe distance, got badly on my nerves. The young Buddhist priests were the worst of all. There were several thousands of them in the town and none of them seemed to have anything to do except stand on street corners and jeer at Europeans.

All this was perplexing and upsetting. For at that time I had already made up my mind that imperialism was an evil thing and the sooner I chucked up my job and got out of it the better. Theoretically—and secretly, of course—I was all for the Burmese and all against their oppressors, the British. As for the job I was doing, I hated it more bitterly than I can perhaps make clear. In a job like that you see the dirty work of Empire at close quarters. The wretched prisoners huddling in the stinking cages of the lock-ups, the gray cowed faces of the long-term convicts, the scarred buttocks of the men who had been flogged with bamboos—all these oppressed me with an intolerable sense of guilt. But I could get nothing into perspective. I was young and ill educated and I had had to think out my problems in the utter silence that is imposed on every Englishman in the East. I did not even know that the British Empire is dying, still less did I know that it is a great deal better than the younger empires that are going to supplant it. All I knew was that I was stuck between my hatred of the empire I served and my rage against the evil-spirited little beast who tried to make my job impossible. With one part of my mind I thought of the British Raj as an unbreakable tyranny, as something clamped down, in *saecula saeculorum,* upon the will of prostrate peoples; with another part I thought that the greatest joy in the world would be to drive a bayonet into a Buddhist priest's gut. Feelings like these are the normal by-products of imperialism; ask any Anglo-Indian official, if you catch him off duty.

One day something happened which in a roundabout way was enlightening. It was a tiny incident in itself, but it gave me a better glimpse than I had had before of the real nature of imperialism—the real motives for which despotic governments act. Early one morning the sub-inspector at a police station the other end of town rang me up on the phone and said that an elephant was ravaging the bazaar. Would I please come and do something about it? I did not know what I could do, but I wanted to see what was happening and I got onto a pony and started out. I took my rifle, an old .44 Winchester and much too small to kill an elephant, but I thought the noise might be useful in *terrorem*. Various Burmans stopped me on the way and told me about the elephant's doing. It was not, of course, a wild elephant, but a tame one which had gone "must." It had been chained up, as tame elephants always are when their attack of "must" is due, but on the previous night it had broken its chain and escaped. Its mahout, the only person who could manage it when it was in that state, had set out in pursuit, but had taken the wrong direction and was now twelve hours' journey away, and in the morning the elephant had suddenly reappeared in the town. The Burmese population had no weapons and were quite helpless against it. It had already destroyed somebody's bamboo hut, killed a cow and raided some fruit stalls and devoured the stock; also it had met the municipal rubbish van and, when the driver jumped out and took to his heels, had turned the van over and inflicted violences upon it.

The Burmese sub-inspector and some Indian constables were waiting for me in the quarter where the elephant had been seen. It was a very poor quarter, a labyrinth of squalid bamboo huts, thatched with palm-leaf, winding all over a steep hillside.

> *The Burmese population had no weapons and were quite helpless against it.*

I remember that it was a cloudy, stuffy morning at the beginning of the rains. We began questioning the people as to where the elephant had gone and, as usual, failed to get any definite information. That is invariably the case in the East; a story always sounds clear enough at a distance, but the nearer you get to the scene of the events the vaguer it becomes. Some of the people said that the elephant had gone in one direction, some said that he had gone in another, some professed not even to have heard of any elephant. I had almost made up my mind that the whole story was a pack of lies, when we heard yells a little distance away. There was a loud, scandalized cry of "Go away, child! Go away this instant!" and an old woman with a switch in her hand came round the corner of a hut, violently shooing away a crowd of naked children. Some more women followed, clicking their tongues and exclaiming; evidently there was something that the children ought not to have seen. I rounded the hut and saw a man's dead body sprawling in the mud. He was an Indian, a black Davidian coolie, almost naked, and he could not have been dead many minutes. The people said that the elephant had come suddenly upon him round the corner of the hut, caught him with its trunk, put its foot on his back and ground him into the earth. This was the rainy season and the ground was soft, and his face had scored a trench a foot deep and a couple of yards long. He was lying on his belly with arms crucified and head sharply twisted to one side. His face was coated with mud, the eyes wide open, the teeth bared and grinning with an

(cont'd on next page)

expression of unendurable agony. (Never tell me, by the way, that the dead look peaceful. Most of the corpses I have seen looked devilish.) The friction of the great beast's foot had stripped the skin from his back as neatly as one skins a rabbit. As soon as I saw the dead man I sent an orderly to a friend's house nearby to borrow an elephant rifle. I had already sent back the pony, not wanting it to go mad with fright and throw me if it smelt the elephant.

The orderly came back in a few minutes with a rifle and five cartridges, and meanwhile some Burmans had arrived and told us that the elephant was in the paddy fields below, only a few hundred yards away. As I started forward practically the whole population of the quarter flocked out of the houses and followed me. They had seen the rifle and were all shouting excitedly that I was going to shoot the elephant. They had not shown much interest in the elephant when he was ravaging their homes, but it was different now that he was going to be shot. It was a bit of fun to them, as it would be to an English crowd; besides they wanted the meat. It made me vaguely uneasy. I had no intention of shooting the elephant—I had merely sent for the rifle to defend myself if necessary—and it is always unnerving to have a crowd following you. I marched down the hill, looking and feeling a fool, with the rifle over my shoulder and an ever-growing army of people jostling at my heels. At the bottom, when you got away from the huts, there was a metalled road and beyond that a miry waste of paddy fields a thousand yards across, not yet ploughed but soggy from the first rains

and dotted with coarse grass. The elephant was standing eight yards from the road; his left side toward us. He took not the slightest notice of the crowd's approach. He was tearing up bunches of grass, beating them against his knees to clean them, and stuffing them into his mouth.

I had halted on the road. As soon as I saw the elephant I knew with perfect certainty that I ought not to shoot him. It is a serious matter to shoot a working elephant—it is comparable to destroying a huge and costly piece of machinery—and obviously one ought not to do it if it can possibly be avoided. And at that distance, peacefully eating, the elephant looked no more dangerous than a cow. I thought then and I think now that his attack of "must" was already passing off; in which case he would merely wander harmlessly about until the mahout came back and caught him. Moreover, I did not in the least want to shoot him. I decided that I would watch him for a little while to make sure that he did not turn savage again, and then go home.

But at that moment I glanced round at the crowd that had followed me. It was an immense crowd, two thousand at the least and growing every minute. It blocked the road for a long distance on either side. I looked at the sea of yellow faces above the garish clothes—faces all happy and excited over this bit of fun, all certain that the elephant was going to be shot. They were watching me as they would watch a conjurer about to perform a trick. They did not like me, but with the magical rifle in my hands I was momentarily worth

> *They were watching me as they would watch a conjurer about to perform a trick.*

watching. And suddenly I realized that I should have to shoot the elephant after all. The people expected it of me and I had got to do it; I could feel their two thousand wills pressing me forward, irresistibly. And it was at this moment, as I stood there with the rifle in my hands, that I first grasped the hollowness, the futility of the white man's dominion in the East. Here was I, the white man with his gun, standing in front of the unarmed native crowd—seemingly the leading actor of the piece, but in reality I was only an absurd puppet pushed to and fro by the will of those yellow faces behind. I perceived in this moment that when the white man turns tyrant it is his own freedom that he destroys. He becomes a sort of hollow, posing dummy, the conventionalized figure of a sahib. For it is the condition of his rule that he shall spend his life in trying to impress the "natives," and so in every crisis he has got to do what the "natives" expect of him. He wears a mask, and his face grows to fit it. I had got to shoot the elephant. I had committed myself to doing it when I sent for the rifle. A sahib has got to act like a sahib; he has got to appear resolute, to know his own mind and do definite things. To come all that way, rifle in hand, with two thousand people marching at my heels, and then to trail feebly away, having done nothing—no, that was impossible. The crowd would laugh at me. And my whole life, every white man's life in the East, was one long struggle not to be laughed at.

But I did not want to shoot the elephant. I watched him beating his bunch of grass

> *. . . I had never shot an elephant and never wanted to.*

against his knees with that preoccupied grandmotherly air that elephants have. It seemed to me that it would be murder to shoot him. At that age I was not squeamish about killing animals, but I had never shot an elephant and never wanted to. (Somehow it always seems worse to kill a large animal.) Besides, there was the beast's owner to be considered. Alive, the elephant was worth at least a hundred pounds; dead, he would only be worth the value of his tusks, five pounds, possibly. But I had got to act quickly. I turned to some experienced-looking Burmans who had been there when we arrived, and asked them how the elephant had been behaving. They all said the same thing: he took no notice of you if you left him alone, but he might charge if you went too close to him.

It was perfectly clear to me what I ought to do. I ought to walk up to within, say, twenty-five yards of the elephant and test his behavior. If he charged, I could shoot; if he took no notice of me, it would be safe to leave him until the mahout came back. But also I knew that I was going to do no such thing. I was a poor shot with a rifle and the ground was soft mud into which one would sink at every step. If the elephant charged and I missed him, I should have about as much chance as a toad under a steam-roller. But even then I was not thinking particularly of my own skin, only of the watchful yellow faces behind. For at that moment, with the crowd watching me, I was not afraid in the ordinary sense, as I would have been if I had been alone. A white man mustn't be frightened in front of the "natives"; and so, in general, he isn't frightened. The sole

(cont'd on next page)

thought in my mind was that if anything went wrong those two thousand Burmans would see me pursued, caught, trampled on, and reduced to a grinning corpse like that Indian on the hill. And if that happened it was quite probable that some of them would laugh. That would never do. There was only one alternative. I shoved the cartridges into the magazine and lay down on the road to get a better aim.

> *He neither stirred nor fell, but every line of his body had altered.*

The crowd grew very still, and a deep, low, happy sigh, as of people who see the theater curtain go up at last, breathed from innumerable throats. They were going to have their bit of fun after all. The rifle was a beautiful German thing with cross-hair sights. I did not then know that in shooting an elephant one would shoot to cut an imaginary bar running from ear-hole to ear-hole. I ought, therefore, as the elephant was sideways on, to have aimed straight at his earhole; actually I aimed several inches in front of this, thinking the brain would be further forward.

When I pulled the trigger I did not hear the bang or feel the kick—one never does when a shot goes home—but I heard the devilish roar of glee that went up from the crowd. In that instant, in too short a time, one would have thought, even for the bullet to get there, a mysterious, terrible change had come over the elephant. He neither stirred nor fell, but every line of his body had altered. He looked suddenly stricken, shrunken, immensely old, as though the frightful impact of the bullet had paralyzed him without knocking him down. At last, after what seemed a long time—it might have been five seconds, I

dare say—he sagged flabbily to his knees. His mouth slobbered. An enormous senility seemed to have settled upon him. One could have imagined him thousands of years old. I fired again into the same spot. At the second shot he did not collapse but climbed with desperate slowness to his feet and stood weakly upright with legs sagging and head dropping. I fired a third time. That was the shot that did for him. You could see the agony of it jolt his whole body and knock the last remnant of strength from his legs. But in falling he seemed for a moment to rise, for as his hind legs collapsed beneath him he seemed to tower upward like a huge rock toppling, his trunk reaching skyward like a tree. He trumpeted, for the first and only time. And then down he came, his belly toward me, with a crash that seemed to shake the ground even where I lay.

I got up. The Burmans were already racing past me across the mud. It was obvious that the elephant would never rise again, but he was not dead. He was breathing very rhythmically with long rattling gasps, his great mound of a side painfully rising and falling. His mouth was wide open—I could see far down into caverns of pale pink throat. I waited a long time for him to die, but his breathing did not weaken. Finally I fired my two remaining shots into the spot where I thought his heart must be. The thick blood welled out of him like red velvet, but still he did not die. His body did not even jerk when the shots hit him, the tortured breathing continued without a pause. He was dying very slowly and in great agony, but in some world remote from me where not even a bullet could damage him further. I felt that I had got to put an end to that dreadful noise. It seemed dreadful to see the great beast lying there, powerless to move and yet powerless to die, and not even to be able to finish him. I sent back for my small rifle and poured shot after shot into his heart and down his throat. They seemed to make no impression. The tortured gasps continued as steadily as the ticking of a clock.

In the end I could not stand it any longer and went away. I heard later that it took him half an hour to die. Burmans were bringing dahs and baskets even before I left, and I was told they had stripped his body almost to the bones by afternoon.

Afterward, of course, there were endless discussions about the shooting of the

> *. . . I had done it solely to avoid looking like a fool.*

elephant. The owner was furious, but he was only an Indian and could do nothing. Besides, legally I had done the right thing, for a mad elephant has to be killed, like a mad dog, if its owner fails to control it. Among the Europeans opinion was divided. The older men said I was right, the younger men said it was a damn shame to shoot an elephant for killing a coolie, because an elephant was worth more than any damn Coringhee coolie. And afterward I was very glad that the coolie had been killed; it put me legally in the right and it gave me a sufficient pretext for shooting the elephant. I often wondered whether any of the others grasped that I had done it solely to avoid looking like a fool.

—George Orwell

Start-Up: Orwell allowed himself to be persuaded to shoot the elephant even though he was totally against the act. The crowd was able to pressure Orwell into taking this action because he put too much importance on how others perceived him. He did not stand up for what he believed was the right thing to do.

Connection: Cite a similar experience of being persuaded by two or more people to do something that you thought was wrong. What methods did they use to influence you?

DIGITAL VISION

"I don't like work—no man does—but I like what is in work—the chance to find yourself. Your own reality—for yourself, not for others—what no other man can ever know."

—JOSEPH CONRAD, POLISH-BORN ENGLISH NOVELIST

Top 10 Reasons for Rejecting Job Applicants

10. Vagueness (being evasive or misleading)
9. Lack of confidence or overconfidence
8. Sloppy resume
7. Uninformed about the organization
6. Lack of courtesy, maturity, or tact
5. Too interested in salary or benefits
4. Lack of interest in the job
3. Poor personal appearance
2. Uncertainty about goals
1. Inability to express oneself clearly

Applying for a Job

You have been preparing for your first career position since you were young. The skills, talents, and personality traits that you bring to your first real job are not handed to you on graduation day along with your diploma—you have been developing them all through your life. On the soccer field, in the third-grade production of *The Wizard of Oz,* or in hundreds of hours of video games, you found out what you like—and what you can do well. Are you happiest when you're alone outdoors? When you're at the mall with a group of friends? When you've created something entirely original? The answers to those and many other questions form the heart of your career plan.

Part-time jobs held during school teach you about being dependable, working with others, taking direction, and getting through those hours when you'd rather be doing anything *but* working.

This chapter is not about how to land that type of job. This chapter is about how to land a *career* position—a challenging job with opportunities for learning and advancement; a job related to your talents, interests, and occupational training; a job that pays enough to cover rent, transportation, utilities, food, and other necessities, with enough left over for having fun and for savings; a job that includes benefits, such as health insurance and paid vacations. There is a great deal of competition for these jobs, often from people who may have more training and experience than you have. The first step is to locate potential employers.

Job Leads

Most job openings are never advertised; they are filled from within the organization or by word of mouth. When you are in the market for a job, tell everyone you know what you can do and what type of job you are looking for.

Practice 11–1: Job Leads

1. Do you know anyone who has the type of job you're looking for? Do you know anyone who works for an organization where you might like to work? List at least ten names, giving the names of companies, job titles, telephone numbers, and e-mail addresses for people who might be sources of leads for career positions. Include teachers and counselors, neighbors, family members, family members of your friends, friends of your family, etc.

2. You can turn job leads into good resume references. Choose five leads from Item 1 of this Practice—people who know your skills and work habits. Complete the Job Lead Reference Card on *Student Workbook* page 11-A. Do not choose your peers or your relatives.

Helpful Sources of Information

Start reading the help wanted ads in the newspaper. People often find good jobs this way. Even if the classified ads do not lead directly to a job, you can still learn a lot from reading them, as shown in Figure 11-1. For instance, the ads may answer these questions:

- What jobs are available in this area for people with my training?

- What is the demand?

---

by the way...

SERVICE TECHNICIANS

Reprographics company has opening for one full-time and one part-time copier repair technician. Requires copier service and electro/mechanical experience. Must be customer-oriented, reliable, self-motivated. Capable of scheduling service calls, filling out reports, maintaining a parts inventory. Full medical, tuition reimb. program. Send resume to EMH, 684 Mills Drive, Laurel, MD 20725-1426.

FIGURE 11-1   Read help wanted ads carefully and follow instructions.

Career *Connection*

The Bureau of Labor Statistics predicts large numbers of openings and above-average earnings for these occupations. None requires a bachelor's degree. All require additional training beyond standard high school courses.

- Registered nurses
- Licensed practical nurses
- Auto service technicians and mechanics
- Preschool teachers
- Computer support specialists
- Hairstylists and cosmetologists
- Medical secretaries
- Fitness trainers and instructors
- Legal secretaries
- Emergency medical technicians and paramedics

© GETTY IMAGES/PHOTODISC, INC.

Help wanted ads are good sources of information.

- What do these jobs pay?
- What qualities do the employers expect?

Always follow the instructions given in the ad. For example, if the ad asks for a resume, do not call instead.

The *Occupational Outlook Handbook (OOH)* is a publication of the U.S. Department of Labor that gives detailed descriptions of hundreds of jobs. The Bureau of Labor Statistics web site, http://bls.gov, has the complete *OOH* online. Also, the print edition is available in many libraries. By reading descriptions of jobs you have held and jobs you may apply for, you can find the following types of information:

- What work the job involves
- Estimated future job openings
- Necessary skills and training
- Working conditions
- Earnings
- Essential personal characteristics

Practice 11–2: Researching a Position

Tomorrow begin checking the help wanted ads in the newspaper or on the many Internet sites that post ads. Find an ad that closely matches your training and skills. But don't expect an exact match, since that rarely happens. When you find an ad that gives an address to write to, clip it or print it out and attach it to a sheet of paper. You will use it later in this chapter.

Computer, Automated Teller, and Office Machine Repairers

Computer repairers, also known as *computer service technicians or data-processing equipment repairers,* service mainframe, server, and personal computers; printers; and disc drives. These workers perform primarily hands-on repair, maintenance, and installation of computers and related equipment. Workers who provide technical assistance, in person or by telephone, to computer system users are known as computer support specialists or computer support technicians.

Office machine and cash register servicers work on photocopiers, cash registers, mail-processing equipment, and fax machines. Newer models of office machinery include computerized components that allow them to function more effectively than earlier models.

When equipment breaks down, many repairers travel to customers' workplaces or to other locations to make the necessary repairs. In small companies, repairers may work in repair shops and at customer locations.

Office machine repairers usually work on machinery at the customer's workplace; alternatively, if the machines are small enough, customers may bring them to a repair shop for maintenance. Common malfunctions include paper misfeeds, due to worn or dirty parts, and poor-quality copy, due to problems with lamps, lenses, or mirrors. These malfunctions usually can be resolved simply by cleaning the necessary components. Breakdowns also may result from the failure of commonly used parts. For example, heavy usage of a photocopier may wear down the printhead, which applies ink to the final copy. In such cases, the repairer usually replaces the part instead of repairing it.

Workers use a variety of tools for diagnostic tests and repair. To diagnose malfunctions, they use multimeters to measure voltage, current, resistance, and other electrical properties; signal generators to provide test signals; and oscilloscopes to monitor equipment signals. To diagnose computerized equipment, repairers use software programs. To repair or adjust equipment, workers use hand tools, such as pliers, screwdrivers, and soldering irons.

FIGURE 11-2 Excerpts from the *Occupational Outlook Handbook* description of computer, automated teller, and office machine repairers

Preparing a Resume

Take a look at a brochure advertising any product—a car stereo system, for instance. The brochure lists the features of the system, gives data about its performance, and lets you know where to find one. The brochure is eye-catching, well organized, and easy to read. The most important information jumps out at you. The purpose of the brochure, of course, is to interest you in buying the system. Chances are you won't place an order based on the brochure, but you might visit a store that sells the system so you can listen to it for yourself and get more information in person.

Your **resume** is like a sales brochure, but the product is *you*. Of course, your resume will not be colorful or flashy like the brochure. But it will be attractive, and it will include essentially the same kinds of information. It summarizes the job hunter's features and performance data—education, skills, training, and experience. No one is hired based only on the information in a resume. However, after reviewing resumes, many employers do make decisions about whom to call for an interview.

A decent resume cannot be prepared in a day, so it's a good idea to have one ready at all times. As is true for any other important communication, preparing a resume takes planning, organizing, writing, editing, revising, and more revising. If an employer has a large stack of resumes sitting on a desk, he or she is looking for ways to reduce this load of paperwork. Since interviews are time-consuming and the employer will schedule only a few of them, one error on your resume may be enough to cause an employer to discard it. You may lose your chance at getting a job interview.

Gathering Information

The entire job-seeking process requires a lot of information. Finding that information can take time. For instance, exact dates, names, and addresses for the jobs that you have held are required. You also have to take a good look at yourself and identify your own strengths and skills. Unless you know what you can offer employers, how will they know?

When you are looking for a job, you must match your experience, skills, training, and personal qualities to the type of job that you want. You need to point out to employers that you have what it takes to be a valuable employee.

Ask your teacher for a list of skills that are covered in your educational program curriculum. Talk to people who have or have had the type of job you're looking for. You must be able to show an employer what you know and what you can do. This information can make the difference between being considered for a job or being rejected.

Look for ways your education and experience have prepared you for the career position you want. Honestly examine your own skills and personal characteristics.

by the way...

Today a considerable amount of work gets done in teams. Find opportunities to show employers that you have accomplished things in cooperation with other people.

by the way...

Do let employers know when you are proficient in a second language. It's a definite plus!

Practice 11–3: Preparation for Writing a Resume

Complete the Personal Inventory form on *Student Workbook* pages 11-B through 11-E. The information that you write on this form will be useful not only as you plan your resume, but also as you write letters, complete applications, and prepare for interviews. Take your time filling it out. You will need to look up addresses and phone numbers, check the spelling of names, and request permission from references to list their names.

Do not treat this as just another classroom exercise. You will use the information from this form to prepare a resume to send to potential employers. Taking the time now to be thorough and exact will make the job of writing a resume much easier. An example of a completed Personal Inventory form is shown in Figure 11-3.

PERSONAL INFORMATION

FIRST NAME _Marcus_	MIDDLE NAME _H._ OR INITIAL	LAST NAME _Davis_

STREET ADDRESS _87 Ross Ave._	CITY _Laurel_	STATE _MD_	ZIP CODE _20726-2723_	NO. OF YEARS _16_

PREVIOUS ADDRESS _NA_	CITY	STATE	ZIP CODE	NO. OF YEARS

PHONE # _301-555-0172_	DATE OF BIRTH _5-3-90_

	MARITAL STATUS _SINGLE_	SOCIAL SECURITY # _202-44-8763_	DRIVER'S LICENSE # _PW68742_

IN AN EMERGENCY, NOTIFY: NAME _Benina Davis_ PHONE # _301-555-0153_

HOW MANY DAYS DID YOU MISS AT SCHOOL OR WORK DURING THE PAST 12 MONTHS? _0_

HEALTH: ☑ EXCELLENT ☐ GOOD ☐ POOR (IF POOR, EXPLAIN):

HAVE YOU EVER BEEN CONVICTED OF A FELONY? ☑ NO ☐ YES IF YES, EXPLAIN:

REFERENCES

NAME	JOB TITLE	ADDRESS	PHONE #	# OF YEARS
Marla Jones	manager	Shop 'n' Save 1007 Laurel Blvd. Laurel, MD 20723-1130	301-555-0132	5 mo.
Tom Hunter	head of maintenance	Laurel Public Schools 805 Pine Rd. Laurel, MD 20724-5423	301-555-0107 x 201	4
Lessa Hass	sales rep	EMH 684 Mills Dr. Laurel, MD 20725-1426	301-555-0141	5
Girard Watkins	head football coach	Laurel High School 801 Pine Rd. Laurel, MD 20724-5423	301-555-0107	4
Arlene Cooper	EMS instructor	Laurel Career Center 803 Pine Rd. Laurel, MD 20724-5423	301-555-0107 x 114	2

FIGURE 11-3 A sample Personal Inventory form

I AM: PERSONAL QUALITIES — Check as many as apply to you.

☑ accurate	☐ adaptable	☑ competent
☑ alert	☐ assertive	☑ conscientious
☑ calm	☑ careful	☑ cooperative
☐ competitive	☐ confident	☑ energetic
☐ considerate	☑ consistent	☑ hardworking
☐ creative	☑ dependable	☑ honest
☑ flexible	☑ friendly	☐ intelligent
☑ healthy	☑ helpful	☐ open-minded
☐ imaginative	☐ independent	☐ patient
☐ loyal	☐ mature	☑ punctual
☑ organized	☐ outgoing	☐ resourceful
☑ persistent	☐ practical	☑ self-reliant
☑ quick	☑ reliable	☐ tactful
☑ responsible	☑ self-motivated	☐ thoughtful
☑ steady	☐ strong	
☑ teachable	☐ thorough	

LIST YOUR FIVE STRONGEST QUALITIES WITH EVIDENCE BELOW:

1. reliable - perfect attendance. Trusted to maintain and repair school copiers.
2. teachable - A-B grade average
3. self-motivated - work unsupervised at Shop 'n' Save
4. honest - returned 3 wallets at Shop 'n' Save
5. friendly - enjoy helping customers. Lots of friends.

I CAN: SKILLS — Check as many as apply to you.

☑ listen	☑ read
☑ speak clearly	☑ write clearly
☑ follow instructions	☐ give instructions
☐ train others	☑ learn quickly
☐ learn from mistakes	☐ accept criticism
☑ take responsibility	☑ understand
☐ ask questions	☐ ask for help
☐ persuade	☐ sell
☑ cooperate	☑ help people
☐ handle complaints	☑ work with a team
☐ work safely	☐ organize time
☑ organize information	☐ organize people
☐ organize materials	☐ plan ahead
☑ follow through	☑ meet deadlines
☑ solve problems	☐ handle money
☑ calculate	☑ assemble
☑ construct	☑ inspect
☑ maintain	☑ repair
☑ install	☑ operate
☑ drive	☐ process

LIST YOUR FIVE STRONGEST SKILLS WITH EVIDENCE BELOW:

1. work with a team - played football for 3 years
2. calculate - A-B average in math
3. solve problems - I'll work with copier problems until I solve them.
4. operate computers - have used computers for 6 years
5. organize information - accurate stock & inventory, troubleshooting reports

TWO JOBS YOU'D LIKE TO HAVE:

1. copier service tech
2. pro football player

QUALITIES & SKILLS YOU HAVE FOR EACH JOB:

1. accurate, persistent, reliable, honest, competent
2. strong, quick, good team player

FIGURE 11-3 (cont'd)

EDUCATION

MOST RECENT SCHOOL ATTENDED

NAME Laurel Career Center

ADDRESS 803 Pine Rd. Laurel, MD 20724-5423

DATES: FROM 8-04 TO present

DIPLOMA/CERTIFICATE/DEGREE 6-06

GRADE POINT AVERAGE 3.2

CLASS RANK ?

FAVORITE CLASS EMS

LEAST FAVORITE CLASS Social Studies

MOST VALUABLE CLASS EMS

SPECIAL COURSES
Calculus
Physics
Technical communication

ACTIVITIES, HONORS, AWARDS
Skills USA member

First place - Skills USA Electronics Technology
Perfect attendance

SPECIAL SKILLS LEARNED
Troubleshooting, diagnosing, repairing, servicing of office machines
Reading blueprints & schematics
ID components
Radio & stereo circuits

SECOND MOST RECENT SCHOOL ATTENDED

NAME Laurel High School

ADDRESS 801 Pine Rd. Laurel, MD 20724-5423

DATES: FROM 2002 TO 2004

DIPLOMA/CERTIFICATE/DEGREE 2004

GRADE POINT AVERAGE 2.5

CLASS RANK ?

FAVORITE CLASS math

LEAST FAVORITE CLASS English

MOST VALUABLE CLASS Computer Science

SPECIAL COURSES
general studies

ACTIVITIES, HONORS, AWARDS
football - 3 years
Spanish Club - 2 years

SPECIAL SKILLS LEARNED
word processing, database, spreadsheet, computer graphics

FIGURE 11-3 (cont'd)

EXPERIENCE

CURRENT OR MOST RECENT JOB

JOB TITLE stock clerk

DATES OF EMPLOYMENT: FROM 10 / 05 TO / present

NAME OF BUSINESS Shop 'n' Save

NAME OF SUPERVISOR Marla Jones PHONE # 301-555-0132

ADDRESS 1007 Laurel Blvd., Laurel, MD 20723-1130

DUTIES Unpack, check, shelve products. Mark codes. Keep records, inventory. Help customers.

SECOND MOST RECENT JOB

JOB TITLE Groundskeeper

DATES OF EMPLOYMENT: FROM 6 / 03 & 04 TO 8 / 03 & 04
Two summers

NAME OF BUSINESS Laurel Public Schools

NAME OF SUPERVISOR Tom Hunter PHONE # 301-555-0107 x201

ADDRESS 805 Pine Rd., Laurel, MD 20724-5423

DUTIES Plant sod, maintain athletic fields, build & repair bleachers

THIRD MOST RECENT JOB

JOB TITLE Yard maintenance

DATES OF EMPLOYMENT: FROM 5 / 00 TO 9 / 00

NAME OF BUSINESS

NAME OF SUPERVISOR Ms. Lessa Haas PHONE # 301-555-0154

ADDRESS 27 Fair Oaks Ct., Laurel, MD 20725-1428

DUTIES Plant & maintain lawn & garden. Perform simple household repairs. Do errands.

OTHER RELEVANT EXPERIENCES & ACTIVITIES

Details of volunteer work, hobbies, interests, and other activities that apply to a career position

Install car stereos   Carpentry
Computers   Play guitar

FIGURE 11-3 (cont'd)

CHAPTER 11: Applying for a Job   375

Drafting the Resume

Use a computer for drafting the resume; there simply is no other way to do it. Resume-writing software, web sites and word processing programs make it easy to correct errors, move sections, and improve page design. You can even create slightly different resumes for different employers. If your address or job changes after you have completed your resume, you can easily revise it if it has been saved on a disk or your hard drive. A resume is never finished; it is a work in progress. Once you have a good, basic resume prepared, you can modify it for years without having to start over.

Your resume will be as unique as your fingerprint. The resumes in Figures 11-4 and 11-5 will give you some ideas; however, you need to adapt those ideas to fit your situation. Make sure that your resume says what you want it to say about you. Take advantage of this opportunity to tell the reader what you know and what you can do. It is not enough to list where and when you worked or attended school. Provide information that will tell the reader how dependable, hardworking, and trainable you are. What skills do you already have that this employer is looking for? List your accomplishments and their results. If you don't tell the reader, who will?

Even though your resume will be unique, it should include the following sections:

Name, Address, and Phone Number

This information appears at the top of the resume. Use your full name (you may use a middle initial) and your full mailing address. Write out words such as *Street* and *Avenue*. Include the area code with your phone number and make sure an answering machine or a person will answer at that number during business hours. If you have an answering machine, make sure your greeting is brief and businesslike. Include your e-mail address; you can create a free account at sites such as http://www.yahoo.com and http://www.hotmail.com.

Job Objective

The **job objective** is a brief statement of your employment goal. If you are applying for a specific opening, make that job your objective. You can change your objective slightly for different jobs. Don't try to get by with something general such as "A rewarding position with opportunities for growth and advancement." That just says that you have no objective. Besides, who actually *wants* a dead-end job with no rewards?

Education

Since school has been your main job so far, your education is probably the most important section of your resume. Give the name of your school, your graduation date, and the name of any special course of study that would interest employers. List special job-related skills and relevant honors and awards. Include school activities, especially those in which you took leadership or demonstrated your value as a team player. If you are proud of your grade point average, include it as well.

Marcus H. Davis

87 Ross Avenue
Laurel, Maryland 20726-2723
301-555-0172

Objective: Service technician with a reprographics company specializing in copiers

Education
2002 to 2004

LAUREL CAREER CENTER
Laurel, Maryland

Program: Electro-Mechanical Systems Maintenance

Activities: First place, Skills USA
State Electronics Technologycompetition
Perfect Attendance Award

Skills:
- Troubleshooting, rebuilding, and adjusting copiers
- Reading blueprints and schematics
- Performing preventive maintenance on all office machines
- Identifying electrical/electronic components
- Operating power tools safely
- Using instruments for diagnosing and servicing
- Redesigning circuitry, replacing components, and servicing alignment of tuned circuits in radios and stereo systems
- Using word processing, spreadsheet, and database software

2004 to 2006

LAUREL HIGH SCHOOL
Laurel, Maryland
Diploma, June 2006

Activities: Varsity football, three years
Spanish Club, two years

Experience
October 2005 to Present

SHOP 'N' SAVE
Laurel Boulevard, Laurel, Maryland
Stock Clerk, part-time. Unpacking, checking, marking, and shelving products. Keeping detailed stock and inventory records. Helping customers.

2003 to 2004

LAUREL PUBLIC SCHOOLS
Laurel, Maryland

Groundskeeper. Temporary summer employment. Planted and maintained sod, shrubs, and trees. Built and repaired bleachers.

FIGURE 11-4 A sample chronological resume

Experience

Give the names of organizations you worked for, when you worked there, and your job title. Briefly describe job duties. List jobs in **reverse chronological order**—with your present job first. Write about your current job in the present tense; describe other jobs in the past tense. If you have no paid work experience, consider describing volunteer work or other valuable, relevant experiences.

Anne T. Barrientos

112 North Barrington Road
Salt Lake City, UT 84116-0504
801/555-0109

Job Target

A position as an administrative assistant in a business office

Office Skills

- Experience with MS Word
- Experience with WordPerfect
- Knowledge of office procedures
- Strong interpersonal skills
- Knowledge of accounting ledgers
- Experience with Excel spreadsheets
- Experience with PowerPoint
- Keying speed of 60 wpm
- Operation of switchboard
- Excellent math skills

Administrative Activities

- Assisted with clerical duties in family-owned business
- Treasurer, Sycamore High School Business Professionals of America
  Maintained account ledger, created annual budget, balanced budget
- Cochairperson, Business Professionals candy sale
  Directed sales staff, planned advertising campaign, sold candy

Education

Sycamore High School, Salt Lake City, Utah
Swim team, two years
Assistant editor of school newspaper, three years

Experience

Freese's Flowers, Layton, Utah
Salesclerk and clerical assistant, part-time

Mr. and Mrs. Wardell Sampson, Spring, Utah
Baby-sitter for three children, part-time

FIGURE 11-5 A sample functional resume

Culture *Connection*

Training employees is taken seriously in Japan. New employees spend up to six months in intensive training programs, which are usually held outside of the job in special training centers. On April 1, most companies observe *nyusha-shiki,* a ceremony for receiving newly hired employees into a company.

Practice 11–4: Revising Resumes

1. One key to designing an effective resume is consistency. For example, format all of your headings and dates the same way throughout your resume. You must also be consistent with the wording of items in lists; the wording must be **parallel.** The following list of restaurant management duties is from the resume of a person who had worked in the family restaurant business for several years. Revise the list so that all items have the same grammatical structure. Use concise phrases, not complete sentences.

Ch11–04.doc

   • Prepared payroll for staff of 10
   • Cash registers—opening and closing
   • decorating and cleaning of the restaurant
   • Have trained 15 servers
   • Greeted and served customers
   • stockroom organization and maintaining inventory
   • Menu planning
   • I made sure that the food deliveries were of acceptable quality and that they were accurate.
   • I checked to make sure that the food preparation areas were orderly and clean.
   • Supervise the preparation, arrangement, and serving of food

2. Many verbs in English are followed by an adverb or a preposition; the two-word phrase is a type of **idiom.** However, since the fewer words used in a resume the better, the idiom should be replaced by one word. Using *Student Workbook* page 11-F, change each idiom to one word.

Organizational Plans

The two most common organizational plans for resumes are chronological and functional. The **chronological resume** (see Figure 11-4) lists background information in chronological (time) sequence, starting with the most recent experience first and working backward. This is the most common form and the one that most employers expect to see.

In the **functional resume** (see Figure 11-5), work experience and abilities are listed by skill areas. Resumes in this style are more difficult to put together and tend to be longer. The functional resume is most often used by people with a great deal of experience.

Resume Guidelines

When preparing a resume, follow these guidelines:

- Tell the truth. Nothing is more important than accuracy.

- Limit the resume to one page.

- Give only positive information. Do not include a photo or personal information about health or family. Do not give salary requirements or reasons for leaving other jobs. Include only hobbies and interests that relate to your ability to do the job for which you are applying. Your readers are not interested in you personally; they are interested in how you can benefit their organization.

- Avoid using technical jargon or acronyms on resumes. If the reader doesn't understand them, they're just wasting space.

- Don't use the word *I* in the resume. It's not necessary because the resume is obviously about you.

- Decide whether your education or work experience will be more valuable to the reader. Put the most valuable section first.

- Use short sentences or lists with parallel structure to describe skills or responsibilities. Begin sentences in resumes by describing work experience with **active verbs**, such as the ones listed here.

Past-Tense Active Verbs

achieved	handled	performed	selected
analyzed	helped	planned	served
arranged	improved	prepared	sold
assembled	installed	presented	solved
assisted	learned	processed	sorted
built	maintained	produced	studied
coordinated	managed	provided	trained
demonstrated	operated	recorded	won
designed	organized	repaired	worked
developed	participated	scheduled	wrote

- Use **keywords**, nouns and noun phrases, rather than active verbs for resumes that will be sent electronically (over the Internet) or **scanned**. Some companies use special software that searches the resume for keywords that match the requirements for particular positions. For example, an electrician might include the following keyword section:

Career *Connection*

When you send your resume to a medium-size or large company today, a computer, not a person, will probably be the first to look at it. At some companies, resume-scanning software reads resumes and stores keywords in databases. The software then uses keywords to match resumes with positions. That means the resumes must be computer-friendly. This same procedure is also used when you send your resume as an e-mail attachment or post your resume on the Internet. If you know your resume will be scanned, follow these guidelines:

- Use nouns, rather than active verbs, to emphasize specific talents.
- Use industry keywords.
- Do not use fancy fonts, type smaller than 12 points, italics, underlining, lines and borders, bullets, or multiple columns. Begin all text at the left margin.
- Send originals printed on white paper.
- Do not fold or staple.
- Triple-check spelling.
- Include your e-mail address, but not your address and phone number, on a resume sent via the Internet.

KEYWORD SUMMARY: Commercial wiring. Use of hand and hydraulic benders. Experience with EMT and rigid conduit. Fire alarm experience. Blueprint reading and layout. Two years experience. Good problem-solving skills.

- Don't be creative. There's no such thing as a cute, hip, or flashy resume. Don't even consider using adorable clip art, clever bullets, or snazzy borders. Resumes should have a businesslike, dignified appearance.

- Use a plain, readable typeface, such as Times New Roman, Palatino, or Arial.

- Use white space, headings, bold print, and bullets to make the resume attractive and easy to read.

- Balance the resume between margins.

- Do not include "References available upon request" on your resume. The employer assumes you have references. List them on a separate page so that, if an interviewer asks for this list, you have it ready. The best references are school personnel and former supervisors who can say good things about your skills and work habits. Don't ask your peers or relatives to be references.

- Use every proofreading trick you know. Ask several people to proofread for you. Keep at it until the resume is perfect.

- Stand several feet away from your resume to check its overall appearance and use of white space.

by the way...

True story! From a resume: "College, August 1880–May 1984."

Career *Connection*

Good references give you an edge in a competitive job market. To get more from your references, do the following:

• Choose people who are enthusiastic when they talk about you.
• Select a variety of people. Comments from clergy or family friends don't give employers much information, unless you worked for them.
• Ask permission when choosing a reference. Give each reference a copy of your resume.
• If you don't want your current employer to know you're job hunting, find peers who can discuss your job performance.
• If you don't list supervisors from past jobs, you seem to be hiding references. Find someone from a previous job who can verify your performance.

• Use high-quality paper in a conservative color—white or off-white—and a high-quality ink-jet or laser printer. Send originals if you can. However, if you must send photocopies, make sure they are clear and clean.

How would you feel as an employer if you received a resume like the one shown in Figure 11-6?

Miki Lin

543 St. Claire Ave. ☆ Little Rock, Ark. ☆ 501-555-0162

JOB OBJECTIVE
I am looking for a any type good radio, television, or video production job with good pay and good benefits.

EDUCATION
Princeton High School, Little Rock, Arkansas

I took two years of special classes in Radio and Television Production and I learned how to:
☆ read transmiter
☆ doing on-location shoots
☆ positioning & operating studio lights
☆ audio board & microphones
☆ script writing
☆ I can operate studio cameras

DECA, Honor Role (Two Quarters), Sound Director For Talent Show, Junior High Track Team, Certificate Of Participation In Speech Contest, 2.4 GPA, Member Of Thespian Society, Participated In S.A.A.A.

EXPERIENCE
MOM'S   SHOE WORLD
February 2005 to present   Sales Clerk
Cook   November 2004 to December 2004

Personnel Information

Age: 17   Height: 5'11"   Weight: 185 lbs.   Heath: good
I like to listen to the radio, ride mountain bikes, play video games

Referecnes
Refereces are available upon request.

FIGURE 11-6   A negative resume example

A hiring manager spends ten seconds on a resume to decide whether to interview you. These ten seconds *include* your cover letter. Don't let your cover letter waste your ten-second opportunity. The rule of a resume is that every line sells you as a potential employee. The same rule applies to the cover letter. In fact, the cover letter is shorter, so it should sell your qualifications more powerfully. Every sentence in the cover letter should offer a specific reason for hiring you. You never know which sentence will catch the hiring manager's eye during your precious ten seconds.

Practice 11–5: Analyzing Resumes

teamwork

1. Imagine that you are an employer. After receiving in the mail the resumes shown in Figures 11-4, 11-5, and 11-6 on pages 377, 378, and 382 respectively, you immediately toss one in the trash. Why? In a group of two or three students, list ten reasons. How would you improve the other two resumes?

2. What advice would you give Marcus Davis for producing an

Preparing a Cover Letter

by the way...

True story! From a cover letter: "Here are my qualifications for you to overlook."

Always send **cover letters** with resumes. This is your opportunity to demonstrate your qualifications for and interest in a particular job. Figure 11-7 shows the information that is included in a cover letter, and Figure 11-8 shows the letter that Marcus Davis sent with his resume. Cover letters are short and focused—no more than three or four paragraphs. Don't try to write a one-size-fits-all form letter. You may be able to recycle a few sentences, but you'll have to write a different cover letter for each job.

Communicate enthusiasm throughout your letter. Try to include some information that will cause the reader to take notice and to pause and think "I'd like to know more about this person." If you know of any name to mention, such as that of a current employee of the organization, include it in your cover letter. Use a polite, professional tone and only recent information about yourself.

If you have the phone number, call to ask the name of the appropriate person or search the company web site. Address the cover letter to a specific person.

Career *Connection*

You will not be able to learn the name of the person to whom to address the cover letter when the job posting is a blind-box ad. The help wanted ad is either on a web site with only a company description, not the company's name, or the ad provides the only address as being in care of a post office box or the newspaper itself.

When you respond to a blind-box ad, you can address your letter (or e-mail if the web site requests) to the following:

• Dear Boxholder
• Dear Hiring Manager or Human Resource Professional

After the inside address, skip two lines and key: *Re: [Title of Advertised Position].* Skip two more lines and begin the body of the cover letter. Or if you are writing an e-mail, put the title of the advertised position in the subject line.

Your Street Address
City, State ZIP Code
Date

Reader's Name
Reader's Job Title
Company Name
Street Address
City, State ZIP Code

Dear Title and Last Name:

The first paragraph explains who you are and why you are writing. If you are responding to an ad, tell where you saw it. If someone referred you, give the name and your relationship. Name the position for which you want to apply.

The next section summarizes your qualifications. Let the reader know why you want to work for this particular organization and what you can contribute to it. Don't waste space repeating the information included in your resume.

The closing provides a courteous, friendly ending. Include an action statement. For example, ask the reader for an interview or indicate when you will call to make an appointment. Include a polite ending.

Sincerely,

Your Signature

Your Name

Enclosure

FIGURE 11-7 Suggested content for cover letters

87 Ross Avenue
Laurel, MD 20726-2723
March 3, 200-

Mr. Manuel Cardena
Human Resources Manager
EMH Company
684 Mills Drive
Laurel, MD 20725-1426

Dear Mr. Cardena:

I am a high school senior attending the Laurel Career Center in the Electro-Mechanical Systems Maintenance program. I would very much like to apply for the position of part-time service technician, which I read about in Sunday's *Laurel Press*.

I learned about your company during a school field trip last spring. I also recently discussed EMH with your sales representative, Ms. Lessa Haas, who encouraged me to apply. She hired me to do odd jobs for her a few years ago and has agreed to be one of my references.

My training at the Career Center has prepared me for this position, and my present job has given me experience in dealing with customers, which I enjoy. My technical skills, especially my copier repair skills, are excellent; but I plan to expand them by attending college part-time in either computer science or electrical engineering.

Because I believe my qualifications meet your needs, I would like to schedule an interview to discuss them with you. Please call me any day after 2:30.

Sincerely,

Marcus Davis

Marcus Davis

Enclosure

FIGURE 11-8 A sample cover letter

Completing Job Applications

If you are called for an interview, you will be asked to fill out a job application form. You must read and follow instructions on the job application. If you fail to follow instructions, what will the potential employer assume about your ability to follow instructions on the job? Write clearly, respond to all questions, and be honest. Bring along your resume and your Personal Inventory form from Practice 11-3.

Application forms are typically designed with tiny spaces for answers. Print as small as you can, but make sure your responses are legible. If the question does not apply to you, write *NA* (for "not applicable"). Study the example of a job application in Figure 11-9 on the next page.

Assume that you received an application from the organization that ran the ad that you found for Practice 11-2. Carefully complete the job application on *Student Workbook* pages 11-G and 11-H. Use information from your Personal Inventory for Practice 11-3 and follow all instructions carefully. You may need to turn back to Chapter 8 to review guidelines for filling out forms.

APPLICATION FOR EMPLOYMENT

Please Print

We are an equal opportunity employer, dedicated to a policy of nondiscrimination in employment on any basis including race, color, age, sex, religion, or national origin.

PERSONAL INFORMATION   Date **March 8, 2006**   Social Security Number **202-44-8763**

Name	**Davis**	**Marcus**	**H.**		
	Last	First	Middle		
Present Address	**87 Ross Avenue**	**Laurel**	**Maryland**	**20726-1723**	
	Street	City	State	ZIP	
Permanent Address	Street	City	State	ZIP	

Phone No. **(301) 555-0172**

ARE YOU A U.S. CITIZEN? YES ✔ NO м	ANY RESTRICT. ON TRAVEL YES м NO ✔	IF YES, EXPLAIN ___	
HAVE YOU EVER BEEN CONVICTED FOR OTHER THAN м YES ✔ NO MINOR TRAFFIC VIOLATIONS?	IF YES, WHEN? ___	WHERE? ___	REASON ___

EMPLOYMENT DESIRED

Position **service technician**	Date You Can Start **3/15/06**
Are You Employed Now? **yes**	If So, May We Inquire of Your Present Employer? **yes**
Ever Applied to This Company Before? **no**	Where? ___ When? ___

EDUCATION

	Name and Location of School	Circle Last Year Completed	Did You Graduate?	Subjects Studied or Degree?
High School	**Laurel High School** **801 Pine Rd. Laurel, MD**	1 ②3 4	м YES ✔NO	**General Studies** **Diploma 6/06**
College	___	1 2 3 4	м YES м NO	
Trade, Business, or Correspondence School	**Laurel Career Center** **803 Pine Rd. Laurel, MD**	①2 3 4	м YES ✔NO	**Two-Year Electro-Mechanical Systems Maintenance Program**

SPECIALIZED TECHNICAL SKILLS (e.g., Computer Programmer/Language, Equipment Operation, Special Tools or Machines Used)

Troubleshooting, maintenance, and repair of all office equipment, including copiers.

Able to use a computer and all diagnostic and servicing equipment.

Activities Other Than Religious (civic, athletic, etc.) Exclude organizations the name or character of which indicates the race, age, sex, color, or national origin of their members.

Skills USA student organization

(Continued)

FIGURE 11-9 A sample job application

PHYSICAL RECORD

Do you have any disability that would substantially interfere with your ability to perform the essential duties of the job for which you have applied? If so, what can be done to accomodate your limitations?

No

WORK EXPERIENCE

(List below your last four employers, starting with your present or last employer.)

Date Mo./Yr.	Name and Address of Employer	Salary	Position	Name of Supervisor	Reason for Leaving
Fr. 10/05 To Present	Shop 'n' Save 1007 Laurel Blvd.	$6.00 per hour	Stock Clerk	Marla Jones	I wish to work in my trade.
Fr. Summers To 03-04	Laurel Public Schools 805 Pine Rd.	$5.50 per hour	Grounds-keeper	Tom Hunter	Temporary summer employment
Fr. 5/00 To 9/00	Ms. Lessa Haas 27 Fair Oaks Ct.	$25.00 per week	Yard Maintenance/ General Helper	————	Temporary employment
Fr. To	————				

May we contact your present employer?   YES ☑   NO ☐

REFERENCES

Give the names of three persons not related to you, whom you have known for at least two years.

	Name and Occupation	Address	Telephone Number	Years Known
1.	Ms. Lessa Haas, Sales Representative.	EMH 684 Mills Dr. Laurel, MD 20725-1426	301-555-0141	5
2.	Ms. Arlene Cooper, EMS Instructor.	Laurel Career Center 803 Pine Rd. Laurel, MD 20714-5423	301-555-0107, x114	2
3.	Mr. Tom Hunter, Maintenance Supervisor.	Laurel Public Schools 805 Pine Rd. Laurel, MD 20714-5423	301-555-0107, x201	4

I authorize investigation of all statements contained in this application. I understand that misrepresentation or omission of facts called for is cause for dismissal. Further, I understand and agree that my employment is for no definite period and may, regardless of the date of payment of my wages and salary, be terminated at any time without any previous notice.

Date   March 8, 2005   Signature   Marcus H. Davis

DO NOT WRITE BELOW THIS LINE.

Interviewed by _____   Date _____

Remarks _____

_____

_____

_____

Neatness		Ability	

Hired	For Dept.	Position	Will Report	Salary or Wages

Approved: 1. _____   2. _____   3. _____

Employment Manager	Dept. Head	General Manager

FIGURE 11-9 (cont'd)

CHAPTER 11: Applying for a Job   387

Preparing for a Job Interview

Filling out the Personal Inventory form and the job application is good preparation for an interview. The employer will ask about your background, education, experience, skills, and goals.

You also need to find out about the organization to which you are applying. This shows that you are interested in working for the company. Follow these guidelines for successful interviews:

- Get plenty of rest the night before and think positively.

- Arrive clean and well groomed for the interview. Dress as you would for a day on the job, only better. Do not try to look cute, sexy, or trendy; dress conservatively and neatly. This advice also applies to hairstyle, makeup, fragrance, jewelry, and other accessories. Look as if you will fit in.

- Arrive about ten minutes early. Take a pen with black ink, one or more copies of your resume, and the contents of your career portfolio if you've created one.

- Most interviewers make their decision within the first three minutes, so make a terrific first impression. Listen carefully to the pronunciation of the name of the person who will interview you so that you can greet him or her by name. Respond to a move to shake hands with a firm grip and a smile. Don't sit down until you're invited to do so.

- Use common courtesy and good sense. No gum or tobacco products.

- Think about your body language. Sit up straight and keep your hands still. Smile when appropriate. Use frequent, direct eye contact, but don't stare.

- Listen carefully to questions and answer them directly and honestly. Speak up and don't talk too fast or give one-word answers. Remember, you are trying to sell yourself.

- Most interviews last about 30 minutes. When the interviewer moves to end the interview, let him or her know you are interested in the job, say thank you, and leave.

Be prepared to answer questions about your background, education, experience, skills, and goals.

© GETTY IMAGES/PHOTODISC, INC.

Career *Connection*

Most businesses share similar problems and want similar benefits from employees. By understanding how businesses operate, you will be in a better position to figure out ways to convince potential employers that you can make a contribution.

What You Should Know About Business

• The purpose of any business is to make a profit through creating and keeping customers.

• Any company makes a profit by offering something of value to its customers.

• To survive, companies must meet and exceed customer expectations.

• All companies require innovation to stay ahead of the competition—new products, new markets, and improvements to existing products.

Before every interview, ask yourself these questions:

• What can I do to help the organization get or keep customers?

• How can I help the organization deliver value to its customers?

by the way...

When Thomas Edison interviewed job applicants, he would always have them over for lunch and serve them soup. Applicants who salted the soup without tasting it were rejected. Edison was looking for people who challenged assumptions instead of acting on them.

by the way...

"One of the best ways to persuade others is with your ears—by listening to them."

DEAN RUSK, U.S. DEMOCRATIC POLITICIAN

Interview Questions

Because every interviewer has his or her own style, you cannot predict the exact questions you will be asked. There are four basic interview questions, according to Richard Nelson Bolles, author of the book *What Color Is Your Parachute? A Practical Manual for Job-Hunters and Career Changers.*

Basic Questions	Examples
• Why did you choose this organization?	What do you know about our company?

• What can you offer us?	Questions about specific, job-related skills:
	    Are you familiar with . . .
	    Do you know how to . . .
	    Have you received training in . . .

Who are you?	How are your grades? Why did you leave your last job?
Are you affordable?	How much does your current (or did your last) job pay?

Practice 11–7: Preparing Answers to Interview Questions

Memorizing interview questions is not a good idea. However, thinking about possible questions ahead of time *is* a good idea. Write possible answers to the following interview questions:

1. Tell me about yourself.
2. How did you choose your school (program, major, etc.)?
3. Where do you see yourself ten years from now?
4. What are your greatest strengths and weaknesses?
5. What have you learned from your mistakes?
6. Why would you like to work for our organization?
7. How can you make our organization more successful?
8. Do you prefer working by yourself or with others?
9. How do you handle conflicts that develop at work?
10. What kind of work do you enjoy the most? The least?
11. How much would you expect to be paid?
12. Why should I hire you?

Inappropriate Job Interview Questions

Along with questions about your qualifications for the job, some interviewers occasionally ask questions related to applicants' personal lives. These questions have nothing to do with their ability to do the job. Most interviewers avoid these questions, since it is illegal to discriminate against applicants because of marital status, number of children, disability, age, method of transportation to work, religion, race and national origin. By law, you do not need to answer these questions. Some of these questions may be asked once a person is hired, though. Of course, you can refuse to answer the question. A more effective approach, however, if you are truly interested in the job, is to give a positive "nonanswer." For example:

Question: Who will take care of your children while you are at work?
Answer: I've made arrangements so that my family life will interfere as little as possible with my work.
Question: How would you feel about working for a woman (or man)?
Answer: I have worked with both men and women while in school.
Question: Where were you born?
Answer: I'm a permanent resident of the United States and have legal permission to work here.

Ethics *Connection*

You're about to run out the door to go to a doctor's appointment, to take your little sister to soccer practice, or to go to a job interview, and the phone rings. The hiring manager wants to interview you over the phone for a job you really want. What can you do? You have to leave, but you don't want to miss this opportunity. You need to have a prepared response so you won't be caught off guard. A suggested reply would be "I'm sorry, but I have to leave for an appointment. I really would like to talk to you, though. May I call you back later today? What time would be best for you?"

Many organizations use a telephone interview at different stages in the hiring process, especially for an initial interview. In fact, some companies conduct telephone screenings to judge how prepared and professional an applicant is.

⦿ Practice 11–8: Responding to Inappropriate Questions

teamwork

Ch011-08.doc

You may work on this Practice with one or two partners.

How might you respond to the following interview questions? Assume that you do not want to answer directly. Instead, give a positive nonanswer for each question.

1. Would you mind sending us a photo?

2. Do you have any disabilities?

3. What church do you attend?

4. Do you believe that national origin will be a problem in performing your job?

5. How will you get to work? Do you own a car?

6. Are you planning to get married?

7. Do you plan to have children?

by the way...

True story! An extremely nervous young man arrived for an interview wearing a beautiful new suit—with all of the tags still attached to the sleeve.

Questions from the Applicant

Most interviewers ask applicants if they have any questions. If you don't have any, the interviewer may assume you're not interested in the job. Instead of asking about pay or benefits, prepare questions such these:

• What would a normal workday be like?

• What are the opportunities for advancement?

• Are there opportunities for on-the-job training or further education?

• What are you looking for in an entry-level worker?

Ask two or three questions as a way to convey that you have options. Your questions should suggest "I'm trying to find out more about this position to decide whether I'm interested." One way to prepare for the interview is by participating in practice interviews.

Most people go through many interviews before they are hired. In rare

Practice 11-9: Interviewing for a Job

For this Practice, work with two other students. All three of you will take turns acting as applicant, interviewer, and observer. You need your help wanted ad, resume, completed job application form, and a pen or pencil.

Interviewer

1. Quickly read the applicant's help wanted ad, resume, and application.

2. Shake hands with the applicant and introduce yourself. Ask the applicant to be seated.

3. Ask the applicant general interview questions and questions about the information on the resume and application.

4. Ask follow-up questions to clarify the applicant's answers.

5. End the interview by saying, "We'll call to let you know next week."

Applicant

1. The interviewer will extend his or her hand. Shake it firmly, smile, and introduce yourself. Use the interviewer's name; for example, "I'm pleased to meet you, Ms. Woods."

2. After you have been offered a seat, sit down.

3. Think about your posture and body language.

4. Speak clearly, loudly, and slowly enough to be easily understood.

5. Answer questions directly and honestly. Do not give one-word answers, but don't ramble on too long either.

6. Don't be afraid to pause and think before answering a question. Refer to your resume for facts when necessary.

7. Ask the interviewer at least one question.

8. The interviewer will let you know when the interview is over. Express your thanks and your interest in the job. Shake hands.

Observer

Do not participate directly in the interview. Silently watch and listen to the interview while you complete the observation form on *Student Workbook* page 11-I. Share your completed form with the applicant.

Ch11-09.mp3

People *Connection*

Dauna Easley owned the Learning Station, a private school for toddlers through fourth graders, for 15 years. When she listed a position in the newspaper, she took only the first 100 calls. Here's what she said about that important initial contact:

> Make no mistake about it, the phone call is an interview, so get your resume out before calling. I ask ten open-ended questions to find out if the callers would fit in with my staff and if they really want *this* job, not just *a* job. One grammatical error from callers and they are eliminated because teachers must be role models for the children. Since I only invite ten callers in for interviews, I have to find out if the parents, my *customers,* will "buy" this person. One applicant arrived with poison ivy blisters all over her face and arms. I hired her because she showed a sense of humor about the situation and *she showed up,* both essential qualities for any employee.

Preparing the Follow-Up Letter

by the way...

True story! From a follow-up letter: "Thank you for your consideration. Hope to hear from you shorty."

cases, you may be hired on the spot or you may be immediately rejected. Usually, though, the interviewer closes by saying that there are still applicants to interview and that you will receive a call by a certain date. If that day goes by and you hear nothing, you may call the interviewer a few days later.

As soon as you get home from the interview, it's time to start writing again. The **follow-up letter** lets the employer know that you want the job and thanks the interviewer for talking to you. Send this brief, polite letter no later than two days after the interview. Even if you decide that the job for which you interviewed is not for you or if you know that you will not receive a job offer, send a follow-up letter.

You must do one more thing. Call or write to all of the people who helped you get the interview. Thank them and give them the results of the interview. Chances are, you'll be interviewing again and may need more help.

Figure 11-10 on the next page suggests information to include in a follow-up letter. Figure 11-11 on page 395 shows an example of a follow-up letter.

Being Evaluated on the Job

Finding a job can be a frustrating process. Eventually, though, efforts will pay off with an offer of a good job. The new employee must then apply all of his or her skills to that job and learn new skills and procedures.

The new employee will also have to learn what the employer expects. Most employers make their expectations clear. If your boss does not, ask for a complete explanation of the expectations and the evaluation process.

Your Street Address
City, State ZIP Code
Date

Reader's Name
Reader's Job Title
Company Name
Street Address
City, State ZIP Code

Dear Title and Last Name:

Remind the reader when you interviewed and for what position. Express appreciation for the interviewer's time and interest.

Briefly restate your qualifications and your interest in the job. If you have any additional information that the reader may need, mention it.

Let the reader know you are looking forward to hearing from him or her again.

Sincerely,

Your Signature

Your Name

FIGURE 11-10 Suggested content for follow-up letters

All employees are periodically evaluated. Whether the process is informal or formal, within the first few weeks or months, your supervisor will decide whether you fit in with the organization and whether you have potential for making a positive contribution.

To rate employees, some organizations use a form similar to the one found in Figure 11–12 on the next page. Employers make decisions about rate of pay and job classification based on the criteria listed on the form. Even in organizations where this type of form is not used, employers use similar criteria to evaluate employees.

87 Ross Avenue
Laurel, MD 20726-2723
March 10, 200-

Mr. Manuel Cardena
Human Resources Manager
EMH Company
684 Mills Drive
Laurel, MD 20725-1426

Dear Mr. Cardena:

Thank you for taking the time to talk with me on March 9 about the position of service technician with EMH.

I also appreciated having the opportunity of talking with Ms. Mateo. She explained the training program in detail and tested my technical skills. Ms. Mateo said that with my training and interest, I should be able to fit right in with the team and make a real contribution.

I look forward to hearing from you. Thanks again for your interest and encouragement.

Sincerely,

Marcus Davis

Marcus Davis

FIGURE 11-11   A sample follow-up letter

EMPLOYEE PERFORMANCE EVALUATION

Characteristics	UNSATISFACTORY (1)	SATISFACTORY (2)	EXCEPTIONAL (3)
ACCURACY	High error level.	Makes average number of mistakes.	Rarely commits errors.
ATTENDANCE	Frequently absent or late.	Satisfactory attendance level.	Rarely absent or late. Offers to work overtime.
CONSISTENCY	Displays emotion, temper. Disrupts work.	Even temper. Manages normal job stress.	Performs well under pressure.
COOPERATION	Often uncooperative with reasonable requests.	Cooperates well with coworkers and customers.	Very cooperative. Often offers help.
COURTESY	Often rude to others.	Usually polite. Does not offend others.	Respectful of the rights and feelings of others. Polite.
CREATIVITY	Rarely or never offers suggestions.	Occasionally offers positive suggestions.	Often offers positive, innovative suggestions.
DECISION MAKING	Frequently makes unsound decisions.	Usually shows good judgment.	Shows exceptional judgment. Excellent reasoning ability.
DEPENDABILITY	Unreliable and untrustworthy.	Can be depended on to complete work.	Works with little supervision. Self-motivated.
DETERMINATION	Quits when encountering problems.	Overcomes most problems.	Shows perseverance. Reaches most goals.
HABITS AND APPEARANCE	Displays offensive habits and careless appearance.	Acceptable appearance and habits.	Properly dressed and groomed. Shows good taste in behavior.
INITIATIVE	Rarely volunteers. Does only what is demanded.	Shows initiative.	Self-starter. Accepts unpleasant jobs willingly.
LEARNING ABILITY	Slow to learn new ideas and procedures.	Understands most new ideas and procedures.	Fast, independent learner.
ORGANIZATION	Work and work area in disarray.	Usually organized and orderly.	Organized, precise, and efficient.
PRODUCTIVITY	Below-average output.	Acceptable level of output.	Very productive. Exceeds expectations.
PROFICIENCY	Lacking in job skills.	Understands the job.	Complete understanding of all job aspects.

RATING

15 20 25 30 35 40 45

UNSATISFACTORY   SATISFACTORY   EXCEPTIONAL

FIGURE 11-12   An employee performance evaluation form

No matter what evaluation system is used, the employee is usually informed about its results and is given a chance to respond. A list of tips for responding to an employee performance evaluation follows:

- Do not let compliments or positive comments make you feel uncomfortable. Accept praise with thanks.

- Ask questions to clarify any information in your evaluation that you do not understand.

- Respond in writing to any negative remarks that you believe are inaccurate. Make your response specific, factual, clear, and complete. Include documentation (proof) to support your objection.

- Ask for specific advice for improving your performance.

- Thank your supervisor for the opportunity to discuss your job performance.

Summary

Job application materials present the qualifications of the applicant, including work experience, education, and personal information. This information may be presented as a resume, in a letter or an application form, or in an interview. Whatever the format, the purpose is to persuade the audience to hire the applicant. Follow these guidelines whenever you prepare job application materials:

- Begin by collecting all relevant information about education, employment, references, skills, and personal qualities.

- Carefully draft a resume that is informative, positive, and attractive.

- Send an effective cover letter with your resume.

- Fill out application forms accurately, neatly, and completely.

- Practice interviewing skills so that you can competently participate in actual interviews.

- Write and send a follow-up letter after an interview, thanking the interviewer and expressing your interest in the job.

- Carefully proofread and revise all job application materials until they are as clear and correct as possible.

by the way...

Since communication skills are important to many employers, consider the resume, letters, and job interview as tests of how well you express yourself. Make sure you pass.

review and research activities visit
communicating.swlearning.com

Writing a Resume

1. Use the Project Plan on *Student Workbook* page 11-J to plan a resume so you'll be ready the next time you look for a job. Select the information from your Personal Inventory form.

2. Use a computer for the rough draft. Experiment with fonts, spacing, and organization until the resume looks attractive and easy to read.

3. List three to five references on a separate page under the heading "References." Key your name; then block the addresses for references as you would an inside address. Center the information.

4. Using the Rough Draft column of the Project Guide, *Student Workbook* page 11-K, check your rough draft with two other students. Have them record all of their comments and changes on your Project Guide and rough draft. Ask them to write a constructive comment on the rough draft and sign it. Ask your teacher and an adult outside the classroom for feedback as well.

5. Revise the resume and have your teacher check it.

6. Prepare the final draft. Proofread until your resume is perfect, using the Final Draft column of the Project Guide. Turn your resume in with the Project Guide.

Writing a Cover Letter

1. Review information about and examples of business letters in Chapter 9.

2. Using the Project Plan, *Student Workbook* page 11-L, plan a cover letter addressed to the ad that you found for Practice 11-2. Remember that this letter will be sent with the resume, so don't repeat information from the resume.

3. Use a computer for the rough draft. With one or more classmates, use the Rough Draft column of the Project Guide, *Student Workbook* page 11-M, to check your work. Have them record all of their comments and changes on your Project Guide and rough draft. Ask them to write a constructive comment on the rough draft and sign it. Ask your teacher to check it. Cover letters must be free of errors.

4. Revise the letter, check it using the Final Draft column of the Project Guide, and turn it in with the Project Guide.

Writing a Follow-Up Letter

1. Assume that an interview has taken place and that you have decided you want the position for which you wrote the cover letter. Using the Project Plan on *Student Workbook* page 11-N, plan the follow-up letter. If the ad did not include a person's name, supply one for this letter, since you would have met by this time.

2. Draft the letter. Using the Rough Draft column of the Project Guide on *Student Workbook* page 11-O, check your work with one or more classmates. Have them record all of their comments and changes on your Project Guide and rough draft. Ask them to write a constructive comment on the rough draft and sign it. Ask your teacher to check the rough draft.

3. Revise your letter, check it using the Final Draft column of the Project Guide, and turn it in with the Project Guide.

literature

Overview

In 1949, Arthur Miller became a famous playwright overnight when his play *Death of a Salesman* premiered in New York. The play is a Henrik Ibsen-influenced social-problem type of drama. (An excerpt from *A Doll's House* by Ibsen appears on pages 244-245.) The tragedy is a story of a father, Willy Loman, a failure at the age of 63, who has imparted to his sons his own values in material success.

In the following scene near the end of the play, Biff (Willy's son) tries to explain to his brother Happy why he failed to see an employer, whom he worked for years ago, about a chance to borrow some money and start a new business and a new life.

from Death of a Salesman

Happy: Did you see Oliver?

Biff: I saw him all right. Now look, I want to tell Dad a couple of things and I want you to help me.

Happy: What? Is he going to back you?

Biff: Are you crazy? You're out of your head, you know that?

Happy: Why? What happened?

Biff (breathlessly): I did a terrible thing today, Hap. It's been the strangest day I ever went through. I'm all numb, I swear.

Happy: You mean he wouldn't see you?

Biff: Well, I waited six hours for him, see? All day. Kept sending my name in. Even tried to date his secretary so she'd get me to him, but no soap.

Happy: Because you're not showin' the old confidence, Biff. He remembered you, didn't he?

Biff (stopping Happy with a gesture): Finally, about five o'clock, he comes out. Didn't remember who I was or anything. I felt like such an idiot, Hap.

Happy: Did you tell him my Florida idea?

Biff: He walked away. I saw him for one minute. I got so mad I could've torn the walls down! How the hell did I ever get the idea I was a salesman there? I even

> "... I realized what a ridiculous lie my whole life has been!"

believed myself that I'd been a salesman for him! And then he gave me one look and—I realized what a ridiculous lie my whole life has been! We've been talking in a dream for fifteen years. I was a shipping clerk.

Happy: What'd you do?

Biff (with great tension and wonder): Well, he left, see. And the secretary went out. I was all alone in the waiting room. I don't know what came over me, Hap. The next thing I know, I'm in his office—paneled walls, everything.

I can't explain it. I—Hap, I took his fountain pen.

Happy: Geez, did he catch you?

Biff: I ran out. I ran down all eleven flights. I ran and ran and ran.

—Arthur Miller

Start-Up: Biff had fooled himself for 15 years, convincing himself that he had worked for Bill Oliver as a salesman, when in actuality he had been a shipping clerk. Based on his delusion, he went to see Oliver about borrowing a substantial sum of money to start a sporting goods business. In the scene in the excerpt, Biff realizes what he actually is. A few lines later he says that he's got to explain to his father that "I'm not the man somebody lends that kind of money to."

Connection: Assume that Biff has applied for a job with your company. You are an assistant personnel manager who has just interviewed Biff. Your supervisor wants a written explanation for your reason(s) when you reject any applicant.

1. Based on the scene above (or on the entire play if you have seen it or read it), why is Biff *not* the kind of person you would hire if he were applying for a job? State your reasons in a grammatically correct paragraph. Be sure to support your reasons.

2. Using good judgment and tact, write a letter from the assistant personnel manager to Biff, rejecting Biff's job application.

Overview

A folktale is a story composed orally and then passed from person to person by word of mouth by illiterate or semiliterate people. Some of these stories are based on actual events. The folktale preserves a culture's ideas and customs. This Swedish folktale teaches a lesson in a humorous way.

"The Old Man and Woman Who Switched Jobs" from Swedish Folktales and Legends

Once there was an old man, just like any other old man. This old man worked in the forest, chopping wood, and burning charcoal, while his old woman stayed at home spinning, cooking, and taking care of the house. In this way their days passed one after another. But the old man always complained that he had to labor and toil all day long to support both of them while the old woman merely sat at home cooking porridge, eating, and enjoying herself. Even though the old

> *. . . he was convinced that he alone was pulling their entire load.*

woman told him that there was plenty to do at home as well and that the old man would be badly fed and clothed if she did

not look after the house, the old man turned a deaf ear; he was convinced that he alone was pulling their entire load.

© GETTY IMAGES/PHOTODISC, INC.

One day, after they'd bickered longer than usual, the old woman said, "Have it your way! Tomorrow we'll switch jobs. I'll go to the forest and cut wood for the fire, and you'll stay home and do my chores."

This suited the old man just fine. "I'll take good care of the house," he said. "But how you'll fare in the woods is another story."

Early the next morning the old woman said, "Don't forget to bake the bread, churn the butter, watch the cow, and cook the greens for dinner."

These were all mere trifles, thought the old man, and soon they parted. The old woman took the old man's axe and went off to the forest while the old man began to build a fire under the oven and make the dough. When he thought it was ready, he began to bake it. But what sort of bread it was going to be was hard to say, for he forgot the yeast and put the loaves into the oven without first sweeping away the ashes.

The old man thought he'd managed the baking very well, and the thought of fresh bread awakened his appetite.

"Fresh bread is fine," he said to himself, "but if you have some bacon to go along with it, it tastes even better."

So the next moment he went to the storehouse to fetch their last piece of bacon. But since the bacon was salty, he wanted something to drink with it. He put the bacon on the cellar steps and went downstairs.

"If only I'd let mother stay at home!"

Just as he was taking the plug out of the beer barrel, a dog came by and grabbed the bacon. The old man certainly didn't want to lose it, so he jumped up and ran off after the dog. But as he was running he discovered that he still had the plug in his hand, and he abandoned the bacon and ran back so that he could at least save the beer.

But it was too late. The barrel was empty and all the good beer had run out. This made him very unhappy, but he comforted himself with the thought that the old woman probably wasn't doing any better in the forest. Even if he had to do without bacon and beer, at least he still had the nice fresh-baked bread. With bread to eat, life is complete! as the saying goes.

How on earth was he going to manage it all?

But his comfort was short-lived. When he got inside the hut he found the bread burned to a crisp. Not a single bite was left for him to taste. It was a terrible state of affairs.

"This is no good at all," he moaned. "If only I'd let mother stay at home! If I'm doing this badly, how might she be doing in the forest? By now she may have chopped off both arms and legs!"

But there was no time for thinking. The sun was already high in the sky, and he had to cook greens for dinner. For greens one must have something green, the old man said to himself, and as he couldn't find anything else green, he took the old woman's homespun jacket, chopped it into little bits, and put the pieces in the pot.

He realized that he couldn't cook greens without water, but the spring was so far away. And besides, he also had to churn butter! How on earth was he going to manage it all?

"If I put the churn on my back and shake it while I'm running to the spring, it'll probably turn to butter by the time I get back," he thought.

(cont'd on next page)

And that is what he did. But in his haste he forgot to put the lid on, and when he bent to haul up the water bucket, the cream poured over his shoulders and head and down into the spring.

Disheartened, he returned with the soupy, creamy water.

Now he had to tend to the cow, and since he couldn't be both inside and outside at the same time, how was he going to manage? On top of the house's sod roof, the grass shone a bright green in the sunshine; *there* was a juicy pasture! He tied a long rope around the cow's neck and pulled her up onto the roof, then threw the other end of the rope down the chimney.

Feeling a little happier, he went back inside the cottage and tied the tether hanging down through the chimney around his own waist so that the cow wouldn't get away from him. Then he started blowing on the fire under the pot. But while he was occupied blowing, the cow fell off the roof and pulled him up into the chimney!

At that very moment the old woman came home with a big bundle of firewood on her back. When she saw the cow hanging alongside the cottage wall, she hurried as fast as she could and cut the rope. Then she went inside. There on the floor lay the old man, smoked, burned, and half suffocated.

"God preserve us!" she exclaimed. "Is this how you've been managing at home?"

The poor old man couldn't utter a word; he just moaned and groaned. But it didn't take the old woman long to see how he'd managed: the bacon was gone, the beer run out, the bread burned to coal. The cream was in the spring and her jacket chopped up in the pot. The cow was hanged and the old man himself badly bruised and burned.

What happened later is not hard to guess. The old woman was allowed to care for her house in peace and quiet while the old man went off to the forest. Never again was he heard to complain of his lot.

—retold by Lone Thygesen Blecher and George Blecher

> *Never again was he heard to complain of his lot.*

Start-Up: People are busy at work every day. Since most people spend more hours working than doing anything else, choosing a career and preparing for it should be very important. One way to choose the right career is to be aware of different jobs that are available. Observe people working in your community, paying close attention to the jobs they do.

Connection: This project will take some time to complete. Your teacher will give you instructions and a deadline.

1. Divide into groups of two or three. Each group should use a camera to take pictures of people doing their job in the workplace. Candid shots and pictures of men and women doing nontraditional jobs should be the goal of each group.

2. Use pictures to create a classroom display of the various types of work in your community.

Working with Literature: Refer to *Student Workbook* page 11-P for an activity that will help you prepare for finding a fulfilling job.

Chapter 12

DIGITAL VISION

"There are many thousands of individuals on this planet more intelligent than I. I, however, work at it eighteen hours a day."

—ALBERT EINSTEIN, GERMAN-BORN U.S. SCIENTIST

* "Didn't the Buckeyes play better this year?"

* "When I eat burritos at Habanero, I feel like I'm eating in Mexico."

* "Moving the couch against the far wall makes the room look so much bigger."

* "You look healthier since you started working out regularly."

Comparing and Contrasting

You constantly hear remarks pointing out similarities and differences in your everyday conversation. For example,

Marlon brags about his retuned engine compared to its formerly

sluggish condition; you talk about how the spring weather is great

compared to the winter's ice and snow. "There's nothing good for

lunch today" compares today's lunch to yesterday's feast.

In Chapters 5 and 6, you learned how to use analogies to show similarities. One of the best, and easiest, tools for analyzing and evaluating is comparison and contrast. This chapter will help you organize data with this tool and use it to draw conclusions and make logical recommendations.

Everyday comparison decisions

Often, to make personal decisions, you will compare and contrast your options, perhaps without even realizing what you are doing. **Comparison** shows how things are alike; **contrast** shows how things are different. When comparing your athletic shoes endorsed by a basketball star to the star's actual shoes, you are talking about how both pairs of shoes are alike. When you contrast last year's grades with this year's, you emphasize the improvement, or difference, over your grades last year.

In the workplace, you often must analyze, evaluate, and/or justify your decisions to your supervisor, to coworkers, and to customers. For example, a new procedure is more efficient than one currently used, one person is better qualified for a promotion than another, or the preferred product is superior to the competitor's. You must be aware of using the comparing and contrasting process in the workplace.

Purposes for Comparison and Contrast

Comparison and contrast are used to make the unfamiliar more familiar, to analyze features, or to help make decisions. After you use comparison and contrast to analyze, you can draw conclusions and make recommendations based on that analysis.

Becoming Familiar

When you are faced with something unfamiliar, you can understand it more easily if you compare it with something familiar. Try comparing or contrasting the familiar everyday object with the new object. The similarities will make the new object a more familiar one. Here are some examples:

Soldering circuits

- A snake sheds its skin inside out, the way you take off your sweater.
- To begin soldering, hold the soldering iron as you hold a pen.
- Spreadsheets and databases have similar components; however, some of their uses are completely different.
- The amount of carpeting needed for the floor of a room is not computed the same way as the amount of wall covering needed for the walls of the same room.

Looking at the Details

People tend to look at the whole and often not at individual details or parts. Use comparison and contrast to focus the audience's attention on contrasting details in similar mechanisms. Here are some examples:

Technology *Connection*

Aquaculture research specialist Kevin Fitzsimmons uses the very limited water resources of the desert to grow fish in water designated to grow crops. Fish deposit a natural fertilizer in the water; then the same water is used for growing vegetables. Thus, two crops use the same water, making the scarce resource more efficient.

- The basic difference between an omelet and scrambled eggs is the presentation.

- The horses are identical except for the colors of their manes and tails.

- Those two teachers have the same classroom rules except that one allows you to use electronic spelling checkers.

- The only way the child-care teacher can tell the twins apart is that one has blue eyes and one has green eyes.

Making Decisions

Customers want the greatest benefit they can get for what they are willing to pay. Comparison and contrast will provide the tools for making the best choice.

- The hybrid car's engine is smaller and more fuel-efficient than a gasoline-powered engine.
- Carpenters use a circular saw on a construction site because the table saw is not portable.
- Should you upgrade your computer's memory or buy a new computer with more features?
- Clarissa received the gold medal from the Restaurant Association because her béarnaise sauce was more difficult to prepare than Beck's brown gravy.

© GETTY IMAGES/PHOTODISC, INC.

Welder at work

Organizing Comparison and Contrast

Subjects are the topics of comparison and contrast. First, you must have at least two subjects to analyze likenesses and differences. Next, you need to have ways to analyze the subjects, called **points of comparison**. For example, if you are comparing two types of welding, the *subjects* would be MIG welding and TIG welding. Some *points of comparison* would be technique, materials, equipment, use, etc.

Comparison and contrast discussions need to be in parallel order. In other words, the points for Subject A must be the same points—and in the same order—as the points for Subject B. If you discuss MIG welding techniques first, then you must discuss TIG welding techniques first.

Practice 12–1: Discovering Similarities and Differences

Use *Student Workbook* page 12-A to complete this Practice. List similar subjects to compare from your career cluster and note the points of comparison for each subject. Then arrange the points in a logical order.

career

Organizing Data with a Table

When faced with large quantities of data, a reader frequently does one of two things: stops reading or becomes confused. In comparing or contrasting, a writer may use facts, numbers, and statistics to draw conclusions and to make recommendations. However, too often technical data ends up not being read at all, or at the very least, the meaning is lost. Creating a **table** to organize and compare large quantities of data helps eliminate the confusion of wordy, fact-filled paragraphs by displaying the data visually. The table emphasizes the importance of the information and saves time for the reader.

Using a Table to Display Data

Isabel needed to make some metric conversions at her construction site. The statistical information in the reference book that her supervisor gave Isabel only served to confuse her. Try as she would, she kept getting the numbers confused in the conversion formulas. Here is an example of the information from the reference book:

To convert feet into centimeters, multiply the feet by 30.48; to convert centimeters into feet, multiply the centimeters by 0.03281. To convert inches into centimeters, multiply the inches by 2.54; to convert meters into inches, multiply the meters by 39.37. To convert feet into meters, multiply the feet by 0.3048; to convert meters into feet, multiply the meters by 3.281.

When Isabel saw the same information arranged in a table, her confusion cleared and she easily made the conversions. Table 12-1 organizes the same data as in the example paragraph; however, it makes the task of converting numbers much easier. The table puts the data into categories that form the columns of the table.

TABLE I
Simplified Conversion Table

To Convert	Into	Multiply by
centimeters	feet	0.03281
feet	centimeters	30.48
feet	meters	0.3048
inches	centimeters	2.54
meters	feet	3.281
meters	inches	39.37

TABLE 12-1

by the way...

Online news versus traditional news media—Will the Internet kill newspapers and TV news? Online news can be delivered as soon as stories are written and coded. However, critics of Internet news question the bias and credibility of web sites. Television and print news offer custom coverage of more than one viewpoint, letting the audience draw their own conclusions. But the instant coverage of online news is exciting. Radio didn't put an end to newspapers, and TV didn't put an end to radio. A variety of news sources is necessary.

Using a Table to Compare and Contrast

Besides organizing data visually, tables also serve another important purpose—to assist you in analyzing or evaluating data. In these situations, you can use the table setup to compare and contrast data for purposes of making the unfamiliar familiar, looking at details, and making decisions. Using the table allows you to draw conclusions from the data and make a recommendation.

For example, Finney decided that he wanted to continue his education after graduating with his dental assistant certification. He and his parents are trying to determine which school he should attend to become a dental hygienist. One of the factors in their decision is the annual cost of his education at his three choices of schools. To decide which amount of money to borrow, Finney created Table 12-2 to show typical monthly loan payments over a ten-year period. Another factor in Finney's decision-making process is the source of the loan. The Stafford Loan for students and the parent PLUS Loan are federal loans with lower interest, but State Bank is locally owned and convenient for completing paperwork and asking questions. Table 12-2 visually displays the information to help Finney decide the amount to borrow and the source of the loan.

TABLE II
Monthly Payments for Education Loans
(10-Year Replacement Period)

Loan Amount	Stafford Student Loan	PLUS Loan	State Bank Loan
$2,000	$25	$26	$25
4,000	50	52	48
5,000	75	77	76
7,500	99	103	97

TABLE 12-2

Source: http://loansaver.us.com

Career *Connection*

The secretaries of the past are the managers of today. In the past, secretaries typed correspondence, took dictation, and answered the phones for many executives and managers. Now those same secretaries, often titled administrative assistants, are assuming the duties of downsized middle managers. The new secretaries format and organize the correspondence, coordinate department meetings and appointments, and handle record keeping. The majority of secretaries supervise and train others, something their predecessors never would have done. Even though projected overall employment growth is slowing, the average salary for the secretary has increased more in the last 20 years than the average salaries of other white-collar workers.

Constructing a Table

Constructing a table takes some planning; however, once you do the preliminary work, the rest is relatively simple. If a computer is available, table construction becomes even easier, but, again, planning is essential. Table 12-3 is an example of a well-constructed table to be used for a comparison and contrast discussion. If you decide that an audience will benefit from seeing data visually in a table, you must carefully plan, draft, and revise the data arrangement.

TABLE III
Costs of Business Communication

	Written Memo	E-mail Memos
Number Written per Week	1	145
Production in Minutes	54	3
Cost per Message	$15.75	$.05
Annual Cost per Employee	$4,095.00	$750.00

TABLE 12-3

Source: Personnel Journal Enterprise Network & Servers

The Label and the Title

The title introduces the table to the reader and implies the table's meaning. Number the tables when referring to them in text or within a presentation.

- Label the table with the word *TABLE*, in capital letters and bold or normal print, centered over the data. (Tables sometimes have an informative heading instead of the word *TABLE*.)

- Give the table an informative title that will help the audience understand what is in the table, using as few words as possible. Use title case (see page 47) in bold or normal print and center the title directly above the table data.

- Number tables consecutively when there is more than one table; for example, "TABLE 1," "TABLE 2," etc.

The Layout

The layout of the table is as important as the format of a business letter. Planning is the key.

- Make a pencil sketch of the table before beginning its construction on the computer or on the paper used for the final copy..

- Construct the table in such a way that it is wide enough not to crowd the data; include adequate white space with a neat appearance. The table must be easy to read. If you have access to a word processing program, use one of the automatic table formats.

- Frame the table to add emphasis. Also, if necessary for easier reading, separate the columns with vertical lines. Use horizontal lines only if they make the table easier to read.

- Label each column of data with a brief heading in bold or normal type and in title case. Headings are flush left or centered in the columns. Arrange the rows logically (alphabetically or numerically, for example). Rows are arranged horizontally; columns, vertically.

- Make the units of measurement the same within all columns, including lining up the decimal points within each column. This alignment makes the table appear neat and clean. (See Table 12-1 on page 411.)

- Draw a short centered line in any blank table cells.

- Double-space between rows. (Tables are sometimes single-spaced.)

by the way...

According to psychology studies reported by career development speaker Randy Dorn, readers in Western cultures (United States, European, etc.) find illustrations in landscape orientation easier to read and use. Eastern cultures have positive reactions to portrait orientation.

Ethics *Connection*

Answering a phone call during a meeting announces to those present that the phone is more important than they are. During a meeting, have voice mail or someone else take your calls. Use silent or vibrating mode for a cell phone. Allow an interruption only when you're expecting an urgent call—and then, before the meeting starts, warn those in attendance that you might be interrupted during the meeting.

by the way...

I'm a great believer in luck, and I find that the harder I work, the more I have of it.

Thomas Jefferson, U.S. president

The Source Line

Credit the author of the information used to construct the table by including a source line at the bottom of the table at the left margin. Use the table illustrations in this chapter as examples.

Common knowledge requires no documentation. It consists of widely known facts that are available from many sources. The fact that President John F. Kennedy was assassinated in 1963 is common knowledge. The fact that Congress adopted the Declaration of Independence on July 4, 1776, is common knowledge. If you base your table information on common knowledge, no source line is necessary.

Practice 12–2: Constructing Tables

The information in the following paragraphs is very confusing. The information could be more effective if displayed visually in tables. First, read each paragraph carefully and decide what subjects are being compared. Next, list the **points** of comparison in the first column in alphabetical order. To make the data clear, construct a table using the **details** of all of the information in the paragraphs. Then add a **label**, a **title**, and the **source** of the information.

Paragraph 1
To compare his construction company with the competition, Doug Lowe researched the number of building permits given by the Building Inspector's Office in Herbert County for plumbing, electrical, and construction work this year. According to this data, DHB Construction had 341 electrical permit applications, 555 plumbing permit applications, and 1,112 construction permit applications. Bires Builders had 410 electrical permit applications, 689 plumbing permit applications, and 929 construction permit applications. Then there was Creative Creations with 434 electrical applications, 121 plumbing applications, and 655 construction applications. Peter Fisher received 714 electrical, 615 plumbing, and 992 construction applications. Last of all, Matthews Materials obtained 327 electrical, 615 plumbing, and 871 construction applications.

Paragraph 2

When should Jannah call Rodrigo? Even though she runs the Midwest Division of Bart Graphics, she must call after office hours and interrupt sleep schedules to save money. However, sometimes asking questions is more important than saving money. To help with her decision, she consulted the telephone directory for direct-dial, one-minute rates for long distance. On Monday from 8 a.m. to 5 p.m., the weekday full rate applies; from 5 p.m. to 11 p.m., the evening 40 percent discount rate applies; and from 11 p.m. to 8 a.m., the night and weekend 60 percent discount applies. The weekday full rate is in effect from 8 a.m. to 5 p.m. on Tuesday; the evening 40 percent discount, from 5 p.m. to 11 p.m.; and the night and weekend 60 percent rate, from 11 p.m. to 8 a.m. Callers on Wednesday from 8 a.m. to 5 p.m. are charged the weekday full rate; from 5 p.m. to 11 p.m., the evening 40 percent discount rate; and from 11 p.m. to 8 a.m., the night and weekend 60 percent discount rate. Rates on Thursdays and Fridays are similar to the weekday full rate in existence from 8 a.m. to 5 p.m.; the evening 40 percent discount rate, from 5 p.m. to 11 p.m.; and the night and weekend 60 percent discount, from 11 p.m. to 8 a.m. The schedule changes from 8 a.m. Saturday to 8 a.m. Sunday, when the night and weekend 60 percent discount applies. The night and weekend 60 percent discount rate is in effect Sunday from 8 a.m. to 5 p.m. and from 11 p.m. to 8 a.m. The evening 40 percent discount rate applies from 5 p.m. to 11 p.m. Sunday.

Preparing a Comparison and Contrast Analysis

A comparison and contrast analysis helps you examine and make decisions about two or more subjects. The discussion includes an introduction, the central section (body), conclusions, and recommendations. Whether the discussion is a written analysis or an oral presentation, each section should blend into the next.

The Introduction

This brief section sets up the comparison and contrast analysis. It prepares the reader by referring to the following:

1. The subjects that are being compared and contrasted.

2. The ways the subjects are alike and/or different.

3. Any necessary background information.

4. A general description of the conclusion and recommendation.

Career *Connection*

Before comparing his brand with the competition and expanding his business, Starbucks's founder, Howard Schultz, believed he needed his employees' allegiance. He hired workers who were enthusiastic and knowledgeable about his coffee. Consequently, brand loyalty overflowed from the workers to the customers, building up a devoted following for Starbucks Coffee.

The conservation research firm Sanders Laboratories is changing its uniforms. A Uniform Committee was formed from its employees to choose the company that will supply the new uniforms. A subcommittee has narrowed the uniform choice to two brands—Utilitywear and StarService. Here is the first part of the subcommittee's report to the Uniform Committee:

> After researching more than eight uniform companies, the subcommittee narrowed the choices to two—the Utilitywear and the StarService uniform companies. These companies have the type of uniforms that Sanders requires, and both companies have offices here in Minneapolis—good for service needs. Now the Uniform Committee must choose which uniform company to use based on the variety of sizes offered, stain resistance, durability of the uniforms, and price.

The Analysis

When you are planning a comparison and contrast analysis, consider the subjects that are being compared, the points of comparison, and the audience. These three factors will help you choose the most effective organization for the analysis. Discussing several points of one subject and then the same several points of another subject is one method of arrangement. Another method is to discuss one point for the first subject, then the same point for the other subject, the second point for the first subject, etc. One of these two options of organization becomes the body of your comparison and contrast analysis.

Order of importance determines the order of the points. You may choose to start with the strongest point or the weakest, depending on your audience and the purpose for the analysis. In the Sanders' uniform decision example, the company needs to compare the two brands, using four different points: varieties of sizes, stain resistance, durability, and price. When the uniforms are compared, details and examples will then support the points of comparison. The committee believes that having uniforms to fit all employees is the most important factor in recommending a company, followed by stain resistance and durability. Price is the least important factor for Sanders.

The Subject-by-Subject Method

When choosing two subjects to compare and/or contrast, you show how the subjects are alike or different. First, you analyze one topic; then you discuss the other topic. With subject-by-subject comparison and contrast, you select points of comparison (and/or contrast) to analyze the first subject; then you analyze the same points in the same order for the other subject.

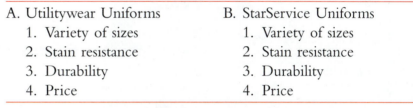

Subjects:	Points of Comparison:
A. Utilitywear Uniforms	1. Variety of sizes
B. StarService Uniforms	2. Stain resistance
	3. Durability
	4. Price

Here is the subject-by-subject organization:

A. Utilitywear Uniforms	B. StarService Uniforms
1. Variety of sizes	1. Variety of sizes
2. Stain resistance	2. Stain resistance
3. Durability	3. Durability
4. Price	4. Price

The Point-by-Point Method

Choose several points to compare this uniform with another.

Comparison and contrast explanations are used every day, not only with subject-by-subject analysis, but also with point-by-point analysis. In point-by-point analysis, you choose three or more points to discuss for each subject. Using the previous example, one section would discuss how Utilitywear's and StarService's uniforms compare in variety of sizes offered. The second section would explain how the companies' uniforms compare in stain resistance; the third, in durability; and the fourth, in price.

Here is the point-by-point organization:

A. Variety of Sizes	C. Durability
1. Utilitywear uniforms	1. Utilitywear uniforms
2. StarService uniforms	2. StarService uniforms
B. Stain Resistance	D. Price
1. Utilitywear uniforms	1. Utilitywear uniforms
2. StarService uniforms	2. StarService uniforms

People *Connection*

Landscape architect Margarette Beckwith designed the specific garden areas of the Alois Alzheimer Center in Cincinnati, Ohio, according to the stages of the disease. The most active residents are in the gardens on their own, in an enclosed, looped unit with scattered benches and tables for strolling and visiting. The next level of patients tends to wander and become easily disoriented, so the garden for these patients is more contained. Since those in the last stages of the disease are generally wheelchair-bound, their gardens have raised planters so that patients can touch and smell the vegetation. The arrangement of the gardens keeps the patients safe, but offers them glimpses of the world beyond, giving them a sense of being in control.

BECKWITH CHAPMAN ASSOCIATES

Courtyard Garden, Alois Alzheimer Center, Cincinnati, Ohio

The Conclusions and the Recommendations

After hearing or reading all of the facts and figures of the comparison and contrast analysis, you may say "Now what?" The speaker or the writer must tie all of the points together and draw conclusions. The conclusions will lead to recommendations—the purpose of the analysis.

Tables will add to the analysis if they are used to draw conclusions based on the information analyzed and offer recommendations to make the unfamiliar familiar, examine details, or make decisions.

After inspecting all of the statements, facts, figures, and tables, the speaker or writer will point out the relationships among the data in the analysis that explains the deductions in the conclusions. The following statements are examples of conclusions for the Sanders' uniform analysis:

- Utilitywear has the full size range of uniforms needed for Sanders' employees; StarService does not have the full range of sizes in stock.
- Since the prices for both companies' uniforms are very similar, cost should not be a consideration in choosing a uniform company.
- When tests of various weather conditions and spills of commonly used chemical agents were conducted, StarService's uniforms lasted more than 50 percent longer than Utilitywear's uniforms.

by the way...

Better to see once than hear 100 times.

MIKHAIL GORBACHEV, FORMER SOVIET UNION PRESIDENT

After the conclusions are stated based on the evidence, the committee must make recommendations to the company. These recommendations will endorse further action based on the conclusions and will solve the problem. The Sanders Uniform Committee made the following recommendation:

> The Sanders Uniform Committee recommends the purchase of StarService uniforms to replace the existing uniforms of Sanders' employees.

Using the evidence in the analysis for support, the speaker or writer can elaborate on the reasons for the conclusions and the recommendations. However, these two sections, like the introduction, are much briefer than the analysis itself.

Practice 12–3: Drawing Conclusions and Making Recommendations

1. Examine the following tables and reread any introductory information given: Tables 12-2 and 12-3 on pages 411 and 412, respectively, and at least one of the tables you created for Practice 12-2 on pages 414 and 415. For each of the three tables, write two conclusions and one recommendation based on the information. Your teacher may have you work with a partner or in small groups.

2. You use **comparative degree** to compare two items, one of which is superior or inferior to the other in some way; for example, an elephant is heavier than a lion, and chocolate mousse has more calories than peach sorbet. However, you must create logical comparisons so that similar things are compared. Using *Student Workbook* page 12-C, rewrite each of the illogical comparisons so that like things are compared. Explain the reason for each revision.

Transitional Signals

If an audience hears a comparison and contrast discussion without transitional signals, it can easily miss the points that you want to stress. Using transitions helps the audience discover the relationships between important facts. Transitional words and phrases also help to connect or blend thoughts.

Culture *Connection*

One stumbling block to communication between cultures is that many people assume that enough similarities exist to make communication simple. The belief that "people are people" emphasizes similarities and seemingly makes any differences wrong. These misinformed people believe that because humans have the common needs of food, shelter, and security, everyone is alike. However, the differences among cultures are often broader than the similarities, making living and working together more difficult.

Another assumption is that words in one language, when translated, have a comparative meaning in another language. Not only is this supposition often not true, but its results can be disastrous!

To signal a similarity, use

also	each of	likewise
and	in addition	neither
as well as	in the same way	similarly
besides	just as . . . so	too
both	like	

To signal a difference or opposition, use

although	however	on the contrary
at the same time	in contrast	whereas
besides	nevertheless	while this may be
but	notwithstanding	true
but still	on one hand; on	yet
conversely	the other hand	

The transitions point out the relationships within the paragraph and make the reading smoother. In addition, transitions help connect the sections of the comparison and contrast analysis—from the introduction to the recommendation.

Practice 12–4: Comparing and Contrasting with Transitions

1. Use the information in Table 12-3 on page 412 to write an analysis paragraph. Use transitions from the preceding list to compare and/or contrast the types of messages sent, as reported in the table. Then underline the transitions you used before handing in your work.

2. Do the same for Practice 12-2, Paragraph 2, on page 415.

Ethics *Connection*

The Better Business Bureau (BBB) is the ethical watchdog of business. It helps consumers by acting as a clearinghouse for complaints, posting notices of scams, and actually negotiating differences with businesses. As a business owner, you can receive tips from the BBB for starting or strengthening your business. The BBB's Core Services include business reliability reports, dispute resolution, truth-in-advertising, consumer and business education, and review of charities. For more information, access http://www.bbb.org.

Summary

Comparing and contrasting are processes used to analyze and evaluate likenesses and differences. These tools can be used to make decisions. Follow these guidelines whenever you prepare a comparison and contrast discussion:

- Determine the points and supporting details of the subjects of comparison and contrast.
- Organize your comparison and contrast discussion with either the subject-by-subject or the point-by-point method.
- Construct a table, when appropriate, to illustrate the comparison and contrast conclusions and recommendations for the audience.
- Use transitions to connect the comparison and contrast discussion into one unit.

by the way...

77% of U.S. workers drive to work.

10% carpool.

5% use public transportation.

The average commute is 25 minutes.

U.S. CENSUS BUREAU

review and research activities visit
communicating.swlearning.com

project-based assessment

Comparing and Contrasting

Comparing and Contrasting Products or Procedures

Your teacher, Mr. Marcos, wants your class to learn more about new procedures and products in your career cluster. Rather than duplicate many articles for you to read or lecture to the class for several days, Mr. Marcos wants the class to give presentations. He suggests that you begin by researching. For this presentation, you will be analyzing two or more processes or products from your career cluster. Keep your audience in mind when choosing the subjects to compare and contrast.

From sources such as web searches, magazines, and journals, you will have numbers, statistics, and data regarding the two or more different procedures or products. To organize and analyze the information, you need to complete this Project effectively. Show your research results or data in a table. Then, through a presentation, draw conclusions from your analysis and make one or more recommendations based on the data.

You will need to do the following:

• Research your processes or products.

• Construct a table of details to support your conclusion and recommendation(s).

• Present your analysis orally.

Some suggestions for subjects to compare and contrast follow:

• Closed versus open magnetic resonance imaging (MRI) procedure

• Three types of window construction

• Physical filter, activated carbon, and reverse osmosis water filtration systems

• Ice cream, frozen yogurt, or sorbet

• Apple versus Windows operating systems

• Relaxing hair versus getting a perm

• Emergency procedures for first aid

• Troubleshooting a defective piece of equipment

1. Review the examples of comparison and contrast analyses and tables in this chapter. Examine Linda Hockenberry's Sample Project Plan on page 425. Then listen to the recorded CD sample presentation based on this plan. Your teacher will show you the table that accompanies the presentation.

2. After consulting reference materials, choose what you are analyzing through comparison and contrast. List *at least six to ten points* to analyze *at least two* subjects. (Your teacher may specify exact numbers.) The items on this list are the points of comparison and contrast. Locate and record details on all points of the topics as you did for Practice 12-1.

3. Complete the Project Plan, *Student Workbook* page 12-D.

4. Using the information from your Project Plan, construct a rough draft of your table, showing the details of your analysis. If a computer is available, use it to construct the table. Include a title and the source of information, using as few words as possible.

5. Prepare notes for your presentation. Write out the introduction and the closing completely. Briefly outline the body of the talk, including transitions to link the analysis points and details. Discuss both similarities and differences.

6. Study the Project Guide, *Student Workbook* page 12-E, criteria for your table and for your presentation. Using the Rough Draft column of the Project Guide, check your table and your presentation notes with one or more classmates. Each of you should mark the Project Guide in all categories except the last four steps and note any changes on the rough draft. Have your teacher check your rough draft.

7. Revise your table and presentation notes, incorporating the changes that your classmate(s) and your teacher suggested. Rehearse the presentation, referring to your table. Practice with another student, preferably a classmate who checked your table and presentation notes with the Project Guide. During the rehearsal, have the class member use the last four steps of the Rough Draft column of the Project Guide to evaluate the presentation.

8. Using the Final Draft column of the Project Guide, proofread your work. Make needed corrections.

9. Present your analysis to the class. Using the last four steps of the Final Draft column of the Project Guide, your teacher and possibly your classmates will evaluate your presentation.

10. After your presentation, turn in the final draft along with the Project Guide.

Presentation Guidelines:

1. Present your analysis and table to the class on the day assigned by your teacher.

2. Explain your analysis thoroughly by including the following:
   - All necessary information
   - Source(s) of your information
   - A valid conclusion and recommendation(s)

3. Do not read your presentation. Have the introduction, main points, and closing written. Use a maximum of three note cards that contain phrases only, not sentences. Include transitions in your notes.

Sample Project Plan

Plan for Comparing and Contrasting

SUBJECTS	(At least two)
	A. Perch fillets cooked by baking
	B. Perch fillets cooked by frying
	C. Perch fillets cooked by steaming
AUDIENCE	Class members and teacher
	Reason(s) for choosing the subjects: Teach about new procedures
PURPOSE	**Conclusions:** Less healthy — frying
	More expertise needed, less taste — steaming
	Recommendations: Choose method best fits your lifestyle, health, expertise, taste
FORMAT	☐ written ☒ oral ☐ other Table for visual
SOURCES	Clark County Extension Service
	U.S. Department of Agriculture
	United Dairy Council
METHOD	**Organize by subjects**
	Or
	(Organize by points)

CONTENTS OF TABLE

Points (number may be specified by your teacher):

— yes

1. Calories
2. Cholesterol content
3. Fats
4. Proteins
5. Sodium
6. Added ingredients
7. Preparation time

Analysis (details to compare and contrast):

Nutritional value

Cooking skill

Lifestyle of cook

literature

Overview

In the two paragraphs you are about to read from *Life on the Mississippi*, Mark Twain compares the way he saw the river as an innocent apprentice to the way he saw it as an experienced pilot.

"Two Views of the River" from *Life on the Mississippi*

Now when I had mastered the language of this water, and had come to know every trifling feature that bordered the great river as familiarly as I knew the letters of the alphabet, I had made a valuable acquisition. But I had lost something, too. I had lost something which could never be restored to me while I lived. All the grace, the beauty, the poetry, had gone out of the majestic river! I still keep in mind a certain wonderful sunset which I witnessed when steamboating was new to me. A broad expanse of the river was turned to blood; in the middle distance the red hue brightened into gold, through which a solitary log came floating black and conspicuous; in one place a long, slanting mark lay sparkling upon the water; in another the surface was broken by boiling, tumbling rings that were as many-tinted as an opal; where the ruddy flush was faintest, was a smooth spot that was covered with graceful circles and radiating lines, ever so delicately traced; the shore on our left was densely wooded, and the somber shadow that fell from this forest was broken in one place by a long, ruffled trail that shone like silver; and high above the forest wall a clean-stemmed dead tree waved a single leafy bough that glowed like a flame in the unobstructed splendor that was flowing from the sun. There were graceful curves, reflected images, woody heights, soft distances; and over the whole scene, far and near, the dissolving lights drifted steadily, enriching it every passing moment with new marvels of coloring.

© GETTY IMAGES/PHOTODISC, INC.

I stood like one bewitched. I drank it in, in a speechless rapture. The world was new to me, and I had never seen anything like this at home. But as I have said, a day came when I began to cease from noting the glories and the charms which the moon and the sun and the twilight wrought upon the river's face; another day came when I ceased altogether to note them.

Then, if that sunset scene had been repeated, I should have looked upon it without rapture, and should have commented upon it, inwardly, after this fashion: "This sun means that we are going to have wind tomorrow; that floating log means that the river is rising, small thanks to it; that slanting mark on the water refers to a bluff reef which is going to kill somebody's steamboat one of these nights, if it keeps on stretching out like that; those tumbling 'boils' show a dissolving bar and a changing channel there; the lines and circles in the slick water over yonder are a warning that that troublesome place is shoaling up dangerously; that silver streak in the shadow of the forest is the 'break' from a new snag, and he has located himself in the very best place he could have found to fish for steamboats; that tall dead tree, with a single living branch, is not going to last long, and then how is a body ever going to get through this blind place at night without the friendly old landmark?"

> *Then, if that sunset scene had been repeated, I should have looked upon it without rapture.. . .*

—Mark Twain (pseudonym for Samuel Langhorne Clemens)

Start-Up: All individuals experience a change in the way they view people, places, and things as they grow older, become more knowledgeable and experienced, and set different goals in life. In this literary selection, Twain looks at the same scenes on the river from two perspectives: one when he was a young dreamer of adventure and one when he had become an experienced steamboat captain.

Connection: (1) Format a sheet of paper or a word processing file in three columns. (You may wish to use the table feature of your software.) In the first column, make a list of the items or scenes that Twain notes in "Two Views of the River." In the second column, list what he says about the scenes or items from the young dreamer's viewpoint. In the third column, list what he says about them from the experienced captain's viewpoint. See the following example:

Scene	Young Dreamer's Viewpoint	Steamboat Captain's Viewpoint
Sunset	"brightened into gold . . ." ". . . wonderful sunset . . ."	" 'This sun means that we are going to have wind. . . .' "

(2) Imagine a situation in the workplace in which you have a beginner and an experienced employee involved in the same task. Make a similar

three-columned list for that situation. Using those details, write two paragraphs: one paragraph in which you describe the process from the point of view of the new employee and a second paragraph in which you describe the process from the point of view of the experienced employee.

Working with Literature: Refer to *Student Workbook* page 12-F for an activity on comparing and contrasting.

Overview

Born in Poland in 1923, Wislawa Szymborska is known as one of the best representatives, since World War II, of the ancient art of poetry in Poland.

When she started writing, her poetry dealt with political themes and the war. Her first volume of poetry, completed in 1948, was not published for four years because the government did not approve of her political views. She rewrote her volume of poetry; she tried to raise a poetic voice in tune with the revolutionary era in Poland. Her work was not up to expectations. Her later poems have dealt with lyrical subjects (expressing direct and usually intense personal emotions), new themes, and new poetic techniques. Undeniably, her poetry bears the stamp of originality!

"Possibilities"

I prefer movies.
I prefer cats.

I prefer oaks along the Warta River.

I prefer Dickens to Dostoyevsky.

I prefer liking people
to loving mankind.

I prefer having a needle and thread handy.

I prefer the color green.

I prefer not to assert
that reason should be blamed for everything.

I prefer exceptions.

I prefer to leave earlier.

I prefer to talk with doctors about something else.

I prefer old-fashioned, striped illustrations.

I prefer the foolishness of writing poems
to the foolishness of not writing them.

I prefer, in love, those anniversaries which are not so big,
which can be celebrated every day.

I prefer moralists
who do not promise me anything.

I prefer a crafty rather than a too credulous kindness.

I prefer the earth in civilian clothes.

I prefer the conquered to the conquering countries.

I prefer to hold doubts.

I prefer the hell of chaos to the hell of order.

I prefer tales of the Brothers Grimm to the front
    pages of newspapers.

I prefer leaves without flowers to flowers without leaves.

I prefer dogs with uncut tails.

I prefer light-colored eyes, because I have dark.

I prefer drawers.

I prefer many things which I have not specified here
to many other things also unspecified.

I prefer zeros on the loose
to those standing in line behind the number.

I prefer insects' time to stellar time.

I prefer to knock on wood.

I prefer not to ask how much longer and when.

I prefer to take into consideration even this possibility, that
life has meaning.

—Wislawa Szymborska (translated by
Grazyna Drabik and Austin Flynt)

Start-Up: All people have preferences. Making choices in life based on these preferences helps make people different from one another. It would be a stale, dull world if all people preferred the same things in life. The French say "Vive la différence." Americans say "Different strokes for different folks."

In her poem "Possibilities," the poet briefly explains her own preferences.

Connection: Reread the poem. Write a list of your own preferences in life. Try to balance your preferences as the poet does in this example: "I prefer the foolishness of writing poems / to the foolishness of not writing them."

Chapter 13

© GETTY IMAGES/PHOTODISC, INC.

The most difficult part of an interview is gaining the trust and confidence of the interviewee.

"My cousin Frances educated me about the press. She had been the AP White House correspondent during the Nixon and Ford administrations, and was now working for CNN. Frances would tell me stories of guys running out back doors because they're afraid of the press. From her I got the idea that the press isn't doing anything evil; the reporters are simply trying to help people know what's going on, and it doesn't do any harm to be courteous to them.

"I found out that they're really quite friendly, if you give them a chance. So I wasn't afraid of the press, and I would always answer their questions."

—Richard P. Feynman, Nobel Prize-winning physicist, regarding interviews with the press while serving on the commission to investigate the *Challenger* disaster in 1986

Interviewing for Information

In 1968, Eliot Wigginton, a teacher, and two classes of his high school English students in the mountains of Georgia took pencils, paper, and cameras and went out to talk to people who had spent their lives in those mountains. Then they came back and put together a series of articles based on what they had seen and heard. The stories were published in a magazine and later, due to their popularity, in *The Foxfire Book*, named after foxfire, the glowing blue-green lichen that grows on logs in the forests in that part of Georgia.

Each year, as new students continued the *Foxfire* project, they published a regular quarterly magazine, the contents of which fed the publication of a series of books. Each book after the first one was entitled *Foxfire* followed by a number: *Foxfire 2, Foxfire 3,* etc. Once the name caught on, each new volume was like an old friend returning for another visit. By 2004, the 12th book was in print and the series was selling by the thousands.

A man who has many stories of the past to share

© GETTY IMAGES/PHOTODISC, INC.

The appeal of the *Foxfire* books was twofold: The series of stories touched readers' souls by taking them into the everyday lives of people who had been in those mountains all of their lives, and the stories told the historic details of an almost forgotten way of life. They were filled with folklore—with explanations of how quilts were made and how illnesses were cured and details of living that had been passed on from parent to child for hundreds of years but were now almost forgotten.

Were these student authors marvelous writers who had spent years practicing their writing until, in high school, they finally perfected their craft? No. They were just normal students who had learned a big lesson from their teacher, which they then learned to pass along to others. They understood the importance of listening to what other people had to say.

These Georgia students gathered their material not only by sitting in the classroom and brainstorming, but also by going into the mountains and interviewing people—asking them to tell the stories of their childhood, explain how they built a wagon or made a fiddle, or talk about the religious customs they learned from their grandparents. And as these people talked, the students listened, took notes, took pictures, and made tape recordings. Then they went back to school to piece it all together. The results were better than most teachers could ever dream that their students would produce.

Interviewing for information is nothing new—it's just that few students think of it as an approach to writing or research. In fact, most of the time, students go to the library to gather material for a term paper. They seldom think of the possibility of interviewing experts, as the *Foxfire* writers did, to get their information.

by the way...

"The greatest mistake you can make in life is to be continually fearing you will make one."

ELBERT HUBBARD, U.S. AUTHOR

Using an Expert

The world is filled with all kinds of experts. These people do not include the "person on the street" interviewed so often at the end of the nightly news. Such interviews do no more than reveal the collective opinion (not necessarily knowledge) of five or six people about a question such as "Which NBA team will win the championship?"

Instead, to get good information, think about the following:

An expert is someone who knows how to do something well.

- An in-depth interview with a trial lawyer to find out how juries are selected
- An interview with a police officer on the positive and negative sides of her job
- An interview with the safety directors of several manufacturing firms on the types and causes of injuries in their workplaces and how often they occur
- An interview with a man who is a registered nurse in a large hospital to find out how his patients and their families accept him in this nontraditional role

In these examples, experts are practitioners in their fields, dealing with activities, skills, or concerns that others want to know more about.

Interviewing in a Workplace Situation

You may find many situations in your future work life when a personal interview is necessary. That's why this skill is important to learn. Often students say "That's something I'll never use." But five years later, these same students ask "Why didn't anyone teach me how to do these things?" This chapter will teach you how to do "these things."

Interviewing is part of a variety of jobs. Some interviews are informal; some are very formal. An interview doesn't necessarily require three hours, a large notebook, and planned questions. But it is better to be prepared for such an interview in case you are ever involved in one. Also note that one interview may be just talking and listening, while another may involve someone showing you how to do a particular task and letting you practice doing it yourself.

An interview at work might be necessary when someone needs to:

- Find out what witnesses observed about a major accident.
- Research all phases of a sale or purchase to find out what went wrong—for example, talking to each person who signed or handled a purchase order, an invoice, or a shipment when tracking down a missing item.
- Learn a new job from another worker in order to be able to take over in case of emergency—for example, an accounting clerk responsible for handling purchase order payments may have to learn to do payroll in case the payroll clerk is away from work for several days.
- Get tips from a knowledgeable horse trainer on the fine points of training Arabians after working only with quarter horses for many years.
- Understand how a trauma center differs from a typical emergency room when starting work in an urban trauma center after a year of working in a suburban hospital emergency room.
- Discuss the design and layout of an advertisement with the owner of a small business, finding out what kind of business the person owns, what impression he or she wants to give, and what audience he or she is trying to reach.

Practice 13–1: Brainstorming Situations That Would Require an Interview

teamwork

In a small group, brainstorm additional workplace situations that would require an interview. The interview may or may not include a show-and-tell of how to perform a task.

The Positive Side of Interviewing an Expert

When compared to other ways of gathering information, interviewing has certain advantages that other forms of research do not have.

- Meeting an expert helps put reality into what might otherwise be an abstract topic.
- You can ask clarifying questions and get answers as you go along.
- An expert can give you his or her personal insights—the kind that books rarely provide.

© COMSTOCK IMAGES

Interviewing experts is a valuable approach to gathering information.

The Negative Side of Interviewing an Expert

On the other hand, everything about interviewing isn't always positive. It does, at times, have disadvantages. Here are some examples:

- A potential interviewee may be shy or unwilling to talk.
- It may be difficult to make appointments with experts, especially if you have trouble meeting strangers.
- It's impossible to go back and reread what someone says. You must pay constant attention during an interview. (This is where recording the interview would help.)

Pinpointing Your Topic

by the way...

"Designing a bridge or any other large structure is not unlike planning a trip or a vacation. The end may be clear and simple: to go from here to there. But the means may be limited only by our imaginations."

HENRY PETROSKI IN *To Engineer Is Human: The Role of Failure in Successful Design*

You won't be able to find the right expert to provide the information you need if you're not sure what that information is. For instance, suppose you're interested in the medical field and decide to do a report on cancer, since it is a disease that has touched nearly every family you know. Whom should you interview to get accurate information?

First of all, you must narrow your topic to one of the many forms of cancer that exist. Then narrow the topic further until you pinpoint a part of it that you can manage. (See Figure 13-1.) You cannot pick an expert until you first decide what aspect of the disease you want to know about—symptoms, treatments, or the effects of the disease and treatments on individuals suffering from cancer. One person is not likely to know all of the details about all aspects of all types of cancer.

GENERAL TOPIC	NARROWED TOPIC	PINPOINTED TOPIC
All cancers	One type of cancer	One person's experience with one type of cancer
CANCER	**LUNG CANCER**	**LIVING WITH LUNG CANCER: ONE PATIENT'S POINT OF VIEW**
Includes all aspects of all types of cancers, such as lung cancer, bone cancer, brain cancer, and breast cancer, with their known causes, symptoms, treatments, side effects, survival rates, effects on family life/ workplace, etc.	Narrowed to one type of cancer. Still includes causes, symptoms, treatments, rates of cure, and effects on families and the workplace.	
Experts needed: several cancer specialists, therapists, family members, insurance or business representatives and cancer patient	*Experts needed:* lung cancer specialist, therapist, family members, business representatives, and cancer patient	*One expert needed:* person who has lung cancer
Too broad a topic for a single interview	Still too broad a topic for a single interview of one or two people	Manageable for an in-depth interview with one person

FIGURE 13-1 Narrowing and pinpointing a topic

Practice 13-2: Narrowing and Pinpointing Your Topic

1. Use *Student Workbook* page 13-A to decide what individual items in a group have in common. Then write a descriptive category for each group.

2. Look at the following example. The general topic is "Automobile Collisions," a very broad topic. Four examples of a narrowed focus on the subject of auto collisions are given. You could probably think of several others without too much difficulty. Each narrowed topic is then more finely pinpointed in the second column.

Example:

General Topic: Automobile Collisions

Narrowed Topics:	Pinpointed Topics:
1. Two major causes of auto collisions	1-a. Speeding as a major cause of auto collisions
2. Some of the most dangerous highways in our state	2-a. Highway 101: our state's most dangerous highway
3. Methods for reducing auto fatalities	3-a. The argument for seat belts as life savers
4. Some special problems repairing automobiles after a collision	4-a. Repairing a fiberglass auto body after a front-end collision

3. Page 13-B in your *Student Workbook* consists of a list of general topics. Each general topic has one narrowed topic. Work with a partner to pinpoint each of the narrowed topics as was done with the topic "Automobile Collisions." Try to relate at least one of the pinpointed topics to a career or an occupational field that interests you.

Preparing for an Interview: Finding an Expert Who Knows Your Topic

After you have pinpointed your topic, you need to find an expert who can answer your questions. For example, to learn the fine points of training a thoroughbred horse, you would have to talk to (interview) a trainer of thoroughbreds. You might ask a few knowledgeable people to recommend someone who would be a good source of information for you. This person does not have to be well educated about other matters, but he or she does have to know a great deal about the subject you are researching. For example, your father may be a great cook. He may use an old family recipe for making spaghetti sauce that always gets compliments from guests. Someone could interview him about how to make spaghetti sauce and learn a great deal. Whether your father has a high school diploma or a college degree has nothing to do with how good his spaghetti sauce is.

So you have two tasks: not only carefully pinpointing your topic, but also finding one or more people who can provide you with enough reliable information to explore the topic adequately.

Practice 13–3: Finding an Expert

For each of the following pinpointed topics, give a type of expert who could provide the kind of information required. Be prepared to discuss your choices with the class.

Pinpointed Topics:

1. The planting and managing of a peach tree orchard

2. Computerized libraries in schools

3. The making of a cheese soufflé

4. On-site experiences in the war with Iraq

5. New designs for safer batting helmets for Little League ballplayers

6. Effects of chemical insecticides on flowering plants

7. Efficiency of seat belts as safety devices

8. Dog food as a billion-dollar industry

9. The making of a dulcimer

10. Head lice epidemics in child-care centers

11. Safety tips for in-line skaters

12. The creation of an advertising campaign (print, TV, or other)

by the way...

A small percentage of individuals may experience epileptic seizures when exposed to certain light patterns or flashing lights. Exposure to certain patterns or backgrounds on a television screen or while playing video games may induce an epileptic seizure in these individuals.

FROM A WARNING ON A VIDEO GAME

People *Connection*

Oliver Sacks is a neurologist who deals with differences in behaviors and abilities caused by anomalies in the brain. Part of his life was dramatized in the movie *Awakenings*, starring Robin Williams (Dr. Sacks) and Robert de Niro (a patient).

Dr. Sacks is interested not only in the person's affliction, but also in how it manifests itself and how the person copes with it. In his book *An Anthropologist on Mars*, he describes a surgeon with Tourette's Syndrome; an autistic woman with a Ph.D. who designs more humane cattle pens based on her innate understanding of the animals; and an artist who has lost all ability to see color, but who continues to paint in leaden tones. Sacks says, "I have taken off my white coat [and] deserted, by and large, the hospitals where I have spent the last twenty-five years, to explore my subjects' lives as they live in the real world, feeling in part like a naturalist examining rare forms of life . . . but most of all like a physician, called here and there to make house calls . . . at the far borders of human experience."

© MURRAY ANDREW/CORBIS SYGMA

Oliver Sacks, neurologist, expert in the study of people with brain and nervous system disorders

Setting Up the Interview

Once you figure out the type of expert you need and get a lead or two from a reliable person such as a friend, family member, coworker, or teacher, be sure to get the expert's address, phone number, and e-mail address (if possible). Then get your thoughts together so that you know what you want to say. Jot down a few notes that you can use to introduce yourself to this person and explain why you want to interview him or her. This way you won't waste the person's time or risk being turned down because you sound unsure of what you want. Also have a calendar handy so that you can set the date during your conversation.

Contacting a Potential Interviewee

Call, introduce yourself, and set up an appointment. Don't just walk in. Your expert is probably a busy person. Show courtesy by setting a meeting time that he or she selects as most convenient. This touch of courtesy will impress the expert with your professionalism and may result in greater willingness to spend time on the interview.

If the person does not have a telephone or works outdoors or for some other reason can't be reached by phone, drop by his or her place of work. Briefly explain your need to get information from an expert and ask for a convenient time and place to meet. Some people are shy and need to be encouraged. But most are flattered to be called an expert and will agree to talk with you.

Researching the Interviewee's Background

Do some background work on the interviewee before going to the scheduled appointment. Find out what this person does and what other interests the person has. Sometimes talking about other things—children, pets, sports, or mutual acquaintances, for example—gives both of you time to relax and feel more comfortable with each other.

Keeping an Open Mind

© SHELLEY GAZIN/CORBIS

Nobel Prize-winning physicist Richard Feynman

Go into the interview with an open mind. Do not allow **preconceived notions** or stereotypes to affect your opinion of this person or your behavior toward the person. If you discover that your expert is far different than you expected, have the good sense to adjust your thinking and perhaps even refocus your interview.

For example, perhaps you've decided to interview a physicist, but you've somewhere gotten the idea that all physicists are men, are boring, and are lost in the world of their theories. Maybe you've never met the female physicist who plays the tuba, the male physicist who leads his church choir, or his coworker who designs hang gliders and spends her weekends testing out different designs. Perhaps you haven't read *"Surely You're Joking, Mr. Feynman!": Adventures of a Curious Character,* a biography that consists largely of transcriptions of taped interviews with Feynman, so you don't know that he played the bongos for years, just for the fun of it, and once took second place in an international musical competition. If you had had the opportunity to learn about all of these people, you might have changed your viewpoint to "What amazingly interesting and varied lives some physicists lead."

The point is that you have to suspend your judgment and make the assumption that most people lead varied and interesting lives, even when they don't realize it themselves. Your job as an interviewer is to appreciate your expert's personal uniqueness as well as learn what he or she knows about your topic.

Preparing Questions for the Interview

Write down some key questions about your topic that you want to be sure to ask. Leave a space for notes after each question. Most of the questions should be open-ended, not questions that can be answered with a simple yes or no.

Here are some questions that might be used in an interview on the topic "Cocaine Use During Pregnancy and Its Effects on the Child."

- Have you ever witnessed the birth of infants to women who are addicted to cocaine?
- What differences have you observed between these infants and infants of mothers who do not consume drugs during pregnancy?
- Are there any lasting effects on the infant because of the mother's addiction, or are the effects just temporary? What are these effects? Can they be overcome? If so, how?
- What are the chances of a female cocaine addict having a normal baby?
- Is there any evidence that a father's cocaine addiction can affect the baby?

Conducting the Interview

Your interviewee will rely on you to ask appropriate questions that provide you with the information you need. You will have to keep the interview on the topic, ask appropriate questions, get clarification on your expert's answers if you don't understand something that is said, and record your information.

Staying on the Topic During the Interview

It's easy to get caught up in the excitement of meeting an interesting or famous person and hearing stories about his or her life. However, even professionals can wander off the topic. You may need to keep bringing yourself and/or your expert back to the subject.

Example

You are interviewing someone about emergency medical teams. You want to know what kind of training is essential to be an effective EMT (emergency medical technician).

You: "Where did you get your training?"

Member of life squad: "I started out as a volunteer with the Sycamore Branch Emergency Medical Team and took a night class twice a week. I remember one time, right after I started, when we answered a call and this kid was lying facedown in a pool of blood in the kitchen. His dad was hysterical. Kept yelling at us the whole time. It was crazy."

Technology *Connection*

Digital cameras and scanners are excellent tools for someone who wants to publish an interview in a magazine or newspaper, at school, or elsewhere. These two tools allow interviewers to take still photos of their subjects and incorporate the pictures into the article, using an interface program that imports the photos into word processing or desktop publishing software. The digital camera uses no film, so the photographs don't have to be developed. If you do not have a digital camera, you can take a photograph with an ordinary camera and scan the picture, saving it on the computer's hard drive or on a CD. You can then place this picture anywhere in your document.

Note that your interviewee's answer, while interesting, is getting away from the point of your question. Gently get him back on topic.

> *You:* "How did you learn to deal with a situation like that? Did the night classes help prepare you for it?"

This subtle refocusing of the conversation back to the question of training will hardly be noticed by the interviewee, but it will ensure that you get the information you need. In the meantime, you will have picked up a greater awareness of the kinds of things your expert has to endure, which adds to your understanding of your subject.

Taking Effective Notes

Don't rely on your memory to remind you of what was said during the interview. Effective notes are very important.

- *Take down some phrases* **verbatim**, *even if you are recording the interview.* Enclose them in quotes or circle them in your notes to show that they are the exact words of the speaker.

- *Read quotes or general explanations back to the interviewee to check accuracy* and to avoid recording a slip of the tongue. Remember, you are going after accurate information; you are not trying to catch the interviewee in a mistake.

- *Listen carefully and ask clarifying questions.* (Remember what you learned about the use of **clarifying questions** in Chapter 3.)

Example
Interviewee: "I worked on the Columbus squad for a while."
You (clarifying): "Was that in Columbus, Ohio?"
Interviewee: "No. Columbus, Georgia. It's a college town."

Using Alternatives to Note Taking

If you're not the note-taking type, there a lot of other ways to do an interview. Be inventive about it. You might want to try an Internet interview, or you may want to record a personal interview in case you can't keep up with note taking.

Using the Internet for Online Interviews

If you and your interviewee both have the necessary equipment, a face-to-face interview is possible via the Internet. If your expert agrees to the interview, you will have to arrange a time. If you do not have the capability of conducting such an interview, you can still talk to your expert via e-mail. You can also communicate through real-time correspondence if you know that a recognized expert is open for questions in a particular chat room and you can get in on the conversation and record the answers to your questions. This last alternative may be a bit tricky due to possible interference by others on the line.

Recording Interviews

Some interviewees may allow you to record personal interviews, using an audiocassette tape recorder or video camera. This procedure allows you to listen and think during the interview rather than concentrate on getting responses on paper. Be sure to test the microphone before starting the interview, not only to be certain that it is functioning, but also to set it properly so that it will pick up the person's voice clearly.

If you have access to a video camera and if your interviewee is not uncomfortable with the idea and grants you permission, you can videotape the interview. It would be best to have someone with you who can do the videotaping while you conduct the interview. This allows you to concentrate on the interview and not on the technicalities of recording. Later you can review not only the words, but also the subtle body language and facial reactions of the interviewee to the questions you asked. You may see things that you did not notice as you were concentrating on your interviewee's words. You may note a frown, a vacant stare, an energetic walking back and forth, or other body language that can help you edit the interviewee's words with more realism and accuracy.

Record the date and time of your interview and the full name of each person you are interviewing. Write this information on the label of each tape or disk to avoid a mix-up later and to make it easy to access information as needed.

Culture *Connection*

PHOTO COURTESY OF SUSAN L. KEMP

Amish doll

Start your interview by stating the full name of each person interviewed and the date of the interview just as you begin to record. You can easily forget details or misplace notes by the time you start to work on your written version.

When the interview is ended, thank your interviewee and follow up with a thank-you note a day or two after the interview.

Editing the Interview: Making the Voice Come Through on Paper

When you begin to turn your interview into a report, let the person's voice come through as much as possible in your writing. In other words, don't try to make someone sound better or worse. What you're looking for is **authenticity**, the authentic response of the individual. Let the person speak for himself or herself.

Replay in your mind the way the person looked, sat, and moved. If you videotaped the interview, watch it several times to catch aspects of the person that you may have failed to notice as you were taking notes or sorting out your thoughts. As you edit, you may want to add a word or phrase that describes something the person is doing as he or she speaks. But this should be done rarely. The most important reason for remembering the person's behavior during the interview is so that you can edit for the right tone, the right emphasis.

Depending on the effect that you want (or the way the interview turns out), you will have to decide whether to put your questions and comments into the written interview or leave them out. If the interviewee began by speaking freely, providing many points of information in a smooth flow of talk without your having to ask many questions, the job is much easier. Then you can leave the questions out.

But if the person gave rather short answers to your questions and the answers provide little or no clue to what was asked, then the questions will have to be included. For example, look at the following quote from an interview:

> "No, I don't believe that's true. He wouldn't have said something like that."

This quote tells you absolutely nothing about the subject of the interview. Was the interviewee being asked about:

- How a mortician addressed the family of an accident victim?
- Whether an actor criticized the writer of a television show?
- Whether a teacher used vulgar language in the classroom?
- Whether an employee accused his boss of neglect in a workplace accident?

The quotation is so general that it could have been the answer to any one of those questions. Therefore, it cannot be used without including the following question, which was asked in the actual interview:

> "Do you believe that the personnel director told Ms. Turner that her children would probably cause her to miss too much work?"

© GETTY IMAGES/PHOTODISC, INC.

An interview in progress

Once you have copied all notes and/or **transcribed** the tape, it's time to make decisions about exactly what to include in your report, what words, phrases, sentences, spacing, and punctuation are essential to the message you want to pass on to your audience. One good rule of thumb: Never omit any word or phrase, whether standard English or slang, that is essential to your interviewee's character or message.

Handling Repetition

A good rule is to omit unnecessary or repetitious words. However, you may want to keep them if they help give a clearer picture of the subject or the speaker, as is true in the following quotation:

> "Why? Why? I keep asking myself why I didn't pick up that phone. For the rest of my life, I'll regret not hearing my brother's voice that one last time."

The repeated word *why* indicates the speaker's frustration with himself or herself. If communicating that frustration is important, removing the repeated *why* would dilute the message and give a slightly different impression of the speaker.

On the other hand, in the following quotation, the repeated phrase *you know* simply distracts from the message:

> "It was pretty scary, you know, being on duty by myself. It was, you know, like one of those Halloween movies you see, you know?"

Using Inserts

Sometimes the interviewee uses an abbreviated name, a set of initials, or some reference that is unclear to the average reader or listener—or that is unclear even to the person conducting the interview. In this case, a clarifying question or statement is in order. The clarification could be made in the printed report by using brackets [ ].

Brackets can help the reader understand what the speaker meant. Using brackets tells the reader that you have added something, but only to help clarify what the speaker meant, not to change the meaning or intent of the speaker.

Say, for example, that it is time to edit the previously quoted section of an interview with a member of an emergency medical team. The actual interview went like this:

> *Interviewee:* "I worked on the Columbus squad for a while."
> *You (clarifying):* "Was that in Columbus, Ohio?"
> *Interviewee:* "No. Columbus, Georgia. It's a college town."

A simple way to edit this exchange is to write the following:

> "I worked on the Columbus [Georgia] squad for a while."

This approach allows you to use information from your clarifying question where it is needed and to avoid unnecessary verbiage.

Brackets can also be used to indicate movements or facial expressions, as you've seen them described in a play:

> "We had a team of ironworkers checking out that girder [he points], but they didn't find any weak spots. We even installed cameras. Nothing. We found nothing."

Using Spacing and Punctuation

Listen to the voice. If you are working from notes only, try to hear the interviewee's voice in your mind as you reread your notes. If you have an audiocassette or videotape, listen for pauses, questions, or exclamations that might give you clues as to how to punctuate and space your sentences.

Remember that the meaning drives the editing. Strive to get on paper the meaning that the person was trying to convey by using commas, question marks, exclamation points, colons, dashes, periods, or other marks of punctuation to help convey the interviewee's intent. Also decide where to start new paragraphs.

If your interviewee gets emotionally overwrought or confused and stammers or unnecessarily repeats a word, use an ellipsis (. . .). An ellipsis shows that you left out one or more words, but that leaving them out does not change the meaning intended by the speaker. Never omit a word, however, that will change a speaker's meaning.

Practice 13-4: Editing an Interview

Your teacher will play a CD selection for you. Listen to the voice of the man being interviewed as he tells part of his story. Then, using page 13-C in your *Student Workbook*, read along as you listen to the interview a second time. Edit the interview, using the proofreading marks found on page 572 to show where you need to delete a word, insert an explanation, capitalize, insert a period or other punctuation marks, etc.

The assignment was to interview an older worker who was fired or laid off late in his or her career. Four questions were given to the interviewee, Bill Steinemann, and he was asked to tell his story and to include these points as he talked. The results are a personal story in the manner of the literature selection "Nick Salerno" on page 462. The questions asked were as follows:

1. How did it feel to be fired or laid off late in life?

2. How did it affect you?

3. How did you react?

4. Did you ever get another job?

Conducting a Survey

A survey is a way to get information or opinions from a large number of people. For a survey to be effective, you have to ask all of the people exactly the same questions, or there will be no basis for comparing their answers.

For example, maybe you need to find out what 20 dentists know about TMJ (temporomandibular joint syndrome—a misalignment of the lower jaw joint). Which dentists treat it? Do any consider it a psychosomatic disorder? Do they recognize common symptoms of TMJ? Are they aware of proven methods of treatment? Do they refer TMJ patients to surgeons? Do they refer patients to other professionals? Instead of having a general list of questions to keep you (the interviewer) on track, you need a very specific, carefully worded list of questions. When each person you survey doesn't answer exactly the same questions, you have no basis for comparing their answers.

You also must have a means of recording responses so that you can tally and compare the results with relative ease. One way to do this is to use a carefully prepared questionnaire.

Preparing an Appropriate Type of Questionnaire

A questionnaire makes it possible to ask a series of questions of either a select or random group of people in order to learn how they think or feel about a particular topic. A questionnaire requires careful attention to words. Exactly what are you asking? What do you want to know?

Next, you have to think about how you are going to record all of the answers (maybe ten or more) from of the people you survey. Directing people to reply in a certain way makes it possible to tally results. Of course, the way people are required to reply will vary with the type of information you are looking for. This is why you may see one or more of the following types of questions and response patterns on different questionnaires.

"Would you say Atilla is doing an excellent job, a good job, a fair job, or a poor job?"

Reprinted by permission www.howstuffworks.com

Type 1: Recording What People Think or Feel

On a scale of 1 to 10, how would you rate the Green Bay Packers? We've all heard this kind of question. When a stopwatch or game score cannot be used to judge an Olympic event, for example, judges are asked to rate the competitors on a scale of 1 to 10 (or 1 to 6 in the case of figure skaters). Judges in such events have guidelines to follow in arriving at their judgments, something not always possible on a survey. But the ultimate method of replying is the same—by using a number. Strictly speaking, the numbers used in this way cannot be added or subtracted, though people sometimes do so anyway. The numbers merely represent an opinion or a judgment. One should tally how many people answered with a 7, a 6, etc. to report results.

To find out what people think or feel and to have an efficient way of recording their answers, many surveyors use a similar scale of five to seven numbers and ask people to rate items.

SAMPLE 1 (Rating scale)

Directions: Indicate how you rate the following media as a way of staying informed by circling the number that best reflects your response (5 = excellent, 1 = poor). If you have never used a particular medium, circle *NA*.

Medium	Excellent	Very Good	Average	Below Average	Poor	NA
Radio	5	4	3	2	1	NA
Television	5	4	3	2	1	NA
Newspapers	5	4	3	2	1	NA
The Internet	5	4	3	2	1	NA

SAMPLE 2 (Agree-Disagree scale)

Directions: Indicate your response to the following statements about products. Circle one number from 7 (strongly agree) to 1 (strongly disagree) for each product.

	Strongly Agree	Agree		No Opinion	Disagree		Strongly Disagree
No-pain is an effective painkiller.	7	6	5	4	3	2	1
Windoclear eliminates streaking.	7	6	5	4	3	2	1

SAMPLE 3 (Nonnumerical yes and no response)

Directions: Answer each question by circling either YES or NO.

1. Do you think No-pain is an effective painkiller? YES NO

2. Have you ever used Windoclear? YES NO
   If you answered YES, does it eliminate streaks? YES NO

Type 2: Recording Actual Amounts

When you need to know actual amounts, set up your questionnaire so that actual amounts can be obtained and survey only knowledgeable people. The responses you get from such a questionnaire may not be exact, but they will give you a better idea than you would have gotten by estimating without asking.

SAMPLE 4 (Indicating an actual numerical range)

Directions: Check the amount that most accurately answers each question.

What percentage of your patients' insurance companies provide 100% coverage for multiple surgical procedures?

_____80% to 100% _____60% to 79% _____40% to 59% _____20% to 39% _____1% to 19%

SAMPLE 5 (Indicating exact amounts)

How many televisions are in your home? (Check answer.)

_____1　　　　_____2　　　　_____3　　　　_____4 or more

Note that the arrangement of blanks and numbers can be confusing in Sample 4. People often tend to place the check mark or X after a number. If you want respondents to place the check mark before each number, as is shown in Sample 5, use appropriate spacing so respondents know where to place their mark. Otherwise, your results may be inaccurate.

Be sure to set up response patterns and test them on a sample group first. This allows you to correct any problems in the questionnaire format that you may not have anticipated.

Type 3: Using a Nonnumerical Checklist

In a nonnumerical checklist, actual counts are not needed. Facts or feelings may be indicated by placing a check mark next to the word or phrase that answers the question.

SAMPLE 6 (Indicating objective facts)

Where did you learn about this computer? Check all sources that apply.

_____ television commercial　　　　_____ friend or neighbor

_____ radio commercial　　　　_____ store display

_____ newspaper or magazine ad　　　　_____ other

> **SAMPLE 7 (Indicating subjective responses)**
>
> How did you feel when you were told that your prospective employer ran a closed shop and that to work there you would have to join a labor union?
>
> _____ No reaction   _____ Angry   _____ Pleased

You may set up a questionnaire in a variety of ways. The seven examples provided give you a few to choose from. The important point to remember is that you need to consider what you want to know in order to choose an appropriate format.

Avoiding Pitfalls of Questionnaire Design

Every part of a questionnaire must be absolutely clear in its meaning—from the directions to the questions to the choices of answers. Unclear directions can result in unusable information. Unclear words or phrases of any kind in a questionnaire can cause your entire project to be worthless.

But is Zappo extraordinarily effective?

Choosing Words That Say Exactly What You Mean

The following are illustrations of some dos and don'ts in wording a questionnaire:

- Don't say *Zappo is an extraordinary roach killer.* (What does *extraordinary* mean? Interpretations may range from "extraordinarily bad" to "extraordinarily good.")

- Don't say *Zappo is a different kind of roach killer.* (Is *different* better or worse? Does *different* mean a spray, as opposed to powder or glue boards?)

Instead, say:

- Zappo kills roaches effectively.

- Zappo kills roaches better than any other roach killers.

- Zappo kills roaches without harming pets.

Avoiding Open-Ended or Essay Answers

Suppose you wanted to know whether most students like to drive American or foreign-made cars. So you asked,

"What kind of car do you like to drive?"

Think about the nightmare of tallying the responses. The respondents wouldn't know whether you were asking them to give the make, model, or style (convertible, sedan, etc.). You would have to spend hours writing down all of the different answers you received. Some respondents may have said they liked two-seater sports models; others may have referred to an SUV or a truck. Some may have said they liked Japanese- or American-made vehicles. Some may simply have said "fast" or "loud."

The responses probably wouldn't focus on any one aspect of comparing cars because the question was so unfocused. To prevent this problem, limit the choices of the respondents. Doing so will show them the kind of answer you are looking for, as in the following example.

"What is your favorite type of radio show?" (Check one)

_____ country-western	_____ open talk	_____ bluegrass/
_____ hip-hop	_____ New Wave	country
_____ sports/sports talk	_____ jazz	_____ soft rock
_____ classical	_____ hard rock/	_____ religious
_____ oldies	heavy metal	_____ other

Avoiding Loaded Statements

Statements such as "I like Springbok running shoes because . . ." are a problem because they assume that the respondent does, indeed, like the product. In fact, advertisers often use such an opening line in promotional contests.

A survey, however, is not a promotional contest. It is an attempt to gather material in an unbiased manner. If you assume that someone likes or dislikes something and you word your statements accordingly, the results will be biased. The survey will be worthless.

Seeking Responses from Reliable Sources

Your respondents in a survey do not have to be experts in order to be reliable. Marketing surveys are a prime illustration of this fact. If a shoe manufacturer wants to know why people prefer a particular kind of shoe, it doesn't need a shoe expert. (The company is full of shoe experts.) It needs to find out which people buy shoes and why they buy them. Then it can look at the responses for ideas on what kinds of shoes to make more or fewer of in the future.

Career *Connection*

Dean Schoenewald was struck by the advice of a teacher to "Find out what you love and figure out how to make a living at it." Schoenewald loved acting. He also had a good head for business and wanted to make money without working for somebody else. He may have been the most famous person to don a mascot costume, known for his death-defying stunts and his ingenuity.

Before Schoenewald began training other mascots, he was the unofficial mascot of the Philadelphia Eagles, the official mascot of the San Jose Sharks, and the NHL's first official mascot. In an interview on *CBS Morning News*, he was asked what kind of person he looks for. He said the person must first be entertaining—a ham or hot-dog personality. If you are such a person, you then have to (1) cease being yourself, (2) become the character you portray, and (3) give that character a personality. You must be able to please a crowd because your job is to entertain thousands of sports fans in a stadium, especially when there is a lull in the action.

However, if you were to survey people about their choice of shoes in a country where only sandals or bare feet were common, you might get only puzzled looks instead of answers. The responses about shoes from those people would be unreliable.

Likewise, if you asked the fathers of 18-year-olds what their sons and daughters thought about environmental concerns, the information would not be as reliable as it would have been if you had asked the 18-year-olds.

Constructing the Survey Questionnaire

The survey questionnaire is similar to the interview questionnaire. Both types of questionnaires:

- Seek information for a purpose.

- Require a limited topic.

- Help to direct the thoughts of the person who is responding.

The survey questionnaire, however, has to ask for specific information about the respondents before getting to the topic at hand. For example, for purposes of comparison, you may want to know:

- Whether the respondent is male or female.

- How old the person is.

- Whether the person is married.

- How much education the person has.

- What other information might affect the responses (size of family, major in school, etc.).

This collection of facts about age, income, educational level, and other subjects for a group of people is called **demographic data**.

Caution: Protect Anonymity

Never ask for the names of the respondents. Protect their anonymity so that they feel free to answer any question without fear of someone knowing how they answered.

Practice 13–5: Completing a Questionnaire

Fill in the questionnaire on page 13-D in your *Student Workbook*. It is also the sample Project at the end of this chapter. It is important to see how usable and appropriate a well-written and well-designed form can be before attempting one of your own. After completing the questionnaire, answer these questions.

1. Who do you think wants the information on this questionnaire?

2. Why do they want the information?

3. Why might a company that advertises in the newspaper be interested in the results of this survey?

Tallying the Survey Responses

Today massive surveys are tallied on computers. But if you circulate up to only 50 surveys, the tallying can be done by hand.

Working in pairs is best. One person reads the answer while the other marks down responses. A smaller number of responses can be tallied on a blank copy of the questionnaire itself. Larger numbers should be tallied on a separate sheet of paper. Do not write out all of the questions. Write only the number and, in cases such as the newspaper survey you just completed, the category.

Example

1. Yes   ~~THL~~ ~~THL~~ ~~THL~~ ~~THL~~ ~~THL~~ ~~THL~~ I   = 31
    No   ~~THL~~ ~~THL~~ ~~THL~~ IIII   = 19
    (Tally 2 and 3 the same way.)

4. front page   ~~THL~~ ~~THL~~ ~~THL~~   = 15
    sports   ~~THL~~ ~~THL~~ ~~THL~~ ~~THL~~ IIII   = 24
    classified ads   ~~THL~~ ~~THL~~ I   = 11

Proceed this way for all questions. Then add up the totals for each answer.

If you want to see how each age group answers, separate the papers into stacks by age group (all 10- to 15-year-olds in one stack, all 16- to 21-year-olds in another stack, etc.). Then tally totals for each age group.

Reporting the Information

After tallying all of the responses on the questionnaire, the next step is to write a short report summarizing the responses. Use the following format for your report.

REPORT FORMAT

I. INTRODUCTION—STATE THE PURPOSE OF THE QUESTIONNAIRE.

II. BODY—STATE THE KINDS OF QUESTIONS ASKED.

   A. Number of Respondents

     1. Number of males

     2. Number of females

     (Note: You may want to keep the questionnaires of males and females separate and then tally all responses of males and females separately for purposes of comparison.)

   B. Ages of Respondents—Number in Each Age Category

   C. Educational Level of Respondents

   D. Income of Respondents

   E. Number of Respondents Who Receive a Newspaper in Household Each Day

   F. Number of Respondents Who Receive a Newspaper in Household at Least Once a Week

   G. Number of Respondents Who Read All or Part of a Newspaper at Least Once a Week

   H. Part of Paper Read First by Majority of Respondents

   I. Part of Newspaper Read Occasionally by Majority of Respondents

   J. How Newspaper Is Obtained by Majority

III. CONCLUSIONS

Look at your results. What picture do you now have of your respondents? What conclusions can you draw?

Details on how to write reports containing results of your research are in Chapter 15.

Practice 13-6: Word Search

To review key terms used in this chapter, complete the word search puzzle on *Student Workbook* page 13-E.

Summary

Interviews are an important way to gather information. In this chapter, you had a chance to practice personal interviews as well as interviews of groups (commonly known as surveys). Follow these guidelines when the need or opportunity for an interview arises:

- Narrow your topic and be ready with questions that keep you focused on that topic during an interview.

- Arrange an interview with an expert who can shed light on your topic.

- Take careful notes or, with permission, record an interview so that the full meaning of the interviewee's responses is not lost or misinterpreted.

- Represent each interviewee accurately and fairly when writing and presenting the results of an interview.

- Carefully prepare a set of questions and ask each person the same questions when seeking information or opinions from a group, using a survey.

- Tally, summarize, and report the results of your survey.

review and research activities visit
communicating.swlearning.com

Works Cited

Feynman, Richard P., as told to Ralph Leighton. *"What Do YOU Care What Other People Think?": Further Adventures of a Curious Character.* New York: Norton, 1988.

Petroski, Henry. *To Engineer Is Human: The Role of Failure in Successful Design.* New York: St. Martin's, 1985.

Sacks, Oliver. *An Anthropologist on Mars: Seven Paradoxical Tales.* New York: Knopf, 1995.

Woodhouse, Barbara. *Dog Training My Way.* New York: Stein and Day, 1982.

http://citypaper.net/articles/1129ol/cs.cover1.shtml

project-based assessment

Project 1—Interview

Reporting the Results of an Interview

Before beginning this Project, study the Sample Project Plan on page 457 and the Sample Presentation, "Reporting the Results of an Interview," on page 458. Listen to the oral presentation of that interview on the Student CD.

Then prepare a three- to five-minute oral presentation of an interview, following these steps:

1. Choose a specific (pinpointed) topic that interests you and that you think will interest others.

2. Interview an expert who can give you interesting details about the topic. Arrange a time for an interview and think about specific questions you can ask your expert.

3. Conduct the interview. Keep the interview reasonably short (less than an hour). Record all or part of it if possible. (Be sure to get equipment ready in advance, including an extra audiocassette or videocassette.)

4. Use the Project Plan on page 13-F of the *Student Workbook* to organize your oral presentation. Choose an interesting quote or fact from the interview to use in beginning your talk. End with what you learned from the interview (a closing statement).

5. Choose a partner with whom to practice your presentation. Your partner should use the Rough Draft column of the Project Guide, *Student Workbook* page 13-G, to evaluate your practice presentation.

6. Do another rehearsed presentation. Have your partner evaluate it, using the Final Draft column of the Project Guide.

7. Give your presentation. Turn in your Project Guide.

Sample Project Plan

Plan for Presentation of an Interview

SUBJECT	Man who lost job late in life—impact on his life		CONTENT
AUDIENCE	General audience—classmates		"I thank God. I thank him every day that that kid and I got together." Tell how Bill survived because of faith in God and in people. Tell story from interview: —Younger guy (friend) got fired. —Bill got him hired back. —Later when Bill was 53—lost job when his boss sold the business. —Guy he once rehired offered him a job. That was 10 years ago. Now Bill is a happy man. (Load digital photos of Bill in pressroom into laptop computer to show class.)
PURPOSE	**What actions should the audience take?** Understand what the person went through and how he felt.		
FORMAT	☐ written ☒ oral ☐ other		
SOURCES	a 62-year-old printing press operator who was laid off work without warning when he was 53		
VISUALS	**What visuals, if any, will make the presentation more effective?** pictures of Bill Steinemann showing him at work in the pressroom		
PREPARE	Get LCD projector and extension cord to use with laptop. Project pictures on screen in classroom. Set up during study hall before presentation.		

Sample Presentation

Reporting the Results of an Interview

This presentation is based on an interview of a 62-year-old printing press operator. Notice that it starts with a quote from the interview you edited in Practice 13-4.

"I thank God. I thank him every day that that kid and I got together."

These are the words of a man who is very grateful and relieved to be able to support his family again. They tell you what kind of man Bill Steinemann is. He has lived by faith in God and faith in people. He has always believed that if you treat people right, they will treat you right.

When Bill was young and working in a large printing company that produced nationally known magazines and comic books, he found out through the rumor mill that a younger guy in another department had been fired. Bill knew the guy and liked him, even though he was hot-headed, which got him into trouble. This guy was only 20 years old, and his wife was pregnant. They were living on practically nothing, and now he didn't even have a job. Bill put in a good word and got the guy rehired.

The two men remained friends, and their families visited one another even after each was hired by different companies a hundred miles from one another in the Midwest. Suddenly, without any warning, the owner of the company Bill worked for told him that the business had been sold. He gave Bill two weeks' notice, which meant that after two weeks and two paychecks, Bill would have no income.

Bill and his wife did not know what to do. But they couldn't stay depressed for long. They still had two teenagers at home—a girl in high school and a boy who had worked for a year and just finished a semester of college. So they were desperate to find a way to get through this disaster. Bill called his old friend and asked if he knew of any openings among the printing plants that were scattered throughout the Midwest. Within days, his old friend had found him a place in his own label-making plant. The new job required Bill's family to move 100 miles, but they knew they had to do it.

When I talked to Bill, he had been working with his old friend for nearly nine years. He was proud to let me take his picture beside his new printing press, where thousands of labels are printed each day. [Project photo on screen in front of room using LCD projector.] He is proud of what he does and grateful for the power of the friendship that helped him put his life back together.

project-based assessment

Project 2—Questionnaire

Creating a Questionnaire

Review the Sample Project Plan for Designing a Questionnaire (on page 460) that was used in designing the questionnaire on page 13-D of your *Student Workbook*. Does the questionnaire reflect the plan? Does it do what the plan says it should do?

In this final chapter Project, use the Project Plan and Project Guide on pages 13-H and 13-I of your *Student Workbook*. Working in a group, develop a solid questionnaire of your own. Follow these steps:

1. Find a topic or an issue on which conducting a survey could provide helpful information. (Be sure that you have access to enough people who can relate to this issue.)

2. Pinpoint what you want to know about that topic.

3. Work through the Project Plan for Designing a Questionnaire (*Student Workbook* page 13-H). Decide who your audience will be (whom you need to survey) and what questions should ask to get the information you need.

4. Design the questionnaire for your survey based on your plan.

5. Ask a classmate to fill out and evaluate your questionnaire, using the Rough Draft column of the Project Guide on page 13-I of your *Student Workbook*.

6. Revise the questionnaire, if necessary, based on your classmate's feedback.

7. Have another classmate fill out the questionnaire and evaluate it, using the Final Draft column of the Project Guide.

8. Considering your classmate's comments, make any final adjustments to the questionnaire that are needed.

9. Conduct a survey of 25 to 50 people in your target audience.

10. Tally the surveys.

Save your questionnaires and tally sheets for possible interpretation and reporting in Chapters 14 and 15.

Sample Project Plan

Plan for Designing a Questionnaire

SUBJECT	Find out who reads a newspaper, what parts of the newspaper they read, and where they get their paper.	**CONTENT** Need questions that will tell us —how old the person is —how much education the person has —how much income the person has —what part of the paper the person reads and how often Write clear directions at the top of the questionnnaire so that people fill it out right.
AUDIENCE	Anyone over age 10	
PURPOSE	Design an effective questionnaire for this subject.	
FORMAT	☒ written ☐ oral ☐ other	
SOURCES	Ideas of team members in class. Brainstorm questions to put on questionnaire.	
DESIGN	What layout will make the questionnaire most effective (easy to read and respond to)?	

Sample Questionnaire

Please check one reply for each piece of information requested.

Are you

male? _____

female? _____

Your age:

10–15 _____

16-21 _____

22-35 _____

36-50 _____

over 50 _____

Highest education completed by anyone in your household:

grade school _____

some high school _____

high school graduate _____

some college _____

college graduate _____

Your family's approximate income:

under $12,000 _____

$12,000 to $20,000 _____

$21,000 to $30,000 _____

$31,000 to $40,000 _____

$41,000 to $60,000 _____

over $60,000 _____

Answer the first three questions below by <u>circling the answer</u>.

1. Is there a newspaper in your household each day? YES NO

2. Is there a newspaper in your household at least once a week? YES NO

3. Do you read all or part of a newspaper at least once a week? YES NO

_____ **If you answered NO to ALL THREE questions, STOP HERE.** _____

4. What part of the newspaper do you read first?

front page _____

sports _____

classified ads _____

editorial page _____

puzzles/games _____

comics _____

other _____

5. What parts of the newspaper do you read occasionally? (Check all that apply to you.)

front page _____

sports _____

classified ads _____

editorial page _____

puzzles/games _____

comics _____

other _____

6. What best describes how you get your newspaper?

Delivered to your house _____

Buy it on the newsstand _____

Read a copy you find at work _____

Pick up a used copy elsewhere _____

Overview

Studs Terkel, a writer, an actor, a theater manager, and a television and radio show host, is an interviewer extraordinaire. Instead of interviewing celebrities, the infamous, and the heroes who make the news, he interviews the noncelebrated.

Terkel's interviews with everyday people have been published in several books, such as *Hard Times: An Oral History of the Great Depression* (1970) and *Working: People Talk About What They Do All Day and How They Feel About What They Do* (1974). In 1993, he wrote *Race: How Blacks and Whites Think and Feel About the American Obsession.*

"Nick Salerno"

He has been driving a city garbage truck for eighteen years. He is forty-one, married, has three daughters. He works a forty-hour, five-day week, with occasional overtime. He has a crew of three laborers.

I usually get up at five-fifteen. I get to the city parking lot, you check the oil, your water level, then proceed for the ward yard. I meet the men, we pick up our work sheet.

© GETTY IMAGES/PHOTODISC, INC.

You get just like the milkman's horse, you get used to it. If you remember the milkman's horse, all he had to do was whistle and whooshhh! That's it. He knew just where to stop, didn't he? You pull up until you finish the alley. Usually thirty homes on each side. You have thirty stops in an alley. I have nineteen alleys a week. They're called units. Sometimes I can't finish 'em, that's how heavy they are, this bein' an old neighborhood . . . .

Maybe you got a problem at home. Maybe one of the children aren't feeling too good. Like my second one, she's a problem with homework. Am I doin' the right thing with her? Pressing her a little bit with math. Or you'll read the paper. You always daydream.

Some stops, there's one can, they'll throw that on, then we proceed to the next can. They signal with a buzzer or a whistle or they'll yell. The pusher blade pushes the garbage in. A good solid truckload will hold anywhere from eight thousand to twelve thousand pounds. If it's wet, it weighs more. Years ago you had people burning, a lot of people had garbage burners. You would pick up a lot of ashes. Today most of 'em have converted to gas. In place of ashes, you've got cardboard boxes, you've got wood that people aren't burning anymore. It's not like years ago, when people used everything. They're not too economy-wise today. They'll throw anything away. You'll see whole packages of meat just thrown into the garbage can without being opened. I don't know if it's spoiled from the store or not. When I first started here, I had nearly thirty alleys in this ward. Today I'm down to nineteen. And we got better trucks today. Just the way things are packaged today. Plastic. You see a lot of plastic bottles, cardboard boxes.

We try to give 'em twice-a-week service, but we can't complete the ward twice a week. Maybe I can go four alleys over. If I had an alley Monday. I might go in that alley Friday. What happens over the weekend? It just lays there.

After you dump your garbage in the hopper, the sweeper goes around to sweep it up, and the push blade pushes it in. This is where you get your sound. Does that sound bother you in the morning? (Laughs.) Sometimes it's irritating to me. If someone comes up to you to talk, and the

"Other people just don't care or maybe they don't know any better."

men are working in the back, and they press the lever, you can't hear them. It's aggravating but you get used to it. We come around seven-twenty. Not too many complaints. Usually you're in the same alley the same day, once a week. The people know that you're coming and it doesn't bother them that much.

Some people will throw, will literally throw garbage out of the window—right in the alley. We have finished an alley in the morning and that same afternoon it will be like it wasn't even done. They might have a cardboard carton in the can and garbage all over the alley. People are just not takin' care of it. You get some people that takes care of their property, they'll come out and sweep around their cans. Other people just don't care or maybe they don't know any better.

Some days it's real nice. Other days, when you get off that truck you're tired, that's it! You say all you do is drive all day, but driving can be pretty tiresome—especially when the kids are out of school. They'll run through a gangway into the alley. This is what you have to watch for. Sitting in that cab, you have a lot of blind spots around the truck. This is what gets you. You watch out that you don't hit any of them.

At times you get aggravated, like your truck breaks down and you get a junk as a replacement. This, believe me, you could take home with you. Otherwise, working

(cont'd on next page)

here, if there's something on your mind, you don't hold anything in. You discuss anything with these guys. Golf, whatever. One of my laborers just bought a new home and I helped him move some of his stuff. He's helped me around my house, plumbing and painting.

We've got spotters now. It's new. (Laughs.) They're riding around in unmarked cars. They'll turn you in for stopping for coffee. I can't see that. If you have a coffee break in the alley, it's just using a little psychology. You'll get more out of them. But if you're watched continually, you're gonna lay down. There's definitely more watching today, because there was a lot of layin' down on the job. Truthfully, I'd just as soon put in my eight hours a day as easy as possible. It's hard enough comin' to work. I got a good crew, we get along together, but we have our days . . . .

People ask me what I do, I say, "I drive a garbage truck for the city." They call you

> *"I don't like too have my salary compared to anybody else's."*

G-man, or, "How's business, picking up?" Just the standard . . . . Or sanitary engineer. I have nothing to be ashamed of. I put in my eight hours. We make a pretty good salary. I feel I earn my money. I can go any place I want. I conduct myself as a gentleman any place I go. My wife is happy, this is the big thing. She doesn't look down at me. I think that's more important than the white-collar guy looking down at me.

They make a crack to my children at school. My kids would just love to see me do something else. I tell 'em, "Honey, this is a good job. There's nothing to be ashamed of. We're not stealin' money. You have everything you need."

I don't like to have my salary compared to anybody else's. I don't like to hear that we're makin' more than a schoolteacher. I earn my money just as well as they do. A teacher should get more money, but don't take it away from me.

—Studs Terkel

Start-Up: Studs Terkel's interview produces an in-depth look into Nick Salerno's life as a garbage truck driver. The reader learns about Salerno and his job. Imagine what sorts of questions would encourage Salerno to give such a glimpse of himself.

Connection: What questions do you think Terkel asked Salerno to obtain the information he needed to write this interview? Write your own questions. In groups of three, share these questions. Critique them. Make a list of the best questions.

As a class, discuss ways that Terkel lets the interviewee's voice come through in the article.

Overview

One of America's greatest authors (and a printer and lecturer), Mark Twain has the reputation of being a great humorist. In this excerpt from his essay "How To Tell a Story," Mark Twain's responses to the interviewer are a put-on. Twain creates an absurd, comical situation.

Mark Twain, in his essay, maintains that humor in stories depends on the manner in which the stories are told or on the story content.

from "How To Tell a Story"

I used to tell a story about a man who came to interview me once to get a sketch of my life. I consulted with a friend—a practical man—before he came, to know how I should treat him.

"Whenever you give the interviewer a fact," he said, "give him another fact that will contradict it. Then he'll go away with a jumble that he can't use at all. Be gentle, be sweet, smile like an idiot—just be natural." That's what my friend told me to do, and I did it.

The nervous, dapper young man took the chair I offered him, and said he was connected with the *Daily Thunderstorm*, and added:

"Hoping it's no harm, I've come to interview you."

"Come to what?"

"*Interview* you."

"Ah! I see. Yes—yes. Um! Yes—yes."

I was not feeling bright that morning. Indeed, my powers seemed a bit under a cloud. However, I went to the bookcase, and when I had been looking six or seven minutes, I said:

"How do you spell it?"

"Spell what?"

"Interview."

"Oh, my goodness! What do you want to spell it for?"

"I don't want just to spell it; I want to spell it to see what it means."

(cont'd on next page)

"In, *in*, ter, *ter*, *inter*—"

"Then you spell it with an *I*?"

"Why, certainly!"

"Oh, that is what took me so long."

"Why, my *dear* sir, what did *you* propose to spell it with?"

"Well, I—I—hardly know. I had the Unabridged, and I was looking around in the back end, among the pictures. But it's a very old edition."

"Why, my friend, they wouldn't have a *picture* of it in even the latest e— My dear sir, I beg your pardon, I mean no harm in the world, but you do not look as—as—intelligent as I had expected you would. No harm—I mean no harm at all."

"Oh, don't mention it! It has often been said, and by people who would not flatter me, that I am quite remarkable in that way. Yes—yes; they always speak of it with pleasure."

"I can easily imagine it. But about this interview. You know it is the custom, now, to interview any man who has become famous."

"Indeed, I had not heard of it before. It must be very interesting. What do you do it with?"

"Ah, well—well—well—it *ought* to be done with a club in some cases. But usually the interviewer asks questions and the interviewed answers them. It is all the rage now. Will you let me ask you certain questions to bring out the salient points of your public and private history?"

"Oh, with pleasure—with pleasure. I have a very bad memory, but I hope you will not mind that. That is to say, it is an irregular memory—very irregular. Sometimes it goes in a gallop, and then again it will be as much as a week passing a given point. This is a great grief to me."

"Oh, it is no matter, so you will try to do the best you can."

"I will. I will put my whole mind on it."

"Thanks. Are you ready to begin?"

"Ready."

Q. How old are you?

A. Nineteen, in June.

Q. Indeed. I would have taken you to be thirty-five or -six. Where were you born?

A. In Missouri.

Q. When did you begin to write?

A. In 1836.

Q. Why, how could that be, if you are only nineteen now?

A. I don't know. It does seem curious, somehow.

Q. It does, indeed. Whom do you consider the most remarkable man you ever met?

A. Aaron Burr.

Q. But you never could have met Aaron Burr, if you are only nineteen years—

A. Now, if you know more about me than I do, what do you ask me for?

Q. Well, it was only a suggestion; nothing more. How did you happen to meet Burr?

A. Well, I happened to be at his funeral one day, and he asked me to make less noise, and—

Q. But, good heavens! If you were at his funeral, he must have been dead, and if he was dead how could he care whether you made a noise or not?

A. I don't know. He was always a particular kind of man that way.

© BETTMANN/CORBIS

Q. Still, I don't understand it at all. You say he spoke to you, and that he was dead.

A. I didn't say he was dead.

Q. But wasn't he dead?

A. Well, some said he was, some said he wasn't.

Q. What did you think?

A. Oh, it was none of my business! It wasn't any of my funeral.

Q. Did you—However, we can never get this matter straight. Let me ask about something else. What was the date of your birth?

A. Monday, October 31, 1693.

Q. What! Impossible! That would make you a hundred and eighty years old. How do you account for that?

A. I don't account for it at all.

Q. But you said at first you were only nineteen, and now you make yourself out to be one hundred and eighty. It is an awful discrepancy.

A. Why, have you noticed that? (Shaking hands.) Many a time it has seemed to me like a discrepancy, but somehow I couldn't make up my mind. How quick you notice a thing!

Q. Thank you for the compliment, as far as it goes. Had you, or have you, any brothers or sisters?

A. Eh! I—I—I think so—yes—but I don't remember.

Q. Well, that is the most extraordinary statement I ever heard!

A. Why, what makes you think that?

Q. How could I think otherwise? Why, look here! Who is this a picture of on the wall? Isn't that a brother of yours?

A. Oh, yes, yes, yes! Now you remind me of it; that *was* a brother of mine. That's William—*Bill* we called him. Poor old Bill!

Q. Why? Is he dead, then?

A. Ah! Well, I suppose so. We never could tell. There was a great mystery about it.

Q. That is sad, very sad. He disappeared, then?

A. Well, yes, in a sort of general way. We buried him.

(cont'd on next page)

Q. *Buried* him! *Buried* him, without knowing whether he was dead or not?

A. Oh, no! Not that. He was dead enough.

Q. Well, I confess that I can't understand this. If you buried him, and you knew he was dead—

A. No! no! We only thought he was.

Q. Oh, I see! He came to life again?

A. I bet he didn't.

Q. Well, I never heard anything like this. *Somebody* was dead. *Somebody* was buried. Now, where was the mystery?

A. Ah! That's just it! That's it exactly. You see, we were twins—defunct and I—and we got mixed in the bathtub when we were only two weeks old, and one of us was drowned. But we didn't know which. Some think it was Bill. Some think it was me.

Q. Well, this *is* remarkable. What do *you* think?

A. Goodness knows! I would give whole worlds to know. This solemn, this awful mystery has cast a gloom over my whole life. But I will tell you a secret now, which I never have revealed to any creature before. One of us had a peculiar mark—a large mole on the back of his left hand; that was *me. That child was the one that was drowned!*

Q. Very well, then, I don't see that there is any mystery about it, after all.

A. You don't? Well, I do. Anyway, I don't see how they could ever have been such a blundering lot as to go and bury the wrong child. But, 'sh!—don't mention it where the family can hear of it. Heaven knows they have heartbreaking troubles enough without adding this.

Q. Well, I believe I have got material enough for the present, and I am very much obliged to you for the pains you have taken. But I was a good deal interested in that account of Aaron Burr's funeral. Would you mind telling me what it was that made you think Burr was such a remarkable man?

A. Oh! It was a mere trifle! Not one man in fifty would have noticed it at all. When the sermon was over, and the procession all ready to start for the cemetery, and the body all arranged nice in the hearse, he said he wanted to take a last look at the scenery, and so he got up and *rode with the driver.*

Then the young man reverently withdrew. He was very pleasant company, and I was sorry to see him go.

—Mark Twain (pseudonym for Samuel Langhorne Clemens)

Start-Up: The interviewer should be prepared for the positive and negative sides of interviewing. On the positive side, interviews are an excellent source of primary (firsthand) information. The interviewee can provide a unique angle on a topic, something few reference books can do. On the negative side, not all interviewees give good interviews; for many different reasons, some of them are reluctant to answer the interviewer's questions.

Nevertheless, the interviewer has a job to do. Twain gave his interviewer some ridiculous answers, but the young man must still write an article about Twain for his newspaper.

Connection: Assume you are the young interviewer. Write an article about Twain for your paper based on the information in the excerpt you just read.

Working with Literature: Refer to *Student Workbook* page 13-J for an activity on preparing for an interview.

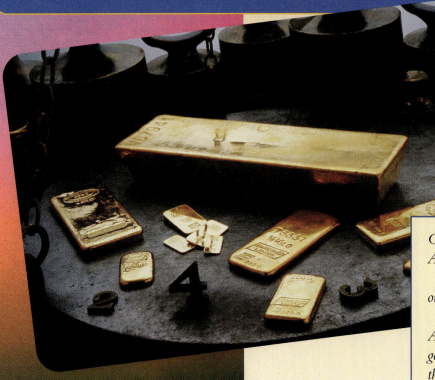

Chapter 14

© GETTY IMAGES/PHOTODISC, INC.

Gold is amazing.
A mere cubic inch of it can be pulled
*   into a wire 43 miles long*
or beaten into a thin sheet that covers
*   1,400 square feet.*
Although one of the heaviest of metals,
gold can be pounded so thin
that the slightest breath
will send it floating like a cobweb into
*   the air.*

"It is true that the income of the average household has been increasing. But averages often obscure the important details. After all, Shaquille O'Neal and I have an average height of six feet."

—ROBERT REICH, FORMER SECRETARY OF LABOR

© GIANNI DAGLI ORTI/CORBIS

Using Numbers and Statistics

Gold has fascinated human beings for thousands of years. It is rare and beautiful and, hence, expensive; but it also has great strength and **ductility**.

It can be stretched and pounded into extremely fine wires and transparently thin sheets without breaking.

It can hold its shape and function even when it is so thin that a **micrometer** is needed to measure it. Some people have spent their entire lifetime working with gold. They have weighed and measured it very precisely to arrive at the measurements and observations that opened this chapter. A small part of the numerical data they have calculated can be summed up in one equation that applies uniquely to gold: 1 cubic inch = 43 miles = 1,400 square feet.

Numerical Data Fills Our Lives

Have you ever stopped to realize how many times a day you are confronted with numerical data? Numbers are so much a part of your life that you probably pay little attention to them. But if you listen closely, you may find dozens of numbers in just one evening news program.

"The unemployment rate stands at 6.8 percent nationwide."

"Housing starts are down 19 percent since last April."

Many investors read the stock market report daily

"Odds are 1 in 100 that a baby born to a woman over 40 will have Down syndrome.

"In 1991, approximately 200,000 people in the United States were suffering from AIDS. By 2002, the number exceeded 886,000."

These comments are fairly straightforward. What isn't seen is the tremendous amount of research—statistical research—behind what they say. Teams of people had to collect data from throughout the United States. The facts were then compiled, sorted, and analyzed, usually with the aid of computers. (Gathering, sorting, and analyzing numerical data is what statistics is all about.) News writers and analysts then looked through the pages and pages of information to come up with a few short, simple-sounding sentences that were slotted into the news for listeners to digest.

As you know from math classes, numbers can be put together in many different ways—some simple and some extremely difficult to decipher. In this chapter, you will look at simple kinds of statistics and how they can be used not only to inform, but also to persuade people to think in certain ways. You will practice explaining facts in statistical terms, illustrating them with charts and graphs, and making them understandable to an audience.

Making Numerical Data Understandable

Businesses and government agencies spend a great deal of time trying to make numerical data understandable to their employees and customers, to other businesses and governments, and to the average person. The numerical data that they gather and analyze is referred to as statistics. Statistics are used to clarify information and to help make predictions.

Career *Connection*

Tool and die makers in Detroit take blueprints of a tool needed to mass-produce a part such as a torque converter or a piston, and they create a prototype tool that an automobile manufacturer uses to make the parts. According to the *Detroit News*, Michigan alone lost 16,000 tool and die makers between 1997 and 2004. About 4,000 (one-third) of the U.S. tool and die shops were closed between 2000 and 2004, leaving about 100,000 toolmakers without jobs.

There are two major reasons for the loss of these jobs. One reason is that American tool and die makers can make up to $80,000 a year, but they are losing out to foreign workers who may earn as little as $2 a day. Another reason is that many U.S. manufacturers haven't kept up with the computer age. Companies that invest in computer-based machinery and other up-to-date equipment are successfully competing in the world market. But many of those firms are in construction and computers, not in the auto industry.

Some people (for example, advertisers and political activists) use statistics when trying to convince people that they should vote, contribute, or act a certain way (*their* way). So they become expert at setting up the numbers to sway people one way or another. Sometimes the numbers are arranged somewhat deceptively. But once you understand a few basic techniques about using statistics, you're less likely to be fooled by those who use them to try to manipulate you.

Reporting Actual Numbers

When no attempt is made to influence the reader, to make predictions, or to generalize, the facts are reported just as they occur.

- Of the 65 married couples surveyed, 57 owned a dog.
- The results of the vote showed that 21 members of the senior class want to open student council meetings to all students.
- Of the 314 students in our graduating class, 11 were home-schooled until ninth grade.

These are straightforward statements of fact.

Editorializing with Numbers

Since numerical data are usually gathered for a specific purpose and not just for the pure joy of gathering information, those using the data often adds words and phrases that attempt to make a certain point or influence the audience in some way. Journalists call this practice **editorializing**—trying to do more than simply inform. Editorializing is used when someone is trying to sway the thinking of an audience in some way. A writer or speaker who editorializes wants the audience to make an inference about the information by picking up on certain cue words. Notice the difference when such words are added to the same three sentences that were cited previously. The editorializing is underlined.

• Of the 65 married couples surveyed, <u>nearly every one of them</u> (57) owned a dog.

(Inference the writer or speaker wanted you to make: Almost all married couples own a dog; that is, dogs are popular with married couples.)

• The results of the vote showed that <u>only</u> 21 members of the <u>entire</u> senior class want to open student council meetings to all students.

(Inference: The senior class is overwhelmingly against opening student council meetings to all students.)

What might the inference be if someone instead said, "<u>A solid voting block</u> of 21 seniors wants to open student council meetings to all students"? In either case, knowing the size of the senior class would put those 21 members into a clearer perspective.

• Of the 314 students in our graduating class, 11, including 3 honors students , were home-schooled until ninth grade.

(Inference: Having been educated at home doesn't limit a student's ability to achieve honors if he or she decides to return to school.)

Notice that the basic numerical facts have not been changed. But editorializing has subtly—and sometimes not so subtly—told readers how the writer wants them to think about those facts.

Practice 14–1: Editorializing with Numbers

teamwork

1. Each of the following ten sentences is simply and factually stated. Working with a partner, figure out how you can rewrite each sentence, adding words or phrases to put a different focus or slant on the facts to influence the thinking of an audience in some way, either positively or negatively. Hint: You may want to change some of the numbers to percents or fractions to make your point stronger.

Example:

Statement of fact: In 2000, the average earnings of experienced brake and front-end auto technicians in medium-sized cities (populations between 100,000 and 499,999) was $34,398. In 2002, the average earnings of those technicians was $40,222.

In October 2004, the Bureau of
Labor Statistics reported that the
unemployment rate was 8 percent
for those without a high school
diploma, 4.3 percent for those with a
high school diploma, and only 2.6
percent for those with a college
degree.

Editorialized statement: In the two short years between 2002 and 2004, the average earnings of experienced brake and front end auto technicians jumped from $34,398 to $40,222.

a. Two out of three married women will outlive their husbands.

b. The average man in the United States is 5 feet 10 inches tall.

c. Banks are paying 2 percent interest on money in savings accounts.

d. Daytime preschool has 20 five-year-olds enrolled, and 12 of them can recite their ABCs.

e. In a career/technical student organization calculator contest, 38 percent of the students missed the second problem.

f. A national study using the U.S. Department of Education's 2001 data showed that 70 percent of all seniors in public high schools graduated. Of those graduates, 32 percent qualified to attend a four-year college.

g. The Bureau of Labor Statistics reported that in 2003, union members accounted for 12.9 percent of wage and salary employees. In 1983, it was 20.1 percent.

h. Aurelia can enter data into the computer at the rate of 300 keystrokes per minute. The average rate is 200.

i. Thirty years ago VCRs cost approximately $2,600. Today a DVD player can cost less than $80.

2. Complete *Student Workbook* page 14-A by giving examples of how people in different careers use numbers.

Rounding Numbers

Rounding is used to simplify numbers and make them more understandable to the general public.

Numbers such as 527,611,432,112 are unwieldy to use. Unless you are recording or researching information, you probably have no need for such an exact quantity. What is important to a general audience is to have an idea of what this number means. In a headline, the number might be reported as "more than 525 billion" or "nearly 530 billion," both of which are close enough to inform people in a factual way and to impress them with the quantity.

Which amount would be the rounded number for each of the following?

Sample:
Round 62 to the nearest ten. (Think of counting by tens: 10, 20, 30, 40, 50, 60, 70. Is 62 closer to 60 or 70?) Remember: If your number is halfway or more than halfway between 60 and 70, the answer is 70. Is it?

1. Round 56 to the nearest 10. (Is 56 closer to 50 or 60?)

2. Round 432 to the nearest hundred. (Is 432 closer to 400 or 500?)

3. Round 9.1 to the nearest whole number. (Think: Is 9.1 closer to 9.0 or 10.0?)

Notice the way that numbers are rounded in the news, in sportscasts, and in conversations. Usually, some editorializing is done when the rounded number is reported.

For example, when speaking of someone with a salary of $19,850, you could say either of the following:

She's making nearly $20,000 to start.
She's making just under $20,000 to start.

In both cases, however, you rounded the salary to the nearest thousand when reporting it.

On certain occasions, even smaller numbers are rounded. When figuring your federal taxes, for example, rounding to the nearest dollar is acceptable. If you owe less than a dollar, you don't have to pay anything.

Using Ratios and Percentages

A simple way of expressing the relationship between two sets of numbers is by using a ratio. The ratio of men to women in the United States is approximately 49 to 51. For every 49 men, there are 51 women.

A percentage is actually a ratio in which everything is compared to 100. (*Percent* means "per hundred.") If about 49 out of every 100 people in the United States are male, you can say that 49 percent of the U.S. population is male. With that information, you can easily figure that 51 percent of the population is female. Those numbers came from adding the millions of people in the 2000 U.S. census, comparing the numbers of males and females, and reducing those numbers to percents.

by the way...

"Ten men in our country could buy the whole world and ten million can't buy enough to eat."

WILL ROGERS, AMERICAN PERSONALITY AND POLITICAL COMMENTATOR (1931)

Culture *Connection*

Dogs have a unique place in the lives of Americans. Dogs are companions, and the bond between human and dog is valued by many. In *The Intelligence of Dogs*, Stanley Coren takes a popular theory of human intelligence and relates it to dogs. He also ranks dogs from most to least intelligent. How did he figure out how to rank them? He sent a questionnaire to more than 400 dog obedience judges, asking them to rate the 75 most popular breeds on working and obedience intelligence.

Which breeds were judged worst and best? Of the 199 judges, 121 ranked the Afghan hound one of the ten worst breeds for obedience; 99, the basenji; and 81, the chow chow. For the top ten, 190 named the border collie; 171, the shetland sheepdog; 169, the poodle; and 167, the German shepherd and golden retriever. For your dog's rank, check out Coren's book.

Care and attention keep dogs happy.

Sometimes the ratios and percentages are reduced to a smaller number (like reducing fractions) and then expressed in a different way. For example:

-25% = 25/100, or 25 out of every 100

25/100 can be reduced to 1/4 by dividing both numbers (25 and 100) by the same number: 25.

$$\frac{25}{100} \div \frac{25}{25} = \frac{1}{4}$$

Thus, 25 out of 100 is the same as 1 out of 4.

Generalizing from a Sample Group

Public opinion polls are good examples of using smaller numbers of people to represent larger groups. It is usually impossible to count everyone or everything needed to get the desired information, especially if it is needed in a short amount of time. So in news magazines and on radio and television news shows, reporting the results of a poll is a common occurrence. The agency that conducts the poll is mentioned; then a piece of information is often added that readers and listeners may not notice. The information goes something like this:

In this opinion poll, a representative sampling of 1,000 people were asked whether they believed that women's professional sports will attract large enough crowds and sufficient media coverage within the next ten years to pay the athletes competitive salaries and to provide sports careers for large numbers of young women in the United States. (Margin of error is ± 4 percent.)

In this case, a **representative sample** of 1,000 people would have to represent a cross section of people in the United States in order to get an idea of how the American people felt. That means that the men and women surveyed would have to be from all walks of life; from high, middle, and low income levels; and from a variety of ethnic and religious backgrounds. Then their responses would be generalized to the rest of the population (which means that if this group believes something, chances are that the rest of Americans do, too). This technique is acceptable and is fairly accurate when a large enough sample is used and appropriate statistical formulas are followed.

Often, again unnoticed by the average reader or listener, the sampling error is given. The report may say, "The sampling error was plus or minus 5 percent"—a way of saying that the data aren't guaranteed to be 100 percent accurate. In fact, generalizations can never account for 100 percent of reality. To find out how all

DILBERT reprinted by permission of United Feature Syndicate, INC.

American people feel or think about anything would require asking every one of them the same question and recording the answer. Of course, that is impossible to do.

A **random sample** is different from a representative sample. How is a random sample obtained? One old-fashioned way is by lot. To get an idea of how students at a certain school with an enrollment of 850 felt about a certain issue, you could put the name of each student on a small token or card and place it in a large bin. After the bin was shaken or turned many times and all of the names were thoroughly mixed, names of students could be drawn from the bin one at a time until, say, 150 students' names were on a list. This 17.6 percent of the student body could be used to predict how the rest of the students feel about the same issue. Chances are that every grade would be represented, as would both sexes. Students from a variety of neighborhoods and family backgrounds would probably also be represented. Some would be active in sports, and some would not. Some would be active in clubs, and some would not. The point is that all students would have had an equal chance of having their names drawn.

A random sample doesn't have to equal 17.6 percent of the total group researched. The required percentage depends on a number of mathematical considerations. The important point is that random samples are designed to provide fairly reliable data because they provide a cross section of the society they represent.

Some researchers use the telephone directory as the basis for a kind of random sampling of a particular city. The researchers pick a name at random and then pick every 50th or 150th name after that. (The number used would depend on the number of names in the phone book and the total number needed for the sampling.) Then the researchers survey those people by telephone. This method is called a ==systematic sample with a random start==.

With today's modern technology, computers using large databases can produce true random lists for research purposes. However, not everyone has access to such databases. And chances are that you do not. Instead, you will have to use sample groups that are available to you and describe what is true of those groups, without trying to make generalizations.

Claims Based on Questionable Generalizations

In the fictitious report on the poll of 1,000 people cited on page 477, suppose that the following results were obtained:

- Seventy percent of adults surveyed said that women's professional sports would continue to draw crowds and to gain in popularity in the United States.

- Sixty-five percent said that female athletes' salaries would increase, but would not be on a par with male athletes' salaries, in the next ten years.

- Thirty-seven percent said that they would buy tickets for and attend games played by female athletes.

- Fifty-two percent agreed that women would have more opportunities to advance in sports careers in the next ten years.

Compare these data and the way they were obtained to the advertising claim in Figure 14-1.

In this advertisement, is any information given as to how many dentists were surveyed about their preferences? Is it possible that only four dentists were surveyed and that two of those four said they preferred Glossy toothpaste? After all, 2 out of 4 is 50 percent.

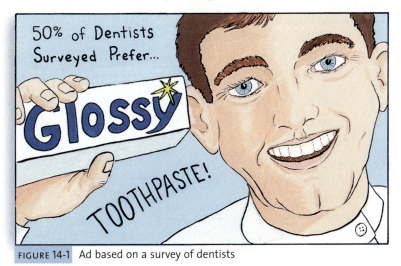

FIGURE 14-1   Ad based on a survey of dentists

Do you think that many readers, not being as critical as you, might read such a statement and believe that 50 percent of all dentists actually prefer this toothpaste? Does the fictitious poll information you just read regarding women's professional sports and opportunities for female athletes answer these kinds of questions?

Technology *Connection*

Is agriculture a sticky business? Well, when you discover where glue comes from, you may say yes. Many common glues have for years come from plants and animals, but new high-tech methods have, in many cases, resulted in more dependability and versatility in glues.

Are old horses really sent to the glue factory? Yes. Animal bones are still part of the glues used in cartons and boxes. Other agricultural products are used to produce different kinds of glue. Tapioca is used on stamps, envelopes, and labels. Soybean glue holds plywood together. Fish glue is used in photo mounting, gummed paper, and paints. But not all glue comes from plants and animals. One of the strongest, most heat-resistant glues comes from porcelain enamel grit combined with iron oxide and stainless steel powder. It is heat-resistant to 1,500°F, which is not true of plant and animal glues. (Glover 258–263)

Identifying a Target Group

A **target group** is a subset of the population who would be most likely to provide useful information about the topic in question—so-called because they are targeted by poll takers or surveyors as a group that has special knowledge or opinions about a subject. If you want to find out how 13-year-olds feel about being a teenager, you don't ask their parents; you ask the 13-year-olds. They are your target group for that particular subject. On the other hand, if you want to find out about the concerns that parents have about their teen-aged children, parents of teens would be your target group. In the example of the survey of dentists cited previously, dentists are the target group.

Practice 14–2: Target Groups: Finding the Best Source

Students would be the target group surveyed to find out what students believe about an issue. Dentists would be the target group surveyed to learn which dental cleaner dentists prefer. Target groups must be carefully selected to get accurate answers to questions.

Eight research questions follow. For the first five questions, write the letter of the specific group (the target group) that would be the most reliable to survey to get the most accurate responses to each question. Starting with Question 6, there are no choices. You must come up with the choice yourself. Be prepared to defend your answers.

1. How do middle-aged Republicans in Midtown, Iowa, feel about enforced retirement at the age of 65?

   Best target group:
   a. registered Republicans
   b. Republicans between the ages of 40 and 60
   c. registered voters
   d. Republican men between the ages of 35 and 50

2. How many health care workers in your town are smokers?

   Best target group:
   a. tobacco companies' sales staff
   b. local hospital and medical office workers
   c. personnel in Smoke-Stoppers' Clinic
   d. doctors' spouses

3. What kind of training does the average home health care worker in your town or city have?

   Best target group:
   a. people who have hired home health care workers
   b. human resources staff in a local technical college that has a home health care program
   c. home health care workers in your town
   d. representatives from agencies in your town that supply home health care workers

4. How many workers in the local textile mill are satisfied with their jobs?

   Best target group:
   a. high school students whose parents work in the textile mill
   b. supervisors of each department at the mill
   c. workers from each department at the mill
   d. union stewards at the mill

5. How do incoming ninth-grade girls in your school feel about studying math?

   Best target group:
   a. math teachers at your school
   b. incoming ninth-graders
   c. your school counselors
   d. incoming ninth-grade girls

6. How do teenage fathers feel about helping to raise their children?

   Best target group:

7. Do parents of 15- to 18-year-olds trust their children?

   Best target group:

8. Do coaches push high school athletes to train beyond what should be physically allowed?

   Best target group:

People *Connection*

In 1964, when Lee Iacocca was general manager of the Ford Division of Ford Motor Company, the Mustang was introduced to the American public. It was small, sporty, strong in performance, and inexpensive, while other cars had gotten longer, wider, and more expensive every year.

After a great deal of publicity, including pictures on the covers of both *Time* and *Newsweek*, the little car showed up in dealers' showrooms to record crowds of potential buyers. During its first year on the market, it broke all sales records for new Ford automobiles. It is now a collector's classic.

Iacocca notes in his autobiography that many people observed that the horse symbol on the front of the car was running the wrong way, because horses on a track run counterclockwise. His response: "The Mustang was a wild horse, not a domesticated race horse. And no matter which way it was running, I felt increasingly sure that it was headed in the right direction."

Ways of Looking at Groups of Numbers

When large groups of numbers are gathered, three types of simple analyses help to reveal certain facts or trends about the group:

- Figuring the mean (the average)
- Finding the median (the midpoint)
- Looking at the mode (the most common number)

The Mean

The **mean** is simply the average, as in "The mean (average) age of the group is 25" or "The mean (average) score on the test in this class was 82 percent."

The mean test score for a given group is obtained by adding all of the scores and dividing by the total number of scores. For example, here are 21 scores that students received on an American government test:

TEST SCORES FOR AMERICAN GOVERNMENT CLASS, SECTION 402

54	82	86
66	84	88
66	84	88
72	84	94
74	84	98
74	84	100
82	86	100

Table 14-1

When the scores from all three columns in Table 14–1 are added, the total is 1,730.

Divide the total by 21:

The mean is 82.38.

$$\begin{array}{r} 82.38 \\ 21\overline{)\ 1730.00} \end{array}$$

What is the mean for each of the following groups of numbers? Round your answers to the nearest tenth.

Group X: 6, 6, 7, 9, 2, 8, 1, 5, 6

Group Y: 54, 66, 71, 73, 84, 87, 88, 91

The Median

The **median** is the midpoint. This is not the same as an average. To find the median, you simply arrange the scores in numerical order, as has been done in the list of American government test scores in Table 14-1. Then you count down to the exact middle of the list.

List all of the scores, either from low to high or from high to low. (The answer will be the same.) Then count to the halfway point in the class. That point is the median.

Identify the median in each of the following sets of numbers. The first one is identified with a circle.

1. 1, 2, ③, 4, 5

2. 0, 1, 2, 2, 5, 55, 90, 98, 98

3. 96, 88, 86, 80, 76, 74, 72

4. 121, 110, 79, 61, 42, 33, 19

You've probably noticed that every set contained an odd number of numbers. How would you figure the median if there were an even number of numbers in the set (as in the following example)?

1, 2, 2, 5, 55, 90, 98, 98

The median is between the 5 and the 55.

Add the 5 and the 55 together (5 + 55 = 60).

The median is 30 (midway between 5 and 55).

Can you identify the median in each of the following sets of numbers?

1. 16, 16, 19, 20, 21, 22, 23, 23, 24

2. 79, 77, 68, 42, 34, 22, 10, 8

3. 33, 34, 35, 38, 40, 44, 46, 51, 55, 60

4. 33, 34, 34, 38, 41, 44, 46, 51, 55, 60

The Mode

The **mode** is defined as the most common number; that is, the one that occurs most frequently. What is the most common number in this list: 1, 2, 2, 2, 3, 4, 5, 5? The answer is 2. There are more 2s than any other number. Therefore, 2 is the mode.

In the following list, there is no mode:

1, 2, 3, 4, 5, 6, 7, 8

Fact: Every group of numbers has a mean and a median. Not every group has a mode.

What is the mode in the following groups of numbers?

1. 97, 98, 99, 100, 101, 101, 101, 102, 103

2. 3, 4, 4, 5, 6, 6, 7, 7, 7, 7, 7, 7, 8, 8, 9, 10

Sometimes there is more than one mode, as in the following set of numbers:

③③, 4⑤⑤, 6, 7

Is there a mode in the list of American government test scores in Table 14–1?

Using Numerals When No Quantity Is Involved

Numerals can be used to indicate real quantities, as in

Count them. There are four.

Numerals can also be used in **performance ratings** and in reporting **subjective data**.

Performance Ratings

Look at Figure 14-2. Can you count the 8.5 in Mary Jo's performance rating? No, because it does not represent 8.5 things. The 8.5 that the judges gave her is not a real numerical quantity, even though people act as though it is. It is simply a judgment as to where Mary Jo ranks on a scale of 1 to 10 in her performance. We add up all of the judges' ratings and divide by the number of judges to get the mean (average) number of rating points for her performance. This procedure is followed for each gymnast. The one with the highest mean score wins.

Similarly, grades of A, B, C, D, and F cannot be averaged without some number to accompany them. That is why someone developed the idea of quality points. Depending

FIGURE 14-2 The judges gave Mary Jo an 8.5 rating on her balance beam performance.

on where you go to school, an A may receive three, four, or five quality points. An A in an advanced placement college prep class may receive one or two extra quality points.

Assume that your school is on a four-point system and that you have the following grades:

History	B
Physical Education	B
English	C
Algebra II	A
CAD Lab	A
	??? Impossible to average

With quality points, your average looks like this:

History	B = 3	
Physical Education	B = 3	$\begin{array}{r} 3.2 \\ 5\overline{)16.0} \\ 15 \\ \overline{10} \\ 10 \\ \overline{0} \end{array}$
English	C = 2	
Algebra II	A = 4	
CAD Lab	A = 4	
	16	

In figuring class rank, a B with a 3.2 quality-point average would outrank a 3.0. Thus, several students can have B averages but be higher or lower than one another in class rank. Class rank could not be figured unless some numerical value were given to the letter grades. (Some schools do not have to calculate quality points since they use percentage grades. The percentages can be averaged.)

Subjective Data

Subjective data are clusters of information obtained about how people feel or think. Often, as in the case of the judges of Mary Jo's balance beam performance, those judgments are given a number.

However, judges of performances are not the only sources of subjective, nonnumerical data. In testing their clients, psychologists often use attitude scales, which involve using a number to indicate a response. A sample follows.

SAMPLE ATTITUDE SCALE

Circle the number on each scale that best describes how you feel right now.

Happy	1	2	3	4	5	6	7	Sad
Optimistic	1	2	3	4	5	6	7	Pessimistic
Wise	1	2	3	4	5	6	7	Foolish

Table 14-2

Notice in Table 14-2 that all of the positive descriptive words are on the left, nearest the 1, and all of the negative words are on the right, nearest the 7. If the average of all answers is 2.5, is the person feeling more positive or more negative today?

Accurate conclusions cannot be made by comparing 30 people's attitudes numerically, because attitudes are not measurable quantities. The numbers on the scale may represent something completely different to each person who participates in the survey. Special care must be taken in interpreting and using such data.

Using Tables, Charts, and Graphs

Tables, charts, and graphs are organized, attention-getting ways to present information. After surveys or other forms of research are concluded, some type of summary or report is usually made. Tables, pie charts, line graphs, and bar graphs are clear, easy-to-read ways of summarizing data.

Tables

Tables contain organized lists of information, arranged in columns and rows. For example, a student in animal science or wildlife management might find the following table of reproductive cycles of selected animals familiar:

HEAT AND GESTATION PERIODS OF SMALL MAMMALS

Mammal	Duration of Heat	Gestation Period (in days)
Ferret	Continuous, March to August	42
Guinea pig	6–11 days	67
Gerbil	4 days	24–26
Hamster	20 hours	18
Rat	13–15 hours	22
Mouse	10 hours	19

Table 14-3

All tables do not have to have three columns. The number of columns you use is dictated by the information and how it can best be arranged. Notice in Table 14-3 that each column is given a heading that describes the data in it. Selecting the right heading is important in helping the reader understand information at a glance. Tables like this may be used for handy reference when you are asking questions such as "What is the gestation period for a guinea pig?" They may also be used for comparison purposes, to answer a question such as "Do smaller animals have shorter gestation periods than larger animals have?"

The most important column, or the one that is designed to be the comparison point or focal point for the reader, is put into some order—chronological, alphabetical, numerical (high to low or low to high), or some other logical arrangement. If the writer wanted to make it easier for the reader to find the animals' names, listing them in alphabetical order would be a good idea. Then, of course, the order of the information in the second and third columns would change. In Table 14-3, which column was the basis for arranging the rest of the information and thus was placed in a particular order?

Also notice that Table 14-3 uses technical terms such as *gestation*, since it is designed to be read by specialists, students of animal science. What changes would have to be made for a general audience?

Tables are labeled sequentially, beginning with "Table 1." If you're doing a research paper in animal science and including information on birds in Chapter 1, small mammals in Chapter 2, and reptiles in Chapter 3, you could label the table on small mammals "Table 2-1" (for Chapter 2, Table 1).

Practice 14–3: Putting Information into a Table

Read the following paragraph of detailed information and decide how it can be organized into three columns. Then make a descriptive title for each column. Finally, using table construction software, if available, (as you did in Chapter 12) or the table form on *Student Workbook* page 14-B, arrange the information in a logical, readable way. (A table title and setup have already been provided for you on *Student Workbook* page 14-B.)

Road construction fatalities in the Tri-State area from 2000 through 2005 often involved trucks. Causes of some of the deaths and the places and times they occurred are as follows: struck by on-site truck, West Village (2000); on-site truck backed into victim, Sussex County (2001); fell off truck, Washington (2002); on-site truck backed into victim, Bluefield (2002); dump box fell from truck onto victim, Washington (2004); truck backed into victim, Mt. Storm (2004); hit by side of truck, Bills County (2005); truck ran through barricade, Jefferson County (2005).

Pie Charts

Pie charts, also known as circle graphs, get their name because they look like pies cut into slices. Pie charts start with a circle. The circle represents 100 percent of something—the whole thing. The slices represent the parts of the whole.

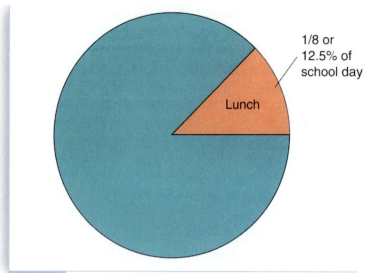

FIGURE 14-3 Portion of lunch period in school day

Pie charts are important tools that are used to illustrate, persuade, or compare. For example, you already know what a small portion of time your lunch period is compared to the rest of the day. But when it is illustrated in a pie chart, as shown in Figure 14-3, the lunch break appears as small as it seems to you.

The circle in Figure 14-4 represents Ronald D'Amato's monthly income of $2,000. To figure out how to divide the circle, each expense was listed and then divided by his total monthly income of $2,000. (See Table 14-4.) This told us what percentage of Ronald's income is used for each expense. Every dollar had to be accounted for, since the pie chart had to show 100 percent of his income.

Every month $400 is withheld from Ronald's pay to cover taxes and social security. Ronald then has to spend $500 on rent and make a $200 car payment. He usually spends about $400 a month on food. To begin saving money, he is putting $50 a month into his savings account. He makes monthly installment payments on car and medical insurance, totaling $150 each month. The rest of his income is left for clothes, entertainment, and other expenses (for example, household supplies and car upkeep). What percent does he have left for clothes, entertainment, and other expenses?

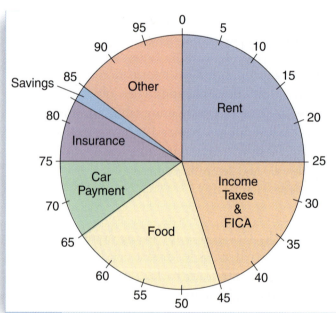

FIGURE 14-4 Distribution of Ronald's income

Practice 14–4: Constructing a Pie Chart

Using page 14-C of your *Student Workbook*, complete the following:

1. Make a list of your activities for one day (24 hours). Include sleeping, eating, studying, working at a part-time job, playing basketball, or anything else you do.

2. Figure out how many hours or what part of an hour each activity takes. Some activities, such as sleeping, may take eight hours. Others, such as washing your car, may take only half an hour.

FIGURING RONALD D'AMATO'S EXPENSES
AS PERCENTAGES OF HIS INCOME

Item	Cost (Part of Income)	÷	Whole Income	=	Percentage of Income
Taxes & Social Security	$400	÷	$2,000	=	20%
Rent	500	÷	2,000	=	25%
Car payment	200	÷	2,000	=	10%
Food	400	÷	2,000	=	20%
Insurance	150	÷	2,000	=	7.5%
Savings	50	÷	2,000	=	2.5%
Clothes and other expenses	300	÷	$2,000	=	15%
Total	$2,000				100%

Table 14-4

3. Figure what percent of your day each activity represents. Divide the number of hours spent on the activity by 24 (the number of hours in a day). If these numbers do not divide evenly, carry your answer to one decimal place.

Example:

Sleeping may take 8 hours out of 24 hours.

Divide 24 into 8.

$$24\overline{)8.000} = .333 = 33.3\%$$

4. Construct a pie chart showing the percentage of time you spend on each activity. Each line on the rim of the circle represents 5 percent of your day.

Line Graphs

Line graphs, like pie charts, turn numbers into drawings. The use of a line graph helps make the numbers more meaningful to the reader because it makes a visual comparison between two kinds of change. In business, a line graph often shows change in dollars earned from month to month or from year to year, so the comparison is between money and time.

Technology *Connection*

Bloodless surgery? Yes, it's possible. In the past, surgery could be as bad as the illness it was meant to cure. Patients required long recovery periods and sometimes died from loss of blood due to large incisions used to remove even small cysts and tumors. Thanks to lasers, sound waves, cryogenics, and other inventions, many types of surgeries and medical treatments are now almost bloodless. When, for example, coronary arteries are blocked by plaque (built-up cholesterol and other substances in the artery's inner lining), a thin plastic tube with a laser at its tip is inserted into the artery. The laser emits pulses of light beams, which vaporize the plaque, allowing blood to flow freely. Cryosurgery, the medical use of liquid nitrogen, is used to remove tumors and some skin cancers by literally freezing them.

FIGURE 14-5 Line graph showing weight gain over time

In Figure 14-5, the comparison is between a child's size (in this case, weight) and time (age in years). So the graph shows gain in weight over time.

Each vertical line that cuts through the baseline represents a number—in this case, a child's age in years: .5, 1.0, 1.5, etc., up to 5 years. Each space between the lines, then, stands for a half year (6 months).

Each horizontal line that cuts through the vertical lines represents 5 pounds of the child's weight. Notice that a dark dot marking the child's weight at birth is placed at 0 on the horizontal line (because he or she is 0 years old) and just past the 5 on the vertical line (to indicate a weight of 6.5 pounds). The child's weight at 6 months is 12 pounds, so the dot is placed on the spot where the half-year (.5) line crosses the 12 line (between the 10- and 15-pound lines). The remainder of the dots show the amount of weight gain every 6 months until the child reaches 5 years of age.

Both increases and decreases can be illustrated well with a line graph. But line graphs can be misleading. Compare the two graphs in Figure 14-6. Which company is growing faster, based on employees on payroll? What do these two graphs tell you about the use of line graphs?

● Practice 14–5: Drawing a Line Graph

Using graph paper, create a line graph to illustrate the following data: Westport Technical College had enrollments over a ten-year period as follows: 1,378 in 1995; 1,401 in 1996; 1,412 in 1997; 1,802 in 1998; 2,203 in 1999; 2,264 in 2000; 3,003 in 2001; 3,561 in 2002; 3,997 in 2003; and 4,610 in 2004.

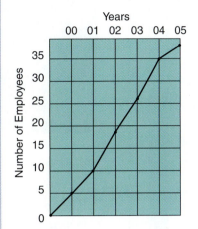

Quail Company Growth, 2000–2005
Based on Number of Employees

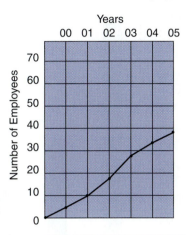

Xenon Company Growth, 2000–2005
Based on Number of Employees

FIGURE 14-6 Two ways to illustrate the same data

Bar Graphs

Bar graphs usually compare two or more things in relation to time or space. The bars may be either vertical or horizontal. Vertical bars are used in the bar graph in Figure 14-7 on page 492, which compares income per capita for four regions of the United States for 1993 and for 2003. A different-colored bar is used for each of the years for easier visual comparison.

Practice 14–6: Creating a Bar Graph

Using a computer with a software program such as Microsoft Word, create a bar graph, using the information in Table 14-5. The table compares five cars, showing the EPA average of fuel consumption. If a computer is not available, use graph paper to construct your graph.

FUEL CONSUMPTION OF FIVE SMALL, INEXPENSIVE CARS

Miles per Gallon

Make and Model	City	Highway
2004 Honda Civic	23	28
2004 Toyota Corolla	24	38
2004 Volkswagen Golf	28	37
2004 Ford Focus	24	30
2004 Hyundai Accent	29	33

Table 14-5

Source: http://www.edmunds.com

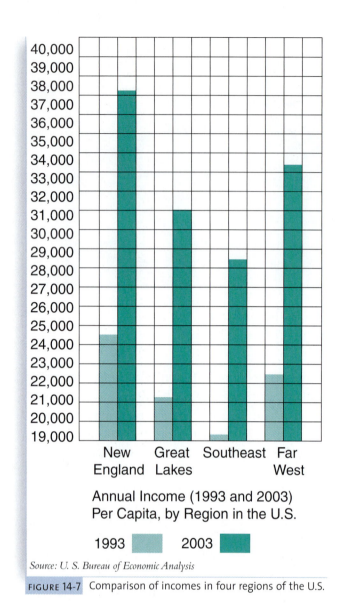

Annual Income (1993 and 2003)
Per Capita, by Region in the U.S.

| 1993 | | 2003 | |

Source: U. S. Bureau of Economic Analysis

FIGURE 14-7 Comparison of incomes in four regions of the U.S.

Summary

Numerical data is everywhere. It can be informative, but it can also be misleading. When gathering and reporting information, it is important to be able to use statistics and other numerical information to your advantage, especially in the following ways:

- Recognize when numbers are used accurately or inaccurately.

- Understand and use common terms such as *sample group, mean,* and *median.*

- Recognize that all numbers used do not represent real numerical quantities—some are merely ratings.

- Read charts and graphs.

- Design charts and graphs to illustrate numerical information you have collected.

For review and research activities visit
communicating.swlearning.com

Works Cited

Glover, Thomas J. *Pocket Ref.* Littleton, Colorado: Sequoia Publishing, 1995.

Iacocca, Lee. *Iacocca: An Autobiography.* New York: Bantam, 1984.

http://www.detnews.com/2004/specialreport/0407/11

http://www.americanheart.org

http://www.sciencedaily.com/Health/Medicine/Surgery/Cryosurgery

http://www.bea.gov/ARTICLES/2004/05May

project-based assessment

Table and Chart or Graph

Illustrating Statistical Information

For this Project, you will use either (1) the data from your customer satisfaction questionnaire Project in Chapter 13 ("Interviewing for Information") or (2) information that you research for this purpose on the Internet, in an almanac, or in other sources.

1. Fill out the Project Plan on Student Workbook page 14-D.

2. Illustrate accurately and neatly the data for a general audience by first putting the data into a table. (Use table construction software if available.) If you do not have access to table construction software, use the table format on page 14-E of your *Student Workbook* to set up your information.

3. Convert the table into (1) a pie chart, (2) a line graph, or (3) a bar graph. Use computer software if at all possible. It will give your Project a more professional look. If you do not have access to software with graphing capabilities, use either the pie chart forms on page 14-F of your *Student Workbook* or graph paper to illustrate your data. If necessary, refer to appropriate parts of this chapter for assistance on how to set up each of these illustrations.

4. Write a short explanation telling the following:

   • How you gathered the information

   • Why you illustrated it the way you did

   • What conclusions can be drawn from the illustration

5. Ask a classmate to check your work and use the Rough Draft column of your Project Guide (page 14-G in your *Student Workbook*) to evaluate the entire Project, including the explanation, the table, and the graph or chart.

6. After making adjustments as needed on your Project, check it again, using the Final Draft column of your Project Guide.

7. Give your Project and the Project Guide to your teacher for final evaluation.

You may wish to save this Project to use as part of your report Project in Chapter 15.

literature

Overview

W. H. Auden often wrote against the grain of Modernism and the technology that he feared would dehumanize society. Modernism is a series of artistic movements in the 20th century. The movements have characteristics in common: to be new and different, to experiment with new forms, to innovate, to startle, and sometimes to shock. Modernistic literature often uses previously taboo subjects, gives attention to psychological insights, and uses imaginative symbols to evoke an emotional response in readers. The stream-of-consciousness technique of telling a story that tries to duplicate the inner workings of the characters' minds is an example of this movement in literature.

Auden wrote this poem in 1935 when he returned to England after living in Europe for a period of time. The poem is autobiographical, and the unknown citizen in the poem is Auden himself in the act of rediscovering his homeland. "The Unknown Citizen" is a satirical view of the tendency of modern society to depersonalize its citizens. Notice the use of words such as *normal*, *sensible*, and *necessary*. The poem asks two important questions about the citizen: "Was he free? Was he happy?"

"The Unknown Citizen"

(To JS/07/M/378
This Marble Monument
Is Erected by the State)

He was found by the Bureau of Statistics to be
    One against whom there was no official complaint.
    And all the reports on his conduct agree
        That, in the modern sense of an old-fashioned word, he was a saint.
For in everything he did he served the Greater Community.
Except for the War till the day he retired
He worked in a factory and never got fired,
But satisfied his employers, Fudge Motors Inc.
Yet he wasn't a scab or odd in his views,
For his Union reports that he paid his dues.
(Our report on his Union shows it was sound.)
And our Social Psychology workers found

That he was popular with his mates and liked a drink.

The Press are convinced that he bought a paper every day

And that his reactions to advertisements were normal in every way.

Policies taken out in his name prove that he was fully insured.

And his Health-card shows he was once in hospital but left it cured.

Both Producers Research and High-Grade Living declare

He was fully sensible to the advantages of the Installment Plan

And had everything necessary to the Modern Man,

A phonograph, a radio, a car and a frigidaire.

Our researchers into Public Opinion are content

That he held the proper opinions for the time of year;

When there was peace, he was for peace; when there was war, he went.

He was married and added five children to the population,

Which our Eugenist says was the right number for a parent of his generation,

And our teachers report that he never interfered with their education.

Was he free? Was he happy? The question is absurd:

Had anything been wrong, we should certainly have heard.

—W. H. Auden

Start-Up: The citizen in the poem is identified by all of the records available to define who he was, what he did, and how he compared to others living at the same time. The specifics of his life were a matter of public record. But what can you infer from these facts? What might you conclude about him as a person because he was for peace during peaceful times and volunteered to fight during war? Look at the other "facts on record" and see what additional conclusions about the unknown citizen you might draw.

Connection: Today people are identified by numbers as well as facts of public record. Take five minutes and list in a column all of the numbers by which you can be identified (driver's license, social security, credit card, etc.). Your list should contain at least 20 numbers. Next to the numbers, write at least one conclusion that might be made about you from the numbers you've listed (for example, a library card number might lead someone to conclude that you enjoy reading). Then write a paragraph about yourself as revealed by the numbers and their implications. Write a second paragraph in which you describe yourself in ways that no numbers or facts of public record could ever reveal. Use specific examples to support your points.

Overview

From July 4, 1845, to September 6, 1847, Henry David Thoreau lived alone in a house he built for himself on the shore of Walden Pond, near his home in Concord, Massachusetts. Thoreau argued the validity of the simple life in *Walden*, a book of his essays.

In the following excerpt from his chapter on economy, Thoreau says that "The mass of men lead lives of quiet desperation" because they are in such a hurry that they never stop to ask what is really necessary for their lives. He says that people need, after food, a shelter to keep themselves warm, but a shelter that requires all of their energy simply to pay for it is not necessary. According to Thoreau, people should struggle to free themselves from such a condition. His experiment on Walden Pond was to free himself. In March, he started building himself a house by cutting some tall white pine trees for timber. By April, the house was standing, costing a grand total of 28.12\frac{1}{2}$.

from *Walden*

By the words, *necessary of life,* I mean whatever, of all that man obtains by his own exertions, has been from the first, or from long use has become, so important to human life that few, if any, whether from savageness, or poverty, or philosophy, ever attempt to do without it. To many creatures there is in this sense but one necessary of life, Food. To the bison of the prairie it is a few inches of palatable grass, with water to drink; unless he seeks the Shelter of the forest or the mountain's shadow. None of the brute creation requires more than Food and Shelter. The necessaries of life for man in this climate may, accurately enough, be distributed under the several heads of Food, Shelter, Clothing, and Fuel; for not till we have secured these are we prepared to entertain the true problems of life with freedom and a prospect of success. Man has invented, not only houses, but clothes and cooked food; and possibly from the accidental discovery of the warmth of fire, and the consequent use of it, at first a luxury, arose the present necessity to sit by it. We observe cats and dogs acquiring the same second nature. By proper Shelter and Clothing we legitimately retain our own internal heat; but with an excess of these, or Fuel, that is, with an external heat greater than our own internal, may not cookery properly be said to begin? . . .

© LEE SNIDER/CORBIS

As for Shelter, I will not deny that this is now a necessary of life, though there are instances of men having done without it for long periods in colder countries than this. . . .

Near the end of March, 1845, I borrowed an axe and went down to the woods by Walden Pond, nearest to where I intended to build my house, and began to cut down some tall, arrowy white pines, still in their youth, for timber. It is difficult to begin without borrowing, but perhaps it is the most generous course thus to permit your fellow-men to have an interest in your enterprise. The owner of the axe, as he released his hold on it, said that it was the apple of his eye; but I returned it sharper than I received it. . . .

I hewed the main timbers six inches square, most of the studs on two sides only, and the rafters and floor timbers on one side, leaving the rest of the bark on, so that they were just as straight and much stronger than sawed ones. Each stick was carefully mortised or tenoned by its stump, for I had borrowed other tools by this time. My days in the woods were not very long ones; yet I usually carried my dinner of bread and butter, and read the newspaper in which it was wrapped, at noon, sitting amid the green pine boughs which I had cut off, and to my bread was

> "*. . . with the help of some of my acquaintances, rather to improve so good an occasion for neighborliness than from any necessity, I set up the frame of my house.*"

imparted some of their fragrance, for my hands were covered with a thick coat of pitch. Before I had done I was more the friend than the foe of the pine tree, though I had cut down some of them, having become better acquainted with it. Sometimes a rambler in the wood was attracted by the sound of my axe, and we chatted pleasantly over the chips which I had made. . . .

By the middle of April, for I made no haste in my work, but rather made the most of it, my house was framed and ready for the raising. . . .

At length, in the beginning of May, with the help of some of my acquaintances, rather to improve so good an occasion for neighborliness than from any necessity, I set up the frame of my house. No man was ever more honored in the character of his raisers than I. They are destined, I trust, to assist at the raising of loftier structures one day. I began to occupy my house on the 4th of July, as soon as it was boarded and roofed, for the boards were carefully feather-edged and lapped, so that it was perfectly impervious to rain, but before boarding I laid the foundation of a chimney at one end, bringing two cartloads of stones up the hill from the pond in my arms. I built the chimney after my hoeing in the fall, before a fire became necessary for warmth, doing my cooking the meanwhile out of doors on the ground,

(cont'd on next page)

early in the morning: which mode I still think is in some respects more convenient and agreeable than the usual one. . . .

I have thus a tight shingled and plastered house, ten feet wide by fifteen long, and eight-feet posts, with a garret and a closet, a large window on each side, two trap-doors, one door at the end and a brick fireplace opposite. The exact cost of my house, paying the usual price for such materials as I used, but not counting the work, all of which was done by myself, was as follows; and I give the details because very few are able to tell exactly what their houses cost, and fewer still, if any, the separate cost of the various material which compose them:

Boards . . . .8.03\frac{1}{2}$
Mostly shanty boards.

Refuse shingles for roof
   and sides 4.00

Laths 1.25

Two second-hand windows
   with glass 2.43

One thousand old brick 4.00

Two casks of lime 2.40

Hair 0.31
That was high. More than I needed.

Mantle-tree iron 0.15

Nails 3.90

Hinges and screws 0.14

Latch 0.10

Chalk 0.01

Transportation 1.40
I carried a good part on my back.

In all . . . .28.12\frac{1}{2}$

These are all the materials, excepting the timber, stones, and sand, which I claimed by squatter's right. I have also a small woodshed adjoining, made chiefly of the stuff which was left after building the house.

I intend to build me a house which will surpass any on the main street in Concord in grandeur and luxury, as soon as it pleases me as much and will cost me no more than my present one.

I thus found that the student who wishes for a shelter can obtain one for a lifetime at an expense not greater than the rent which he now pays annually.

—Henry David Thoreau

Start-Up: Having the ability to work effectively with numbers is important throughout your life. Number puzzles are fun to solve and help you develop your mathematics skills.

Connection: Make this activity a competitive one. Work in pairs to solve the puzzles on the following page.

Puzzle 1: If Bill Gates of Microsoft, who was reportedly worth $48 billion in the first half of 2004 (after giving away $28 billion to charity), spent $97 million building his house, how much would Thoreau have been worth if the $28.13 he spent building his house was equally proportionate to Bill Gates's worth?

Puzzle 2: *A Horse and a Pig*
Thoreau bought a horse and a pig for $85. The horse cost $55 more than the pig. How much did Thoreau pay for the pig?

Puzzle 3: *Thoreau's Jarring Experience*
There are two jars of equal capacity. In the first jar is one amoeba. In the second jar are two amoebas. An amoeba can reproduce itself in three minutes. It takes the two amoebas in the second jar three hours to fill the jar to capacity. How long will it take the one amoeba in the first jar to fill that jar to capacity?

Puzzle 4: *Thoreau's Zoo Story*
Thoreau: How many birds and how many beasts do you have in your zoo?
Zookeeper: There are 30 heads and 100 feet.
Thoreau: I can't tell from that!
Zookeeper: Oh, yes, you can!
Can you?

Working with Literature: Refer to *Student Workbook* page 14-H for an activity on using numbers to create a graphic.

Chapter 15

"The last thing one discovers in composing a work is what to put first."

—BLAISE PASCAL, FRENCH SCIENTIST AND PHILOSOPHER

"As the group [of students] hiked along a private field road on the Don Ney Farm, they noticed many frogs hopping about. . . . At one point, students accused each other of injuring the frogs because their legs were 'weird.' However, it wasn't long before they realized that this was not an injury problem—it was a developmental problem!

"Immediately, students pulled out notebooks and began collecting data about the frogs they were catching. Fully 50% of the frogs caught that day had deformities of their hind legs."

—Ryan Fisher, when in 10th grade at Minnesota New Country School

Presenting Reports

Students always seem to be writing reports—book reports, research papers, history reports, etc. Why? To let their

teachers know that they have learned something

and that they can write effectively about it.

In the world of business, industry, and science, reports are not designed to prove what you know or have learned, unless you are in training. They are simply ways of organizing information that will help a business, an industry, or a scientific organization succeed in some way. They pull together information that someone needs.

Reports may be designed to inform, persuade, or justify a position. They convey information specific to a particular task. Reports sometimes involve original research, but they may also involve gathering information from research done by others and making it available to those who need it.

Reports can take many forms. They can be formal or informal, handwritten or laser-printed. They can be extensive and full of footnotes or succinct and illustrated with original diagrams, charts, or photographs. They can be produced to be shown in full color on a computer screen, using presentation software. They can be launched on the Internet. But in all cases, they contain information that someone—or a group of someones—needs.

The importance of well-researched reports is illustrated in two real-life examples. In each case, a situation exists that demands extensive, specialized research and reporting. In the first case, the demand was met and a large business venture succeeded. In the second, the demand was not met and a near-disaster ensued.

Example 1: A Fried Chicken Franchise Goes to Japan

A fried chicken franchise plans to open a restaurant in Japan. However, the owners know that the average person in Japan is used to different kinds of seasonings on food than are commonly used in the southern United States, where the chicken seasoning recipe was developed. The owners also realize that other countries have different habits and customs. For their restaurant, the owners want to know what kind of external appearance, interior decorating, seating arrangement, manner of ordering food, and use of signs and symbols would be most attractive to the Japanese. So market researchers from the fried chicken company are sent to Japan to find the answers to these questions. Then, because the owners of the business want to attract customers and make money, they adjust the way they cook, design their restaurants, and serve their food to suit their potential Japanese customers. The fast-food restaurant is a success.

Example 2: Hillside Disaster

A civil engineer is hired by a major city in the Midwest to design a new bridge and highway linkages for the downtown area. Unfortunately, though the engineer is familiar with the solid bedrock of his home state in the Northeast, he is unfamiliar with the shale under the surface of the midwestern city that has hired him. Worse still, he either fails to require sufficient research or ignores important parts of the research report warning him of the effects the shale may have on his project. As a result,

© GETTY IMAGES/PHOTODISC, INC.

A hillside disaster

part of his roadbed is cut through the toe of a hill, releasing loose shale, and an entire historic neighborhood is endangered as homes begin to slide down the hill with the loosened soil.

These two examples represent large-scale needs for **field research** and reports that may take months or years to complete. In smaller businesses, information is needed and reports are made every day. These reports may range from those informal enough to be included as part of a memo, letter, or conversation to printed booklets dozens of pages in length that contain elaborate and expensive photographs, graphs, and charts.

Regardless of how elaborate or how simple reports may be, they tend to fall into categories. In this chapter, you will find four types of reports, with examples of each, that are used in a variety of job settings. Even early in your career, you may be asked to present reports like these, particularly if you are hired by a small- to medium-sized business. If you become familiar with these types of reports, you will recognize them when you encounter them at work.

This chapter will focus on the field report, the laboratory report, the proposal (a type of persuasive report), and the progress report.

Field Reports

Field reporting literally means reporting information found in the field. *The field* is a general term for the world outside a particular department or business headquarters—perhaps a construction site, an automobile test track, a shopping mall, an oil field, a pond, or a pasture. The field is wherever you have to go to get the answers you need.

Questions That Require Field Research and Reports

In completing the survey Project in Chapter 13, you were actually doing a field study. You asked a variety of people what they thought about something and then tallied their responses. Surveying is one way of getting information, but other ways are possible. If the government wants to know how many people are in the country, it can conduct a census and count the number of people. But to find out how many sets of quadruplets were born in a certain hospital in the past ten years, a person would have to search birth records. If someone is looking for the names of his or her ancestors, he or she can explore genealogical records containing information on many generations of families, including birth, marriage, and death dates.

by the way...

The Mormon's Family History Library (FHL) has the most complete genealogical records in the world. They are accessible on the Internet and on CD-ROM at Mormon temples in many cities and in many public libraries. If you want to know more about your family tree, you can search these records free of charge.

An Example of a Student Group's Field Study That Gained National Attention

An excellent example of a field study that resulted in many other studies and reports is described in the following information published on the Internet.

The Discovery

The discovery occurred on an intended hike through the Ney Woods, which is part of a Wildlife Game Refuge near Henderson, MN. As the group hiked along a private field road on the Don Ney Farm, they noticed many frogs hopping about. As kids are prone to do, the students began catching frogs for fun. At one point, students accused each other of injuring the frogs because their legs were "weird." However, it wasn't long before they realized that this was not an injury problem—it was a developmental problem!

Immediately, students pulled out notebooks and began collecting data about the frogs they were catching. Fully 50% of the frogs caught that day had deformities of their hind legs. Many had one leg which was underdeveloped and webbed together, preventing normal function. One frog captured that day had only one hind leg, while another had two feet on one leg and a bony protrusion from the spine.

Following their return to school, students developed a list of questions to pursue. Frogs were photographed with a QuickTake camera to put on the Internet. Phone calls were made regarding types of farm chemicals used in the area. Cindy Reinitz, the teacher, made a series of phone calls which would eventually lead her to Judy Helgen, a research scientist at the Minnesota Pollution Control Agency.

The excerpt above tells about the accidental discovery of deformed frogs by students in a Nature Studies class in August of 1995 and the field research that resulted from that discovery. More than seven years after the discovery of the deformed frogs, no one was yet certain as to the cause of the deformities. (See "Deformed frogs in Minnesota" at *http://www.pca.state.mn.us/hot/frogs.html.*)

Regarding methods pursued in the study, then ninth grader Betsy Kroon added, "I have been part of the group who [h]as tested water and I have taken part in gathering vertebrate[s], gathering frogs and recording deformities. I have also set 'traps' in Nye Pond to catch small creatures and used large nets to gather snails, leaches, and any other animal that lives in the mucky weeds that float at the top of the water."

Betsy Kroon then raised serious questions: "I'm concerned that having these frogs in the condition they are may have a great effect on other animals in the Eco system. What happens to the animals that eat frogs? What about the animals that frogs eat? Is the insect population going to be different because they aren't at such a risk of being eaten? Are the plants around the pond [a]ffected in any way?"

Students from the frog project won first place in the sixth- to eighth-grade category in the Anheuser-Busch Theme Parks' "A Pledge and a Promise Environmental Awards." Several state and federal studies related to the Minnesota frogs are still under way and may lead to years of further field research in several states.

Practice 15–1: Identifying Methods to Use in Field Research

teamwork

In the Minnesota frog project, research methods included catching, photographing, and recording data about malformed frogs and collecting and testing samples of the pond water in which the frogs lived. What methods could be used to answer each of the following questions? Brainstorm with a partner or small group until you have at least two methods for finding the answer to each question.

1. Are there any health hazards in the fat substitutes found in certain brands of potato chips, cake mixes, and other foods?

2. What types of grasses grow best along interstate highways in this state?

3. How safe are working conditions in this company's Tennessee plant?

4. What, if any, are the serious environmental hazards at this site?

5. How can ammonia levels created by pig urine in a farrowing barn be controlled to protect newborn pigs from toxic fumes?

6. Which of the new truck models really performs best on winding mountain roads?

---

by the way...

The average home is filled with toxic substances that cause air pollution. Laboratory experiments have indicated that eight to ten spider plants in a five-room house could absorb impurities and restore clean oxygen to the house, thus providing a healthier environment for the residents.

Laboratory Reports

Although similar to field reports, laboratory reports are based on research in a highly controlled environment. The laboratory is not always like the chemistry lab at a school; instead, it may be a greenhouse or a test area within a manufacturing plant—in short, anyplace where the environment can be controlled while the subject is studied.

Laboratory reports answer questions such as the following:

Can this animal be taught a language?

- Which of these two foods is better for producing healthier gerbils?
- How fast does the virus grow under these conditions?
- Can this animal be taught a language?
- What effect does water of varying acidity levels have on this paint?
- Where is the flaw in this metal alloy that causes it to crack under severe wind conditions?
- How effective is Detergent X compared to Detergent Y?
- What antibodies will kill these bacteria?

Both laboratory and field reports provide the results of an investigation, so they follow a similar reporting format. A common reporting format that can be used for field reports and lab reports follows. It can be used when testing one item or when comparing two or more items.

A Lab or Field Report Format

1. State Your Purpose.

(We set out to test Item X **or** to compare Item X with Item Y.)

2. Give Background Information.

(We tell why we chose Item X and/or Item Y. On what points did we test or compare them: ease of use, efficiency, comfort, cost . . . ?)

3. Explain How the Investigation Was Conducted.

(We tell how we tested and gathered facts about the product's ease of use, durability, efficiency, cost, etc.)

4. Explain the Results.

(What qualities were found in each brand? Which item was better? In what ways? For example, if Item Y was more efficient, did it also cost less?)

5. State Your Conclusions.

(What conclusions can be drawn after looking at the results of our investigation into these products?)

6. Discuss Your Conclusions and What They Mean.

(We found Item X to have . . . qualities and Brand Y to have . . . qualities. **Or** We recommend Item X because . . .)

Adapted from Mathes and Stevenson

A Good Source for Lab and Field Reports

One popular and informative magazine that specializes in laboratory and field-test reports is *Consumer Reports*. This magazine is known for being fair and objective. Its tests and reports cover consumer products as diverse as:

- Cell phones.
- Household appliances.
- Disposable diapers.
- Electronic equipment.
- Software for children.
- Power tools.
- New cars, trucks, and SUVs.

Brands are compared and models are rated on various criteria, depending on the types of items being tested. The reports include pictures of the products, as well as comparison charts ranking the products on various points, and are written to appeal to a general adult audience.

Consumer Reports also contains informational articles that are not lab-test reports, such as a list of automobile recalls, facts about changes in income tax law, readers' rating of movies, and more. But every issue has several major articles devoted to lab- or field-test reports designed to inform the consumer of the merit of certain products.

One reason people tend to respect what they read in this magazine may be that the Consumers Union, which publishes *Consumer Reports,* does not sell advertising space in the magazine and accepts no money from the manufacturers of products it tests.

Other magazines—such as *Motor Trend, Popular Photography & Imaging,* and *DVD News*—are special-interest magazines that publish comparisons of automobiles, camera equipment, and stereo equipment, respectively. These magazines do contain advertising related to their readers' interests.

Practice 15–2: Analyzing a Field or Laboratory Report

1. Using a copy of a trade journal or special-interest magazine such as *Consumer Reports* from your school library, public library, or some other source, find an article critiquing a product or comparing two or more products or services.

   Trade and professional journals are usually reliable sources of information, since they were designed to help people do their work better. A list of such journals, along with some special-interest magazines, follows. Most are accessible on the Internet.

List of Selected Trade and Special-Interest Periodicals

American Artist	*Childhood Education*
American Fitness	*Computer Videomaker*
American Forests	*Consumer Reports*
American Gardener	*DVD News*
American Journal of Nursing	*Flying*
American Machinist	*Motor Trend*
American Woodworker	*National Wildlife*
Architectural Digest	*Nursing*
Aviation Week & Space Technology	*Occupational Hazards*
	The Office Professional
Boating	*PC Magazine*
Broadcasting & Cable	*Popular Photography*
BusinessWeek	*Popular Mechanics*
Car and Driver	*Sales & Marketing Management*
Car Audio and Electronics	*Sporting News*

2. Read the article you have selected.

3. Fill in *Student Workbook* page 15-A to find out whether the article really follows the field or lab report format. A sample analysis is provided for you on page 509.

Technology *Connection*

For decades, men and women in uniforms walked from house to house reading meters—gas meters, electric meters, and water meters. If no one was home to let them in, the meter readers would leave a card, requesting a time to reschedule the meter reading.

One company figured that 15 meter readers, walking door to door, would read an average of 5,000 to 8,000 meters a day. Now small meters are wired to a box that is attached to the outside of houses. As a result, in an eight-hour day, an employee in a drive-by van can read 12,000 meters via radio waves. And utility companies can figure gas, water, and electric bills without estimating or sending out another meter reader to verify usage.

However, some questions remain. How many meter readers will lose their jobs? Are the radio waves affecting the health of people and animals? Do the radio waves interfere with other waves that carry information? Only time will tell.

4. Complete *Student Workbook* page 15–B to identify various occupations/professions and the information that these professionals gather or report on.

SUBJECT	Title of the article: "A Second Look at Minivans"	**CONCLUSIONS** **What conclusions can be drawn from this article about the better product or method? How was it better?**
AUDIENCE	General—adult	Revavan—best fuel economy at 21 m.p.g.—more headroom and legroom—more reliable antilock brakes—dual air conditioners in Deluxe model—good support in driver's seat—better (safer) rear door latches.
PURPOSE	**What actions should the audience take after reading?** Make better decision about which minivan to buy when looking at the Transtar, Aerovan, and Revavan.	
FORMAT	☒ written ☐ oral ☐ other	
SOURCES	**Magazine title and date:** Cars Galore March 2005	
VISUALS	**Visuals used to make the article effective:** Photos of each van. Close-ups of rear door latches and new side doors on Aerovan.	**What do the conclusions mean for the reader?** You'll save money and be safer and more comfortable in the Revavan.
RESULTS	**Which item or method was better?** Revavan rated "best buy"	

Proposals (Persuasive Reports)

"Look into it."

"Let me know what you think."

"Check it out and see what we can use to get what we need for the best price."

All of the statements you just read are ways people in authority might tell you to investigate the best way to do something—and then to submit a proposal for doing it.

What, exactly, is a proposal? It is a report in which you try to persuade someone to do something based on information you have provided. A proposal is designed to be the answer to a question or problem.

A proposal might start with an idea such as the following:

- Here are some ways to tackle the attendance problem.
- Our work area needs to be rearranged.
- We need to advertise on the radio rather than in the newspaper.
- We should add goat's milk and tofu to the dairy case.
- Our department needs a new accounting software program.
- We should replace our old delivery trucks.

Of course, there is always a *because* after these opening statements. One must state the reason for the needed change in order to make the proposal persuasive.

Then research is done to determine the best way to accomplish the needed change, by talking with knowledgeable people (interviewing), reading written materials, gathering raw data, doing Internet searches, or attending informational workshops or seminars.

And, finally, a cost must be calculated. The bottom line in business is profit, and if the proposal is not likely to help the company be more profitable, it will be rejected. Keep in mind that investing money in a large piece of equipment, for example, may involve a very large expense. A large expense may reap even larger profits—or it may not. Your proposal must show that it will. If you're wrong, you'll have to face the consequences. So do your homework or drop the proposal!

by the way...

During the 1984–1985 school year, the National Collegiate Athletic Association (NCAA) had 89,062 women and 197,446 men participating in championship sports. During the 1994–1995 school year, 107,605 women and 186,607 men were taking part in sports. By 2002–2003, there were 158,469 women and 214,464 men participating in sports. This type of data can be used to support proposals for increasing the number and quality of high school programs for female athletes, as well as for increasing the number of college scholarships for female athletes.

A Proposal Format

A common reporting format that can be used for a proposal follows.

1. Start with Your Conclusion.

State what needs to be done. (You've made up your mind. That's why you are writing the proposal.)

2. State Your Reasons.

Tell why you think your proposal should be done and how to do it. (State your most important reasons first, followed by less important reasons.) Include facts; don't just state your opinions. Find information to support your position and state where you found it.

3. Answer Possible Objections.

Anticipate what your reader or listener may object to and answer those objections. For example, "I know we've never done this, but market research shows that 40 percent of our customers want it."

4. Restate Your Conclusion.

"So it is clear that . . . needs to be done."

Adapted from Mathes and Stevenson

How to Handle a Situation Requiring a Persuasive Report

Assume, for example, that you are in charge of maintenance in a 60-bed hospital in a medium-sized town. The hospital floors have to be clean at all times, yet never slippery. Many cleaning solutions have powerful chemicals that act as disinfectants but also irritate membranes in the nasal passages. The use of these chemicals may cause additional breathing problems in patients who are already having trouble remaining comfortable. These and other concerns have been called to your attention by a hospital administrator who was not pleased with the previous maintenance supervisor's work at the hospital.

As a new employee, you have begun by using the supplies that were purchased before you came. In your previous job, you didn't have to deal with sick people, sterile conditions, and constant traffic, so these are new issues for you.

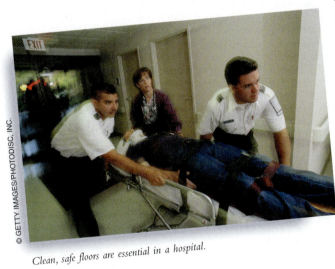

Clean, safe floors are essential in a hospital.

You go to your hospital administrator to discuss your shared concerns, knowing that solving the many facets of this floor-care problem could add to your costs. You may need a bigger budget to get the job done right. New cleaners and waxes may require special equipment. The administrator responds, "Check out the details and bring me some facts. We'll talk about them."

You know that the hospital operates on a tight budget. You are also aware that the administrator doesn't know you well enough yet to trust your judgment. What do you do?

Use the Expertise of Others

This is no time for original research, but you are going to have to put some facts and figures together for your administrator fairly quickly. Where do you get them?

First, look at the kinds of questions that need to be answered. You'll have to know which types of floor cleaners and waxes are available for the terrazzo tile flooring and vinyl tile floors in your hospital. Which are most effective for disinfecting and preserving the floors? Which are the safest? Which have fewer hazardous chemicals in them? How are they applied? What equipment is necessary to use them most effectively?—buckets and mops or electric floor scrubbers and high-speed polishers?

What is the cost of each floor cleaner and wax? What quantity will be needed to take care of the floors in your building for one year? Considering all factors (effectiveness, safety, availability of equipment to apply the products, and cost), what needs to be purchased?

How do you get answers to those questions? Where do you look? Whom do you ask? Are letters needed, or will a phone call do?

Approaching a task like this cold (without previous knowledge or preparation) can be quite a challenge. That's why people in almost every line of work develop networks; that is, they get to know other people in their field of work, people who do the same kinds of jobs they do. They may join trade or professional organizations, many of which publish trade journals, from which they receive written information on topics pertaining to their jobs. They attend workshops on the latest products, methods, and OSHA (Occupational Safety and Health Administration) regulations.

Use the expertise of others to gather information for a proposal.

In the case of the hospital floors, you could begin by calling the supervisors of maintenance at several other hospitals in your area or in nearby towns. Have they had the same problems? What have they done about the problems? Can they recommend a product? Where can you buy it? Check the Internet for descriptions of floor maintenance products used in hospitals. Most businesses have a web site, which contains information about the company and its products.

Technology *Connection*

In the early 1990s, Garth Brooks was an ordinary country singer, mostly ignored by those in the music business. Suddenly, his name was at the top of the charts, almost overnight. The reason was a change that was made in the way the recording industry reported sales. When complete sales information was available, thanks to scanners and bar codes, and a data gathering system from a company named SoundScan was put into place, the true popularity of Garth Brooks was suddenly evident. And the Top 200 chart began to show which recordings were really selling, as opposed to what a number of store clerks had been reporting in questionable telephone surveys. Now high-stakes charts are no longer based on sketchy and unreliable information; a truer picture is available through the *zap!* of a bar code reader. Marketing practices in the music recording business can now be accurately tailored to what is actually happening in sales.

Once you get a promising lead, call the manufacturer for details about the ingredients of the products that have been recommended or about the availability of other products that might solve your problem. Most large companies today have 800 numbers, which can be dialed free of charge.

Compare Products

Ask for a detailed description of each product: specifications, methods of application, and warnings related to application or use. Be sure to request the names and addresses of vendors (preferably local) from whom the product can be purchased.

Usually, a vendor is happy to supply you with the names and addresses of others who use a product. You can visit them and see for yourself how the product really works.

Compare Costs, Not Just Prices

When you have found one or two products that look promising, check with the vendor(s) for prices and shipping costs, but don't stop there. Figure the costs of using the products for one year. The new products may last longer and may not have to be stripped from the floor as often as the old ones, thus saving both time and money in the long run.

Organize Your Information

Now you are ready to put together a proposal for your administrator. Your job will be to persuade him or her to accept your recommendations, invest in special floor scrubbers (which may cost several thousands of dollars each), or do whatever else is needed.

You'll need to compare the old cleaners and waxes with several new products and then:

- Recommend the purchase and use of one or more of the products.
- Give several reasons for your recommendations.
- Tell where you got your information.
- Explain what using the new products will involve (for example, cost, new equipment, and training of your staff in how to apply them).
- Tell why you rejected other products. Restate your conviction that the hospital will benefit by using these new floor-care products. (You may be able to recommend using some of the old products in nonpatient areas of the hospital, such as storage areas, business offices, or gift shops, until they are used up. This will cut down on initial expense and eliminate waste.)
- Anticipate objections and concerns. Be ready to answer questions.
- Restate your conclusions in your closing.

Offer More Than One Plan

Show how much the total cost would be if you gradually phased in new equipment and materials instead of buying everything new at once. Or suggest the purchase of rebuilt or reconditioned equipment, which would lower costs.

Prepare Your Thoughts in Writing

Get your thoughts together by writing down your main points. Then you can make your most convincing presentation. You can use these notes initially as a guide to help you speak persuasively about your conclusions; that is, what needs to be done regarding floor care in this hospital. Then you can leave the notes for your administrator to use for future reference. (Do not give away your only copy; keep one for yourself.)

Make an Appointment to Present the Information

At the meeting, use your written information as a backup. Remember, the more knowledgeable and convincing you are, the more likely your proposal will be accepted.

Culture *Connection*

Everyone is familiar with the small shopping centers that have been built along major roads and highways and that dot the American landscape. They often contain a grocery store, one or more clothing stores, a pharmacy, perhaps an electronics store, a hair salon, a video rental store, and two or more food stands or restaurants. The location of such a shopping center typically starts with a proposal that includes information from population surveys, studies of traffic patterns, analyses of buying habits, and other sources that support the kinds of retail or service centers that would be frequented by people in the area. Investors who build such centers must be persuaded in advance that they will make money.

Practice 15–3: Writing Conclusions for a Proposal

The conclusion you reach after gathering the facts for your proposal must be worded clearly, concisely, and convincingly. A proposal may contain wonderful information, but it will not be persuasive if you cannot construct a strong conclusion.

Read the following weak conclusion and decide what's wrong with it. Be specific about what makes it sound weak. Which words were changed or deleted to produce a better conclusion?

Weak Conclusion (Sample)
(*Audience:* Office manager)

We could really use some kind of a program that's more user-friendly, like, maybe, Softwrite. This new word processing program will also work along with a spreadsheet—like you can go from one to the other—back and forth—and put stuff from your spreadsheet into what you're writing.

Improved Conclusion (Sample)
The new word processing program Softwrite is exactly what we need. It is user-friendly, and it interfaces with a spreadsheet, allowing information from the spreadsheet to be efficiently incorporated into any report.

This Practice contains three rambling and indistinct conclusions. After reading them carefully, write an improved version of each one. This Practice will help you learn to eliminate fuzzy thoughts, use appropriate words, and present an idea convincingly. The type of audience is specified for each conclusion.

Ch15–03.doc

(cont'd on next page)

Career *Connection*

When David Ho came to Los Angeles from Taiwan at age 12, he could not speak English. His classmates thought he was dumb. But after six months of instruction in English as a second language and a lot of TV, Ho learned the language. Working intensely, he began to leave his classmates behind, getting straight A's in everything, including English.

Ho went to Harvard Medical School, where his training led him to the focal point of his career: how to stop HIV (the human immunodeficiency virus) from multiplying and how to eliminate it from the body.

Dr. Ho is scientific director of the Aaron Diamond AIDS Research Center. He hopes to eradicate AIDS (acquired immunodeficiency syndrome) by using protease inhibitors with other antiviral medications. Thanks to his research, many people with HIV not only have survived, but also have not developed full-blown AIDS. He was named *TIME* magazine's Man of the Year in 1996. Needless to say, no one thinks he's dumb anymore.

by the way...

Judge Deidra Hair is good at stating strong conclusions, often using analogies to soften them with humor. Referring to a day's work in Municipal Court, she writes, "The pace in Room A is grueling. Three hundred cases in one day is the approximate equivalent of a fourteen-hour stint in the ER, with no assisting physicians."

Weak Conclusion 1
(*Audience:* Coworkers at Designs Plus)

To improve our safety at Designs Plus, it would probably be better if we did something about all of the suggestions, such as not plugging in electrical cords across the aisle from our computers because we wouldn't want someone to trip over them. If we ask, the electrical maintenance department might be able to put outlets closer to our desks. Or we could move our desks. Maybe we could get somebody to figure out how to rearrange our area. And it would be better, I guess, not to plug three or four electrical plugs into the same extension cord if we want to avoid fires.

Weak Conclusion 2
(*Audience:* Professional day-care-center workers)

We should feed the kids in the day-care center only the kind of food that doesn't have a whole lot of sugar and salt. Like fruit and stuff. Some kids get hyperactive when they get too much sugar and caffeine, like when they drink cola drinks. You have to be careful what you feed them. That's what Dr. Feingold says in his book. And it's what we've noticed ourselves with a lot of kids.

Progress Reports

Progress reports tell what has happened so far in a project or job. Progress reports answer questions such as these:

- Are plans being followed?
- Are we making a profit?
- Are we improving our products and services?
- Is the work proceeding as planned?
- How much money did we make this year?
- How many customers came back a second time this year?
- Have we been able to decrease our workdays lost due to absenteeism over the past three years?

An on-site oral progress report

Progress reports vary depending on the purpose, location, job, and degree of technology available within a company. Sometimes progress reports are written out, but often they are placed on a specially designed form. In most schools, the grade card is used as a progress report. On some jobs that require personal inspections, a checklist is used, with space for notations. (Some companies call these checklists "field reports," since they are done in the field. But they are not the same as the field reports discussed earlier in this chapter.)

A Progress Report Format

Formats for progress reports vary. One simple format follows:

1. **Summary of What's Been Done to Date**
2. **Details of Step 1**
3. **Problems Encountered So Far (If Any)**
4. **What Will Be Done Next**
5. **Recommendations**

Anyone in charge of a project that is expected to take more than a few days will gain the confidence and respect of an employer or a customer by writing or calling in informal reports that indicate how the job is progressing.

A Sample Progress Report

A remodeling contractor had estimated that it would take one month for three workers to dismantle a rotting greenhouse located behind the kitchen, to remodel a second-floor bathroom, and to add a second-floor deck off the bathroom of a 130-year-old house. After one week of work, the carpenter left the handwritten note shown in Figure 15-1.

The note was left on a table just outside the entrance to the bathroom, since the carpenter knew that his customer would be checking to see how the work was progressing as soon as she came home from work.

Obviously, this carpenter knew that the homeowner was anxious about what was being done to her house and how unforeseen problems could add to both the cost and the inconvenience. He also knew that he would stay on good terms with his customer by keeping her fully informed and letting her know what to expect.

Although the carpenter's note is well-written, it doesn't appear at first glance to follow a progress report format. In fact, Don probably never thought of his note as more than just keeping the customer informed.

4-4-04

We're already behind schedule. The greenhouse looked rickety, but it was built to stay. It took an extra half day to remove all the #10 nails in those 2 x 4's.

We're ready for the bathroom. Hope all the brick and plaster dust isn't too bad. Leave the mop in the bucket and we'll try to clean up as we go.

PROBLEMS: It took us a full day to get the ceiling in. Old houses settle and aren't square to begin with.

The wrong color lavatory was shipped. It's going to take two weeks to get the Monroe 6 you ordered.

Meanwhile, we'll get the walls done. We won't be here till after 10:00 a.m. Wednesday. Have to pick up lumber on the way.

Call Steve if you have concerns. He'll track me down.

—Don

FIGURE 15-1   Don's report

Practice 15–4: Critiquing Don's Report

Reread the steps in the progress report format reprinted in this Practice. See if Don's note contains everything in that format. What did he write in order to:

1. Summarize what's been done to date?

2. Give details of specific tasks accomplished?

3. Explain problems that have been encountered so far?

4. Tell what will be done next?

5. Make recommendations?

Practice 15–5: Writing a Progress Report

Ch15-05.doc

Report cards—with their lists of six or seven grades each report period—do not do justice to all you do as a person with your many other responsibilities, your extracurricular activities, and possibly a part-time job.

Write an informal personal progress report approximately one page in length in the form of a memo. The audience for your progress report memo may be you, a trusted friend, a teacher, a parent, or someone else who is interested in what you do with your life. Include the following steps:

1. A summary of what you've done this school year

2. Details of step 1

3. Problems encountered so far (if any). If there have been none, say so

4. Explanation of what will be done next

5. Recommendations you would make to yourself (for example, "Next time I will . . . ")

Other Types of Progress Reports

In addition to the basic five-step report, there are many specialized types of progress reports. A few of them are listed here.

Annual Reports to Stockholders

Publicly owned companies (those in which the public owns shares of stock in the company) publish annual reports for their shareholders. These reports may be very elaborate publications detailing profits and losses, the effects of new laws (such as those controlling air or water pollution) on their business, major expenditures, new product lines, and other information.

Newsletters and Magazines

Some agencies, such as the Union of Concerned Scientists, regularly publish small magazines or newsletters outlining new projects and updating the public about their ongoing projects, such as their watchdog activities on the regulation and safety of nuclear power plants. Some departments within schools and businesses publish newsletters to keep other departments or outside people aware of the status of certain activities and projects within that department.

Courtesy of Denny McKeown's Landscape & Bloomin Garden Centre, Cincinnati, Ohio

Computerized Inventory Records

Cash registers in most large supermarkets are online to a central computer that keeps track of prices and inventories. This allows managers to know how much has been sold, which items need to be replaced, and what the gross receipts are for a given period of time—for the whole store or for a department within the store. This record can provide management with an ongoing sales progress report.

Electronic Surveillance of Workers

In some businesses, an electronic counter or recorder provides feedback to management on how much work has been accomplished. Thus, if you are a data entry clerk, your keystrokes per minute and total input for the day may be recorded automatically and compared to your work on other days. In other settings, video cameras may be recording the activities of a company's employees. Workers in a variety of industries are questioning the ethics of such surveillance, claiming that it is an invasion of privacy and that it causes severe stress. Managers, however, argue that they can get a better idea of how to project timelines, how to spot possible illness in workers by observing their changing work patterns, and how to curtail theft—either in time or in materials. What do you think?

Culture *Connection*

If you've ever gone into a grocery store outside your neighborhood, you may have noticed differences in the products sold. If a neighborhood has a large concentration of Chinese-Americans, the neighborhood supermarket probably carries, in addition to the basic inventory, a stock of vegetables, spices, and other products preferred by Chinese-Americans in that community. Stores in a Mexican-American or Italian-American neighborhood would stock different items. Stores must know or research their customer base and cater to its needs.

Stores in a low-income neighborhood are less likely to have a large inventory of higher-priced specialty items. Grocery stores typically make only a small margin of profit on each item sold, so to stay in business, they must stock mainly those items that large numbers of local shoppers will buy. The next time you visit a new neighborhood, head for the food mart and do a little personal research on the food you see there. It will give you a snapshot of the neighborhood residents.

Monthly or Annual Meetings

Sometimes progress reports are delivered in meetings as audiovisual presentations to show progress charts, pictures of new machinery, new product packaging, or other information to workers who might not otherwise be aware of these things. Such a regular update can keep all employees aware of the big picture—of what's happening throughout the company—and give them a better understanding of what's going on in the organization beyond their own department.

Tips on Report Writing

Everything you have learned about technical communication in this course comes together in the collection of data and in the presentation of a report.

- *Audience analysis.* Audience analysis is critical. Reports may be written for customers or company managers or with the general public in mind. Adjust word choice and tone accordingly.

- *Clear, concise writing.* Clarity and conciseness are critical. Reports should not be padded. Less is more, provided that no necessary information is left out.

- *Tables, charts, and graphs.* Use of tables, charts, and graphs to help organize information in an attention–getting and logical way helps the reader focus on important points.

- *Layout and design.* In all technical writing, layout and design are very important. The use of headings to label and introduce each section is important, too, as is the use of white space, underlining, boxes, bullets, and other devices that highlight information or help to focus the reader's attention.

Technology *Connection*

"Green" Houses

When environmentally conscious groups refer to green houses, they are not talking about a place for raising flowers and selling potted plants. They are talking about environmentally friendly houses that are designed to use less coal, less electricity, and less gas for heating and cooling. And most especially, green houses don't pollute the environment as much as traditional homes do.

The Scandinavians have been developing and selling environmentally friendly houses since the 1980s. The thick-walled structures are built with heavy timbers from coniferous trees that are purchased from local timber farms. The windows and walls of the houses harness the warmth of the sun, and solar panels on the roof heat tap water. Homeowners find that their heating bills are lowered by as much as 90 percent.

In the United States, the green house industry is growing. Typically, the houses have large panes of glass on the south side to catch the warmth of the sun; some have concrete floors that are heated by rooftop solar panels via hot water tubing. Thick, solid wooden walls are used for maximum energy efficiency. Many of the houses use heat pumps, but at least one company has devised a way to make the house itself a heat pump, using the natural energy of rising solar-heated air.

- *Review for assistance.* If there is a problem with any aspect of your final report, you can get help by using the table of contents of this book and reviewing the concept. If, for example, you are writing a persuasive report in which you are encouraging someone to buy one product instead of another, refer to Chapter 12 to review how to contrast one product with another in your report.

- *Mechanics of report writing.* Start with the topical heading. State what you are writing about. Always indicate to whom the report is addressed, by whom it was written, and what date it was submitted. Sometimes a memo form is preferred. (Refer to Chapter 9 for tips on formatting a memo.)

Usually, the person submitting the report signs or initials and dates the report (sometimes on each page). Follow whatever format your employer prefers.

Key all but the most informal reports. If you write or print an informal report, be sure that every letter and number is clear and legible.

Ch15-06.doc

Practice 15-6: A Scavenger Hunt

How would you like to go on a scavenger hunt? Use your textbook to find answers to the questions on *Student Workbook* page 15-C.

Summary

In all lines of work, reports of various types play important roles. Reports may be presented orally, in writing, or both. They may require a great deal of information gathering, careful organization, and appropriate illustrations. Four types of reports that are commonly used in business and industry are:

- Laboratory reports, which summarize tests done on a product or process under controlled conditions.
- Field reports, which require gathering information "from the field," either in the workplace or outside the workplace, in order to understand or improve something.
- Proposals, which attempt to persuade someone to take action based on information reported and which require the use of convincing language, strong conclusions, and supporting data.
- Progress reports, which show how much was accomplished over a set period of time.

The ability to write and present a top-quality report will place you a notch above the average worker. It is the kind of skill you need to be promoted to management positions, and it requires the use of all of the skills you have learned in this course.

or review and research activities visit
communicating.swlearning.com

Works Cited

Carper, Jean. *The Food Pharmacy.* New York: Bantam, 1988.

Hair, Deidra. *No Shoes, No Shirt, No Trial.* Cincinnati: Symetry Publications, 1987.

Mathes, J. C., and Dwight W. Stevenson. *Designing Technical Reports.* 2d ed. New York: Macmillan, 1991.

http://www.ag.iastate.edu/centers/rdev/newsletter/fall98/digest.html

http://www2.kumc.edu/son/academicinformation/msappdeadlines.html

http://www.bookrags.com/biography/david-da-i-ho

http://www.time.com/time/moy.ho.html

http://www.clarkpublicutilities.com/Residential/meterReading/remoteMeterReading

http://www.in4ma.co.uk./products/in4mapc_remote_meter_reading.html

http://www.ci.kirkwood.mo.us/water/remote-meter.htm

http://www.ncaa.org/library/research/participation-rates/1982-003/2003ParticipationReport.pdf

http://www.scanhome.ie

http://enertia.com

project-based assessment

Presenting a Report

Use the data you collected in Chapter 13 or Chapter 14 or use other data that you collect. Then plan and write one of the following:

• A laboratory report (see format on pages 506–509)

• A field report (same format as laboratory report)

• A proposal (see format on pages 510–517)

1. Carefully read the Sample Project Plan and Sample Project on pages 525–527.

2. Find the two Project Plans in your *Student Workbook:* one for a field or laboratory report (page 15-D) and the other for a proposal (page 15-F). Complete the one appropriate for the report you have chosen to do. There is also a Project Guide for each (pages 15-E and 15-G).

3. Locate facts that will answer the questions in your Project Plan about the topic you have chosen. Do not write complete sentences, just brief notes.

4. Using the information in your Project Plan, write a rough draft. Write quickly without worrying about exact wording. Just get your ideas in roughly the correct form.

5. Use the Rough Draft column of your Project Guide (*Student Workbook* page 15-E for a field or lab report or *Student Workbook* page 15-G for a proposal) and check your work with one or more classmates. Each of you should mark the Project Guide and note any changes on the rough draft.

6. Revise your rough draft, incorporating the changes that your classmate(s) suggested.

7. Use the Final Draft column of the Project Guide to proofread your work. Make needed corrections.

Sample Project Plan

Plan for Field or Laboratory Report

SUBJECT	Report of customer satisfaction survey for Craig Bird's Lawn Care Service.	
AUDIENCE	General (classmates and teachers)	
PURPOSE	**What actions should the audience take?** Inform audience about how a real business survey took place, what the results were, and what the client did with the information.	
FORMAT	☒ written ☐ oral ☐ other	
SOURCES	**How will information be obtained? What methods will be used?** Face-to-face or phone interviews of customers. Recorded responses on questionnaire. Then tallied responses for report.	
VISUALS	**What visuals, if any, will make the report more effective?** Use table to illustrate responses.	
RESULTS	**What are the results of the investigation?** Most customers satisfied with service. Decided to train shrub trimmer and publicize services through flyers.	

CONCLUSIONS

Hired to do customer satisfaction survey.

Total customers: 611

Number surveyed: 109

Breakdown of services used by customers who were surveyed:

1. shrub trimming—33	5. aerating lawn—15
2. grass mowing—95	6. tree stakes—7
3. mulching—7	7. leaf raking—43
4. lawn weed and feed—61	

Additional points on survey:

1. job cleanup

2. friendly, businesslike manner

3. billing procedures

4. pricing

Results of survey (Use notes from survey tally sheet) Highlights: 84% said lawn mowing was very good. Nearly half of shrub trim customers complained of choppy, uneven trim. Need attention to this service. 2 reported mulch piles dropped on lawn. Others rated mulching around shrubs average.

39 liked getting bill on day of service and getting questions answered. Others liked bills left inside storm door or on doorknob in plastic bag. Prices rated as average.

Recommendations: Improve shrub trimming and mulching services. (Train trimmer) Keep current billing practices. Use flyers to help sell less-used services.

Sample Report

Field Report: Customer Satisfaction Survey Analysis

Mr. Craig Bird and his two partners in Craig Bird's Lawn Care Service asked me to do a customer satisfaction survey of at least 100 of their 611 customers, using some questions they had put together.

They thought that if I surveyed about 25 people from each of the four neighborhoods they serve, the results would help them see what they need to improve to keep their customers happy. They were also concerned about why they had lost 15 customers in the last six months and wanted to avoid losing more.

Mr. Bird gave me a list of questions to ask. We agreed that personal contacts either in person or by phone would be best, since very few people will fill out and mail a questionnaire. We decided that since Mr. Bird's company was into the regular spring/summer cycle with its customers here in Memphis, I would go with some of his lawn workers during the spring break and on afternoons and interview people who were at home during the day. I surveyed other customers by phone in the evening. It took a lot of hours. Mr. Bird let the customers know about the survey in advance and gave them my name so they would be expecting my call.

On the chart I put together, you can see that I contacted 109 customers, a few more than Mr. Bird expected, which made him happy. From his customer records, we knew how many he mowed lawns for, trimmed shrubs for, and provided other services for. (Some of them used more than one service.) As it turned out, I did a fair job of reaching people who used all of the lawn services his company provided.

The results show that most customers are satisfied with the service. The strongest satisfaction areas reported were lawn mowing and billing procedures. Customers liked getting their bills on the day of service and having their questions answered. The weakest areas were mulching and shrub trimming, although we didn't have as many responses in those categories. Two people said that mulch was left in their grass and on their sidewalks. Fifteen said that their shrubs got a choppy trimming job, and some said that the old branches weren't removed from the bushes.

We also took a hard look at how few of his customers take advantage of some of his services. Mr. Bird admits that sometimes he speaks to people who are at home when he's working in their yards, and those are the ones who hire him for a wider variety of services, such as mulching in the spring and raking leaves and putting in tree stakes in the fall. I suggested that he create a flyer containing a couple of garden tips, add a list of services and their cost, and leave a copy with the bill as he makes his rounds. He could also leave flyers at neighboring houses. That would save mailing costs. We also decided that he needs to take the time to train the person he hired to do shrub trimming so the worker does a better job. We think that doing these things will help the company get more business and keep it from losing any more customers.

James Godinez
Technical Communication 213
Final Project
May 2005

SURVEY RESULTS

Craig Bird's Lawn Care Service

Item	Number of Customers		Responses		
	# Rec. Svc.	# Surveyed	Very Good	Average	Poor
1. grass mowing	517	95	80	15	0
2. shrub trimming	409	33	0	8	15
3. mulching	45	7	1	3	3
4. lawn weed & feed	387	61	31	24	6
5. aerating	76	15	13	2	0
6. tree stakes	31	7	3	4	0
7. leaf raking & removal	261	43	33	8	2
8. cleanup	611	109	27	71	11
9. friendly, businesslike	611	109	49	59	1
10. pricing	611	109	37	72	0
11. billing procedures	611	109	59	49	1

Total customers: 611. Number surveyed: 109.

Overview

The following proposal by Stephen Budiansky appeared in the magazine *U.S. News & World Report*. The topic of his memo is the U.S. government's attempt to limit immigration to the United States. He writes his proposal as one Native American to another, recommending the denial of asylum to the Pilgrims.

"1620 to 1992: Long Ago But Not So Far Away"

TO: Massasoit, Chief, Wampanoag tribe

FROM: Squanto

RE: Immigration interview report, 26 DEC 1620

One hundred so-called boat people filing claims for political asylum were interviewed. The vast majority of the claims were nonsensical. None could show a justifiable, immediate fear for their lives if they returned to Holland and/or that they had held a sensitive position in a persecuted political or religious organization. In fact, several admitted that they had only several years earlier voluntarily relocated to Holland specifically because it was an open society that would tolerate their sect ("the Separatists"). The obvious contradictions in their stories suggest that these are not bona fide political refugees but rather economic refugees, merely out to better their lives.

Their claim to permanent residency status based on special skills or professional training is likewise unsubstantiated. Most lack even the most basic job skills, as the earlier waves of boat people who were admitted to Jamestown has unfortunately demonstrated. Most of those immigrants were listed on the ship's manifest as "Gentleman," which they themselves define as "whosoever can live without manual labor." They are lazy, prone to acts of violence and unable or unwilling to become productive members of society. Established residents of the area complain of a rash of petty thefts and of outright starvation—and more than two thirds already have starved to death—they are unwilling to find gainful employment. In one well-documented incident, the immigrants chopped down their own houses for firewood. It is perhaps relevant that several prominent authorities in England have explicitly encouraged emigration to America as a way to rid their country of "idle and worthless" persons.

The conditions aboard these boats are horrendous. Interviewees report that five persons in fact died in transit. Smallpox, scurvy and typhus are rampant aboard these crowded ships, which allot a space of only 7 feet by $2\frac{1}{2}$ feet, below decks, for each passenger. More than 150 boat people died of disease on one ship that arrived in Virginia two years ago. The ships are also in poor physical condition. Interviewees reported that a second boat, the *Speedwell,* was forced to turn back twice because of leaks and eventually abandoned the voyage.

Firm action now can effectively discourage other Englishmen from taking to unseaworthy vessels, which will only lead to a further unnecessary and tragic loss of life. . . .

Recommendation on applications for asylum: **DENY.**

—Stephen Budiansky

Start-Up: People write proposals in the workplace to fix a problem, meet a need, or make an improvement. Having a good idea is not enough to bring about a change. Writers must demonstrate that they understand the problem or need, that they are considering the reader's position, and that they have a detailed program for putting their plans into action. A proposal must be persuasive.

In literature, proposals are written for the same reasons. Writers of literature must also plan persuasive proposals. There is no one correct format for a proposal. However, most proposals contain certain basic parts: a conclusion (what needs to be done), the reasons (why it should be done), answers to possible objections, and a restatement of the conclusion.

Pay attention to how a proposal looks. Are headings used to help the reader determine what each paragraph contains? Are lists enumerated or bulleted? Are visuals included to help the reader understand what is being proposed? A careless presentation may result in the rejection of the proposal.

Connection: Meet in groups of four. Brainstorm situations that exist within the school that you would like to see changed. Make a list of these situations. Also brainstorm for solutions to these situations. Each member of the group should write a proposal based on one of the situations. Use the memo format. Key your proposal and submit it to your teacher.

Working with Literature: Refer to *Student Workbook* page 15-H for an activity on report writing.

Overview

Does a pet have a special place in your life? On occasion, you probably have bragged about its unusually smart performances. It is just more intelligent than other pets, right? Just how smart is your pet?

Two dolphin trainers asked this question about dolphins and investigated to find the answer. The following factual report pursues the answer to this question: How smart are dolphins?

"How Smart Are Dolphins?"

Malia was smart. She learned quickly, mastering many tricks after two or three lessons. She seemed to enjoy performing for audiences at Sea Life Park in Hawaii. She was so clever that her trainers, Karen Pryor and Ingrid Kang, decided to try something new.

Pryor and Kang felt that Malia's act had become too slick and polished. The dolphin knew her routines perfectly. She never made mistakes. There were no surprises. To make Malia's act more lively and interesting, Pryor and Kang decided to show their audiences how a dolphin is trained. They would teach Malia a brand-new trick at each show. When she learned the trick, she would be rewarded with a fish.

In the following days, Malia learned one new trick after another. She was rewarded only for learning something new, not for performing her old tricks. After fourteen shows, the dolphin had learned fourteen new tricks. Pryor and Kang were running

© GETTY IMAGES/PHOTODISC, INC.

out of new tricks to teach her. At one show, they couldn't come up with anything new.

Malia solved the problem herself. She began to perform new stunts she made up herself. She swam on her back with her tail in the air. She threw herself into the air backward and made an arching leap upside down. She jumped from the water and spun like a top in mid-air.

Malia had not been taught these tricks and had never performed them before. She had apparently figured out on her own that she would not be rewarded for performing old tricks. She could earn her reward only by doing something new. She seemed to realize that it didn't matter what she did, as long as she hadn't done it before.

In show after show, Malia came up with new and astonishing stunts. She performed tricks on her own that her trainers never would have imagined. The dolphin appeared to understand the abstract principle that only novelty would win a reward. She seemed to be thinking, not just learning tricks in an automatic way.

Inspired by Malia's remarkable behavior, her trainers decided to try the same thing with another dolphin, Hou. They wanted to see if Hou would also catch on to the idea that only novelty would be rewarded. This time they would keep a careful record of everything that happened.

. . . Malia and Hou had performed a feat of intelligence highly unusual in any animal.

It took a while for Hou to understand what the trainers wanted, but she did catch on. Like Malia, she began to make up and perform one new trick after another.

It seemed that Malia and Hou had performed a feat of intelligence highly unusual in any animal. Did the experiments really prove that?

Karen Pryor tried a similar experiment with pigeons. The pigeons were put through the same kind of training as the dolphins. Surprisingly, they responded in the same way.

Karen Pryor concluded that the experiments did not, after all, show how smart dolphins are. Given the same kind of training, pigeons were capable of learning the same lesson—that only new behavior would be rewarded. Apparently, the dolphins' feat did not require super-intelligence.

These experiments show how difficult it is to understand the intelligence of a creature different from ourselves. We can test an animal, but we don't always know how to interpret the results.

Dolphins live in a world of sound. Sounds tell them most of what they need to know about their underwater world. While it is not possible to see very far under water, sounds travel clearly through the water.

Dolphins stay in touch with each other by sending sounds through the water. They also scan the waters around them by means of echo-location. They send out high-frequency sounds, just as bats do. The sounds bounce off objects, and the echoes bring back information about the size of the object, its shape, its texture, and its distance. By means of echo-location, a dolphin can identify a shark that is too far away to be seen.

Dolphins have much keener hearing than humans. They pick up sounds that we can't hear at all. A dolphin's acoustic nerve, which sends information to the brain, is three to four times bigger than the same nerve in humans. And a dolphin has a much larger part of its brain devoted to hearing than a human has.

Because each creature has a different kind of brain and lives in a special world of its own, it is very tricky to compare animals by means of intelligence tests. A test that is fair to one animal might not be fair to

(cont'd on next page)

another. In general, however, intelligence is closely linked to learning ability. An animal's intelligence depends, in part, on how fast it can learn, how much it can learn, and how long it can remember.

We can gain a rough idea of an animal's intelligence by looking at its brain. As a rule, smarter animals have bigger and more complex brains, but a giant brain doesn't always mean a giant intelligence.

The biggest brains on this planet belong to whales and elephants. A sperm whale has a brain that weighs about 9,000 grams, nearly 20 pounds. That's the largest brain that has ever existed on earth. An elephant's brain weighs about 6,000 grams. A bottle-nosed dolphin, a member of the whale family, has a brain of about 1,600 grams. The human brain is somewhat smaller, averaging about 1,400 grams.

Next to humans, then, dolphins have the biggest brains for their size. They also have extremely complex brains—another sign of intelligence. In some ways, the dolphin brain is even more intricate and complex than the human brain. However, it is also quite different. The human brain is longer than it is wide. A dolphin's brain is wider than it is long, and it is quite high. The part of the dolphin brain that receives and analyzes sounds appears to be much larger and more complex than in humans. There are other important differences, too. We have barely begun to understand the workings of the human brain, and we know much less about the dolphin brain. So it's difficult to compare them. There is no question, however, that the dolphin has the brain of a highly intelligent animal.

Another way to judge the dolphin's intelligence is by its behavior. We know surprisingly little about the behavior of the dolphins in the wild. Because they live in the ocean and move rapidly over long distances, human observers have not been able to spend more than brief moments with them. It is extremely difficult to approach a group of dolphins in a boat and stay with them long enough to study their behavior. The animals are visible briefly as they surface to breathe. Then they are lost to view as they move on under the water.

We do know that dolphins travel together in groups of about twenty or more individuals. At certain times of the year, many of these groups come together to form large herds that may number thousands of dolphins.

Dolphins have been seen to cooperate with each other in a number of ways. They often work together when they hunt for food. A group of dolphins will spread out in underwater formation and advance toward a school of anchovies. They herd the anchovies up toward the ocean surface, where they close in to feed on them.

> *Next to humans, then, dolphins have the biggest brains for their size.*

Dolphins also have been seen to aid and protect members of their group. A shark that tries to attack a dolphin may find itself surrounded by other dolphins. One by one, the dolphins charge the shark at high speed, battering it to death with their hard beaks.

If a dolphin is ill or injured and can't rise to the surface for air, other dolphins rush over and take turns lifting the injured animal to the surface, so it can breathe.

These appear to be intelligent acts. Yet many other animals cooperate in similar ways.

The best evidence for dolphins' intelligence comes from their behavior in captivity. Bottle-nosed dolphins are famous as star performers in seaquariums. They can master a wide variety of complex tricks and stunts. They catch on quickly and often learn a trick simply by watching other dolphins perform it. Trainers say that they can learn faster than any other animal.

A standard laboratory test shows just how quickly they can learn. An animal can be trained to push a lever in order to earn a reward. It takes hundreds of trials for a rhesus monkey to learn to do this. Dolphins catch on in about 20 trials.

Besides being quick learners, dolphins are talented mimics—another sign of intelligence. Sometimes they can watch an action only once and then repeat it. One dolphin watched a diver use a mechanical scraper to clean an observation window in its tank. When given the scraper, the dolphin used it just as the diver had.

With their keen hearing, dolphins also are experts at imitating sounds. Some researchers say that not only can they imitate the human voice, but they can actually learn the meaning of certain words.

Do dolphins really communicate in sophisticated ways? Scientists have conducted a number of experiments to find out.

Jarvis Bastian, a psychologist at the University of California at Davis, tried to determine if one dolphin can send specific information to another. Bastian trained two dolphins named Buzz and Doris to push underwater levers. By pushing the correct lever, they would earn their reward, a tasty fish. If they saw a flashing signal light, they had to push the lever on the left. If they saw a steady light, they had to push the lever on the right.

(cont'd on next page)

© GETTY IMAGES/PHOTODISC, INC.

This is an easy lesson for dolphins. Buzz and Doris both learned it quickly.

Despite the years of study, researchers have never come up with convincing evidence that dolphins have a complex language. Although dolphins exchange many sounds, we have no idea what those sounds mean. As one scientist put it, "It's a bit like a man from outer space tapping into the Bell System center trying to make sense of all the beeps and switching."

One dolphin may be able to describe an underwater object to another by re-creating the sounds that bounce back from that object. Instead of "saying" a single word that stands for "sharks," for example, the dolphin would repeat the sounds that bounce back from the shark. It would create a sound-picture of the shark, which it could pass along to other dolphins, telling them how big it is, how far away it is, and possibly even what kind of shark it is.

The dolphin's mind remains a mystery, too.

At the moment, that is an unproven theory. The sounds exchanged by dolphins remain an unsolved mystery.

The dolphin's mind remains a mystery, too. While everyone agrees that dolphins are smart, they don't agree on how smart they really are. Karen Pryor, who trained many dolphins at Sea Life Park, once guessed that dolphins rank in intelligence somewhere between dogs and chimpanzees. John Lilly, a devoted student of dolphins who has written many books about them, believes that they may be as intelligent as humans. "It is possible that their intelligence is comparable to ours," says Lilly, "but in a strange fashion."

Other scientists aren't too sure. According to them, we just don't have enough evidence to understand the dolphin mind or to judge the dolphin's intelligence.

—Russell Freedman

Start-Up: "How Smart Are Dolphins?" does not fit into the reporting format of either the field or the laboratory report you have studied in this chapter. However, the information in this report is ably presented. Many government and business reports are given in various formats. Often an employee is asked to write a report for which no instructions are given, making it necessary to design a format.

Connection: Researchers use two basic types of research for acquiring their information: primary and secondary research. **Primary research** is the gathering of firsthand information. The researcher might perform a series of experiments, conduct interviews with experts on the topic being researched, or use official records and documents. **Secondary research** is the gathering and analyzing of facts and ideas from published sources such as books and articles. The authors of these sources have obtained their data or information from an original source; then they basically do what they want with it. A researcher needs to be careful with secondary research; he or she should check the sources for accuracy.

1. What type of research was used to secure information for this report: primary or secondary?

2. Analyze the literature selection by answering the following questions:

   a. What is the title of the selection?

   b. Who is the audience?

   c. What is the purpose?

   d. What is some background information?

   e. How was the investigation conducted?

   f. What were the results?

   g. What were the conclusions?

   h. Discuss the conclusions. What do they mean?

Chapter 16

© CORBIS

"And life is what we make it, always has been, always will be."

—GRANDMA MOSES, ARTIST

The Store Owner Who Missed Her Sale

Elizabeth told her family that her store was going to have its biggest sale since it opened. The sale was scheduled for Tuesday, the following day. Early Tuesday morning, Elizabeth went out to start the car but found that the car's windshield needed to be cleaned. When she entered the garage to get the windshield washer fluid, she noticed that the garage windows were open. She shut the windows, but then she stopped to clean up the rainwater on the garage floor. Elizabeth also discovered rainwater on the lawnmower, so she tried to start it to make sure it still worked. However, Elizabeth found that the lawnmower needed oil. On her way to get the oil, she heard the dog barking to go outside. . . .

Becoming a Professional

Feel overwhelmed? How can you fit everything you want to do into your week? The presentation is due for English class, your boss needs overtime hours from you this weekend, and the local student organization competition date is fast approaching. Why is everyone asking so much from you?

Becoming a professional doesn't mean that you have to become a doctor, an attorney, or even a teacher—unless you want to become one. Becoming a professional means not only that will you have the knowledge to go out and get a job in your field, but also that you present an image. That polished image reflects the way you will conduct your professional life.

Disorganization causes poor time management.

© GETTY IMAGES/PHOTODISC, INC.

Time is frustrating. You cannot touch time. Try and try again, but you cannot save or change time. Time travels at various speeds. The clock seems to go more slowly on Friday afternoon than it does on Saturday night. The last few pages of the assignment often take longer to read than the first half of the chapter, and sometimes time seems out of control. Then nothing gets done on time. Deadlines are always approaching. You oversleep. You can't find the left shoe that matches the blue outfit you want to wear today.

Remember, you're in charge. You can handle time. Effective **time management** is getting done *what* you want to do *when* you want to do it. It is also finding what you want to find when you're looking for something. Controlling time has nothing to do with being neat or perfect. Taking command of your surroundings puts you in charge of your time; then you get more out of the time you have. However, before you try to manage your time more effectively, you need to discover what you're doing with it now.

Practice 16–1: Monitoring Time

Use *Student Workbook* page 16-A to discover how you use your time. To do this monitoring, you will record your time in 30-minute periods, from 7 a.m. to 11 p.m., for the number of days your teacher tells you.

In the left column for each day, write your general activities. Driving, watching television, taking care of children, exercising, working, sleeping, and going to school are all examples of general ways that you may spend your time. The Grooming section includes taking showers, applying makeup, fixing hair, choosing clothes, etc.

Every two or three hours, record what you've done by darkening the boxes on the chart. Each small section represents 30 minutes.

After you have recorded the time period, total the darkened blocks for each category. Divide the total by 2 to find the number of hours spent on each activity. In the Comments box, record what you discovered about the totals. Save your form for use in Practice 16-2.

Wasting Time

Everyone wastes time at some point in the day. Even the most efficient business executive does not use every minute wisely. Throwing away minutes does add up. Catch the time wasters and save time. Descriptions of four ways to waste time follow.

Career *Connection*

For 55 percent of U.S. workers, the average part of the lunch hour actually spent eating lunch is down to just 25 minutes. The remaining 35 minutes is used for a variety of activities, including the following:

- Socializing (53%)
- Running errands (44%)
- Catching up on work (43%)
- Reading or surfing the Internet (42%)
- Making personal phone calls (28%)
- Shopping (in stores or online) (33%)
- Exercising (14%)
- Going to medical appointments (9%)
- Monitoring child care (6%)
- Interviewing for other jobs (1%)

by the way...

"A big part of sticking to resolutions is getting through bad days. Don't focus on the day when you failed, focus on all of the days when you won. Keep a chart, monitor your success, and don't give up!"

—Robert R. Butterworth, psychologist

The Unproductive Task

Sometimes concentration does not come easily. As a result, other activities often take the place of what should be done. If studying for a test is not a favorite activity, then talking on the phone, making popcorn, and brushing the dog take the place of studying. Unproductive tasks that interrupt work or study time include talking on the phone, surfing the Internet, sending and responding to instant messages, and constantly checking e-mail. Don't spend too much time on activities that are not urgent or that are not important.

The Wrong Task

Guests are coming to the house in one hour, and you have the house nearly straightened. All you have to do is clean the bathroom. Choosing to straighten the desk over cleaning the bathroom may seem like a good choice. However, the bathroom is the problem; the desk is not the solution. Zero in on what is needed, rather than what your preference is.

The Right Task Done the Wrong Way

Lisa's assignment is to frame a window for carpentry class. Unless she attempts the project without measurements, she cannot finish the framing. All the required tasks must be done to complete the goal of finishing on schedule. However, if the details of preparing for the framing take most of the assigned time, then Lisa is not planning her time wisely. Preparation, such as drawing, gathering supplies, and adjusting equipment, becomes more important than the project itself.

© GETTY IMAGES/PHOTODISC, INC.

Preparation details are important.

Career *Connection*

Here are some ways to use time wisely.

In five minutes, I can:

- Write a to-do list.
- Put a load of dirty clothes in the washer.

In 10 minutes, I can:

- Pack a gym bag.
- Answer e-mail.

In 30 minutes (or less), I can:

- Fold and put away two loads of laundry.
- Use a planner to schedule my week's activities.

Too Much Detail

Not every woodworking project is a fine piece of furniture. Not every assignment is a term paper. Not every piece has to be perfect. Sometimes perfection is not necessary.

To test whether you need to be flawless, consider how perfect the task needs to be. A rough draft does not have to be perfectly formatted; it can be handwritten on notebook paper with even a few cross outs. On the other hand, you must correct and key the final draft perfectly.

by the way...

The Procrastinators' Club of America was founded in 1956. The members celebrate National Procrastination Month in March—the month before April 15 (of course).

● Practice 16-2: Discovering Time Wasters

teamwork

With a partner, brainstorm as many time wasters as you can write down in five minutes. Use your time-monitoring form from Practice 16-1 for ideas. Choose two time wasters. Then, on a separate sheet of paper, answer the following three questions about each time waster you chose.

1. Why is the time waster so tempting to use?

   Time Waster A:

   Time Waster B:

2. What is the benefit of using the time waster?

   Time Waster A:

   Time Waster B:

3. What is the problem with using the time waster?

   Time Waster A:

   Time Waster B:

Procrastination

Tim is a procrastinator. He has every intention of doing what he says he will, but Tim does not follow through. He does very little of what he says he will do. In fact, he regrets saying yes ten minutes after he says it. Tim is also a charming man. He wants everyone to like him, so he has a hard time saying no. However, he also has many reasons for not finishing jobs. His excuse is usually "I had so much to do that I didn't know where to start—so I didn't." When caught not finishing tasks, Tim claims that he works best under pressure, so he puts things off until the last minute. However, if he is constantly reminded, Tim feels that he is under too much pressure and decides not to do anything at all. That's the time when Tim looks for a rescuer. He hopes that the job will somehow disappear or someone will take over. Usually, someone does.

Procrastination: A Self-Check

If you find some of yourself in Tim, you may be suffering from **procrastination**, also known as *tomorrowitis*. "I'll think about it tomorrow" is the procrastinator's theme. Procrastinators often use these excuses:

- I've got too much work to start on it now.
- When I have some free time, I'll do it immediately.
- I've had no chance to get to it.
- After I unwind, I'll start on it.
- No problem. I'll do these other things, and then I'll get right on it.
- That's right—I've been planning to do it.

People who procrastinate avoid difficult jobs, though procrastination often takes more energy than doing the job itself.

Procrastination may not be a problem in all parts of your life. For example, you may be very organized at work, but you may forget to pay the bills at home. Procrastination then may be selective because of your own personal choices. You need to do something, but resist doing it. Rather than finding a way to resolve the dilemma, you postpone it.

Practice 16–3: Exploring Procrastination

Fill out *Student Workbook* page 16-B. Answer the questions yes or no by placing a check mark in the correct column. Answer each question honestly. Then total your score according to the instructions provided. (Don't put off doing this Practice!)

Helping to Eliminate Procrastination

Effective time management ensures that you use time wisely. Procrastination becomes controlled, and forgetfulness becomes manageable. The result? More time with less work. Here are some tips to help you manage your time.

- Watch for time wasters. Use Practice 16-2 on page 540 to catch those time wasters and save time.

- Do the most difficult, boring jobs first. When you get those tasks over with, the rest of the day will go more smoothly.

- Determine what is your most productive time of day. Some people work best in the early morning; others do not get motivated to work hard until late afternoon. When do you have the most energy? Make the most of your energy during that time.

- Break a large job into chunks. When you divide a big job into separate parts, it seems smaller.

- Take advantage of electronic devices. Send messages via e-mail to avoid the extra conversation time spent on the telephone. Program frequently called numbers in your cell phone. Scan documents to store them on a CD for easy use and storage.

- Pay attention to your attention. When you find yourself daydreaming, try to take a ten-minute break. You'll come back refreshed, with a more positive attitude. Or make a to-do list and a to-think-about list; then concentrate on them.

- Remember that perfection is not always necessary. If lower standards will be acceptable, allow yourself to use them. If you're a perfectionist, try making one intentional mistake a day.

by the way...

Ask yourself the following question: **Would I pay myself for what I did today?** *If you answered yes, then you're probably effectively managing your time.*

Goal Setting

What do you want out of life? What do you believe in? What are the major goals you want to achieve in a lifetime? Asking yourself a few questions before you begin goal setting is the first step in organizing your life. **Goals** are specific expressions of your **values**. To determine your values and the roles you want them to play in your future, you need to ask what activities have had special significance for you in the past. What are you passionate about doing and sharing? What gave you a sense of confidence and inner peace?

Culture *Connection*

Practice 16–4: From the Past to the Future

The dreams you choose today are probably different from the dreams you chose five years ago. Ten years from now, you'll choose different dreams than today. Using your memories of the past and your dreams of the future, complete the following statements. Do not answer too quickly; take time to consider your remarks.

1. Five years ago my most important dreams were . . .

2. Today my most important dreams are . . .

3. In ten years, my most important dreams will be . . .

Goals

One good way to see if your values and your dreams for the future really matter to you is to fit them into your goals. You can determine truly meaningful ambitions and values by deciding whether you are willing to spend time accomplishing them. After establishing the goals, break them into activities, starting with long-range plans and ending with short-term or even daily activities.

Long-Term Goals

The major targets, or ambitions, of life are **long-term goals**. Reaching those goals takes a long time. Goals such as "I want to own my own business," "I want to learn a second language," or "I want to travel to every one of the 50 states" take a long time to accomplish. Long-term goals may include your career, your financial plans, and your family plans.

COMSTOCK IMAGES

Set your goal before the race.

Midterm Goals

What do you have to do in the next two to five years to achieve your long-term goals? **Midterm goals** are activities or projects that you must accomplish to attain a long-term goal. You can't perform a goal; you perform an activity to reach a goal. To become the owner of a beauty shop, your midterm goal might be to attain your degree in business management, in addition to having your cosmetologist's license. If you want to travel the United States for a long-term goal, plan a midterm goal of visiting a new state every year for five years.

Short-Term Goals

Midterm goals will generate the **short-term goals**. These goals can be reached in one year or less. Start taking action on these goals now or in the very near future. Taking the necessary admission tests, completing school applications, and working out a schedule with your employer are short-term goals for the midterm goal of obtaining that college degree in business management. Completing a travel itinerary for your summer vacation to Arkansas, a state you've never seen, is a short-term goal toward the midterm goal of visiting a new state every year for five years.

Barriers

Goal setting isn't always smooth. Doubts about speaking in public (the number one fear of adults), lack of training, procrastination, or family problems are **barriers** that could prevent you from succeeding if you let them. Planning ahead for high-risk situations helps with the temptations that may get you off track. However, blaming others or feeling sorry for yourself won't help you accomplish your goals. Staying positive helps keep you on the track and tells others that you believe in yourself. Department store owner R. H. Macy had seven businesses fail before his store in New York became a success. Babe Ruth struck out 1,330 times, but he also hit 714 home runs in his career. So perseverance will reward you if you don't quit trying to achieve your goals. Remember, the only way to avoid failing is never to try.

● Practice 16–5: Past Persistence

Think of obstacles you've overcome in the past. Completing a complicated project and coming back from an injury are examples of overcoming barriers to achieve success. List at least three barriers that you have successfully defeated. Beside each barrier, describe the way you conquered it.

Example:

Barrier	Way I Overcame It
Memorizing algebraic formulas	Invented rhymes that start with the first letters or numbers of the formula's parts

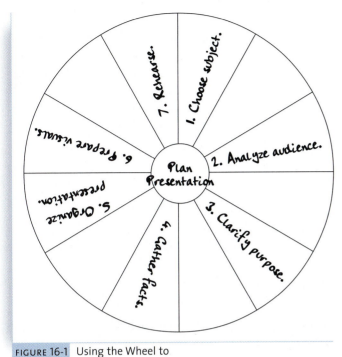

FIGURE 16-1 Using the Wheel to plan a presentation

Goal-Setting Methods

Goal setting is not just a paper-and-pencil activity, but a way of visualizing a goal and the activities you need to perform to achieve it. Each person needs to find his or her best method of putting goals on paper. Here are three practical ways of planning a presentation:

The Wheel

At the center of the Wheel (sometimes known as webbing or a spidergram) is the goal. Each spoke represents an activity needed to reach the goal. You write the activities in the order you need to do them. Place the timelines on the spokes. Figure 16-1 demonstrates the Wheel method.

The Fishbone

On the backbone or at the head of the fish, write the goal. On the bones of the fish, write the activities needed to reach the goal. Using the bones, you can divide activities into each action required. Figure 16-2 shows a Fishbone diagram.

Lists

Numbered lists in a column are the way many people set goals. Listing is not as visual as the Wheel or the Fishbone, which shows that all of the activities support the goal. You can also list tasks in order of importance or in a timeline. Figure 16-3 shows a list used to plan a presentation.

PLANNING A PRESENTATION

1. Choose subject.
2. Analyze audience.
3. Clarify purpose.
4. Gather facts.
5. Organize presentation.
6. Prepare visuals.
7. Rehearse presentation.

FIGURE 16-3 Using a list to plan a presentation

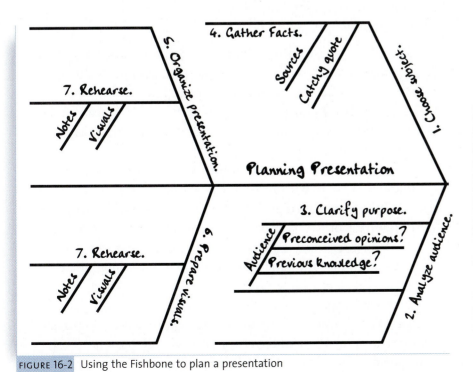

FIGURE 16-2 Using the Fishbone to plan a presentation

Career *Connection*

With the amount of information increasing daily, bookstores are flooded with publications on memory strategies. One of the easiest strategies is **mnemonics**, a technique in which you use devices such as rhymes and formulas to help in remembering. Here are several mnemonic devices:

- To remember how to spell *friend*:

  A *friend* to the **end**.

- To remember how to adjust your clocks for daylight saving or standard time:

  Spring ahead; fall back.

- To remember which way to turn a bolt to tighten or remove it:

  Right is tight, left is loose.

- To remember the order of calculations in algebra:

  Please **E**xcuse **M**y **D**ear **A**unt **S**ally

  Parentheses, **E**xponents, **M**ultiplication, **D**ivision, **A**ddition, **S**ubtraction

- To remember the Great Lakes of North America:

  HOMES—**H**uron, **O**ntario, **M**ichigan, **E**rie, **S**uperior

Practice 16–6: Setting Goals

1. a. During the next five minutes, write down any long-term goals that come to mind. Use *Student Workbook* page 16-C if you prefer to use a Wheel or a Fishbone, adding lines if needed. Long-term goals may involve education, career, personal relationships, travel, possessions, savings, and other areas. When time is up, select the three long-term goals that are most important to you today.

   b. Select one long-term goal from the list you created above. For five minutes, write down midterm goals that will help you reach your chosen long-term goal. These goals should be activities that you can do in the next two to five years. After the five minutes are up, choose the three midterm goals that are most realistic.

   c. Select one midterm goal from the list above. In the next five minutes, write down short-term goals that will help you reach that specific midterm goal. A short-term goal can be achieved in one year or less. A specific action, such as choosing a school or earning a certain amount of money, is necessary for a short-term goal. After the time is up, weed out any inappropriate goals. Then select three short-term goals that you will begin working on today.

2. When writing your goals for the future, you may use comparative or superlative forms of adjectives or adverbs. Use the **comparative** form when comparing two items or events and

by the way...

Try setting your alarm clock one hour earlier in the morning. Studies show that people who work out in the morning are more consistent. The hour of exercise will be more beneficial than the one hour's sleep that you missed.

People *Connection*

Art Mellor had a goal and a plan. At age 27, he had been dreaming of starting his own business for years. To realize this dream, he planned to get a job at the smallest company that would hire him. That company was Cayman Systems Inc., a descendant of the giant Apple Corporation. When Art interviewed with Cayman, he told the maker of networking software and hardware that he intended to get the skills to start his own company. And they hired him!

After three years, Art Mellor gained a considerable amount of on-the-job experience. The principal rules he learned were to be quiet and to listen to customers—and to learn from the company's mistakes. Even the most successful company will make mistakes; the gain is worth the pain. Art Mellor's knowledge enabled him to cofound Midnight Networks Inc., which was bought by Teradyne, Inc., six years after Cayman Systems hired him.

the **superlative** form when comparing three or more things. Using *Student Workbook* page 16-D, write sentences relating to the goals you've created for this Practice, using the comparative and superlative forms of the adjectives and adverbs given.

Priorities

The realistic goals you develop help you set your **priorities** in life. You can use subgoals developed from major goals to schedule tasks. The arrangement of these tasks in order of importance gives you your priorities. Use your priorities to establish your calendars and to develop your own daily system.

Calendars

Calendars overflow bookstore shelves and computer desktops. They are available on web sites and personal data assistants (PDAs). Try using more than one calendar. You can schedule yearly or weekly calendars for different purposes. Develop goals and tasks on yearly calendars, showing the preparation time necessary to achieve a short-term goal in one year's time.

Whether you organize your life electronically or use pen and paper, your daily calendar system should contain a to-do list of daily priorities. The average list should have ten things that you can reasonably expect to accomplish each day. Some of these tasks may occur regularly every day, week, or month. In the list, you set daily priorities in relationship to your long-term, midterm, and short-term goals.

Establish priorities when planning.

© GETTY IMAGES/PHOTODISC, INC.

CATHY © 1991, 1992 Cathy Guisewite.
Reprinted with permission of UNIVERSAL PRESS SYNDICATE. All rights reserved.

A, B, and C Priorities

By breaking larger projects into chunks, you can accomplish assignments more easily. Have a backup plan for emergencies and interruptions that may happen to prevent you from finishing that presentation for tomorrow. By planning for several days or an even longer period of time, you can avoid the problem of pulling an all-nighter or facing your teacher with an incomplete assignment. Review the dates and the timelines, keeping the goal and **objective** (the *why* of the goal) in mind. To be effective, the to-do list must be written with A, B, and C priorities and include specific timelines.

A Priorities

The A items are the most important things to do during the day and must be done immediately. To label these items, ask the question "What will happen if I don't get this done?" If the results are critical, label the item an A.

B Priorities

The B items are important but less critical than the A items and may be postponed for a short time. However, they may become A's if postponed several times.

C Priorities

These items do not need immediate attention. If no time is left, they can wait. Sometimes it's easier to make a list full of C's than to have to cope with A's. To some people, A's seem too difficult or pose a greater chance of failure.

Prioritizing Tasks

How do you decide to prioritize? Learn the 80/20 rule: The important work for the day is only about 20 percent of all of the items you have written down. So focus on the 20 percent that matters.

by the way...

The most productive time of the day for many U.S. workers is during regular working hours. However, business executives are most productive in the office before 9 a.m. and after 5 p.m. Many business leaders arrive at work early in the morning and don't leave until long after the office is closed. They are struggling to be productive while being swamped with office meetings, phone calls, e-mail, and employee issues.

When is the best time to organize the calendar and the to-do list? Slow starters organize the day better in the morning in order to arrange the day in their minds. Those people who begin work energetically in the morning plan best the night before. However, no one can plan for you except you. Planning the schedule ahead of time and following it will make more things go the way you want them to. Reducing chaos helps you overcome any unforeseen obstacles.

Make time for your friends, nurturing the relationships that provide feelings of warmth and fun. Your life will not be made up of just education and work. Think about what you want to accomplish during your life. Will you be doing what you want to be doing?

Assess your best times for privacy and people. When do you work best by yourself? When is the best time for you to interact with people? Discover your most productive time for work and plan creative projects and high-demand A projects during that time in your day.

Practice 16–7: Making a Time Design

Plan your activities for the next three days on the time schedule provided by your teacher. Choose activities you actually want to finish and schedule enough time to complete them. Use a To-Do list to jot down ideas that will fit into your schedule. Mark the items of the To-Do list as A, B, or C priorities. You won't be planning every minute, but make the Time Design as detailed as possible.

In the Actual column, record how you actually spent your time. The purpose of this column is to show you how your activities differed from your original planning.

by the way...

How do people organize themselves? According to time management expert Jeff Davidson, most use to-do lists and sticky notes, but 42 percent use computers and PDAs. Leaving reminders on home answering machines and sending e-mail messages to home computers is common also. At the opposite technological end, 4 percent remind themselves by writing on their hands.

Practice 16–8: Reaching Goals

For this Practice, use the three short-term goals from Practice 16-6, page 546. Choose one of those short-term goals and complete the following statement:

In order to move toward this goal, I will _____ in the next 48 hours.

Example:

study for the biology test a minimum of three hours

Have your teacher check your statement. After two days, share the results with the class.

Teams and Decision Making

Almost any survey of employers ranks teamwork skills as among those skills most necessary for success in today's work environment. In school, groups are important, but as students, you may not agree with their importance. Teams provide constant feedback, a sense of loyalty, and a win-together/lose-together feeling.

A good manager needs to have the team decide what must be done. How will the team finish the task? Who will do it? The team must consider the needs of the members or employees; however, the team must also consider the customer. The customer's needs must determine the outcome. A **customer** is a person who receives and/or uses the work of other people. The customer may be your teacher, your employer, a group member, or even yourself. What is good for the team is good for all— from the lowest-paid worker to the president of the company.

Practice 16-9: Team Production

teamwork

After breaking the class into groups, your teacher will give each group some materials to use in making a product. You will have ten minutes to choose and make the product, using only those supplies. *Beware:* Your teacher will be making changes in each group while the process is taking place.

After completing the team production, you will be discussing the following questions:

1. How did the team choose what product to make? How did production take place?

2. What roles evolved in the process? Did the person who had the idea for the product do the most work? Who provided the most encouragement?

3. What leadership qualities were revealed?

4. What happened when one of the team members was removed?

5. What happened when one team member was present but did not participate?

6. What happened when the working conditions worsened?

7. How could your team have improved?

8. How does this Practice relate to work? To school?

◎ Practice 16–10: Making Choices

Your teacher will divide the class into groups.

1. Brainstorm the choices you have made so far today. Examples may include choosing what time to get out of bed, whether to come to school, what to wear, and what to eat for breakfast and/or lunch. These choices are average, everyday decisions that everyone must make.

2. Your teacher has prepared four small bags. Your group must come to a consensus to decide which bag it will pick. During the decision-making process, you may ask your teacher questions. However, you cannot ask to look inside the bag. Your teacher will give you a time limit for making the group decision.

   Each group should choose a recorder and a leader who will facilitate the group discussion. (See *Student Workbook* page 5-F for an explanation of some of the group roles.) The recorder will write down the positive and negative reasons for choosing each bag. Then after your group has reached a consensus, the recorder will write down the choice that the group made and give the decision to the teacher.

Extravagant touches bring unanticipated quality.

© GETTY IMAGES/PHOTODISC, INC.

Quality

In the past, image was the primary emphasis for most companies, but today the business world emphasizes quality more than image for both the employee and the customer. Generally, quality can be divided into three types:

- *Routine quality.* Routine quality means the level of service that is expected, such as a satisfactory repair and a correct order.

- *Assumed quality.* The customer expects this type of quality. Examples include prompt delivery and clean surroundings.

- *Unanticipated quality.* This type of quality adds value to a business or a product and enhances the self-esteem of the customer. Examples of this unexpected level of service are a follow-up call checking on product satisfaction and a thank-you note for an extra gesture of support or encouragement.

Leadership Styles

A school of fish does not swim without direction, a place to go, and a place to feed. Whether you can see the leader of the group, each school of fish has one. Out of hundreds of fish, the leader appears because it has certain qualities.

The most effective leaders, however, are trained. Professional associations and student organizations offer formal training. Observing successful leaders helps a person gain the necessary skills and confidence for leadership. What leaders do in groups is called their **leadership style**. The style influences an organization, whether the organization is a club, a classroom, or the workplace.

A leader with the **authoritarian style of leadership** maintains strict control of everything the group does. Groups led by authoritarian leaders tend to make decisions more quickly, make fewer mistakes, and get more work done because the leader makes all of the decisions and does most of the work.

As a result, the group depends on the leader more for guidance, rather than trying to make its own decisions. The drawback of an authoritarian group is that the leader is not really part of the group. At times, the authoritarian leader takes the role of a dictator and the group members are the commoners. This type of leader is not a true communicator. In team decision making, the authoritarian leader is generally not accepted. However, in some situations, such as when a building is burning, the person who leads the group to safety has to use the authoritarian leadership style.

Laissez-faire leadership works well with highly trained, very motivated groups whose members are leaders themselves. The leader does not take part in or direct group decisions. The group is actually leading itself, for the members determine its goals, its rules, and the level or amount of participation of each person. Yet care must be taken when using this style since few groups succeed without some leadership.

The **facilitative team leader** produces results. The group does the primary decision making, with the leader providing coaching and encouragement. Although this style takes more time, group members feel a greater sense of participation in problem solving and decision making. The facilitator is open, sincere, and flexible, producing positive results. Business leaders today use less of an authoritarian style of leadership in favor of facilitative or democratic leadership. The leader fosters a feeling of cooperation and enthusiasm, along with mutual respect and interdependence. The result? Increased productivity.

The team leader treats each person on the team as though he or she is the most important member. Through motivation rather than manipulation, the team leader shows the importance of each person's particular job and of him or her personally. When people know that the company cares about them as individuals and about their team and its goals, the leader will find that he or she is thinking more about how to make the team successful than about his or her own self-importance.

Facilitative leadership

DIGITAL VISION

An effective facilitator-leader creates a positive climate for team decision-making and problem-solving situations. The leader whose group has the most success keeps the following observations in mind:

- Groups whose members know each other make better decisions.

- If the group is large, the members contribute less.

- If a member offers feedback, he or she should state the feedback in a positive way; then the group will more readily accept it.

- If members believe their skills are weaker than others', they will be less likely to use those skills.

- A person who sits at the head of the table or in the most central position will often become the leader of the group. The foot of the table is the weakest position. A round table is friendlier, inviting conversation and promoting a spirit of teamwork. With a round table, the leader should be a facilitative team leader.

- A leader's worst words are "I'll get back to you." Such a comment often makes group members feel that their concerns are worthless and that the leader has all of the power. The leader loses the group's confidence.

Practice 16–11: Evaluating Leadership Styles

1. Think about your current supervisor or the supervisor on your last job. Answer the following questions about that person's leadership style:

   a. What leadership style does the supervisor use? Authoritarian? Laissez-faire? Facilitative?
   b. How did you decide which style fit the supervisor?
   c. Give a specific example of the supervisor leadership style.
   d. What do you like or dislike about the supervisor's leadership style? Be specific.
   e. If you were a supervisor, what leadership style would you normally use? Why?

2. Choose an adult outside of your school that you believe is a good leader, such as a family member, businessperson, or community leader. Answer the questions about the person's leadership qualities on *Student Workbook* page 11-F. You may answer the questions based on your experience working with this person or on an interview with him or her.

by the way...

Over 11 million meetings take place in the United States every day. Estimates are that over half of that meeting time is unproductive. In fact, according to an MCI survey of businesspeople who attended meetings regularly, 91 percent of them admitted to daydreaming during meetings, 96 percent intentionally missed at least part of a meeting, 73 percent said they brought other work to meetings, and 39 percent have dozed during meetings. Now do you know why meetings have a bad reputation?

Successful Meetings

Leadership and officer training almost always includes how to run a meeting. **Parliamentary procedure**, the rules for conducting a meeting, may seem overly formal, but many organizations use informal versions of these rules to run a meeting efficiently and fairly. Groups use parliamentary procedure most often in formal meetings and board meetings.

Many meetings are more casual. Groups may form to share information, to decide the theme of Career Day, to hire a new employee, to form a budget, or to go over new rules. **Teleconferences** are meetings in which the participants conduct their business via a conference telephone call or videoconference to save travel. Some groups save time by having meetings during conference calls. Whatever the reason for the meeting, the following basic guidelines will help to ensure its success:

1. Start the meeting on time. If the meeting is scheduled to begin at ten o'clock, be sure to begin at ten o'clock. Otherwise, people will arrive late for the next meeting, and you will lose strength as a leader. End the meeting by or before the set time limit. Promptness encourages future meeting attendance.

Successful meetings start with an agenda.

2. Use an **agenda**. A good agenda is practically a map of the meeting. This map is the list of items to be included in the meeting. Following the list will keep things moving. Send those attending the meeting an agenda as far in advance as possible with roles assigned so that people are prepared to lead parts of the meeting. This meeting style is facilitative leadership; the group members will then consider themselves more a part of the decision-making and problem-solving process.

3. Keep the discussion on topic. The agenda is a guide, but topics often lead to other off-topic ideas. Refer to the agenda and have the group relate the discussion to it to keep on schedule. Another suggestion to keep a meeting within the agenda is to appoint someone in the group to guide the discussion back on track when needed. This allows the leader to be less of a police officer, instead letting him or her concentrate on the issues. When creating the agenda and setting the meeting time limit, try to schedule time for comments at the end of the meeting, as well as a few minutes for off-topic discussion.

4. Encourage all members to participate. Make sure that every member gets a chance to contribute and that no one person dominates the discussion. Also end long-winded discussions. Asking members for agenda items before a meeting encourages participation.

5. Use questions, **paraphrases**, and summaries to keep the meeting moving. Questions enable you to point out the important points of the discussion. Paraphrasing promotes clarity; saying, "Do I understand that you meant . . . ?" invites communication. Summaries emphasize the major items. These positive techniques help keep the group on track.

6. End the meeting by summarizing decisions that were made and discussions that took place during the meeting. Ask for questions to make sure all members understand the results of the meeting.

Ethics *Connection*

To influence negotiation positively, follow these basic rules:

1. Know what you want. Be able to explain that goal easily. Preparation is absolutely essential. Unfortunately, it is not unusual to enter into negotiation without having done your research. For example, is your motivation more money, prestige, or career opportunities? Determine your objective ahead of time.

2. Know what the other person needs. Try to plan a solution that will meet the other person's needs—and your needs. The more you understand the other side, the more likely you are to achieve your goal.

3. Prepare a backup plan ahead of time, an alternative solution that should meet your needs and the needs of others as well. For example, if a raise isn't possible, suggest more vacation days or flexible hours.

4. Don't give up if your plan is rejected. Showing your anger often stops negotiations immediately. If you regroup and offer your alternative solution, at least you are showing your determination. Getting even or getting mad is not the solution—the solution is to achieve your goal.

Conflicts and Negotiation Within Groups

Group members who know one another well may conflict. Conflict may occur even if the group usually agrees on most subjects. Often conflict results from a change in the way things have always been. Why do groups resist change? Well, it is easier not to change. If the group changes, it will have to understand, accept, and use new ideas. If the change doesn't fit the old rules or habits, everyone must make an adjustment.

Moving toward the future causes shifts in thinking. For example, in the early 1980s, a computer was the tool of the accountant and the data processor. If a company made a mistake, it blamed the computer. Today, however, computers are everywhere. Although the computer is still blamed when a mistake is made, people have learned that they can control this invention. The computer is part of society now.

People react to change in four ways:

1. *Do nothing.* People think that if they ignore change, maybe it will go away.

2. *Outwardly rebel.* People who are not consulted about the change often protest the loudest.

3. *Adapt.* People who adapt to change want to keep their jobs—and eventually become part of the change.

4. *Welcome the change.* These people are motivated by the change and eventually become leaders.

by the way...

Supervisors in the United States are spending twice as much time settling employee disputes as they did ten years ago, when they spent 10 percent of their time resolving personality conflicts.

by the way...

Suggesting a seating arrangement may relieve a conflict situation. If a member is in conflict with someone, try not to have the opponents sit across from each other. Instead, seat opponents next to each other. Having the two people closer to each other makes both of them more vulnerable and results in less conflict.

When group members make an effort to see one another's viewpoint, less conflict results. Members may not always agree, but at least they will try to shift their thinking. The successful facilitative leader will help them.

Practice 16-12: Running a Meeting

1. After reviewing the following questions in small groups, access the Student CD to listen to the audio recording of a meeting. Take notes to prepare for discussion.

   a. Do the group members have an agenda before the meeting date? Is an agenda used during the meeting?
   b. Does the meeting start on time? Explain.
   c. Who is the leader of the discussion? How can you tell?
   d. Is the meeting a decision-making situation? Why or why not?
   e. In a decision-making situation, the leader gives specific instructions to the group. What are the instructions given?
   f. Does the leader take part in the discussion? How?
   g. Is the leader in charge of the group? Is the group listening to the leader? Give some examples.
   h. How does the leader encourage all of the participants to become involved?
   i. Does the leader give positive feedback to each group member? What are some of the leader's statements?
   j. Does the discussion stay on topic? When does it stray off topic?
   k. How does the leader keep the discussion moving? Give examples of questions, summaries, and comments used for this purpose.
   l. What decision is made? How is the decision made?
   m. Does the leader end with a summary?
   n. How does the group display confidence in the final decision?
   o. What leadership style is displayed in this meeting? Why did you choose this style?

2. After discussing the first meeting, listen to the next selection, taking notes on the second meeting. Then discuss and answer the same questions concerning the second meeting.

Student Organizations

In a workforce development or career/technical program, participating in **student organizations** is part of the curriculum. Those organizations promote student involvement and education. The workforce development lab, the academic classroom, and student organizations are all parts of the educational picture. (See Figure 16-4.) The classroom work cannot exist without the student organizations; the student organizations cannot exist without the classroom work.

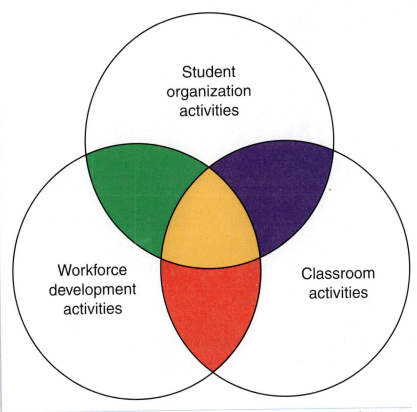

FIGURE 16-4 The related parts of workforce development (career/technical) education

Specific Student Organizations

Which student organization you belong to depends on your career cluster and educational program. The primary student organizations are described in the following sections. A chapter begins at the local level; has regional or district divisions; and then branches into the state, national, and international parts of the organization. Both high schools (secondary) and postsecondary schools participate in student organizations, for they are the professional organizations for students in training. Many student organizations also have **alumni** organizations for graduates.

Business Professionals of America, Future Business Leaders of America (FBLA), and Phi Beta Lambda

These organizations are designed to meet the needs of high school and postsecondary students enrolled in business and office education programs. The organizations are part of the business student's education; they develop leadership, interest in American business, and competency in business occupations. Phi Beta Lambda is for postsecondary students.

DECA

Marketing education has DECA as its student organization. The club develops students' skills in marketing, management, and entrepreneurship. Events sponsored by DECA stress the needs of business and industry, as well as excellence in school and work, as the basis for a successful career.

Courtesy of the National
FFA Organization © 2004

Reprinted with permission from
FCCLA. Inc. ®

Reprinted with permission
from Future Business Leaders
of America—Phi Beta Lambda

FFA

The oldest student organization, FFA, is the national association of students preparing for careers in the science, business, and technology of agriculture. The group's activities, honors, and awards provide incentives and practical experience. Formerly known as the Future Farmers of America, this organization has many time-honored traditions and provides excellent leadership training.

Reprinted with permission from Business
Professionals of America www.bpa.org

Reprinted with permission from DECA, Inc.

Family, Career and Community Leaders of America (FCCLA)

The chapters for this organization emphasize consumer and home

Reprinted with permission of SkillsUSA

Reprinted with permission
of HOSA

FIGURE 16-5 Logos of major student organizations

economics, now called family and consumer sciences. Projects focus on student concerns, including nutrition and fitness, career exploration, preparation for employment, parenting skills, family relationships, teen pregnancy, substance abuse, peer pressure, and communication among different age groups.

Health Occupations Students of America (HOSA)

Health Occupations Students of America is the organization that promotes health care careers and education. The organization is concerned with health care issues, leadership development, career enrichment, and environmental problems. The activities include community health projects.

Skills USA

The organization for trade, industrial, technical, dental assisting, cosmetology, and medical occupation students, Skills USA (formerly VICA) offers leadership, citizenship, and character-development programs, as well as activities to expand student skill training related to its career clusters. This organization emphasizes respect for the dignity of work, high standards, trade ethics, workmanship, scholarship, and safety, as well as partnerships with businesses in trade and industrial careers.

Student Organization Responsibilities

Student organizations are more than clubs that collect dues and give out membership cards. The student organization is the specialized organization that helps in your transition from school to work. The national and state student organization divisions operate along with local chapters to improve skills; strengthen interest in careers; provide appropriate information for the profession; and offer guidance through advisers, training, leadership, and reading materials. Encouraging various areas of professionalism, the student organization promotes professional growth, service learning, and competition through its chapter meetings, activities, and social events.

Professional Development

Developing leadership skills is an important part of the student organization's activities. Educational programs offer training in character development, leadership training, self-esteem, officer training, and citizenship. Leadership opportunities vary from running for office to being an active member of a committee.

Service Learning

Helping others is another facet of student organizations. Chapters of student organizations have been involved in toy, food, and blood drives; Red Cross aid; voter registration; school functions; recycling; and campus cleanup. Service learning not only helps citizens, but also earns recognition for both the club and the school.

Competition

Competitive events are a primary part of student organizations. However, remember that the experience and education that you gain from competing are well worth the effort, regardless of winning or losing. Competitive events are classified as either skills or leadership contests.

- Skills contests use the knowledge gained in the workforce development program. One type of contest is to have a project completed to exact specifications within a certain time period. For example, in the Skills USA Residential Wiring skills competition, Woody was given a schematic diagram of a circuit with standard wiring symbols. Using only the required tools and provided materials, he had to install residential wiring and electrical devices to the specifications of the in-circuit design within a $2\frac{1}{2}$-hour time period.

PHOTO COURTESY OF DECA INC.

Student organizations build professionalism.

The other type of skills contest is a demonstration. In the FCCLA Focus on Children competition, Tracey demonstrated a sound box that teaches preschoolers a game and the alphabet at the same time.

- Leadership contests are events that are not related to a specific career program. One of the two major types of leadership events is directly associated with leadership skills. Running a meeting using parliamentary procedure, giving a prepared or extemporaneous speech, and participating in job interviews are examples of such an event.

The other leadership competitive event includes knowledge tests for teams or individuals. These events can be tests on subjects indirectly related to the cluster, such as math, science, or health. Other knowledge tests cover information about the club itself, current events, or general knowledge.

Your teachers will help you prepare for competition. In skills events, your lab teacher can boost your confidence and help you acquire the knowledge you need to compete. Other teachers, especially in your academic subjects, can help by listening to your speech, proofreading, and coaching team practices. Just ask; they'll be glad to help.

Your school may have other student organizations that are or are not related to workforce development. Some groups, such as the National Honor Society, the National Art Honor Society, and the National Technical Honor Society, have selection criteria that may include grade point average, attendance record, activities, and teacher recommendations. Other formal student groups may encourage interests in careers, such as the Future Educators of America, which explores careers in education, and Student Health Professionals, which helps prepare for health careers. Some student career organizations may find members in schools, but they are really community organizations. An example is Exploring Scouting, part of the Boy Scouts of America. Exploring is a worksite-based program that gives students an opportunity to visit community organizations and explore the dynamics of various careers, such as law enforcement, fire service, and aviation.

by the way...

Great leaders have one thing in common—passion! If you're not excited about what you're doing, then your team won't be either. Show team members you're enthusiastic and watch them get motivated.

Practice 16–13: Investigating Leadership Activities

Each student organization has leadership training, activities that teach the leadership qualities discussed in the previous sections of this chapter. In small groups, research your particular organization's leadership opportunities. You may have to go to the media center, to the organization's web site, to your chapter adviser, or to your organization's officers. After finding the answers, your group will report to the class.

Professional Organizations

Professional organizations serve their members through networking. The professional organization provides a **network**, a way of connecting with information, jobs, and other individuals in the field. Whether a formalized structure or an informal group, a network is a supplement for the usual information gained from coworkers.

by the way...

"Leadership is the ability to get other people to do what they don't want to do, and like it."

Harry S. Truman, U.S. President

Advantages of Professional Organizations

To represent the interests of members to the community, professional associations convey information through meetings and publicity. The benefits of professional organizations include the following:

Services

Organizations offer special services for their members only, such as job placement and professional consultation. The organization may also have a **clearinghouse** for resource material; if a member needs information in a specific area, the organization can provide this service. The groups also support **lobbyists** who work to influence legislators on behalf of the organizations.

Journals, Web Sites, and Other Publications

An organization's **journal** and website provides brief evaluations of recent developments and government actions. New products, research, and theories are introduced to members. The beliefs and ethics of an organization are presented, along with information on conferences, **seminars**, scholarships, courses, and jobs.

Conferences, Seminars, and Courses

During conferences or conventions, members of a professional organization gather to share ideas, work for legislation, and conduct business. The membership or its representatives can discuss problems concerning the association and plans for the future. These meetings can be local, regional, state, or national.

The dues paid to professional organizations are an investment in the future of an occupation. Besides the contacts and friendships offering valuable support, the associations may offer scholarships or job listings. Professional organizations provide opportunities for improvement in trade and professional areas.

When you enter the working world, you should join one or more professional organizations. It is your responsibility to keep up with advances in your trade or profession. With the knowledge that you gain, you may be president of the company someday.

Mentors

Through networking in your organization, you can find and develop mentors who will support you and expand your thinking as you grow within a career and an organization. A **mentor** is similar to a coach, a person who will share his or her expertise, insights, ideas, and experiences. That person will offer you support along the education and career process. Giving guidance, the mentor teaches, shares resources and information, and helps lead you to the next step. Coaches, teachers, family members, and parents may be mentors, but mentors are not limited to those people.

When choosing mentors, find people whom you respect, people with whom you feel comfortable asking questions and discussing decision-making situations. Then be a good listener, for your mentors will work with you to offer motivation and inspiration for your career path.

Membership in a professional organization is for specialized areas of employment; the contact and membership comes after you are employed in your career major, generally after graduation. These organizations are often similar to student organizations because both promote members' participation and continuing education within career areas. Networking also increases participation and contacts in your career. Frequently organizations with a formalized structure, professional organizations have two basic forms: trade and professional organizations and labor unions.

A mentor can help you in your education or career.

© GETTY IMAGES/PHOTODISC, INC.

Trade and Professional Associations

Anyone with an interest in a specific occupation can be a member of a trade or professional association. These organizations do not require that a member have a certain occupation or place of employment, merely interest. For instance, Women in Construction works for the interests of females in the building industry. Other examples of these types of associations are the American Welding Society and the Business Professional Women of America. The organization 9 to 5 supports the interests of workers in hourly occupations, such as secretaries and cosmetologists.

Labor Unions

Labor unions require being employed in a certain career field and possibly attaining a certain job classification before membership is offered. Members may be skilled in a certain occupation, such as carpentry or food service. The other type of union consists of workers within the same industry, such as automobile manufacturing. These workers may be running machines or supervising—all within the automotive industry.

Labor unions were created to stand behind the rights of workers. The unions not only help negotiate contracts between labor and management, but also advocate workplace safety, legislative issues, and other workplace issues.

Practice 16–14: Using Professional Journals

Ch16-14.doc

In the library, at school, in the community, or on the Internet, find at least one journal pertaining to your career cluster. If trade journals in your program are not available, find a magazine related to your field. Your teacher can provide appropriate titles. You will find a list of career titles in Chapter 15 on page 508.

Write down the following information for each journal. Be as specific as possible. (Chapter 7 will provide additional help in finding the central idea of an article.) Report your information in small groups.

1. The title of the journal

2. The subject area covered by the journal

3. The date of publication

4. The number of pages in the journal (if it is a printed copy)

5. Does the journal include articles on the following topics? If so, identify the name of the article on which it appears.

   a. New products
   b. Government action
   c. Technology
   d. Career opportunities
   e. Book reviews

6. Choose one article and identify the following information:

   a. The title of the article
   b. The author(s)
   c. The page(s) or URL
   d. The central idea of the article

People *Connection*

Louie Brockhoeft has always been involved in sports, starting in elementary school and continuing with football, basketball, and baseball teams in high school and college. After college, Louie had careers as a salesperson and a stockbroker; however, he continued to be involved in sports as a coach and referee. When Louie decided to change careers to give him the opportunity to work toward starting his own business, becoming a personal trainer was a natural fit. He was passionate about fitness, constantly researched the human body's reactions to conditioning, and studied nutrition books and web sites. With his degree in psychology and marketing, Louie had the education to support his work and real-world experiences.

Through the National Academy of Sports Medicine, Louie became a Certified Personal Trainer, which was necessary for his being hired by a national chain of gyms. Becoming certified allowed him to be hired by Mercy HealthPlex, a health and wellness center operated by Mercy Health Partners. Since working for Mercy, Louie chose to broaden his expertise by passing the American Council on Exercise certification as a Clinical Exercise Specialist, enabling him to work with special populations, such as people with back and knee problems. The next step? While gaining experience with a variety of clients, Louie is exploring small-business ownership and investigating possible sites for his own training facility.

Summary

Your behavior is the basis of the professional image others form of you. A professional displays skills required to be successful. Follow these guidelines to be a successful professional:

- Manage your time by analyzing your time wasters and procrastination techniques.
- Set goals by determining your priorities and controlling barriers.
- Choose an effective leadership style when working in groups.
- Use strategies for conducting effective meetings and for conflict resolution.
- Become active in a student organization.
- Read professional journals and join a professional organization.

For review and research activities visit
communicating.swlearning.com

Works Cited

Hagstrom, Jr., Robert J. *The Warren Buffett Way: Investment Strategies of the World's Greatest Investor.* New York: Wiley, 1994.

Linden, Dana Wechsler, and Dyan Machan. "The Disinheritors." *Forbes.* 19 May 1997: 152–154.

Letter Completing Goals

After working with priorities, goals, and schedules, it's time to move toward your life ambitions. This Project will help you make a commitment to accomplish your plans. You will be writing yourself a letter that you will open in six months. The letter will contain three promises you make to yourself to move toward achieving one of your long-term goals. Also, you will include advice and a reward to yourself for completing the promises. Setting goals and carrying out promises are difficult, so you deserve a reward for fulfillment.

1. Complete the Project Plan, *Student Workbook* page 16-G, and have your teacher check it.

2. Complete the rough draft of the letter. Have your teacher check it.

3. Write the final draft of your letter. Have your teacher check it.

4. Place the signed letter inside a stamped, self-addressed envelope. On the back of the envelope, write "Do not open until _____" (a date six months from now). Give the envelope to your teacher.

5. In six months, you will receive the envelope in the mail.

Overview

In the following profile of Nikki Giovanni, Lois Rosenthal describes her as "one of our age's most fearless and influential poets." Rosenthal adds that "she's earned her nickname 'priestess of black poetry.'"

Nikki Giovanni is one of America's most widely read living poets and one of the most outspoken. From the sixties, when she gained recognition as one of the prime forces in the civil rights movement, to the present, when she travels all over the world to teach and to give scores of poetry readings and lectures each year, she speaks out on whatever issues she believes are crucial. Her awards and outstanding achievements are legion.

"Nikki Giovanni"

Says Giovanni: "I use poetry as an outlet for my mind. It's my justification for living. But speaking my mind is an important part of my life as well, even when it's not a popular view. Everyone has a right to the dictates of her own heart. The one thing you cannot take away from people is their own sense of integrity. I don't want my integrity impinged upon nor will I impinge on the integrity of someone else.

"Though you cannot live your life to be intimidated by lesser people under any circumstances, I don't think you should shout people down if you disagree with them—which is what people are doing in the eighties.

"For instance, I don't agree with those who would attend a speech given by Jeanne Kirkpatrick in order to disrupt it. I think you should find out why she has the views she does and debate with her. You don't have to agree with her, but you can't solve a problem by shutting a person up.

> *". . . you can't solve a problem by shutting a person up."*

The integrity of the individual is everything."

About poets, Giovanni says:

"This is a great profession. If everybody became a poet, the world would be so much better. We would all read to each other. It would be an enhancing situation. This is not a restricted profession. There's a living out there, you just have to find it.

"People say poets can't make a living. I tell them to lower their expectations to match their income. Any young artist should stay out of debt so that, for instance, if an opportunity arises in another part of the country, she won't say, 'I can't go because I have a lease on this apartment or car payments to make.' You must be free."

Giovanni feels earning a living as a poet depends on how serious you are about it. She advises staying close to the writing profession—all facets of it. Learn to write magazine articles, book reviews. Give poetry readings to churches, restaurants, for civic organizations, any place that agrees to have them—for free if you have to. And Giovanni recommends doing every job as if it were the most important one you'll ever have. Just because it may not be the audience you dream of, don't think you can let up on the energy you put into your work.

What about all the people who want to be poets but can never hope to reach Giovanni's heights? She has a ready answer.

"Most of them won't try. They won't risk what I did. I had a son, and an apartment, and I decided I was going to try to be a poet and to do it as well as I could. If it didn't work out, I'd have still given it my best shot. Most people won't do that.

"If I have a 36-inch bust, a 24-inch waist, 38-inch hips and I lived in Stillwater, Oklahoma, and I decided to become a ballerina, I'd try. I would never say 'My chest is too big and my behind sticks out, and my measurements are all wrong for a ballerina,' I would get on my toes. Someone would have to stop me because I will not stop myself.

"Whatever I do in life, I want to do it to the absolute maximum. I want to be the best that I can be. I encourage every one of my students to do that. Give yourself the chance to fully realize whatever your dreams are."

—Lois Rosenthal

> *"Give yourself the chance to fully realize whatever your dreams are."*

Start-Up: Nikki Giovanni's philosophy of life encourages the reading audience to take charge of their lives and live them to the maximum. She urges readers to hang on to a sense of integrity. Also, she gives advice to young poets.

What can you draw from Giovanni's remarks that would make a good set of guidelines for becoming a professional?

Connection: First, write what you have learned from Giovanni's remarks that would make a good set of guidelines for becoming a professional. Then write your own guidelines for becoming a professional. Share your guidelines and steps for achieving them with the rest of the class.

Overview

In the summer of 2004, *Forbes* compiled a list of America's wealthiest people. Several names you may recognize—Bill Gates; Warren Buffet; Paul Allen; and the heirs of the founder of Wal-Mart, Sam Walton—were listed as the richest people in the United States. Number one on the list was Bill Gates, with a net worth of $48 billion. He made his billions with Microsoft computer software.

Warren Buffet was number two on the list, having a net worth of $41 billion. He made his billions from astute stock investments and purchases of entire companies, including Berkshire Hathaway, Inc., which became the name of the holding company of which he owns controlling interest. Companies held by Berkshire Hathaway sell a variety of products, including insurance, energy, carpet, jewelry, furniture, paint (Benjamin Moore), apparel (Fruit of the Loom), and food (Dairy Queen).

One final interesting bit of information: There are now 313 billionaires in the United States—the largest number ever. The combined wealth of these people has reached $1 trillion.

from The Warren Buffett Way

Warren Buffett is not easy to describe. Physically he is unremarkable, with looks often described as grandfatherly. Intellectually he is considered a genius, yet his down-to-earth relationship with people is truly uncomplicated. He is simple, straightforward, forthright, and honest. He displays an engaging combination of sophisticated dry wit and cornball humor. He has a profound reverence for those things logical and a foul distaste for imbecility. He embraces the simple and avoids the complicated. . . .

Of the sixty-nine [richest] individuals, Buffett is the only one who obtained his wealth from the stock market. Berkshire Hathaway, Inc., is best understood as a holding company. In addition to . . . insurance companies, it also owns a newspaper, a candy company, a furniture store, a jewelry store, an encyclopedia publisher, a vacuum cleaner business and a company that manufactures and distributes uniforms [and a large amount of Coca Cola stock]. . . .

The story of how Buffett came to acquire these diverse businesses is interesting itself. Perhaps more to the point, the stories collectively give us a valuable insight into Buffett's way of looking at companies. It will come as little surprise that he used the same yardstick to evaluate companies for possible acquisitions as for additions to the Berkshire Hathaway stock portfolio. . . .

Reading the [Berkshire Hathaway] annual reports, one is struck by how comfortable Buffett is quoting the *Bible,* John Maynard Keynes, or Mae West. Of course the operable word is "reading." Each report is sixty to seventy pages of dense information: no pictures, no color graphics, no charts. Those who are disciplined enough to start on page one and continue uninterrupted are rewarded with a healthy dose of financial acumen,

© NELL REDMOND/BLOOMBERG NEWS/LANDOV

folksy humor, and unabashed honesty. Buffett is very candid in his reporting. He emphasizes both the pluses and the minuses of Berkshire's businesses. He believes that people who own stock in Berkshire Hathaway are owners of the company, and he tells them as much as he would like to be told if he were in their shoes. . . .

. . . He is always upbeat and supportive. He is genuinely excited about coming to work every day. "I have in life all I want right here," he says. "I love every day. I mean, I tap dance in here and work with nothing but people I like. There is no job in the world that is more fun than running Berkshire and I count myself lucky to be where I am."

—Robert G. Hagstrom, Jr.

from Gates

William Henry Gates was born October 28, 1955, in Seattle's (Washington) Swedish Hospital. A cheerful infant, dubbed "Happy Boy" by the neighbors, he was the only son, and the second of three children. . . .

Bill was usually also the youngest in his class. . . . School authorities convinced them (classmates) that however slight Bill's physique or immature his personality, his mind was more than capable. . . .

"He knew a lot about a lot of things," Hazel Carlson [Bill's fourth-grade teacher] remembered. His IQ, which she estimated in the 160's or 170's, "was among the higher ones I've ever had. . . ."

> *On the day he was born in 1955, fewer than 500 electronic computers existed in the entire world. . . .*

Bill Gates, co-founder, chairman, chief executive officer of **Microsoft**, number one personal computer software company in the known galaxy. . . . the hyperkinetic, tousel-haired . . . computer programmer, tycoon, Harvard drop-out and multibillionaire was about to deliver the most important presentation of his presentation-filled career. (Bill's) company . . . was about to announce the latest incarnation of **Microsoft Windows**. . . .

. . . back in 1975, Gates and his partner Paul Allen had been the very first to commercialize software for the just-born personal computer. . . . On the day he was born in 1955, fewer than 500 electronic computers existed in the entire world, their total retail value amounted to less than $200 million, and the term "software" had not yet been coined. . . .

Under the able guidance of his public relations counselor, Gates was being propelled into a curious kind of nerdy celebrityhood riddled with contradictory stories about wild womanizing on the one hand and an inability to get a date on the other, about fast cars and speeding tickets mixed with monkish workaholism. Reportedly a voracious reader, he insisted his favorite books were two novels, *The Catcher in the Rye* and *A Separate Peace,* popular largely with . . . adolescents. Described as oblivious to wealth, he was quoted boasting "I have an infinite amount of money." Bill Gates' story was never rags to riches, a Harvard friend once remarked, but riches to riches—though the initial affluence, embellished to include such

© ERIN LUBIN/BLOOMBERG NEWS/LANDOV

fiction as a million-dollar trust fund, was now utterly insignificant. . . .

Bill Gates in his book *The Road Ahead* remarks on the Information Age: ". . . I'm optimistic about the new technology. It will enhance leisure time and enrich culture by expanding the distribution of information. . . . Technology progress will force all of society to confront tough new problems, only some of which we can foresee. . . . Societies are going to be asked to make hard choices in such areas as universal availability, investment in education, regulation, and the balance between individual privacy and community security. . . . Microsoft has been a leader in the PC era. . . . For me, a big part of the fun has always been to hire and work with smart people. I enjoy working with them. . . . They're extraordinarily talented and will contribute new visions. If Microsoft can combine these visions with listening carefully to customers, we have a chance to continue to lead the way. We can certainly keep providing better and better software to make the PC a universally empowering tool. I often say I have the best job in the world, and I mean it."

—Stephen Manes and Paul Andrews

Start-Up: Both of these men have made a mark on the world through a way that most people recognize: making money. Gates and Buffett have many admirable qualities. Also, their goals are quite evident. They are similar yet different individuals.

Since just a little information is presented here, check your school media center, community library, and the Internet for more information on both of these interesting people.

Connection: Compare and contrast these two multibillionaires. Review Chapter 12 for information on comparing and contrasting if needed.

Working with Literature: Refer to *Student Workbook* page 16-H for an activity on skills needed in the work world.

PROOFREADING MARKS

DEFINED		EXAMPLES
Begin new paragraph	¶	¶ Begin a new paragraph at this point. Insᵉrt a letter here.
Insert a character	^	
Delete	ℰ	delete these words. Disregard the previous correction. To
Do not change	stet or	
Transpose	⌒	transpose is to around turn.
Move left	[	[Move this copy to the left.
Move right	]	] Move this copy to the right.
Do not begin new paragraph	no ¶	no ¶ Do not begin a new paragraph here. Delete the hyphen from
Delete and close up	ℰ	pre-empt and close up the space.
Set in caps	≡	a sentence begins with a capital
Lowercase	/	letter. This Word should not
Insert period	⊙	be capitalized. Insert a period⊙
Insert quotation marks	❝ ❞	❝ Quotation marks and a comma
Insert comma	∧	should be placed here❞ he said.
Insert space	#/	Space between these words. An
Insert apostrophe	˅	apostrophe is whats needed here.
Insert hyphen	=/	Add a hyphen to runner up. Close
Close up	⌒	up the extra spa ce.
Use superior figure	˅	Footnote this sentence. Set
Set in italic	ital.	the words sine qua non in italics.
Spell out	sp ◯	Spell out NY. sp

Literature Acknowledgments

Literature Acknowledgments (cont'd)

Author/Title Index

Index

Index

Index